Materials on Commercial Law – Volume IV

Materials on Commercial Law – Volume IV

Arbitration Law, Public International Law and International Investment Law

Third Edition

Editorial Board

Prof. dr. Tobias Cohen Jehoram
Dr. Julia Hörnig
Prof. dr. Gerard Meijer
Prof. dr. Frank Smeele
Dr. Frank Stevens
Mr. Juan Pablo Valdivia Pizarro
Dr. Johan Vannerom
Prof. dr. Maarten Verbrugh
Dr. Federica Violi
Dr. Piotr Wiliński

eleven

Published, sold and distributed by Eleven
P.O. Box 85576
2508 CG The Hague
The Netherlands
Tel.: +31 70 33 070 33
Fax: +31 70 33 070 30
e-mail: sales@elevenpub.nl
www.elevenpub.com

Sold and distributed in USA and Canada
Independent Publishers Group
814 N. Franklin Street
Chicago, IL 60610, USA
Order Placement: +1 800 888 4741
Fax: +1 312 337 5985
orders@ipgbook.com
www.ipgbook.com

Eleven is an imprint of Boom uitgevers Den Haag.

ISBN 978-90-4730-164-6

Table of Contents

Part IX
Arbitration Law

9.1 Conventions

9.1.1 United Nations Convention on the Recognition and Enforcement of Foreign Arbitral Awards (1958)

Article I

1. This Convention shall apply to the recognition and enforcement of arbitral awards made in the territory of a State other than the State where the recognition and enforcement of such awards are sought, and arising out of differences between persons, whether physical or legal. It shall also apply to arbitral awards not considered as domestic awards in the State where their recognition and enforcement are sought.

2. The term "arbitral awards" shall include not only awards made by arbitrators appointed for each case but also those made by permanent arbitral bodies to which the parties have submitted.

3. When signing, ratifying or acceding to this Convention, or notifying extension under article X hereof, any State may on the basis of reciprocity declare that it will apply the Convention to the recognition and enforcement of awards made only in the territory of another Contracting State. It may also declare that it will apply the Convention only to differences arising out of legal relationships, whether contractual or not, which are considered as commercial under the national law of the State making such declaration.

Article II

1. Each Contracting State shall recognize an agreement in writing under which the parties undertake to submit to arbitration all or any differences which have arisen or which may arise between them in respect of a defined legal relationship, whether contractual or not, concerning a subject matter capable of settlement by arbitration.

2. The term "agreement in writing" shall include an arbitral clause in a contract or an arbitration agreement signed by the parties or contained in an exchange of letters or telegrams.

3. The court of a Contracting State, when seized of an action in a matter in respect of which the parties have made an agreement within the meaning of this article, shall, at the request of one of the parties, refer the parties to arbitration, unless it finds that the said agreement is null and void, inoperative or incapable of being performed.

Article III

Each Contracting State shall recognize arbitral awards as binding and enforce them in accordance with the rules of procedure of the territory where the award is relied upon, under the conditions laid down in the following articles. There shall not be imposed substantially more onerous conditions or higher fees or charges on the recognition or enforcement of arbitral awards to which this Convention applies than are imposed on the recognition or enforcement of domestic arbitral awards.

Article IV

1. To obtain the recognition and enforcement mentioned in the preceding article, the party applying for recognition and enforcement shall, at the time of the application, supply:

(a) The duly authenticated original award or a duly certified copy thereof;

(b) The original agreement referred to in article II or a duly certified copy thereof.

2. If the said award or agreement is not made in an official language of the country in which the award is relied upon, the party applying for recognition and enforcement of the award shall produce a translation of these documents into such language. The translation shall be certified by an official or sworn translator or by a diplomatic or consular agent.

Article V

1. Recognition and enforcement of the award may be refused, at the request of the party against whom it is invoked, only if that party furnishes to the competent authority where the recognition and enforcement is sought, proof that:

(a) The parties to the agreement referred to in article II were, under the law applicable to them, under some incapacity, or the said agreement is not valid under the law to which the parties have subjected it or, failing any indication thereon, under the law of the country where the award was made; or

(b) The party against whom the award is invoked was not given proper notice of the appointment of the arbitrator or of the arbitration proceedings or was otherwise unable to present his case; or

(c) The award deals with a difference not contemplated by or not falling within the terms of the submission to arbitration, or it contains decisions on matters beyond the scope of the submission to arbitration, provided that, if the decisions on matters submitted to arbitration can be separated from those not so submitted, that part of the award which contains decisions on matters submitted to arbitration may be recognized and enforced; or

(d) The composition of the arbitral authority or the arbitral procedure was not in accordance with the agreement of the parties, or, failing such agreement, was not in accordance with the law of the country where the arbitration took place; or

(e) The award has not yet become binding on the parties, or has been set aside or suspended by a competent authority of the country in which, or under the law of which, that award was made.

2. Recognition and enforcement of an arbitral award may also be refused if the competent authority in the country where recognition and enforcement is sought finds that:

(a) The subject matter of the difference is not capable of settlement by arbitration under the law of that country; or

(b) The recognition or enforcement of the award would be contrary to the public policy of that country.

Article VI

If an application for the setting aside or suspension of the award has been made to a competent authority referred to in article V (1) (e), the authority before which the award is sought to be relied upon may, if it considers it proper, adjourn the decision on the enforcement of the award and may also, on the application of the party claiming enforcement of the award, order the other party to give suitable security.

Article VII

1. The provisions of the present Convention shall not affect the validity of multilateral or bilateral agreements concerning the recognition and enforcement of arbitral awards entered into by the Contracting States nor deprive any interested party of any right he may have to avail himself of an arbitral award in the manner and to the extent allowed by the law or the treaties of the country where such award is sought to be relied upon.

2. The Geneva Protocol on Arbitration Clauses of 1923 and the Geneva Convention on the Execution of Foreign Arbitral Awards of 1927 shall cease to have effect between Contracting States on their becoming bound and to the extent that they become bound, by this Convention.

Article VIII
1. This Convention shall be open until 31 December 1958 for signature on behalf of any Member of the United Nations and also on behalf of any other State which is or hereafter becomes a member of any specialized agency of the United Nations, or which is or hereafter becomes a party to the Statute of the International Court of Justice, or any other State to which an invitation has been addressed by the General Assembly of the United Nations.
2. This Convention shall be ratified and the instrument of ratification shall be deposited with the Secretary-General of the United Nations.

Article IX
1. This Convention shall be open for accession to all States referred to in article VIII.
2. Accession shall be effected by the deposit of an instrument of accession with the Secretary-General of the United Nations.

Article X
1. Any State may, at the time of signature, ratification or accession, declare that this Convention shall extend to all or any of the territories for the international relations of which it is responsible. Such a declaration shall take effect when the Convention enters into force for the State concerned.
2. At any time thereafter any such extension shall be made by notification addressed to the Secretary-General of the United Nations and shall take effect as from the ninetieth day after the day of receipt by the Secretary-General of the United Nations of this notification, or as from the date of entry into force of the Convention for the State concerned, whichever is the later.
3. With respect to those territories to which this Convention is not extended at the time of signature, ratification or accession, each State concerned shall consider the possibility of taking the necessary steps in order to extend the application of this Convention to such territories, subject, where necessary for constitutional reasons, to the consent of the Governments of such territories.

Article XI
In the case of a federal or non-unitary State, the following provisions shall apply:
(a) With respect to those articles of this Convention that come within the legislative jurisdiction of the federal authority, the obligations of the federal Government shall to this extent be the same as those of Contracting States which are not federal States;
(b) With respect to those articles of this Convention that come within the legislative jurisdiction of constituent states or provinces which are not, under the constitutional system of the federation, bound to take legislative action, the federal Government shall bring such articles with a favourable recommendation to the notice of the appropriate authorities of constituent states or provinces at the earliest possible moment;
(c) A federal State Party to this Convention shall, at the request of any other Contracting State transmitted through the Secretary-General of the United Nations, supply a statement of the law and practice of the federation and its constituent units in regard to any particular provision of this Convention, showing the extent to which effect has been given to that provision by legislative or other action.

Article XII
1. This Convention shall come into force on the ninetieth day following the date of deposit of the third instrument of ratification or accession.
2. For each State ratifying or acceding to this Convention after the deposit of the third instrument of ratification or accession, this Convention shall enter into force on the ninetieth day after deposit by such State of its instrument of ratification or accession.

Article XIII

1. Any Contracting State may denounce this Convention by a written notification to the Secretary-General of the United Nations. Denunciation shall take effect one year after the date of receipt of the notification by the Secretary-General.

2. Any State which has made a declaration or notification under article X may, at any time thereafter, by notification to the Secretary-General of the United Nations, declare that this Convention shall cease to extend to the territory concerned one year after the date of the receipt of the notification by the Secretary-General.

3. This Convention shall continue to be applicable to arbitral awards in respect of which recognition and enforcement proceedings have been instituted before the denunciation takes effect.

Article XIV

A Contracting State shall not be entitled to avail itself of the present Convention against other Contracting States except to the extent that it is itself bound to apply the Convention.

Article XV

The Secretary-General of the United Nations shall notify the States contemplated in article VIII of the following:

(a) Signatures and ratifications in accordance with article VIII;

(b) Accessions in accordance with article IX;

(c) Declarations and notifications under articles I, X and XI;

(d) The date upon which this Convention enters into force in accordance with article XII;

(e) Denunciations and notifications in accordance with article XIII.

Article XVI

1. This Convention, of which the Chinese, English, French, Russian and Spanish texts shall be equally authentic, shall be deposited in the archives of the United Nations.

2. The Secretary-General of the United Nations shall transmit a certified copy of this Convention to the States contemplated in article VIII.

RECOMMENDATION REGARDING THE INTERPRETATION OF ARTICLE II, PARAGRAPH 2, AND ARTICLE VII, PARAGRAPH 1, OF THE CONVENTION ON THE RECOGNITION AND ENFORCEMENT OF FOREIGN ARBITRAL AWARDS (2006)

The United Nations Commission on International Trade Law,

Recalling General Assembly resolution 2205 (XXI) of 17 December 1966,which established the United Nations Commission on International Trade Law with the object of promoting the progressive harmonization and unification of the law of international trade by, inter alia, promoting ways and means of ensuring a uniform interpretation and application of international conventions and uniform laws in the field of the law of international trade,

Conscious of the fact that the different legal, social and economic systems of the world, together with different levels of development, are represented in the Commission,

Recalling successive resolutions of the General Assembly reaffirming the mandate of the Commission as the core legal body within the United Nations system in the field of international trade law to coordinate legal activities in this field,

Convinced that the wide adoption of the Convention on the Recognition and Enforcement of Foreign Arbitral Awards, done in New York on 10 June 1958, has been a significant achievement in the promotion of the rule of law, particularly in the field of international trade,

Recalling that the Conference of Plenipotentiaries which prepared and opened the Convention for signature adopted a resolution, which states, inter alia, that the Conference "considers that greater uniformity of national laws on arbitration would further the effectiveness of arbitration in the settlement of private law disputes",

Bearing in mind differing interpretations of the form requirements under the Convention that result in part from differences of expression as between the five equally authentic texts of the Convention,

Taking into account article VII, paragraph 1, of the Convention, a purpose of which is to enable the enforcement of foreign arbitral awards to the greatest extent, in particular by recognizing the right of any interested party to avail itself of law or treaties of the country where the award is sought to be relied upon, including where such law or treaties offer a regime more favourable than the Convention,

Considering the wide use of electronic commerce,

Taking into account international legal instruments, such as the 1985 UNCITRAL Model Law on International Commercial Arbitration, as subsequently revised, particularly with respect to article 7, the UNCITRAL Model Law on Electronic Commerce, the UNCITRAL Model Law on Electronic Signatures and the United Nations Convention on the Use of Electronic Communications in International Contracts,

Taking into account also enactments of domestic legislation, as well as case law, more favourable than the Convention in respect of form requirement governing arbitration agreements, arbitration proceedings and the enforcement of arbitral awards,

Considering that, in interpreting the Convention, regard is to be had to the need to promote recognition and enforcement of arbitral awards,

1. Recommends that article II, paragraph 2, of the Convention on the Recognition and Enforcement of Foreign Arbitral Awards, done in New York, 10 June 1958, be applied recognizing that the circumstances described there- in are not exhaustive;

2. Recommends also that article VII, paragraph 1, of the Convention on the Recognition and Enforcement of Foreign Arbitral Awards, done in New York, 10 June 1958, should be applied to allow any interested party to avail itself of rights it may have, under the law or treaties of the country where an arbitration agreement is sought to be relied upon, to seek recognition of the validity of such an arbitration agreement.

9.1.2 Vienna Convention on the Law of Treaties (1969)

PART I. INTRODUCTION

Article 1. Scope of the present Convention
The present Convention applies to treaties between States.

Article 2. Use of terms
1. For the purposes of the present Convention:
(a) "treaty" means an international agreement concluded between States in written form and governed by international law, whether embodied in a single instrument or in two or more related instruments and whatever its particular designation;
(b) "ratification", "acceptance", "approval" and "accession" mean in each case the international act so named whereby a State establishes on the international plane its consent to be bound by a treaty;
(c) "full powers" means a document emanating from the competent authority of a State designating a person or persons to represent the State for negotiating, adopting or authenticating the text of a treaty, for expressing the consent of the State to be bound by a treaty, or for accomplishing any other act with respect to a treaty;
(d) "reservation" means a unilateral statement, however phrased or named, made by a State, when signing, ratifying, accepting, approving or acceding to a treaty, whereby it purports to exclude or to modify the legal effect of certain provisions of the treaty in their application to that State;
(e) "negotiating State" means a State which took part in the drawing up and adoption of the text of the treaty;
(f) "contracting State" means a State which has consented to be bound by the treaty, whether or not the treaty has entered into force;
(g) "party" means a State which has consented to be bound by the treaty and for which the treaty is in force;
(h) "third State" means a State not a party to the treaty;
(i) "international organization" means an intergovernmental organization.
2. The provisions of paragraph 1 regarding the use of terms in the present Convention are without prejudice to the use of those terms or to the meanings which may be given to them in the internal law of any State.

Article 3. International agreements not within the scope of the present Convention
The fact that the present Convention does not apply to international agreements concluded between States and other subjects of international law or between such other subjects of international law, or to international agreements not in written form, shall not affect:
(a) the legal force of such agreements;
(b) the application to them of any of the rules set forth in the present Convention to which they would be subject under international law independently of the Convention;
(c) the application of the Convention to the relations of States as between themselves under international agreements to which other subjects of international law are also parties.

Article 4. Non-retroactivity of the present Convention
Without prejudice to the application of any rules set forth in the present Convention to which treaties would be subject under international law independently of the Convention, the Convention applies

only to treaties which are concluded by States after the entry into force of the present Convention with regard to such States.

Article 5. Treaties constituting international organizations and treaties adopted within an international organization
The present Convention applies to any treaty which is the constituent instrument of an international organization and to any treaty adopted within an international organization without prejudice to any relevant rules of the organization.

PART II. CONCLUSION AND ENTRY INTO FORCE OF TREATIES X

SECTION 1. CONCLUSION OF TREATIES

Article 6. Capacity of States to conclude treaties
Every State possesses capacity to conclude treaties.

Article 7. Full powers
1. A person is considered as representing a State for the purpose of adopting or authenticating the text of a treaty or for the purpose of expressing the consent of the State to be bound by a treaty if:
   (a) he produces appropriate full powers; or
   (b) it appears from the practice of the States concerned or from other circumstances that their intention was to consider that person as representing the State for such purposes and to dispense with full powers.
2. In virtue of their functions and without having to produce full powers, the following are considered as representing their State:
   (a) Heads of State, Heads of Government and Ministers for Foreign Affairs, for the purpose of performing all acts relating to the conclusion of a treaty;
   (b) heads of diplomatic missions, for the purpose of adopting the text of a treaty between the accrediting State and the State to which they are accredited;
   (c) representatives accredited by States to an international conference or to an international organization or one of its organs, for the purpose of adopting the text of a treaty in that conference, organization or organ.

Article 8. Subsequent confirmation of an act performed without authorization
An act relating to the conclusion of a treaty performed by a person who cannot be considered under article 7 as authorized to represent a State for that purpose is without legal effect unless afterwards confirmed by that State.

Article 9. Adoption of the text
1. The adoption of the text of a treaty takes place by the consent of all the States participating in its drawing up except as provided in paragraph 2.
2. The adoption of the text of a treaty at an international conference takes place by the vote of two thirds of the States present and voting, unless by the same majority they shall decide to apply a different rule.

Article 10. Authentication of the text
The text of a treaty is established as authentic and definitive:
   (a) by such procedure as may be provided for in the text or agreed upon by the States participating in its drawing up; or

(b) failing such procedure, by the signature, signature ad referendum or initialling by the representatives of those States of the text of the treaty or of the Final Act of a conference incorporating the text.

Article 11. Means of expressing consent to be bound by a treaty
The consent of a State to be bound by a treaty may be expressed by signature, exchange of instruments constituting a treaty, ratification, acceptance, approval or accession, or by any other means if so agreed.

Article 12. Consent to be bound by a treaty expressed by signature
1. The consent of a State to be bound by a treaty is expressed by the signature of its representative when:
   (a) the treaty provides that signature shall have that effect;
   (b) it is otherwise established that the negotiating States were agreed that signature should have that effect; or
   (c) the intention of the State to give that effect to the signature appears from the full powers of its representative or was expressed during the negotiation.
2. For the purposes of paragraph 1:
   (a) the initialling of a text constitutes a signature of the treaty when it is established that the negotiating States so agreed;
   (b) the signature ad referendum of a treaty by a representative, if confirmed by his State, constitutes a full signature of the treaty.

Article 13. Consent to be bound by a treaty expressed by an exchange of instruments constituting a treaty
The consent of States to be bound by a treaty constituted by instruments exchanged between them is expressed by that exchange when:
   (a) the instruments provide that their exchange shall have that effect; or
   (b) it is otherwise established that those States were agreed that the exchange of instruments should have that effect.

Article 14. Consent to be bound by a treaty expressed by ratification, acceptance or approval
1. The consent of a State to be bound by a treaty is expressed by ratification when:
   (a) the treaty provides for such consent to be expressed by means of ratification;
   (b) it is otherwise established that the negotiating States were agreed that ratification should be required;
   (c) the representative of the State has signed the treaty subject to ratification; or
   (d) the intention of the State to sign the treaty subject to ratification appears from the full powers of its representative or was expressed during the negotiation.
2. The consent of a State to be bound by a treaty is expressed by acceptance or approval under conditions similar to those which apply to ratification.

Article 15. Consent to be bound by a treaty expressed by accession
The consent of a State to be bound by a treaty is expressed by accession when:
   (a) the treaty provides that such consent may be expressed by that State by means of accession;
   (b) it is otherwise established that the negotiating States were agreed that such consent may be expressed by that State by means of accession; or
   (c) all the parties have subsequently agreed that such consent may be expressed by that State by means of accession.

Article 16. Exchange or deposit of instruments of ratification, acceptance, approval or accession
Unless the treaty otherwise provides, instruments of ratification, acceptance, approval or accession establish the consent of a State to be bound by a treaty upon:

(a) their exchange between the contracting States;
(b) their deposit with the depositary; or
(c) their notification to the contracting States or to the depositary, if so agreed.

Article 17. Consent to be bound by part of a treaty and choice of differing provisions
1. Without prejudice to articles 19 to 23, the consent of a State to be bound by part of a treaty is effective only if the treaty so permits or the other contracting States so agree.
2. The consent of a State to be bound by a treaty which permits a choice between differing provisions is effective only if it is made clear to which of the provisions the consent relates.

Article 18. Obligation not to defeat the object and purpose of a treaty prior to its entry into force
A State is obliged to refrain from acts which would defeat the object and purpose of a treaty when:

(a) it has signed the treaty or has exchanged instruments constituting the treaty subject to ratification, acceptance or approval, until it shall have made its intention clear not to become a party to the treaty; or
(b) it has expressed its consent to be bound by the treaty, pending the entry into force of the treaty and provided that such entry into force is not unduly delayed.

SECTION 2. RESERVATIONS

Article 19. Formulation of reservations
A State may, when signing, ratifying, accepting, approving or acceding to a treaty, formulate a reservation unless:

(a) the reservation is prohibited by the treaty;
(b) the treaty provides that only specified reservations, which do not include the reservation in question, may be made; or
(c) in cases not failing under subparagraphs (a) and (b), the reservation is incompatible with the object and purpose of the treaty.

Article 20. Acceptance of and objection to reservations
1. A reservation expressly authorized by a treaty does not require any subsequent acceptance by the other contracting States unless the treaty so provides.
2. When it appears from the limited number of the negotiating States and the object and purpose of a treaty that the application of the treaty in its entirety between all the parties is an essential condition of the consent of each one to be bound by the treaty, a reservation requires acceptance by all the parties.
3. When a treaty is a constituent instrument of an international organization and unless it otherwise provides, a reservation requires the acceptance of the competent organ of that organization.
4. In cases not falling under the preceding paragraphs and unless the treaty otherwise provides:

(a) acceptance by another contracting State of a reservation constitutes the reserving State a party to the treaty in relation to that other State if or when the treaty is in force for those States;
(b) an objection by another contracting State to a reservation does not preclude the entry into force of the treaty as between the objecting and reserving States unless a contrary intention is definitely expressed by the objecting State;
(c) an act expressing a State's consent to be bound by the treaty and containing a reservation is effective as soon as at least one other contracting State has accepted the reservation.

5. For the purposes of paragraphs 2 and 4 and unless the treaty otherwise provides, a reservation is considered to have been accepted by a State if it shall have raised no objection to the reservation by the end of a period of twelve months after it was notified of the reservation or by the date on which it expressed its consent to be bound by the treaty, whichever is later.

Article 21. Legal effects of reservations and of objections to reservations

1. A reservation established with regard to another party in accordance with articles 19, 20 and 23:
   (a) modifies for the reserving State in its relations with that other party the provisions of the treaty to which the reservation relates to the extent of the reservation; and
   (b) modifies those provisions to the same extent for that other party in its relations with the reserving State.
2. The reservation does not modify the provisions of the treaty for the other parties to the treaty inter se.
3. When a State objecting to a reservation has not opposed the entry into force of the treaty between itself and the reserving State, the provisions to which the reservation relates do not apply as between the two States to the extent of the reservation.

Article 22. Withdrawal of reservations and of objections to reservations

1. Unless the treaty otherwise provides, a reservation may be withdrawn at any time and the consent of a State which has accepted the reservation is not required for its withdrawal.
2. Unless the treaty otherwise provides, an objection to a reservation may be withdrawn at any time.
3. Unless the treaty otherwise provides, or it is otherwise agreed:
   (a) the withdrawal of a reservation becomes operative in relation to another contracting State only when notice of it has been received by that State;
   (b) the withdrawal of an objection to a reservation becomes operative only when notice of it has been received by the State which formulated the reservation.

Article 23. Procedure regarding reservations

1. A reservation, an express acceptance of a reservation and an objection to a reservation must be formulated in writing and communicated to the contracting States and other States entitled to become parties to the treaty.
2. If formulated when signing the treaty subject to ratification, acceptance or approval, a reservation must be formally confirmed by the reserving State when expressing its consent to be bound by the treaty. In such a case the reservation shall be considered as having been made on the date of its confirmation.
3. An express acceptance of, or an objection to, a reservation made previously to confirmation of the reservation does not itself require confirmation.
4. The withdrawal of a reservation or of an objection to a reservation must be formulated in writing.

SECTION 3. ENTRY INTO FORCE AND PROVISIONAL, APPLICATION OF TREATIES

Article 24. Entry into force

1. A treaty enters into force in such manner and upon such date as it may provide or as the negotiating States may agree.
2. Failing any such provision or agreement, a treaty enters into force as soon as consent to be bound by the treaty has been established for all the negotiating States.
3. When the consent of a State to be bound by a treaty is established on a date after the treaty has come into force, the treaty enters into force for that State on that date, unless the treaty otherwise provides.

4. The provisions of a treaty regulating the authentication of its text, the establishment of the consent of States to be bound by the treaty, the manner or date of its entry into force, reservations, the functions of the depositary and other matters arising necessarily before the entry into force of the treaty apply from the time of the adoption of its text.

Article 25. Provisional application

1. A treaty or a part of a treaty is applied provisionally pending its entry into force if:
   (a) the treaty itself so provides; or
   (b) the negotiating States have in some other manner so agreed.
2. Unless the treaty otherwise provides or the negotiating States have otherwise agreed, the provisional application of a treaty or a part of a treaty with respect to a State shall be terminated if that State notifies the other States between which the treaty is being applied provisionally of its intention not to become a party to the treaty.

PART III. OBSERVANCE, APPLICATION AND INTERPRETATION OF TREATIES

SECTION 1. OBSERVANCE OF TREATIES

Article 26. "Pacta sunt servanda"

Every treaty in force is binding upon the parties to it and must be performed by them in good faith.

Article 27. Internal law and observance of treaties

A party may not invoke the provisions of its internal law as justification for its failure to perform a treaty. This rule is without prejudice to article 46.

SECTION 2. APPLICATION OF TREATIES

Article 28. Non-retroactivity of treaties

Unless a different intention appears from the treaty or is otherwise established, its provisions do not bind a party in relation to any act or fact which took place or any situation which ceased to exist before the date of the entry into force of the treaty with respect to that party.

Article 29. Territorial scope of treaties

Unless a different intention appears from the treaty or is otherwise established, a treaty is binding upon each party in respect of its entire territory.

Article 30. Application of successive treaties relating to the same subject matter

1. Subject to Article 103 of the Charter of the United Nations, the rights and obligations of States Parties to successive treaties relating to the same subject matter shall be determined in accordance with the following paragraphs.
2. When a treaty specifies that it is subject to, or that it is not to be considered as incompatible with, an earlier or later treaty, the provisions of that other treaty prevail.
3. When all the parties to the earlier treaty are parties also to the later treaty but the earlier treaty is not terminated or suspended in operation under article 59, the earlier treaty applies only to the extent that its provisions are compatible with those of the later treaty.
4. When the parties to the later treaty do not include all the parties to the earlier one:
   (a) as between States Parties to both treaties the same rule applies as in paragraph 3;
   (b) as between a State party to both treaties and a State party to only one of the treaties, the treaty to which both States are parties governs their mutual rights and obligations.

5. Paragraph 4 is without prejudice to article 41, or to any question of the termination or suspension of the operation of a treaty under article 60 or to any question of responsibility which may arise for a State from the conclusion or application of a treaty the provisions of which are incompatible with its obligations towards another State under another treaty.

SECTION 3. INTERPRETATION OF TREATIES

Article 31. General rule of interpretation

1. A treaty shall be interpreted in good faith in accordance with the ordinary meaning to be given to the terms of the treaty in their context and in the light of its object and purpose.
2. The context for the purpose of the interpretation of a treaty shall comprise, in addition to the text, including its preamble and annexes:
   (a) any agreement relating to the treaty which was made between all the parties in connection with the conclusion of the treaty;
   (b) any instrument which was made by one or more parties in connection with the conclusion of the treaty and accepted by the other parties as an instrument related to the treaty.
3. There shall be taken into account, together with the context:
   (a) any subsequent agreement between the parties regarding the interpretation of the treaty or the application of its provisions;
   (b) any subsequent practice in the application of the treaty which establishes the agreement of the parties regarding its interpretation;
   (c) any relevant rules of international law applicable in the relations between the parties.
4. A special meaning shall be given to a term if it is established that the parties so intended.

Article 32. Supplementary means of interpretation

Recourse may be had to supplementary means of interpretation, including the preparatory work of the treaty and the circumstances of its conclusion, in order to confirm the meaning resulting from the application of article 31, or to determine the meaning when the interpretation according to article 31:
   (a) leaves the meaning ambiguous or obscure; or
   (b) leads to a result which is manifestly absurd or unreasonable.

Article 33. Interpretation of treaties authenticated in two or more languages

1. When a treaty has been authenticated in two or more languages, the text is equally authoritative in each language, unless the treaty provides or the parties agree that, in case of divergence, a particular text shall prevail.
2. A version of the treaty in a language other than one of those in which the text was authenticated shall be considered an authentic text only if the treaty so provides or the parties so agree.
3. The terms of the treaty are presumed to have the same meaning in each authentic text.
4. Except where a particular text prevails in accordance with paragraph 1, when a comparison of the authentic texts discloses a difference of meaning which the application of articles 31 and 32 does not remove, the meaning which best reconciles the texts, having regard to the object and purpose of the treaty, shall be adopted.

SECTION 4. TREATIES AND THIRD STATES

Article 34. General rule regarding third States

A treaty does not create either obligations or rights for a third State without its consent.

Article 35. Treaties providing for obligations for third States
An obligation arises for a third State from a provision of a treaty if the parties to the treaty intend the provision to be the means of establishing the obligation and the third State expressly accepts that obligation in writing.

Article 36. Treaties providing for rights for third States
1. A right arises for a third State from a provision of a treaty if the parties to the treaty intend the provision to accord that right either to the third State, or to a group of States to which it belongs, or to all States, and the third State assents thereto. Its assent shall be presumed so long as the contrary is not indicated, unless the treaty otherwise provides.
2. A State exercising a right in accordance with paragraph 1 shall comply with the conditions for its exercise provided for in the treaty or established in conformity with the treaty.

Article 37. Revocation or modification of obligations or rights of third States
1. When an obligation has arisen for a third State in conformity with article 35, the obligation may be revoked or modified only with the consent of the parties to the treaty and of the third State, unless it is established that they had otherwise agreed.
2. When a right has arisen for a third State in conformity with article 36, the right may not be revoked or modified by the parties if it is established that the right was intended not to be revocable or subject to modification without the consent of the third State.

Article 38. Rules in a treaty becoming binding on third States through international custom
Nothing in articles 34 to 37 precludes a rule set forth in a treaty from becoming binding upon a third State as a customary rule of international law, recognized as such.

PART IV. AMENDMENT AND MODIFICATION OF TREATIES

Article 39. General rule regarding the amendment of treaties
A treaty may be amended by agreement between the parties. The rules laid down in Part II apply to such an agreement except insofar as the treaty may otherwise provide.

Article 40. Amendment of multilateral treaties
1. Unless the treaty otherwise provides, the amendment of multilateral treaties shall be governed by the following paragraphs.
2. Any proposal to amend a multilateral treaty as between all the parties must be notified to all the contracting States, each one of which shall have the right to take part in:
   (a) the decision as to the action to be taken in regard to such proposal;
   (b) the negotiation and conclusion of any agreement for the amendment of the treaty.
3. Every State entitled to become a party to the treaty shall also be entitled to become a party to the treaty as amended.
4. The amending agreement does not bind any State already a party to the treaty which does not become a party to the amending agreement; article 30, paragraph 4 (b), applies in relation to such State.
5. Any State which becomes a party to the treaty after the entry into force of the amending agreement shall, failing an expression of a different intention by that State:
   (a) be considered as a party to the treaty as amended; and
   (b) be considered as a party to the unamended treaty in relation to any party to the treaty not bound by the amending agreement.

Article 41. Agreements to modify multilateral treaties between certain of the parties only
1. Two or more of the parties to a multilateral treaty may conclude an agreement to modify the treaty as between themselves alone if:
(a) the possibility of such a modification is provided for by the treaty; or
(b) the modification in question is not prohibited by the treaty and:
(i) does not affect the enjoyment by the other parties of their rights under the treaty or the performance of their obligations;
(ii) does not relate to a provision, derogation from which is incompatible with the effective execution of the object and purpose of the treaty as a whole.
2. Unless in a case falling under paragraph 1 (a) the treaty otherwise provides, the parties in question shall notify the other parties of their intention to conclude the agreement and of the modification to the treaty for which it provides.

PART V. INVALIDITY, TERMINATION AND SUSPENSION OF THE OPERATION OF TREATIES

SECTION 1. GENERAL PROVISIONS

Article 42. Validity and continuance in force of treaties
1. The validity of a treaty or of the consent of a State to be bound by a treaty may be impeached only through the application of the present Convention.
2. The termination of a treaty, its denunciation or the withdrawal of a party, may take place only as a result of the application of the provisions of the treaty or of the present Convention. The same rule applies to suspension of the operation of a treaty.

Article 43. Obligations imposed by international law independently of a treaty
The invalidity, termination or denunciation of a treaty, the withdrawal of a party from it, or the suspension of its operation, as a result of the application of the present Convention or of the provisions of the treaty, shall not in any way impair the duty of any State to fulfil any obligation embodied in the treaty to which it would be subject under international law independently of the treaty.

Article 44. Separability of treaty provisions
1. A right of a party, provided for in a treaty or arising under article 56, to denounce, withdraw from or suspend the operation of the treaty may be exercised only with respect to the whole treaty unless the treaty otherwise provides or the parties otherwise agree.
2. A ground for invalidating, terminating, withdrawing from or suspending the operation of a treaty recognized in the present Convention may be invoked only with respect to the whole treaty except as provided in the following paragraphs or in article 60.
3. If the ground relates solely to particular clauses, it may be invoked only with respect to those clauses where:
(a) the said clauses are separable from the remainder of the treaty with regard to their application;
(b) it appears from the treaty or is otherwise established that acceptance of those clauses was not an essential basis of the consent of the other party or parties to be bound by the treaty as a whole; and
(c) continued performance of the remainder of the treaty would not be unjust.
4. In cases falling under articles 49 and 50, the State entitled to invoke the fraud or corruption may do so with respect either to the whole treaty or, subject to paragraph 3, to the particular clauses alone.
5. In cases falling under articles 51, 52 and 53, no separation of the provisions of the treaty is permitted.

Article 45. Loss of a right to invoke a ground for invalidating, terminating, withdrawing from or suspending the operation of a treaty
A State may no longer invoke a ground for invalidating, terminating, withdrawing from or suspending the operation of a treaty under articles 46 to 50 or articles 60 and 62 if, after becoming aware of the facts:

(a) it shall have expressly agreed that the treaty is valid or remains in force or continues in operation, as the case may be; or

(b) it must by reason of its conduct be considered as having acquiesced in the validity of the treaty or in its maintenance in force or in operation, as the case may be.

SECTION 2. INVALIDITY OF TREATIES

Article 46. Provisions of internal law regarding competence to conclude treaties
1. A State may not invoke the fact that its consent to be bound by a treaty has been expressed in violation of a provision of its internal law regarding competence to conclude treaties as invalidating its consent unless that violation was manifest and concerned a rule of its internal law of fundamental importance.
2. A violation is manifest if it would be objectively evident to any State conducting itself in the matter in accordance with normal practice and in good faith.

Article 47. Specific restrictions on authority to express the consent of a State
If the authority of a representative to express the consent of a State to be bound by a particular treaty has been made subject to a specific restriction, his omission to observe that restriction may not be invoked as invalidating the consent expressed by him unless the restriction was notified to the other negotiating States prior to his expressing such consent.

Article 48. Error
1. A State may invoke an error in a treaty as invalidating its consent to be bound by the treaty if the error relates to a fact or situation which was assumed by that State to exist at the time when the treaty was concluded and formed an essential basis of its consent to be bound by the treaty.
2. Paragraph 1 shall not apply if the State in question contributed by its own conduct to the error or if the circumstances were such as to put that State on notice of a possible error.
3. An error relating only to the wording of the text of a treaty does not affect its validity; article 79 then applies.

Article 49. Fraud
If a State has been induced to conclude a treaty by the fraudulent conduct of another negotiating State, the State may invoke the fraud as invalidating its consent to be bound by the treaty.

Article 50. Corruption of a representative of a State
If the expression of a State's consent to be bound by a treaty has been procured through the corruption of its representative directly or indirectly by another negotiating State, the State may invoke such corruption as invalidating its consent to be bound by the treaty.

Article 51. Coercion of a representative of a State
The expression of a State's consent to be bound by a treaty which has been procured by the coercion of its representative through acts or threats directed against him shall be without any legal effect.

Article 52. Coercion of a State by the threat or use of force
A treaty is void if its conclusion has been procured by the threat or use of force in violation of the principles of international law embodied in the Charter of the United Nations.

Article 53. Treaties conflicting with a peremptory norm of general international law ("jus cogens")
A treaty is void if, at the time of its conclusion, it conflicts with a peremptory norm of general international law. For the purposes of the present Convention, a peremptory norm of general international law is a norm accepted and recognized by the international community of States as a whole as a norm from which no derogation is permitted and which can be modified only by a subsequent norm of general international law having the same character.

SECTION 3. TERMINATION AND SUSPENSION OF THE OPERATION OF TREATIES

Article 54. Termination of or withdrawal from a treaty under its provisions or by consent of the parties
The termination of a treaty or the withdrawal of a party may take place:
(a) in conformity with the provisions of the treaty; or
(b) at any time by consent of all the parties after consultation with the other contracting States.

Article 55. Reduction of the parties to a multilateral treaty below the number necessary for its entry into force
Unless the treaty otherwise provides, a multilateral treaty does not terminate by reason only of the fact that the number of the parties falls below the number necessary for its entry into force.

Article 56. Denunciation of or withdrawal from a treaty containing no provision regarding termination, denunciation or withdrawal
1. A treaty which contains no provision regarding its termination and which does not provide for denunciation or withdrawal is not subject to denunciation or withdrawal unless:
(a) it is established that the parties intended to admit the possibility of denunciation or withdrawal; or
(b) a right of denunciation or withdrawal may be implied by the nature of the treaty.
2. A party shall give not less than twelve months' notice of its intention to denounce or withdraw from a treaty under paragraph 1.

Article 57. Suspension of the operation of a treaty under its provisions or by consent of the parties
The operation of a treaty in regard to all the parties or to a particular party may be suspended:
(a) in conformity with the provisions of the treaty; or
(b) at any time by consent of all the parties after consultation with the other contracting States.

Article 58. Suspension of the operation of a multilateral treaty by agreement between certain of the parties only
1. Two or more parties to a multilateral treaty may conclude an agreement to suspend the operation of provisions of the treaty, temporarily and as between themselves alone, if:
(a) the possibility of such a suspension is provided for by the treaty; or
(b) the suspension in question is not prohibited by the treaty and:
(i) does not affect the enjoyment by the other parties of their rights under the treaty or the performance of their obligations;
(ii) is not incompatible with the object and purpose of the treaty.

2. Unless in a case falling under paragraph 1 (a) the treaty otherwise provides, the parties in question shall notify the other parties of their intention to conclude the agreement and of those provisions of the treaty the operation of which they intend to suspend.

Article 59. Termination or suspension of the operation of a treaty implied by conclusion of a later treaty

1. A treaty shall be considered as terminated if all the parties to it conclude a later treaty relating to the same subject matter and:

(a) it appears from the later treaty or is otherwise established that the parties intended that the matter should be governed by that treaty; or

(b) the provisions of the later treaty are so far incompatible with those of the earlier one that the two treaties are not capable of being applied at the same time.

2. The earlier treaty shall be considered as only suspended in operation if it appears from the later treaty or is otherwise established that such was the intention of the parties.

Article 60. Termination or suspension of the operation of a treaty as a consequence of its breach

1. A material breach of a bilateral treaty by one of the parties entitles the other to invoke the breach as a ground for terminating the treaty or suspending its operation in whole or in part.

2. A material breach of a multilateral treaty by one of the parties entitles:

(a) the other parties by unanimous agreement to suspend the operation of the treaty in whole or in part or to terminate it either:

(i) in the relations between themselves and the defaulting State; or

(ii) as between all the parties;

(b) a party specially affected by the breach to invoke it as a ground for suspending the operation of the treaty in whole or in part in the relations between itself and the defaulting State;

(c) any party other than the defaulting State to invoke the breach as a ground for suspending the operation of the treaty in whole or in part with respect to itself if the treaty is of such a character that a material breach of its provisions by one party radically changes the position of every party with respect to the further performance of its obligations under the treaty.

3. A material breach of a treaty, for the purposes of this article, consists in:

(a) a repudiation of the treaty not sanctioned by the present Convention; or

(b) the violation of a provision essential to the accomplishment of the object or purpose of the treaty.

4. The foregoing paragraphs are without prejudice to any provision in the treaty applicable in the event of a breach.

5. Paragraphs 1 to 3 do not apply to provisions relating to the protection of the human person contained in treaties of a humanitarian character, in particular to provisions prohibiting any form of reprisals against persons protected by such treaties.

Article 61. Supervening impossibility of performance

1. A party may invoke the impossibility of performing a treaty as a ground for terminating or withdrawing from it if the impossibility results from the permanent disappearance or destruction of an object indispensable for the execution of the treaty. If the impossibility is temporary, it may be invoked only as a ground for suspending the operation of the treaty.

2. Impossibility of performance may not be invoked by a party as a ground for terminating, withdrawing from or suspending the operation of a treaty if the impossibility is the result of a breach by that party either of an obligation under the treaty or of any other international obligation owed to any other party to the treaty.

Article 62. Fundamental change of circumstances
1. A fundamental change of circumstances which has occurred with regard to those existing at the time of the conclusion of a treaty, and which was not foreseen by the parties, may not be invoked as a ground for terminating or withdrawing from the treaty unless:
   (a) the existence of those circumstances constituted an essential basis of the consent of the parties to be bound by the treaty; and
   (b) the effect of the change is radically to transform the extent of obligations still to be performed under the treaty.
2. A fundamental change of circumstances may not be invoked as a ground for terminating or withdrawing from a treaty:
   (a) if the treaty establishes a boundary; or
   (b) if the fundamental change is the result of a breach by the party invoking it either of an obligation under the treaty or of any other international obligation owed to any other party to the treaty.
3. If, under the foregoing paragraphs, a party may invoke a fundamental change of circumstances as a ground for terminating or withdrawing from a treaty it may also invoke the change as a ground for suspending the operation of the treaty.

Article 63. Severance of diplomatic or consular relations
The severance of diplomatic or consular relations between parties to a treaty does not affect the legal relations established between them by the treaty except insofar as the existence of diplomatic or consular relations is indispensable for the application of the treaty.

Article 64. Emergence of a new peremptory norm of general international law ("jus cogens")
If a new peremptory norm of general international law emerges, any existing treaty which is in conflict with that norm becomes void and terminates.

SECTION 4. PROCEDURE

Article 65. Procedure to be followed with respect to invalidity, termination, withdrawal from or suspension of the operation of a treaty
1. A party which, under the provisions of the present Convention, invokes either a defect in its consent to be bound by a treaty or a ground for impeaching the validity of a treaty, terminating it, withdrawing from it or suspending its operation, must notify the other parties of its claim. The notification shall indicate the measure proposed to be taken with respect to the treaty and the reasons therefor.
2. If, after the expiry of a period which, except in cases of special urgency, shall not be less than three months after the receipt of the notification, no party has raised any objection, the party making the notification may carry out in the manner provided in article 67 the measure which it has proposed.
3. If, however, objection has been raised by any other party, the parties shall seek a solution through the means indicated in Article 33 of the Charter of the United Nations.
4. Nothing in the foregoing paragraphs shall affect the rights or obligations of the parties under any provisions in force binding the parties with regard to the settlement of disputes.
5. Without prejudice to article 45, the fact that a State has not previously made the notification prescribed in paragraph 1 shall not prevent it from making such notification in answer to another party claiming performance of the treaty or alleging its violation.

Article 66. Procedures for judicial settlement, arbitration and conciliation
If, under paragraph 3 of article 65, no solution has been reached within a period of 12 months following the date on which the objection was raised, the following procedures shall be followed:

(a) any one of the parties to a dispute concerning the application or the interpretation of article 53 or 64 may, by a written application, submit it to the International Court of Justice for a decision unless the parties by common consent agree to submit the dispute to arbitration;

(b) any one of the parties to a dispute concerning the application or the interpretation of any of the other articles in part V of the present Convention may set in motion the procedure specified in the Annex to the Convention by submitting a request to that effect to the Secretary-General of the United Nations.

Article 67. Instruments for declaring invalid, terminating, withdrawing from or suspending the operation of a treaty

1. The notification provided for under article 65, paragraph 1, must be made in writing.

2. Any act of declaring invalid, terminating, withdrawing from or suspending the operation of a treaty pursuant to the provisions of the treaty or of paragraphs 2 or 3 of article 65 shall be carried out through an instrument communicated to the other parties. If the instrument is not signed by the Head of State, Head of Government or Minister for Foreign Affairs, the representative of the State communicating it may be called upon to produce full powers.

Article 68. Revocation of notifications and instruments provided for in articles 65 and 67

A notification or instrument provided for in article 65 or 67 may be revoked at any time before it takes effect.

SECTION 5. CONSEQUENCES OF THE INVALIDITY, TERMINATION OR SUSPENSION OF THE OPERATION OF A TREATY

Article 69. Consequences of the invalidity of a treaty

1. A treaty the invalidity of which is established under the present Convention is void. The provisions of a void treaty have no legal force.

2. If acts have nevertheless been performed in reliance on such a treaty:

(a) each party may require any other party to establish as far as possible in their mutual relations the position that would have existed if the acts had not been performed;

(b) acts performed in good faith before the invalidity was invoked are not rendered unlawful by reason only of the invalidity of the treaty.

3. In cases falling under article 49, 50, 51 or 52, paragraph 2 does not apply with respect to the party to which the fraud, the act of corruption or the coercion is imputable.

4. In the case of the invalidity of a particular State's consent to be bound by a multilateral treaty, the foregoing rules apply in the relations between that State and the parties to the treaty.

Article 70. Consequences of the termination of a treaty

1. Unless the treaty otherwise provides or the parties otherwise agree, the termination of a treaty under its provisions or in accordance with the present Convention:

(a) releases the parties from any obligation further to perform the treaty;

(b) does not affect any right, obligation or legal situation of the parties created through the execution of the treaty prior to its termination.

2. If a State denounces or withdraws from a multilateral treaty, paragraph 1 applies in the relations between that State and each of the other parties to the treaty from the date when such denunciation or withdrawal takes effect.

Article 71. Consequences of the invalidity of a treaty which conflicts with a peremptory norm of general international law

1. In the case of a treaty which is void under article 53 the parties shall:
   (a) eliminate as far as possible the consequences of any act performed in reliance on any provision which conflicts with the peremptory norm of general international law; and
   (b) bring their mutual relations into conformity with the peremptory norm of general international law.
2. In the case of a treaty which becomes void and terminates under article 64, the termination of the treaty:
   (a) releases the parties from any obligation further to perform the treaty;
   (b) does not affect any right, obligation or legal situation of the parties created through the execution of the treaty prior to its termination, provided that those rights, obligations or situations may thereafter be maintained only to the extent that their maintenance is not in itself in conflict with the new peremptory norm of general international law.

Article 72. Consequences of the suspension of the operation of a treaty

1. Unless the treaty otherwise provides or the parties otherwise agree, the suspension of the operation of a treaty under its provisions or in accordance with the present Convention:
   (a) releases the parties between which the operation of the treaty is suspended from the obligation to perform the treaty in their mutual relations during the period of the suspension;
   (b) does not otherwise affect the legal relations between the parties established by the treaty.
2. During the period of the suspension the parties shall refrain from acts tending to obstruct the resumption of the operation of the treaty.

PART VI. MISCELLANEOUS PROVISIONS

Article 73. Cases of State succession, State responsibility and outbreak of hostilities

The provisions of the present Convention shall not prejudge any question that may arise in regard to a treaty from a succession of States or from the international responsibility of a State or from the outbreak of hostilities between States.

Article 74. Diplomatic and consular relations and the conclusion of treaties

The severance or absence of diplomatic or consular relations between two or more States does not prevent the conclusion of treaties between those States. The conclusion of a treaty does not in itself affect the situation in regard to diplomatic or consular relations.

Article 75. Case of an aggressor State

The provisions of the present Convention are without prejudice to any obligation in relation to a treaty which may arise for an aggressor State in consequence of measures taken in conformity with the Charter of the United Nations with reference to that State's aggression.

PART VII. DEPOSITARIES, NOTIFICATIONS, CORRECTIONS AND REGISTRATION

Article 76. Depositaries of treaties

1. The designation of the depositary of a treaty may be made by the negotiating States, either in the treaty itself or in some other manner. The depositary may be one or more States, an international organization or the chief administrative officer of the organization.
2. The functions of the depositary of a treaty are international in character and the depositary is under an obligation to act impartially in their performance. In particular, the fact that a treaty has not

entered into force between certain of the parties or that a difference has appeared between a State and a depositary with regard to the performance of the latter's functions shall not affect that obligation.

Article 77. Functions of depositaries

1. The functions of a depositary, unless otherwise provided in the treaty or agreed by the contracting States, comprise in particular:
   (a) keeping custody of the original text of the treaty and of any full powers delivered to the depositary;
   (b) preparing certified copies of the original text and preparing any further text of the treaty in such additional languages as may be required by the treaty and transmitting them to the parties and to the States entitled to become parties to the treaty;
   (c) receiving any signatures to the treaty and receiving and keeping custody of any instruments, notifications and communications relating to it;
   (d) examining whether the signature or any instrument, notification or communication relating to the treaty is in due and proper form and, if need be, bringing the matter to the attention of the State in question;
   (e) informing the parties and the States entitled to become parties to the treaty of acts, notifications and communications relating to the treaty;
   (f) informing the States entitled to become parties to the treaty when the number of signatures or of instruments of ratification, acceptance, approval or accession required for the entry into force of the treaty has been received or deposited;
   (g) registering the treaty with the Secretariat of the United Nations;
   (h) performing the functions specified in other provisions of the present Convention.
2. In the event of any difference appearing between a State and the depositary as to the performance of the latter's functions, the depositary shall bring the question to the attention of the signatory States and the contracting States or, where appropriate, of the competent organ of the international organization concerned.

Article 78. Notifications and communications

Except as the treaty or the present Convention otherwise provide, any notification or communication to be made by any State under the present Convention shall:
   (a) if there is no depositary, be transmitted direct to the States for which it is intended, or if there is a depositary, to the latter;
   (b) be considered as having been made by the State in question only upon its receipt by the State to which it was transmitted or, as the case may be, upon its receipt by the depositary;
   (c) if transmitted to a depositary, be considered as received by the State for which it was intended only when the latter State has been informed by the depositary in accordance with article 77, paragraph 1 (e).

Article 79. Correction of errors in texts or in certified copies of treaties

1. Where, after the authentication of the text of a treaty, the signatory States and the contracting States are agreed that it contains an error, the error shall, unless they decide upon some other means of correction, be corrected:
   (a) by having the appropriate correction made in the text and causing the correction to be initialled by duly authorized representatives;
   (b) by executing or exchanging an instrument or instruments setting out the correction which it has been agreed to make; or
   (c) by executing a corrected text of the whole treaty by the same procedure as in the case of the original text.

2. Where the treaty is one for which there is a depositary, the latter shall notify the signatory States and the contracting States of the error and of the proposal to correct it and shall specify an appropriate time-limit within which objection to the proposed correction may be raised. If, on the expiry of the time-limit:

(a) no objection has been raised, the depositary shall make and initial the correction in the text and shall execute a procès-verbal of the rectification of the text and communicate a copy of it to the parties and to the States entitled to become parties to the treaty;

(b) an objection has been raised, the depositary shall communicate the objection to the signatory States and to the contracting States.

3. The rules in paragraphs I and 2 apply also where the text has been authenticated in two or more languages and it appears that there is a lack of concordance which the signatory States and the contracting States agree should be corrected.

4. The corrected text replaces the defective text ab initio, unless the signatory States and the contracting States otherwise decide.

5. The correction of the text of a treaty that has been registered shall be notified to the Secretariat of the United Nations.

6. Where an error is discovered in a certified copy of a treaty, the depositary shall execute a procès-verbal specifying the rectification and communicate a copy of it to the signatory States and to the contracting States.

Article 80. Registration and publication of treaties

1. Treaties shall, after their entry into force, be transmitted to the Secretariat of the United Nations for registration or filing and recording, as the case may be, and for publication.

2. The designation of a depositary shall constitute authorization for it to perform the acts specified in the preceding paragraph.

PART VIII. FINAL PROVISIONS

Article 81. Signature

The present Convention shall be open for signature by all States Members of the United Nations or of any of the specialized agencies or of the International Atomic Energy Agency or parties to the Statute of the International Court of Justice, and by any other State invited by the General Assembly of the United Nations to become a party to the Convention, as follows: until 30 November 1969, at the Federal Ministry for Foreign Affairs of the Republic of Austria, and subsequently, until 30 April 1970, at United Nations Headquarters, New York.

Article 82. Ratification

The present Convention is subject to ratification. The instruments of ratification shall be deposited with the Secretary-General of the United Nations.

Article 83. Accession

The present Convention shall remain open for accession by any State belonging to any of the categories mentioned in article 81. The instruments of accession shall be deposited with the Secretary- General of the United Nations.

Article 84. Entry into force

1. The present Convention shall enter into force on the thirtieth day following the date of deposit of the thirty-fifth instrument of ratification or accession.

2. For each State ratifying or acceding to the Convention after the deposit of the thirty-fifth instrument of ratification or accession, the Convention shall enter into force on the thirtieth day after deposit by such State of its instrument of ratification or accession.

Article 85. Authentic texts
The original of the present Convention, of which the Chinese, English, French, Russian and Spanish texts are equally authentic, shall be deposited with the Secretary-General of the United Nations.

IN WITNESS WHEREOF the undersigned Plenipotentiaries, being duly authorized thereto by their respective Governments, have signed the present Convention.

DONE at Vienna this twenty-third day of May, one thousand nine hundred and sixty-nine.

ANNEX

1. A list of conciliators consisting of qualified jurists shall be drawn up and maintained by the Secretary-General of the United Nations. To this end, every State which is a Member of the United Nations or a party to the present Convention shall be invited to nominate two conciliators, and the names of the persons so nominated shall constitute the list. The term of a conciliator, including that of any conciliator nominated to fill a casual vacancy, shall be five years and may be renewed. A conciliator whose term expires shall continue to fulfil any function for which he shall have been chosen under the following paragraph.
2. When a request has been made to the Secretary-General under article 66, the Secretary-General shall bring the dispute before a conciliation commission constituted as follows:

The State or States constituting one of the parties to the dispute shall appoint:

(a) one conciliator of the nationality of that State or of one of those States, who may or may not be chosen from the list referred to in paragraph 1; and

(b) one conciliator not of the nationality of that State or of any of those States, who shall be chosen from the list.

The State or States constituting the other party to the dispute shall appoint two conciliators in the same way. The four conciliators chosen by the parties shall be appointed within sixty days following the date on which the Secretary-General receives the request.

The four conciliators shall, within sixty days following the date of the last of their own appointments, appoint a fifth conciliator chosen from the list, who shall be chairman.

If the appointment of the chairman or of any of the other conciliators has not been made within the period prescribed above for such appointment, it shall be made by the Secretary-General within sixty days following the expiry of that period. The appointment of the chairman may be made by the Secretary-General either from the list or from the membership of the International Law Commission. Any of the periods within which appointments must be made may be extended by agreement between the parties to the dispute.

Any vacancy shall be filled in the manner prescribed for the initial appointment.

3. The Conciliation Commission shall decide its own procedure. The Commission, with the consent of the parties to the dispute, may invite any party to the treaty to submit to it its views orally or in writing. Decisions and recommendations of the Commission shall be made by a majority vote of the five members.
4. The Commission may draw the attention of the parties to the dispute to any measures which might facilitate an amicable settlement.
5. The Commission shall hear the parties, examine the claims and objections, and make proposals to the parties with a view to reaching an amicable settlement of the dispute.

6. The Commission shall report within twelve months of its constitution. Its report shall be deposited with the Secretary-General and transmitted to the parties to the dispute. The report of the Commission, including any conclusions stated therein regarding the facts or questions of law, shall not be binding upon the parties and it shall have no other character than that of recommendations submitted for the consideration of the parties in order to facilitate an amicable settlement of the dispute.
7. The Secretary-General shall provide the Commission with such assistance and facilities as it may require. The expenses of the Commission shall be borne by the United Nations.

9.2 *Model Legislation*

9.2.1 UNCITRAL Model Law on International Commercial Arbitration (1985)

(United Nations documents A/40/17, annex I and A/61/17, annex I)

(As adopted by the United Nations Commission on International Trade Law on 21 June 1985, and as amended by the United Nations Commission on International Trade Law on 7 July 2006)

CHAPTER I. GENERAL PROVISIONS

Article 1. Scope of application[1]

(1) This Law applies to international commercial[2] arbitration, subject to any agreement in force between this State and any other State or States.

(2) The provisions of this Law, except articles 8, 9, 17 H, 17 I, 17 J, 35 and 36, apply only if the place of arbitration is in the territory of this State.

(Article 1(2) has been amended by the Commission at its thirty-ninth session, in 2006)

(3) An arbitration is international if:

(a) the parties to an arbitration agreement have, at the time of the conclusion of that agreement, t heir places of business in different States; or

(b) one of the following places is situated outside the State in which the parties have their places of business:

(i) the place of arbitration if determined in, or pursuant to, the arbitration agreement;

(ii) any place where a substantial part of the obligations of the commercial relationship is to be performed or the place with which the subject-matter of the dispute is most closely connected; or

(c) the parties have expressly agreed that the subject matter of the arbitration agreement relates to more than one country.

(4) For the purposes of paragraph (3) of this article:

(a) if a party has more than one place of business, the place of business is that which has the closest relationship to the arbitration agreement;

(b) if a party does not have a place of business, reference is to be made to his habitual residence.

(5) This Law shall not affect any other law of this State by virtue of which certain disputes may not be submitted to arbitration or may be submitted to arbitration only according to provisions other than those of this Law.

---

1 Article headings are for reference purposes only and are not to be used for purposes of interpretation.

2 The term "commercial" should be given a wide interpretation so as to cover matters arising from all relationships of a commercial nature, whether contractual or not. Relationships of a commercial nature include, but are not limited to, the following transactions: any trade transaction for the supply or exchange of goods or services; distribution agreement; commercial representation or agency; factoring; leasing; construction of works; consulting; engineering; licensing; investment; financing; banking; insurance; exploitation agreement or concession; joint venture and other forms of industrial or business cooperation; carriage of goods or passengers by air, sea, rail or road.

Article 2. Definitions and rules of interpretation

For the purposes of this Law:

(a) "arbitration" means any arbitration whether or not administered by a permanent arbitral institution;

(b) "arbitral tribunal" means a sole arbitrator or a panel of arbitrators;

(c) "court" means a body or organ of the judicial system of a State;

(d) where a provision of this Law, except article 28, leaves the parties free to determine a certain issue, such freedom includes the right of the parties to authorize a third party, including an institution, to make that determination;

(e) where a provision of this Law refers to the fact that the parties have agreed or that they may agree or in any other way refers to an agreement of the parties, such agreement includes any arbitration rules referred to in that agreement;

(f) where a provision of this Law, other than in articles 25(a) and 32(2) (a), refers to a claim, it also applies to a counter-claim, and where it refers to a defence, it also applies to a defence to such counter-claim.

Article 2 A. International origin and general principles

(As adopted by the Commission at its thirty-ninth session, in 2006)

(1) In the interpretation of this Law, regard is to be had to its international origin and to the need to promote uniformity in its application and the observance of good faith.

(2) Questions concerning matters governed by this Law which are not expressly settled in it are to be settled in conformity with the general principles on which this Law is based.

Article 3. Receipt of written communications

(1) Unless otherwise agreed by the parties:

(a) any written communication is deemed to have been received if it is delivered to the addressee personally or if it is delivered at his place of business, habitual residence or mailing address; if none of these can be found after making a reasonable inquiry, a written communication is deemed to have been received if it is sent to the addressee's last-known place of business, habitual residence or mailing address by registered letter or any other means which provides a record of the attempt to deliver it;

(b) the communication is deemed to have been received on the day it is so delivered.

(2) The provisions of this article do not apply to communications in court proceedings.

Article 4. Waiver of right to object

A party who knows that any provision of this Law from which the parties may derogate or any requirement under the arbitration agreement has not been complied with and yet proceeds with the arbitration without stating his objection to such non-compliance without undue delay or, if a time-limit is provided therefor, within such period of time, shall be deemed to have waived his right to object.

Article 5. Extent of court intervention

In matters governed by this Law, no court shall intervene except where so provided in this Law.

Article 6. Court or other authority for certain functions of arbitration assistance and supervision

The functions referred to in articles 11(3), 11(4), 13(3), 14, 16(3) and 34(2) shall be performed by ... [Each State enacting this model law specifies the court, courts or, where referred to therein, other authority competent to perform these functions.]

CHAPTER II. ARBITRATION AGREEMENT

Option I

Article 7. Definition and form of arbitration agreement
(As adopted by the Commission at its thirty-ninth session, in 2006)
(1) "Arbitration agreement" is an agreement by the parties to submit to arbitration all or certain disputes which have arisen or which may arise between them in respect of a defined legal relationship, whether contractual or not. An arbitration agreement may be in the form of an arbitration clause in a contract or in the form of a separate agreement.
(2) The arbitration agreement shall be in writing.
(3) An arbitration agreement is in writing if its content is recorded in any form, whether or not the arbitration agreement or contract has been concluded orally, by conduct, or by other means.
(4) The requirement that an arbitration agreement be in writing is met by an electronic communication if the information contained therein is accessible so as to be useable for subsequent reference; "electronic communication" means any communication that the parties make by means of data messages; "data message" means information generated, sent, received or stored by electronic, magnetic, optical or similar means, including, but not limited to, electronic data interchange (EDI), electronic mail, telegram, telex or telecopy.
(5) Furthermore, an arbitration agreement is in writing if it is contained in an exchange of statements of claim and defence in which the existence of an agreement is alleged by one party and not denied by the other.
(6) The reference in a contract to any document containing an arbitration clause constitutes an arbitration agreement in writing, provided that the reference is such as to make that clause part of the contract.

Option II

Article 7. Definition of arbitration agreement
(As adopted by the Commission at its thirty-ninth session, in 2006)
"Arbitration agreement" is an agreement by the parties to submit to arbitration all or certain disputes which have arisen or which may arise between them in respect of a defined legal relationship, whether contractual or not.

Article 8. Arbitration agreement and substantive claim before court
(1) A court before which an action is brought in a matter which is the subject of an arbitration agreement shall, if a party so requests not later than when submitting his first statement on the substance of the dispute, refer the parties to arbitration unless it finds that the agreement is null and void, inoperative or incapable of being performed.
(2) Where an action referred to in paragraph (1) of this article has been brought, arbitral proceedings may nevertheless be commenced or continued, and an award may be made, while the issue is pending before the court.

Article 9. Arbitration agreement and interim measures by court
It is not incompatible with an arbitration agreement for a party to request, before or during arbitral proceedings, from a court an interim measure of protection and for a court to grant such measure.

CHAPTER III. COMPOSITION OF ARBITRAL TRIBUNAL

Article 10. Number of arbitrators

(1) The parties are free to determine the number of arbitrators.
(2) Failing such determination, the number of arbitrators shall be three.

Article 11. Appointment of arbitrators

(1) No person shall be precluded by reason of his nationality from acting as an arbitrator, unless otherwise agreed by the parties.
(2) The parties are free to agree on a procedure of appointing the arbitrator or arbitrators, subject to the provisions of paragraphs (4) and (5) of this article.
(3) Failing such agreement,
(a) in an arbitration with three arbitrators, each party shall appoint one arbitrator, and the two arbitrators thus appointed shall appoint the third arbitrator; if a party fails to appoint the arbitrator within thirty days of receipt of a request to do so from the other party, or if the two arbitrators fail to agree on the third arbitrator within thirty days of their appointment, the appointment shall be made, upon request of a party, by the court or other authority specified in article 6;
(b) in an arbitration with a sole arbitrator, if the parties are unable to agree on the arbitrator, he shall be appointed, upon request of a party, by the court or other authority specified in article 6.
(4) Where, under an appointment procedure agreed upon by the parties,
(a) a party fails to act as required under such procedure, or
(b) the parties, or two arbitrators, are unable to reach an agreement expected of them under such procedure, or
(c) a third party, including an institution, fails to perform any function entrusted to it under such procedure,
any party may request the court or other authority specified in article 6 to take the necessary measure, unless the agreement on the appointment procedure provides other means for securing the appointment.
(5) A decision on a matter entrusted by paragraph (3) or (4) of this article to the court or other authority specified in article 6 shall be subject to no appeal. The court or other authority, in appointing an arbitrator, shall have due regard to any qualifications required of the arbitrator by the agreement of the parties and to such considerations as are likely to secure the appointment of an independent and impartial arbitrator and, in the case of a sole or third arbitrator, shall take into account as well the advisability of appointing an arbitrator of a nationality other than those of the parties.

Article 12. Grounds for challenge

(1) When a person is approached in connection with his possible appointment as an arbitrator, he shall disclose any circumstances likely to give rise to justifiable doubts as to his impartiality or independence. An arbitrator, from the time of his appointment and throughout the arbitral proceedings, shall without delay disclose any such circumstances to the parties unless they have already been informed of them by him.
(2) An arbitrator may be challenged only if circumstances exist that give rise to justifiable doubts as to his impartiality or independence, or if he does not possess qualifications agreed to by the parties. A party may challenge an arbitrator appointed by him, or in whose appointment he has participated, only for reasons of which he becomes aware after the appointment has been made.

Article 13. Challenge procedure
(1) The parties are free to agree on a procedure for challenging an arbitrator, subject to the provisions of paragraph (3) of this article.
(2) Failing such agreement, a party who intends to challenge an arbitrator shall, within fifteen days after becoming aware of the constitution of the arbitral tribunal or after becoming aware of any circumstance referred to in article 12(2), send a written statement of the reasons for the challenge to the arbitral tribunal. Unless the challenged arbitrator withdraws from his office or the other party agrees to the challenge, the arbitral tribunal shall decide on the challenge.
(3) If a challenge under any procedure agreed upon by the parties or under the procedure of paragraph (2) of this article is not successful, the challenging party may request, within thirty days after having received notice of the decision rejecting the challenge, the court or other authority specified in article 6 to decide on the challenge, which decision shall be subject to no appeal; while such a request is pending, the arbitral tribunal, including the challenged arbitrator, may continue the arbitral proceedings and make an award.

Article 14. Failure or impossibility to act
(1) If an arbitrator becomes de jure or de facto unable to perform his functions or for other reasons fails to act without undue delay, his mandate terminates if he withdraws from his office or if the parties agree on the termination. Otherwise, if a controversy remains concerning any of these grounds, any party may request the court or other authority specified in article 6 to decide on the termination of the mandate, which decision shall be subject to no appeal.
(2) If, under this article or article 13(2), an arbitrator withdraws from his office or a party agrees to the termination of the mandate of an arbitrator, this does not imply acceptance of the validity of any ground referred to in this article or article 12(2).

Article 15. Appointment of substitute arbitrator
Where the mandate of an arbitrator terminates under article 13 or 14 or because of his withdrawal from office for any other reason or because of the revocation of his mandate by agreement of the parties or in any other case of termination of his mandate, a substitute arbitrator shall be appointed according to the rules that were applicable to the appointment of the arbitrator being replaced.

CHAPTER IV. JURISDICTION OF ARBITRAL TRIBUNAL

Article 16. Competence of arbitral tribunal to rule on its jurisdiction
(1) The arbitral tribunal may rule on its own jurisdiction, including any objections with respect to the existence or validity of the arbitration agreement. For that purpose, an arbitration clause which forms part of a contract shall be treated as an agreement independent of the other terms of the contract. A decision by the arbitral tribunal that the contract is null and void shall not entail ipso jure the invalidity of the arbitration clause.
(2) A plea that the arbitral tribunal does not have jurisdiction shall be raised not later than the submission of the statement of defence. A party is not precluded from raising such a plea by the fact that he has appointed, or participated in the appointment of, an arbitrator. A plea that the arbitral tribunal is exceeding the scope of its authority shall be raised as soon as the matter alleged to be beyond the scope of its authority is raised during the arbitral proceedings. The arbitral tribunal may, in either case, admit a later plea if it considers the delay justified.
(3) The arbitral tribunal may rule on a plea referred to in paragraph (2) of this article either as a preliminary question or in an award on the merits. If the arbitral tribunal rules as a preliminary question that it has jurisdiction, any party may request, within thirty days after having received notice of that ruling, the court specified in article 6 to decide the matter, which decision shall be subject to

no appeal; while such a request is pending, the arbitral tribunal may continue the arbitral proceedings and make an award.

CHAPTER IV A. INTERIM MEASURES AND PRELIMINARY ORDERS

(As adopted by the Commission at its thirty-ninth session, in 2006)

SECTION 1. INTERIM MEASURES

Article 17. Power of arbitral tribunal to order interim measures
(1) Unless otherwise agreed by the parties, the arbitral tribunal may, at the request of a party, grant interim measures.
(2) An interim measure is any temporary measure, whether in the form of an award or in another form, by which, at any time prior to the issuance of the award by which the dispute is finally decided, the arbitral tribunal orders a party to:
(a) Maintain or restore the status quo pending determination of the dispute;
(b) Take action that would prevent, or refrain from taking action that is likely to cause, current or imminent harm or prejudice to the arbitral process itself;
(c) Provide a means of preserving assets out of which a subsequent award may be satisfied; or
(d) Preserve evidence that may be relevant and material to the resolution of the dispute.

Article 17 A. Conditions for granting interim measures
(1) The party requesting an interim measure under article 17(2)(a), (b) and (c) shall satisfy the arbitral tribunal that:
(a) Harm not adequately reparable by an award of damages is likely to result if the measure is not ordered, and such harm substantially outweighs the harm that is likely to result to the party against whom the measure is directed if the measure is granted; and
(b) There is a reasonable possibility that the requesting party will succeed on the merits of the claim. The determination on this possibility shall not affect the discretion of the arbitral tribunal in making any subsequent determination.
(2) With regard to a request for an interim measure under article 17(2)(d), the requirements in paragraphs (1)(a) and (b) of this article shall apply only to the extent the arbitral tribunal considers appropriate.

SECTION 2. PRELIMINARY ORDERS

Article 17 B. Applications for preliminary orders and conditions for granting preliminary orders
(1) Unless otherwise agreed by the parties, a party may, without notice to any other party, make a request for an interim measure together with an application for a preliminary order directing a party not to frustrate the purpose of the interim measure requested.
(2) The arbitral tribunal may grant a preliminary order provided it considers that prior disclosure of the request for the interim measure to the party against whom it is directed risks frustrating the purpose of the measure.
(3) The conditions defined under article 17A apply to any preliminary order, provided that the harm to be assessed under article 17A(1)(a), is the harm likely to result from the order being granted or not.

Article 17 C. Specific regime for preliminary orders
(1) Immediately after the arbitral tribunal has made a determination in respect of an application for a preliminary order, the arbitral tribunal shall give notice to all parties of the request for the interim

measure, the application for the preliminary order, the preliminary order, if any, and all other communications, including by indicating the content of any oral communication, between any party and the arbitral tribunal in relation thereto.
(2) At the same time, the arbitral tribunal shall give an opportunity to any party against whom a preliminary order is directed to present its case at the earliest practicable time.
(3) The arbitral tribunal shall decide promptly on any objection to the preliminary order.
(4) A preliminary order shall expire after twenty days from the date on which it was issued by the arbitral tribunal. However, the arbitral tribunal may issue an interim measure adopting or modifying the preliminary order, after the party against whom the preliminary order is directed has been given notice and an opportunity to present its case.
(5) A preliminary order shall be binding on the parties but shall not be subject to enforcement by a court. Such a preliminary order does not constitute an award.

SECTION 3. PROVISIONS APPLICABLE TO INTERIM MEASURES AND PRELIMINARY ORDERS

Article 17 D. Modification, suspension, termination

The arbitral tribunal may modify, suspend or terminate an interim measure or a preliminary order it has granted, upon application of any party or, in exceptional circumstances and upon prior notice to the parties, on the arbitral tribunal's own initiative.

Article 17 E. Provision of security

(1) The arbitral tribunal may require the party requesting an interim measure to provide appropriate security in connection with the measure.
(2) The arbitral tribunal shall require the party applying for a preliminary order to provide security in connection with the order unless the arbitral tribunal considers it inappropriate or unnecessary to do so.

Article 17 F. Disclosure

(1) The arbitral tribunal may require any party promptly to disclose any material change in the circumstances on the basis of which the measure was requested or granted.
(2) The party applying for a preliminary order shall disclose to the arbitral tribunal all circumstances that are likely to be relevant to the arbitral tribunal's determination whether to grant or maintain the order, and such obligation shall continue until the party against whom the order has been requested has had an opportunity to present its case. Thereafter, paragraph (1) of this article shall apply.

Article 17 G. Costs and damages

The party requesting an interim measure or applying for a preliminary order shall be liable for any costs and damages caused by the measure or the order to any party if the arbitral tribunal later determines that, in the circumstances, the measure or the order should not have been granted. The arbitral tribunal may award such costs and damages at any point during the proceedings.

SECTION 4. RECOGNITION AND ENFORCEMENT OF INTERIM MEASURES

Article 17 H. Recognition and enforcement

(1) An interim measure issued by an arbitral tribunal shall be recognized as binding and, unless otherwise provided by the arbitral tribunal, enforced upon application to the competent court, irrespective of the country in which it was issued, subject to the provisions of article 17 I.

(2) The party who is seeking or has obtained recognition or enforcement of an interim measure shall promptly inform the court of any termination, suspension or modification of that interim measure.
(3) The court of the State where recognition or enforcement is sought may, if it considers it proper, order the requesting party to provide appropriate security if the arbitral tribunal has not already made a determination with respect to security or where such a decision is necessary to protect the rights of third parties.

Article 17 I. Grounds for refusing recognition or enforcement[3]
(1) Recognition or enforcement of an interim measure may be refused only:
- (a) At the request of the party against whom it is invoked if the court is satisfied that:
  - (i) Such refusal is warranted on the grounds set forth in article 36(1)(a)(i), (ii), (iii) or (iv); or
  - (ii) The arbitral tribunal's decision with respect to the provision of security in connection with the interim measure issued by the arbitral tribunal has not been complied with; or
  - (iii) The interim measure has been terminated or suspended by the arbitral tribunal or, where so empowered, by the court of the State in which the arbitration takes place or under the law of which that interim measure was granted; or
- (b) If the court finds that:
  - (i) The interim measure is incompatible with the powers conferred upon the court unless the court decides to reformulate the interim measure to the extent necessary to adapt it to its own powers and procedures for the purposes of enforcing that interim measure and without modifying its substance; or
  - (ii) Any of the grounds set forth in article 36(1)(b)(i) or (ii), apply to the recognition and enforcement of the interim measure.

(2) Any determination made by the court on any ground in paragraph (1) of this article shall be effective only for the purposes of the application to recognize and enforce the interim measure. The court where recognition or enforcement is sought shall not, in making that determination, undertake a review of the substance of the interim measure.

Section 5. Court-ordered interim measures

Article 17 J. Court-ordered interim measures
A court shall have the same power of issuing an interim measure in relation to arbitration proceedings, irrespective of whether their place is in the territory of this State, as it has in relation to proceedings in courts. The court shall exercise such power in accordance with its own procedures in consideration of the specific features of international arbitration.

CHAPTER V. CONDUCT OF ARBITRAL PROCEEDINGS

Article 18. Equal treatment of parties
The parties shall be treated with equality and each party shall be given a full opportunity of presenting his case.

3 The conditions set forth in article 17 I are intended to limit the number of circumstances in which the court may refuse to enforce an interim measure. It would not be contrary to the level of armonization sought to be achieved by these model provisions if a State were to adopt fewer circumstances in which enforcement may be refused.

Article 19. Determination of rules of procedure

(1) Subject to the provisions of this Law, the parties are free to agree on the procedure to be followed by the arbitral tribunal in conducting the proceedings.

(2) Failing such agreement, the arbitral tribunal may, subject to the provisions of this Law, conduct the arbitration in such manner as it considers appropriate. The power conferred upon the arbitral tribunal includes the power to determine the admissibility, relevance, materiality and weight of any evidence.

Article 20. Place of arbitration

(1) The parties are free to agree on the place of arbitration. Failing such agreement, the place of arbitration shall be determined by the arbitral tribunal having regard to the circumstances of the case, including the convenience of the parties.

(2) Notwithstanding the provisions of paragraph (1) of this article, the arbitral tribunal may, unless otherwise agreed by the parties, meet at any place it considers appropriate for consultation among its members, for hearing witnesses, experts or the parties, or for inspection of goods, other property or documents.

Article 21. Commencement of arbitral proceedings

Unless otherwise agreed by the parties, the arbitral proceedings in respect of a particular dispute commence on the date on which a request for that dispute to be referred to arbitration is received by the respondent.

Article 22. Language

(1) The parties are free to agree on the language or languages to be used in the arbitral proceedings. Failing such agreement, the arbitral tribunal shall determine the language or languages to be used in the proceedings. This agreement or determination, unless otherwise specified therein, shall apply to any written statement by a party, any hearing and any award, decision or other communication by the arbitral tribunal.

(2) The arbitral tribunal may order that any documentary evidence shall be accompanied by a translation into the language or languages agreed upon by the parties or determined by the arbitral tribunal.

Article 23. Statements of claim and defence

(1) Within the period of time agreed by the parties or determined by the arbitral tribunal, the claimant shall state the facts supporting his claim, the points at issue and the relief or remedy sought, and the respondent shall state his defence in respect of these particulars, unless the parties have otherwise agreed as to the required elements of such statements. The parties may submit with their statements all documents they consider to be relevant or may add a reference to the documents or other evidence they will submit.

(2) Unless otherwise agreed by the parties, either party may amend or supplement his claim or defence during the course of the arbitral proceedings, unless the arbitral tribunal considers it inappropriate to allow such amendment having regard to the delay in making it.

Article 24. Hearings and written proceedings

(1) Subject to any contrary agreement by the parties, the arbitral tribunal shall decide whether to hold oral hearings for the presentation of evidence or for oral argument, or whether the proceedings shall be conducted on the basis of documents and other materials. However, unless the parties have agreed that no hearings shall be held, the arbitral tribunal shall hold such hearings at an appropriate stage of the proceedings, if so requested by a party.

(2) The parties shall be given sufficient advance notice of any hearing and of any meeting of the arbitral tribunal for the purposes of inspection of goods, other property or documents.
(3) All statements, documents or other information supplied to the arbitral tribunal by one party shall be communicated to the other party. Also any expert report or evidentiary document on which the arbitral tribunal may rely in making its decision shall be communicated to the parties.

Article 25. Default of a party
Unless otherwise agreed by the parties, if, without showing sufficient cause,
(a) the claimant fails to communicate his statement of claim in accordance with article 23(1), the arbitral tribunal shall terminate the proceedings;
(b) the respondent fails to communicate his statement of defence in accordance with article 23(1), the arbitral tribunal shall continue the proceedings without treating such failure in itself as an admission of the claimant's allegations;
(c) any party fails to appear at a hearing or to produce documentary evidence, the arbitral tribunal may continue the proceedings and make the award on the evidence before it.

Article 26. Expert appointed by arbitral tribunal
(1) Unless otherwise agreed by the parties, the arbitral tribunal
(a) may appoint one or more experts to report to it on specific issues to be determined by the arbitral tribunal;
(b) may require a party to give the expert any relevant information or to produce, or to provide access to, any relevant documents, goods or other property for his inspection.
(2) Unless otherwise agreed by the parties, if a party so requests or if the arbitral tribunal considers it necessary, the expert shall, after delivery of his written or oral report, participate in a hearing where the parties have the opportunity to put questions to him and to present expert witnesses in order to testify on the points at issue.

Article 27. Court assistance in taking evidence
The arbitral tribunal or a party with the approval of the arbitral tribunal may request from a competent court of this State assistance in taking evidence.

The court may execute the request within its competence and according to its rules on taking evidence.

CHAPTER VI. MAKING OF AWARD AND TERMINATION OF PROCEEDINGS

Article 28. Rules applicable to substance of dispute
(1) The arbitral tribunal shall decide the dispute in accordance with such rules of law as are chosen by the parties as applicable to the substance of the dispute. Any designation of the law or legal system of a given State shall be construed, unless otherwise expressed, as directly referring to the substantive law of that State and not to its conflict of laws rules.
(2) Failing any designation by the parties, the arbitral tribunal shall apply the law determined by the conflict of laws rules which it considers applicable.
(3) The arbitral tribunal shall decide *ex aequo et bono* or as *amiable compositeur* only if the parties have expressly authorized it to do so.
(4) In all cases, the arbitral tribunal shall decide in accordance with the terms of the contract and shall take into account the usages of the trade applicable to the transaction.

Article 29. Decision-making by panel of arbitrators
In arbitral proceedings with more than one arbitrator, any decision of the arbitral tribunal shall be made, unless otherwise agreed by the parties, by a majority of all its members. However, questions of procedure may be decided by a presiding arbitrator, if so authorized by the parties or all members of the arbitral tribunal.

Article 30. Settlement
(1) If, during arbitral proceedings, the parties settle the dispute, the arbitral tribunal shall terminate the proceedings and, if requested by the parties and not objected to by the arbitral tribunal, record the settlement in the form of an arbitral award on agreed terms.
(2) An award on agreed terms shall be made in accordance with the provisions of article 31 and shall state that it is an award. Such an award has the same status and effect as any other award on the merits of the case.

Article 31. Form and contents of award
(1) The award shall be made in writing and shall be signed by the arbitrator or arbitrators. In arbitral proceedings with more than one arbitrator, the signatures of the majority of all members of the arbitral tribunal shall suffice, provided that the reason for any omitted signature is stated.
(2) The award shall state the reasons upon which it is based, unless the parties have agreed that no reasons are to be given or the award is an award on agreed terms under article 30.
(3) The award shall state its date and the place of arbitration as determined in accordance with article 20(1). The award shall be deemed to have been made at that place.
(4) After the award is made, a copy signed by the arbitrators in accordance with paragraph (1) of this article shall be delivered to each party.

Article 32. Termination of proceedings
(1) The arbitral proceedings are terminated by the final award or by an order of the arbitral tribunal in accordance with paragraph (2) of this article.
(2) The arbitral tribunal shall issue an order for the termination of the arbitral proceedings when:
- (a) the claimant withdraws his claim, unless the respondent objects thereto and the arbitral tribunal recognizes a legitimate interest on his part in obtaining a final settlement of the dispute;
- (b) the parties agree on the termination of the proceedings;
- (c) the arbitral tribunal finds that the continuation of the proceedings has for any other reason become unnecessary or impossible.

(3) The mandate of the arbitral tribunal terminates with the termination of the arbitral proceedings, subject to the provisions of articles 33 and 34(4).

Article 33. Correction and interpretation of award; additional award
(1) Within thirty days of receipt of the award, unless another period of time has been agreed upon by the parties:
- (a) a party, with notice to the other party, may request the arbitral tribunal to correct in the award any errors in computation, any clerical or typographical errors or any errors of similar nature;
- (b) if so agreed by the parties, a party, with notice to the other party, may request the arbitral tribunal to give an interpretation of a specific point or part of the award.

If the arbitral tribunal considers the request to be justified, it shall make the correction or give the interpretation within thirty days of receipt of the request. The interpretation shall form part of the award.
(2) The arbitral tribunal may correct any error of the type referred to in paragraph (1)(a) of this article on its own initiative within thirty days of the date of the award.

(3) Unless otherwise agreed by the parties, a party, with notice to the other party, may request, within thirty days of receipt of the award, the arbitral tribunal to make an additional award as to claims presented in the arbitral proceedings but omitted from the award. If the arbitral tribunal considers the request to be justified, it shall make the additional award within sixty days.
(4) The arbitral tribunal may extend, if necessary, the period of time within which it shall make a correction, interpretation or an additional award under paragraph (1) or (3) of this article.
(5) The provisions of article 31 shall apply to a correction or interpretation of the award or to an additional award.

CHAPTER VII. RECOURSE AGAINST AWARD

Article 34. Application for setting aside as exclusive recourse against arbitral award

(1) Recourse to a court against an arbitral award may be made only by an application for setting aside in accordance with paragraphs (2) and (3) of this article.
(2) An arbitral award may be set aside by the court specified in article 6 only if:
- (a) the party making the application furnishes proof that:
  - (i) a party to the arbitration agreement referred to in article 7 was under some incapacity; or the said agreement is not valid under the law to which the parties have subjected it or, failing any indication thereon, under the law of this State; or
  - (ii) the party making the application was not given proper notice of the appointment of an arbitrator or of the arbitral proceedings or was otherwise unable to present his case; or
  - (iii) the award deals with a dispute not contemplated by or not falling within the terms of the submission to arbitration, or contains decisions on matters beyond the scope of the submission to arbitration, provided that, if the decisions on matters submitted to arbitration can be separated from those not so submitted, only that part of the award which contains decisions on matters not submitted to arbitration may be set aside; or
  - (iv) the composition of the arbitral tribunal or the arbitral procedure was not in accordance with the agreement of the parties, unless such agreement was in conflict with a provision of this Law from which the parties cannot derogate, or, failing such agreement, was not in accordance with this Law; or
- (b) the court finds that:
  - (i) the subject-matter of the dispute is not capable of settlement by arbitration under the law of this State; or
  - (ii) the award is in conflict with the public policy of this State.

(3) An application for setting aside may not be made after three months have elapsed from the date on which the party making that application had received the award or, if a request had been made under article 33, from the date on which that request had been disposed of by the arbitral tribunal.
(4) The court, when asked to set aside an award, may, where appropriate and so requested by a party, suspend the setting aside proceedings for a period of time determined by it in order to give the arbitral tribunal an opportunity to resume the arbitral proceedings or to take such other action as in the arbitral tribunal's opinion will eliminate the grounds for setting aside.

CHAPTER VIII. RECOGNITION AND ENFORCEMENT OF AWARDS

Article 35. Recognition and enforcement

(1) An arbitral award, irrespective of the country in which it was made, shall be recognized as binding and, upon application in writing to the competent court, shall be enforced subject to the provisions of this article and of article 36.

(2) The party relying on an award or applying for its enforcement shall supply the original award or a copy thereof. If the award is not made in an official language of this State, the court may request the party to supply a translation thereof into such language.[4]

(Article 35(2) has been amended by the Commission at its thirty-ninth session, in 2006)

Article 36. Grounds for refusing recognition or enforcement

(1) Recognition or enforcement of an arbitral award, irrespective of the country in which it was made, may be refused only:

(a) at the request of the party against whom it is invoked, if that party furnishes to the competent court where recognition or enforcement is sought proof that:

(i) a party to the arbitration agreement referred to in article 7 was under some incapacity; or the said agreement is not valid under the law to which the parties have subjected it or, failing any indication thereon, under the law of the country where the award was made; or

(ii) the party against whom the award is invoked was not given proper notice of the appointment of an arbitrator or of the arbitral proceedings or was otherwise unable to present his case; or

(iii) the award deals with a dispute not contemplated by or not falling within the terms of the submission to arbitration, or it contains decisions on matters beyond the scope of the submission to arbitration, provided that, if the decisions on matters submitted to arbitration can be separated from those not so submitted, that part of the award which contains decisions on matters submitted to arbitration may be recognized and enforced; or

(iv) the composition of the arbitral tribunal or the arbitral procedure was not in accordance with the agreement of the parties or, failing such agreement, was not in accordance with the law of the country where the arbitration took place; or

(v) the award has not yet become binding on the parties or has been set aside or suspended by a court of the country in which, or under the law of which, that award was made; or

(b) if the court finds that:

(i) the subject-matter of the dispute is not capable of settlement by arbitration under the law of this State; or

(ii) the recognition or enforcement of the award would be contrary to the public policy of this State.

(2) If an application for setting aside or suspension of an award has been made to a court referred to in paragraph (1)(a)(v) of this article, the court where recognition or enforcement is sought may, if it considers it proper, adjourn its decision and may also, on the application of the party claiming recognition or enforcement of the award, order the other party to provide appropriate security.

4 The conditions set forth in this paragraph are intended to set maximum standards. It would, thus, not be contrary to the harmonization to be achieved by the model law if a State retained even less onerous conditions.

9.3 *Domestic Law*

9.3.1 English Arbitration Act (1996) (UK law)

1996 CHAPTER 23

An Act to restate and improve the law relating to arbitration pursuant to an arbitration agreement; to make other provision relating to arbitration and arbitration awards; and for connected purposes.[17th June 1996]

Be it enacted by the Queen's most Excellent Majesty, by and with the advice and consent of the Lords Spiritual and Temporal, and Commons, in this present Parliament assembled, and by the authority of the same, as follows: -

PART I ARBITRATION PURSUANT TO AN ARBITRATION AGREEMENT

Introductory

1 General principles.

The provisions of this Part are founded on the following principles, and shall be construed accordingly -

(a) the object of arbitration is to obtain the fair resolution of disputes by an impartial tribunal without unnecessary delay or expense;

(b) the parties should be free to agree how their disputes are resolved, subject only to such safeguards as are necessary in the public interest;

(c) in matters governed by this Part the court should not intervene except as provided by this Part.

2 Scope of application of provisions.

(1) The provisions of this Part apply where the seat of the arbitration is in England and Wales or Northern Ireland.

(2) The following sections apply even if the seat of the arbitration is outside England and Wales or Northern Ireland or no seat has been designated or determined -

(a) sections 9 to 11 (stay of legal proceedings, &c.), and

(b) section 66 (enforcement of arbitral awards).

(3) The powers conferred by the following sections apply even if the seat of the arbitration is outside England and Wales or Northern Ireland or no seat has been designated or determined -

(a) section 43 (securing the attendance of witnesses), and

(b) section 44 (court powers exercisable in support of arbitral proceedings);

but the court may refuse to exercise any such power if, in the opinion of the court, the fact that the seat of the arbitration is outside England and Wales or Northern Ireland, or that when designated or determined the seat is likely to be outside England and Wales or Northern Ireland, makes it inappropriate to do so.

(4) The court may exercise a power conferred by any provision of this Part not mentioned in subsection (2) or (3) for the purpose of supporting the arbitral process where -

(a) no seat of the arbitration has been designated or determined, and

(b) by reason of a connection with England and Wales or Northern Ireland the court is satisfied that it is appropriate to do so.

(5) Section 7 (separability of arbitration agreement) and section 8 (death of a party) apply where the law applicable to the arbitration agreement is the law of England and Wales or Northern Ireland even if the seat of the arbitration is outside England and Wales or Northern Ireland or has not been designated or determined.

3 The seat of the arbitration.
In this Part "the seat of the arbitration" means the juridical seat of the arbitration designated –
(a) by the parties to the arbitration agreement, or
(b) by any arbitral or other institution or person vested by the parties with powers in that regard, or
(c) by the arbitral tribunal if so authorised by the parties,
or determined, in the absence of any such designation, having regard to the parties' agreement and all the relevant circumstances.

4 Mandatory and non-mandatory provisions.
(1) The mandatory provisions of this Part are listed in Schedule 1 and have effect notwithstanding any agreement to the contrary.
(2) The other provisions of this Part (the "non-mandatory provisions") allow the parties to make their own arrangements by agreement but provide rules which apply in the absence of such agreement.
(3) The parties may make such arrangements by agreeing to the application of institutional rules or providing any other means by which a matter may be decided.
(4) It is immaterial whether or not the law applicable to the parties' agreement is the law of England and Wales or, as the case may be, Northern Ireland.
(4) The choice of a law other than the law of England and Wales or Northern Ireland as the applicable law in respect of a matter provided for by a non-mandatory provision of this Part is equivalent to an agreement making provision about that matter.
For this purpose an applicable law determined in accordance with the parties' agreement, or which is objectively determined in the absence of any express or implied choice, shall be treated as chosen by the parties.

5 Agreements to be in writing.
(1) The provisions of this Part apply only where the arbitration agreement is in writing, and any other agreement between the parties as to any matter is effective for the purposes of this Part only if in writing.
The expressions "agreement", "agree" and "agreed" shall be construed accordingly.
(2) There is an agreement in writing –
(a) if the agreement is made in writing (whether or not it is signed by the parties),
(b) if the agreement is made by exchange of communications in writing, or
(c) if the agreement is evidenced in writing.
(3) Where parties agree otherwise than in writing by reference to terms which are in writing, they make an agreement in writing.
(4) An agreement is evidenced in writing if an agreement made otherwise than in writing is recorded by one of the parties, or by a third party, with the authority of the parties to the agreement.
(5) An exchange of written submissions in arbitral or legal proceedings in which the existence of an agreement otherwise than in writing is alleged by one party against another party and not denied by the other party in his response constitutes as between those parties an agreement in writing to the effect alleged.
(6) References in this Part to anything being written or in writing include its being recorded by any means.

The arbitration agreement

6 Definition of arbitration agreement.
(1) In this Part an "arbitration agreement" means an agreement to submit to arbitration present or future disputes (whether they are contractual or not).
(2) The reference in an agreement to a written form of arbitration clause or to a document containing an arbitration clause constitutes an arbitration agreement if the reference is such as to make that clause part of the agreement.

7 Separability of arbitration agreement.
Unless otherwise agreed by the parties, an arbitration agreement which forms or was intended to form part of another agreement (whether or not in writing) shall not be

regarded as invalid, non-existent or ineffective because that other agreement is invalid, or did not come into existence or has become ineffective, and it shall for that purpose be treated as a distinct agreement.

8 Whether agreement discharged by death of a party.
(1) Unless otherwise agreed by the parties, an arbitration agreement is not discharged by the death of a party and may be enforced by or against the personal representatives of that party.
(2) Subsection (1) does not affect the operation of any enactment or rule of law by virtue of which a substantive right or obligation is extinguished by death.

Stay of legal proceedings

9 Stay of legal proceedings.
(1) A party to an arbitration agreement against whom legal proceedings are brought (whether by way of claim or counterclaim) in respect of a matter which under the agreement is to be referred to arbitration may (upon notice to the other parties to the proceedings) apply to the court in which the proceedings have been brought to stay the proceedings so far as they concern that matter.
(2) An application may be made notwithstanding that the matter is to be referred to arbitration only after the exhaustion of other dispute resolution procedures.
(3) An application may not be made by a person before taking the appropriate procedural step (if any) to acknowledge the legal proceedings against him or after he has taken any step in those proceedings to answer the substantive claim.
(4) On an application under this section the court shall grant a stay unless satisfied that the arbitration agreement is null and void, inoperative, or incapable of being performed.
(5) If the court refuses to stay the legal proceedings, any provision that an award is a condition precedent to the bringing of legal proceedings in respect of any matter is of no effect in relation to those proceedings.

10 Reference of interpleader issue to arbitration.
(1) Where in legal proceedings relief by way of interpleader is granted and any issue between the claimants is one in respect of which there is an arbitration agreement between them, the court granting the relief shall direct that the issue be determined in accordance with the agreement unless the circumstances are such that proceedings brought by a claimant in respect of the matter would not be stayed.
(2) Where subsection (1) applies but the court does not direct that the issue be determined in accordance with the arbitration agreement, any provision that an award is a condition precedent to the bringing of legal proceedings in respect of any matter shall not affect the determination of that issue by the court.

11 Retention of security where Admiralty proceedings stayed.

(1) Where Admiralty proceedings are stayed on the ground that the dispute in question should be submitted to arbitration, the court granting the stay may, if in those proceedings property has been arrested or bail or other security has been given to prevent or obtain release from arrest –

(a) order that the property arrested be retained as security for the satisfaction of any award given in the arbitration in respect of that dispute, or

(b) order that the stay of those proceedings be conditional on the provision of equivalent security for the satisfaction of any such award.

(2) Subject to any provision made by rules of court and to any necessary modifications, the same law and practice shall apply in relation to property retained in pursuance of an order as would apply if it were held for the purposes of proceedings in the court making the order.

Commencement of arbitral proceedings

12 Power of court to extend time for beginning arbitral proceedings, &c.

(1) Where an arbitration agreement to refer future disputes to arbitration provides that a claim shall be barred, or the claimant's right extinguished, unless the claimant takes within a time fixed by the agreement some step –

(a) to begin arbitral proceedings, or

(b) to begin other dispute resolution procedures which must be exhausted before arbitral proceedings can be begun,

the court may by order extend the time for taking that step.

(2) Any party to the arbitration agreement may apply for such an order (upon notice to the other parties), but only after a claim has arisen and after exhausting any available arbitral process for obtaining an extension of time.

(3) The court shall make an order only if satisfied –

(a) that the circumstances are such as were outside the reasonable contemplation of the parties when they agreed the provision in question, and that it would be just to extend the time, or

(b) that the conduct of one party makes it unjust to hold the other party to the strict terms of the provision in question.

(4) The court may extend the time for such period and on such terms as it thinks fit, and may do so whether or not the time previously fixed (by agreement or by a previous order) has expired.

(5) An order under this section does not affect the operation of the Limitation Acts (see section 13).

(6) The leave of the court is required for any appeal from a decision of the court under this section.

13 Application of Limitation Acts.

(1) The Limitation Acts apply to arbitral proceedings as they apply to legal proceedings.

(2) The court may order that in computing the time prescribed by the Limitation Acts for the commencement of proceedings (including arbitral proceedings) in respect of a dispute which was the subject matter –

(a) of an award which the court orders to be set aside or declares to be of no effect, or

(b) of the affected part of an award which the court orders to be set aside in part, or declares to be in part of no effect,

the period between the commencement of the arbitration and the date of the order referred to in paragraph (a) or (b) shall be excluded.

(3) In determining for the purposes of the Limitation Acts when a cause of action accrued, any provision that an award is a condition precedent to the bringing of legal proceedings in respect of a matter to which an arbitration agreement applies shall be disregarded.

(4) In this Part "the Limitation Acts" means –
  (a) in England and Wales, the Limitation Act 1980, the Foreign Limitation Periods Act 1984 and any other enactment (whenever passed) relating to the limitation of actions;
  (b) in Northern Ireland, the Limitation (Northern Ireland) Order 1989, the Foreign Limitation Periods (Northern Ireland) Order 1985 and any other enactment (whenever passed) relating to the limitation of actions.

14 Commencement of arbitral proceedings.
(1) The parties are free to agree when arbitral proceedings are to be regarded as commenced for the purposes of this Part and for the purposes of the Limitation Acts.
(2) If there is no such agreement the following provisions apply.
(3) Where the arbitrator is named or designated in the arbitration agreement, arbitral proceedings are commenced in respect of a matter when one party serves on the other party or parties a notice in writing requiring him or them to submit that matter to the person so named or designated.
(4) Where the arbitrator or arbitrators are to be appointed by the parties, arbitral proceedings are commenced in respect of a matter when one party serves on the other party or parties notice in writing requiring him or them to appoint an arbitrator or to agree to the appointment of an arbitrator in respect of that matter.
(5) Where the arbitrator or arbitrators are to be appointed by a person other than a party to the proceedings, arbitral proceedings are commenced in respect of a matter when one party gives notice in writing to that person requesting him to make the appointment in respect of that matter.

The arbitral tribunal

15 The arbitral tribunal.
(1) The parties are free to agree on the number of arbitrators to form the tribunal and whether there is to be a chairman or umpire.
(2) Unless otherwise agreed by the parties, an agreement that the number of arbitrators shall be two or any other even number shall be understood as requiring the appointment of an additional arbitrator as chairman of the tribunal.
(3) If there is no agreement as to the number of arbitrators, the tribunal shall consist of a sole arbitrator.

16 Procedure for appointment of arbitrators.
(1) The parties are free to agree on the procedure for appointing the arbitrator or arbitrators, including the procedure for appointing any chairman or umpire.
(2) If or to the extent that there is no such agreement, the following provisions apply.
(3) If the tribunal is to consist of a sole arbitrator, the parties shall jointly appoint the arbitrator not later than 28 days after service of a request in writing by either party to do so.
(4) If the tribunal is to consist of two arbitrators, each party shall appoint one arbitrator not later than 14 days after service of a request in writing by either party to do so.
(5) If the tribunal is to consist of three arbitrators –
  (a) each party shall appoint one arbitrator not later than 14 days after service of a request in writing by either party to do so, and
  (b) the two so appointed shall forthwith appoint a third arbitrator as the chairman of the tribunal.
(6) If the tribunal is to consist of two arbitrators and an umpire –
  (a) each party shall appoint one arbitrator not later than 14 days after service of a request in writing by either party to do so, and

(b) the two so appointed may appoint an umpire at any time after they themselves are appointed and shall do so before any substantive hearing or forthwith if they cannot agree on a matter relating to the arbitration.

(7) In any other case (in particular, if there are more than two parties) section 18 applies as in the case of a failure of the agreed appointment procedure.

17 Power in case of default to appoint sole arbitrator.

(1) Unless the parties otherwise agree, where each of two parties to an arbitration agreement is to appoint an arbitrator and one party ("the party in default") refuses to do so, or fails to do so within the time specified, the other party, having duly appointed his arbitrator, may give notice in writing to the party in default that he proposes to appoint his arbitrator to act as sole arbitrator.

(2) If the party in default does not within 7 clear days of that notice being given –

(a) make the required appointment, and

(b) notify the other party that he has done so,

the other party may appoint his arbitrator as sole arbitrator whose award shall be binding on both parties as if he had been so appointed by agreement.

(3) Where a sole arbitrator has been appointed under subsection (2), the party in default may (upon notice to the appointing party) apply to the court which may set aside the appointment.

(4) The leave of the court is required for any appeal from a decision of the court under this section.

18 Failure of appointment procedure.

(1) The parties are free to agree what is to happen in the event of a failure of the procedure for the appointment of the arbitral tribunal.

There is no failure if an appointment is duly made under section 17 (power in case of default to appoint sole arbitrator), unless that appointment is set aside.

(2) If or to the extent that there is no such agreement any party to the arbitration agreement may (upon notice to the other parties) apply to the court to exercise its powers under this section.

(3) Those powers are –

(a) to give directions as to the making of any necessary appointments;

(b) to direct that the tribunal shall be constituted by such appointments (or any one or more of them) as have been made;

(c) to revoke any appointments already made;

(d) to make any necessary appointments itself.

(4) An appointment made by the court under this section has effect as if made with the agreement of the parties.

(5) The leave of the court is required for any appeal from a decision of the court under this section.

19 Court to have regard to agreed qualifications.

In deciding whether to exercise, and in considering how to exercise, any of its powers under section 16 (procedure for appointment of arbitrators) or section 18 (failure of appointment procedure), the court shall have due regard to any agreement of the parties as to the qualifications required of the arbitrators.

20 Chairman.

(1) Where the parties have agreed that there is to be a chairman, they are free to agree what the functions of the chairman are to be in relation to the making of decisions, orders and awards.

(2) If or to the extent that there is no such agreement, the following provisions apply.

(3) Decisions, orders and awards shall be made by all or a majority of the arbitrators (including the chairman).

(4) The view of the chairman shall prevail in relation to a decision, order or award in respect of which there is neither unanimity nor a majority under subsection (3).

21 Umpire.

(1) Where the parties have agreed that there is to be an umpire, they are free to agree what the functions of the umpire are to be, and in particular –

(a) whether he is to attend the proceedings, and

(b) when he is to replace the other arbitrators as the tribunal with power to make decisions, orders and awards.

(2) If or to the extent that there is no such agreement, the following provisions apply.

(3) The umpire shall attend the proceedings and be supplied with the same documents and other materials as are supplied to the other arbitrators.

(4) Decisions, orders and awards shall be made by the other arbitrators unless and until they cannot agree on a matter relating to the arbitration.

In that event they shall forthwith give notice in writing to the parties and the umpire, whereupon the umpire shall replace them as the tribunal with power to make decisions, orders and awards as if he were sole arbitrator.

(5) If the arbitrators cannot agree but fail to give notice of that fact, or if any of them fails to join in the giving of notice, any party to the arbitral proceedings may (upon notice to the other parties and to the tribunal) apply to the court which may order that the umpire shall replace the other arbitrators as the tribunal with power to make decisions, orders and awards as if he were sole arbitrator.

(6) The leave of the court is required for any appeal from a decision of the court under this section.

22 Decision-making where no chairman or umpire.

(1) Where the parties agree that there shall be two or more arbitrators with no chairman or umpire, the parties are free to agree how the tribunal is to make decisions, orders and awards.

(2) If there is no such agreement, decisions, orders and awards shall be made by all or a majority of the arbitrators.

23 Revocation of arbitrator's authority.

(1) The parties are free to agree in what circumstances the authority of an arbitrator may be revoked.

(2) If or to the extent that there is no such agreement the following provisions apply.

(3) The authority of an arbitrator may not be revoked except –

(a) by the parties acting jointly, or

(b) by an arbitral or other institution or person vested by the parties with powers in that regard.

(4) Revocation of the authority of an arbitrator by the parties acting jointly must be agreed in writing unless the parties also agree (whether or not in writing) to terminate the arbitration agreement.

(5) Nothing in this section affects the power of the court –

(a) to revoke an appointment under section 18 (powers exercisable in case of failure of appointment procedure), or

(b) to remove an arbitrator on the grounds specified in section 24.

24 Power of court to remove arbitrator.

(1) A party to arbitral proceedings may (upon notice to the other parties, to the arbitrator concerned and to any other arbitrator) apply to the court to remove an arbitrator on any of the following grounds –

(a) that circumstances exist that give rise to justifiable doubts as to his impartiality;

(b) that he does not possess the qualifications required by the arbitration agreement;

(c) that he is physically or mentally incapable of conducting the proceedings or there are justifiable doubts as to his capacity to do so;

(d) that he has refused or failed –

(i) properly to conduct the proceedings, or

(ii) to use all reasonable despatch in conducting the proceedings or making an award,

and that substantial injustice has been or will be caused to the applicant.

(2) If there is an arbitral or other institution or person vested by the parties with power to remove an arbitrator, the court shall not exercise its power of removal unless satisfied that the applicant has first exhausted any available recourse to that institution or person.
(3) The arbitral tribunal may continue the arbitral proceedings and make an award while an application to the court under this section is pending.
(4) Where the court removes an arbitrator, it may make such order as it thinks fit with respect to his entitlement (if any) to fees or expenses, or the repayment of any fees or expenses already paid.
(5) The arbitrator concerned is entitled to appear and be heard by the court before it makes any order under this section.
(6) The leave of the court is required for any appeal from a decision of the court under this section.

25 Resignation of arbitrator.
(1) The parties are free to agree with an arbitrator as to the consequences of his resignation as regards –
(a) his entitlement (if any) to fees or expenses, and
(b) any liability thereby incurred by him.
(2) If or to the extent that there is no such agreement the following provisions apply.
(3) An arbitrator who resigns his appointment may (upon notice to the parties) apply to the court –
(a) to grant him relief from any liability thereby incurred by him, and
(b) to make such order as it thinks fit with respect to his entitlement (if any) to fees or expenses or the repayment of any fees or expenses already paid.
(4) If the court is satisfied that in all the circumstances it was reasonable for the arbitrator to resign, it may grant such relief as is mentioned in subsection (3)(a) on such terms as it thinks fit.
(5) The leave of the court is required for any appeal from a decision of the court under this section.

26 Death of arbitrator or person appointing him.
(1) The authority of an arbitrator is personal and ceases on his death.
(2) Unless otherwise agreed by the parties, the death of the person by whom an arbitrator was appointed does not revoke the arbitrator's authority.

27 Filling of vacancy, &c.
(1) Where an arbitrator ceases to hold office, the parties are free to agree –
(a) whether and if so how the vacancy is to be filled,
(b) whether and if so to what extent the previous proceedings should stand, and
(c) what effect (if any) his ceasing to hold office has on any appointment made by him (alone or jointly).
(2) If or to the extent that there is no such agreement, the following provisions apply.
(3) The provisions of sections 16 (procedure for appointment of arbitrators) and 18 (failure of appointment procedure) apply in relation to the filling of the vacancy as in relation to an original appointment.
(4) The tribunal (when reconstituted) shall determine whether and if so to what extent the previous proceedings should stand.

This does not affect any right of a party to challenge those proceedings on any ground which had arisen before the arbitrator ceased to hold office.
(5) His ceasing to hold office does not affect any appointment by him (alone or jointly) of another arbitrator, in particular any appointment of a chairman or umpire.

28 Joint and several liability of parties to arbitrators for fees and expenses.
(1) The parties are jointly and severally liable to pay to the arbitrators such reasonable fees and expenses (if any) as are appropriate in the circumstances.

(2) Any party may apply to the court (upon notice to the other parties and to the arbitrators) which may order that the amount of the arbitrators' fees and expenses shall be considered and adjusted by such means and upon such terms as it may direct.
(3) If the application is made after any amount has been paid to the arbitrators by way of fees or expenses, the court may order the repayment of such amount (if any) as is shown to be excessive, but shall not do so unless it is shown that it is reasonable in the circumstances to order repayment.
(4) The above provisions have effect subject to any order of the court under section 24(4) or 25(3)(b) (order as to entitlement to fees or expenses in case of removal or resignation of arbitrator).
(5) Nothing in this section affects any liability of a party to any other party to pay all or any of the costs of the arbitration (see sections 59 to 65) or any contractual right of an arbitrator to payment of his fees and expenses.
(6) In this section references to arbitrators include an arbitrator who has ceased to act and an umpire who has not replaced the other arbitrators.

29 Immunity of arbitrator.
(1) An arbitrator is not liable for anything done or omitted in the discharge or purported discharge of his functions as arbitrator unless the act or omission is shown to have been in bad faith.
(2) Subsection (1) applies to an employee or agent of an arbitrator as it applies to the arbitrator himself.
(3) This section does not affect any liability incurred by an arbitrator by reason of his resigning (but see section 25).

Jurisdiction of the arbitral tribunal

30 Competence of tribunal to rule on its own jurisdiction.
(1) Unless otherwise agreed by the parties, the arbitral tribunal may rule on its own substantive jurisdiction, that is, as to –

(a) whether there is a valid arbitration agreement,
(b) whether the tribunal is properly constituted, and
(c) what matters have been submitted to arbitration in accordance with the arbitration agreement.

(2) Any such ruling may be challenged by any available arbitral process of appeal or review or in accordance with the provisions of this Part.

31 Objection to substantive jurisdiction of tribunal.
(1) An objection that the arbitral tribunal lacks substantive jurisdiction at the outset of the proceedings must be raised by a party not later than the time he takes the first step in the proceedings to contest the merits of any matter in relation to which he challenges the tribunal's jurisdiction.

A party is not precluded from raising such an objection by the fact that he has appointed or participated in the appointment of an arbitrator.

(2) Any objection during the course of the arbitral proceedings that the arbitral tribunal is exceeding its substantive jurisdiction must be made as soon as possible after the matter alleged to be beyond its jurisdiction is raised.
(3) The arbitral tribunal may admit an objection later than the time specified in subsection (1) or (2) if it considers the delay justified.
(4) Where an objection is duly taken to the tribunal's substantive jurisdiction and the tribunal has power to rule on its own jurisdiction, it may –

(a) rule on the matter in an award as to jurisdiction, or
(b) deal with the objection in its award on the merits.

If the parties agree which of these courses the tribunal should take, the tribunal shall proceed accordingly.

(5) The tribunal may in any case, and shall if the parties so agree, stay proceedings whilst an application is made to the court under section 32 (determination of preliminary point of jurisdiction).

32 Determination of preliminary point of jurisdiction.

(1) The court may, on the application of a party to arbitral proceedings (upon notice to the other parties), determine any question as to the substantive jurisdiction of the tribunal. A party may lose the right to object (see section 73).

(2) An application under this section shall not be considered unless –
- (a) it is made with the agreement in writing of all the other parties to the proceedings, or
- (b) it is made with the permission of the tribunal and the court is satisfied –
  - (i) that the determination of the question is likely to produce substantial savings in costs,
  - (ii) that the application was made without delay, and
  - (iii) that there is good reason why the matter should be decided by the court.

(3) An application under this section, unless made with the agreement of all the other parties to the proceedings, shall state the grounds on which it is said that the matter should be decided by the court.

(4) Unless otherwise agreed by the parties, the arbitral tribunal may continue the arbitral proceedings and make an award while an application to the court under this section is pending.

(5) Unless the court gives leave, no appeal lies from a decision of the court whether the conditions specified in subsection (2) are met.

(6) The decision of the court on the question of jurisdiction shall be treated as a judgment of the court for the purposes of an appeal.

But no appeal lies without the leave of the court which shall not be given unless the court considers that the question involves a point of law which is one of general importance or is one which for some other special reason should be considered by the Court of Appeal.

The arbitral proceedings

33 General duty of the tribunal.

(1) The tribunal shall –
- (a) act fairly and impartially as between the parties, giving each party a reasonable opportunity of putting his case and dealing with that of his opponent, and
- (b) adopt procedures suitable to the circumstances of the particular case, avoiding unnecessary delay or expense, so as to provide a fair means for the resolution of the matters falling to be determined.

(2) The tribunal shall comply with that general duty in conducting the arbitral proceedings, in its decisions on matters of procedure and evidence and in the exercise of all other powers conferred on it.

34 Procedural and evidential matters.

(1) It shall be for the tribunal to decide all procedural and evidential matters, subject to the right of the parties to agree any matter.

(2) Procedural and evidential matters include –
- (a) when and where any part of the proceedings is to be held;
- (b) the language or languages to be used in the proceedings and whether translations of any relevant documents are to be supplied;
- (c) whether any and if so what form of written statements of claim and defence are to be used, when these should be supplied and the extent to which such statements can be later amended;
- (d) whether any and if so which documents or classes of documents should be disclosed between and produced by the parties and at what stage;

(e) whether any and if so what questions should be put to and answered by the respective parties and when and in what form this should be done;
(f) whether to apply strict rules of evidence (or any other rules) as to the admissibility, relevance or weight of any material (oral, written or other) sought to be tendered on any matters of fact or opinion, and the time, manner and form in which such material should be exchanged and presented;
(g) whether and to what extent the tribunal should itself take the initiative in ascertaining the facts and the law;
(h) whether and to what extent there should be oral or written evidence or submissions.

(3) The tribunal may fix the time within which any directions given by it are to be complied with, and may if it thinks fit extend the time so fixed (whether or not it has expired).

35 Consolidation of proceedings and concurrent hearings.
(1) The parties are free to agree –
(a) that the arbitral proceedings shall be consolidated with other arbitral proceedings, or
(b) that concurrent hearings shall be held,
on such terms as may be agreed.
(2) Unless the parties agree to confer such power on the tribunal, the tribunal has no power to order consolidation of proceedings or concurrent hearings.

36 Legal or other representation.
Unless otherwise agreed by the parties, a party to arbitral proceedings may be represented in the proceedings by a lawyer or other person chosen by him.

37 Power to appoint experts, legal advisers or assessors.
(1) Unless otherwise agreed by the parties –
(a) the tribunal may –
(i) appoint experts or legal advisers to report to it and the parties, or
(ii) appoint assessors to assist it on technical matters,
and may allow any such expert, legal adviser or assessor to attend the proceedings; and
(b) the parties shall be given a reasonable opportunity to comment on any information, opinion or advice offered by any such person.
(2) The fees and expenses of an expert, legal adviser or assessor appointed by the tribunal for which the arbitrators are liable are expenses of the arbitrators for the purposes of this Part.

38 General powers exercisable by the tribunal.
(1) The parties are free to agree on the powers exercisable by the arbitral tribunal for the purposes of and in relation to the proceedings.
(2) Unless otherwise agreed by the parties the tribunal has the following powers.
(3) The tribunal may order a claimant to provide security for the costs of the arbitration. This power shall not be exercised on the ground that the claimant is –
(a) an individual ordinarily resident outside the United Kingdom, or
(b) a corporation or association incorporated or formed under the law of a country outside the United Kingdom, or whose central management and control is exercised outside the United Kingdom.
(4) The tribunal may give directions in relation to any property which is the subject of the proceedings or as to which any question arises in the proceedings, and which is owned by or is in the possession of a party to the proceedings –

(a) for the inspection, photographing, preservation, custody or detention of the property by the tribunal, an expert or a party, or
(b) ordering that samples be taken from, or any observation be made of or experiment conducted upon, the property.
(5) The tribunal may direct that a party or witness shall be examined on oath or affirmation, and may for that purpose administer any necessary oath or take any necessary affirmation.
(6) The tribunal may give directions to a party for the preservation for the purposes of the proceedings of any evidence in his custody or control.

39 Power to make provisional awards.
(1) The parties are free to agree that the tribunal shall have power to order on a provisional basis any relief which it would have power to grant in a final award.
(2) This includes, for instance, making –
(a) a provisional order for the payment of money or the disposition of property as between the parties, or
(b) an order to make an interim payment on account of the costs of the arbitration.
(3) Any such order shall be subject to the tribunal's final adjudication; and the tribunal's final award, on the merits or as to costs, shall take account of any such order.
(4) Unless the parties agree to confer such power on the tribunal, the tribunal has no such power.
This does not affect its powers under section 47 (awards on different issues, &c.).

40 General duty of parties.
(1) The parties shall do all things necessary for the proper and expeditious conduct of the arbitral proceedings.
(2) This includes –
(a) complying without delay with any determination of the tribunal as to procedural or evidential matters, or with any order or directions of the tribunal, and
(b) where appropriate, taking without delay any necessary steps to obtain a decision of the court on a preliminary question of jurisdiction or law (see sections 32 and 45).

41 Powers of tribunal in case of party's default.
(1) The parties are free to agree on the powers of the tribunal in case of a party's failure to do something necessary for the proper and expeditious conduct of the arbitration.
(2) Unless otherwise agreed by the parties, the following provisions apply.
(3) If the tribunal is satisfied that there has been inordinate and inexcusable delay on the part of the claimant in pursuing his claim and that the delay –
(a) gives rise, or is likely to give rise, to a substantial risk that it is not possible to have a fair resolution of the issues in that claim, or
(b) has caused, or is likely to cause, serious prejudice to the respondent,
the tribunal may make an award dismissing the claim.
(4) If without showing sufficient cause a party –
(a) fails to attend or be represented at an oral hearing of which due notice was given, or
(b) where matters are to be dealt with in writing, fails after due notice to submit written evidence or make written submissions,
the tribunal may continue the proceedings in the absence of that party or, as the case may be, without any written evidence or submissions on his behalf, and may make an award on the basis of the evidence before it.

(5) If without showing sufficient cause a party fails to comply with any order or directions of the tribunal, the tribunal may make a peremptory order to the same effect, prescribing such time for compliance with it as the tribunal considers appropriate.
(6) If a claimant fails to comply with a peremptory order of the tribunal to provide security for costs, the tribunal may make an award dismissing his claim.
(7) If a party fails to comply with any other kind of peremptory order, then, without prejudice to section 42 (enforcement by court of tribunal's peremptory orders), the tribunal may do any of the following -

(a) direct that the party in default shall not be entitled to rely upon any allegation or material which was the subject matter of the order;
(b) draw such adverse inferences from the act of non-compliance as the circumstances justify;
(c) proceed to an award on the basis of such materials as have been properly provided to it;
(d) make such order as it thinks fit as to the payment of costs of the arbitration incurred in consequence of the non-compliance.

Powers of court in relation to arbitral proceedings

42 Enforcement of peremptory orders of tribunal.
(1) Unless otherwise agreed by the parties, the court may make an order requiring a party to comply with a peremptory order made by the tribunal.
(2) An application for an order under this section may be made -

(a) by the tribunal (upon notice to the parties),
(b) by a party to the arbitral proceedings with the permission of the tribunal (and upon notice to the other parties), or
(c) where the parties have agreed that the powers of the court under this section shall be available.

(3) The court shall not act unless it is satisfied that the applicant has exhausted any available arbitral process in respect of failure to comply with the tribunal's order.
(4) No order shall be made under this section unless the court is satisfied that the person to whom the tribunal's order was directed has failed to comply with it within the time prescribed in the order or, if no time was prescribed, within a reasonable time.
(5) The leave of the court is required for any appeal from a decision of the court under this section.

43 Securing the attendance of witnesses.
(1) A party to arbitral proceedings may use the same court procedures as are available in relation to legal proceedings to secure the attendance before the tribunal of a witness in order to give oral testimony or to produce documents or other material evidence.
(2) This may only be done with the permission of the tribunal or the agreement of the other parties.
(3) The court procedures may only be used if -

(a) the witness is in the United Kingdom, and
(b) the arbitral proceedings are being conducted in England and Wales or, as the case may be, Northern Ireland.

(4) A person shall not be compelled by virtue of this section to produce any document or other material evidence which he could not be compelled to produce in legal proceedings.

44 Court powers exercisable in support of arbitral proceedings.
(1) Unless otherwise agreed by the parties, the court has for the purposes of and in relation to arbitral proceedings the same power of making orders about the matters listed below as it has for the purposes of and in relation to legal proceedings.

(2) Those matters are –

(a) the taking of the evidence of witnesses;

(b) the preservation of evidence;

(c) making orders relating to property which is the subject of the proceedings or as to which any question arises in the proceedings –

(i) for the inspection, photographing, preservation, custody or detention of the property, or

(ii) ordering that samples be taken from, or any observation be made of or experiment conducted upon, the property;

and for that purpose authorising any person to enter any premises in the possession or control of a party to the arbitration;

(d) the sale of any goods the subject of the proceedings;

(e) the granting of an interim injunction or the appointment of a receiver.

(3) If the case is one of urgency, the court may, on the application of a party or proposed party to the arbitral proceedings, make such orders as it thinks necessary for the purpose of preserving evidence or assets.

(4) If the case is not one of urgency, the court shall act only on the application of a party to the arbitral proceedings (upon notice to the other parties and to the tribunal) made with the permission of the tribunal or the agreement in writing of the other parties.

(5) In any case the court shall act only if or to the extent that the arbitral tribunal, and any arbitral or other institution or person vested by the parties with power in that regard, has no power or is unable for the time being to act effectively.

(6) If the court so orders, an order made by it under this section shall cease to have effect in whole or in part on the order of the tribunal or of any such arbitral or other institution or person having power to act in relation to the subject-matter of the order.

(7) The leave of the court is required for any appeal from a decision of the court under this section.

45 Determination of preliminary point of law.

(1) Unless otherwise agreed by the parties, the court may on the application of a party to arbitral proceedings (upon notice to the other parties) determine any question of law arising in the course of the proceedings which the court is satisfied substantially affects the rights of one or more of the parties.

An agreement to dispense with reasons for the tribunal's award shall be considered an agreement to exclude the court's jurisdiction under this section.

(2) An application under this section shall not be considered unless –

(a) it is made with the agreement of all the other parties to the proceedings, or

(b) it is made with the permission of the tribunal and the court is satisfied –

(i) that the determination of the question is likely to produce substantial savings in costs, and

(ii) that the application was made without delay.

(3) The application shall identify the question of law to be determined and, unless made with the agreement of all the other parties to the proceedings, shall state the grounds on which it is said that the question should be decided by the court.

(4) Unless otherwise agreed by the parties, the arbitral tribunal may continue the arbitral proceedings and make an award while an application to the court under this section is pending.

(5) Unless the court gives leave, no appeal lies from a decision of the court whether the conditions specified in subsection (2) are met.

(6) The decision of the court on the question of law shall be treated as a judgment of the court for the purposes of an appeal.

But no appeal lies without the leave of the court which shall not be given unless the court considers that the question is one of general importance, or is one which for some other special reason should be considered by the Court of Appeal.

The award

46 Rules applicable to substance of dispute.

(1) The arbitral tribunal shall decide the dispute –

(a) in accordance with the law chosen by the parties as applicable to the substance of the dispute, or

(b) if the parties so agree, in accordance with such other considerations as are agreed by them or determined by the tribunal.

(2) For this purpose the choice of the laws of a country shall be understood to refer to the substantive laws of that country and not its conflict of laws rules.

(3) If or to the extent that there is no such choice or agreement, the tribunal shall apply the law determined by the conflict of laws rules which it considers applicable.

47 Awards on different issues, &c.

(1) Unless otherwise agreed by the parties, the tribunal may make more than one award at different times on different aspects of the matters to be determined.

(2) The tribunal may, in particular, make an award relating –

(a) to an issue affecting the whole claim, or

(b) to a part only of the claims or cross-claims submitted to it for decision.

(3) If the tribunal does so, it shall specify in its award the issue, or the claim or part of a claim, which is the subject matter of the award.

48 Remedies.

(1) The parties are free to agree on the powers exercisable by the arbitral tribunal as regards remedies.

(2) Unless otherwise agreed by the parties, the tribunal has the following powers.

(3) The tribunal may make a declaration as to any matter to be determined in the proceedings.

(4) The tribunal may order the payment of a sum of money, in any currency.

(5) The tribunal has the same powers as the court –

(a) to order a party to do or refrain from doing anything;

(b) to order specific performance of a contract (other than a contract relating to land);

(c) to order the rectification, setting aside or cancellation of a deed or other document.

49 Interest.

(1) The parties are free to agree on the powers of the tribunal as regards the award of interest.

(2) Unless otherwise agreed by the parties the following provisions apply.

(3) The tribunal may award simple or compound interest from such dates, at such rates and with such rests as it considers meets the justice of the case –

(a) on the whole or part of any amount awarded by the tribunal, in respect of any period up to the date of the award;

(b) on the whole or part of any amount claimed in the arbitration and outstanding at the commencement of the arbitral proceedings but paid before the award was made, in respect of any period up to the date of payment.

(4) The tribunal may award simple or compound interest from the date of the award (or any later date) until payment, at such rates and with such rests as it considers meets the justice of the case, on the outstanding amount of any award (including any award of interest under subsection (3) and any award as to costs).

(5) References in this section to an amount awarded by the tribunal include an amount payable in consequence of a declaratory award by the tribunal.

(6) The above provisions do not affect any other power of the tribunal to award interest.

50 Extension of time for making award.
(1) Where the time for making an award is limited by or in pursuance of the arbitration agreement, then, unless otherwise agreed by the parties, the court may in accordance with the following provisions by order extend that time.
(2) An application for an order under this section may be made –
(a) by the tribunal (upon notice to the parties), or
(b) by any party to the proceedings (upon notice to the tribunal and the other parties),
but only after exhausting any available arbitral process for obtaining an extension of time.
(3) The court shall only make an order if satisfied that a substantial injustice would otherwise be done.
(4) The court may extend the time for such period and on such terms as it thinks fit, and may do so whether or not the time previously fixed (by or under the agreement or by a previous order) has expired.
(5) The leave of the court is required for any appeal from a decision of the court under this section.

51 Settlement.
(1) If during arbitral proceedings the parties settle the dispute, the following provisions apply unless otherwise agreed by the parties.
(2) The tribunal shall terminate the substantive proceedings and, if so requested by the parties and not objected to by the tribunal, shall record the settlement in the form of an agreed award.
(3) An agreed award shall state that it is an award of the tribunal and shall have the same status and effect as any other award on the merits of the case.
(4) The following provisions of this Part relating to awards (sections 52 to 58) apply to an agreed award.
(5) Unless the parties have also settled the matter of the payment of the costs of the arbitration, the provisions of this Part relating to costs (sections 59 to 65) continue to apply.

52 Form of award.
(1) The parties are free to agree on the form of an award.
(2) If or to the extent that there is no such agreement, the following provisions apply.
(3) The award shall be in writing signed by all the arbitrators or all those assenting to the award.
(4) The award shall contain the reasons for the award unless it is an agreed award or the parties have agreed to dispense with reasons.
(5) The award shall state the seat of the arbitration and the date when the award is made.

53 Place where award treated as made.
Unless otherwise agreed by the parties, where the seat of the arbitration is in England and Wales or Northern Ireland, any award in the proceedings shall be treated as made there, regardless of where it was signed, despatched or delivered to any of the parties.

54 Date of award.
(1) Unless otherwise agreed by the parties, the tribunal may decide what is to be taken to be the date on which the award was made.
(2) In the absence of any such decision, the date of the award shall be taken to be the date on which it is signed by the arbitrator or, where more than one arbitrator signs the award, by the last of them.

55 Notification of award.
(1) The parties are free to agree on the requirements as to notification of the award to the parties.
(2) If there is no such agreement, the award shall be notified to the parties by service on them of copies of the award, which shall be done without delay after the award is made.
(3) Nothing in this section affects section 56 (power to withhold award in case of non-payment).

56 Power to withhold award in case of non-payment.

(1) The tribunal may refuse to deliver an award to the parties except upon full payment of the fees and expenses of the arbitrators.

(2) If the tribunal refuses on that ground to deliver an award, a party to the arbitral proceedings may (upon notice to the other parties and the tribunal) apply to the court, which may order that –

(a) the tribunal shall deliver the award on the payment into court by the applicant of the fees and expenses demanded, or such lesser amount as the court may specify,

(b) the amount of the fees and expenses properly payable shall be determined by such means and upon such terms as the court may direct, and

(c) out of the money paid into court there shall be paid out such fees and expenses as may be found to be properly payable and the balance of the money (if any) shall be paid out to the applicant.

(3) For this purpose the amount of fees and expenses properly payable is the amount the applicant is liable to pay under section 28 or any agreement relating to the payment of the arbitrators.

(4) No application to the court may be made where there is any available arbitral process for appeal or review of the amount of the fees or expenses demanded.

(5) References in this section to arbitrators include an arbitrator who has ceased to act and an umpire who has not replaced the other arbitrators.

(6) The above provisions of this section also apply in relation to any arbitral or other institution or person vested by the parties with powers in relation to the delivery of the tribunal's award.

As they so apply, the references to the fees and expenses of the arbitrators shall be construed as including the fees and expenses of that institution or person.

(7) The leave of the court is required for any appeal from a decision of the court under this section.

(8) Nothing in this section shall be construed as excluding an application under section 28 where payment has been made to the arbitrators in order to obtain the award.

57 Correction of award or additional award.

(1) The parties are free to agree on the powers of the tribunal to correct an award or make an additional award.

(2) If or to the extent there is no such agreement, the following provisions apply.

(3) The tribunal may on its own initiative or on the application of a party –

(a) correct an award so as to remove any clerical mistake or error arising from an accidental slip or omission or clarify or remove any ambiguity in the award, or

(b) make an additional award in respect of any claim (including a claim for interest or costs) which was presented to the tribunal but was not dealt with in the award.

These powers shall not be exercised without first affording the other parties a reasonable opportunity to make representations to the tribunal.

(4) Any application for the exercise of those powers must be made within 28 days of the date of the award or such longer period as the parties may agree.

(5) Any correction of an award shall be made within 28 days of the date the application was received by the tribunal or, where the correction is made by the tribunal on its own initiative, within 28 days of the date of the award or, in either case, such longer period as the parties may agree.

(6) Any additional award shall be made within 56 days of the date of the original award or such longer period as the parties may agree.

(7) Any correction of an award shall form part of the award.

58 Effect of award.

(1) Unless otherwise agreed by the parties, an award made by the tribunal pursuant to an arbitration agreement is final and binding both on the parties and on any persons claiming through or under them.

(2) This does not affect the right of a person to challenge the award by any available arbitral process of appeal or review or in accordance with the provisions of this Part.

Costs of the arbitration

59 Costs of the arbitration.
(1) References in this Part to the costs of the arbitration are to –
(a) the arbitrators' fees and expenses,
(b) the fees and expenses of any arbitral institution concerned, and
(c) the legal or other costs of the parties.
(2) Any such reference includes the costs of or incidental to any proceedings to determine the amount of the recoverable costs of the arbitration (see section 63).

60 Agreement to pay costs in any event.
An agreement which has the effect that a party is to pay the whole or part of the costs of the arbitration in any event is only valid if made after the dispute in question has arisen.

61 Award of costs.
(1) The tribunal may make an award allocating the costs of the arbitration as between the parties, subject to any agreement of the parties.
(2) Unless the parties otherwise agree, the tribunal shall award costs on the general principle that costs should follow the event except where it appears to the tribunal that in the circumstances this is not appropriate in relation to the whole or part of the costs.

62 Effect of agreement or award about costs.
Unless the parties otherwise agree, any obligation under an agreement between them as to how the costs of the arbitration are to be borne, or under an award allocating the costs of the arbitration, extends only to such costs as are recoverable.

63 The recoverable costs of the arbitration.
(1) The parties are free to agree what costs of the arbitration are recoverable.
(2) If or to the extent there is no such agreement, the following provisions apply.
(3) The tribunal may determine by award the recoverable costs of the arbitration on such basis as it thinks fit.
If it does so, it shall specify –
(a) the basis on which it has acted, and
(b) the items of recoverable costs and the amount referable to each.
(4) If the tribunal does not determine the recoverable costs of the arbitration, any party to the arbitral proceedings may apply to the court (upon notice to the other parties) which may –
(a) determine the recoverable costs of the arbitration on such basis as it thinks fit, or
(b) order that they shall be determined by such means and upon such terms as it may specify.
(5) Unless the tribunal or the court determines otherwise –
(a) the recoverable costs of the arbitration shall be determined on the basis that there shall be allowed a reasonable amount in respect of all costs reasonably incurred, and
(b) any doubt as to whether costs were reasonably incurred or were reasonable in amount shall be resolved in favour of the paying party.
(6) The above provisions have effect subject to section 64 (recoverable fees and expenses of arbitrators).
(7) Nothing in this section affects any right of the arbitrators, any expert, legal adviser or assessor appointed by the tribunal, or any arbitral institution, to payment of their fees and expenses.

64 Recoverable fees and expenses of arbitrators.

(1) Unless otherwise agreed by the parties, the recoverable costs of the arbitration shall include in respect of the fees and expenses of the arbitrators only such reasonable fees and expenses as are appropriate in the circumstances.

(2) If there is any question as to what reasonable fees and expenses are appropriate in the circumstances, and the matter is not already before the court on an application under section 63(4), the court may on the application of any party (upon notice to the other parties) –

(a) determine the matter, or

(b) order that it be determined by such means and upon such terms as the court may specify.

(3) Subsection (1) has effect subject to any order of the court under section 24(4) or 25(3) (b) (order as to entitlement to fees or expenses in case of removal or resignation of arbitrator).

(4) Nothing in this section affects any right of the arbitrator to payment of his fees and expenses.

65 Power to limit recoverable costs.

(1) Unless otherwise agreed by the parties, the tribunal may direct that the recoverable costs of the arbitration, or of any part of the arbitral proceedings, shall be limited to a specified amount.

(2) Any direction may be made or varied at any stage, but this must be done sufficiently in advance of the incurring of costs to which it relates, or the taking of any steps in the proceedings which may be affected by it, for the limit to be taken into account.

Powers of the court in relation to award

66 Enforcement of the award.

(1) An award made by the tribunal pursuant to an arbitration agreement may, by leave of the court, be enforced in the same manner as a judgment or order of the court to the same effect.

(2) Where leave is so given, judgment may be entered in terms of the award.

(3) Leave to enforce an award shall not be given where, or to the extent that, the person against whom it is sought to be enforced shows that the tribunal lacked substantive jurisdiction to make the award.

The right to raise such an objection may have been lost (see section 73).

(4) Nothing in this section affects the recognition or enforcement of an award under any other enactment or rule of law, in particular under Part II of the M5Arbitration Act 1950 (enforcement of awards under Geneva Convention) or the provisions of Part III of this Act relating to the recognition and enforcement of awards under the New York Convention or by an action on the award.

67 Challenging the award: substantive jurisdiction.

(1) A party to arbitral proceedings may (upon notice to the other parties and to the tribunal) apply to the court –

(a) challenging any award of the arbitral tribunal as to its substantive jurisdiction; or

(b) for an order declaring an award made by the tribunal on the merits to be of no effect, in whole or in part, because the tribunal did not have substantive jurisdiction.

A party may lose the right to object (see section 73) and the right to apply is subject to the restrictions in section 70(2) and (3).

(2) The arbitral tribunal may continue the arbitral proceedings and make a further award while an application to the court under this section is pending in relation to an award as to jurisdiction.

(3) On an application under this section challenging an award of the arbitral tribunal as to its substantive jurisdiction, the court may by order –

(a) confirm the award,

(b) vary the award, or

(c) set aside the award in whole or in part.

(4) The leave of the court is required for any appeal from a decision of the court under this section.

68 Challenging the award: serious irregularity.

(1) A party to arbitral proceedings may (upon notice to the other parties and to the tribunal) apply to the court challenging an award in the proceedings on the ground of serious irregularity affecting the tribunal, the proceedings or the award.

A party may lose the right to object (see section 73) and the right to apply is subject to the restrictions in section 70(2) and (3).

(2) Serious irregularity means an irregularity of one or more of the following kinds which the court considers has caused or will cause substantial injustice to the applicant –

(a) failure by the tribunal to comply with section 33 (general duty of tribunal);

(b) the tribunal exceeding its powers (otherwise than by exceeding its substantive jurisdiction: see section 67);

(c) failure by the tribunal to conduct the proceedings in accordance with the procedure agreed by the parties;

(d) failure by the tribunal to deal with all the issues that were put to it;

(e) any arbitral or other institution or person vested by the parties with powers in relation to the proceedings or the award exceeding its powers;

(f) uncertainty or ambiguity as to the effect of the award;

(g) the award being obtained by fraud or the award or the way in which it was procured being contrary to public policy;

(h) failure to comply with the requirements as to the form of the award; or

(i) any irregularity in the conduct of the proceedings or in the award which is admitted by the tribunal or by any arbitral or other institution or person vested by the parties with powers in relation to the proceedings or the award.

(3) If there is shown to be serious irregularity affecting the tribunal, the proceedings or the award, the court may –

(a) remit the award to the tribunal, in whole or in part, for reconsideration,

(b) set the award aside in whole or in part, or

(c) declare the award to be of no effect, in whole or in part.

The court shall not exercise its power to set aside or to declare an award to be of no effect, in whole or in part, unless it is satisfied that it would be inappropriate to remit the matters in question to the tribunal for reconsideration.

(4) The leave of the court is required for any appeal from a decision of the court under this section.

69 Appeal on point of law.

(1) Unless otherwise agreed by the parties, a party to arbitral proceedings may (upon notice to the other parties and to the tribunal) appeal to the court on a question of law arising out of an award made in the proceedings.

An agreement to dispense with reasons for the tribunal's award shall be considered an agreement to exclude the court's jurisdiction under this section.

(2) An appeal shall not be brought under this section except –

(a) with the agreement of all the other parties to the proceedings, or

(b) with the leave of the court.

The right to appeal is also subject to the restrictions in section 70(2) and (3).

(3) Leave to appeal shall be given only if the court is satisfied –

(a) that the determination of the question will substantially affect the rights of one or more of the parties,

(b) that the question is one which the tribunal was asked to determine,

(c) that, on the basis of the findings of fact in the award –

(i) the decision of the tribunal on the question is obviously wrong, or

(ii) the question is one of general public importance and the decision of the tribunal is at least open to serious doubt, and

(d) that, despite the agreement of the parties to resolve the matter by arbitration, it is just and proper in all the circumstances for the court to determine the question.

(4) An application for leave to appeal under this section shall identify the question of law to be determined and state the grounds on which it is alleged that leave to appeal should be granted.

(5) The court shall determine an application for leave to appeal under this section without a hearing unless it appears to the court that a hearing is required.

(6) The leave of the court is required for any appeal from a decision of the court under this section to grant or refuse leave to appeal.

(7) On an appeal under this section the court may by order –

(a) confirm the award,

(b) vary the award,

(c) remit the award to the tribunal, in whole or in part, for reconsideration in the light of the court's determination, or

(d) set aside the award in whole or in part.

The court shall not exercise its power to set aside an award, in whole or in part, unless it is satisfied that it would be inappropriate to remit the matters in question to the tribunal for reconsideration.

(8) The decision of the court on an appeal under this section shall be treated as a judgment of the court for the purposes of a further appeal.

But no such appeal lies without the leave of the court which shall not be given unless the court considers that the question is one of general importance or is one which for some other special reason should be considered by the Court of Appeal.

70 Challenge or appeal: supplementary provisions.

(1) The following provisions apply to an application or appeal under section 67, 68 or 69.

(2) An application or appeal may not be brought if the applicant or appellant has not first exhausted –

(a) any available arbitral process of appeal or review, and

(b) any available recourse under section 57 (correction of award or additional award).

(3) Any application or appeal must be brought within 28 days of the date of the award or, if there has been any arbitral process of appeal or review, of the date when the applicant or appellant was notified of the result of that process.

(4) If on an application or appeal it appears to the court that the award –

(a) does not contain the tribunal's reasons, or

(b) does not set out the tribunal's reasons in sufficient detail to enable the court properly to consider the application or appeal,

the court may order the tribunal to state the reasons for its award in sufficient detail for that purpose.

(5) Where the court makes an order under subsection (4), it may make such further order as it thinks fit with respect to any additional costs of the arbitration resulting from its order.

(6) The court may order the applicant or appellant to provide security for the costs of the application or appeal, and may direct that the application or appeal be dismissed if the order is not complied with.

The power to order security for costs shall not be exercised on the ground that the applicant or appellant is –

(a) an individual ordinarily resident outside the United Kingdom, or

(b) a corporation or association incorporated or formed under the law of a country outside the United Kingdom, or whose central management and control is exercised outside the United Kingdom.

(7) The court may order that any money payable under the award shall be brought into court or otherwise secured pending the determination of the application or appeal, and may direct that the application or appeal be dismissed if the order is not complied with.
(8) The court may grant leave to appeal subject to conditions to the same or similar effect as an order under subsection (6) or (7).
This does not affect the general discretion of the court to grant leave subject to conditions.

71 Challenge or appeal: effect of order of court.
(1) The following provisions have effect where the court makes an order under section 67, 68 or 69 with respect to an award.
(2) Where the award is varied, the variation has effect as part of the tribunal's award.
(3) Where the award is remitted to the tribunal, in whole or in part, for reconsideration, the tribunal shall make a fresh award in respect of the matters remitted within three months of the date of the order for remission or such longer or shorter period as the court may direct.
(4) Where the award is set aside or declared to be of no effect, in whole or in part, the court may also order that any provision that an award is a condition precedent to the bringing of legal proceedings in respect of a matter to which the arbitration agreement applies, is of no effect as regards the subject matter of the award or, as the case may be, the relevant part of the award.

Miscellaneous

72 Saving for rights of person who takes no part in proceedings.
(1) A person alleged to be a party to arbitral proceedings but who takes no part in the proceedings may question –
(a) whether there is a valid arbitration agreement,
(b) whether the tribunal is properly constituted, or
(c) what matters have been submitted to arbitration in accordance with the arbitration agreement,
by proceedings in the court for a declaration or injunction or other appropriate relief.
(2) He also has the same right as a party to the arbitral proceedings to challenge an award –
(a) by an application under section 67 on the ground of lack of substantive jurisdiction in relation to him, or
(b) by an application under section 68 on the ground of serious irregularity (within the meaning of that section) affecting him;
and section 70(2) (duty to exhaust arbitral procedures) does not apply in his case.

73 Loss of right to object.
(1) If a party to arbitral proceedings takes part, or continues to take part, in the proceedings without making, either forthwith or within such time as is allowed by the arbitration agreement or the tribunal or by any provision of this Part, any objection –
(a) that the tribunal lacks substantive jurisdiction,
(b) that the proceedings have been improperly conducted,
(c) that there has been a failure to comply with the arbitration agreement or with any provision of this Part, or
(d) that there has been any other irregularity affecting the tribunal or the proceedings,
he may not raise that objection later, before the tribunal or the court, unless he shows that, at the time he took part or continued to take part in the proceedings, he did not know and could not with reasonable diligence have discovered the grounds for the objection.

(2) Where the arbitral tribunal rules that it has substantive jurisdiction and a party to arbitral proceedings who could have questioned that ruling –

(a) by any available arbitral process of appeal or review, or

(b) by challenging the award,

does not do so, or does not do so within the time allowed by the arbitration agreement or any provision of this Part, he may not object later to the tribunal's substantive jurisdiction on any ground which was the subject of that ruling.

74 Immunity of arbitral institutions, &c.

(1) An arbitral or other institution or person designated or requested by the parties to appoint or nominate an arbitrator is not liable for anything done or omitted in the discharge or purported discharge of that function unless the act or omission is shown to have been in bad faith.

(2) An arbitral or other institution or person by whom an arbitrator is appointed or nominated is not liable, by reason of having appointed or nominated him, for anything done or omitted by the arbitrator (or his employees or agents) in the discharge or purported discharge of his functions as arbitrator.

(3) The above provisions apply to an employee or agent of an arbitral or other institution or person as they apply to the institution or person himself.

75 Charge to secure payment of solicitors' costs.

The powers of the court to make declarations and orders under section 73 of the M6Solicitors Act 1974 or Article 71H of the M7Solicitors (Northern Ireland) Order 1976 (power to charge property recovered in the proceedings with the payment of solicitors' costs) may be exercised in relation to arbitral proceedings as if those proceedings were proceedings in the court.

Supplementary

76 Service of notices, &c.

(1) The parties are free to agree on the manner of service of any notice or other document required or authorised to be given or served in pursuance of the arbitration agreement or for the purposes of the arbitral proceedings.

(2) If or to the extent that there is no such agreement the following provisions apply.

(3) A notice or other document may be served on a person by any effective means.

(4) If a notice or other document is addressed, pre-paid and delivered by post –

(a) to the addressee's last known principal residence or, if he is or has been carrying on a trade, profession or business, his last known principal business address, or

(b) where the addressee is a body corporate, to the body's registered or principal office,

it shall be treated as effectively served.

(5) This section does not apply to the service of documents for the purposes of legal proceedings, for which provision is made by rules of court.

(6) References in this Part to a notice or other document include any form of communication in writing and references to giving or serving a notice or other document shall be construed accordingly.

77 Powers of court in relation to service of documents.

(1) This section applies where service of a document on a person in the manner agreed by the parties, or in accordance with provisions of section 76 having effect in default of agreement, is not reasonably practicable.

(2) Unless otherwise agreed by the parties, the court may make such order as it thinks fit –

(a) for service in such manner as the court may direct, or

(b) dispensing with service of the document.

(3) Any party to the arbitration agreement may apply for an order, but only after exhausting any available arbitral process for resolving the matter.
(4) The leave of the court is required for any appeal from a decision of the court under this section.

78 Reckoning periods of time.
(1) The parties are free to agree on the method of reckoning periods of time for the purposes of any provision agreed by them or any provision of this Part having effect in default of such agreement.
(2) If or to the extent there is no such agreement, periods of time shall be reckoned in accordance with the following provisions.
(3) Where the act is required to be done within a specified period after or from a specified date, the period begins immediately after that date.
(4) Where the act is required to be done a specified number of clear days after a specified date, at least that number of days must intervene between the day on which the act is done and that date.
(5) Where the period is a period of seven days or less which would include a Saturday, Sunday or a public holiday in the place where anything which has to be done within the period falls to be done, that day shall be excluded.

In relation to England and Wales or Northern Ireland, a "public holiday" means Christmas Day, Good Friday or a day which under the M8Banking and Financial Dealings Act 1971 is a bank holiday.

79 Power of court to extend time limits relating to arbitral proceedings.
(1) Unless the parties otherwise agree, the court may by order extend any time limit agreed by them in relation to any matter relating to the arbitral proceedings or specified in any provision of this Part having effect in default of such agreement.

This section does not apply to a time limit to which section 12 applies (power of court to extend time for beginning arbitral proceedings, &c.).
(2) An application for an order may be made –
(a) by any party to the arbitral proceedings (upon notice to the other parties and to the tribunal), or
(b) by the arbitral tribunal (upon notice to the parties).
(3) The court shall not exercise its power to extend a time limit unless it is satisfied –
(a) that any available recourse to the tribunal, or to any arbitral or other institution or person vested by the parties with power in that regard, has first been exhausted, and
(b) that a substantial injustice would otherwise be done.
(4) The court's power under this section may be exercised whether or not the time has already expired.
(5) An order under this section may be made on such terms as the court thinks fit.
(6) The leave of the court is required for any appeal from a decision of the court under this section.

80 Notice and other requirements in connection with legal proceedings.
(1) References in this Part to an application, appeal or other step in relation to legal proceedings being taken "upon notice" to the other parties to the arbitral proceedings, or to the tribunal, are to such notice of the originating process as is required by rules of court and do not impose any separate requirement.
(2) Rules of court shall be made –
(a) requiring such notice to be given as indicated by any provision of this Part, and
(b) as to the manner, form and content of any such notice.
(3) Subject to any provision made by rules of court, a requirement to give notice to the tribunal of legal proceedings shall be construed –
(a) if there is more than one arbitrator, as a requirement to give notice to each of them; and
(b) if the tribunal is not fully constituted, as a requirement to give notice to any arbitrator who has been appointed.

(4) References in this Part to making an application or appeal to the court within a specified period are to the issue within that period of the appropriate originating process in accordance with rules of court.
(5) Where any provision of this Part requires an application or appeal to be made to the court within a specified time, the rules of court relating to the reckoning of periods, the extending or abridging of periods, and the consequences of not taking a step within the period prescribed by the rules, apply in relation to that requirement.
(6) Provision may be made by rules of court amending the provisions of this Part –
  (a) with respect to the time within which any application or appeal to the court must be made,
  (b) so as to keep any provision made by this Part in relation to arbitral proceedings in step with the corresponding provision of rules of court applying in relation to proceedings in the court, or
  (c) so as to keep any provision made by this Part in relation to legal proceedings in step with the corresponding provision of rules of court applying generally in relation to proceedings in the court.
(7) Nothing in this section affects the generality of the power to make rules of court.

81 Saving for certain matters governed by common law.
(1) Nothing in this Part shall be construed as excluding the operation of any rule of law consistent with the provisions of this Part, in particular, any rule of law as to –
  (a) matters which are not capable of settlement by arbitration;
  (b) the effect of an oral arbitration agreement; or
  (c) the refusal of recognition or enforcement of an arbitral award on grounds of public policy.
(2) Nothing in this Act shall be construed as reviving any jurisdiction of the court to set aside or remit an award on the ground of errors of fact or law on the face of the award.

82 Minor definitions.
(1) In this Part –

"arbitrator", unless the context otherwise requires, includes an umpire; "available arbitral process", in relation to any matter, includes any process

of appeal to or review by an arbitral or other institution or person vested by the parties with powers in relation to that matter;

"claimant", unless the context otherwise requires, includes a counterclaimant, and related expressions shall be construed accordingly;

"dispute" includes any difference;

"enactment" includes an enactment contained in Northern Ireland legislation;

"legal proceedings" means civil proceedings [F1 in England and Wales in the High Court or the county court or in Northern Ireland] in the High Court or a county court;

"peremptory order" means an order made under section 41(5) or made in exercise of any corresponding power conferred by the parties;

"premises" includes land, buildings, moveable structures, vehicles, vessels, aircraft and hovercraft;

"question of law" means –
  (a) for a court in England and Wales, a question of the law of England and Wales, and
  (b) for a court in Northern Ireland, a question of the law of Northern Ireland;

"substantive jurisdiction", in relation to an arbitral tribunal, refers to the matters specified in section 30(1)(a) to (c), and references to the tribunal exceeding its substantive jurisdiction shall be construed accordingly.

(2) References in this Part to a party to an arbitration agreement include any person claiming under or through a party to the agreement.

83 Index of defined expressions: Part I.
In this Part the expressions listed below are defined or otherwise explained by the provisions indicated –

agreement, agree and agreed	section 5(1)
agreement in writing	section 5(2) to (5)
arbitration agreement	sections 6 and 5(1)
arbitrator	section 82(1)
available arbitral process	section 82(1)
claimant	section 82(1)
commencement (in relation to arbitral proceedings)	section 14
costs of the arbitration	section 59
the court	section 105
dispute	section 82(1)
enactment	section 82(1)
legal proceedings	section 82(1)
Limitation Acts	section 13(4)
notice (or other document)	section 76(6)
party –	
– in relation to an arbitration agreement	section 82(2)
– where section 106(2) or (3) applies	section 106(4)
peremptory order	section 82(1) (and see section 41(5))
premises	section 82(1)
question of law	section 82(1)
recoverable costs	sections 63 and 64
seat of the arbitration	section 3
serve and service (of notice or other document)	section 76(6)
substantive jurisdiction (in relation to an arbitral tribunal)	section 82(1) (and see section 30(1)(a) to (c))
upon notice (to the parties or the tribunal)	section 80
written and in writing	section 5(6)

84 Transitional provisions.
(1) The provisions of this Part do not apply to arbitral proceedings commenced before the date on which this Part comes into force.
(2) They apply to arbitral proceedings commenced on or after that date under an arbitration agreement whenever made.
(3) The above provisions have effect subject to any transitional provision made by an order under section 109(2) (power to include transitional provisions in commencement order).

PART II OTHER PROVISIONS RELATING TO ARBITRATION

Domestic arbitration agreements

[PROSPECTIVE]

85 Modification of Part I in relation to domestic arbitration agreement.
(1) In the case of a domestic arbitration agreement the provisions of Part I are modified in accordance with the following sections.

(2) For this purpose a "domestic arbitration agreement" means an arbitration agreement to which none of the parties is –

(a) an individual who is a national of, or habitually resident in, a state other than the United Kingdom, or

(b) a body corporate which is incorporated in, or whose central control and management is exercised in, a state other than the United Kingdom,

and under which the seat of the arbitration (if the seat has been designated or determined) is in the United Kingdom.

(3) In subsection (2) "arbitration agreement" and "seat of the arbitration" have the same meaning as in Part I (see sections 3, 5(1) and 6).

[PROSPECTIVE]

86 Staying of legal proceedings.

(1) In section 9 (stay of legal proceedings), subsection (4) (stay unless the arbitration agreement is null and void, inoperative, or incapable of being performed) does not apply to a domestic arbitration agreement.

(2) On an application under that section in relation to a domestic arbitration agreement the court shall grant a stay unless satisfied –

(a) that the arbitration agreement is null and void, inoperative, or incapable of being performed, or

(b) that there are other sufficient grounds for not requiring the parties to abide by the arbitration agreement.

(3) The court may treat as a sufficient ground under subsection (2)(b) the fact that the applicant is or was at any material time not ready and willing to do all things necessary for the proper conduct of the arbitration or of any other dispute resolution procedures required to be exhausted before resorting to arbitration.

(4) For the purposes of this section the question whether an arbitration agreement is a domestic arbitration agreement shall be determined by reference to the facts at the time the legal proceedings are commenced.

[PROSPECTIVE]

87 Effectiveness of agreement to exclude court's jurisdiction.

(1) In the case of a domestic arbitration agreement any agreement to exclude the jurisdiction of the court under –

(a) section 45 (determination of preliminary point of law), or

(b) section 69 (challenging the award: appeal on point of law),

is not effective unless entered into after the commencement of the arbitral proceedings in which the question arises or the award is made.

(2) For this purpose the commencement of the arbitral proceedings has the same meaning as in Part I (see section 14).

(3) For the purposes of this section the question whether an arbitration agreement is a domestic arbitration agreement shall be determined by reference to the facts at the time the agreement is entered into.

88 Power to repeal or amend sections 85 to 87.

(1) The Secretary of State may by order repeal or amend the provisions of sections 85 to 87.

(2) An order under this section may contain such supplementary, incidental and transitional provisions as appear to the Secretary of State to be appropriate.

(3) An order under this section shall be made by statutory instrument and no such order shall be made unless a draft of it has been laid before and approved by a resolution of each House of Parliament.

Consumer arbitration agreements

89 Application of unfair terms regulations to consumer arbitration agreements.
(1) The following sections extend the application of Part 2 (unfair terms) of the Consumer Rights Act 2015 in relation to a term which constitutes an arbitration agreement.
For this purpose "arbitration agreement" means an agreement to submit to arbitration present or future disputes or differences (whether or not contractual).
(2) In those sections "the Part" means Part 2 (unfair terms) of the Consumer Rights Act 2015.
(3) Those sections apply whatever the law applicable to the arbitration agreement.

90 Part applies where consumer is a legal person
The Part applies where the consumer is a legal person as it applies where the consumer is an individual.

91 Arbitration agreement unfair where modest amount sought.
(1) A term which constitutes an arbitration agreement is unfair for the purposes of the Part so far as it relates to a claim for a pecuniary remedy which does not exceed the amount specified by order for the purposes of this section.
(2) Orders under this section may make different provision for different cases and for different purposes.
(3) The power to make orders under this section is exercisable –

(a) for England and Wales, by the Secretary of State with the concurrence of the Lord Chancellor,
(b) for Scotland, by the Secretary of State. . ., and
(c) for Northern Ireland, by the Department of Economic Development for Northern Ireland with the concurrence of the Lord Chancellor.

(4) Any such order for England and Wales or Scotland shall be made by statutory instrument which shall be subject to annulment in pursuance of a resolution of either House of Parliament.
(5) Any such order for Northern Ireland shall be a statutory rule for the purposes of the Statutory Rules (Northern Ireland) Order 1979 and shall be subject to negative resolution, within the meaning of section 41(6) of the Interpretation Act (Northern Ireland) 1954.

Small claims arbitration in the county court

92 Exclusion of Part I in relation to small claims arbitration in the county court.
Nothing in Part I of this Act applies to arbitration under section 64 of the County Courts Act 1984.

Appointment of judges as arbitrators

93 Appointment of judges as arbitrators.
(1) An eligible High Court judge or an official referee may, if in all the circumstances he thinks fit, accept appointment as a sole arbitrator or as umpire by or by virtue of an arbitration agreement.
(2) An eligible High Court judge shall not do so unless the Lord Chief Justice has informed him that, having regard to the state of business in the High Court and the Crown Court, he can be made available.
(3) An official referee shall not do so unless the Lord Chief Justice has informed him that, having regard to the state of official referees' business, he can be made available.
(4) The fees payable for the services of an eligible High Court judge] or official referee as arbitrator or umpire shall be taken in the High Court.

(4A) The Lord Chief Justice may nominate a senior judge (as defined in section 109(5) of the Constitutional Reform Act 2005) to exercise functions of the Lord Chief Justice under this section.
(5) In this section –

"arbitration agreement" has the same meaning as in Part I;...

"eligible High Court judge" means –

(a) a puisne judge of the High Court, or

(b) a person acting as a judge of the High Court under or by virtue of section 9(1) of the Senior Courts Act 1981;]

"official referee" means a person nominated under section 68(1)(a) of the Senior Courts Act 1981 to deal with official referees' business.
(6) The provisions of Part I of this Act apply to arbitration before a person appointed under this section with the modifications specified in Schedule 2.

Statutory arbitrations

94 Application of Part I to statutory arbitrations.
(1) The provisions of Part I apply to every arbitration under an enactment (a "statutory arbitration"), whether the enactment was passed or made before or after the commencement of this Act, subject to the adaptations and exclusions specified in sections 95 to 98.
(2) The provisions of Part I do not apply to a statutory arbitration if or to the extent that their application –

(a) is inconsistent with the provisions of the enactment concerned, with any rules or procedure authorised or recognised by it, or

(b) is excluded by any other enactment.

(3) In this section and the following provisions of this Part "enactment" –

(a) in England and Wales, includes an enactment contained in subordinate legislation within the meaning of the Interpretation Act 1978;

(b) in Northern Ireland, means a statutory provision within the meaning of section 1(f) of the Interpretation Act (Northern Ireland) 1954.

95 General adaptation of provisions in relation to statutory arbitrations.
(1) The provisions of Part I apply to a statutory arbitration –

(a) as if the arbitration were pursuant to an arbitration agreement and as if the enactment were that agreement, and

(b) as if the persons by and against whom a claim subject to arbitration in pursuance of the enactment may be or has been made were parties to that agreement.

(2) Every statutory arbitration shall be taken to have its seat in England and Wales or, as the case may be, in Northern Ireland.

96 Specific adaptations of provisions in relation to statutory arbitrations.
(1) The following provisions of Part I apply to a statutory arbitration with the following adaptations.
(2) In section 30(1) (competence of tribunal to rule on its own jurisdiction), the reference in paragraph (a) to whether there is a valid arbitration agreement shall be construed as a reference to whether the enactment applies to the dispute or difference in question.
(3) Section 35 (consolidation of proceedings and concurrent hearings) applies only so as to authorise the consolidation of proceedings, or concurrent hearings in proceedings, under the same enactment.
(4) Section 46 (rules applicable to substance of dispute) applies with the omission of subsection (1)(b) (determination in accordance with considerations agreed by parties).

97 Provisions excluded from applying to statutory arbitrations.

The following provisions of Part I do not apply in relation to a statutory arbitration –

(a) section 8 (whether agreement discharged by death of a party);

(b) section 12 (power of court to extend agreed time limits);

(c) sections 9(5), 10(2) and 71(4) (restrictions on effect of provision that award condition precedent to right to bring legal proceedings).

98 Power to make further provision by regulations.

(1) The Secretary of State may make provision by regulations for adapting or excluding any provision of Part I in relation to statutory arbitrations in general or statutory arbitrations of any particular description.

(2) The power is exercisable whether the enactment concerned is passed or made before or after the commencement of this Act.

(3) Regulations under this section shall be made by statutory instrument which shall be subject to annulment in pursuance of a resolution of either House of Parliament.

PART III RECOGNITION AND ENFORCEMENT OF CERTAIN FOREIGN AWARDS

Enforcement of Geneva Convention awards

99 Continuation of Part II of the Arbitration Act 1950.

Part II of the Arbitration Act 1950 (enforcement of certain foreign awards) continues to apply in relation to foreign awards within the meaning of that Part which are not also New York Convention awards.

Recognition and enforcement of New York Convention awards

100 New York Convention awards.

(1) In this Part a "New York Convention award" means an award made, in pursuance of an arbitration agreement, in the territory of a state (other than the United Kingdom) which is a party to the New York Convention.

(2) For the purposes of subsection (1) and of the provisions of this Part relating to such awards –

(a) "arbitration agreement" means an arbitration agreement in writing, and

(b) an award shall be treated as made at the seat of the arbitration, regardless of where it was signed, despatched or delivered to any of the parties.

In this subsection "agreement in writing" and "seat of the arbitration" have the same meaning as in Part I.

(3) If Her Majesty by Order in Council declares that a state specified in the Order is a party to the New York Convention, or is a party in respect of any territory so specified, the Order shall, while in force, be conclusive evidence of that fact.

(4) In this section "the New York Convention" means the Convention on the Recognition and Enforcement of Foreign Arbitral Awards adopted by the United Nations Conference on International Commercial Arbitration on 10th June 1958.

101 Recognition and enforcement of awards.

(1) A New York Convention award shall be recognised as binding on the persons as between whom it was made, and may accordingly be relied on by those persons by way of defence, set-off or otherwise in any legal proceedings in England and Wales or Northern Ireland.

(2) A New York Convention award may, by leave of the court, be enforced in the same manner as a judgment or order of the court to the same effect.

As to the meaning of "the court" see section 105.

(3) Where leave is so given, judgment may be entered in terms of the award.

102 Evidence to be produced by party seeking recognition or enforcement.

(1) A party seeking the recognition or enforcement of a New York Convention award must produce –

(a) the duly authenticated original award or a duly certified copy of it, and

(b) the original arbitration agreement or a duly certified copy of it.

(2) If the award or agreement is in a foreign language, the party must also produce a translation of it certified by an official or sworn translator or by a diplomatic or consular agent.

103 Refusal of recognition or enforcement.

(1) Recognition or enforcement of a New York Convention award shall not be refused except in the following cases.

(2) Recognition or enforcement of the award may be refused if the person against whom it is invoked proves –

(a) that a party to the arbitration agreement was (under the law applicable to him) under some incapacity;

(b) that the arbitration agreement was not valid under the law to which the parties subjected it or, failing any indication thereon, under the law of the country where the award was made;

(c) that he was not given proper notice of the appointment of the arbitrator or of the arbitration proceedings or was otherwise unable to present his case;

(d) that the award deals with a difference not contemplated by or not falling within the terms of the submission to arbitration or contains decisions on matters beyond the scope of the submission to arbitration (but see subsection (4));

(e) that the composition of the arbitral tribunal or the arbitral procedure was not in accordance with the agreement of the parties or, failing such agreement, with the law of the country in which the arbitration took place;

(f) that the award has not yet become binding on the parties, or has been set aside or suspended by a competent authority of the country in which, or under the law of which, it was made.

(3) Recognition or enforcement of the award may also be refused if the award is in respect of a matter which is not capable of settlement by arbitration, or if it would be contrary to public policy to recognise or enforce the award.

(4) An award which contains decisions on matters not submitted to arbitration may be recognised or enforced to the extent that it contains decisions on matters submitted to arbitration which can be separated from those on matters not so submitted.

(5) Where an application for the setting aside or suspension of the award has been made to such a competent authority as is mentioned in subsection (2)(f), the court before which the award is sought to be relied upon may, if it considers it proper, adjourn the decision on the recognition or enforcement of the award.

It may also on the application of the party claiming recognition or enforcement of the award order the other party to give suitable security.

104 Saving for other bases of recognition or enforcement.

Nothing in the preceding provisions of this Part affects any right to rely upon or enforce a New York Convention award at common law or under section 66.

PART IV GENERAL PROVISIONS

105 Meaning of "the court": jurisdiction of High Court and county court.

(1) In this Act "the court" in relation to England and Wales means the High Court or the county court and in relation to Northern Ireland means the High Court or a county court, subject to the following provisions.

(2) The Lord Chancellor may by order make provision –

(za) allocating proceedings under this Act in England and Wales to the High Court or the county court;

(a) allocating proceedings under this Act in Northern Ireland to the High Court or to county courts; or

(b) specifying proceedings under this Act which may be commenced or taken only in the High Court or in the county court or (as the case may be) a county court.

(3) The Lord Chancellor may by order make provision requiring proceedings of any specified description under this Act in relation to which a county court in Northern Ireland has jurisdiction to be commenced or taken in one or more specified county courts.

Any jurisdiction so exercisable by a specified county court is exercisable throughout Northern Ireland.

(3A) The Lord Chancellor must consult the Lord Chief Justice of England and Wales or the Lord Chief Justice of Northern Ireland (as the case may be) before making an order under this section.

(3B) The Lord Chief Justice of England and Wales may nominate a judicial office holder (as defined in section 109(4) of the Constitutional Reform Act 2005) to exercise his functions under this section.

(3C) The Lord Chief Justice of Northern Ireland may nominate any of the following to exercise his functions under this section –

(a) the holder of one of the offices listed in Schedule 1 to the Justice (Northern Ireland) Act 2002;

(b) a Lord Justice of Appeal (as defined in section 88 of that Act).

(4) An order under this section –

(a) may differentiate between categories of proceedings by reference to such criteria as the Lord Chancellor sees fit to specify, and

(b) may make such incidental or transitional provision as the Lord Chancellor considers necessary or expedient.

(5) An order under this section for England and Wales shall be made by statutory instrument which shall be subject to annulment in pursuance of a resolution of either House of Parliament.

(6) An order under this section for Northern Ireland shall be a statutory rule for the purposes of the Statutory Rules (Northern Ireland) Order 1979 which shall be subject to negative resolution (within the meaning of section 41(6) of the Interpretation Act (Northern Ireland) 1954).

106 Crown application.

(1) Part I of this Act applies to any arbitration agreement to which Her Majesty, either in right of the Crown or of the Duchy of Lancaster or otherwise, or the Duke of Cornwall, is a party.

(2) Where Her Majesty is party to an arbitration agreement otherwise than in right of the Crown, Her Majesty shall be represented for the purposes of any arbitral proceedings –

(a) where the agreement was entered into by Her Majesty in right of the Duchy of Lancaster, by the Chancellor of the Duchy or such person as he may appoint, and

(b) in any other case, by such person as Her Majesty may appoint in writing under the Royal Sign Manual.

(3) Where the Duke of Cornwall is party to an arbitration agreement, he shall be represented for the purposes of any arbitral proceedings by such person as he may appoint.

(4) References in Part I to a party or the parties to the arbitration agreement or to arbitral proceedings shall be construed, where subsection (2) or (3) applies, as references to the person representing Her Majesty or the Duke of Cornwall.

107 Consequential amendments and repeals.
(1) The enactments specified in Schedule 3 are amended in accordance with that Schedule, the amendments being consequential on the provisions of this Act.
(2) The enactments specified in Schedule 4 are repealed to the extent specified.

108 Extent.
(1) The provisions of this Act extend to England and Wales and, except as mentioned below, to Northern Ireland.
(2) The following provisions of Part II do not extend to Northern Ireland –
section 92 (exclusion of Part I in relation to small claims arbitration in the county court), and
section 93 and Schedule 2 (appointment of judges as arbitrators).
(3) Sections 89, 90 and 91 (consumer arbitration agreements) extend to Scotland and the provisions of Schedules 3 and 4 (consequential amendments and repeals) extend to Scotland so far as they relate to enactments which so extend, subject as follows.
(4) The repeal of the Arbitration Act 1975 extends only to England and Wales and Northern Ireland.

109 Commencement.
(1) The provisions of this Act come into force on such day as the Secretary of State may appoint by order made by statutory instrument, and different days may be appointed for different purposes.
(2) An order under subsection (1) may contain such transitional provisions as appear to the Secretary of State to be appropriate.

110 Short title.
This Act may be cited as the Arbitration Act 1996.

SCHEDULE 1 SECTION 4(1).

MANDATORY PROVISIONS OF PART I

sections 9 to 11 (stay of legal proceedings);
section 12 (power of court to extend agreed time limits); section 13 (application of Limitation Acts);
section 24 (power of court to remove arbitrator);
section 26(1) (effect of death of arbitrator);
section 28 (liability of parties for fees and expenses of arbitrators); section 29 (immunity of arbitrator);
section 31 (objection to substantive jurisdiction of tribunal); section 32 (determination of preliminary point of jurisdiction); section 33 (general duty of tribunal);
section 37(2) (items to be treated as expenses of arbitrators); section 40 (general duty of parties);
section 43 (securing the attendance of witnesses);
section 56 (power to withhold award in case of non-payment);
section 60 (effectiveness of agreement for payment of costs in any event); section 66 (enforcement of award);
sections 67 and 68 (challenging the award: substantive jurisdiction and serious irregularity), and sections 70 and 71 (supplementary provisions; effect of order of court) so far as relating to those sections;

section 72 (saving for rights of person who takes no part in proceedings); section 73 (loss of right to object);
section 74 (immunity of arbitral institutions, &c.); section 75 (charge to secure payment of solicitors' costs).

9.3.2 Dutch Arbitration Act (2015) (Dutch law, unofficial English translation)[1]

DUTCH CODE OF CIVIL PROCEDURE BOOK FOUR – ARBITRATION

TITLE ONE – ARBITRATION IN THE NETHERLANDS

SECTION ONE – ARBITRATION AGREEMENT

Article 1020

(1) The parties may agree to submit to arbitration disputes which have arisen or may arise between them out of a defined legal relationship, whether contractual or not.
(2) The arbitration agreement referred to in paragraph (1) includes both the submission agreement by which the parties bind themselves to submit to arbitration an existing dispute between them and an arbitration clause under which parties bind themselves to submit to arbitration disputes which may arise between them.
(3) The arbitration agreement shall not serve to determine legal consequences that may not be freely determined by the parties.
(4) Parties may also agree to submit the following matters to arbitration:

- (a) the determination only of the quality or condition of goods;
- (b) the determination only of the quantum of damages or monetary debt;
- (c) the filling of gaps, or modification of, the legal relationship between the parties referred to in paragraph (1).

(5) The term 'arbitration agreement' includes an arbitration clause which is contained in Articles of association or rules which bind the parties.
(6) Arbitration rules referred to in an arbitration agreement shall be deemed to form part of that agreement.

Article 1021

The arbitration agreement shall be proven by an instrument in writing. For this purpose an instrument in writing which provides for arbitration or which refers to standard conditions providing for arbitration is sufficient, provided that this instrument is expressly or impliedly accepted by or on behalf of the other party. The arbitration agreement may also be proven by electronic data. Article 227a(1) of Book 6 of the Civil Code shall apply mutatis mutandis.

SECTION ONE A – ARBITRATION AGREEMENT AND JURISDICTION OF THE COURTS

Article 1022

A court seized of a dispute in respect of which an arbitration agreement has been concluded shall declare that it has no jurisdiction if a party invokes the existence of said agreement before submitting a defence, unless the agreement is invalid.

1 This English translation of the Dutch Arbitration Act is reproduced by kind permission of the Netherlands Arbitration Institute and is available at: www.nai-nl.org.

Article 1022a
An arbitration agreement shall not preclude a party from requesting the court to grant conservatory measures, or from applying to the provisional relief judge of the district court or the cantonal judge for a decision in summary proceedings in accordance with the provisions of Article 254.

Article 1022b
An arbitration agreement shall not preclude a party from requesting the court to order a preliminary witness examination, a preliminary expert report, a preliminary on-site examination and viewing, or inspection of, a copy of or an extract from specific documents.

Article 1022c
If, in the events mentioned in Articles 1022a and 1022b, a party invokes the existence of an arbitration agreement before submitting a defence, the court shall only declare that it has jurisdiction if the requested decision cannot, or cannot in a timely manner, be obtained in arbitration.

SECTION ONE B – ARBITRAL TRIBUNAL

Article 1023
Any natural person of legal capacity may be appointed as arbitrator. Unless the parties have agreed otherwise with a view to the impartiality and the independence of the arbitral tribunal, no person shall be precluded from appointment by reason of his nationality.

Article 1024
(1) The submission agreement shall describe the matters which the parties wish to submit to arbitration.
(2) The arbitration shall be deemed to have been commenced by the conclusion of the submission agreement, unless the parties have agreed another manner of commencement.

Article 1025
(1) In the event of an arbitration clause, the arbitration shall be deemed to have been commenced on the day of receipt of a notice in writing in which a party informs the other party that it is commencing arbitration. Said notice shall contain a description of the matters which the party commencing the arbitration wishes to submit to arbitration.
(2) The parties may agree that the arbitration shall be commenced in another manner than as for in this article.

Article 1026
(1) The arbitral tribunal shall be composed of an uneven number of arbitrators. It may also consist of a sole arbitrator.
(2) If the parties have not agreed the number of arbitrators, or if an agreed method of determining that number is not carried out and the parties cannot reach agreement on the number, the number shall, at the request of the most diligent party, be determined by the provisional relief judge of the district court.
(3) If the parties have agreed an even number of arbitrators, the arbitrators shall appoint an additional arbitrator who shall act as the chairman of the arbitral tribunal.
(4) Failing agreement between the arbitrators such arbitrator shall, unless the parties have agreed otherwise, be appointed at the request of the most diligent party by the provisional relief judge of the district court.
(5) Article 1027(4) shall apply mutatis mutandis to the provisions in the second and fourth paragraphs.

Article 1027

(1) The arbitrator or arbitrators shall be appointed by any method agreed by the parties. The parties may charge a third person with the appointment of the arbitrator or arbitrators of any of them. If no method of appointment is agreed, the arbitrator or arbitrators shall be appointed by the parties jointly.
(2) The appointment shall be made within three months after the commencement of the arbitration, unless the arbitrator or arbitrators have already been appointed. In any of the events referred to in Article 1026(2), however, the time-limit of three months shall start to run on the day on which the number of arbitrators is determined. These time-limits may be shortened or extended by agreement between the parties.
(3) If the appointment of the arbitrator or arbitrators is not made within the time-limit referred to in the preceding paragraph, the lacking arbitrator or arbitrators shall, at the request of the most diligent party, be appointed by the provisional relief judge of the district court. The other party shall be given the opportunity to be heard.
(4) The provisional relief judge or the third person shall appoint the arbitrator or arbitrators without regard to the question of whether or not the arbitration agreement is valid. By cooperating in the appointment of the arbitrator or arbitrators, the parties shall not forfeit the right to challenge the jurisdiction of the arbitral tribunal on the ground of non-existence of a valid arbitration agreement.

Article 1028

(1) If by agreement or otherwise one party is given a privileged position with regard to the appointment of the arbitrator or arbitrators, either party may, in derogation of the agreed method of appointment, request the provisional relief judge of the district court to appoint the arbitrator or arbitrators.
(2) A party must present the request referred to in the first paragraph within three months from the commencement of the proceedings, on pain of forfeiting the right to invoke the privileged position with regard to the appointment of the arbitrator or arbitrators in the arbitral proceedings or before the court. The parties may extend the time-limit by agreement.
(3) The other party to the requesting party shall be given the opportunity to be heard. Article 1027(4) shall apply mutatis mutandis.

Article 1029

(1) An arbitrator shall accept his mandate in writing. An arbitrator may only be dismissed in the events referred to in the second to fifth paragraphs, inclusive, of this article, unless the parties have agreed otherwise.
(2) An arbitrator who has accepted his mandate may, at his own request, be released from his mandate either with the consent of the parties or by a third person designated by the parties, or in the absence thereof, by the provisional relief judge of the district court.
(3) An arbitrator who has accepted his mandate may be released from his mandate by the parties jointly.
(4) An arbitrator who has accepted his mandate and who has become unable de jure or de facto to perform his mandate, may, at the request of any party, be released from his mandate by a third person designated by the parties, or in the absence of such third person, by the provisional relief judge of the district court.
(5) An arbitral tribunal that has accepted its mandate may, at the request of any of the parties, be released from its mandate by the third person designated by the parties, or absent the same, by the provisional relief judge of the district court, if, taking account of all the circumstances, it performs its mandate in an unacceptably slow manner despite reminders.

Article 1030
(1) Unless the parties have agreed another manner of replacement, an arbitrator who has been released from his mandate in accordance with the provisions of Article 1029(2), (3) or (4), or an arbitral tribunal that has been released from its mandate in accordance with the provisions of Article 1029(5), shall be replaced pursuant to the rules applicable to the original appointment. The same shall apply in the event of the death of an arbitrator.
(2) If the parties designated the arbitrator or arbitrators in the arbitration agreement by name, their replacement shall also take place in the events referred to in paragraph (1) above, unless the parties have agreed that the arbitration agreement shall then end.
(3) Unless the parties have agreed otherwise, the proceedings shall be suspended by operation of law in case of replacement. Unless the parties have agreed otherwise, the arbitral proceedings shall, after the suspension ceases, continue from the stage they had reached.

Article 1031
The parties may jointly terminate the mandate of the arbitral tribunal.

Article 1032
[Deleted]

Article 1033
(1) An arbitrator may be challenged if there are justifiable doubts as to his impartiality or independence.
(2) A party may only challenge an arbitrator appointed by that party for reasons of which that party became aware after the appointment was made.
(3) A party may not challenge an arbitrator appointed by a third person or the provisional relief judge of the district court if he has acquiesced in this appointment, unless that party only became aware of the ground for the challenge afterwards.

Article 1034
(1) A person approached to be engaged as arbitrator who has reason to suspect that he could be challenged, shall communicate the same in writing to the person who approached him, stating the suspected reasons for challenge.
(2) A person who has been appointed as arbitrator shall send the communication referred to in the previous paragraph to the parties upon having been appointed, unless they have already received said communication.
(3) An arbitrator who, during the arbitral proceedings, suspects that he could be challenged, shall communicate the same in writing to the parties, mentioning the suspected reasons for challenge, and, if the arbitral tribunal consists of multiple arbitrators, to the co-arbitrators.

Article 1035
(1) The challenging party shall give written notice of the reasons for challenge to the arbitrator concerned, the other party and, if the arbitral tribunal consists multiple arbitrators, the co- arbitrators. The notice shall be given within four weeks after the day of receipt of the communication referred to in Article 1034 or, in the absence thereof, within four weeks after the reason for challenge becomes known to the challenging party.
(2) If a challenged arbitrator does not resign within two weeks after the day of receipt of a timely notice as referred to in the first paragraph, the provisional relief judge of the district court shall, at the request of the most diligent party, decide whether the challenge is well-founded. The request shall be submitted within two weeks after the day of receipt of the written notice from the challenged arbitrator that he will not resign, or, in the absence thereof, within six weeks after the date of receipt of the notice.

(3) If the challenged arbitrator resigns or the provisional relief judge of the district court finds the challenge to be well- founded, the challenged arbitrator shall be replaced in accordance with the rules that governed his original appointment, unless the parties have agreed another manner of replacement. Article 1030(2) and (3) shall apply mutatis mutandis.
(4) If a challenged arbitrator resigns, this does not imply acceptance that the reasons for the challenge are well-founded.
(5) The arbitral tribunal may suspend the arbitral proceedings from the day of receipt of the timely notice, as referred to in the first paragraph, or afterwards, pending the challenge procedure, from the moment that the arbitral tribunal considers appropriate. If the challenge is found to be inadmissible or is not upheld, the proceedings, if suspended, shall resume from the stage they had reached.
(6) The parties may, by agreement, shorten or extend the time-limits referred to in the first and second paragraphs of this article.
(7) The parties may provide by agreement for the handling of a challenge request by an independent third person other than the provisional relief judge of the district court.
(8) A party that has reasons to challenge an arbitrator shall base a challenge request in accordance with the provisions in this article on these reasons, on pain of forfeiture of the right to invoke them later in the arbitral proceedings or in court.

Article 1035a
If the arbitral tribunal is assisted by a secretary, Articles 1033 to 1035, inclusive, shall apply mutatis mutandis.

SECTION TWO – THE ARBITRAL PROCEEDINGS

Article 1036
(1) Without prejudice to the provisions of mandatory law in this title, the arbitral proceedings shall be conducted in the manner agreed by the parties. Insofar as the parties have not made provision for the arbitral proceedings, they shall, without prejudice to the provisions in this title, be conducted in the manner determined by the arbitral tribunal.
(2) The arbitral tribunal shall treat the parties equally. The arbitral tribunal shall give the parties the opportunity mutually to set out and explain their positions and to comment on each other's positions and on all documents and other information brought to the attention of the arbitral tribunal during the proceedings. The arbitral tribunal shall not base its decision, where it is unfavourable for one party, upon documents and other information on which that party was not sufficiently able to comment.
(3) The arbitral tribunal shall guard against unreasonable delay of the proceedings and, if necessary, at the request of a party or of its own motion, take measures. The parties shall mutually be obliged to prevent unreasonable delay of the proceedings.

Article 1037
(1) The place of arbitration shall be determined by agreement of the parties, or in the absence thereof, by the arbitral tribunal. The place where the award is made shall also be determined by the determination of the place of arbitration.
(2) If the place of arbitration has been determined neither by the parties nor by the arbitral tribunal, the place where the award is made, as stated by the arbitral tribunal in the award, shall be deemed to be the place of arbitration.
(3) The arbitral tribunal may hold hearings, deliberate, and hear witnesses and experts at any other place, within or outside the Netherlands, it considers appropriate, unless the parties have agreed otherwise. The arbitral tribunal shall have the power to appoint one of its members to hold the hearing referred to in the previous sentence, unless the parties have agreed otherwise.

Article 1038
(1) The parties may appear in the proceedings in person, be represented by a practising lawyer, or by a representative expressly authorised in writing for this purpose.
(2) The parties may be assisted in the proceedings by any persons of their choice.

Article 1038a
(1) Unless the parties have agreed otherwise, the arbitral tribunal shall give the claimant and the respondent the opportunity to present a statement of claim and a statement of defence, respectively.
(2) Unless the parties have agreed otherwise, the arbitral tribunal shall be free to determine whether any further statements may be presented.

Article 1038b
The arbitral tribunal shall, at the request of any of the parties or of its own motion, give the parties the opportunity to explain their case at an oral hearing, unless the parties have agreed otherwise.

Article 1038c
(1) A counterclaim shall be admissible if it is subject to the same arbitration agreement as the one on which the claim is based or if that same arbitration agreement has been expressly or tacitly declared applicable by the parties.
(2) Unless the parties have agreed otherwise, a counterclaim as referred to in the first paragraph shall be presented directly with the statement of defence.

Article 1038d
A party may amend or increase its claim or counterclaim, respectively, or the grounds thereof, during the arbitral procedure, on the condition that the other party will not be unreasonably hindered in its defence or that the proceedings will not be unreasonably delayed.

Article 1039
(1) The arbitral tribunal shall be free to determine the rules of evidence, the admissibility of evidence, the division of the burden of proof and the assessment of evidence, unless the parties have agreed otherwise.
(2) The arbitral tribunal shall have the power to designate one of its members to hear witnesses or experts or to conduct an on-site examination or viewing, unless the parties have agreed otherwise.

Article 1040
(1) Unless the parties have agreed otherwise, the statements referred to in Article 1038a shall, insofar as possible, be accompanied by the documents relied upon by the parties.
(2) The arbitral tribunal may, at the request of any of the parties or of its own motion, order the inspection of, a copy of or an extract from specific documents related to the dispute from the party which has these documents at its disposal, unless the parties have agreed otherwise. The arbitral tribunal shall determine the conditions under which and the manner in which inspection of, a copy of or an extract from documents are provided.

Article 1041
(1) The arbitral tribunal may, at the request of any of the parties or of its own motion, order parties to furnish evidence by hearing witnesses and experts, unless the parties have agreed otherwise.
(2) The arbitral tribunal may determine the form in which the statements of the witnesses and the experts are given, unless the parties have agreed otherwise.

(3) If an oral hearing of witnesses or experts takes place, the arbitral tribunal shall determine the time and place for the hearing and the manner in which the hearing will be conducted.
(4) If the arbitral tribunal considers it necessary, it shall hear the witnesses after they have sworn, in the manner prescribed by law, that they will tell the whole truth and nothing but the truth.

Article 1041a
(1) If a witness does not voluntarily appear, or having appeared, refuses to make a statement, the arbitral tribunal may allow the party requesting that the witness be heard, within a time- limit of time fixed by the arbitral tribunal, to apply to the provisional relief judge of the district court with the request that an examining judge be appointed before whom the examination of the witness will take place.
(2) The examination shall take place in the same manner as in ordinary cases, it being understood that the arbitrator or arbitrators, through the registry of the district court, will be given the opportunity to be present and to pose questions to the witness.
(3) The registry of the district court shall send the official report of the examination to the arbitral tribunal and the parties as quickly as possible.
(4) The arbitral tribunal may suspend the proceedings until the day that the arbitral tribunal has received the report of the examination.

Article 1042
(1) Unless the parties have agreed otherwise, the arbitral tribunal may appoint one or more experts to give advice. The arbitral tribunal may consult the parties regarding the terms of reference to be issued to the experts. The arbitral tribunal shall send the parties a copy of the appointment and the terms of reference of the experts as soon as possible.
(2) The arbitral tribunal may require a party to provide the requisite information and necessary cooperation to the expert.
(3) At the request of any of the parties, the experts shall be heard at a hearing of the arbitral tribunal. If a party wishes to make such a request, it shall so notify the arbitral tribunal and the other party as soon as possible.
(4) Without prejudice to the provisions in paragraph (3), the arbitral tribunal shall give the parties the opportunity to be heard regarding the advice of the experts appointed by the arbitral tribunal, unless the parties have agreed otherwise.

Article 1042a
The arbitral tribunal may, at the request of any of the parties or of its own motion, examine a local situation or conduct a viewing, within or outside the Netherlands, unless the parties have agreed otherwise. The arbitral tribunal shall give the parties the opportunity to be present at the on-site examination or viewing.

Article 1043
At any stage of the proceedings, the arbitral tribunal may order the parties to appear in person for the purpose of providing information or attempting to arrive at a settlement.

Article 1043a
(1) If the claimant, although reasonably given the opportunity to do so, fails to assert or reasonably explain its claims, without asserting well-founded reasons, the arbitral tribunal may, by award, or in another manner it considers appropriate, bring an end to the arbitral proceedings.
(2) If the respondent, although reasonably given the opportunity to do so, fails to submit its defence, without asserting well-founded reasons, the arbitral tribunal may immediately make an award.

(3) In the award referred to in the second paragraph, the claim shall be awarded, unless it appears to the arbitral tribunal to be unlawful or unfounded. The arbitral tribunal may, before making its award, require proof from the claimant of one or more of its assertions.

Article 1043b

(1) During pending arbitral proceedings on the merits, the arbitral tribunal may, at the request of any of the parties, grant provisional relief, except for conservatory measures as referred to in the Fourth Title of the Third Book. The provisional relief must be related to the claim or counterclaim in the pending arbitral proceedings.

(2) By agreement, the parties may authorise an arbitral tribunal separately appointed for that purpose, irrespective of whether the arbitral proceedings on the merits are pending within the limits set by Article 254(1), to grant provisional relief at the request of any of the parties, except for conservatory measures as referred to in the Fourth Title of the Third Book.

(3) The arbitral tribunal referred to in the first and second paragraphs may, in conjunction with the provisional relief, require any party to provide sufficient security.

(4) Unless the arbitral tribunal determines otherwise, a decision by the arbitral tribunal on the request to grant provisional relief shall constitute an arbitral award to which the provisions of Sections Three to Five inclusive of this Title shall be applicable.

(5) The arbitral tribunal may, at the unanimous request of the parties, instead of taking a decision on provisional relief, immediately take a decision on the merits, in which it shall state the request. Such a decision on the merits shall constitute an arbitral award to which the provisions of Sections Three to Five, inclusive, of this Title shall be applicable.

(6) The arbitral tribunal may, at the unanimous request of the parties, convert an arbitral award as referred to in the fourth paragraph into an arbitral award as referred to in the fifth paragraph, in which it shall state the request.

Article 1044

(1) Unless the parties have agreed otherwise, the arbitral tribunal may, through the intervention of the provisional relief judge of the district court at The Hague, request information as referred to in Article 3 of the European Convention on Information on Foreign Law, done at London, 7 June 1968 (Dutch Treaty Series 1968, 142). The provisional relief judge shall send the request, unless it appears to him to be unfounded, to the agency referred to in Article 2 of said Convention as soon as possible and notify the arbitral tribunal thereof.

(2) The arbitral tribunal may suspend the proceedings until the day on which it has received the answer to its request for information.

Article 1045

(1) Unless the parties have agreed otherwise, at the written request of a third person who has an interest in arbitral proceedings, the arbitral tribunal may allow that person to join or intervene in the proceedings, provided that the same arbitration agreement as between the original parties applies or enters into force between the parties and the third person.

(2) The arbitral tribunal shall send a copy of the request to the parties as soon as possible.

(3) The arbitral tribunal shall give the parties the opportunity to make their opinions known. The arbitral tribunal may give the third person the opportunity to make its opinion known

(4) By the allowance of the joinder or intervention, the third person shall become a party to the arbitral proceedings.

(5) After the allowance of a joinder or an intervention, the arbitral tribunal shall arrange the further course of the proceedings, unless the parties have made provision for this by agreement.

Article 1045a

(1) At the written request of a party the arbitral tribunal may allow that party to implead a third person, provided that the same arbitration agreement as between the original parties applies or enters into force between the interested party and the third person.
(2) A copy of the notice of impleader shall be sent to the arbitral tribunal and the other party as soon as possible.
(3) The arbitral tribunal shall give the parties and the third person the opportunity to make their opinions known.
(4) The arbitral tribunal shall not allow the impleader if the arbitral tribunal finds it implausible, in advance, that the third person will be required to bear the adverse consequences of a possible judgment against the interested party or is of the opinion that impleader proceedings are likely to cause unreasonable or unnecessary delay of the proceedings.
(5) After allowing the impleader the arbitral tribunal shall determine the further course of proceedings, unless the parties have made provision for this by agreement.

Article 1046

(1) In respect of arbitral proceedings pending in the Netherlands, a party may request that a third person designated to that end by the parties order consolidation with other arbitral proceedings pending within or outside the Netherlands, unless the parties have agreed otherwise. In the absence of a third person designated to that end by the parties, the provisional relief judge of the district court of Amsterdam may be requested to order consolidation of arbitral proceedings pending in the Netherlands with other arbitral proceedings pending in the Netherlands, unless the parties have agreed otherwise.
(2) Consolidation may be ordered insofar as it does not cause unreasonable delay in the pending proceedings, also in view of the stage they have reached, and the two arbitral proceedings are so closely connected that good administration of justice renders it expedient to hear and determine them together to avoid the risk of irreconcilable decisions resulting from separate proceedings.
(3) The third person or the provisional relief judge may grant or refuse the request, after he has given all the parties and, if appointed, the arbitrators, an opportunity to make their opinions known. His decision shall be communicated in writing to all the parties and the arbitral tribunals concerned.
(4) If the third person or the provisional relief judge orders consolidation, the parties shall, in mutual consultation, appoint the arbitrator or arbitrators, in an uneven number, and determine the rules which shall apply to the consolidated proceedings. If, within a time-limit fixed by the third person or the provisional relief judge, the parties fail to reach agreement in this regard, the third person or the provisional relief judge shall, at the request of the most diligent party, appoint the arbitrator or arbitrators and, if necessary, determine the rules which shall apply to the consolidated proceedings. The third person or the provisional relief judge shall, if necessary, determine the remuneration for the work already carried out by the arbitrators whose mandate is terminated by reason of the consolidation. Article 1027(4) shall apply mutatis mutandis.

Article 1047

With the exception of the provisions of Articles 1037 and 1048, the provisions of this Section shall not apply to arbitrations concerning the matters referred to in Article 1020(4)(a). In that event the proceedings shall be conducted in the manner agreed by the parties or, insofar as the parties have not made provision for this, as determined by the arbitral tribunal.

Article 1048

The determination of the date on which the award will be made shall be at the exclusive discretion of the arbitral tribunal.

Article 1048a
A party that has appeared in the proceedings shall make objection to the arbitral tribunal without unreasonable delay, sending a copy thereof to the other party, as soon as it knows or reasonably should know of any act contrary to, or failure to act in accordance with, any provisions in the Second Section of this Title, the arbitration agreement, or any order, decision or measure of the arbitral tribunal. If a party fails to do so, then the right to rely on this later in the arbitral proceedings or before the court shall be forfeited.

SECTION THREE – THE ARBITRAL AWARD

Article 1049
(1) The arbitral tribunal may render a final award, a partial final award, or an interim award. A final award or a partial final award exists if the claim is wholly or partially settled in the operative part of an award.
(2) If an arbitral tribunal makes an award that, as evidenced by the operative part, partially forms an interim award and partially a final award, such an award is a partial final award.

Article 1050
[Deleted as of 01-01-2015]

Article 1051
[Deleted as of 01-01-2015]

Article 1052
(1) The arbitral tribunal shall have the power to rule on its own jurisdiction.
(2) A party that has appeared in the arbitral proceedings must raise a plea that the arbitral tribunal does not have jurisdiction on the ground of non-existence of a valid arbitration agreement before submitting a defence, on pain of forfeiting its right to rely on this later, in the arbitral proceedings or before the court, unless this plea is made on the ground that the dispute is not capable of settlement by arbitration according to Article 1020(3).
(3) A party who has cooperated in the composition of the arbitral tribunal may not, in the arbitral proceedings or before the court, raise the plea that the arbitral tribunal does not have jurisdiction on the ground that the arbitral tribunal was composed in violation of the applicable rules. A party that has appeared in the arbitral proceedings and that has not cooperated in the composition of the arbitral tribunal shall raise the plea that the arbitral tribunal does not have jurisdiction on the ground that the arbitral tribunal was composed in violation of the applicable rules before submitting a defence, on pain of forfeiting its right to rely on this later, in the arbitral proceedings or before the court.
(4) The decision in which the arbitral tribunal declares that it has jurisdiction can only be challenged simultaneously with a subsequent final or partial final award using the legal remedies mentioned in Article 1064.
(5) If and insofar as the arbitral tribunal has declared that it has no jurisdiction on the ground of non-existence of a valid arbitration agreement as referred to in the second paragraph, the court shall have jurisdiction to hear the case. If and insofar as the arbitral tribunal has no jurisdiction on another ground, the arbitration agreement shall remain valid, unless the parties have agreed otherwise.
(6) The declaration of no jurisdiction referred to in the previous paragraph shall constitute an arbitral award to which the First Section B to the Fifth Section of this Title, inclusive, are applicable.

Article 1053
An arbitration agreement shall be considered and decided upon as a separate agreement. The arbitral tribunal shall have the power to decide on the existence and the validity of the main contract of which the arbitration agreement forms part or to which it is related.

Article 1054
(1) The arbitral tribunal shall decide in accordance with the rules of law.
(2) If a choice of law has been made by the parties, the arbitral tribunal shall decide in accordance with the rules of law designated by the parties. Failing such designation of law, the arbitral tribunal shall decide in accordance with the rules of law which it considers appropriate.
(3) The arbitral tribunal shall decide as *amiable compositeur* if the parties, by agreement, have authorised it to do so.
(4) In any event the arbitral tribunal shall take into account any applicable trade usages.

Article 1055
[Deleted as of 01-01-2015]

Article 1056
In any event where the court has the power to impose a penalty for non-compliance, the arbitral tribunal shall have such power as well. Without prejudice to the applicability of Articles 611a to 611h inclusive, in the events referred to in Article 611d, the revocation, the suspension or the reduction of the penalty must be requested from the arbitral tribunal, and if the mandate of the arbitral tribunal is not still in effect, from the provisional relief judge of the district court within whose district the place of arbitration is located.

Article 1057
(1) Unless the parties have agreed otherwise, if the arbitral tribunal consists of multiple arbitrators, it shall decide by a majority of votes. If the arbitral tribunal consists of multiple arbitrators, procedural matters of minor importance may be decided by the chairman of the arbitral tribunal if he has been so authorised by the co-arbitrators, unless the parties have agreed otherwise.
(2) The award shall be made in writing and signed by the arbitrator or arbitrators.
(3) If a minority of the arbitrators refuses to sign, this shall be stated by the other arbitrators in the award signed by them. A similar statement shall be made if a minority is incapable of signing and it is unlikely that the impediment will cease to exist shortly.
(4) In addition to the decision, the award shall in any event contain:
- (a) the name and place of residence of the arbitrator or each of the arbitrators;
- (b) the name and place of residence of each of the parties;
- (c) the date on which the award is made;
- (d) the place where the award is made;
- (e) the reasons for the decision given in the award.

(5) In derogation of the fourth paragraph, subsection (e), the award shall contain no grounds for the decision given if:
- (a) the award exclusively concerns the determination only of the quality or condition of goods as referred to in Article 1020(4) (a);
- (b) the recording of a settlement as referred to in Article 1069; or
- (c) in all other events, after the arbitration has been commenced, the parties agree in writing that no grounds shall be given for the decision.

Article 1058

(1) The arbitral tribunal shall ensure that, as soon as possible:

(a) the original of the award, or a copy thereof certified by an arbitrator or a third person designated by the parties, is sent to the parties.

(b) the original of a final or partial final award is deposited with the registry of the district court within whose district the place of arbitration is located, insofar as the parties have so agreed.

(2) The award shall be deemed to have been sent if four weeks have elapsed after the date of the award.

(3) Without prejudice to the provisions of Articles 1060, 1061 and 1065a, the mandate of the arbitral tribunal shall terminate when the last final award is sent to the parties or, in the event referred to in the first paragraph under (b), upon the deposit of the last final award with the registry of the district court.

(4) No copy of or extract from a deposited award shall be issued to third persons.

(5) Unless the parties have agreed other time-limits as referred to in Articles 1060, 1061, and 1061c, a time-limit of three months from the date of the deposit of the award with the registry of the district court shall apply, if the parties have agreed such deposit.

Article 1059

(1) Decisions concerning the legal relationship in dispute and contained in an arbitral award in relation to which ordinary means of recourse are no longer available shall have res judicata effect in other proceedings between the same parties from the day on which they have been given. Article 236(2) and (3) shall apply mutatis mutandis.

(2) The first paragraph shall not apply to decisions as referred to in Article 1043b concerning provisional relief.

(3) An arbitral award in relation to which ordinary means of recourse are no longer available as referred to in the first paragraph shall have binding force between the same parties in another proceeding from the day on which it has been made.

Article 1060

(1) A party may, within a time-limit as agreed by the parties or within three months after the day the award was sent, request in writing that the arbitral tribunal correct a manifest computing error, clerical error, or other manifest error that lends itself to simple rectification in the award.

(2) If the particulars referred to in Article 1057(4)(a) to (d) inclusive are stated incorrectly or are partially or wholly absent from the award, a party may, within a time-limit as agreed by the parties or within three months after the day the award was sent, request in writing that the arbitral tribunal correct such particulars.

(3) A copy of a request as referred to in the first or second paragraph shall be sent to the other party by the arbitral tribunal.

(4) The arbitral tribunal may, within a time-limit as agreed by the parties or within three months after the day the award was sent, also of its own motion proceed to the correction referred to in the first or second paragraph.

(5) Before the arbitral tribunal decides on a request referred to in the first or second paragraph, or decides of its own motion to proceed to the correction as referred to in the fourth paragraph, it shall give the parties the opportunity to comment on the matter.

(6) If the arbitral tribunal proceeds to the correction, it shall be made by the arbitral tribunal on the original and the copies of the award and be signed by it, or mentioned in a separate document signed by the arbitral tribunal, which document shall be considered to be a part of the award. Articles 1057(1) to (3) inclusive and Article 1058(1) shall apply mutatis mutandis.

(7) If the arbitral tribunal denies the request for correction, then it shall communicate this to the parties in writing.

(8) The request, referred to in the first and second paragraphs, shall not suspend the possibility of enforcement, unless the provisional relief judge finds that important reasons exist to suspend this possibility until a decision has been made on the request. The provisions in Article 1070 shall apply mutatis mutandis to the decision of the provisional relief judge. The same shall apply if the arbitral tribunal proceeds to the correction of its own motion in accordance with the fourth paragraph.

Article 1061
(1) Within a time-limit agreed by the parties or within three months after the day the award was sent, the most diligent party may request the arbitral tribunal to make an additional award as to any one or more claims or counterclaims presented to the arbitral tribunal but not decided by it.
(2) A copy of the request shall be sent by the arbitral tribunal to the other party.
(3) The arbitral tribunal shall give the parties an opportunity to comment on the request before deciding on it.
(4) An additional award shall constitute an arbitral award to which the provisions of Sections Three to Five inclusive of this Title shall be applicable.
(5) If the arbitral tribunal denies a request for an additional award, it shall so notify the parties in writing. A copy of this notice, signed by an arbitrator or the secretary of the arbitral tribunal, may be deposited with the registry of the district court in accordance with the provisions of Article 1058(1)(b).

SECTION THREE A – ARBITRAL APPEAL

Article 1061a
If the parties have agreed to arbitral appeal, the provisions in this Title shall be applicable insofar as not otherwise provided in this Section or insofar as the nature of the arbitral appeal does not preclude this.

Article 1061b
Arbitral appeal against an arbitral award is only possible if the parties have made provision for this by agreement. Said agreement must comply with the requirements of Articles 1020 and 1021 as well as the requirements of Articles 166 and 167 of Book 10 of the Civil Code.

Article 1061c
The parties may institute arbitral appeal within a time-limit as agreed between the parties or within three months after the day the award was sent.

DUTCH CODE OF CIVIL PROCEDURE

Article 1061d
(1) Arbitral appeal may be instituted against a final award and a last partial final award.
(2) Unless the parties have agreed otherwise, arbitral appeal may also be instituted against other partial final awards.
(3) Arbitral appeal against an interim award, except an award based on Article 1043b(1), may only be instituted simultaneously with arbitral appeal against a final or partial final award, unless the parties have agreed otherwise.

Article 1061e
Arbitral appeal shall be available against an arbitral award made under Article 1046(4) if and insofar as all the parties to the consolidated proceedings have made provision for such arbitral appeal by agreement. Said agreement must comply with the requirements of Articles 1020 and 1021 as well as with the requirements of Articles 166 and 167 of Book 10 of the Civil Code.

Article 1061f

(1) In the event that the arbitral tribunal declares that it has no jurisdiction as referred to in the second sentence of Article 1052(5), arbitral appeal shall be allowed.

(2) In the event that the arbitral tribunal declares that it has jurisdiction or declares that it has no jurisdiction, the provisions in Article 1052(4) and (5) shall be applicable after a decision has been made on appeal, or the time-limit for such appeal has expired without being used, or earlier, if either party has waived the possibility of appeal in writing, or later, at the moment of premature termination of the appeal.

Article 1061g

(1) The penalty for non-compliance as referred to in Article 1056 may also be claimed for the first time on arbitral appeal.

(2) In derogation of the provisions in Article 1056, in the events referred to in Article 611d the lifting, suspension, or reduction of the penalty for non-compliance must be requested from the arbitral tribunal on appeal, if and as long as the mandate of that arbitral tribunal is still in effect.

DUTCH CODE OF CIVIL PROCEDURE

Article 1061h

The arbitral award made at the first instance may only be supplemented in accordance with Article 1061. The request to that end must be made within the time-limit applicable for arbitral appeal. The parties may deviate from the provisions of this article by agreement.

Article 1061i

(1) Unless the law or the nature of the case requires otherwise, the arbitral tribunal at first instance may, if this is claimed, declare that its award shall be immediately enforceable notwithstanding arbitral appeal. The declaration of immediate enforceability may relate to the entire award or any part thereof. The arbitral tribunal may attach as a condition to the declaration of immediate enforceability that an amount of security as determined by the arbitral tribunal be provided.

(2) If the award is not declared immediately enforceable by the arbitral tribunal at the first instance and arbitral appeal is instituted against that award, a claim for a declaration of immediate enforceability may be presented to the arbitral tribunal on arbitral appeal. Said claim, the other party having been heard, shall be decided immediately. The second and third sentences of the first paragraph shall apply mutatis mutandis.

(3) If the award is declared immediately enforceable by the arbitral tribunal at first instance, however without attaching the condition that security be provided, and if arbitral appeal is instituted against that award, a claim to that end may be presented to the arbitral tribunal on appeal. Said claim, the other party having been heard, shall be decided immediately.

Article 1061j

In derogation of the provisions in Article 1059(3), an arbitral award made at first instance has binding force between the same parties in other proceedings from the day on which the time-limit for arbitral appeal has expired without being used, or earlier, from the day on which the possibility of appeal has been waived in writing, or later, at the moment of premature termination of the appeal, or from the day on which a decision has been made on appeal, if and insofar as the award at first instance has been confirmed in that appeal.

Article 1061k

(1) An arbitral award granted at first instance that has been declared immediately enforceable, and an arbitral award that has been made on appeal, may be executed in accordance with the provisions in the Fourth Section of this Title. In addition to Article 1063(1), the provisional relief judge of the district court may also deny enforcement if immediate enforceability has been ordered contrary to Article 1061i.

(2) An arbitral award made at first instance that has not been declared immediately enforceable may only be enforced in accordance with the provisions of the Fourth Section of this Title after the time-limit for instituting arbitral appeal has expired without being used, or if and insofar as it has been confirmed on appeal, or earlier, if the possibility of appeal has been waived in writing, or later, at the moment of premature termination of the appeal.

Article 1061l

(1) Only the legal remedies of setting aside and revocation based on the Fifth Section of this Title are open against a final or partial final award made on arbitral appeal.

(2) The setting aside or revocation of an arbitral award made on arbitral appeal entails, by operation of law, the setting aside or revocation of the arbitral award made at first instance, unless the court decides that the arbitral award made at first instance shall be upheld.

(3) Only the legal remedies of setting aside and revocation based on the Fifth Section of this Title are open against a final or a partial final arbitral award made at first instance if the time-limit for arbitral appeal has expired without being used or earlier if each of the parties has waived the possibility of appeal in writing. In derogation of Article 1064a(2), the possibility of presenting a claim for setting aside such an award expires three months after the day on which the time-limit which applies for arbitral appeal has expired.

(4) In regard to an arbitral interim award made at first instance or on appeal, Article 1064a(3) shall, in accordance with the provisions in this article, apply mutatis mutandis.

SECTION FOUR – ENFORCEMENT OF THE ARBITRAL AWARD

Article 1062

(1) An arbitral award may only be enforced in the Netherlands after the provisional relief judge of the district court within whose district the place of arbitration is located has granted leave to do so at the request of any of the parties.

(2) The leave for enforcement shall be recorded on the original of the award or, if the award has not been deposited, shall be laid down in a decision. The registry of the district court shall as soon as possible send to the parties a certified copy of the award on which the leave for enforcement has been recorded or a certified copy of the decision in which the leave for enforcement has been granted.

(3) If the provisional relief judge of the district court grants the leave for enforcement, then only the legal remedies provided for in Article 1064 are open to the other party.

(4) Setting aside or revocation of the arbitral award entails, by operation of law, the setting aside or revocation of the leave for enforcement.

Article 1063

(1) Enforcement of the arbitral award may only be refused by the provisional relief judge of the district court if it appears plausible to him after a summary investigation that the award will be set aside based on one of the grounds mentioned in Article 1065(1), or revoked based on one of the grounds mentioned in Article 1068(1), or if a penalty for non-compliance has been imposed contrary to Article 1056. In this last event the refusal shall concern only the enforcement of the penalty for non- compliance.

(2) If the time-limit for presenting a claim for setting aside as referred to in Article 1064a has expired without being used, then the provisional relief judge of the district court may only refuse the request for leave for enforcement if it appears plausible to him after a summary investigation that the award is contrary to Article 1065(1)(e).
(3) The registry of the district court shall as soon as possible send to the parties a certified copy of the decision of the provisional relief judge of the district court in which the leave for enforcement is refused.
(4) Appeal against the decision in which the request for leave for enforcement is refused may be instituted before the Court of Appeal.
(5) If the leave for enforcement is also not granted on appeal, appeal in cassation may be instituted.
(6) If on appeal, or after appeal in cassation, the request for leave for enforcement is granted, the provisions in Article 1062(3) shall apply mutatis mutandis.

SECTION FIVE – SETTING ASIDE AND REVOCATION OF THE ARBITRAL AWARD

Article 1064
Only the legal remedies of setting aside and revocation based on the provisions in this Section shall be open against a final or a partial final arbitral award.

Article 1064a
(1) The claim for setting aside shall be presented to the Court of Appeal in whose judicial district the place of arbitration is located. If the place of arbitration is in the judicial district of Amsterdam and the parties have expressly agreed to this place of arbitration, the claim for setting aside may be presented to the Amsterdam Court of Appeal ("Netherlands Commercial Court of Appeal"). Article 30r shall apply mutatis mutandis.
(2) The possibility to present the claim for setting aside shall expire three months after the day the award was sent. If the parties have agreed to make use of the provision in Article 1058(1)(b), this possibility shall expire three months after the deposit of the award. If, however, the award with leave for enforcement is served on the other party, then that party may, notwithstanding the expiry of the time-limit of three months mentioned in the previous sentence, still present a claim for setting aside within three months after such service.
(3) The claim for setting aside an interim award may only be presented together with the claim for setting aside a final of partial final award.
(4) All grounds for setting aside must, on pain of being barred, be presented in the writ of summons.
(5) Appeal to the Supreme Court may be instituted against a judgment based on the first paragraph. The parties may agree that no appeal to the Supreme Court may be instituted against a judgment based on the first paragraph, unless any of them is a natural person not acting in the conduct of a trade or business.

Article 1065
(1) An award may only be set aside on one or more of the following grounds:
- (a) non-existence of a valid arbitration agreement;
- (b) the arbitral tribunal was composed in violation of the applicable rules;
- (c) the arbitral tribunal did not comply with its mandate;
- (d) the award was not signed or did not contain reasons in accordance with the provisions of Article 1057;
- (e) the award, or the manner in which it was made, violates public policy.

(2) The ground referred to in paragraph (1)(a) above shall not constitute a ground for setting aside in the event mentioned in Article 1052(2).

(3) The ground referred to in paragraph (1)(b) above shall not constitute a ground for setting aside in the event mentioned in Articles 1028(2) and 1052(3).
(4) The ground referred to in paragraph (1)(c) shall not constitute a ground for setting aside if the deviation from the mandate is not of a serious nature. Nor shall the ground referred to in (1)(c) constitute a ground for setting aside if the party advancing this ground has failed to make an objection in the matter in accordance with Article 1048a.
(5) If a ground for setting aside only concerns a part of the arbitral award, then the award shall not be set aside in respect of the remaining part, insofar as this, taking into account the content and purport of the award, is not inseparably connected with the part to be set aside.
(6) If and insofar as the arbitral tribunal has not decided one or more claims or counterclaims presented to it, the claim for setting aside on the ground referred to in paragraph (1)(c) above shall be admissible only if an additional award referred to in Article 1061(1) has been made, or the request for an additional award referred to in Article 1061(1) has wholly or partially been denied.
(7) In derogation of the provisions of Article 1064a(2), the time-limit for presenting a claim for setting aside referred to in the preceding paragraph shall expire three months after the day the additional award or the notice of denial referred to in Article 1061(5) was sent. If the parties have agreed to make use of the provision in Article 1058(1)(b), the time-limit for presenting the claim for setting aside referred to in the preceding paragraph shall expire three months after the day of the deposit of the additional award or of the notice of denial referred to in Article 1061(5). The provisions in the first and second sentence shall apply mutatis mutandis to the correction of the award referred to in Article 1060.

Article 1065a
(1) The Court of Appeal may, at the request of a party or of its own motion, suspend the setting aside proceedings for a period of time to be determined by the Court of Appeal to put the arbitral tribunal in a position to reverse the ground for setting aside by reopening the arbitral proceedings or by taking other measures as the arbitral tribunal considers appropriate. No appeal is open against a decision of the Court of Appeal.
(2) Before the arbitral tribunal makes a decision, it shall give the parties an opportunity to be heard.
(3) If the arbitral tribunal finds that the ground for setting aside may be reversed, it shall make an award accordingly that takes the place of the award for which a claim for setting aside has been presented.
(4) After the suspension of the setting aside proceedings, the Court of Appeal shall decide as it considers, taking into account the circumstances.

Article 1066
(1) A claim for setting aside shall not suspend the enforcement of the award.
(2) However, the court which decides on a claim for setting aside may, at the request of the most diligent party, if there are grounds to do so, suspend enforcement until a final decision has been made on the claim for setting aside.
(3) A copy of the request for suspension shall be communicated by the registry of the Court of Appeal to the other party as soon as possible.
(4) The court shall not decide on the request until the other party has been given an opportunity to comment on the matter.
(5) When granting the request, the court may order the petitioner to provide security. When denying the request, the court may order the other party to provide security.
(6) In the event that enforcement is suspended, the most diligent party may request the court to lift the suspension. The provisions of paragraphs (3) to (5) inclusive shall apply mutatis mutandis.

Article 1067
As soon as the decision setting aside the award has become final, the jurisdiction of the court shall be revived if and insofar as the arbitral award has been set aside on the ground of non-existence of a valid arbitration agreement. If and insofar as the arbitral award is set aside on any other ground, the arbitration agreement shall remain in force, unless the parties have agreed otherwise.

Article 1068
(1) The award may only be revoked on one or more of the following grounds:
(a) the award is wholly or partially based on fraud discovered after the award was made and committed during the arbitral proceedings by or with the knowledge of the other party;
(b) the award is wholly or partially based on documents which, after the award was made, are discovered to have been forged;
(c) after the award was made, a party obtains documents which would have had an influence on the decision of the arbitral tribunal and which were withheld as a result of the acts of the other party.
(2) A claim for revocation shall be brought before the Court of Appeal in whose judicial district the place of arbitration is located, within three months after the fraud or forgery of documents has become known or the party has obtained the new documents. The provisions of Article 1066 shall apply mutatis mutandis.
(3) If the court finds the ground or grounds for revocation presented to have merit, it shall set aside the award wholly or in part. Articles 1065a and 1067 shall apply mutatis mutandis.

SECTION SIX – ARBITRAL AWARD ON AGREED TERMS

Article 1069
(1) If the parties reach a settlement during the arbitral proceedings, the arbitral tribunal may, at their joint request, record the contents of the settlement in an arbitral award. The arbitral tribunal may refuse this request without giving reasons.
(2) An arbitral award on agreed terms shall be regarded as an arbitral award to which the provisions of Sections Three to Five inclusive of this Title shall be applicable, it being understood that:
(a) the award may be set aside only on the ground that it is contrary to public policy, and
(b) in derogation of the provisions of Article 1057, the award need not contain the grounds on which it is based.

SECTION SEVEN- FINAL PROVISIONS

Article 1070
No appeal is open against decisions of the provisional relief judge of the district court as referred to in Sections One to Three inclusive of this Title.

Article 1071
In the events referred to in Articles 1026(2) and (4), 1027(3), 1028(1), 1029(2), (4) and (5), 1041a(1), 1044(1) and 1062(1), the petition and, insofar as applicable, the defence need not be presented by an attorney.

Article 1072
The parties may designate by agreement the provisional relief judge of a specific district court as the provisional relief judge competent for the matters as referred to in Articles 1026(2) and (4), 1027(3), 1028(1), 1029(2), (4) and (5), 1035(2), and 1041a(1).

Article 1072a
Insofar as not otherwise provided in this Title, Articles 261 to 291 inclusive shall apply mutatis mutandis to cases which are instituted with a petition in accordance with the provisions of this Title.

Article 1072b
(1) Insofar as any provision of this Title requires an agreement, a submission, a notice, a request or an action to take written form, these may also take electronic form if the addressee has communicated that it may be reached for these purposes by such means and the arbitral tribunal agrees thereto. The availability by such means shall be valid for the duration of the arbitral proceedings, unless the addressee communicates that it modifies, or, insofar as the parties have agreed to this possibility, withdraws this possibility. This paragraph does not apply to actions in judicial proceedings.
(2) Documents as referred to in this Title shall also be understood to be data on a data carrier as well as data presented by electronic means.
(3) The award referred to in Article 1057(2) may also be made in electronic form by providing it with a qualified electronic signature as referred to in Article 3(12) of Regulation (EU) No 910/2014 of the European Parliament and of the Council of 23 July 2014 on electronic identification and trust services for electronic transactions in the internal market repealing Directive 1999/93/EC (OJ 2014 L 257).
(4) Instead of a personal appearance of a witness, an expert or a party, the arbitral tribunal may determine that the relevant person have direct contact with the arbitral tribunal and, insofar as applicable, with others, by electronic means. The arbitral tribunal shall determine, in consultation with those concerned, which electronic means shall be used to this end and in which manner this shall occur.
(5) A notice or action that occurs by electronic means or a procedural document which is presented by electronic means shall be deemed to have been sent at the time at which the message has reached a data processing system for which the sender is not responsible.

Article 1072c
(1) The death of a party shall terminate neither the arbitration agreement nor the mandate of the arbitral tribunal, unless the parties have agreed otherwise.
(2) The arbitral tribunal shall suspend the proceedings for a period of time determined by it. The arbitral tribunal may, at the request of the legal successors of a deceased party, extend this period. The arbitral tribunal shall give the other party, at its request, the opportunity to be heard.
(3) After the suspension the proceedings shall be continued from the stage they had reached, unless the parties have agreed otherwise.
(4) If the party which has grounds to apply for setting aside or revocation of an arbitral award dies within the time-limits mentioned in Article 1064a(2), Article 1065(7) or Article 1068(2), Article 341 shall apply mutatis mutandis.

Article 1073
(1) The provisions of this Title shall apply if the place of arbitration is located within the Netherlands.
(2) If the parties have not determined the place of arbitration, the appointment or the challenge of the arbitrator or arbitrators or the secretary engaged by an arbitral tribunal may take place in accordance with the provisions in Section One B of this Title if at least one of the parties is domiciled or has his actual residence in the Netherlands.

TITLE TWO – ARBITRATION OUTSIDE THE NETHERLANDS

Article 1074
A court in the Netherlands seized of a dispute in respect of which an arbitration agreement has been concluded and which entails that arbitration must take place outside the Netherlands shall declare that it has no jurisdiction if a party invokes the existence of said agreement before submitting a defence, unless the agreement is invalid under the law applicable to said agreement.

Article 1074a
The agreement which entails that arbitration must take place outside the Netherlands shall not preclude a party from requesting a court in the Netherlands to grant provisional conservatory measures, or from applying to the provisional relief judge of the district court or the cantonal judge for a decision in summary proceedings in accordance with the provisions of Article 254.

Article 1074b
An arbitration agreement which entails that arbitration must take place outside the Netherlands shall not preclude a party from requesting a court in the Netherlands to order a preliminary witness hearing, a preliminary expert report or a preliminary on-site examination and viewing in the Netherlands.

Article 1074c
An arbitration agreement which entails that arbitration must take place outside the Netherlands shall not preclude a party from requesting the court to appoint an examining magistrate if a witness who is domiciled or has his actual residence in the Netherlands does not voluntarily appear. In that event the provisions of Article 1041a(1) to (3) inclusive shall apply mutatis mutandis.

Article 1074d
If, in the events mentioned in Articles 1047a to 1074c inclusive, a party invokes the existence of an arbitration agreement before submitting a defence, the court shall only declare that it has jurisdiction if the requested decision cannot or cannot in a timely manner be obtained in arbitration.

Article 1075
(1) An arbitral award made in a foreign State to which a treaty concerning recognition and enforcement is applicable may, at the request of any of the parties, be recognised and enforced in the Netherlands.
(2) Articles 985 to 991 inclusive shall apply mutatis mutandis insofar as the treaty does not contain provisions in derogation thereof and it being understood that the Court of Appeal shall be substituted for the district court and the time-limit for appeal in cassation shall be three months.
(3) Articles 261 to 291 inclusive shall apply mutatis mutandis to the request insofar as not otherwise provided in paragraph two of this article.

Article 1076
(1) If no treaty concerning recognition and enforcement is applicable, or if an applicable treaty allows a party to rely upon the law of the country in which recognition and enforcement is sought, an arbitral award made in a foreign State may be recognised in the Netherlands and its enforcement may be sought in the Netherlands by any of the parties, upon submission of the original or a certified copy of the arbitration agreement and arbitral award, unless:

- (A) the party against whom recognition or enforcement is sought, asserts and proves that:
  - (a) no valid arbitration agreement under the law applicable thereto exists;
  - (b) the arbitral tribunal was composed in violation of the applicable rules;
  - (c) the arbitral tribunal did not comply with its mandate;

(d) the arbitral award is open to appeal to arbitrators or the courts in the country in which the award was made;
(e) the arbitral award was set aside by a competent authority of the country in which that award was made;

(B) the court finds that the recognition or enforcement would be contrary to public policy.

(2) The ground mentioned in paragraph (l)(A)(a) above shall not constitute a ground for refusal of recognition or enforcement if the party invoking this ground has appeared in the arbitral proceedings and, before submitting a defence, has not raised the plea that the arbitral tribunal has no jurisdiction on the ground of non-existence of a valid arbitration agreement.

(3) The ground mentioned in paragraph (l)(A)(b) above shall not constitute a ground for refusal of recognition or enforcement if the party invoking this ground has cooperated in the composition of the arbitral tribunal, or if it has not cooperated in the composition of the arbitral tribunal, has appeared in the arbitral proceedings and, before submitting a defence, has not raised the plea that the arbitral tribunal has no jurisdiction on the ground that the arbitral tribunal was composed in violation of the applicable rules.

(4) The ground mentioned in paragraph (1)(A)(c) above shall not constitute a ground for refusal of recognition or enforcement if the deviation from the mandate is not of a serious nature. Nor shall the ground mentioned in paragraph (1)(A)(c) above constitute a ground for refusal of recognition or enforcement if the party invoking this ground has participated in the arbitral proceedings without raising it in a timely manner, although it was known to it that the arbitral tribunal did not comply with its mandate.

(5) If the award is in excess of, or different from, the relief sought, the arbitral award shall be capable of partial recognition or enforcement insofar as the part of the award which is in excess of or different from the relief sought may be separated from the remaining part of the award.

(6) The provisions of Articles 985 to 991 inclusive shall apply mutatis mutandis, it being understood that the Court of Appeal shall be substituted for the district court, the time-limit for appeal to the Supreme Court shall be three months, and no documents need be submitted evidencing the enforceability of the arbitral award in the country in which it is made.

(7) Articles 261 to 291 inclusive shall apply mutatis mutandis to the request insofar as not otherwise provided in the sixth paragraph of this article.

(8) If a claim for setting aside an award made in a foreign State is made to a competent authority of the country in which the award was made, the provisions of Article 1066(2) to (6) inclusive shall apply mutatis mutandis when recognition or enforcement is sought in the Netherlands.

9.3.3 Swiss Private International Law Act (1987) (Swiss law, unofficial English translation)[1]

CHAPTER 1: GENERAL PROVISIONS (EXCERPT)

VI. ARBITRATION AGREEMENT

Art. 7. If parties have concluded an arbitration agreement with respect to an arbitrable dispute, a Swiss court before which an action is brought shall decline its jurisdiction, unless:

(a) the respondent has submitted to the procedure without reservation;
(b) the court finds that the arbitration agreement is invalid, inoperable or incapable of being performed; or
(c) the arbitral tribunal cannot be constituted for reasons for which the respondent in the arbitration is manifestly responsible.

CHAPTER 12: INTERNATIONAL ARBITRATION

I. SCOPE OF APPLICATION; SEAT OF THE ARBITRAL TRIBUNAL

Art. 176. (1) The provisions of this Chapter shall apply to arbitrations with their seat in Switzerland if at least one of the parties to the arbitration agreement, at the time of its conclusion, did not have its domicile, habitual residence or seat in Switzerland.
(2) The parties may, either in the arbitration agreement or in a subsequent agreement, exclude the application of this Chapter and agree on the application of Part 3 of the CCP. The exclusion shall meet the conditions as to form set out in Article 178(1).
(3) The seat of the arbitration shall be determined by the parties or by the arbitral institution designated by the parties, or, failing which, by the arbitral tribunal.

II. ARBITRABILITY

Art. 177. (1) Any claim involving a financial interest may be the subject-matter of an arbitration.
(2) Where a party to the arbitration agreement is a State, or an enterprise held by, or an organisation controlled by, a State, it may not invoke its own law in order to contest the arbitrability of a dispute or its capacity to be a party to an arbitration.

III. ARBITRATION AGREEMENT AND ARBITRATION CLAUSE

Art. 178. (1) The arbitration agreement shall be valid if made in writing or in any other manner that can be evidenced by text.
(2) As regards its substance, the arbitration agreement shall be valid if it conforms to the law chosen by the parties, or to the law applicable to the dispute, in particular the law governing the main contract, or to Swiss law.

---

1 This English translation of the Swiss International Law Act is reproduced with kind permission of the Swiss Arbitration Association (www.swissarbitration.org).

(3) The validity of an arbitration agreement cannot be contested on the grounds that the main contract may not be valid or that the arbitration agreement relates to a dispute that has not yet arisen.
(4) The provisions of this Chapter shall apply by analogy to an arbitration clause set out in a unilateral legal act or in articles of association.

IV. ARBITRATORS

1. APPOINTMENT AND REPLACEMENT

Art. 179. (1) The arbitrators shall be appointed and replaced in accordance with the parties' agreement. Unless the parties have agreed otherwise, the arbitral tribunal shall consist of three arbitrators, whereby two of the arbitrators are appointed by each of the parties and the two arbitrators so appointed unanimously select the third arbitrator as the president of the tribunal.
(2) In the absence of an agreement or if the arbitrators cannot be appointed or replaced for other reasons, the matter may be referred to the state court at the seat of the arbitration. If the parties have not designated a seat or have merely agreed that the seat of the arbitration shall be in Switzerland, the state court first seized shall have jurisdiction.
(3) If a state court is called upon to appoint or replace an arbitrator, it shall grant such request, unless a summary examination shows that no arbitration agreement exists between the parties.
(4) At the request of a party, the state court shall take the necessary action to constitute the arbitral tribunal if the parties or arbitrators fail to fulfil their obligations within 30 days of being called upon to do so.
(5) In the case of a multi-party arbitration, the state court may appoint all arbitrators.
(6) A person who has been approached to serve as arbitrator must promptly disclose any circumstances that may give rise to justifiable doubts as to his or her independence or impartiality. This obligation shall persist for the duration of the proceedings.

2. CHALLENGE

a. Grounds

Art. 180. (1) An arbitrator may be challenged:
- (a) if that arbitrator does not meet the qualifications agreed upon by the parties;
- (b) if a ground for challenge exists under the arbitration rules agreed upon by the parties;
- (c) if circumstances exist that give rise to justifiable doubts as to that arbitrator's independence or impartiality.

(2) A party may challenge an arbitrator whom it has appointed or in whose appointment it has participated only for reasons of which, despite having exercised due diligence, it became aware of only after the appointment.

b. Procedure

Art. 180a. (1) Unless the parties have agreed otherwise and if the arbitral proceedings are not yet concluded, the request for challenge shall be addressed, with reasons and in writing, to the challenged arbitrator and notified to the other arbitrators within 30 days of the requesting party becoming aware, or exercising due diligence ought to have become aware, of the ground for challenge.
(2) The requesting party may, within 30 days of the submission of the request for challenge, challenge the arbitrator before the state court. The decision of the state court is final.

(3) Unless the parties have agreed otherwise, during the challenge procedure the arbitral tribunal may proceed with the arbitration and render an award, with the participation of the challenged arbitrator.

3. REMOVAL

Art. 180b. (1) Any arbitrator may be removed by agreement of the parties.
(2) Unless the parties have agreed otherwise, if an arbitrator is unable to perform his or her duties within a reasonable time or with due diligence, a party may apply, with reasons and in writing, to the state court for the arbitrator's removal. The decision of the state court is final.

V. LIS PENDENS

Art. 181. The arbitral proceedings shall be pending from the time when a party submits a claim with the arbitrator or arbitrators designated in the arbitration agreement or, in the absence of such designation, from the time when a party initiates the procedure for the constitution of the arbitral tribunal.

VI. PROCEDURE

1. PRINCIPLE

Art. 182. (1) The parties may determine the arbitral procedure, directly or by reference to arbitration rules; they may also submit it to a procedural law of their choice.
(2) If the parties have not determined the procedure, the arbitral tribunal shall determine it to the extent necessary, either directly or by reference to a law or to arbitration rules.
(3) Regardless of the chosen procedure, the arbitral tribunal shall ensure equal treatment of the parties and their right to be heard in adversarial proceedings.
(4) A party that proceeds with the arbitration without immediately raising an objection to a violation of procedural rules which it knew or, exercising due diligence, ought to have known, may not subsequently raise such objection.

2. PROVISIONAL AND CONSERVATORY MEASURES

Art. 183. (1) Unless the parties have agreed otherwise, the arbitral tribunal may, at the request of a party, order provisional or conservatory measures.
(2) If the party concerned does not voluntarily comply with the measure so ordered, the arbitral tribunal or a party may request the assistance of the state court; such court shall apply its own law.
(3) The arbitral tribunal or the state court may make the order of provisional or conservatory measures conditional on the provision of appropriate security.

3. TAKING OF EVIDENCE

Art. 184. (1) The arbitral tribunal shall conduct the taking of evidence itself.
(2) If the assistance of state judicial authorities is required for the taking of evidence, the arbitral tribunal, or a party with the consent of the arbitral tribunal, may request the assistance of the state court at the seat of the arbitration.
(3) The state court shall apply its own law. Upon request, it may apply or consider other forms of procedure.

4. OTHER CASES OF JUDICIAL ASSISTANCE

Art. 185. If any other judicial assistance is required, the state court at the seat of the arbitration shall have jurisdiction.

5. JUDICIAL ASSISTANCE IN SUPPORT OF FOREIGN ARBITRATIONS

Art. 185a. (1) An arbitral tribunal sitting abroad or a party to a foreign arbitration may request the assistance of the state court at the place where a provisional or conservatory measure is to be enforced. Article 183(2) and (3) shall apply by analogy.
(2) An arbitral tribunal sitting abroad or, with the consent of the arbitral tribunal, a party to a foreign arbitration may request the assistance of the state court at the place where the taking of evidence is to be carried out. Article 184(2) and (3) shall apply by analogy.

VII. JURISDICTION

Art. 186. (1) The arbitral tribunal shall decide on its own jurisdiction.
(1bis) It shall decide on its jurisdiction notwithstanding any pending action before a state court or another arbitral tribunal on the same subject-matter between the same parties, unless there are substantial reasons to stay the proceedings.
(2) Any plea of lack of jurisdiction must be raised prior to any defence on the merits.
(3) The arbitral tribunal shall, in general, decide on its jurisdiction by means of a preliminary award.

VIII. ARBITRAL AWARD

1. APPLICABLE LAW

Art. 187. (1) The arbitral tribunal shall decide the dispute according to the rules of law chosen by the parties or, in the absence thereof, according to the rules of law with which the dispute has the closest connection.
(2) The parties may authorise the arbitral tribunal to decide ex aequo et bono.

2. PARTIAL AWARD

Art. 188. Unless the parties have agreed otherwise, the arbitral tribunal may render partial awards.

3. PROCEDURE AND FORM

Art. 189. (1) The award shall be rendered in conformity with the rules of procedure and in the form agreed upon by the parties.
(2) In the absence of such agreement, the award shall be made by a majority decision or, in the absence of a majority, by the presiding arbitrator alone. The award shall be made in writing, with reasons, dated and signed. The signature of the presiding arbitrator is sufficient.

4. CORRECTION AND INTERPRETATION OF THE AWARD; AND SUPPLEMENTAL AWARD

Art. 189a. (1) Unless the parties have agreed otherwise, either party may, within 30 days of the notification of the award, request the arbitral tribunal to correct any clerical or computational errors

in the award, to interpret certain parts of the award or to issue a supplement to the award on claims which were raised in the arbitral proceedings but not dealt with in the award. Within the same time limit, the arbitral tribunal may, on its own initiative, correct, interpret or supplement the award.
(2) The request does not suspend the time limits for recourse against the award. With respect to the corrected, interpreted or supplemented part of the award, the time limit for recourse shall start anew.

IX. FINALITY, CHALLENGE, REVISION

1. CHALLENGE

Art. 190. (1) The award is final from the time when it is notified.
(2) The award can only be challenged on the grounds that:
- (a) the sole arbitrator was not properly appointed or the arbitral tribunal was not properly constituted;
- (b) the arbitral tribunal wrongly accepted or declined jurisdiction;
- (c) the arbitral tribunal decided claims which were not submitted to it or failed to decide claims submitted to it;
- (d) the principle of equal treatment of the parties or their right to be heard in adversarial proceedings was violated;
- (e) the award is incompatible with public policy.

(3) Preliminary awards can only be challenged on the grounds of paragraph 2(a) and (b); the time limit runs from the notification of the preliminary award.
(4) The time limit for the challenge is 30 days from the notification of the award.

2. REVISION

Art. 190a. (1) A party may request the revision of an award:
- (a) if it subsequently discovers material facts or conclusive evidence which, despite having exercised due diligence, it was unable to invoke in the previous proceedings; facts and evidence which postdate the award are excluded;
- (b) if criminal proceedings have established that the award was influenced, to the detriment of the challenging party, by a crime or misdemeanour, even in the absence of any conviction; if criminal proceedings cannot be pursued, proof can be furnished by other means;
- (c) if, despite having exercised due diligence, a ground for challenge under Article 180(1)(c) was not discovered until after the conclusion of the arbitration and no other remedy is available.

(2) The request for revision must be filed within 90 days of the discovery of the ground for revision. Except in cases provided for by paragraph 1(b), the right to request revision shall expire ten years from the date on which the award has come into force.

3. JUDICIAL AUTHORITY FOR RECOURSE

Art. 191. The Swiss Federal Supreme Court is the sole judicial authority for recourse against an award. The procedure is governed by Articles 77 and 119b of the Federal Supreme Court Act of 17 June 2005.

X. WAIVER OF RECOURSE

Art. 192. (1) If none of the parties has its domicile, habitual residence, or seat in Switzerland, the parties may, either in the arbitration agreement or in a subsequent agreement, exclude in whole or in

part recourse against arbitral awards; the right to revision under Article 190a(1)(b) cannot be waived. The agreement shall meet the conditions as to form set out in Article 178(1).
(2) If the parties have excluded any recourse against arbitral awards and such awards are to be enforced in Switzerland, the New York Convention of 10 June 1958 on the Recognition and Enforcement of Foreign Arbitral Awards shall apply by analogy.

XI. DEPOSIT AND CERTIFICATE OF ENFORCEABILITY

Art. 193. (1) Any party may, at its own expense, deposit a copy of the award with the state court at the seat of the arbitration.
(2) At the request of a party, the state court at the seat of the arbitration shall certify the enforceability of the award.
(3) At the request of a party, the arbitral tribunal shall certify that the award has been rendered in conformity with the provisions of this Act; such certificate has the same effect as the deposit of the award.

XII. FOREIGN ARBITRAL AWARDS

Art. 194. The recognition and enforcement of a foreign arbitral award is governed by the New York Convention of 10 June 1958 on the Recognition and Enforcement of Foreign Arbitral Awards.

FEDERAL SUPREME COURT ACT (EXCERPT)

CHAPTER 3 THE FEDERAL SUPREME COURT AS AN ORDINARY COURT OF APPEAL SECTION 1 APPEAL IN CIVIL MATTERS

Art. 77 Arbitration. (1) An appeal in civil matters is admissible, regardless of the amount in dispute, against the decisions of arbitral tribunals:

- (a) in international arbitrations, under the conditions set out in Articles 190-192 of the Private International Law Act of 18 December 1987;
- (b) in domestic arbitrations, under the conditions set out in Articles 389 to 395 of the Code of Civil Procedure of 19 December 2008.

(2) Articles 48(3), 90 to 98, 103(2), 105(2) and 106(1), as well as Article 107(2), to the extent that the latter provision allows the Federal Supreme Court to rule on the merits of the case, do not apply in these cases.
(2bis) Written submissions may be in English.
(3) The Federal Supreme Court only examines grounds for challenge that have been raised and substantiated by the challenging party.

CHAPTER 5A REVISION OF INTERNATIONAL ARBITRAL AWARDS

Art. 119a. (1) The Federal Supreme Court decides on requests for revision of international arbitral awards under the conditions set out in Article 190a of the Private International Law Act of 18 December 1987.
(2) The revision procedure is governed by Articles 77(2bis) and 126. Unless the Federal Supreme Court determines the request for revision to be manifestly inadmissible or unfounded, it shall notify it to the opposing party and the arbitral tribunal for comment.
(3) If the Federal Supreme Court grants the request for revision, it shall set the award aside and remand the case to the arbitral tribunal for a new decision or make the necessary findings.

(4) If the arbitral tribunal no longer comprises the required number of arbitrators, Article 179 of the Private International Law Act shall apply.

9.3.4 French Arbitration Act (French law, unofficial English translation)

(Decree no. 2011-48 of 13 January 2011 on arbitration reform)

Article 1. Articles 1508 to 1519 of the Code of Civil Procedure become articles 1570 to 1582 respectively.

Article 2. Book IV of the Code of Civil Procedure is worded as follows:

BOOK IV. ARBITRATION

TITLE I. DOMESTIC ARBITRATION

CHAPTER I. THE ARBITRATION AGREEMENT

Art. 1442. The arbitration agreement shall take the form of an arbitration clause or an arbitration agreement.

An arbitration clause is an agreement whereby the parties to one or more contracts undertake to submit to arbitration any disputes that may arise in connection with that contract or those contracts.

An arbitration agreement is a contract by which the parties to a dispute submit the dispute to arbitration.

Art. 1443. Under pain of being declared null and void, the arbitration agreement shall be in writing. It may result from an exchange of writings or from a document to which reference is made in the main agreement.

Art. 1444. The arbitration agreement shall designate the arbitrator or arbitrators, if applicable by reference to the arbitration rules, or provide for the manner in which they are to be appointed. Failing this, the arbitration shall proceed in accordance with the provisions of Articles 1451 to 1454.

Art. 1445. Under pain of being null and void, the arbitration agreement shall determine the subject-matter of the dispute.

Art. 1446. The parties may submit their dispute to arbitration even during proceedings already instituted before a court.

Art. 1447. An arbitration agreement is independent of the contract to which it relates. It is not affected by the voidness of the contract.

If the arbitration clause is null and void, is will be deemed not to have been written.

Art. 1448. Where a dispute arising under an arbitration agreement is brought before a court, the latter shall declare that it has no jurisdiction unless the Arbitral Tribunal has not yet been seised and the arbitration agreement is manifestly null and void or manifestly inapplicable.

The court may not of its own motion declare that it does not have jurisdiction.

Any stipulation contrary to this article shall be deemed unwritten.

Art. 1449. The existence of an arbitration agreement shall not prevent a party, as long as the Arbitral Tribunal has not been constituted, from bringing an action before a court for the purpose of obtaining an investigative measure or an interim or protective measure.

Subject to the provisions governing protective attachments and judicial sureties, the claim shall be brought before the President of the Tribunal de Grande Instance or the Tribunal de Commerce, who shall rule on the measures of inquiry under the conditions set out in Article 145 and, in urgent cases, on the interim or protective measures requested by the parties to the arbitration agreement.

CHAPTER II. THE ARBITRAL TRIBUNAL

Art. 1450. The office of arbitrator may only be held by a natural person enjoying the full exercise of his rights.

If the arbitration agreement designates a legal entity, that entity only has the power to organise the arbitration.

Art. 1451. The Arbitral Tribunal shall be composed of one or more arbitrators in an uneven number.

If the arbitration agreement provides for the appointment of an even number of arbitrators, an additional one must be appointed.

If the parties do not agree on the appointment of an additional arbitrator, he will be appointed by the other arbitrators within one month of the acceptance of their appointment, failing that, by the supporting judge referred to in Article 1459.

Art. 1452. In the absence of an agreement by the parties on the method of appointing the arbitrator or arbitrators:

1. In the event of arbitration by a sole arbitrator, if the parties do not agree on the choice of arbitrator, the arbitrator shall be appointed by the person responsible for organising the arbitration or, failing this, by the supporting judge;
2. In the event of arbitration by three arbitrators, each party shall choose one arbitrator and the two arbitrators so chosen shall appoint the third arbitrator; if a party fails to choose an arbitrator within one month of receipt of the request to do so from the other party or if the two arbitrators fail to agree on the choice of the third arbitrator within one month of acceptance of their appointment, the person responsible for organising the arbitration or, failing this, the supporting judge shall make the appointment.

Art. 1453. Where the dispute is between more than two parties and the parties are unable to agree on how the Arbitral Tribunal should be constituted, the person responsible for organising the arbitration or, failing that, the supporting judge, shall appoint the arbitrator or arbitrators.

Art. 1454. Any other dispute relating to the constitution of the Arbitral Tribunal shall be settled, in the absence of agreement by the parties, by the person responsible for organising the arbitration or, failing that, by the supporting judge.

Art. 1455. If the arbitration agreement is manifestly null and void or manifestly unenforceable, the supporting judge shall declare that there are no grounds for appointment.

Art. 1456. The Arbitral Tribunal is constituted when the arbitrator or arbitrators have accepted the assignment entrusted to them. The dispute shall then be referred to it.

It is the arbitrator's responsibility, before accepting his assignment, to disclose any circumstances likely to affect his independence or impartiality. He is also required to disclose without delay any similar circumstances that may arise after accepting his assignment.

In the event of a dispute over the removal of the arbitrator, the issue shall be settled by the person responsible for organising the arbitration or, failing this, by the supporting judge who shall refer the matter to the court within one month of the disclosure or discovery of the disputed fact.

Art. 1457. The arbitrator must carry out his mandate until it is completed, unless he is prevented from doing so or has a legitimate reason for abstaining or resigning.

In the event of a dispute as to whether the reason given is genuine, the matter shall be settled by the person responsible for organising the arbitration or, failing that, by the supporting judge to whom the matter is referred within one month of the impediment, abstention or resignation.

Article 1458. The arbitrator may only be removed from office with the unanimous consent of the parties. In the absence of such consent, the last paragraph of Article 1456 shall apply.

Art. 1459. The President of the Tribunal de Grande Instance is the competent supporting judge.

However, if the arbitration agreement expressly so provides, the President of the Commercial Court shall have jurisdiction to hear claims brought pursuant to Articles 1451 to 1454. In this case, he may apply article 1455.

The court having territorial jurisdiction shall be the court designated in the arbitration agreement or, failing that, the court within whose jurisdiction the seat of the Arbitral Tribunal has been set. In the absence of any stipulation in the arbitration agreement, the court having territorial jurisdiction shall be that of the place where the defendant or one of the defendants to the dispute resides or, if the defendant does not reside in France, the place where the claimant resides.

Art. 1460. A matter is referred to the supporting judge either by a party or by the Arbitral Tribunal or one of its members.

The application is lodged, investigated and judged in the same way as an application for interim relief.

The supporting judge shall give his decision in an order that is not subject to appeal. However, this order may be appealed when the judge declares that there are no grounds for appointment for one of the reasons set out in Article 1455.

Art. 1461. Subject to the provisions of the first paragraph of Article 1456, any stipulation contrary to the rules laid down in this chapter is deemed to be unwritten.

CHAPTER III. ARBITRATION PROCEEDINGS

Art. 1462. The dispute shall be submitted to the Arbitral Tribunal either jointly by the parties or by the most diligent party.

Art. 1463. If the arbitration agreement does not specify a time limit, the term of office of the Arbitral Tribunal shall be limited to six months from the date on which the case is referred to it.

The legal or contractual time limit may be extended by agreement between the parties or, failing that, by the supporting judge.

Art. 1464. Unless the parties have agreed otherwise, the Arbitral Tribunal shall determine the arbitral procedure without being bound to follow the rules established for state courts.

However, the guiding principles of the proceedings set out in Articles 4 to 10, the first paragraph of Article 11, the second and third paragraphs of Article 12 and Articles 13 to 21, 23 and 23-1 shall continue to apply.

The parties and the arbitrators shall act promptly and fairly in the conduct of the proceedings.

Subject to legal obligations and unless the parties agree otherwise, the arbitration proceedings are subject to the principle of confidentiality.

Art. 1465. The Arbitral Tribunal shall have exclusive jurisdiction to rule on disputes relating to its jurisdictional powers.

Art. 1466. A party who, knowingly and without legitimate reason, fails to raise an irregularity before the Arbitral Tribunal in a timely manner shall be deemed to have waived its right to do so.

Art. 1467. The Arbitral Tribunal shall carry out the necessary investigative acts unless the parties authorize it to appoint one of its members.

The Arbitral Tribunal may hear any person. Such hearings shall be held without the taking of an oath.

If a party is in possession of evidence, the Arbitral Tribunal may order it to produce it in the manner it shall determine and, if necessary, subject to a penalty payment.

Art. 1468. The Arbitral Tribunal may order the parties to take any protective or provisional measures that it considers appropriate, subject to such conditions as it shall determine and, if necessary, subject to a fine. However, only courts shall have jurisdiction to order protective measures and judicial securities.

The Arbitral Tribunal may modify or supplement the interim measure of protection that it has ordered.

Art. 1469. If a party to the arbitral proceedings intends to rely on an authentic instrument or a private document to which he was not a party or on a document in the possession of a third party, he may, at the request of the Arbitral Tribunal, summon such third party before the President of the Tribunal de Grande Instance in order to obtain the delivery of a copy or the production of the instrument or document.

The territorial jurisdiction of the President of the Tribunal de Grande Instance shall be determined in accordance with Articles 42 to 48.

The application is lodged, investigated and judged in the same way as an application for interim relief.

If the President deems the application to be well-founded, he shall order that the original, copy or extract, as the case may be, of the document be issued or produced under the conditions and subject to the guarantees that he shall determine, if necessary subject to a penalty payment.

This decision is not automatically enforceable.

It may be appealed within fifteen days of the decision being served.

Art. 1470. Unless otherwise agreed, the Arbitral Tribunal shall have the power to rule on the request for verification of handwriting or forgery in accordance with the provisions of Articles 287 to 294 and Article 299.

In the event of a claim of forgery article 313 shall apply.

Art. 1471. The interruption of proceedings is governed by the provisions of articles 369 to 372.

Art. 1472. The Arbitral Tribunal may, if appropriate, stay the proceedings. Such decision shall suspend the course of the proceedings for the time set in the stay order or until the occurrence of such event as it shall determine.

The Arbitral Tribunal may, depending on the circumstances, revoke the stay or shorten its duration.

Art. 1473. Unless otherwise agreed, the arbitral proceedings shall also be suspended in the event of the death, incapacity, abstention, resignation, challenge or revocation of an arbitrator until the arbitrator appointed to replace him accepts his office.

The new arbitrator shall be appointed in accordance with the procedures agreed between the parties or, failing that, in accordance with those that governed the appointment of the arbitrator he replaces.

Art. 1474. The interruption or suspension of the proceedings shall not relieve the Arbitral Tribunal of its jurisdiction.

The Arbitral Tribunal may invite the parties to inform it of their initiatives to resume the proceedings or to put an end to the causes of interruption or suspension. If the parties fail to do so, it may terminate the proceedings.

Art. 1475. Proceedings resume in the state in which they were at the time they were interrupted or suspended when the causes of their interruption or suspension cease to exist.

Upon resumption of the proceedings and by way of exception to Article 1463, the Arbitral Tribunal may decide that the time limit for the proceedings shall be extended for a period not exceeding six months.

Art. 1476. The Arbitral Tribunal shall fix the date on which the deliberation is to be delivered.

During the deliberations, no claim may be made, no plea raised and no document produced, except at the request of the Arbitral Tribunal.

Art. 1477. The expiry of the arbitration period shall result in the termination of the arbitral proceedings.

CHAPTER IV. THE ARBITRATION AWARD

Art. 1478. The Arbitral Tribunal shall decide the dispute in accordance with the rules of law, unless the parties have entrusted it with the task of deciding the case in amiable composition.

Art. 1479. The deliberations of the Arbitral Tribunal shall be secret.

Art. 1480. The arbitral award shall be made by a majority of votes.

It is signed by all the arbitrators.

If a minority of the arbitrators refuse to sign the award, the award shall state so and shall have the same effect as if it had been signed by all the arbitrators.

Art. 1481. The arbitral award shall state:

1. The full names of the parties and their domicile or registered office;
2. Where applicable, the names of the lawyers or any other person who represented or assisted the parties;
3. The names of the arbitrators who rendered the decision;
4. Its date;
5. The place where the award was made.

Art. 1482. The arbitral award shall succinctly state the respective claims of the parties and their pleas in law.

It shall contain the reasons upon which it is based.

Art. 1483. The provisions of Article 1480, those of Article 1481 relating to the names of the arbitrators and the date of the award and those of Article 1482 relating to the statement of reasons for the award are prescribed under pain of nullity of the award.

However, the omission or inaccuracy of a statement intended to establish the regularity of the award shall not render the award null and void if it is established, by the documents of the proceedings or by any other means, that the legal requirements have in fact been complied with.

Art. 1484. As soon as it is made, an arbitral award has the force of res judicata in relation to the dispute which it resolves.

It may be enforced provisionally.

It shall be notified by service unless the parties agree otherwise.

Art. 1485. The award relieves the Arbitral Tribunal of jurisdiction over the dispute which it resolves.

However, at the request of a party, the Arbitral Tribunal may interpret the award, make good any material errors or omissions in it or supplement it where it has omitted to rule on a claim. It shall give its decision after hearing the parties or after hearing them on appeal.

If the Arbitral Tribunal cannot be reconvened and the parties cannot agree to constitution of a new one, this power shall be vested in the court which would have had jurisdiction in the absence of arbitration.

Art. 1486. Applications under the second paragraph of Article 1485 shall be made within three months of notification of the award.

Unless otherwise agreed, the corrected or completed award shall be made within three months of the referral of the case to the Arbitral Tribunal. This period may be extended in accordance with the second paragraph of Article 1463.

The corrected or completed award shall be notified in the same manner as the original award.

CHAPTER V. EXEQUATUR

Art. 1487. An arbitral award may only be enforced by virtue of an exequatur order issued by the Tribunal de Grande Instance within whose jurisdiction the award was made.

The exequatur procedure is not adversarial.

The application shall be filed by the most diligent party at the court registry together with the original award and a copy of the arbitration agreement or copies thereof which meet the conditions required for authenticity.

The exequatur is affixed to the original or, if this is not produced, to the copy of the arbitration award that meets the conditions set out in the previous paragraph.

Art. 1488. Enforceability may not be granted if the award is manifestly contrary to public policy.

The order refusing enforcement shall state the reasons on which it is based.

CHAPTER VI. LEGAL REMEDIES

SECTION 1. APPEAL

Art. 1489. An award may not be appealed unless the parties have agreed otherwise.

Art. 1490 An appeal may seek to have the award reversed or annulled.

The court shall rule in accordance with the law or by amicable composition within the limits of the Arbitral Tribunal's terms of reference.

SECTION 2. ACTIONS FOR ANNULMENT

Art. 1491. The award may be the subject of an action for annulment unless the parties have agreed that the award can be appealed.

Any stipulation to the contrary is deemed unwritten.

Art. 1492. An action for annulment may only be brought if:
1. The Arbitral Tribunal has wrongly declared itself competent or incompetent, or
2. The Arbitral Tribunal was improperly constituted or
3. The Arbitral Tribunal has ruled without complying with the terms of reference entrusted to it, or
4. The principle of contradiction has not been respected or
5. The award is contrary to public policy or
6. The award does not state the reasons on which it is based, does not indicate the date on which it was made or the name(s) of the arbitrator(s) who made it, does not bear the required signature(s) or was not made by a majority of votes.

Art. 1493. Where the court annuls the arbitral award, it shall rule on the merits within the limits of the arbitrator's terms of reference, unless otherwise agreed by the parties.

SECTION 3. PROVISIONS COMMON TO APPEALS AND ACTIONS FOR ANNULMENT

Art. 1494. Appeals and actions for annulment shall be brought before the Court of Appeal in whose jurisdiction the award was made.

Such appeals shall be admissible as soon as the award has been made. They cease to be admissible if they have not been lodged within one month of notification of the award.

Art. 1495. Appeals and actions for annulment are lodged, investigated and judged in accordance with the rules relating to procedure in contentious matters set out in Articles 900 to 930-1.

Art. 1496. The time limit for lodging an appeal or an action for annulment, as well as any appeal or action lodged within such time limit, shall stay the enforcement of the arbitral award unless it is provisionally enforceable.

Art. 1497. The First President, acting in summary proceedings or, as soon as the matter has been referred to him, the judge assigned to the case, may:
1. Where the award is subject to provisional enforcement, stay or modify its enforcement where it is likely to entail manifestly excessive consequences, or
2. Where the award is not subject to provisional enforcement, order the provisional enforcement of all or part of the award.

Art. 1498. Where the award is subject to provisional enforcement or where Article 1497 (2) is applied, the First President or, as soon as the matter is referred to him, the judge assigned to the case, may grant exequatur to the arbitral award.

Dismissal of the appeal or of the action for annulment confers exequatur on the arbitration award or on those of its provisions which are not affected by the court's censure.

SECTION 4. APPEAL AGAINST THE ORDER RULING ON THE APPLICATION FOR ENFORCEMENT

Art. 1499. The order granting the exequatur is not subject to appeal.

However, an appeal or an action for annulment of the award shall, within the limits of the jurisdiction of the court, automatically entail an appeal against the order of the judge who ruled on the enforcement or the jurisdiction of that judge.

Art. 1500. An appeal may be lodged against an order refusing enforceability within one month of service of the order.

In such a case, the Court of Appeal shall, at the request of a party, hear the appeal or the application to annul the arbitral award, if the time limit for doing so has not expired.

SECTION 5. OTHER REMEDIES

Art. 1501. Subject to the provisions of the first paragraph of Article 588, an arbitral award may be subject to third-party proceedings before the court which would have had jurisdiction had there been no arbitration.

Article 1502. An application for revision may be made against an arbitration award in the cases provided for in Article 595 and under the conditions provided for in Articles 594, 596, 597 and 601 to 603.

The appeal is lodged with the Arbitral Tribunal.

However, if the Arbitral Tribunal cannot be reconvened, the appeal shall be brought before the Court of Appeal which would have had jurisdiction to hear the other appeals against the award.

Art. 1503. The arbitral award may not be contested or appealed to the Supreme Court.

TITLE II. INTERNATIONAL ARBITRATION

Art. 1504. Arbitration involving the interests of international commerce is international.

Art. 1505. In international arbitration proceedings, the judge in charge of the arbitration proceedings shall, unless otherwise provided, be the President of the Tribunal de Grande Instance de Paris where:
1. The arbitration takes place in France or
2. The parties have agreed that the arbitration shall be governed by French procedural law, or
3. The parties have expressly conferred jurisdiction on the French courts to hear disputes relating to the arbitration or arbitration proceedings.
4. One of the parties is exposed to a risk of a denial of justice.

Art. 1506. Unless the parties have agreed otherwise and subject to the provisions of this Title, the following Articles shall apply to international arbitration:
1. 1446, 1447, 1448 (paragraphs 1 and 2) and 1449, relating to the arbitration agreement;

2. 1452 to 1458 and 1460, relating to the constitution of the arbitration tribunal and the procedure applicable before the supporting judge;
3. 1462, 1463 (paragraph 2), 1464 (paragraph 3), 1465 to 1470 and 1472 relating to arbitration proceedings;
4. 1479, 1481, 1482, 1484 (paragraphs 1 and 2), 1485 (paragraphs 1 and 2) and 1486 relating to arbitral awards;
5. 1502 (paragraphs 1 and 2) and 1503 relating to remedies other than appeals and actions for annulment.

CHAPTER I. THE INTERNATIONAL ARBITRATION AGREEMENT

Art. 1507. The arbitration agreement is not subject to any formal requirements.

Art. 1508. The arbitration agreement may, directly or by reference to arbitration rules or rules of procedure, appoint the arbitrator or arbitrators or provide for the manner of their appointment.

CHAPTER II. ARBITRATION PROCEEDINGS AND AWARDS

Art. 1509. The arbitration agreement may, directly or by reference to arbitration rules or rules of procedure, regulate the procedure to be followed in the arbitral proceedings.

If the arbitration agreement is silent, the Arbitral Tribunal shall regulate the procedure to the extent necessary, either directly or by reference to arbitration rules or rules of procedure.

Art. 1510 Whichever procedure is chosen, the Arbitral Tribunal shall guarantee the equality of the parties and shall respect the principle of adversarial proceedings.

Art. 1511. The Arbitral Tribunal shall decide the dispute in accordance with the rules of law chosen by the parties or, failing that, in accordance with those it considers appropriate.

In all cases, it takes account of trade practices.

Art. 1512. The Arbitral Tribunal shall decide in amiable composition if the parties have entrusted it with this task.

Art. 1513. If the arbitration agreement is silent, the award shall be made by a majority of votes. It shall be signed by all the arbitrators.

However, if a minority of them refuse to sign it, the others mention this in the award..

In the absence of a majority, the Chairman of the Arbitral Tribunal shall decide alone. If the other arbitrators refuse to sign the award, the chairman shall record this fact in the award, which he shall then sign alone.

An award made in accordance with either of the two preceding paragraphs shall have the same effect as if it had been signed by all the arbitrators or made by a majority of votes.

CHAPTER III. RECOGNITION AND ENFORCEMENT OF ARBITRAL AWARDS MADE ABROAD OR IN INTERNATIONAL ARBITRATION PROCEEDINGS

Art. 1514. Arbitral awards shall be recognised or enforced in France if their existence is established by the party relying on them and if such recognition or enforcement is not manifestly contrary to international public policy.

Art. 1515. The existence of an arbitral award shall be established by the production of the original accompanied by the arbitration agreement or copies of such documents which satisfy the conditions required for their authenticity.

If these documents are not in French, the requesting party must produce a translation. The requesting party may be asked to provide a translation prepared by a translator registered on a list of legal experts or by a translator authorised to work for the judicial or administrative authorities of another Member State of the European Union, of a State party to the Agreement on the European Economic Area or of the Swiss Confederation.

Art. 1516. An arbitral award may only be enforced by virtue of an exequatur order issued by the Tribunal de Grande Instance in whose jurisdiction it was made or by the Tribunal de Grande Instance of Paris if it was made abroad.

The exequatur procedure is not adversarial.

The application shall be filed by the earliest party at the court registry together with the original award and a copy of the arbitration agreement or copies thereof which meet the conditions required for authenticity.

Article 1517. The exequatur is affixed to the original or, if this is not produced, to the copy of the arbitral award that meets the conditions set out in the last paragraph of Article 1516.

Where the arbitral award is not drawn up in French, the exequatur shall also be affixed to the translation made under the conditions provided for in Article 1515.

Reasons shall be given for any order refusing to grant enforceability to the arbitration award.

CHAPTER IV. APPEAL PROCEDURES

SECTION 1: AWARDS MADE IN FRANCE

Art. 1518. An award made in France in international arbitration proceedings may only be the subject of an action for annulment.

Art. 1519. An action for annulment shall be brought before the Court of Appeal within whose jurisdiction the award was made.

This recourse is admissible as soon as the award is made. It ceases to be admissible if it is not lodged within one month of notification of the award.

Notification is done by service unless the parties agree otherwise.

Art. 1520. An action for annulment may be brought only if:
1. The Arbitral Tribunal has wrongly declared itself competent or incompetent, or
2. The Arbitral Tribunal was improperly constituted, or
3. The Arbitral Tribunal has ruled without complying with the terms of reference entrusted to it, or
4. The principle of contradiction has not been respected or
5. The recognition or enforcement of the award is contrary to international public policy.

Art. 1521. The First President or, as soon as the matter has been referred to him, the judge assigned to the case, may grant enforceability to the award.

Art. 1522. By special agreement, the parties may at any time expressly waive the right to an action for annulment.

In this case, they may always appeal against the enforcement order on one of the grounds set out in Article 1520.

The appeal shall be lodged within one month of the notification of the enforceable award. The notification shall be done by service unless the parties agree otherwise.

Art. 1523. A decision refusing recognition or enforcement of an international arbitration award made in France may be appealed.

The appeal must be lodged within one month of service of the decision.

In such a case, the Court of Appeal shall, at the request of a party, hear the application to set aside the award unless that party has waived its right to do so or the time limit for doing so has expired.

Art. 1524. The order granting the exequatur is not subject to appeal except in the case provided for in the second paragraph of Article 1522.

However, an action to annul the award shall, within the limits of the jurisdiction of the Court, automatically entail an action against the order of the judge who ruled on the exequatur or the relinquishment of jurisdiction of that judge.

SECTION 2. FOREIGN AWARDS

Art. 1525. A decision on an application for recognition or enforcement of an arbitration award made abroad may be appealed.

The appeal must be lodged within one month of service of the decision.

The parties may, however, agree on another method of notification when the appeal is lodged against an award that has been granted exequatur.

The Court of Appeal may refuse to recognise or enforce an arbitral award only in the cases provided for in Article 1520.

SECTION 3. PROVISIONS COMMON TO AWARDS MADE IN FRANCE AND ABROAD

Art. 1526. An action to annul an award and an appeal against an order granting enforcement shall not have suspensive effect.

However, the First President, acting in summary proceedings, or, as soon as the matter has been referred to him, the judge assigned to the case, may halt or adjust the enforcement of the award if such enforcement is likely to seriously prejudice the rights of one of the parties.

Art. 1527. An appeal against an order granting enforcement and an application to set aside an award shall be lodged, heard and determined in accordance with the rules relating to contentious proceedings set out in Articles 900 to 930-1.

The rejection of the appeal or of the application to set aside confers exequatur on the arbitration award or on those of its provisions which are not affected by the court's censure.

Article 3. The provisions of this decree come into force on the first day of the fourth month following its publication, subject to the following provisions:

1. The provisions of Articles 1442 to 1445, 1489 and 2. and 3. of Article 1505 of the Code of Civil Procedure apply where the arbitration agreement was concluded after the date mentioned in the first paragraph;
2. The provisions of Articles 1456 to 1458, 1486, 1502, 1513 and 1522 of the same Code apply where the court was constituted after the date mentioned in the first paragraph;

3. The provisions of Article 1526 of the same Code apply to arbitration awards made after the date mentioned in the first paragraph.

Article 4. This decree is applicable in the Wallis and Futuna Islands.

Article 5. The Keeper of the Seals, Minister of Justice and Freedoms, and the Minister of the Interior, Overseas Territories, Local Authorities and Immigration are each responsible for the execution of this decree, which will be published in the Official Journal of the French Republic.

9.4 *Arbitration Rules*

9.4.1 UNCITRAL Arbitration Rules (as revised in 2021)

The General Assembly,

Recalling its resolution 2205 (XXI) of 17 December 1966, by which it established the United Nations Commission on International Trade Law with a mandate to further the progressive harmonization and unification of the law of international trade and in that respect to bear in mind the interests of all peoples, in particular those of developing countries, in the extensive development of international trade,

Recalling also its resolution 31/98 of 15 December 1976 recommending the use of the Arbitration Rules of the United Nations Commission on International Trade Law[1] and its resolution 65/22 of 6 December 2010 recommending the use of the Arbitration Rules as revised in 2010,[2]

Mindful of the value of arbitration as a method of settling disputes that may arise in the context of international commercial relations,

Noting the value of expedited arbitration as a streamlined and simplified procedure for settling disputes that arise in the context of international commercial relations within a shortened time frame, and its increased use in international and domestic commercial practice for parties to reach a final resolution of the dispute in a cost-and time-effective manner,

Aware of the need to balance the efficiency of the arbitral proceedings and the rights of the disputing parties to due process and fair treatment,

Noting that the preparation of the UNCITRAL Expedited Arbitration Rules and the accompanying explanatory note benefited greatly from consultations with Governments and interested intergovernmental and international non-governmental organizations,

Noting also that the Expedited Arbitration Rules were adopted by the United Nations Commission on International Trade Law at its fifty-fourth session, after due deliberations,[3]

1. Expresses its appreciation to the United Nations Commission on International Trade Law for having formulated and adopted the Expedited Arbitration Rules, the text of which is contained in annex IV to the report of the United Nations Commission on International Trade Law on the work of its fifty-fourth session[4] and which came into effect on 19 September 2021;

2. Recommends the use of the UNCITRAL Expedited Arbitration Rules in the settlement of disputes arising in the context of international commercial relations;

3. Requests the Secretary-General to make all efforts to ensure that the UNCITRAL Expedited Arbitration Rules become generally known and available.

1 Official Records of the General Assembly, Thirty-first Session, Supplement No. 17 (A/31/17), chap. V, sect. C.
2 Ibid., Sixty-fifth Session, Supplement No. 17 (A/65/17), annex I.
3 Ibid., Seventy-sixth Session, Supplement No. 17 (A/76/17), chap. VII.
4 Ibid., annex IV.

SECTION I. INTRODUCTORY RULES

Scope of application

Article 1

1. Where parties have agreed that disputes between them in respect of a defined legal relationship, whether contractual or not, shall be referred to arbitration under the UNCITRAL Arbitration Rules, then such disputes shall be settled in accordance with these Rules subject to such modification as the parties may agree.
2. The parties to an arbitration agreement concluded after 15 August 2010 shall be presumed to have referred to the Rules in effect on the date of commencement of the arbitration, unless the parties have agreed to apply a particular version of the Rules. That presumption does not apply where the arbitration agreement has been concluded by accepting after 15 August 2010 an offer made before that date.
3. These Rules shall govern the arbitration except that where any of these Rules is in conflict with a provision of the law applicable to the arbitration from which the parties cannot derogate, that provision shall prevail.

Notice and calculation of periods of time

Article 2

1. A notice, including a notification, communication or proposal, may be transmitted by any means of communication that provides or allows for a record of its transmission.
2. If an address has been designated by a party specifically for this purpose or authorized by the arbitral tribunal, any notice shall be delivered to that party at that address, and if so delivered shall be deemed to have been received. Delivery by electronic means such as facsimile or e-mail may only be made to an address so designated or authorized.
3. In the absence of such designation or authorization, a notice is:
   (a) Received if it is physically delivered to the addressee; or
   (b) Deemed to have been received if it is delivered at the place of business, habitual residence or mailing address of the addressee.
4. If, after reasonable efforts, delivery cannot be effected in accordance with paragraphs 2 or 3, a notice is deemed to have been received if it is sent to the addressee's last-known place of business, habitual residence or mailing address by registered letter or any other means that provides a record of delivery or of attempted delivery.
5. A notice shall be deemed to have been received on the day it is delivered in accordance with paragraphs 2, 3 or 4, or attempted to be delivered in accordance with paragraph 4. A notice transmitted by electronic means is deemed to have been received on the day it is sent, except that a notice of arbitration so transmitted is only deemed to have been received on the day when it reaches the addressee's electronic address.
6. For the purpose of calculating a period of time under these Rules, such period shall begin to run on the day following the day when a notice is received. If the last day of such period is an official holiday or a non-business day at the residence or place of business of the addressee, the period is extended until the first business day which follows. Official holidays or non-business days occurring during the running of the period of time are included in calculating the period.

Notice of arbitration

Article 3

1. The party or parties initiating recourse to arbitration (hereinafter called the "claimant") shall communicate to the other party or parties (hereinafter called the "respondent") a notice of arbitration.
2. Arbitral proceedings shall be deemed to commence on the date on which the notice of arbitration is received by the respondent.
3. The notice of arbitration shall include the following:
   (a) A demand that the dispute be referred to arbitration;
   (b) The names and contact details of the parties;
   (c) Identification of the arbitration agreement that is invoked;
   (d) Identification of any contract or other legal instrument out of or in relation to which the dispute arises or, in the absence of such contract or instrument, a brief description of the relevant relationship;
   (e) A brief description of the claim and an indication of the amount involved, if any;
   (f) The relief or remedy sought;
   (g) A proposal as to the number of arbitrators, language and place of arbitration, if the parties have not previously agreed thereon.
4. The notice of arbitration may also include:
   (a) A proposal for the designation of an appointing authority referred to in article 6, paragraph 1;
   (b) A proposal for the appointment of a sole arbitrator referred to in article 8, paragraph 1;
   (c) Notification of the appointment of an arbitrator referred to in article 9 or 10.
5. The constitution of the arbitral tribunal shall not be hindered by any controversy with respect to the sufficiency of the notice of arbitration, which shall be finally resolved by the arbitral tribunal.

Response to the notice of arbitration

Article 4

1. Within 30 days of the receipt of the notice of arbitration, the respondent shall communicate to the claimant a response to the notice of arbitration, which shall include:
   (a) The name and contact details of each respondent;
   (b) A response to the information set forth in the notice of arbitration, pursuant to article 3, paragraphs 3 *(c)* to *(g)*.
2. The response to the notice of arbitration may also include:
   (a) Any plea that an arbitral tribunal to be constituted under these Rules lacks jurisdiction;
   (b) A proposal for the designation of an appointing authority referred to in article 6, paragraph 1;
   (c) A proposal for the appointment of a sole arbitrator referred to in article 8, paragraph 1;
   (d) Notification of the appointment of an arbitrator referred to in article 9 or 10;
   (e) A brief description of counterclaims or claims for the purpose of a set-off, if any, including where relevant, an indication of the amounts involved, and the relief or remedy sought;
   (f) A notice of arbitration in accordance with article 3 in case the respondent formulates a claim against a party to the arbitration agreement other than the claimant.
3. The constitution of the arbitral tribunal shall not be hindered by any controversy with respect to the respondent's failure to communicate a response to the notice of arbitration, or an incomplete or late response to the notice of arbitration, which shall be finally resolved by the arbitral tribunal.

Representation and assistance

Article 5
Each party may be represented or assisted by persons chosen by it. The names and addresses of such persons must be communicated to all parties and to the arbitral tribunal. Such communication must specify whether the appointment is being made for purposes of representation or assistance. Where a person is to act as a representative of a party, the arbitral tribunal, on its own initiative or at the request of any party, may at any time require proof of authority granted to the representative in such a form as the arbitral tribunal may determine.

Designating and appointing authorities

Article 6
1. Unless the parties have already agreed on the choice of an appointing authority, a party may at any time propose the name or names of one or more institutions or persons, including the Secretary-General of the Permanent Court of Arbitration at The Hague (hereinafter called the "PCA"), one of whom would serve as appointing authority.
2. If all parties have not agreed on the choice of an appointing authority within 30 days after a proposal made in accordance with paragraph 1 has been received by all other parties, any party may request the Secretary-General of the PCA to designate the appointing authority.
3. Where these Rules provide for a period of time within which a party must refer a matter to an appointing authority and no appointing authority has been agreed on or designated, the period is suspended from the date on which a party initiates the procedure for agreeing on or designating an appointing authority until the date of such agreement or designation.
4. Except as referred to in article 41, paragraph 4, if the appointing authority refuses to act, or if it fails to appoint an arbitrator within 30 days after it receives a party's request to do so, fails to act within any other period provided by these Rules, or fails to decide on a challenge to an arbitrator within a reasonable time after receiving party's request to do so, any party may request the Secretary-General of the PCA to designate a substitute appointing authority.
5. In exercising their functions under these Rules, the appointing authority and the Secretary-General of the PCA may require from any party and the arbitrators the information they deem necessary and they shall give the parties and, where appropriate, the arbitrators, an opportunity to present their views in any manner they consider appropriate. All such communications to and from the appointing authority and the Secretary-General of the PCA shall also be provided by the sender to all other parties.
6. When the appointing authority is requested to appoint an arbitrator pursuant to articles 8, 9, 10 or 14, the party making the request shall send to the appointing authority copies of the notice of arbitration and, if it exists, any response to the notice of arbitration.
7. The appointing authority shall have regard to such considerations as are likely to secure the appointment of an independent and impartial arbitrator and shall take into account the advisability of appointing an arbitrator of a nationality other than the nationalities of the parties.

SECTION II. COMPOSITION OF THE ARBITRAL TRIBUNAL

Number of arbitrators

Article 7
1. If the parties have not previously agreed on the number of arbitrators, and if within 30 days after the receipt by the respondent of the notice of arbitration the parties have not agreed that there shall be only one arbitrator, three arbitrators shall be appointed.

2. Notwithstanding paragraph 1, if no other parties have responded to a party's proposal to appoint a sole arbitrator within the time limit provided for in paragraph 1 and the party or parties concerned have failed to appoint a second arbitrator in accordance with article 9 or 10, the appointing authority may, at the request of a party, appoint a sole arbitrator pursuant to the procedure provided for in article 8, paragraph 2, if it determines that, in view of the circumstances of the case, this is more appropriate.

Appointment of arbitrators (articles 8 to 10)

Article 8
1. If the parties have agreed that a sole arbitrator is to be appointed and if within 30 days after receipt by all other parties of a proposal for the appointment of a sole arbitrator the parties have not reached agreement thereon, a sole arbitrator shall, at the request of a party, be appointed by the appointing authority.
2. The appointing authority shall appoint the sole arbitrator as promptly as possible. In making the appointment, the appointing authority shall use the following list-procedure, unless the parties agree that the list-procedure should not be used or unless the appointing authority determines in its discretion that the use of the list-procedure is not appropriate for the case:
(a) The appointing authority shall communicate to each of the parties an identical list containing at least three names;
(b) Within 15 days after the receipt of this list, each party may return the list to the appointing authority after having deleted the name or names to which it objects and numbered the remaining names on the list in the order of its preference;
(c) After the expiration of the above period of time the appointing authority shall appoint the sole arbitrator from among the names approved on the lists returned to it and in accordance with the order of preference indicated by the parties;
(d) If for any reason the appointment cannot be made according to this procedure, the appointing authority may exercise its discretion in appointing the sole arbitrator.

Article 9
1. If three arbitrators are to be appointed, each party shall appoint one arbitrator. The two arbitrators thus appointed shall choose the third arbitrator who will act as the presiding arbitrator of the arbitral tribunal.
2. If within 30 days after the receipt of a party's notification of the appointment of an arbitrator the other party has not notified the first party of the arbitrator it has appointed, the first party may request the appointing authority to appoint the second arbitrator.
3. If within 30 days after the appointment of the second arbitrator the two arbitrators have not agreed on the choice of the presiding arbitrator, the presiding arbitrator shall be appointed by the appointing authority in the same way as a sole arbitrator would be appointed under article 8.

Article 10
1. For the purposes of article 9, paragraph 1, where three arbitrators are to be appointed and there are multiple parties as claimant or as respondent, unless the parties have agreed to another method of appointment of arbitrators, the multiple parties jointly, whether as claimant or as respondent, shall appoint an arbitrator.
2. If the parties have agreed that the arbitral tribunal is to be composed of a number of arbitrators other than one or three, the arbitrators shall be appointed according to the method agreed upon by the parties.

3. In the event of any failure to constitute the arbitral tribunal under these Rules, the appointing authority shall, at the request of any party, constitute the arbitral tribunal and, in doing so, may revoke any appointment already made and appoint or reappoint each of the arbitrators and designate one of them as the presiding arbitrator.

Disclosures by and challenge of arbitrators[5]

Article 11
When a person is approached in connection with his or her possible appointment as an arbitrator, he or she shall disclose any circumstances likely to give rise to justifiable doubts as to his or her impartiality or independence. An arbitrator, from the time of his or her appointment and throughout the arbitral proceedings, shall without delay disclose any such circumstances to the parties and the other arbitrators unless they have already been informed by him or her of these circumstances.

Article 12
1. Any arbitrator may be challenged if circumstances exist that give rise to justifiable doubts as to the arbitrator's impartiality or independence.
2. A party may challenge the arbitrator appointed by it only for reasons of which it becomes aware after the appointment has been made.
3. In the event that an arbitrator fails to act or in the event of the de jure or de facto impossibility of his or her performing his or her functions, the procedure in respect of the challenge of an arbitrator as provided in article 13 shall apply.

Article 13
1. A party that intends to challenge an arbitrator shall send notice of its challenge within 15 days after it has been notified of the appointment of the challenged arbitrator, or within 15 days after the circumstances mentioned in articles 11 and 12 became known to that party.
2. The notice of challenge shall be communicated to all other parties, to the arbitrator who is challenged and to the other arbitrators. The notice of challenge shall state the reasons for the challenge.
3. When an arbitrator has been challenged by a party, all parties may agree to the challenge. The arbitrator may also, after the challenge, withdraw from his or her office. In neither case does this imply acceptance of the validity of the grounds for the challenge.
4. If, within 15 days from the date of the notice of challenge, all parties do not agree to the challenge or the challenged arbitrator does not withdraw, the party making the challenge may elect to pursue it. In that case, within 30 days from the date of the notice of challenge, it shall seek a decision on the challenge by the appointing authority.

Replacement of an arbitrator

Article 14
1. Subject to paragraph 2, in any event where an arbitrator has to be replaced during the course of the arbitral proceedings, a substitute arbitrator shall be appointed or chosen pursuant to the procedure provided for in articles 8 to 11 that was applicable to the appointment or choice of the arbitrator being replaced. This procedure shall apply even if during the process of appointing the arbitrator to be replaced, a party had failed to exercise its right to appoint or to participate in the appointment.
2. If, at the request of a party, the appointing authority determines that, in view of the exceptional circumstances of the case, it would be justified for a party to be deprived of its right to appoint a

5 Model statements of independence pursuant to article 11 can be found in the annex to the Rules.

substitute arbitrator, the appointing authority may, after giving an opportunity to the parties and the remaining arbitrators to express their views: *(a)* appoint the substitute arbitrator; or *(b)* after the closure of the hearings, authorize the other arbitrators to proceed with the arbitration and make any decision or award.

Repetition of hearings in the event of the replacement of an arbitrator

Article 15
If an arbitrator is replaced, the proceedings shall resume at the stage where the arbitrator who was replaced ceased to perform his or her functions, unless the arbitral tribunal decides otherwise.

Exclusion of liability

Article 16
Save for intentional wrongdoing, the parties waive, to the fullest extent permitted under the applicable law, any claim against the arbitrators, the appointing authority and any person appointed by the arbitral tribunal based on any act or omission in connection with the arbitration.

SECTION III. ARBITRAL PROCEEDINGS

General provisions

Article 17
1. Subject to these Rules, the arbitral tribunal may conduct the arbitration in such manner as it considers appropriate, provided that the parties are treated with equality and that at an appropriate stage of the proceedings each party is given a reasonable opportunity of presenting its case. The arbitral tribunal, in exercising its discretion, shall conduct the proceedings so as to avoid unnecessary delay and expense and to provide a fair and efficient process for resolving the parties' dispute.
2. As soon as practicable after its constitution and after inviting the parties to express their views, the arbitral tribunal shall establish the provisional timetable of the arbitration. The arbitral tribunal may, at any time, after inviting the parties to express their views, extend or abridge any period of time prescribed under these Rules or agreed by the parties.
3. If at an appropriate stage of the proceedings any party so requests, the arbitral tribunal shall hold hearings for the presentation of evidence by witnesses, including expert witnesses, or for oral argument. In the absence of such a request, the arbitral tribunal shall decide whether to hold such hearings or whether the proceedings shall be conducted on the basis of documents and other materials.
4. All communications to the arbitral tribunal by one party shall be communicated by that party to all other parties. Such communications shall be made at the same time, except as otherwise permitted by the arbitral tribunal if it may do so under applicable law.
5. The arbitral tribunal may, at the request of any party, allow one or more third persons to be joined in the arbitration as a party provided such person is a party to the arbitration agreement, unless the arbitral tribunal finds, after giving all parties, including the person or persons to be joined, the opportunity to be heard, that joinder should not be permitted because of prejudice to any of those parties. The arbitral tribunal may make a single award or several awards in respect of all parties so involved in the arbitration.

Place of arbitration

Article 18
1. If the parties have not previously agreed on the place of arbitration, the place of arbitration shall be determined by the arbitral tribunal having regard to the circumstances of the case. The award shall be deemed to have been made at the place of arbitration.
2. The arbitral tribunal may meet at any location it considers appropriate for deliberations. Unless otherwise agreed by the parties, the arbitral tribunal may also meet at any location it considers appropriate for any other purpose, including hearings.

Language

Article 19
1. Subject to an agreement by the parties, the arbitral tribunal shall, promptly after its appointment, determine the language or languages to be used in the proceedings. This determination shall apply to the statement of claim, the statement of defence, and any further written statements and, if oral hearings take place, to the language or languages to be used in such hearings.
2. The arbitral tribunal may order that any documents annexed to the statement of claim or statement of defence, and any supplementary documents or exhibits submitted in the course of the proceedings, delivered in their original language, shall be accompanied by a translation into the language or languages agreed upon by the parties or determined by the arbitral tribunal.

Statement of claim

Article 20
1. The claimant shall communicate its statement of claim in writing to the respondent and to each of the arbitrators within a period of time to be determined by the arbitral tribunal. The claimant may elect to treat its notice of arbitration referred to in article 3 as a statement of claim, provided that the notice of arbitration also complies with the requirements of paragraphs 2 to 4 of this article.
2. The statement of claim shall include the following particulars:
   (a) The names and contact details of the parties;
   (b) A statement of the facts supporting the claim;
   (c) The points at issue;
   (d) The relief or remedy sought;
   (e) The legal grounds or arguments supporting the claim.
3. A copy of any contract or other legal instrument out of or in relation to which the dispute arises and of the arbitration agreement shall be annexed to the statement of claim.
4. The statement of claim should, as far as possible, be accompanied by all documents and other evidence relied upon by the claimant, or contain references to them.

Statement of defence

Article 21
1. The respondent shall communicate its statement of defence in writing to the claimant and to each of the arbitrators within a period of time to be determined by the arbitral tribunal. The respondent may elect to treat its response to the notice of arbitration referred to in article 4 as a statement of defence, provided that the response to the notice of arbitration also complies with the requirements of paragraph 2 of this article.

2. The statement of defence shall reply to the particulars *(b)* to *(e)* of the statement of claim (art. 20, para. 2). The statement of defence should, as far as possible, be accompanied by all documents and other evidence relied upon by the respondent, or contain references to them.
3. In its statement of defence, or at a later stage in the arbitral proceedings if the arbitral tribunal decides that the delay was justified under the circumstances, the respondent may make a counterclaim or rely on a claim for the purpose of a set-off provided that the arbitral tribunal has jurisdiction over it.
4. The provisions of article 20, paragraphs 2 to 4, shall apply to a counterclaim, a claim under article 4, paragraph 2 *(f)*, and a claim relied on for the purpose of a set-off.

Amendments to the claim or defence

Article 22
During the course of the arbitral proceedings, a party may amend or supplement its claim or defence, including a counterclaim or a claim for the purpose of a set-off, unless the arbitral tribunal considers it inappropriate to allow such amendment or supplement having regard to the delay in making it or prejudice to other parties or any other circumstances. However, a claim or defence, including a counterclaim or a claim for the purpose of a set-off, may not be amended or supplemented in such a manner that the amended or supplemented claim or defence falls outside the jurisdiction of the arbitral tribunal.

Pleas as to the jurisdiction of the arbitral tribunal

Article 23
1. The arbitral tribunal shall have the power to rule on its own jurisdiction, including any objections with respect to the existence or validity of the arbitration agreement. For that purpose, an arbitration clause that forms part of a contract shall be treated as an agreement independent of the other terms of the contract. A decision by the arbitral tribunal that the contract is null shall not entail automatically the invalidity of the arbitration clause.
2. A plea that the arbitral tribunal does not have jurisdiction shall be raised no later than in the statement of defence or, with respect to a counterclaim or a claim for the purpose of a set-off, in the reply to the counterclaim or to the claim for the purpose of a set-off. A party is not precluded from raising such a plea by the fact that it has appointed, or participated in the appointment of, an arbitrator. A plea that the arbitral tribunal is exceeding the scope of its authority shall be raised as soon as the matter alleged to be beyond the scope of its authority is raised during the arbitral proceedings. The arbitral tribunal may, in either case, admit a later plea if it considers the delay justified.
3. The arbitral tribunal may rule on a plea referred to in paragraph 2 either as a preliminary question or in an award on the merits. The arbitral tribunal may continue the arbitral proceedings and make an award, notwithstanding any pending challenge to its jurisdiction before a court.

Further written statements

Article 24
The arbitral tribunal shall decide which further written statements, in addition to the statement of claim and the statement of defence, shall be required from the parties or may be presented by them and shall fix the periods of time for communicating such statements.

Periods of time

Article 25

The periods of time fixed by the arbitral tribunal for the communication of written statements (including the statement of claim and statement of defence) should not exceed 45 days. However, the arbitral tribunal may extend the time limits if it concludes that an extension is justified.

Interim measures

Article 26

1. The arbitral tribunal may, at the request of a party, grant interim measures.
2. An interim measure is any temporary measure by which, at any time prior to the issuance of the award by which the dispute is finally decided, the arbitral tribunal orders a party, for example and without limitation, to:
   (a) Maintain or restore the status quo pending determination of the dispute;
   (b) Take action that would prevent, or refrain from taking action that is likely to cause,
      (i) current or imminent harm or
      (ii) prejudice to the arbitral process itself;
   (c) Provide a means of preserving assets out of which a subsequent award may be satisfied; or
   (d) Preserve evidence that may be relevant and material to the resolution of the dispute.
3. The party requesting an interim measure under paragraphs 2 *(a)* to *(c)* shall satisfy the arbitral tribunal that:
   (a) Harm not adequately reparable by an award of damages is likely to result if the measure is not ordered, and such
   harm substantially outweighs the harm that is likely to result to the party against whom the measure is directed if the measure is granted; and
   (b) There is a reasonable possibility that the requesting party will succeed on the merits of the claim. The determination on this possibility shall not affect the discretion of the arbitral tribunal in making any subsequent determination.
4. With regard to a request for an interim measure under paragraph 2 *(d)*, the requirements in paragraphs 3 *(a)* and *(b)* shall apply only to the extent the arbitral tribunal considers appropriate.
5. The arbitral tribunal may modify, suspend or terminate an interim measure it has granted, upon application of any party or, in exceptional circumstances and upon prior notice to the parties, on the arbitral tribunal's own initiative.
6. The arbitral tribunal may require the party requesting an interim measure to provide appropriate security in connection with the measure.
7. The arbitral tribunal may require any party promptly to disclose any material change in the circumstances on the basis of which the interim measure was requested or granted.
8. The party requesting an interim measure may be liable for any costs and damages caused by the measure to any party if the arbitral tribunal later determines that, in the circumstances then prevailing, the measure should not have been granted. The arbitral tribunal may award such costs and damages at any point during the proceedings.
9. A request for interim measures addressed by any party to a judicial authority shall not be deemed incompatible with the agreement to arbitrate, or as a waiver of that agreement.

Evidence

Article 27

1. Each party shall have the burden of proving the facts relied on to support its claim or defence.
2. Witnesses, including expert witnesses, who are presented by the parties to testify to the arbitral tribunal on any issue of fact or expertise may be any individual, notwithstanding that the individual is a party to the arbitration or in any way related to a party. Unless otherwise directed by the arbitral tribunal, statements by witnesses, including expert witnesses, may be presented in writing and signed by them.
3. At any time during the arbitral proceedings the arbitral tribunal may require the parties to produce documents, exhibits or other evidence within such a period of time as the arbitral tribunal shall determine.
4. The arbitral tribunal shall determine the admissibility, relevance, materiality and weight of the evidence offered.

Hearings

Article 28

1. In the event of an oral hearing, the arbitral tribunal shall give the parties adequate advance notice of the date, time and place thereof.
2. Witnesses, including expert witnesses, may be heard under the conditions and examined in the manner set by the arbitral tribunal.
3. Hearings shall be held in camera unless the parties agree otherwise. The arbitral tribunal may require the retirement of any witness or witnesses, including expert witnesses, during the testimony of such other witnesses, except that a witness, including an expert witness, who is a party to the arbitration shall not, in principle, be asked to retire.
4. The arbitral tribunal may direct that witnesses, including expert witnesses, be examined through means of telecommunication that do not require their physical presence at the hearing (such as videoconference).

Experts appointed by the arbitral tribunal

Article 29

1. After consultation with the parties, the arbitral tribunal may appoint one or more independent experts to report to it, in writing, on specific issues to be determined by the arbitral tribunal. A copy of the expert's terms of reference, established by the arbitral tribunal, shall be communicated to the parties.
2. The expert shall, in principle before accepting appointment, submit to the arbitral tribunal and to the parties a description of his or her qualifications and a statement of his or her impartiality and independence. Within the time ordered by the arbitral tribunal, the parties shall inform the arbitral tribunal whether they have any objections as to the expert's qualifications, impartiality or independence. The arbitral tribunal shall decide promptly whether to accept any such objections. After an expert's appointment, a party may object to the expert's qualifications, impartiality or independence only if the objection is for reasons of which the party becomes aware after the appointment has been made. The arbitral tribunal shall decide promptly what, if any, action to take.
3. The parties shall give the expert any relevant information or produce for his or her inspection any relevant documents or goods that he or she may require of them. Any dispute between a party and such expert as to the relevance of the required information or production shall be referred to the arbitral tribunal for decision.

4. Upon receipt of the expert's report, the arbitral tribunal shall communicate a copy of the report to the parties, which shall be given the opportunity to express, in writing, their opinion on the report. A party shall be entitled to examine any document on which the expert has relied in his or her report.
5. At the request of any party, the expert, after delivery of the report, may be heard at a hearing where the parties shall have the opportunity to be present and to interrogate the expert. At this hearing, any party may present expert witnesses in order to testify on the points at issue. The provisions of article 28 shall be applicable to such proceedings.

Default

Article 30
1. If, within the period of time fixed by these Rules or the arbitral tribunal, without showing sufficient cause:
   (a) The claimant has failed to communicate its statement of claim, the arbitral tribunal shall issue an order for the termination of the arbitral proceedings, unless there are remaining matters that may need to be decided and the arbitral tribunal considers it appropriate to do so;
   (b) The respondent has failed to communicate its response to the notice of arbitration or its statement of defence, the arbitral tribunal shall order that the proceedings continue, without treating such failure in itself as an admission of the claimant's allegations; the provisions of this subparagraph also apply to a claimant's failure to submit a defence to a counterclaim or to a claim for the purpose of a set-off.
2. If a party, duly notified under these Rules, fails to appear at a hearing, without showing sufficient cause for such failure, the arbitral tribunal may proceed with the arbitration.
3. If a party, duly invited by the arbitral tribunal to produce documents, exhibits or other evidence, fails to do so within the established period of time, without showing sufficient cause for such failure, the arbitral tribunal may make the award on the evidence before it.

Closure of hearings

Article 31
1. The arbitral tribunal may inquire of the parties if they have any further proof to offer or witnesses to be heard or submissions to make and, if there are none, it may declare the hearings closed.
2. The arbitral tribunal may, if it considers it necessary owing to exceptional circumstances, decide, on its own initiative or upon application of a party, to reopen the hearings at any time before the award is made.

Waiver of right to object

Article 32
A failure by any party to object promptly to any non-compliance with these Rules or with any requirement of the arbitration agreement shall be deemed to be a waiver of the right of such party to make such an objection, unless such party can show that, under the circumstances, its failure to object was justified.

SECTION IV. THE AWARD

Decisions

Article 33
1. When there is more than one arbitrator, any award or other decision of the arbitral tribunal shall be made by a majority of the arbitrators.
2. In the case of questions of procedure, when there is no majority or when the arbitral tribunal so authorizes, the presiding arbitrator may decide alone, subject to revision, if any, by the arbitral tribunal.

Form and effect of the award

Article 34
1. The arbitral tribunal may make separate awards on different issues at different times.
2. All awards shall be made in writing and shall be final and binding on the parties. The parties shall carry out all awards without delay.
3. The arbitral tribunal shall state the reasons upon which the award is based, unless the parties have agreed that no reasons are to be given.
4. An award shall be signed by the arbitrators and it shall contain the date on which the award was made and indicate the place of arbitration. Where there is more than one arbitrator and any of them fails to sign, the award shall state the reason for the absence of the signature.
5. An award may be made public with the consent of all parties or where and to the extent disclosure is required of a party by legal duty, to protect or pursue a legal right or in relation to legal proceedings before a court or other competent authority.
6. Copies of the award signed by the arbitrators shall be communicated to the parties by the arbitral tribunal.

Applicable law, amiable compositeur

Article 35
1. The arbitral tribunal shall apply the rules of law designated by the parties as applicable to the substance of the dispute. Failing such designation by the parties, the arbitral tribunal shall apply the law which it determines to be appropriate.
2. The arbitral tribunal shall decide as *amiable compositeur* or *ex aequo et bono* only if the parties have expressly authorized the arbitral tribunal to do so.
3. In all cases, the arbitral tribunal shall decide in accordance with the terms of the contract, if any, and shall take into account any usage of trade applicable to the transaction.

Settlement or other grounds for termination

Article 36
1. If, before the award is made, the parties agree on a settlement of the dispute, the arbitral tribunal shall either issue an order for the termination of the arbitral proceedings or, if requested by the parties and accepted by the arbitral tribunal, record the settlement in the form of an arbitral award on agreed terms. The arbitral tribunal is not obliged to give reasons for such an award.
2. If, before the award is made, the continuation of the arbitral proceedings becomes unnecessary or impossible for any reason not mentioned in paragraph 1, the arbitral tribunal shall inform the parties of its intention to issue an order for the termination of the proceedings. The arbitral tribunal shall have

the power to issue such an order unless there are remaining matters that may need to be decided and the arbitral tribunal considers it appropriate to do so.
3. Copies of the order for termination of the arbitral proceedings or of the arbitral award on agreed terms, signed by the arbitrators, shall be communicated by the arbitral tribunal to the parties. Where an arbitral award on agreed terms is made, the provisions of article 34, paragraphs 2, 4 and 5, shall apply.

Interpretation of the award

Article 37
1. Within 30 days after the receipt of the award, a party, with notice to the other parties, may request that the arbitral tribunal give an interpretation of the award.
2. The interpretation shall be given in writing within 45 days after the receipt of the request. The interpretation shall form part of the award and the provisions of article 34, paragraphs 2 to 6, shall apply.

Correction of the award

Article 38
1. Within 30 days after the receipt of the award, a party, with notice to the other parties, may request the arbitral tribunal to correct in the award any error in computation, any clerical or typographical error, or any error or omission of a similar nature. If the arbitral tribunal considers that the request is justified, it shall make the correction within 45 days of receipt of the request.
2. The arbitral tribunal may within 30 days after the communication of the award make such corrections on its own initiative.
3. Such corrections shall be in writing and shall form part of the award. The provisions of article 34, paragraphs 2 to 6, shall apply.

Additional award

Article 39
1. Within 30 days after the receipt of the termination order or the award, a party, with notice to the other parties, may request the arbitral tribunal to make an award or an additional award as to claims presented in the arbitral proceedings but not decided by the arbitral tribunal.
2. If the arbitral tribunal considers the request for an award or additional award to be justified, it shall render or complete its award within 60 days after the receipt of the request. The arbitral tribunal may extend, if necessary, the period of time within which it shall make the award.
3. When such an award or additional award is made, the provisions of article 34, paragraphs 2 to 6, shall apply.

Definition of costs

Article 40
1. The arbitral tribunal shall fix the costs of arbitration in the final award and, if it deems appropriate, in another decision.
2. The term "costs" includes only:
   (a) The fees of the arbitral tribunal to be stated separately as to each arbitrator and to be fixed by the tribunal itself in accordance with article 41;
   (b) The reasonable travel and other expenses incurred by the arbitrators;

(c) The reasonable costs of expert advice and of other assistance required by the arbitral tribunal;
(d) The reasonable travel and other expenses of witnesses to the extent such expenses are approved by the arbitral tribunal;
(e) The legal and other costs incurred by the parties in relation to the arbitration to the extent that the arbitral tribunal determines that the amount of such costs is reasonable;
(f) Any fees and expenses of the appointing authority as well as the fees and expenses of the Secretary-General of the PCA.

3. In relation to interpretation, correction or completion of any award under articles 37 to 39, the arbitral tribunal may charge the costs referred to in paragraphs 2 *(b)* to *(f)*, but no additional fees.

Fees and expenses of arbitrators

Article 41

1. The fees and expenses of the arbitrators shall be reasonable in amount, taking into account the amount in dispute, the complexity of the subject matter, the time spent by the arbitrators and any other relevant circumstances of the case.

2. If there is an appointing authority and it applies or has stated that it will apply a schedule or particular method for determining the fees for arbitrators in international cases, the arbitral tribunal in fixing its fees shall take that schedule or method into account to the extent that it considers appropriate in the circumstances of the case.

3. Promptly after its constitution, the arbitral tribunal shall inform the parties as to how it proposes to determine its fees and expenses, including any rates it intends to apply. Within 15 days of receiving that proposal, any party may refer the proposal to the appointing authority for review. If, within 45 days of receipt of such a referral, the appointing authority finds that the proposal of the arbitral tribunal is inconsistent with paragraph 1, it shall make any necessary adjustments thereto, which shall be binding upon the arbitral tribunal.

4. (a) When informing the parties of the arbitrators' fees and expenses that have been fixed pursuant to article 40, paragraphs 2 *(a)* and *(b)*, the arbitral tribunal shall also explain the manner in which the corresponding amounts have been calculated;
(b) Within 15 days of receiving the arbitral tribunal's determination of fees and expenses, any party may refer for review such determination to the appointing authority. If no appointing authority has been agreed upon or designated, or if the appointing authority fails to act within the time specified in these Rules, then the review shall be made by the Secretary-General of the PCA;
(c) If the appointing authority or the Secretary-General of the PCA finds that the arbitral tribunal's determination is inconsistent with the arbitral tribunal's proposal (and any adjustment thereto) under paragraph 3 or is otherwise manifestly excessive, it shall, within 45 days of receiving such a referral, make any adjustments to the arbitral tribunal's determination that are necessary to satisfy the criteria in paragraph 1. Any such adjustments shall be binding upon the arbitral tribunal;
(d) Any such adjustments shall either be included by the arbitral tribunal in its award or, if the award has already been issued, be implemented in a correction to the award, to which the procedure of article 38, paragraph 3, shall apply.

5. Throughout the procedure under paragraphs 3 and 4, the arbitral tribunal shall proceed with the arbitration, in accordance with article 17, paragraph 1.

6. A referral under paragraph 4 shall not affect any determination in the award other than the arbitral tribunal's fees and expenses; nor shall it delay the recognition and enforcement of all parts of the award other than those relating to the determination of the arbitral tribunal's fees and expenses.

Allocation of costs

Article 42

1. The costs of the arbitration shall in principle be borne by the unsuccessful party or parties. However, the arbitral tribunal may apportion each of such costs between the parties if it determines that apportionment is reasonable, taking into account the circumstances of the case.
2. The arbitral tribunal shall in the final award or, if it deems appropriate, in any other award, determine any amount that a party may have to pay to another party as a result of the decision on allocation of costs.

Deposit of costs

Article 43

1. The arbitral tribunal, on its establishment, may request the parties to deposit an equal amount as an advance for the costs referred to in article 40, paragraphs 2 *(a)* to *(c)*.
2. During the course of the arbitral proceedings the arbitral tribunal may request supplementary deposits from the parties.
3. If an appointing authority has been agreed upon or designated, and when a party so requests and the appointing authority consents to perform the function, the arbitral tribunal shall fix the amounts of any deposits or supplementary deposits only after consultation with the appointing authority, which may make any comments to the arbitral tribunal that it deems appropriate concerning the amount of such deposits and supplementary deposits. If the required deposits are not paid in full within 30 days after the receipt of the request, the arbitral tribunal shall so inform the parties in order that one or more of them may make the required payment. If such payment is not made, the arbitral tribunal may order the suspension or termination of the arbitral proceedings.
5. After a termination order or final award has been made, the arbitral tribunal shall render an accounting to the parties of the deposits received and return any unexpended balance to the parties.

ANNEX

Model arbitration clause for contracts

Any dispute, controversy or claim arising out of or relating to this contract, or the breach, termination or invalidity thereof, shall be settled by arbitration in accordance with the UNCITRAL Arbitration Rules.

Note. Parties should consider adding:
(a) The appointing authority shall be . . . [name of institution or person];
(b) The number of arbitrators shall be [one or three];
(c) The place of arbitration shall be . . . [town and country];
(d) The language to be used in the arbitral proceedings shall be . . . .

Possible waiver statement

Note. If the parties wish to exclude recourse against the arbitral award that may be available under the applicable law, they may consider adding a provision to that effect as suggested below, considering, however, that the effectiveness and conditions of such an exclusion depend on the applicable law.

Waiver

The parties hereby waive their right to any form of recourse against an award to any court or other competent authority, insofar as such waiver can validly be made under the applicable law.

MODEL STATEMENTS OF INDEPENDENCE PURSUANT TO ARTICLE 11 OF THE RULES

No circumstances to disclose

I am impartial and independent of each of the parties and intend to remain so. To the best of my knowledge, there are no circumstances, past or present, likely to give rise to justifiable doubts as to my impartiality or independence. I shall promptly notify the parties and the other arbitrators of any such circumstances that may subsequently come to my attention during this arbitration.

Circumstances to disclose
I am impartial and independent of each of the parties and intend to remain so. Attached is a statement made pursuant to article 11 of the UNCITRAL Arbitration Rules of (a) my past and present professional, business and other relationships with the parties and (b) any other relevant circumstances. [Include statement.] I confirm that those circumstances do not affect my independence and impartiality. I shall promptly notify the parties and the other arbitrators of any such further relationships or circumstances that may subsequently come to my attention during this arbitration.

Note. Any party may consider requesting from the arbitrator the following addition to the statement of independence:

I confirm, on the basis of the information presently available to me, that I can devote the time necessary to conduct this arbitration diligently, efficiently and in accordance with the time limits in the Rules.

APPENDIX – UNCITRAL EXPEDITED ARBITRATION RULES

SCOPE OF APPLICATION

Article 1
Where parties have agreed that disputes between them in respect of a defined legal relationship, whether contractual or not, shall be referred to arbitration under the UNCITRAL Expedited Arbitration Rules ("Expedited Rules"), then such disputes shall be settled in accordance with the UNCITRAL Arbitration Rules as modified by these Expedited Rules and subject to such modification as the parties may agree.[6]

Article 2
1. At any time during the proceedings, the parties may agree that the Expedited Rules shall no longer apply to the arbitration.
2. At the request of a party, the arbitral tribunal may, in exceptional circumstances and after inviting the parties to express their views, determine that the Expedited Rules shall no longer apply to the arbitration. The arbitral tribunal shall state the reasons upon which that determination is based.

6 Unless otherwise agreed by the parties, the following articles in the UNCITRAL Arbitration Rules do not apply to expedited arbitration: article 3(4)(a) and (b); article 6(2); article 7; article 8(1); first sentence of article 20(1); first sentence of article 21(1); article 21(3); article 22; and second sentence of article 27(2).

3. When the Expedited Rules no longer apply to the arbitration pursuant to paragraph 1 or 2, the arbitral tribunal shall remain in place and conduct the arbitration in accordance with the UNCITRAL Arbitration Rules.

CONDUCT OF THE PARTIES AND THE ARBITRAL TRIBUNAL

Article 3

1. The parties shall act expeditiously throughout the proceedings.
2. The arbitral tribunal shall conduct the proceedings expeditiously taking into account the fact that the parties agreed to refer their dispute to expedited arbitration and the time frames in the Expedited Rules.
3. The arbitral tribunal may, after inviting the parties to express their views and taking into account the circumstances of the case, utilize any technological means as it considers appropriate to conduct the proceedings, including to communicate with the parties and to hold consultations and hearings remotely.

NOTICE OF ARBITRATION AND STATEMENT OF CLAIM

Article 4

1. A notice of arbitration shall also include:
   (a) A proposal for the designation of an appointing authority, unless the parties have previously agreed thereon; and
   (b) A proposal for the appointment of an arbitrator.
2. When communicating its notice of arbitration to the respondent, the claimant shall also communicate its statement of claim.
3. The claimant shall communicate the notice of arbitration and the statement of claim to the arbitral tribunal as soon as it is constituted.

RESPONSE TO THE NOTICE OF ARBITRATION AND STATEMENT OF DEFENCE

Article 5

1. Within 15 days of the receipt of the notice of arbitration, the respondent shall communicate to the claimant a response to the notice of arbitration, which shall also include responses to the information set forth in the notice of arbitration pursuant to article 4(1)(a) and (b) of the Expedited Rules.
2. The respondent shall communicate its statement of defence to the claimant and the arbitral tribunal within 15 days of the constitution of the arbitral tribunal.

DESIGNATING AND APPOINTING AUTHORITIES

Article 6

1. If all parties have not agreed on the choice of an appointing authority 15 days after a proposal for the designation of an appointing authority has been received by all other parties, any party may request the Secretary-General of the Permanent Court of Arbitration (hereinafter called the "PCA") to designate the appointing authority or to serve as appointing authority.
2. When making the request under article 6(4) of the UNCITRAL Arbitration Rules, a party may request the Secretary-General of the PCA to serve as appointing authority.
3. If requested to serve as appointing authority in accordance with paragraph 1 or 2, the Secretary-General of the PCA will serve as appointing authority unless it determines that in view of the circumstances of the case, it is more appropriate to designate an appointing authority.

NUMBER OF ARBITRATORS

Article 7
Unless otherwise agreed by the parties, there shall be one arbitrator.

APPOINTMENT OF A SOLE ARBITRATOR

Article 8
1. A sole arbitrator shall be appointed jointly by the parties.
2. If the parties have not reached agreement on the appointment of a sole arbitrator 15 days after a proposal has been received by all other parties, a sole arbitrator shall, at the request of a party, be appointed by the appointing authority in accordance with article 8(2) of the UNCITRAL Arbitration Rules.

CONSULTATION WITH THE PARTIES

Article 9
Promptly after and within 15 days of its constitution, the arbitral tribunal shall consult the parties, through a case management conference or otherwise, on the manner in which it will conduct the arbitration.

DISCRETION OF THE ARBITRAL TRIBUNAL WITH REGARD TO PERIODS OF TIME

Article 10
Subject to article 16 of the Expedited Rules, the arbitral tribunal may at any time, after inviting the parties to express their views, extend or abridge any period of time prescribed under the UNCITRAL Arbitration Rules and the Expedited Rules or agreed by the parties.

HEARINGS

Article 11
The arbitral tribunal may, after inviting the parties to express their views and in the absence of a request to hold hearings, decide that hearings shall not be held.

COUNTERCLAIMS OR CLAIMS FOR THE PURPOSE OF SET-OFF

Article 12
1. A counterclaim or a claim for the purpose of a set-off shall be made no later than in the statement of defence provided that the arbitral tribunal has jurisdiction over it.
2. The respondent may not make a counterclaim or rely on a claim for the purpose of a set-off at a later stage in the arbitral proceedings, unless the arbitral tribunal considers it appropriate to allow such claim having regard to the delay in making it or prejudice to other parties or any other circumstances.

AMENDMENTS AND SUPPLEMENTS TO A CLAIM OR DEFENCE

Article 13
During the course of the arbitral proceedings, a party may not amend or supplement its claim or defence, including a counterclaim or a claim for the purpose of a set-off, unless the arbitral tribunal considers it appropriate to allow such amendment or supplement having regard to when it is requested

or prejudice to other parties or any other circumstances. However, a claim or defence, including a counterclaim or a claim for the purpose of a set-off, may not be amended or supplemented in such a manner that the amended or supplemented claim or defence falls outside the jurisdiction of the arbitral tribunal.

FURTHER WRITTEN STATEMENTS

Article 14
The arbitral tribunal may, after inviting the parties to express their views, decide whether any further written statement shall be required from the parties or may be presented by them.

EVIDENCE

Article 15
1. The arbitral tribunal may decide which documents, exhibits or other evidence the parties should produce. The arbitral tribunal may reject any request, unless made by all parties, to establish a procedure whereby each party can request another party to produce documents.
2. Unless otherwise directed by the arbitral tribunal, statements by witnesses, including expert witnesses, shall be presented in writing and signed by them.
3. The arbitral tribunal may decide which witnesses, including expert witnesses, shall testify to the arbitral tribunal if hearings are held.

PERIOD OF TIME FOR MAKING THE AWARD

Article 16
1. The award shall be made within six months from the date of the constitution of the arbitral tribunal unless otherwise agreed by the parties.
2. The arbitral tribunal may, in exceptional circumstances and after inviting the parties to express their views, extend the period of time established in accordance with paragraph 1. The extended period of time shall not exceed a total of nine months from the date of the constitution of the arbitral tribunal.
3. If the arbitral tribunal concludes that it is at risk of not rendering an award within nine months from the date of the constitution of the arbitral tribunal, it shall propose a final extended time limit, state the reasons for the proposal, and invite the parties to express their views within a fixed period of time. The extension shall be adopted only if all parties express their agreement to the proposal within the fixed period of time.
4. If there is no agreement to the extension in paragraph 3, any party may make a request that the Expedited Rules no longer apply to the arbitration. After inviting the parties to express their views, the arbitral tribunal may determine to continue to conduct the arbitration in accordance with the UNCITRAL Arbitration Rules

ANNEX TO THE UNCITRAL EXPEDITED ARBITRATION RULES

MODEL ARBITRATION CLAUSE FOR CONTRACTS

Any dispute, controversy or claim arising out of or relating to this contract, or the breach, termination or invalidity thereof, shall be settled by arbitration in accordance with the UNCITRAL Expedited Arbitration Rules.

Note: Parties should consider adding:

(a) The appointing authority shall be . . . [name of institution or person];
(b) The place of arbitration shall be . . . [town and country];
(c) The language to be used in the arbitral proceedings shall be ...;

Model statement

Note. Parties should consider requesting from the arbitrator the following addition to the statement of independence pursuant to article 11 of the UNCITRAL Arbitration Rules:

I confirm, on the basis of the information presently available to me, that I can devote the time necessary to conduct this arbitration diligently, efficiently, expeditiously and in accordance with the time limits in the UNCITRAL Arbitration Rules and the UNCITRAL Expedited Arbitration Rules.

9.4.2 UNCITRAL Rules on Transparency in Treaty-based Investor-State Arbitration (2014)

New York, 2015

Resolution adopted by the General Assembly on 10 December 2014
[on the report of the Sixth Committee (A/69/496)]

69/116. United Nations Convention on Transparency in Treaty-based Investor-State Arbitration

The General Assembly,

Recalling its resolution 2205 (XXI) of 17 December 1966, by which it established the United Nations Commission on International Trade Law with a mandate to further the progressive harmonization and unification of the law of international trade in the interests of all peoples, in particular those of developing countries, in the extensive development of international trade,

Recalling also its resolution 68/109 of 16 December 2013, in which it recommended the use of the United Nations Com- mission on International Trade Law Rules on Transparency in Treaty-based Investor-State Arbitration1 and Arbitration Rules (as revised in 2010, with new article 1, paragraph 4, as adopted in 2013),

Recognizing the need for provisions on transparency in the settlement of treaty-based investor-State disputes to take account of the public interest involved in such arbitrations,

Believing that the Rules on Transparency contribute significantly to the establishment of a harmonized legal framework for a fair and efficient settlement of international investment disputes, increase transparency and accountability and promote good governance,

Recalling that, at its forty-sixth session, in 2013, the Commission recommended that the Rules on Transparency be applied through appropriate mechanisms to investor-State arbitration initiated pursuant to investment treaties concluded before the coming into effect of the Rules on Transparency, to the extent that such application is consistent with those investment treaties, and that the Commission decided to pre- pare a convention that was intended to give those States that wished to make the Rules on Transparency applicable to their existing investment treaties concluded before 1 April 2014 an efficient mechanism to do so, without creating any expectation that other States would use the mechanism offered by the convention,

Acknowledging that the Rules on Transparency might be made applicable to investor-State arbitration initiated pursuant to investment treaties concluded before 1 April 2014, the date of coming into effect of the Rules on Transparency, by means other than a convention,

Recognizing that all States and interested international organizations were invited to participate in the preparation of the draft convention either as members or as observers during the forty-seventh session of the Commission, with full opportunity to speak and make proposals,

Noting that the preparation of the draft convention was the subject of due deliberation in the Commission and that the draft convention benefited from consultations with Governments and interested intergovernmental and international non-governmental organizations,

Noting with satisfaction that the text of the draft convention was circulated for comment to all States Members of the United Nations and intergovernmental organizations invited to attend the meetings of the Commission as observers, and that the comments received were before the Commission at its forty-seventh session,

Taking note with satisfaction of the decision of the Commission at its forty-seventh session to submit the draft convention to the General Assembly for its consideration,

Taking note of the draft convention approved by the Commission,

Expressing its appreciation to the Government of Mauritius for its offer to host a signing ceremony for the Convention in Port Louis,

1. *Commends* the United Nations Commission on Inter- national Trade Law for preparing the draft convention on transparency in treaty-based investor-State arbitration;6

2. *Adopts* the United Nations Convention on Transparency in Treaty-based Investor-State Arbitration, contained in the annex to the present resolution;

3. *Authorizes* a ceremony for the opening for signature of the Convention to be held in Port Louis on 17 March 2015, and recommends that the Convention be known as the "Mauritius Convention on Transparency";

4. *Calls upon* those Governments and regional economic integration organizations that wish to make the United Nations Commission on International Trade Law Rules on Transparency in Treaty-based Investor-State Arbitration1 applicable to arbitrations under their existing investment treaties to consider becoming a party to the Convention.

UNITED NATIONS CONVENTION ON TRANSPARENCY IN TREATY-BASED INVESTOR-STATE ARBITRATION

Preamble

The Parties to this Convention,

Recognizing the value of arbitration as a method of settling disputes that may arise in the context of international relations, and the extensive and wide-ranging use of arbitration for the settlement of investor-State disputes,

Also recognizing the need for provisions on transparency in the settlement of treaty-based investor-State disputes to take account of the public interest involved in such arbitrations,

Believing that the Rules on Transparency in Treaty-based Investor-State Arbitration adopted by the United Nations Commission on International Trade Law on 11 July 2013 ("UNCITRAL Rules on Transparency"), effective as of 1 April 2014, would contribute significantly to the establishment of a harmonized legal framework for a fair and efficient settlement of international investment disputes,

Noting the great number of treaties providing for the protection of investments or investors already in force, and the practical importance of promoting the application of the UNCITRAL Rules on Transparency to arbitration under those already concluded investment treaties,

Noting also article 1(2) and (9) of the UNCITRAL Rules on Transparency,

Have agreed as follows:

Article 1. Scope of application

1. This Convention applies to arbitration between an investor and a State or a regional economic integration organization conducted on the basis of an investment treaty concluded before 1 April 2014 ("investor-State arbitration").

2. The term "investment treaty" means any bilateral or multilateral treaty, including any treaty commonly referred to as a free trade agreement, economic integration agreement, trade and investment framework or cooperation agreement, or bilateral investment treaty, which contains provisions on the protection of investments or investors and a right for investors to resort to arbitration against contracting parties to that investment treaty.

Article 2. Application of the UNCITRAL Rules on Transparency

Bilateral or multilateral application

1. The UNCITRAL Rules on Transparency shall apply to any investor-State arbitration, whether or not initiated under the UNCITRAL Arbitration Rules, in which the respondent is a Party that has not made a relevant reservation under article 3(1)(a) or (b), and the claimant is of a State that is a Party that has not made a relevant reservation under article 3(1)(a).

Unilateral offer of application

2. Where the UNCITRAL Rules on Transparency do not apply pursuant to paragraph 1, the UNCITRAL Rules on Transparency shall apply to an investor-State arbitration, whether or not initiated under the UNCITRAL Arbitration Rules, in which the respondent is a Party that has not made a reservation relevant to that investor-State arbitration under article 3(1), and the claimant agrees to the application of the UNCITRAL Rules on Transparency.

Applicable version of the UNCITRAL Rules on Transparency

3. Where the UNCITRAL Rules on Transparency apply pursuant to paragraph 1 or 2, the most recent version of those Rules as to which the respondent has not made a reservation pursuant to article 3(2) shall apply.

Article 1(7) of the UNCITRAL Rules on Transparency

4. The final sentence of article 1(7) of the UNCITRAL Rules on Transparency shall not apply to investor-State arbitrations under paragraph 1.

Most favoured nation provision in an investment treaty

5. The Parties to this Convention agree that a claimant may not invoke a most favoured nation provision to seek to apply, or avoid the application of, the UNCITRAL Rules on Transparency under this Convention.

Article 3. Reservations

1. A Party may declare that:
   - (a) It shall not apply this Convention to investor-State arbitration under a specific investment treaty, identified by title and name of the contracting parties to that investment treaty;
   - (b) Article 2(1) and (2) shall not apply to investor-State arbitration conducted using a specific set of arbitration rules or procedures other than the UNCITRAL Arbitration Rules, and in which it is a respondent;
   - (c) Article 2(2) shall not apply in investor-State arbitration in which it is a respondent.

2. In the event of a revision of the UNCITRAL Rules on Transparency, a Party may, within six months of the adoption of such revision, declare that it shall not apply that revised version of the Rules.

3. Parties may make multiple reservations in a single instrument. In such an instrument, each declaration made:

(a) In respect of a specific investment treaty under para- graph (1)(a);

(b) In respect of a specific set of arbitration rules or procedures under paragraph (1)(b);

(c) Under paragraph (1)(c); or

(d) Under paragraph (2);

shall constitute a separate reservation capable of separate withdrawal under article 4(6).

4. No reservations are permitted except those expressly authorized in this article.

Article 4. Formulation of reservations

1. Reservations may be made by a Party at any time, save for a reservation under article 3(2).

2. Reservations made at the time of signature shall be subject to confirmation upon ratification, acceptance or approval. Such reservations shall take effect simultaneously with the entry into force of this Convention in respect of the Party concerned.

3. Reservations made at the time of ratification, acceptance or approval of this Convention or accession thereto shall take effect simultaneously with the entry into force of this Convention in respect of the Party concerned.

4. Except for a reservation made by a Party under article 3(2), which shall take effect immediately upon deposit, a reservation deposited after the entry into force of the Convention for that Party shall take effect twelve months after the date of its deposit.

5. Reservations and their confirmations shall be deposited with the depositary.

6. Any Party that makes a reservation under this Convention may withdraw it at any time. Such withdrawals are to be deposited with the depositary, and shall take effect upon deposit.

Article 5. Application to investor-State arbitrations

This Convention and any reservation, or withdrawal of a reservation, shall apply only to investor-State arbitrations that are commenced after the date when the Convention, reservation, or withdrawal of a reservation, enters into force or takes effect in respect of each Party concerned.

Article 6. Depositary

The Secretary-General of the United Nations is hereby designated as the depositary of this Convention.

Article 7. Signature, ratification, acceptance, approval, accession

1. This Convention is open for signature in Port Louis, Mauritius, on 17 March 2015, and thereafter at United Nations Headquarters in New York by any (a) State; or (b) regional economic integration organization that is constituted by States and is a contracting party to an investment treaty.

2. This Convention is subject to ratification, acceptance or approval by the signatories to this Convention.

3. This Convention is open for accession by all States or regional economic integration organizations referred to in para- graph 1 which are not signatories as from the date it is open for signature.

4. Instruments of ratification, acceptance, approval or accession are to be deposited with the depositary.

Article 8. Participation by regional economic integration organizations

1. When depositing an instrument of ratification, acceptance, approval or accession, a regional economic integration organization shall inform the depositary of a specific investment treaty to which it is a contracting party, identified by title and name of the contracting parties to that investment treaty.

2. When the number of Parties is relevant in this Convention, a regional economic integration organization does not count as a Party in addition to its member States which are Parties.

Article 9. Entry into force
1. This Convention shall enter into force six months after the date of deposit of the third instrument of ratification, acceptance, approval or accession.
2. When a State or a regional economic integration organization ratifies, accepts, approves or accedes to this Convention after the deposit of the third instrument of ratification, acceptance, approval or accession, this Convention enters into force in respect of that State or regional economic integration organization six months after the date of the deposit of its instrument of ratification, acceptance, approval or accession.

Article 10. Amendment
1. Any Party may propose an amendment to the present Convention by submitting it to the Secretary-General of the United Nations. The Secretary-General shall thereupon communicate the proposed amendment to the Parties to this Convention with a request that they indicate whether they favour a conference of Parties for the purpose of considering and voting upon the proposal. In the event that within four months from the date of such communication at least one third of the Parties favour such a conference, the Secretary-General shall convene the conference under the auspices of the United Nations.
2. The conference of Parties shall make every effort to achieve consensus on each amendment. If all efforts at consensus are exhausted and no consensus is reached, the amendment shall, as a last resort, require for its adoption a two-thirds majority vote of the Parties present and voting at the conference.
3. An adopted amendment shall be submitted by the Secretary-General of the United Nations to all the Parties for ratification, acceptance or approval.
4. An adopted amendment enters into force six months after the date of deposit of the third instrument of ratification, acceptance or approval. When an amendment enters into force, it shall be binding on those Parties which have expressed consent to be bound by it.
5. When a State or a regional economic integration organization ratifies, accepts or approves an amendment that has already entered into force, the amendment enters into force in respect of that State or that regional economic integration organization six months after the date of the deposit of its instrument of ratification, acceptance or approval.
6. Any State or regional economic integration organization which becomes a Party to the Convention after the entry into force of the amendment shall be considered as a Party to the Convention as amended.

Article 11. Denunciation of this Convention
1. A Party may denounce this Convention at any time by means of a formal notification addressed to the depositary. The denunciation shall take effect twelve months after the notification is received by the depositary.
2. This Convention shall continue to apply to investor-State arbitrations commenced before the denunciation takes effect.

DONE in a single original, of which the Arabic, Chinese, English, French, Russian and Spanish texts are equally authentic.

IN WITNESS WHEREOF, the undersigned plenipotentiaries, being duly authorized by their respective Governments, have signed the present Convention.

9.4.3 Rules of Arbitration of the International Chamber of Commerce ('ICC') (2021)

In force as from 1 January 2021

INTRODUCTORY PROVISIONS

Article 1 International Court of Arbitration

1. The International Court of Arbitration (the "Court") of the International Chamber of Commerce ("ICC") is the independent arbitration body of ICC. The statutes of the Court are set forth in Appendix I.
2. The Court does not itself resolve disputes. It administers the resolution of disputes by arbitral tribunals, in accordance with the Rules of Arbitration of ICC (the "Rules"). The Court is the only body authorized to administer arbitrations under the Rules, including the scrutiny and approval of awards rendered in accordance with the Rules. It draws up its own internal rules, which are set forth in Appendix II (the "Internal Rules").
3. The President of the Court (the "President") shall have the power to take urgent decisions on behalf of the Court, provided that any such decision is reported to the Court at one of its next sessions. At the President's request, in the President's absence or otherwise where the President is unable to act, one of the Vice-Presidents shall have the same power.
4. As provided for in the Internal Rules, the Court may delegate to one or more committees composed of its members the power to take certain decisions, provided that any such decision is reported to the Court at one of its next sessions.
5. The Court is assisted in its work by the Secretariat of the Court (the "Secretariat") under the direction of its Secretary General (the "Secretary General").

Article 2 Definitions

In the Rules:

(i) "arbitral tribunal" includes one or more arbitrators;
(ii) "claimant" includes one or more claimants, "respondent" includes one or more respondents, and "additional party" includes one or more additional parties;
(iii) "party" or "parties" include claimants, respondents or additional parties;
(iv) "claim" or "claims" include any claim by any party against any other party;
(v) "award" includes, inter alia, an interim, partial, final, or additional award.

Article 3 Written Notifications or Communications; Time Limits

1. Save as otherwise provided in Articles 4(4)(b) and 5(3), all pleadings and other written communications submitted by any party, as well as all documents annexed thereto, shall be sent to each party, each arbitrator, and the Secretariat. Any notification or communication from the arbitral tribunal to the parties shall also be sent in copy to the Secretariat.
2. All notifications or communications from the Secretariat and the arbitral tribunal shall be made to the last address of the party or its representative for whom the same are intended, as notified either by the party in question or by any other party. Such notification or communication may be made by delivery against receipt, registered post, courier, email, or any other means of telecommunication that provides a record of the sending thereof.

3. A notification or communication shall be deemed to have been made on the day it was received by the party itself or by its representative, or would have been received if made in accordance with Article 3(2).
4. Periods of time specified in or fixed under the Rules shall start to run on the day following the date a notification or communication is deemed to have been made in accordance with Article 3(3). When the day next following such date is an official holiday, or a non-business day in the country where the notification or communication is deemed to have been made, the period of time shall commence on the first following business day. Official holidays and non-business days are included in the calculation of the period of time. If the last day of the relevant period of time granted is an official holiday or a non-business day in the country where the notification or communication is deemed to have been made, the period of time shall expire at the end of the first following business day.

COMMENCING THE ARBITRATION

Article 4 Request for Arbitration

1. A party wishing to have recourse to arbitration under the Rules shall submit its Request for Arbitration (the "Request") to the Secretariat at any of the offices specified in the Internal Rules. The Secretariat shall notify the claimant and respondent of the receipt of the Request and the date of such receipt.
2. The date on which the Request is received by the Secretariat shall, for all purposes, be deemed to be the date of the commencement of the arbitration.
3. The Request shall contain the following information:
  (a) the name in full, description, address and other contact details of each of the parties;
  (b) the name in full, address and other contact details of any person(s) representing the claimant in the arbitration;
  (c) a description of the nature and circumstances of the dispute giving rise to the claims and of the basis upon which the claims are made;
  (d) a statement of the relief sought, together with the amounts of any quantified claims and, to the extent possible, an estimate of the monetary value of any other claims;
  (e) any relevant agreements and, in particular, the arbitration agreement(s);
  (f) where claims are made under more than one arbitration agreement, an indication of the arbitration agreement under which each claim is made;
  (g) all relevant particulars and any observations or proposals concerning the number of arbitrators and their choice in accordance with the provisions of Articles 12 and 13, and any nomination of an arbitrator required thereby; and
  (h) all relevant particulars and any observations or proposals as to the place of the arbitration, the applicable rules of law and the language of the arbitration.

The claimant may submit such other documents or information with the Request as it considers appropriate or as may contribute to the efficient resolution of the dispute.

4. Together with the Request, the claimant shall:
  (a) make payment of the filing fee required by Appendix III ("Arbitration Costs and Fees") in force on the date the Request is submitted; and
  (b) submit a sufficient number of copies of the Request for each other party, each arbitrator and the Secretariat where the claimant requests transmission of the Request by delivery against receipt, registered post or courier.

In the event that the claimant fails to comply with either of these requirements, the Secretariat may fix a time limit within which the claimant must comply, failing which the file shall be closed without prejudice to the claimant's right to submit the same claims at a later date in another Request.

5. The Secretariat shall transmit a copy of the Request and the documents annexed thereto to the respondent for its Answer to the Request once the Secretariat has sufficient copies of the Request and the required filing fee.

Article 5 Answer to the Request; Counterclaims

1. Within 30 days from receipt of the Request from the Secretariat, the respondent shall submit an Answer (the "Answer") which shall contain the following information:

(a) its name in full, description, address and other contact details;

(b) the name in full, address and other contact details of any person(s) representing the respondent in the arbitration;

(c) its comments as to the nature and circumstances of the dispute giving rise to the claims and the basis upon which the claims are made;

(d) its response to the relief sought;

(e) any observations or proposals concerning the number of arbitrators and their choice in light of the claimant's proposals and in accordance with the provisions of Articles 12 and 13, and any nomination of an arbitrator required thereby; and

(f) any observations or proposals as to the place of the arbitration, the applicable rules of law and the language of the arbitration.

The respondent may submit such other documents or information with the Answer as it considers appropriate or as may contribute to the efficient resolution of the dispute.

2. The Secretariat may grant the respondent an extension of the time for submitting the Answer, provided the application for such an extension contains the respondent's observations or proposals concerning the number of arbitrators and their choice and, where required by Articles 12 and 13, the nomination of an arbitrator. If the respondent fails to do so, the Court shall proceed in accordance with the Rules.

3. The Answer shall be submitted in a sufficient number of copies for each other party, each arbitrator and the Secretariat where the respondent requests transmission thereof by delivery against receipt, registered post or courier.

4. The Secretariat shall communicate the Answer and the documents annexed thereto to all other parties.

5. Any counterclaims made by the respondent shall be submitted with the Answer and shall provide:

(a) a description of the nature and circumstances of the dispute giving rise to the counterclaims and of the basis upon which the counterclaims are made;

(b) a statement of the relief sought together with the amounts of any quantified counterclaims and, to the extent possible, an estimate of the monetary value of any other counterclaims;

(c) any relevant agreements and, in particular, the arbitration agreement(s); and

(d) where counterclaims are made under more than one arbitration agreement, an indication of the arbitration agreement under which each counterclaim is made.

The respondent may submit such other documents or information with the counterclaims as it considers appropriate or as may contribute to the efficient resolution of the dispute.

6. The claimant shall submit a reply to any counterclaim within 30 days from receipt of the counterclaims communicated by the Secretariat. Prior to the transmission of the file to the arbitral tribunal, the Secretariat may grant the claimant an extension of time for submitting the reply.

Article 6 Effect of the Arbitration Agreement

1. Where the parties have agreed to submit to arbitration under the Rules, they shall be deemed to have submitted ipso facto to the Rules in effect on the date of commencement of the arbitration, unless they have agreed to submit to the Rules in effect on the date of their arbitration agreement.

2. By agreeing to arbitration under the Rules, the parties have accepted that the arbitration shall be administered by the Court.
3. If any party against which a claim has been made does not submit an Answer, or if any party raises one or more pleas concerning the existence, validity or scope of the arbitration agreement or concerning whether all of the claims made in the arbitration may be determined together in a single arbitration, the arbitration shall proceed and any question of jurisdiction or of whether the claims may be determined together in that arbitration shall be decided directly by the arbitral tribunal, unless the Secretary General refers the matter to the Court for its decision pursuant to Article 6(4).
4. In all cases referred to the Court under Article 6(3), the Court shall decide whether and to what extent the arbitration shall proceed. The arbitration shall proceed if and to the extent that the Court is prima facie satisfied that an arbitration agreement under the Rules may exist. In particular:

(i) where there are more than two parties to the arbitration, the arbitration shall proceed between those of the parties, including any additional parties joined pursuant to Article 7(1), with respect to which the Court is prima facie satisfied that an arbitration agreement under the Rules that binds them all may exist; and

(ii) where claims pursuant to Article 9 are made under more than one arbitration agreement, the arbitration shall proceed as to those claims with respect to which the Court is prima facie satisfied

(a) that the arbitration agreements under which those claims are made may be compatible, and

(b) that all parties to the arbitration may have agreed that those claims can be determined together in a single arbitration.

The Court's decision pursuant to Article 6(4) is without prejudice to the admissibility or merits of any party's plea or pleas.
5. In all matters decided by the Court under Article 6(4), any decision as to the jurisdiction of the arbitral tribunal, except as to parties or claims with respect to which the Court decides that the arbitration cannot proceed, shall then be taken by the arbitral tribunal itself.
6. Where the parties are notified of the Court's decision pursuant to Article 6(4) that the arbitration cannot proceed in respect of some or all of them, any party retains the right to ask any court having jurisdiction whether or not, and in respect of which of them, there is a binding arbitration agreement.
7. Where the Court has decided pursuant to Article 6(4) that the arbitration cannot proceed in respect of any of the claims, such decision shall not prevent a party from reintroducing the same claim at a later date in other proceedings.
8. If any of the parties refuses or fails to take part in the arbitration or any stage thereof, the arbitration shall proceed notwithstanding such refusal or failure.
9. Unless otherwise agreed, the arbitral tribunal shall not cease to have jurisdiction by reason of any allegation that the contract is non-existent or null and void, provided that the arbitral tribunal upholds the validity of the arbitration agreement. The arbitral tribunal shall continue to have jurisdiction to determine the parties' respective rights and to decide their claims and pleas even though the contract itself may be non-existent or null and void.

MULTIPLE PARTIES, MULTIPLE CONTRACTS AND CONSOLIDATION

Article 7 Joinder of Additional Parties

1. A party wishing to join an additional party to the arbitration shall submit its request for arbitration against the additional party (the "Request for Joinder") to the Secretariat. The date on which the Request for Joinder is received by the Secretariat shall, for all purposes, be deemed to be the date of the commencement of arbitration against the additional party. Any such joinder shall be subject to the provisions of Articles 6(3)–6(7) and 9. Unless all parties, including the additional party, otherwise agree, or as provided for in Article 7(5), no additional party may be joined after the confirmation or

appointment of any arbitrator. The Secretariat may fix a time limit for the submission of a Request for Joinder.

2. The Request for Joinder shall contain the following information:
   (a) the case reference of the existing arbitration;
   (b) the name in full, description, address and other contact details of each of the parties, including the additional party; and
   (c) the information specified in Article 4(3), subparagraphs c), d), e) and f).

The party filing the Request for Joinder may submit therewith such other documents or information as it considers appropriate or as may contribute to the efficient resolution of the dispute.

3. The provisions of Articles 4(4) and 4(5) shall apply,
mutatis mutandis, to the Request for Joinder.

4. The additional party shall submit an Answer in accordance, mutatis mutandis, with the provisions of Articles 5(1)–5(4). The additional party may make claims against any other party in accordance with the provisions of Article 8.

5. Any Request for Joinder made after the confirmation or appointment of any arbitrator shall be decided by the arbitral tribunal once constituted and shall be subject to the additional party accepting the constitution of the arbitral tribunal and agreeing to the Terms of Reference, where applicable. In deciding on such a Request for Joinder, the arbitral tribunal shall take into account all relevant circumstances, which may include whether the arbitral tribunal has prima facie jurisdiction over the additional party, the timing of the Request for Joinder, possible conflicts of interests and the impact of the joinder on the arbitral procedure. Any decision to join an additional party is without prejudice to the arbitral tribunal's decision as to its jurisdiction with respect to that party.

Article 8 Claims Between Multiple Parties

1. In an arbitration with multiple parties, claims may be made by any party against any other party, subject to the provisions of Articles 6(3)–6(7) and 9 and provided that no new claims may be made after the Terms of Reference are signed or approved by the Court without the authorization of the arbitral tribunal pursuant to Article 23(4).

2. Any party making a claim pursuant to Article 8(1) shall provide the information specified in Article 4(3), subparagraphs c), d), e) and f).

3. Before the Secretariat transmits the file to the arbitral tribunal in accordance with Article 16, the following provisions shall apply, mutatis mutandis, to any claim made: Article 4(4) subparagraph b); Article 4(5); Article 5(1) except for subparagraphs a), b), e) and f); Article 5(2); Article 5(3) and Article 5(4). Thereafter, the arbitral tribunal shall determine the procedure for making a claim.

Article 9 Multiple Contracts

Subject to the provisions of Articles 6(3)–6(7) and 23(4), claims arising out of or in connection with more than one contract may be made in a single arbitration, irrespective of whether such claims are made under one or more than one arbitration agreement under the Rules.

Article 10 Consolidation of Arbitrations

The Court may, at the request of a party, consolidate two or more arbitrations pending under the Rules into a single arbitration, where:
(a) the parties have agreed to consolidation; or
(b) all of the claims in the arbitrations are made under the same arbitration agreement or agreements; or
(c) the claims in the arbitrations are not made under the same arbitration agreement or agreements, but the arbitrations are between the same parties, the disputes in the arbitrations arise in connection with the same legal relationship, and the Court finds the arbitration agreements to be compatible.

In deciding whether to consolidate, the Court may take into account any circumstances it considers to be relevant, including whether one or more arbitrators have been confirmed or appointed in more than one of the arbitrations and, if so, whether the same or different persons have been confirmed or appointed.

When arbitrations are consolidated, they shall be consolidated into the arbitration that commenced first, unless otherwise agreed by all parties.

THE ARBITRAL TRIBUNAL

Article 11 General Provisions

1. Every arbitrator must be and remain impartial and independent of the parties involved in the arbitration.
2. Before appointment or confirmation, a prospective arbitrator shall sign a statement of acceptance, availability, impartiality and independence. The prospective arbitrator shall disclose in writing to the Secretariat any facts or circumstances which might be of such a nature as to call into question the arbitrator's independence in the eyes of the parties, as well as any circumstances that could give rise to reasonable doubts as to the arbitrator's impartiality. The Secretariat shall provide such information to the parties in writing and fix a time limit for any comments from them.
3. An arbitrator shall immediately disclose in writing to the Secretariat and to the parties any facts or circumstances of a similar nature to those referred to in Article 11(2) concerning the arbitrator's impartiality or independence which may arise during the arbitration.
4. The decisions of the Court as to the appointment, confirmation, challenge or replacement of an arbitrator shall be final.
5. By accepting to serve, arbitrators undertake to carry out their responsibilities in accordance with the Rules.
6. Insofar as the parties have not provided otherwise, the arbitral tribunal shall be constituted in accordance with the provisions of Articles 12 and 13.
7. In order to assist prospective arbitrators and arbitrators in complying with their duties under Articles 11(2) and 11(3), each party must promptly inform the Secretariat, the arbitral tribunal and the other parties, of the existence and identity of any non-party which has entered into an arrangement for the funding of claims or defences and under which it has an economic interest in the outcome of the arbitration.

Article 12 Constitution of the Arbitral Tribunal

Number of Arbitrators

1. The disputes shall be decided by a sole arbitrator or by three arbitrators.
2. Where the parties have not agreed upon the number of arbitrators, the Court shall appoint a sole arbitrator, save where it appears to the Court that the dispute is such as to warrant the appointment of three arbitrators. In such case, the claimant shall nominate an arbitrator within 15 days from receipt of the notification of the decision of the Court, and the respondent shall nominate an arbitrator within 15 days from receipt of the notification of the nomination made by the claimant. If a party fails to nominate an arbitrator, the appointment shall be made by the Court.

Sole Arbitrator

3. Where the parties have agreed that the dispute shall be resolved by a sole arbitrator, they may, by agreement, nominate the sole arbitrator for confirmation. If the parties fail to nominate a sole arbitrator within 30 days from the date when the claimant's Request for Arbitration has been received

by the other party or parties, or within such additional time as may be allowed by the Secretariat, the sole arbitrator shall be appointed by the Court.

Three Arbitrators

4. Where the parties have agreed that the dispute shall be resolved by three arbitrators, each party shall nominate in the Request and the Answer, respectively, one arbitrator for confirmation. If a party fails to nominate an arbitrator, the appointment shall be made by the Court.

5. Where the dispute is to be referred to three arbitrators, the third arbitrator, who will act as president of the arbitral tribunal, shall be appointed by the Court, unless the parties have agreed upon another procedure for such appointment, in which case the nomination will be subject to confirmation pursuant to Article 13. Should such procedure not result in a nomination within 30 days from the confirmation or appointment of the co-arbitrators or any other time limit agreed by the parties or fixed by the Court, the third arbitrator shall be appointed by the Court.

6. Where there are multiple claimants or multiple respondents, and where the dispute is to be referred to three arbitrators, the multiple claimants, jointly, and the multiple respondents, jointly, shall nominate an arbitrator for confirmation pursuant to Article 13.

7. Where an additional party has been joined (Article 7(1)), and where the dispute is to be referred to three arbitrators, the additional party may, jointly with the claimant(s) or with the respondent(s), nominate an arbitrator for confirmation pursuant to Article 13 and subject to Article 7(5).

8. In the absence of a joint nomination pursuant to Articles 12(6) or 12(7) and where all parties are unable to agree to a method for the constitution of the arbitral tribunal, the Court may appoint each member of the arbitral tribunal and shall designate one of them to act as president. In such cases, the Court shall be at liberty to choose any person it regards as suitable to act as arbitrator, applying Article 13 when it considers this appropriate.

9. Notwithstanding any agreement by the parties on the method of constitution of the arbitral tribunal, in exceptional circumstances the Court may appoint each member of the arbitral tribunal to avoid a significant risk of unequal treatment and unfairness that may affect the validity of the award.

Article 13 Appointment and Confirmation of the Arbitrators

1. In confirming or appointing arbitrators, the Court shall consider the prospective arbitrator's nationality, residence and other relationships with the countries of which the parties or the other arbitrators are nationals and the prospective arbitrator's availability and ability to conduct the arbitration in accordance with the Rules. The same shall apply where the Secretary General confirms arbitrators pursuant to Article 13(2).

2. The Secretary General may confirm as co- arbitrators, sole arbitrators and presidents of arbitral tribunals persons nominated by the parties or pursuant to their particular agreements, provided that the statement they have submitted contains no qualification regarding impartiality or independence or that a qualified statement regarding impartiality or independence has not given rise to objections. Such confirmation shall be reported to the Court at one of its next sessions. If the Secretary General considers that a co-arbitrator, sole arbitrator or president of an arbitral tribunal should not be confirmed, the matter shall be submitted to the Court.

3. Where the Court is to appoint an arbitrator, it shall make the appointment upon proposal of an ICC National Committee or Group that it considers to be appropriate. If the Court does not accept the proposal made, or if the National Committee or Group fails to make the proposal requested within the time limit fixed by the Court, the Court may repeat its request, request a proposal from another National Committee or Group that it considers to be appropriate, or appoint directly any person whom it regards as suitable.

4. The Court may also appoint directly to act as arbitrator any person whom it regards as suitable where:

(a) one or more of the parties is a state or may be considered to be a state entity;
(b) the Court considers that it would be appropriate to appoint an arbitrator from a country or territory where there is no National Committee or Group; or
(c) the President certifies to the Court that circumstances exist which, in the President's opinion, make a direct appointment necessary and appropriate.

5. Where the Court is to appoint the sole arbitrator or the president of the arbitral tribunal, such sole arbitrator or president of the arbitral tribunal shall be of a nationality other than those of the parties. However, in suitable circumstances and provided that none of the parties objects within the time limit fixed by the Secretariat, the sole arbitrator or the president of the arbitral tribunal may be chosen from a country of which any of the parties is a national.

6. Whenever the arbitration agreement upon which the arbitration is based arises from a treaty, and unless the parties agree otherwise, no arbitrator shall have the same nationality of any party to the arbitration.

Article 14 Challenge of Arbitrators

1. A challenge of an arbitrator, whether for an alleged lack of impartiality or independence, or otherwise, shall be made by the submission to the Secretariat of a written statement specifying the facts and circumstances on which the challenge is based.

2. For a challenge to be admissible, it must be submitted by a party either within 30 days from receipt by that party of the notification of the appointment or confirmation of the arbitrator, or within 30 days from the date when the party making the challenge was informed of the facts and circumstances on which the challenge is based if such date is subsequent to the receipt of such notification.

3. The Court shall decide on the admissibility and, at the same time, if necessary, on the merits of a challenge after the Secretariat has afforded an opportunity for the arbitrator concerned, the other party or parties and any other members of the arbitral tribunal to comment in writing within a suitable period of time. Such comments shall be communicated to the parties and to the arbitrators.

Article 15 Replacement of Arbitrators

1. An arbitrator shall be replaced upon death, upon acceptance by the Court of the arbitrator's resignation, upon acceptance by the Court of a challenge, or upon acceptance by the Court of a request of all the parties.

2. An arbitrator shall also be replaced on the Court's own initiative when it decides that the arbitrator is prevented de jure or de facto from fulfilling the arbitrator's functions, or that the arbitrator is not fulfilling those functions in accordance with the Rules or within the prescribed time limits.

3. When, on the basis of information that has come to its attention, the Court considers applying Article 15(2), it shall decide on the matter after the arbitrator concerned, the parties and any other members of the arbitral tribunal have had an opportunity to comment in writing within a suitable period of time. Such comments shall be communicated to the parties and to the arbitrators.

4. When an arbitrator is to be replaced, the Court has discretion to decide whether or not to follow the original nominating process. Once reconstituted, and after having invited the parties to comment, the arbitral tribunal shall determine if and to what extent prior proceedings shall be repeated before the reconstituted arbitral tribunal.

5. Subsequent to the closing of the proceedings, instead of replacing an arbitrator who has died or been removed by the Court pursuant to Articles 15(1) or 15(2), the Court may decide, when it considers it appropriate, that the remaining arbitrators shall continue the arbitration. In making such determination, the Court shall take into account the views of the remaining arbitrators and of the parties and such other matters that it considers appropriate in the circumstances.

THE ARBITRAL PROCEEDINGS

Article 16 Transmission of the File to the Arbitral Tribunal

The Secretariat shall transmit the file to the arbitral tribunal as soon as it has been constituted, provided the advance on costs requested by the Secretariat at this stage has been paid.

Article 17 Party Representation

1. Each party must promptly inform the Secretariat, the arbitral tribunal and the other parties of any changes in its representation.
2. The arbitral tribunal may, once constituted and after it has afforded an opportunity to the parties to comment in writing within a suitable period of time, take any measure necessary to avoid a conflict of interest of an arbitrator arising from a change in party representation, including the exclusion of new party representatives from participating in whole or in part in the arbitral proceedings.
3. At any time after the commencement of the arbitration, the arbitral tribunal or the Secretariat may require proof of the authority of any party representatives.

Article 18 Place of the Arbitration

1. The place of the arbitration shall be fixed by the Court, unless agreed upon by the parties.
2. The arbitral tribunal may, after consulting the parties, conduct hearings and meetings at any location it considers appropriate, unless otherwise agreed by the parties.
3. The arbitral tribunal may deliberate at any location it considers appropriate.

Article 19 Rules Governing the Proceedings

The proceedings before the arbitral tribunal shall be governed by the Rules and, where the Rules are silent, by any rules which the parties or, failing them, the arbitral tribunal may settle on, whether or not reference is thereby made to the rules of procedure of a national law to be applied to the arbitration.

Article 20 Language of the Arbitration

In the absence of an agreement by the parties, the arbitral tribunal shall determine the language or languages of the arbitration, due regard being given to all relevant circumstances, including the language of the contract.

Article 21 Applicable Rules of Law

1. The parties shall be free to agree upon the rules of law to be applied by the arbitral tribunal to the merits of the dispute. In the absence of any such agreement, the arbitral tribunal shall apply the rules of law which it determines to be appropriate.
2. The arbitral tribunal shall take account of the provisions of the contract, if any, between the parties and of any relevant trade usages.
3. The arbitral tribunal shall assume the powers of an *amiable compositeur* or decide *ex aequo et bono* only if the parties have agreed to give it such powers.

Article 22 Conduct of the Arbitration

1. The arbitral tribunal and the parties shall make every effort to conduct the arbitration in an expeditious and cost effective manner, having regard to the complexity and value of the dispute.
2. In order to ensure effective case management, after consulting the parties, the arbitral tribunal shall adopt such procedural measures as it considers appropriate, provided that they are not contrary to any agreement of the parties. Such measures may include one or more of the case management techniques described in Appendix IV.

3. Upon the request of any party, the arbitral tribunal may make orders concerning the confidentiality of the arbitration proceedings or of any other matters in connection with the arbitration and may take measures for protecting trade secrets and confidential information.
4. In all cases, the arbitral tribunal shall act fairly and impartially and ensure that each party has a reasonable opportunity to present its case.
5. The parties undertake to comply with any order made by the arbitral tribunal.

Article 23 Terms of Reference
1. As soon as it has received the file from the Secretariat, the arbitral tribunal shall draw up, on the basis of documents or in the presence of the parties and in the light of their most recent submissions, a document defining its Terms of Reference. This document shall include the following particulars:
(a) the names in full, description, address and other contact details of each of the parties and of any person(s) representing a party in the arbitration;
(b) the addresses to which notifications and communications arising in the course of the arbitration may be made;
(c) a summary of the parties' respective claims and of the relief sought by each party, together with the amounts of any quantified claims and, to the extent possible, an estimate of the monetary value of any other claims;
(d) unless the arbitral tribunal considers it inappropriate, a list of issues to be determined;
(e) the names in full, address and other contact details of each of the arbitrators;
(f) the place of the arbitration; and
(g) particulars of the applicable procedural rules and, if such is the case, reference to the power conferred upon the arbitral tribunal to act as *amiable compositeur* or to decide *ex aequo et bono*.
2. The Terms of Reference shall be signed by the parties and the arbitral tribunal. Within 30 days from the date on which the file has been transmitted to it, the arbitral tribunal shall transmit to the Court the Terms of Reference signed by it and by the parties. The Court may extend this time limit pursuant to a reasoned request from the arbitral tribunal or on its own initiative if it decides it is necessary to do so.
3. If any of the parties refuses to take part in the drawing up of the Terms of Reference or to sign the same, they shall be submitted to the Court for approval. When the Terms of Reference have been signed in accordance with Article 23(2) or approved by the Court, the arbitration shall proceed.
4. After the Terms of Reference have been signed or approved by the Court, no party shall make new claims which fall outside the limits of the Terms of Reference unless it has been authorized to do so by the arbitral tribunal, which shall consider the nature of such new claims, the stage of the arbitration and other relevant circumstances.

Article 24 Case Management Conference and Procedural Timetable
1. When drawing up the Terms of Reference or as soon as possible thereafter, the arbitral tribunal shall hold a case management conference to consult the parties on procedural measures that may be adopted pursuant to Article 22(2).
2. During such conference, or as soon as possible thereafter, the arbitral tribunal shall establish the procedural timetable that it intends to follow for the efficient conduct of the arbitration. The procedural timetable and any modifications thereto shall be communicated to the Court and the parties.
3. To ensure continued effective case management, the arbitral tribunal, after consulting the parties by means of a further case management conference or otherwise, may adopt further procedural measures or modify the procedural timetable.
4. Case management conferences may be conducted through a meeting in person, by video conference, telephone or similar means of communication. In the absence of an agreement of the parties, the arbitral tribunal shall determine the means by which the conference will be conducted. The

arbitral tribunal may request the parties to submit case management proposals in advance of a case management conference and may request the attendance at any case management conference of the parties in person or through an internal representative.

Article 25 Establishing the Facts of the Case

1. The arbitral tribunal shall proceed within as short a time as possible to establish the facts of the case by all appropriate means.
2. The arbitral tribunal may decide to hear witnesses, experts appointed by the parties or any other person, in the presence of the parties, or in their absence provided they have been duly summoned.
3. The arbitral tribunal, after consulting the parties, may appoint one or more experts, define their terms of reference and receive their reports. At the request of a party, the parties shall be given the opportunity to question at a hearing any such expert.
4. At any time during the proceedings, the arbitral tribunal may summon any party to provide additional evidence.
5. The arbitral tribunal may decide the case solely on the documents submitted by the parties unless any of the parties requests a hearing.

Article 26 Hearings

1. A hearing shall be held if any of the parties so requests or, failing such a request, if the arbitral tribunal on its own motion decides to hear the parties. When a hearing is to be held, the arbitral tribunal, giving reasonable notice, shall summon the parties to appear before it on the day and at the place fixed by it. The arbitral tribunal may decide, after consulting the parties, and on the basis of the relevant facts and circumstances of the case, that any hearing will be conducted by physical attendance or remotely by videoconference, telephone or other appropriate means of communication.
2. If any of the parties, although duly summoned, fails to appear without valid excuse, the arbitral tribunal shall have the power to proceed with the hearing.
3. The arbitral tribunal shall be in full charge of the hearings, at which all the parties shall be entitled to be present. Save with the approval of the arbitral tribunal and the parties, persons not involved in the proceedings shall not be admitted.
4. The parties may appear in person or through duly authorized representatives. In addition, they may be assisted by advisers.

Article 27 Closing of the Proceedings and Date for Submission of Draft Awards

As soon as possible after the last hearing concerning matters to be decided in an award or the filing of the last authorized submissions concerning such matters, whichever is later, the arbitral tribunal shall:

(a) declare the proceedings closed with respect to the matters to be decided in the award; and

(b) inform the Secretariat and the parties of the date by which it expects to submit its draft award to the Court for approval pursuant to Article 34.

After the proceedings are closed, no further submission or argument may be made, or evidence produced, with respect to the matters to be decided in the award, unless requested or authorized by the arbitral tribunal.

Article 28 Conservatory and Interim Measures

1. Unless the parties have otherwise agreed, as soon as the file has been transmitted to it, the arbitral tribunal may, at the request of a party, order any interim or conservatory measure it deems appropriate. The arbitral tribunal may make the granting of any such measure subject to appropriate security being furnished by the requesting party. Any such measure shall take the form of an order, giving reasons, or of an award, as the arbitral tribunal considers appropriate.

2. Before the file is transmitted to the arbitral tribunal, and in appropriate circumstances even thereafter, the parties may apply to any competent judicial authority for interim or conservatory measures. The application of a party to a judicial authority for such measures or for the implementation of any such measures ordered by an arbitral tribunal shall not be deemed to be an infringement or a waiver of the arbitration agreement and shall not affect the relevant powers reserved to the arbitral tribunal. Any such application and any measures taken by the judicial authority must be notified without delay to the Secretariat. The Secretariat shall inform the arbitral tribunal thereof.

Article 29 Emergency Arbitrator

1. A party that needs urgent interim or conservatory measures that cannot await the constitution of an arbitral tribunal ("Emergency Measures") may make an application for such measures pursuant to the Emergency Arbitrator Rules in Appendix V. Any such application shall be accepted only if it is received by the Secretariat prior to the transmission of the file to the arbitral tribunal pursuant to Article 16 and irrespective of whether the party making the application has already submitted its Request for Arbitration.

2. The emergency arbitrator's decision shall take the form of an order. The parties undertake to comply with any order made by the emergency arbitrator.

3. The emergency arbitrator's order shall not bind the arbitral tribunal with respect to any question, issue or dispute determined in the order. The arbitral tribunal may modify, terminate or annul the order or any modification thereto made by the emergency arbitrator.

4. The arbitral tribunal shall decide upon any party's requests or claims related to the emergency arbitrator proceedings, including the reallocation of the costs of such proceedings and any claims arising out of or in connection with the compliance or non- compliance with the order.

5. Articles 29(1)–29(4) and the Emergency Arbitrator Rules set forth in Appendix V (collectively the "Emergency Arbitrator Provisions") shall apply only to parties that are either signatories of the arbitration agreement under the Rules that is relied upon for the application or successors to such signatories.

6. The Emergency Arbitrator Provisions shall not apply if:

(a) the arbitration agreement under the Rules was concluded before 1 January 2012;

(b) the parties have agreed to opt out of the Emergency Arbitrator Provisions; or

(c) the arbitration agreement upon which the application is based arises from a treaty.

7. The Emergency Arbitrator Provisions are not intended to prevent any party from seeking urgent interim or conservatory measures from a competent judicial authority at any time prior to making an application for such measures, and in appropriate circumstances even thereafter, pursuant to the Rules. Any application for such measures from a competent judicial authority shall not be deemed to be an infringement or a waiver of the arbitration agreement. Any such application and any measures taken by the judicial authority must be notified without delay to the Secretariat.

Article 30 Expedited Procedure

1. By agreeing to arbitration under the Rules, the parties agree that this Article 30 and the Expedited Procedure Rules set forth in Appendix VI (collectively the "Expedited Procedure Provisions") shall take precedence over any contrary terms of the arbitration agreement.

2. The Expedited Procedure Rules set forth in Appendix VI shall apply if:

(a) the amount in dispute does not exceed the limit set out in Article 1(2) of Appendix VI at the time of the communication referred to in Article 1(3) of that Appendix; or

(b) the parties so agree.

3. The Expedited Procedure Provisions shall not apply if:

(a) the arbitration agreement under the Rules was concluded before the date on which the Expedited Procedure Provisions came into force;

(b) the parties have agreed to opt out of the Expedited Procedure Provisions; or
(c) the Court, upon the request of a party before the constitution of the arbitral tribunal or on its own motion, determines that it is inappropriate in the circumstances to apply the Expedited Procedure Provisions.

AWARDS

Article 31 Time Limit for the Final Award
1. The time limit within which the arbitral tribunal must render its final award is six months. Such time limit shall start to run from the date of the last signature by the arbitral tribunal or by the parties of the Terms of Reference or, in the case of application of Article 23(3), the date of the notification to the arbitral tribunal by the Secretariat of the approval of the Terms of Reference by the Court. The Court may fix a different time limit based upon the procedural timetable established pursuant to Article24(2).
2. The Court may extend the time limit pursuant to a reasoned request from the arbitral tribunal or on its own initiative if it decides it is necessary to do so.

Article 32 Making of the Award
1. When the arbitral tribunal is composed of more than one arbitrator, an award is made by a majority decision. If there is no majority, the award shall be made by the president of the arbitral tribunal alone.
2. The award shall state the reasons upon which it is based.
3. The award shall be deemed to be made at the place of the arbitration and on the date stated therein.

Article 33 Award by Consent
If the parties reach a settlement after the file has been transmitted to the arbitral tribunal in accordance with Article 16, the settlement shall be recorded in the form of an award made by consent of the parties, if so requested by the parties and if the arbitral tribunal agrees to do so.

Article 34 Scrutiny of the Award by the Court
Before signing any award, the arbitral tribunal shall submit it in draft form to the Court. The Court may lay down modifications as to the form of the award and, without affecting the arbitral tribunal's liberty of decision, may also draw its attention to points of substance. No award shall be rendered by the arbitral tribunal until it has been approved by the Court as to its form.

Article 35 Notification, Deposit and Enforceability of the Award
1. Once an award has been made, the Secretariat shall notify to the parties the text signed by the arbitral tribunal, provided always that the costs of the arbitration have been fully paid to ICC by the parties or by one of them.
2. Additional copies certified true by the Secretary General shall be made available on request and at any time to the parties, but to no one else.
3. By virtue of the notification made in accordance with Article 35(1), the parties waive any other form of notification or deposit on the part of the arbitral tribunal.
4. An original of each award made in accordance with the Rules shall be deposited with the Secretariat.
5. The arbitral tribunal and the Secretariat shall assist the parties in complying with whatever further formalities may be necessary.
6. Every award shall be binding on the parties. By submitting the dispute to arbitration under the Rules, the parties undertake to carry out any award without delay and shall be deemed to have waived their right to any form of recourse insofar as such waiver can validly be made.

Article 36 Correction and Interpretation of the Award; Additional Award; Remission of Awards

1. On its own initiative, the arbitral tribunal may correct a clerical, computational or typographical error, or any errors of similar nature contained in an award, provided such correction is submitted for approval to the Court within 30 days from notification of the award by the Secretariat pursuant to Article 35(1).

2. Any application of a party for the correction of an error of the kind referred to in Article 36(1), or for the interpretation of an award, must be made to the Secretariat within 30 days from receipt of the award by such party.

3. Any application of a party for an additional award as to claims made in the arbitral proceedings which the arbitral tribunal has omitted to decide must be made to the Secretariat within 30 days from receipt of the award by such party.

4. After transmission of an application pursuant to Articles 36(2) or 36(3) to the arbitral tribunal, the latter shall grant the other party or parties a short time limit, normally not exceeding 30 days, from receipt of the application by that party or parties, to submit any comments thereon. The arbitral tribunal shall submit its decision on the application in draft form to the Court not later than 30 days from expiry of the time limit for the receipt of any comments from the other party or parties or within such other period as the Court may decide. A decision to correct or to interpret the award shall take the form of an addendum and shall constitute part of the award. A decision to grant the application under paragraph 3 shall take the form of an additional award. The provisions of Articles 32, 34 and 35 shall apply mutatis mutandis.

5. Where a court remits an award to the arbitral tribunal, the provisions of Articles 32, 34, 35 and this Article 36 shall apply mutatis mutandis to any addendum or award made pursuant to the terms of such remission. The Court may take any steps as may be necessary to enable the arbitral tribunal to comply with the terms of such remission and may fix an advance to cover any additional fees and expenses of the arbitral tribunal and any additional ICC administrative expenses.

COSTS

Article 37 Advance to Cover the Costs of the Arbitration

1. After receipt of the Request, the Secretary General may request the claimant to pay a provisional advance in an amount intended to cover the costs of the arbitration

(a) until the Terms of Reference have been drawn up; or

(b) when the Expedited Procedure Provisions apply, until the case management conference.

Any provisional advance paid will be considered as a partial payment by the claimant of any advance on costs fixed by the Court pursuant to this Article 37.

2. As soon as practicable, the Court shall fix the advance on costs in an amount likely to cover the fees and expenses of the arbitrators, the ICC administrative expenses and any other expenses incurred by ICC related to the arbitration for the claims which have been referred to it by the parties, unless any claims are made under Article 7 or 8 in which case Article 37(4) shall apply. The advance on costs fixed by the Court pursuant to this Article 37(2) shall be payable in equal shares by the claimant and the respondent.

3. Where counterclaims are submitted by the respondent under Article 5 or otherwise, the Court may fix separate advances on costs for the claims and the counterclaims. When the Court has fixed separate advances on costs, each of the parties shall pay the advance on costs corresponding to its claims.

4. Where claims are made under Article 7 or 8, the Court shall fix one or more advances on costs that shall be payable by the parties as decided by the Court. Where the Court has previously fixed any advance on costs pursuant to this Article 37, any such advance shall be replaced by the advance(s) fixed pursuant to this Article 37(4), and the amount of any advance previously paid by any party will

be considered as a partial payment by such party of its share of the advance(s) on costs as fixed by the Court pursuant to this Article 37(4).
5. The amount of any advance on costs fixed by the Court pursuant to this Article 37 may be subject to readjustment at any time during the arbitration. In all cases, any party shall be free to pay any other party's share of any advance on costs should such other party fail to pay its share.
6. When a request for an advance on costs has not been complied with, and after consultation with the arbitral tribunal, the Secretary General may direct the arbitral tribunal to suspend its work and set a time limit, which must be not less than 15 days, on the expiry of which the relevant claims shall be considered as withdrawn. Should the party in question wish to object to this measure, it must make a request within the aforementioned period for the matter to be decided by the Court. Such party shall not be prevented, on the ground of such withdrawal, from reintroducing the same claims at a later date in another proceeding.
7. If one of the parties claims a right to a set-off with regard to any claim, such set-off shall be taken into account in determining the advance to cover the costs of the arbitration in the same way as a separate claim insofar as it may require the arbitral tribunal to consider additional matters.

Article 38 Decision as to the Costs of the Arbitration
1. The costs of the arbitration shall include the fees and expenses of the arbitrators and the ICC administrative expenses fixed by the Court, in accordance with the scales in force at the time of the commencement of the arbitration, as well as the fees and expenses of any experts appointed by the arbitral tribunal and the reasonable legal and other costs incurred by the parties for the arbitration.
2. The Court may fix the fees of the arbitrators at a figure higher or lower than that which would result from the application of the relevant scale should this be deemed necessary due to the exceptional circumstances of the case.
3. At any time during the arbitral proceedings, the arbitral tribunal may make decisions on costs, other than those to be fixed by the Court, and order payment.
4. The final award shall fix the costs of the arbitration and decide which of the parties shall bear them or in what proportion they shall be borne by the parties.
5. In making decisions as to costs, the arbitral tribunal may take into account such circumstances as it considers relevant, including the extent to which each party has conducted the arbitration in an expeditious and cost-effective manner.
6. In the event of the withdrawal of all claims or the termination of the arbitration before the rendering of a final award, the Court shall fix the fees and expenses of the arbitrators and the ICC administrative expenses. If the parties have not agreed upon the allocation of the costs of the arbitration or other relevant issues with respect to costs, such matters shall be decided by the arbitral tribunal. If the arbitral tribunal has not been constituted at the time of such withdrawal or termination, any party may request the Court to proceed with the constitution of the arbitral tribunal in accordance with the Rules so that the arbitral tribunal may make decisions as to costs.

MISCELLANEOUS

Article 39 Modified Time Limits
1. The parties may agree to shorten the various time limits set out in the Rules. Any such agreement entered into subsequent to the constitution of an arbitral tribunal shall become effective only upon the approval of the arbitral tribunal.
2. The Court, on its own initiative, may extend any time limit which has been modified pursuant to Article 39(1) if it decides that it is necessary to do so in order that the arbitral tribunal and the Court may fulfil their responsibilities in accordance with the Rules.

Article 40 Waiver
A party which proceeds with the arbitration without raising its objection to a failure to comply with any provision of the Rules, or of any other rules applicable to the proceedings, any direction given by the arbitral tribunal, or any requirement under the arbitration agreement relating to the constitution of the arbitral tribunal or the conduct of the proceedings, shall be deemed to have waived its right to object.

Article 41 Limitation of Liability
The arbitrators, any person appointed by the arbitral tribunal, the emergency arbitrator, the Court and its members, ICC and its employees, and the ICC National Committees and Groups and their employees and representatives shall not be liable to any person for any act or omission in connection with the arbitration, except to the extent such limitation of liability is prohibited by applicable law.

Article 42 General Rule
In all matters not expressly provided for in the Rules, the Court and the arbitral tribunal shall act in the spirit of the Rules and shall make every effort to make sure that the award is enforceable at law.

Article 43 Governing Law and Settlement of Disputes
Any claims arising out of or in connection with the administration of the arbitration proceedings by the Court under the Rules shall be governed by French law and settled by the Paris Judicial Tribunal (*Tribunal Judiciaire de Paris*) in France, which shall have exclusive jurisdiction.

APPENDIX I - STATUTES OF THE INTERNATIONAL COURT OF ARBITRATION

Article 1. Function
1. The function of the International Court of Arbitration of the International Chamber of Commerce (the "Court") is to ensure the application of the Rules of Arbitration of ICC, and it has all the necessary powers for that purpose.
2. As an autonomous body, it carries out these functions in complete independence from ICC and its organs.
3. Its members are independent from the ICC National Committees and Groups.

Article 2. Composition of the Court
The Court shall consist of a President, Vice-Presidents, and members and alternate members (collectively designated as members). In its work it is assisted by its Secretariat (Secretariat of the Court).

Article 3. Appointment
1. The President is elected by the ICC World Council upon the recommendation of the Executive Board of ICC based on the proposal of an independent selection committee which includes highly distinguished arbitration practitioners.
2. On the proposal of the President, the ICC World Council appoints the Vice-Presidents of the Court from among the members of the Court or otherwise. The President and the Vice-Presidents of the Court form the Bureau of the Court.
3. The members of the Court are appointed by the ICC World Council on the proposal of ICC National Committees or Groups, one member for each National Committee or Group. On the proposal of the President, the World Council may appoint alternate members.

4. On the proposal of the President, the ICC World Council may appoint members and alternate members in countries and territories:

a) where there is no National Committee or Group; or

b) where the National Committee or Group is suspended.

5. The term of office of all members, including, for the purposes of this paragraph, the President and Vice- Presidents, is three years and may be renewed once. If a member is no longer in a position to exercise the member's functions, a successor is appointed by the World Council for the remainder of the term.

6. No Court member shall serve for more than two full consecutive terms, unless the World Council decides otherwise upon the recommendation of the Executive Board further to the proposal of the President, in particular where a Court member is proposed for election as Vice-President.

Article 4. Committees

1. Save as provided in Articles 5(1), 6 and 7 of this Appendix, the Court conducts its work in Committees of three members.

2.Members of the Committees consist of a president and two other members.

Article 5. Special Committees

1. The Court may conduct its work in Special Committees:

a) to decide on matters under Articles 14 and 15(2) of the Rules;

b) to scrutinise draft awards in the presence of dissenting opinions;

c) to scrutinise draft awards in cases where one or more of the parties is a state or may be considered to be a state entity;

d) to decide on matters transferred to a Special Committee by a Committee which did not reach a decision or deemed it preferable to abstain, having made any suggestions it deemed appropriate; or

e) upon request of the President.

2. Members of the Special Committee consist of a president and at least six other members.

Article 6. Single-member Committees

The Court may scrutinize draft awards under the Expedited Procedure Provisions in Single-member Committees.

Article 7. Plenary of the Court

1. The Court meets in plenary during its annual working session. It also meets in plenary whenever so convened by the President.

2. The plenary of the Court may take any decision under Articles 4(1), 5(1) and 6 of this Appendix.

3. Members of the plenary consist of the President, the Vice-Presidents and all Court members who have accepted to attend and are in attendance.

Article 8. Confidentiality

The work of the Court is of a confidential nature which must be respected by everyone who participates in that work in whatever capacity. The Court lays down the rules regarding the persons who can attend the meetings of the Court and its Committees and who are entitled to have access to materials related to the work of the Court and its Secretariat.

Article 9. Modification of the Rules of Arbitration

Any proposal of the Court for a modification of the Rules is laid before the Commission on Arbitration and ADR before submission to the Executive Board of ICC for approval, provided, however, that the

Court, in order to take account of developments in information technology, may propose to modify or supplement the provisions of Article 3 of the Rules or any related provisions in the Rules without laying any such proposal before the Commission.

Article 10.
The decisions of the Court shall be deemed to be made in Paris, France.

APPENDIX II - INTERNAL RULES OF THE INTERNATIONAL COURT OF ARBITRATION

Article 1. Confidential Character of the Work of the International Court of Arbitration
1. For the purposes of this Appendix, members of the Court include the President and Vice-Presidents of the Court.
2. The sessions of the Court are open only to its members and to the Secretariat.
3. However, in exceptional circumstances, the President of the Court may invite other persons to attend. Such persons must respect the confidential nature of the work of the Court.
4.The documents submitted to the Court, or drawn up by it or the Secretariat in the course of the Court's proceedings, are communicated only to the members of the Court, to the Secretariat and to persons authorized by the President to attend Court sessions.
5. The President or the Secretary General of the Court may authorize researchers undertaking work of an academic nature to acquaint themselves with awards and other documents of general interest, with the exception of memoranda, notes, statements and documents remitted by the parties within the framework of arbitration proceedings.
6. Such authorization shall not be given unless the beneficiary has undertaken to respect the confidential character of the documents made available and to refrain from publishing anything based upon information contained therein without having previously submitted the text for approval to the Secretary General of the Court.
7. The Secretariat will in each case submitted to arbitration under the Rules retain in the archives of the Court all awards, Terms of Reference and decisions of the Court, as well as copies of the pertinent correspondence of the Secretariat.
8. Any documents, communications or correspondence submitted by the parties or the arbitrators may be destroyed unless a party or an arbitrator requests in writing within a period fixed by the Secretariat the return of such documents, communications or correspondence. All related costs and expenses for the return of those documents shall be paid by such party or arbitrator.

Article 2. Participation of Members of the International Court of Arbitration in ICC Arbitration
1. The President and the members of the Secretariat of the Court may not act as arbitrators or as counsel in cases submitted to ICC Arbitration.
2. The Court shall not appoint Vice-Presidents or members of the Court as arbitrators. They may, however, be proposed for such duties by one or more of the parties, or pursuant to any other procedure agreed upon by the parties, subject to confirmation.
3. When the President, a Vice-President or a member of the Court or of the Secretariat is involved in any capacity whatsoever in proceedings pending before the Court, such person must inform the Secretary General of the Court upon becoming aware of such involvement.
4. Such person must be absent from the Court session whenever the matter is considered by the Court and shall not participate in the discussions or in the decisions of the Court.
5. Such person will not receive any material documentation or information pertaining to such proceedings.

Article 3. Relations Between the Members of the Court and the ICC National Committees and Groups

1. By virtue of their capacity, the members of the Court are independent of the ICC National Committees and Groups which proposed them for appointment by the ICC World Council.
2. Furthermore, they must regard as confidential, vis- à-vis the said National Committees and Groups, any information concerning individual cases with which they have become acquainted in their capacity as members of the Court, except when they have been requested by the President of the Court, by a Vice-President of the Court authorized by the President of the Court, or by the Court's Secretary General to communicate specific information to their respective National Committees or Groups.

Article 4. Constitution, Quorum and Decision-Making

1. The members of Committees, Special Committees and Single-member Committees are appointed by the President from among the Vice-Presidents or the other members of the Court. In the President's absence or otherwise where the President is unable to act, they are appointed by a Vice-President at the request of the Secretary General or the Deputy Secretary General of the Court.
2. Committees and Special Committees meet whenever convened by their president.
3. The President of the Court acts as the president of the Committee, the Special Committee and the plenary. A Vice-President of the Court may act as president of a Committee, Special Committee or the plenary (i) at the request of the President or (ii) in the President's absence or otherwise where the President is unable to act, at the request of the Secretary General or the Deputy Secretary General of the Court. In exceptional circumstances, another member of the Court may act as president of a Committee or Special Committee following the same procedure.
4. The President of the Court, a Vice-President and any Court member may act in, and convene, the Single- member Committee.
5. Decisions on the constitution of Committees, Special Committees and Single-member Committees are reported to the Court at one of its next sessions.
6. Deliberations shall be valid:
   a) At the Committee, when at least two members are present.
   b) At the Special Committee and plenary, when at least six members, and the President or designated Vice-President, are present.
7. Decisions at Committees are taken unanimously. When a Committee cannot reach a unanimous decision or deems it preferable to abstain, it transfers the case to a Special Committee, making any suggestions it deems appropriate.
8. Decisions at Special Committees and the plenary are taken by majority, the President or Vice-President, as the case may be, having a casting vote in the event of a tie.

Article 5. Communication of Reasons of Decisions

1. Upon request of any party, the Court will communicate the reasons for Articles 6(4), 10, 12(8), 1.2(9), 14 and 15(2).
2. Any request for the communications of reasons must be made in advance of the decision in respect of which reasons are sought. For decisions pursuant to Article 15(2), a party shall address its request to the Court when invited to comment pursuant to Article 15(3).
3. In exceptional circumstances, the Court may decide not to communicate the reasons for any of the above decisions.

Article 6. Court Secretariat

1. In the Secretary General's absence or otherwise at the Secretary General's request, the Deputy Secretary General and/or the General Counsel shall have the authority to refer matters to the Court, confirm arbitrators, certify true copies of awards, request the payment of a provisional advance and

authorize the payment of advances in instalments, respectively provided for in Articles 6(3), 13(2), 35(2) and 37(1) of the Rules and Article 1(6) of Appendix III, as well as to take the measure provided for in Article 37(6).
2. The Secretariat may, with the approval of the Court, issue notes and other documents for the information of the parties and the arbitrators, or as necessary for the proper conduct of the arbitral proceedings.
3. Offices of the Secretariat may be established outside the headquarters of ICC. The Secretariat shall keep a list of offices designated by the Secretary General. Requests for Arbitration may be submitted to the Secretariat at any of its offices, and the Secretariat's functions under the Rules may be carried out from any of its offices, as instructed by the Secretary General, Deputy Secretary General or General Counsel.

Article 7. Scrutiny of Arbitral Awards
When the Court scrutinizes draft awards in accordance with Article 34 of the Rules, it considers, to the extent practicable, the requirements of mandatory law at the place of the arbitration.

APPENDIX III - ARBITRATION COSTS AND FEES

Article 1. Advance on Costs
1. Each request to commence an arbitration pursuant to the Rules must be accompanied by a filing fee of US$ 5,000. Such payment is non-refundable and shall be credited to the claimant's portion of the advance on costs.
2. The provisional advance fixed by the Secretary General according to Article 37(1) of the Rules shall normally not exceed the amount obtained by adding together the ICC administrative expenses, the minimum of the fees (as set out in the scales hereinafter) based upon the amount of the claim and the expected reimbursable expenses of the arbitral tribunal incurred with respect to the drafting of the Terms of Reference or the holding of the case management conference. If such amount is not quantified, the provisional advance shall be fixed at the discretion of the Secretary General. Payment by the claimant shall be credited to its share of the advance on costs fixed by the Court.
3. In general, the arbitral tribunal shall, in accordance with Article 37(6) of the Rules, proceed only with respect to those claims or counterclaims in regard to which the whole of the advance on costs has been paid.
4. The advance on costs fixed by the Court according to Articles 37(2) or 37(4) of the Rules comprises the fees of the arbitrator or arbitrators (hereinafter referred to as "arbitrator"), any arbitration-related expenses of the arbitrator and the ICC administrative expenses.
5. Each party shall pay its share of the total advance on costs in cash. However, if a party's share of the advance on costs is greater than US$ 500,000 (the "Threshold Amount"), such party may post a bank guarantee for any amount above the Threshold Amount. The Court may modify the Threshold Amount at any time at its discretion.
6. The Secretary General may authorize the payment of advances on costs, or any party's share thereof, in instalments, subject to such conditions as the Court thinks fit.
7. A party that has already paid in full its share of the advance on costs fixed by the Court may, in accordance with Article 37(5) of the Rules, pay the unpaid portion of the advance owed by the defaulting party by posting a bank guarantee.
8. When the Court has fixed separate advances on costs pursuant to Article 37(3) of the Rules, the Secretariat shall invite each party to pay the amount of the advance corresponding to its respective claim(s).
9. When, as a result of the fixing of separate advances on costs, the separate advance fixed for the claim of either party exceeds one half of such global advance as was previously fixed (in respect of the same

claims and counterclaims that are the subject of separate advances), a bank guarantee may be posted to cover any such excess amount. In the event that the amount of the separate advance is subsequently increased, at least one half of the increase shall be paid in cash.
10. The Secretariat shall establish the terms governing all bank guarantees which the parties may post pursuant to the above provisions.
11. As provided in Article 37(5) of the Rules, the advance on costs may be subject to readjustment at any time during the arbitration, in particular to take into account fluctuations in the amount in dispute, changes in the amount of the estimated expenses of the arbitrator, or the evolving difficulty or complexity of arbitration proceedings.
12.Before any expertise ordered by the arbitral tribunal can be commenced, the parties, or one of them, shall pay an advance on costs fixed by the arbitral tribunal sufficient to cover the expected fees and expenses of the expert as determined by the arbitral tribunal. The arbitral tribunal shall be responsible for ensuring the payment by the parties of such fees and expenses.
13. The amounts paid as advances on costs do not yield interest for the parties or the arbitrator.

Article 2. Costs and Fees
1. Subject to Article 38(2) of the Rules, the Court shall fix the fees of the arbitrator in accordance with the scales hereinafter set out or, where the amount in dispute is not stated, at its discretion.
2. In setting the arbitrator's fees, the Court shall take into consideration the diligence and efficiency of the arbitrator, the time spent, the rapidity of the proceedings, the complexity of the dispute and the timeliness of the submission of the draft award, so as to arrive at a figure within the limits specified or, in exceptional circumstances (Article 38(2) of the Rules), at a figure higher or lower than those limits.
3. When a case is submitted to more than one arbitrator, the Court, at its discretion, shall have the right to increase the total fees up to a maximum which shall normally not exceed three times the fees of one arbitrator.
4. The arbitrator's fees and expenses shall be fixed exclusively by the Court as required by the Rules. Separate fee arrangements between the parties and the arbitrator are contrary to the Rules.
5. The Court shall fix the ICC administrative expenses of each arbitration in accordance with the scales hereinafter set out or, where the amount in dispute is not stated, at its discretion. Where the parties have agreed upon additional services, or in exceptional circumstances, the Court may fix the ICC administrative expenses at a lower or higher figure than that which would result from the application of such scale, provided that such expenses shall normally not exceed the maximum amount of the scale.
6. At any time during the arbitration, the Court may fix as payable a portion of the ICC administrative expenses corresponding to services that have already been performed by the Court and the Secretariat.
7. The Court may require the payment of administrative expenses in addition to those provided in the scale of administrative expenses as a condition for holding an arbitration in abeyance at the request of the parties or of one of them with the acquiescence of the other.
8. If an arbitration terminates before the rendering of a final award, the Court shall fix the fees and expenses of the arbitrators and the ICC administrative expenses at its discretion, taking into account the stage attained by the arbitral proceedings and any other relevant circumstances.
9. Any amount paid by the parties as an advance on costs exceeding the costs of the arbitration fixed by the Court shall be reimbursed to the parties having regard to the amounts paid.
10. In the case of an application under Articles 36(2) or 36(3) of the Rules, or of a remission pursuant to Article 36(5) of the Rules, the Court may fix an advance to cover additional fees and expenses of the arbitral tribunal and additional ICC administrative expenses and may make the transmission of such application to the arbitral tribunal subject to the prior cash payment in full to ICC of such advance. The Court shall fix at its discretion the costs of the procedure following an application or a

remission, which shall include any possible fees of the arbitrator and ICC administrative expenses, when approving the decision of the arbitral tribunal.

11. The Secretariat may require the payment of administrative expenses in addition to those provided in the scale of administrative expenses for any expenses arising in relation to a request pursuant to Article 35(5) of the Rules.

12. When an arbitration is preceded by proceedings under the ICC Mediation Rules, one half of the ICC administrative expenses paid for such proceedings shall be credited to the ICC administrative expenses of the arbitration.

13. Amounts paid to the arbitrator do not include any possible value added tax (VAT) or other taxes or charges and imposts applicable to the arbitrator's fees. Parties have a duty to pay any such taxes or charges; however, the recovery of any such charges or taxes is a matter solely between the arbitrator and the parties.

14. ICC administrative expenses do not include VAT, taxes, imposts or any other charges of a similar nature. They may be increased by the amount of VAT, taxes, imposts or any charges of a similar nature at the prevailing rate. Parties have a duty to pay any such charges pursuant to invoices issued by ICC.

Article 3. Scales of Administrative Expenses and Arbitrator's Fees

1. The scales of administrative expenses and arbitrator's fees set forth below shall be effective as of 1 January 2017 in respect of all arbitrations commenced on or after such date, irrespective of the version of the Rules applying to such arbitrations.

2. To calculate the ICC administrative expenses and the arbitrator's fees, the amounts calculated for each successive tranche of the amount in dispute must be added together, except that where the amount in dispute is over US$ 500 million, a flat amount of US$ 150,000 shall constitute the entirety of the ICC administrative expenses.

3. The scales of administrative expenses and arbitrator's fees for the expedited procedure set forth below shall be effective as of 1 March 2017 in respect of all arbitrations commenced on or after such date, irrespective of the version of the Rules applying to such arbitrations. When parties have agreed to the expedited procedure pursuant to Article 30(2), subparagraph b), the scales for the expedited procedure will apply.

4. All amounts fixed by the Court or pursuant to any of the appendices to the Rules are payable in US$ except where prohibited by law or decided otherwise by the Court, in which case ICC may apply a different scale and fee arrangement in another currency.

SCALES OF ADMINISTRATIVE EXPENSES AND ARBITRATOR'S FEES

Amount in dispute (in US Dollars)	Administrative expenses* (in US Dollars)
up to 50,000	5,000
from 50,001 to 100,000	5,000 + 1.53% of amt. over 50,000
from 100,001 to 200,000	5,765 + 2.72% of amt. over 100,000
from 200,001 to 500,000	8,485 + 2.25% of amt. over 200,000
from 500,001 to 1,000,000	15,235 + 1.62% of amt. over 500,000
from 1,000,001 to 2,000,000	23,335 + 0.788% of amt. over 1,000,000
from 2,000,001 to 5,000,000	31,215 + 0.46% of amt. over 2,000,000
from 5,000,001 to 10,000,000	45,015 + 0.25% of amt. over 5,000,000
from 10,000,001 to 30,000,000	57,515 + 0.10% of amt. over 10,000,000
from 30,000,001 to 50,000,000	77,515 + 0.09% of amt. over 30,000,000
from 50,000,001 to 80,000,000	95,515 + 0.01% of amt. over 50,000,000
from 80,000,001 to 500,000,000	98,515 + 0.0123% of amt. over 80,000,000
over 500,000,000	150,000
* Amounts excluding VAT.	

Amount in dispute (in US Dollars)	Arbitrator's Fees (in US Dollars)	
	Minimum	**Maximum**
up to 50,000	3,000	18.0200% of amount in dispute
from 50,001 to 100,000	3,000 + 2.6500% of amt. over 50,000	9,010 + 13.5680% of amt. over 50,000
from 100,001 to 200,000	4,325 + 1.4310% of amt. over 100,000	15,794 + 7.6850% of amt. over 100,000
from 200,001 to 500,000	5,756 + 1.3670% of amt. over 200,000	23,479 + 6.8370% of amt. over 200,000
from 500,001 to 1,000,000	9,857 + 0.9540% of amt. over 500,000	43,990 + 4.0280% of amt. over 500,000
from 1,000,001 to 2,000,000	14,627 + 0.6890% of amt. over 1,000,000	64,130 + 3.6040% of amt. over 1,000,000
from 2,000,001 to 5,000,000	21,517 + 0.3750% of amt. over 2,000,000	100,170 + 1.3910% of amt. over 2,000,000
from 5,000,001 to 10,000,000	32,767 + 0.1280% of amt. over 5,000,000	141,900 + 0.9100% of amt. over 5,000,000
from 10,000,001 to 30,000,000	39,167 + 0.0640% of amt. over 10,000,000	187,400 + 0.2410% of amt. over 10,000,000
from 30,000,001 to 50,000,000	51,967 + 0.0590% of amt. over 30,000,000	235,600 + 0.2280% of amt. over 30,000,000
from 50,000,001 to 80,000,000	63,767 + 0.0330% of amt. over 50,000,000	281,200 + 0.1570% of amt. over 50,000,000
from 80,000,001 to 100,000,000	73,667 + 0.0210% of amt. over 80,000,000	328,300 + 0.1150% of amt. over 80,000,000
from 100,000,001 to 500,000,000	77,867 + 0.0110% of amt. over 100,000,000	351,300 + 0.0580% of amt. over 100,000,000
over 500,000,000	121,867 + 0.0100% of amt. over 500,000,000	583,300 + 0.0400% of amt. over 500,000,000

SCALES OF ADMINISTRATIVE EXPENSES AND ARBITRATOR'S FEES FOR THE EXPEDITED PROCEDURE

Amount in dispute (in US Dollars)	Administrative expenses* (in US Dollars)
up to 50,000	5,000
from 50,001 to 100,000	5,000 + 1.53% of amt. over 50,000
from 100,001 to 200,000	5,765 + 2.72% of amt. over 100,000
from 200,001 to 500,000	8,485 + 2.25% of amt. over 200,000
from 500,001 to 1,000,000	15,235 + 1.62% of amt. over 500,000
from 1,000,001 to 2,000,000	23,335 + 0.788% of amt. over 1,000,000
from 2,000,001 to 5,000,000	31,215 + 0.46% of amt. over 2,000,000
from 5,000,001 to 10,000,000	45,015 + 0.25% of amt. over 5,000,000
from 10,000,001 to 30,000,000	57,515 + 0.10% of amt. over 10,000,000

Amount in dispute (in US Dollars)	Administrative expenses* (in US Dollars)
from 30,000,001 to 50,000,000	77,515 + 0.09% of amt. over 30,000,000
from 50,000,001 to 80,000,000	95,515 + 0.01% of amt. over 50,000,000
from 80,000,001 to 500,000,000	98,515 + 0.0123% of amt. over 80,000,000
over 500,000,000	150,000
* Amounts excluding VAT.	

Amount in dispute (in US Dollars)	Arbitrator's Fees (in US Dollars)	
	Minimum	Maximum
up to 50,000	2,400	14.4160% of amount in dispute
from 50,001 to 100,000	2,400 + 2.1200% of amt. over 50,000	7,208 + 10.8544% of amt. over 50,000
from 100,001 to 200,000	3,460 + 1.1448% of amt. over 100,000	12,635 + 6.1480% of amt. over 100,000
from 200,001 to 500,000	4,605 + 1.0936% of amt. over 200,000	18,783 + 5.4696% of amt. over 200,000
from 500,001 to 1,000,000	7,886 + 0.7632% of amt. over 500,000	35,192 + 3.2224% of amt. over 500,000
from 1,000,001 to 2,000,000	11,702 + 0.5512% of amt. over 1,000,000	51,304 + 2.8832% of amt. over 1,000,000
from 2,000,001 to 5,000,000	17,214 + 0.3000% of amt. over 2,000,000	80,136 + 1.1128% of amt. over 2,000,000
from 5,000,001 to 10,000,000	26,214 + 0.1024% of amt. over 5,000,000	113,520 + 0.7280% of amt. over 5,000,000
from 10,000,001 to 30,000,000	31,334 + 0.0512% of amt. over 10,000,000	149,920 + 0.1928% of amt. over 10,000,000
from 30,000,001 to 50,000,000	41,574 + 0.0472% of amt. over 30,000,000	188,480 + 0.1824% of amt. over 30,000,000
from 50,000,001 to 80,000,000	51,014 + 0.0264% of amt. over 50,000,000	224,960 + 0.1256% of amt. over 50,000,000
from 80,000,001 to 100,000,000	58,934 + 0.0168% of amt. over 80,000,000	262,640 + 0.0920% of amt. over 80,000,000
from 100,000,001 to 500,000,000	62,294 + 0.0088% of amt. over 100,000,000	281,040 + 0.0464% of amt. over 100,000,000
over 500,000,000	97,494 + 0.0080% of amt. over 500,000,000	466,640 + 0.0320% of amt. over 500,000,000

APPENDIX IV - CASE MANAGEMENT TECHNIQUES

The following are examples of case management techniques that can be used by the arbitral tribunal and the parties for controlling time and cost. Appropriate control of time and cost is important in all cases. In cases of low complexity and low value, it is particularly important to ensure that time and costs are proportionate to what is at stake in the dispute.

a) Bifurcating the proceedings or rendering one or more partial awards on key issues, when doing so may genuinely be expected to result in a more efficient resolution of the case.

b) Identifying issues that can be resolved by agreement between the parties or their experts.
c) Identifying issues to be decided solely on the basis of documents rather than through oral evidence or legal argument at a hearing.
d) Production of documentary evidence:
   (i) requiring the parties to produce with their submissions the documents on which they rely;
   (ii) avoiding requests for document production when appropriate in order to control time and cost;
   (iii) in those cases where requests for document production are considered appropriate, limiting such requests to documents or categories of documents that are relevant and material to the outcome of the case;
   (iv) establishing reasonable time limits for the production of documents;
   (v) using a schedule of document production to facilitate the resolution of issues in relation to the production of documents.
e) Limiting the length and scope of written submissions and written and oral witness evidence (both fact witnesses and experts) so as to avoid repetition and maintain a focus on key issues.
f) Using telephone or video conferencing for procedural and other hearings where attendance in person is not essential and use of IT that enables online communication among the parties, the arbitral tribunal and the Secretariat of the Court.
g) Organizing a pre-hearing conference with the arbitral tribunal at which arrangements for a hearing can be discussed and agreed and the arbitral tribunal can indicate to the parties issues on which it would like the parties to focus at the hearing.
h) Settlement of disputes:
   (i) encouraging the parties to consider settlement of all or part of the dispute either by negotiation or through any form of amicable dispute resolution methods such as, for example, mediation under the ICC Mediation Rules;
   (ii) where agreed between the parties and the arbitral tribunal, the arbitral tribunal may take steps to facilitate settlement of the dispute, provided that every effort is made to ensure that any subsequent award is enforceable at law.

Additional techniques are described in the ICC publication entitled "Controlling Time and Costs in Arbitration".

APPENDIX V - EMERGENCY ARBITRATOR RULES

Article 1. Application for Emergency Measures

1. A party wishing to have recourse to an emergency arbitrator pursuant to Article 29 of the Rules of Arbitration of ICC (the "Rules") shall submit its Application for Emergency Measures (the "Application") to the Secretariat at any of the offices specified in the Internal Rules of the Court in Appendix II to the Rules.
2. The Application shall be supplied in a number of copies sufficient to provide one copy for each party, plus one for the emergency arbitrator, and one for the Secretariat where the party submitting the Application requests transmission thereof by delivery against receipt, registered post or courier.
3. The Application shall contain the following information:
   a) the name in full, description, address and other contact details of each of the parties;
   b) the name in full, address and other contact details of any person(s) representing the applicant;
   c) a description of the circumstances giving rise to the Application and of the underlying dispute referred or to be referred to arbitration;
   d) a statement of the Emergency Measures sought;
   e) the reasons why the applicant needs urgent interim or conservatory measures that cannot await the constitution of an arbitral tribunal;

f) any relevant agreements and, in particular, the arbitration agreement;
g) any agreement as to the place of the arbitration, the applicable rules of law or the language of the arbitration;
h) proof of payment of the amount referred to in Article 7(1) of this Appendix; and
i) any Request for Arbitration and any other submissions in connection with the underlying dispute, which have been filed with the Secretariat by any of the parties to the emergency arbitrator proceedings prior to the making of the Application.

The Application may contain such other documents or information as the applicant considers appropriate or as may contribute to the efficient examination of the Application.
4. The Application shall be drawn up in the language of the arbitration if agreed upon by the parties or, in the absence of any such agreement, in the language of the arbitration agreement.
5. If and to the extent that the President of the Court (the "President") considers, on the basis of the information contained in the Application, that the Emergency Arbitrator Provisions apply with reference to Article 29(5) and Article 29(6) of the Rules, the Secretariat shall transmit a copy of the Application and the documents annexed thereto to the responding party. If and to the extent that the President considers otherwise, the Secretariat shall inform the parties that the emergency arbitrator proceedings shall not take place with respect to some or all of the parties and shall transmit a copy of the Application to them for information.
6. The President shall terminate the emergency arbitrator proceedings if a Request for Arbitration has not been received by the Secretariat from the applicant within 10 days from the Secretariat's receipt of the Application, unless the emergency arbitrator determines that a longer period of time is necessary.

Article 2. Appointment of the Emergency Arbitrator; Transmission of the File
1. The President shall appoint an emergency arbitrator within as short a time as possible, normally within two days from the Secretariat's receipt of the Application.
2. No emergency arbitrator shall be appointed after the file has been transmitted to the arbitral tribunal pursuant to Article 16 of the Rules. An emergency arbitrator appointed prior thereto shall retain the power to make an order within the time limit permitted by Article 6(4) of this Appendix.
3. Once the emergency arbitrator has been appointed, the Secretariat shall so notify the parties and shall transmit the file to the emergency arbitrator. Thereafter, all written communications from the parties shall be submitted directly to the emergency arbitrator with a copy to each other party and the Secretariat. A copy of any written communications from the emergency arbitrator to the parties shall be submitted to the Secretariat.
4. Every emergency arbitrator shall be and remain impartial and independent of the parties involved in the dispute.
5. Before being appointed, a prospective emergency arbitrator shall sign a statement of acceptance, availability, impartiality and independence. The Secretariat shall provide a copy of such statement to the parties.
6. An emergency arbitrator shall not act as an arbitrator in any arbitration relating to the dispute that gave rise to the Application.

Article 3. Challenge of an Emergency Arbitrator
1. A challenge against the emergency arbitrator must be made within three days from receipt by the party making the challenge of the notification of the appointment or from the date when that party was informed of the facts and circumstances on which the challenge is based if such date is subsequent to the receipt of such notification.
2. The challenge shall be decided by the Court after the Secretariat has afforded an opportunity for the emergency arbitrator and the other party or parties to provide comments in writing within a suitable period of time.

Article 4. Place of the Emergency Arbitrator Proceedings

1. If the parties have agreed upon the place of the arbitration, such place shall be the place of the emergency arbitrator proceedings. In the absence of such agreement, the President shall fix the place of the emergency arbitrator proceedings, without prejudice to the determination of the place of the arbitration pursuant to Article 18(1) of the Rules.
2. Any meetings with the emergency arbitrator may be conducted through a meeting in person at any location the emergency arbitrator considers appropriate or by video conference, telephone or similar means of communication.

Article 5. Proceedings

1. The emergency arbitrator shall establish a procedural timetable for the emergency arbitrator proceedings within as short a time as possible, normally within two days from the transmission of the file to the emergency arbitrator pursuant to Article 2(3) of this Appendix.
2. The emergency arbitrator shall conduct the proceedings in the manner which the emergency arbitrator considers to be appropriate, taking into account the nature and the urgency of the Application. In all cases, the emergency arbitrator shall act fairly and impartially and ensure that each party has a reasonable opportunity to present its case.

Article 6. Order

1. Pursuant to Article 29(2) of the Rules, the emergency arbitrator's decision shall take the form of an order (the "Order").
2. In the Order, the emergency arbitrator shall determine whether the Application is admissible pursuant to Article 29(1) of the Rules and whether the emergency arbitrator has jurisdiction to order Emergency Measures.
3. The Order shall be made in writing and shall state the reasons upon which it is based. It shall be dated and signed by the emergency arbitrator.
4. The Order shall be made no later than 15 days from the date on which the file was transmitted to the emergency arbitrator pursuant to Article 2(3) of this Appendix. The President may extend the time limit pursuant to a reasoned request from the emergency arbitrator or on the President's own initiative if the President decides it is necessary to do so.
5. Within the time limit established pursuant to Article 6(4) of this Appendix, the emergency arbitrator shall send the Order to the parties, with a copy to the Secretariat, by any of the means of communication permitted by Article 3(2) of the Rules that the emergency arbitrator considers will ensure prompt receipt.
6. The Order shall cease to be binding on the parties upon:
    a) the President's termination of the emergency arbitrator proceedings pursuant to Article 1(6) of this Appendix;
    b) the acceptance by the Court of a challenge against the emergency arbitrator pursuant to Article 3 of this Appendix;
    c) the arbitral tribunal's final award, unless the arbitral tribunal expressly decides otherwise; or
    d) the withdrawal of all claims or the termination of the arbitration before the rendering of a final award.
7. The emergency arbitrator may make the Order subject to such conditions as the emergency arbitrator thinks fit, including requiring the provision of appropriate security.
8. Upon a reasoned request by a party made prior to the transmission of the file to the arbitral tribunal pursuant to Article 16 of the Rules, the emergency arbitrator may modify, terminate or annul the Order.

Article 7. Costs of the Emergency Arbitrator Proceedings

1. The applicant must pay an amount of US$ 40,000, consisting of US$ 10,000 for ICC administrative expenses and US$ 30,000 for the emergency arbitrator's fees and expenses. Notwithstanding Article 1(5) of this Appendix, the Application shall not be notified until the payment of US$ 40,000 is received by the Secretariat.
2. The President may, at any time during the emergency arbitrator proceedings, decide to increase the emergency arbitrator's fees or the ICC administrative expenses taking into account, inter alia, the nature of the case and the nature and amount of work performed by the emergency arbitrator, the Court, the President and the Secretariat. If the party which submitted the Application fails to pay the increased costs within the time limit fixed by the Secretariat, the Application shall be considered as withdrawn.
3. The emergency arbitrator's Order shall fix the costs of the emergency arbitrator proceedings and decide which of the parties shall bear them or in what proportion they shall be borne by the parties.
4. The costs of the emergency arbitrator proceedings include the ICC administrative expenses, the emergency arbitrator's fees and expenses and the reasonable legal and other costs incurred by the parties for the emergency arbitrator proceedings.
5. In the event that the emergency arbitrator proceedings do not take place pursuant to Article 1(5) of this Appendix or are otherwise terminated prior to the making of an Order, the President shall determine the amount to be reimbursed to the applicant, if any. An amount of US$ 5,000 for ICC administrative expenses is non- refundable in all cases.

Article 8. General Rule

1. The President shall have the power to decide, at the President's discretion, all matters relating to the administration of the emergency arbitrator proceedings not expressly provided for in this Appendix.
2. In the President's absence or otherwise at the President's request, any of the Vice-Presidents of the Court shall have the power to take decisions on behalf of the President.
3. In all matters concerning emergency arbitrator proceedings not expressly provided for in this Appendix, the Court, the President and the emergency arbitrator shall act in the spirit of the Rules and this Appendix.

APPENDIX VI - EXPEDITED PROCEDURE RULES

Article 1. Application of the Expedited Procedure Rules

1. Insofar as Article 30 of the Rules of Arbitration of ICC (the "Rules") and this Appendix VI do not provide otherwise, the Rules shall apply to an arbitration under the Expedited Procedure Rules.
2. The amount referred to in Article 30(2), subparagraph a) of the Rules is:
   a) US$ 2,000,000 if the arbitration agreement under the Rules was concluded on or after 1 March 2017 and before 1 January 2021; or
   b) US$ 3,000,000 if the arbitration agreement under the Rules was concluded on or after 1 January 2021.
3. Upon receipt of the Answer to the Request pursuant to Article 5 of the Rules, or upon expiry of the time limit for the Answer or at any relevant time thereafter and subject to Article 30(3) of the Rules, the Secretariat will inform the parties that the Expedited Procedure Provisions shall apply in the case.
4. The Court may, at any time during the arbitral proceedings, on its own motion or upon the request of a party, and after consultation with the arbitral tribunal and the parties, decide that the Expedited Procedure Provisions shall no longer apply to the case. In such case, unless the Court considers that it is appropriate to replace and/or reconstitute the arbitral tribunal, the arbitral tribunal shall remain in place.

Article 2. Constitution of the Arbitral Tribunal

1. The Court may, notwithstanding any contrary provision of the arbitration agreement, appoint a sole arbitrator.

2. The parties may nominate the sole arbitrator within a time limit to be fixed by the Secretariat. In the absence of such nomination, the sole arbitrator shall be appointed by the Court within as short a time as possible.

Article 3. Proceedings

1. Article 23 of the Rules shall not apply to an arbitration under the Expedited Procedure Rules.

2. After the arbitral tribunal has been constituted, no party shall make new claims, unless it has been authorized to do so by the arbitral tribunal, which shall consider the nature of such new claims, the stage of the arbitration, any cost implications and any other relevant circumstances.

3. The case management conference convened pursuant to Article 24 of the Rules shall take place no later than 15 days from the date on which the file was transmitted to the arbitral tribunal. The Court may extend this time limit pursuant to a reasoned request from the arbitral tribunal or on its own initiative if it decides it is necessary to do so.

4. The arbitral tribunal shall have discretion to adopt such procedural measures as it considers appropriate. In particular, the arbitral tribunal may, after consultation with the parties, decide not to allow requests for document production or to limit the number, length and scope of written submissions and written witness evidence (both fact witnesses and experts).

5. The arbitral tribunal may, after consulting the parties, decide the dispute solely on the basis of the documents submitted by the parties, with no hearing and no examination of witnesses or experts.

Article 4. Award

1. The time limit within which the arbitral tribunal must render its final award is six months from the date of the case management conference. The Court may extend the time limit pursuant to Article 31(2) of the Rules.

2. The fees of the arbitral tribunal shall be fixed according to the scales of administrative expenses and arbitrator's fees for the expedited procedure set out in Appendix III.

Article 5. General Rule

In all matters concerning the expedited procedure not expressly provided for in this Appendix, the Court and the arbitral tribunal shall act in the spirit of the Rules and this Appendix.

9.4.4 The London Court of International Arbitration Rules ('LCIA') (2020)

Preamble

Where any agreement, submission or reference howsoever made or evidenced in writing (whether signed or not) provides in whatsoever manner for arbitration under the rules of or by the LCIA, the London Court of International Arbitration, the London Court of Arbitration or the London Court, the parties thereto shall be taken to have agreed in writing that any arbitration between them shall be conducted in accordance with the LCIA Rules or such amended rules as the LCIA may have adopted hereafter to take effect before the commencement of the arbitration and that such LCIA Rules form part of their agreement (collectively, the "Arbitration Agreement"). These LCIA Rules comprise this Preamble, the Articles and the Index, together with the Annex to the LCIA Rules and the Schedule of Costs as both from time to time may be separately amended by the LCIA (the "LCIA Rules").

Article 1 Request for Arbitration

1.1 Any party wishing to commence arbitration under the LCIA Rules (the "Claimant") shall deliver to the Registrar of the LCIA Court (the "Registrar") a written request for arbitration (the "Request"), containing or accompanied by:

- (i) the full name, nationality and all contact details (including email address, postal address and telephone number) of the Claimant for the purpose of receiving delivery of all documentation in the arbitration in accordance with Article 4; and the same particulars of the Claimant's authorised representatives (if any) and of all other parties to the arbitration;
- (ii) the full terms of the Arbitration Agreement (excepting the LCIA Rules) invoked by the Claimant to support its claim, together with a copy of any contractual or other documentation in which those terms are contained and to which the Claimant's claim relates;
- (iii) a statement briefly summarising the nature and circumstances of the dispute, its estimated monetary amount or value, the transaction(s) at issue and the claim advanced by the Claimant against any other party to the arbitration (each such other party being here separately described as a "Respondent");
- (iv) a statement of any procedural matters for the arbitration (such as the arbitral seat, the language(s) of the arbitration, the number of arbitrators, their qualifications and identities) upon which the parties have already agreed in writing or in respect of which the Claimant makes any proposal under the Arbitration Agreement;
- (v) if the Arbitration Agreement (or any other written agreement) howsoever calls for any form of party nomination of arbitrators, the full name, email address, postal address and telephone number of the Claimant's nominee;
- (vi) confirmation that the registration fee prescribed in the Schedule of Costs has been or is being paid to the LCIA, without actual receipt of which the Request shall be treated by the Registrar as not having been delivered and the arbitration as not having been commenced under the Arbitration Agreement; and
- (vii) confirmation that copies of the Request (including all accompanying documents) have been or are being delivered to all other parties to the arbitration in accordance with Article 4 by one or more means to be identified specifically in such confirmation, to be supported then or as soon as possible thereafter by documentary proof satisfactory to the LCIA Court of actual delivery (including the date of delivery) or, if actual delivery is demonstrated to be impossible to the LCIA Court's satisfaction, sufficient information as to any other effective form of notification.

1.2 A Claimant wishing to commence more than one arbitration under the LCIA Rules (whether against one or more Respondents and under one or more Arbitration Agreements) may serve a composite Request in respect of all such arbitrations, provided that the requirements of Article 1.1 are complied with to the satisfaction of the LCIA Court in respect of each arbitration. In particular, in any composite Request the Claimant must identify separately the estimated monetary amount or value in dispute, the transaction(s) at issue and the claim advanced by the Claimant against any other party in each arbitration. Each arbitration so commenced shall proceed separately and in accordance with the LCIA Rules, subject to the LCIA Court or the Arbitral Tribunal determining otherwise.

1.3 The Request (including all accompanying documents) shall be submitted to the Registrar in electronic form in accordance with Article 4.1.

1.4 The arbitration shall be treated as having commenced for all purposes on the date upon which the Request (including all accompanying documents) is received electronically by the Registrar (the "Commencement Date"), provided that the LCIA has received the registration fee. Where the registration fee is received subsequently the Commencement Date will be the date of the LCIA's actual receipt of the registration fee.

1.5 At any time after the Commencement Date but prior to the appointment of the Arbitral Tribunal the LCIA Court may allow a Claimant to supplement, modify or amend its Request to correct any error in computation, any clerical or typographical error, any ambiguity or any mistake of a similar nature, after giving the parties a reasonable opportunity to state their views and upon such terms as the LCIA Court may decide.

1.6 There may be one or more Claimants (whether or not jointly represented); and in such event, where appropriate, the term "Claimant" shall be so interpreted under the Arbitration Agreement.

Article 2 Response

2.1 Within 28 days of the Commencement Date, or such lesser or greater period to be determined by the LCIA Court upon application by any party or upon its own initiative (pursuant to Article 22.5), the Respondent shall deliver to the Registrar a written response to the Request (the "Response"), containing or accompanied by:

- (i) the Respondent's full name, nationality and all contact details (including email address, postal address and telephone number) for the purpose of receiving delivery of all documentation in the arbitration in accordance with Article 4 and the same particulars of its authorised representatives (if any);
- (ii) confirmation or denial of all or part of the claim advanced by the Claimant in the Request, including the Claimant's invocation of the Arbitration Agreement in support of its claim;
- (iii) if not full confirmation, a statement briefly summarising the nature and circumstances of the dispute, its estimated monetary amount or value, the transaction(s) at issue and the defence advanced by the Respondent, and also indicating any counterclaim advanced by the Respondent against any Claimant and any cross-claim against any other Respondent;
- (iv) a response to any statement of procedural matters for the arbitration contained in the Request under Article 1.1(iv), including the Respondent's own statement relating to the arbitral seat, the language(s) of the arbitration, the number of arbitrators, their qualifications and identities and any other procedural matter upon which the parties have already agreed in writing or in respect of which the Respondent makes any proposal under the Arbitration Agreement;
- (v) if the Arbitration Agreement (or any other written agreement) howsoever calls for party nomination of arbitrators, the full name, email address, postal address and telephone number of the Respondent's nominee; and
- (vi) confirmation that copies of the Response (including all accompanying documents) have been or are being delivered to all other parties to the arbitration in accordance with Article 4 by one or more means of delivery to be identified specifically in such confirmation, to be supported

then or as soon as possible thereafter by documentary proof satisfactory to the LCIA Court of actual delivery (including the date of delivery) or, if actual delivery is demonstrated to be impossible to the LCIA Court's satisfaction, sufficient information as to any other effective form of notification.

2.2 Where the Request is a composite Request, the Respondent may serve a composite Response in respect of all or any of the arbitrations, provided that the requirements of Article 2.1 are complied with to the satisfaction of the LCIA Court in respect of each arbitration to which the Response responds. In particular, in any composite Response the Respondent must identify separately the estimated monetary amount or value in dispute, the transaction(s) at issue and the defence, counterclaim or cross-claim advanced by the Respondent against any other party to each arbitration.

2.3 The Response (including all accompanying documents) shall be submitted to the Registrar in electronic form in accordance with Article 4.1.

2.4 Failure to nominate or propose any arbitrator candidate within the time for delivery of a Response or such other time period as is agreed by the parties shall constitute an irrevocable waiver of that party's opportunity to nominate or propose any arbitrator candidate. Failure to deliver any or any part of a Response within time or at all shall not (by itself) preclude the Respondent from denying any claim or from advancing any defence, counterclaim or cross-claim in the arbitration.

2.5 Subject to Article 2.4, at any time prior to the appointment of the Arbitral Tribunal the LCIA Court may allow a party to supplement, modify or amend its Response to correct any error in computation, any clerical or typographical error, any ambiguity or any mistake of a similar nature, after giving the parties a reasonable opportunity to state their views and upon such terms as the LCIA Court may decide.

2.6 There may be one or more Respondents (whether or not jointly represented); and in such event, where appropriate, the term "Respondent" shall be so interpreted under the Arbitration Agreement.

Article 3 LCIA Court and Registrar

3.1 The functions of the LCIA Court under the Arbitration Agreement shall be performed in its name by the President of the LCIA Court (or any of its Vice Presidents, Honorary Vice Presidents or former Vice Presidents) or by a division of three or more members of the LCIA Court appointed by its President or any Vice President (the "LCIA Court").

3.2 The functions of the Registrar under the Arbitration Agreement shall be performed under the supervision of the LCIA Court by the Registrar or any deputy Registrar.

3.3 All communications in the arbitration to the LCIA Court from any party, authorised representative of a party, arbitrator, tribunal secretary or expert to the Arbitral Tribunal shall be addressed to the Registrar. All such communications with the Registrar from any party or authorised representative of a party shall be copied to all other parties.

Article 4 Written Communications and Periods of Time

4.1 The Claimant shall submit the Request under Article 1.3 and the Respondent the Response under Article 2.3 in electronic form, either by email or other electronic means including via any electronic filing system operated by the LCIA. Prior written approval should be sought from the Registrar, acting on behalf of the LCIA Court, to submit the Request or the Response by any alternative method.

4.2 Save with the prior written approval or direction of the Arbitral Tribunal, or, prior to the constitution of the Arbitral Tribunal, the Registrar acting on behalf of the LCIA Court, any written communication in relation to the arbitration shall be delivered by email or any other electronic means of communication that provides a record of its transmission.

4.3 Delivery by email or other electronic means of communication shall be as agreed or designated by a party for the purpose of receiving any communication in regard to the Arbitration Agreement. Any written communication (including the Request and Response) delivered to such party by that electronic means shall be treated as having been received by such party. In the absence of such agreement or designation or order by the Arbitral Tribunal, if delivery by electronic means has been regularly used in the parties' previous dealings, any written communication (including the Request and Response) may be delivered to a party by that electronic means and shall be treated as having been received by such party, subject to the LCIA Court or the Arbitral Tribunal being informed of any reason why the communication will not actually be received by such party including electronic delivery failure notification. Notwithstanding the above, the LCIA Court or the Arbitral Tribunal may direct that any written communication be delivered to a party at any address and by any means it considers appropriate.

4.4 For the purpose of determining the commencement of any time limit, unless otherwise ordered by the Arbitral Tribunal or the Registrar acting on behalf of the LCIA Court, a written communication sent by electronic means shall be treated as having been received by a party on the day it is transmitted (such time to be determined by reference to the recipient's time zone). If delivery by any other means is permitted or directed under this Article 4, a written communication shall be treated as having been received by a party on the day it is delivered (such time to be determined by reference to the recipient's time zone).

4.5 For the purpose of determining compliance with a time limit, unless otherwise ordered by the Arbitral Tribunal or the Registrar acting on behalf of the LCIA Court, a written communication shall be treated as having been made by a party if transmitted or delivered prior to or on the date of the expiration of the time limit (such time to be determined by reference to the sender's time zone).

4.6 For the purpose of calculating a period of time, such period shall begin to run on the day following the day when a written communication is received by the addressee. If the last day of such period is an official holiday or non-business day at the place of that addressee (or the place of the party against whom the calculation of time applies), the period shall be extended until the first business day which follows that last day. Official holidays and non-business days occurring during the running of the period of time shall be included in calculating that period.

4.7 A party shall inform the Registrar, the Arbitral Tribunal and all other parties as soon as reasonably practical of any changes to its full name and contact details (including email address, postal address and telephone number) or to those of its authorised representatives.

Article 5 Formation of Arbitral Tribunal

5.1 The formation of the Arbitral Tribunal by the LCIA Court shall not be impeded by any controversy between the parties relating to the sufficiency of the Request or the Response. The LCIA Court may also proceed with the arbitration notwithstanding that the Request is incomplete or the Response is missing, late or incomplete.

5.2 The expression the "Arbitral Tribunal" includes a sole arbitrator (including, where appropriate, an Emergency Arbitrator) or all the arbitrators where more than one.

5.3 All arbitrators shall be and remain at all times impartial and independent of the parties; and none shall act in the arbitration as advocate for or authorised representative of any party. No arbitrator shall give advice to any party on the parties' dispute or the conduct or outcome of the arbitration.

5.4 Before appointment by the LCIA Court, each arbitrator candidate shall furnish to the Registrar (upon the latter's request) a brief written summary of his or her qualifications and professional positions (past and present); the candidate shall also agree in writing fee rates conforming to the Schedule of Costs; the candidate shall sign a written declaration stating: (i) whether there are any circumstances currently known to the candidate which are likely to give rise in the mind of any party to any justifiable doubts as to his or her impartiality or independence and, if so, specifying in full such circumstances in the declaration; and (ii) whether the candidate is ready, willing and able to devote sufficient time, diligence and industry to ensure the expeditious and efficient conduct of the arbitration. The candidate shall promptly furnish such agreement and declaration to the Registrar.

5.5 Each arbitrator shall assume a continuing duty, until the arbitration is finally concluded, forthwith to disclose in writing any circumstances becoming known to that arbitrator after the date of his or her written declaration (under Article 5.4) which are likely to give rise in the mind of any party to any justifiable doubts as to his or her impartiality or independence, to be delivered to the LCIA Court, any other members of the Arbitral Tribunal and all parties in the arbitration.

5.6 The LCIA Court shall appoint the Arbitral Tribunal promptly following delivery to the Registrar of the Response or, if no Response is received, promptly after 28 days from the Commencement Date (or such other lesser or greater period to be determined by the LCIA Court pursuant to Article 22.5).

5.7 No party or third person may appoint any arbitrator under the Arbitration Agreement: the LCIA Court alone is empowered to appoint arbitrators (albeit taking into account any written agreement or joint nomination by the parties or nomination by the other candidates or arbitrators).

5.8 A sole arbitrator shall be appointed unless the parties have agreed in writing otherwise or the LCIA Court determines that in the circumstances a three-member tribunal is appropriate (or, exceptionally, more than three).

5.9 The LCIA Court shall appoint arbitrators with due regard for any particular method or criteria of selection agreed in writing by the parties. The LCIA Court shall also take into account the transaction(s) at issue, the nature and circumstances of the dispute, its monetary amount or value, the location and languages of the parties, the number of parties and all other factors which it may consider relevant in the circumstances.

5.10 The President of the LCIA Court shall only be eligible to be appointed as an arbitrator if the parties agree in writing to nominate him or her as the sole or presiding arbitrator; and the Vice Presidents of the LCIA Court and the Chair of the LCIA Board of Directors (the latter being ex officio a member of the LCIA Court) shall only be eligible to be appointed as arbitrators if nominated in writing by a party or parties or by the other candidates or arbitrators – provided that no such nominee shall have taken or shall take thereafter any part in any function of the LCIA Court or LCIA relating to such arbitration.

Article 6 Nationality of Arbitrators and Parties

6.1 Upon request of the Registrar, the parties shall each inform the Registrar and all other parties of their nationality. Where the parties are of different nationalities, a sole arbitrator or the presiding arbitrator shall not have the same nationality as any party unless the parties who are not of the same nationality as the arbitrator candidate all agree in writing otherwise.

6.2 For the purposes of Article 6.1, in the case of a natural person, nationality shall mean citizenship, whether acquired by birth or naturalisation or other requirements of the nation concerned. In the case of a legal person, nationality shall mean the jurisdiction in which it is incorporated and has its seat of effective management. A legal person that is incorporated in one jurisdiction but has its seat of effective management in another shall be treated as a national of both jurisdictions. The nationality of a party that is a legal person shall be treated as including the nationalities of its controlling shareholders or interests.

6.3 A person who is a citizen of two or more States shall be treated as a national of each State; citizens of the European Union shall be treated as nationals of its different Member States and shall not be treated as having the same nationality; a citizen of a State's overseas territory shall be treated as a national of that territory and not of that State; and a legal person incorporated in a State's overseas territory shall be treated as such and not (by such fact alone) as a national of or a legal person incorporated in that State.

Article 7 Party and Other Nominations

7.1 If the parties have agreed howsoever that any arbitrator is to be appointed by one or more of them or by any third person (other than the LCIA Court), that agreement shall be treated under the Arbitration

Agreement as an agreement to nominate an arbitrator for all purposes. Such nominee may only be appointed by the LCIA Court as arbitrator subject to that nominee's compliance with Articles 5.3 to 5.5; and the LCIA Court shall refuse to appoint any nominee if it determines that the nominee is not so compliant or is otherwise unsuitable.

7.2 Where the parties have howsoever agreed that the Claimant or the Respondent or any third person (other than the LCIA Court) is to nominate an arbitrator and such nomination is not made within time (in the Request, Response or otherwise), the LCIA Court may appoint an arbitrator notwithstanding the absence of a nomination. The LCIA Court may, but shall not be obliged to, take into consideration any late nomination.

7.3 In the absence of written agreement between the Parties, no party may unilaterally nominate a sole arbitrator or presiding arbitrator.

Article 8 Three or More Parties

8.1 Where the Arbitration Agreement entitles each party howsoever to nominate an arbitrator, the parties to the dispute number more than two and such parties have not all agreed in writing that the disputant parties represent collectively two separate "sides" for the formation of the Arbitral Tribunal (as Claimants on one side and Respondents on the other side, each side nominating a single arbitrator), the LCIA Court shall appoint the Arbitral Tribunal without regard to any party's entitlement or nomination.

8.2 In such circumstances, the Arbitration Agreement shall be treated for all purposes as a written agreement by the parties for the nomination and appointment of the Arbitral Tribunal by the LCIA Court alone.

Article 9A Expedited Formation of Arbitral Tribunal

9.1 In the case of exceptional urgency, any party may apply to the LCIA Court for the expedited formation of the Arbitral Tribunal under Article 5.

9.2 Such an application shall be made to the Registrar in writing by electronic means, together with a copy of the Request (if made by a Claimant) or a copy of the Response (if made by a Respondent), and shall be delivered or notified forthwith to all other parties to the arbitration. The application shall set out the specific grounds for exceptional urgency requiring the expedited formation of the Arbitral Tribunal.

9.3 The LCIA Court shall determine the application as expeditiously as possible in the circumstances. If the application is granted, for the purpose of forming the Arbitral Tribunal the LCIA Court may set or abridge any period of time under the Arbitration Agreement or other agreement of the parties (pursuant to Article 22.5).

Article 9B Emergency Arbitrator

9.4 Subject always to Article 9.16 below, in the case of emergency at any time prior to the formation or expedited formation of the Arbitral Tribunal (under Articles 5 or 9A), any party may apply to the LCIA Court for the immediate appointment of a temporary sole arbitrator to conduct emergency proceedings pending the formation or expedited formation of the Arbitral Tribunal (the "Emergency Arbitrator").

9.5 Such an application shall be made to the Registrar in writing by electronic means, together with a copy of the Request (if made by a Claimant) or a copy of the Response (if made by a Respondent), delivered or notified forthwith to all other parties to the arbitration. The application shall set out, together with all relevant documentation: (i) the specific grounds for requiring, as an emergency, the appointment of an Emergency Arbitrator; and (ii) the specific claim, with reasons, for emergency relief. The application shall be accompanied by the applicant's written confirmation that the applicant has paid or is paying to the LCIA the Special Fee under Article 9B, without actual receipt of which the application shall be dismissed by the LCIA Court. The Special Fee shall be subject to the terms of the Schedule of Costs. Its amount is prescribed in the Schedule, covering the fees and expenses of the Emergency Arbitrator and the administrative charges and expenses of the LCIA, with additional charges (if any) of the LCIA Court. After the appointment of the Emergency Arbitrator, the amount of the Special Fee payable by the applicant may be increased by the LCIA Court in accordance with the Schedule. Save as provided in Section 5(vi) of the Schedule of Costs, Article 24 shall not apply to any Special Fee paid to the LCIA.

9.6 The LCIA Court shall determine the application as soon as possible in the circumstances. If the application is granted, an Emergency Arbitrator shall be appointed by the LCIA Court within three days of the Registrar's receipt of the application (or as soon as possible thereafter). Articles 5.1, 5.7, 5.9, 5.10, 6, 9C, 10 and 16.2 (last sentence) shall apply to such appointment. The Emergency Arbitrator shall comply with the requirements of Articles 5.3, 5.4 and (until the emergency proceedings are finally concluded) Article 5.5.

9.7 The Emergency Arbitrator may conduct the emergency proceedings in any manner determined by the Emergency Arbitrator to be appropriate in the circumstances, taking account of the nature of such emergency proceedings, the need to afford to each party, if possible, an opportunity to be consulted on the claim for emergency relief (whether or not it avails itself of such opportunity), the claim and reasons for emergency relief and the parties' further submissions (if any). The Emergency Arbitrator is not required to hold any hearing with the parties whether in person, or virtually by conference call, videoconference or using other communications technology and may decide the claim for emergency relief on available documentation. In the event of a hearing, which may consist of several part-hearings (as decided by the Emergency Arbitrator), Articles 16.3, 19.2, 19.3 and 19.4 shall apply.

9.8 The Emergency Arbitrator shall decide the claim for emergency relief as soon as possible, but no later than 14 days following the Emergency Arbitrator's appointment. This deadline may only be extended by the LCIA Court in exceptional circumstances (pursuant to Article 22.5) or by the written agreement of all parties to the emergency proceedings. The Emergency Arbitrator may make any order or award which the Arbitral Tribunal could make under the Arbitration Agreement; and, in addition, may make any order adjourning the consideration of all or any part of the claim for emergency relief to the proceedings conducted by the Arbitral Tribunal (when formed).

9.9 An order of the Emergency Arbitrator shall be made in writing, with reasons. An award of the Emergency Arbitrator shall comply with Article 26.2 and, when made, take effect as an award under Article 26.8 (subject to Articles 9.11 and 9.12). The Emergency Arbitrator shall be responsible for delivering any order or award to the Registrar, who shall transmit the same promptly to the parties by electronic means.

9.10 The Special Fee paid shall form a part of the Arbitration Costs under Article 28.1, the amount of which shall be determined by the LCIA Court. Any legal or other expenses incurred by any party during the emergency proceedings shall form a part of the Legal Costs under Article 28.3. The Emergency Arbitrator may determine the amount of the Legal Costs relating to the emergency proceedings and the proportions in which the parties shall bear the Legal Costs and the Arbitration Costs of the emergency proceedings. Alternatively, the Emergency Arbitrator may leave such determination of all or part of the costs of the emergency proceedings to be decided by the Arbitral Tribunal.

9.11 Any order or award of the Emergency Arbitrator (apart from any order adjourning to the Arbitral Tribunal, when formed, any part of the claim for emergency relief) may be confirmed, varied, discharged or revoked, in whole or in part, by order or award made by the Arbitral Tribunal upon application by any party or upon its own initiative.

9.12 Prior to the formation of the Arbitral Tribunal, the Emergency Arbitrator may, upon application by any party or upon its own initiative:

(i) confirm, vary, discharge or revoke, in whole or in part, any order of the Emergency Arbitrator and/or issue an additional order;

(ii) correct any error in computation, any clerical or typographical error, any ambiguity or any mistake of a similar nature in any award of the Emergency Arbitrator; and/or
(iii) make an additional award as to any claim for emergency relief presented in the emergency proceedings but not decided in any award of the Emergency Arbitrator.

9.13 Notwithstanding Article 9B, a party may apply to a competent state court or other legal authority for any interim or conservatory measures before the formation of the Arbitral Tribunal; and Article 9B shall not be treated as an alternative to or substitute for the exercise of such right. During the emergency proceedings, any application to and any order by such court or authority shall be communicated promptly in writing to the Emergency Arbitrator, the Registrar and all other parties.

9.14 Articles 3.3, 4, 13.1-13.4, 14.1-14.2, 14.5, 14A, 16, 17, 18, 22.3-22.4, 23, 24A, 25.1, 25.3, 28, 29, 30, 30A, 31 and 32 and the Annex shall apply to emergency proceedings. In addition to the provisions expressly set out there and in this Article 9B, the Emergency Arbitrator and the parties to the emergency proceedings shall also be guided by other provisions of the Arbitration Agreement, whilst recognising that several such provisions may not be fully applicable or appropriate to emergency proceedings. Wherever relevant, the LCIA Court may set or abridge any period of time under any such provisions (pursuant to Article 22.5).

9.15 The LCIA Court shall have the power to decide, at its discretion, all matters relating to the administration of the emergency proceedings not expressly provided for in this Article 9B.

9.16 Article 9B shall not apply if either: (i) the parties have concluded their arbitration agreement before 1 October 2014 and the parties have not agreed in writing to 'opt in' to Article 9B; or (ii) the parties have agreed in writing at any time to 'opt out' of Article 9B.

Article 9C Expedited Appointment of Replacement Arbitrator

9.17 Any party may apply to the LCIA Court to expedite the appointment of a replacement arbitrator under Article 11.

9.18 Such an application shall be made in writing to the Registrar by electronic means, delivered or notified forthwith to all other parties to the arbitration; and it shall set out the specific grounds requiring the expedited appointment of the replacement arbitrator.

9.19 The LCIA Court shall determine the application as expeditiously as possible in the circumstances. If the application is granted, for the purpose of expediting the appointment of the replacement arbitrator the LCIA Court may set or abridge any period of time in the Arbitration Agreement or any other agreement of the parties (pursuant to Article 22.5).

Article 10 Revocation and Challenges

10.1 The LCIA Court may revoke any arbitrator's appointment upon its own initiative, at the written request of all other members of the Arbitral Tribunal or upon a written challenge by any party if: (i) that arbitrator gives written notice to the LCIA Court of his or her intent to resign as arbitrator, to be copied to all parties and all other members of the Arbitral Tribunal (if any); (ii) that arbitrator falls seriously ill, refuses or becomes unable or unfit to act; or (iii) circumstances exist that give rise to justifiable doubts as to that arbitrator's impartiality or independence.

10.2 The LCIA Court may determine that an arbitrator is unfit to act under Article 10.1 if that arbitrator: (i) acts in deliberate violation of the Arbitration Agreement; (ii) does not act fairly or impartially as between the parties; or (iii) does not conduct or participate in the arbitration with reasonable efficiency, diligence and industry.

10.3 A party challenging an arbitrator under Article 10.1 shall, within 14 days of the formation of the Arbitral Tribunal or (if later) within 14 days of becoming aware of any grounds described in Article 10.1 or 10.2, deliver a written statement of the reasons for its challenge to the LCIA Court, the Arbitral Tribunal and all other parties. A party may challenge an arbitrator whom it has nominated, or in whose appointment it has participated, only for reasons of which it becomes aware after the appointment has been made by the LCIA Court.

10.4 If all other parties agree in writing to the challenge within 14 days of receipt of the written statement, the LCIA Court shall revoke that arbitrator's appointment (without reasons).

10.5 Unless the parties so agree or the challenged arbitrator resigns in writing within 14 days of receipt of the written statement, the LCIA Court shall decide the challenge. The LCIA Court may conduct the challenge proceedings in any manner it considers to be appropriate in the circumstances but shall in any event provide the other parties and the challenged arbitrator a reasonable opportunity to comment on the challenging party's written statement. The LCIA Court may require at any time further information and materials from the challenging party, the challenged arbitrator, other parties, any authorised representative of a party, other members of the Arbitral Tribunal and the tribunal secretary (if any).

10.6 The LCIA Court's decision shall be made in writing, with reasons; and a copy shall be transmitted by the Registrar to the parties, the challenged arbitrator and other members of the Arbitral Tribunal (if any). If the challenge is upheld, the LCIA Court shall revoke that arbitrator's appointment. A challenged arbitrator who resigns in writing prior to the LCIA Court's decision shall not be considered as having admitted any part of the written statement.

10.7 The LCIA Court shall determine the amount of fees and expenses (if any) to be paid for the former arbitrator's services, as it may consider appropriate in the circumstances. The LCIA Court may also determine whether, in what amount and to whom any party should pay all or any part of the costs of the challenge; and the LCIA Court may also refer all or any part of such costs to the later decision of the Arbitral Tribunal and/or the LCIA Court under Article 28.

Article 11 Nomination and Replacement

11.1 In the event that the LCIA Court determines that justifiable doubts exist as to any arbitrator candidate's suitability, independence or impartiality, or if a nominee declines appointment as arbitrator, or if an arbitrator is to be replaced for any reason, the LCIA Court may determine whether or not to follow the original nominating process for such arbitral appointment.

11.2 The LCIA Court may determine that any opportunity given to a party to make any re-nomination (under the Arbitration Agreement or otherwise) shall be waived if not exercised within 14 days (or such lesser or greater time as the LCIA Court may determine), after which the LCIA Court shall appoint the replacement arbitrator without such re-nomination.

11.3 Save for any award rendered, the Arbitral Tribunal (when reconstituted) shall determine whether, and if so to what extent, the previous proceedings in the arbitration shall stand.

Article 12 Majority Power to Continue Deliberations

12.1 Where an arbitrator without good cause refuses or persistently fails to participate in the deliberations of an Arbitral Tribunal, the remaining arbitrators jointly may give written notice of such refusal or failure to the LCIA Court, the parties and the absent arbitrator. In exceptional circumstances, the remaining arbitrators may decide to continue the arbitration (including the making of any award) notwithstanding the absence of that other arbitrator, subject to the written approval of the LCIA Court.

12.2 In deciding whether to continue the arbitration, the remaining arbitrators shall take into account the stage of the arbitration, any explanation made by or on behalf of the absent arbitrator for his or her refusal or failure to participate, the likely effect upon the legal recognition or enforceability of any award at the seat of the arbitration and such other matters as they consider appropriate in the circumstances. The reasons for such decision shall be stated in any award made by the remaining arbitrators without the participation of the absent arbitrator.

12.3 In the event that the remaining arbitrators decide at any time after giving written notice of such refusal or failure not to continue the arbitration without the participation of the absent arbitrator, the remaining arbitrators shall notify in writing the parties and the LCIA Court of such decision; and, in that event, the remaining arbitrators or any party may refer the matter to the LCIA Court for the revocation of the absent arbitrator's appointment and the appointment of a replacement arbitrator under Articles 10 and 11.

Article 13 Communications between Parties and Arbitral Tribunal

13.1 Following the formation of the Arbitral Tribunal, all communications shall take place directly between the Arbitral Tribunal and the parties (to be copied to the Registrar), unless the Arbitral Tribunal decides that communications should continue to be made through the Registrar.

13.2 Where the Registrar sends any written communication to one party on behalf of the Arbitral Tribunal or the LCIA Court, he or she shall send a copy to each of the other parties.

13.3 Where any party delivers to the Arbitral Tribunal any communication (including statements and documents under Article 15) it shall deliver a copy to each arbitrator, all other parties and the Registrar; and it shall confirm to the Arbitral Tribunal in writing that it has done or is doing so.

13.4 During the arbitration proceedings, no party shall deliberately initiate or attempt to initiate any unilateral contact relating to the arbitration or the parties' dispute with any member of the LCIA Court exercising any function in regard to the arbitration or, from the Arbitral Tribunal's formation onwards, any member of the Arbitral Tribunal or the tribunal secretary (if any), which has not been disclosed in writing prior to or shortly after the time of such contact to all other parties, all members of the Arbitral Tribunal and the Registrar. Notwithstanding Article 3.3, a party may, however, have unilateral contact with the Registrar regarding administrative matters.

13.5 Prior to the Arbitral Tribunal's formation, unless the parties agree otherwise in writing, any arbitrator, candidate or nominee who is required to participate in the selection of a presiding arbitrator may consult any party in order to obtain the views of that party as to the suitability of any candidate or nominee as presiding arbitrator, provided that such arbitrator, candidate or nominee promptly informs any other arbitrator, candidate or nominee involved in the selection process and the Registrar of such consultation.

Article 14 Conduct of Proceedings

14.1 Under the Arbitration Agreement, the Arbitral Tribunal's general duties at all times during the arbitration shall include:

(i) a duty to act fairly and impartially as between all parties, giving each a reasonable opportunity of putting its case and dealing with that of its opponent(s); and

(ii) a duty to adopt procedures suitable to the circumstances of the arbitration, avoiding unnecessary delay and expense, so as to provide a fair, efficient and expeditious means for the final resolution of the parties' dispute.

14.2 The Arbitral Tribunal shall have the widest discretion to discharge these general duties, subject to the mandatory provisions of any applicable law or any rules of law the Arbitral Tribunal may decide to be applicable; and at all times the parties shall do everything necessary in good faith for the fair, efficient and expeditious conduct of the arbitration, including the Arbitral Tribunal's discharge of its general duty.

14.3 The parties and the Arbitral Tribunal shall make contact (whether by a hearing in person or virtually by conference call, videoconference or using other communications technology or exchange of correspondence) as soon as practicable but no later than 21 days from receipt of the Registrar's written notification of the formation of the Arbitral Tribunal.

14.4 The parties may agree on joint proposals for the conduct of their arbitration for consideration by the Arbitral Tribunal.

14.5 Without prejudice to the generality of the Arbitral Tribunal's discretion, after giving the parties a reasonable opportunity to state their views, the Arbitral Tribunal may, subject to the LCIA Rules, make any procedural order it considers appropriate with regard to the fair, efficient and expeditious conduct of the arbitration.

14.6 The Arbitral Tribunal's power under Article 14.5 includes the making of any procedural order with a view to expediting the procedure to be adopted in the arbitration by:

(i) limiting the length or content of, or dispensing with, any written statement to be delivered under Article 15;
(ii) limiting the written and oral testimony of any witness in accordance with Article 20.4;
(iii) employing technology to enhance the efficiency and expeditious conduct of the arbitration (including any hearing);
(iv) deciding the stage of the arbitration at which any issue or issues shall be determined, and in what order, in accordance with Article 22.1(vii) below;
(v) dispensing with a hearing, subject always to Article 19;
(vi) exercising its powers of Early Determination under Article 22.1(viii);
(vii) setting an appropriate period of time for any stage of, or step to be taken in, the arbitration including with regard to the conduct of any hearing;
(viii) abridging any period of time in accordance with Article 22.1(ii); and
(ix) making any other order that the Arbitral Tribunal considers appropriate in the circumstances of the arbitration.

14.7 In the case of an Arbitral Tribunal other than a sole arbitrator, the presiding arbitrator, with the prior agreement of its other members and all parties, may make procedural decisions alone.

Article 14A Tribunal Secretary

14.8 Subject to Articles 14.9 to 14.15, and to any applicable law, an Arbitral Tribunal may obtain assistance from a tribunal secretary in relation to an arbitration. Under no circumstances may an Arbitral Tribunal delegate its decision-making function to a tribunal secretary. All tasks carried out by a tribunal secretary shall be carried out on behalf of, and under the supervision of, the Arbitral Tribunal which shall retain its responsibility to ensure that all tasks are performed to the standard required by the LCIA Rules.

14.9 Before assisting an Arbitral Tribunal, each tribunal secretary candidate shall sign a written declaration stating: (i) whether there are any circumstances currently known to the candidate which are likely to give rise in the mind of any party to any justifiable doubts as to his or her impartiality or independence and, if so, specifying in full such circumstances in the declaration; and (ii) whether the candidate is ready, willing and able to devote sufficient time, diligence and industry to ensure the expeditious and efficient conduct of the tasks to be performed by the tribunal secretary. The candidate shall furnish promptly such written declaration to the Arbitral Tribunal and to the Registrar.

14.10 An Arbitral Tribunal may only obtain assistance from a tribunal secretary once the tribunal secretary has been approved by all parties. A tribunal secretary is approved once:

(i) the parties have agreed the tasks that may be carried out by the tribunal secretary;
(ii) if an hourly rate is to be charged and the tribunal secretary is to be entitled to have expenses reimbursed, the parties have agreed to this hourly rate and entitlement to reimbursement;
(iii) the written declaration referred to in Article 14.9 has been provided to the parties; and
(iv) the parties have agreed to the particular person filling the role of tribunal secretary.

14.11 If additional tasks to those agreed under Article 14.10(i) are to be undertaken by the tribunal secretary, or the hourly rate to be charged by the tribunal secretary is to increase, the Arbitral Tribunal must obtain prior agreement from all parties.

14.12 A party will be deemed to have agreed to the matters set out in Articles 14.10 and 14.11 if that party has not objected within such reasonable time as is set by the Arbitral Tribunal.

14.13 Any fees charged by, or expenses reimbursed to, a tribunal secretary shall form a part of the Arbitration Costs determined by the LCIA Court (as to the amount of Arbitration Costs) under Article 28.1.

14.14 A tribunal secretary shall assume a continuing duty, until the arbitration is finally concluded, forthwith to disclose in writing any circumstances becoming known to that tribunal secretary after the date of his or her written declaration (under Article 14.9) which are likely to give rise in the mind of any party to any justifiable doubts as to his or her impartiality or independence, to be delivered to the LCIA Court, the Arbitral Tribunal and all parties in the arbitration.

14.15 A tribunal secretary may be removed by the Arbitral Tribunal at its discretion. Article 10 above shall also apply, with necessary changes, to any tribunal secretary.

Article 15 Written Stage of the Arbitration

15.1 Unless the parties have agreed or jointly proposed in writing otherwise or the Arbitral Tribunal should decide differently, the written stage of the arbitration and its procedural timetable shall be as set out in this Article 15.

15.2 Within 28 days of receipt of the Registrar's written notification of the Arbitral Tribunal's formation, the Claimant shall deliver to the Arbitral Tribunal and all other parties either: (i) its written election to have its Request treated as its Statement of Case complying with this Article 15.2; or (ii) its written Statement of Case setting out in sufficient detail the relevant facts and legal submissions on which it relies, together with the relief claimed against all other parties, and all documents relied upon.

15.3 Within 28 days of receipt of the Claimant's Statement of Case or the Claimant's election to treat the Request as its Statement of Case, the Respondent shall deliver to the Arbitral Tribunal and all other parties either: (i) its written election to have its Response treated as its Statement of Defence and (if applicable) Counterclaim complying with this Article 15.3; or (ii) its written Statement of Defence and (if applicable) Statement of Counterclaim setting out in sufficient detail the relevant facts and legal submissions on which it relies, together with the relief claimed against all other parties, and all documents relied upon.

15.4 Within 28 days of receipt of the Respondent's Statement of Defence and (if applicable) Statement of Counterclaim or the Respondent's election to treat the Response as its Statement of Defence and (if applicable) Counterclaim, the Claimant shall deliver to the Arbitral Tribunal and all other parties a written Statement of Reply which, where there is any counterclaim, shall also include a Statement of Defence to Counterclaim in the same manner required for a Statement of Defence, together with all documents relied upon.

15.5 If the Statement of Reply contains a Statement of Defence to Counterclaim, within 28 days of its receipt the Respondent shall deliver to the Arbitral Tribunal and all other parties its written Statement of Reply to the Defence to Counterclaim, together with all documents relied upon.

15.6 No party may submit any further written statement following the last of these Statements, unless otherwise ordered by the Arbitral Tribunal.

15.7 The Arbitral Tribunal may provide additional or alternative directions as to any part of the written stage of the arbitration, including but not limited to directions for:

(i) further written submissions;
(ii) written statements with respect to any party's cross-claims;
(iii) the service of written evidence from any fact or expert witness;
(iv) the service of any other form of written evidence; and
(v) the sequence, timing and composition of the written stage of the arbitration.

15.8 If the Respondent fails to submit a Statement of Defence or the Claimant a Statement of Defence to Counterclaim, or if at any time any party fails to avail itself of the opportunity to present its written case in the manner required under this Article 15 or as otherwise ordered by the Arbitral Tribunal, the Arbitral Tribunal may nevertheless proceed with the arbitration (with or without a hearing) and make one or more awards.

15.9 As soon as practicable following the written stage of the arbitration, the Arbitral Tribunal shall proceed in such manner as has been agreed in writing by the parties or pursuant to its authority under the Arbitration Agreement.

15.10 In any event, the Arbitral Tribunal shall seek to make its final award as soon as reasonably possible and shall endeavour to do so no later than three months following the last submission from the parties (whether made orally or in writing), in accordance with a timetable notified to the parties and the Registrar as soon as practicable (if necessary, as revised and re-notified from time to time). When the Arbitral Tribunal (not being a sole arbitrator) establishes a time for what it contemplates shall be the last submission from the parties (whether written or oral), it shall set aside adequate time for deliberations (whether in person or otherwise) as soon as possible after that last submission and notify the parties of the time it has set aside.

Article 16 Seat of Arbitration, Place(s) of Hearing and Applicable Law

16.1 The parties may agree in writing the seat (or legal place) of their arbitration at any time before the formation of the Arbitral Tribunal and, after such formation, with the prior written consent of the Arbitral Tribunal.

16.2 In default of any such agreement, the seat of the arbitration shall be London (England), unless and until the Arbitral Tribunal orders, in view of the circumstances and after having given the parties a reasonable opportunity to make written comments to the Arbitral Tribunal, that another arbitral seat is more appropriate. Such default seat shall not be considered as a relevant circumstance by the LCIA Court in appointing any arbitrator or Emergency Arbitrator under Articles 5, 9A, 9B, 9C and 11.

16.3 If any hearing is to be held in person, the Arbitral Tribunal may hold such hearing at any convenient geographical place in consultation with the parties. If the Arbitral Tribunal is to meet in person to hold its deliberations, it may do so at any geographical place of its own choice. If such place(s) should be elsewhere than the seat of the arbitration, or if any hearing or deliberation takes place otherwise than in person (in whole or in part), the arbitration shall nonetheless be treated for all purposes as an arbitration conducted at the arbitral seat and any order or award as having been made at that seat.

16.4 Subject to Article 16.5 below, the law applicable to the Arbitration Agreement and the arbitration shall be the law applicable at the seat of the arbitration, unless and to the extent that the parties have agreed in writing on the application of other laws or rules of law and such agreement is not prohibited by the law applicable at the arbitral seat.

16.5 Notwithstanding Article 16.4, the LCIA Rules shall be interpreted in accordance with the laws of England.

Article 17 Language(s) of Arbitration

17.1 The initial language of the arbitration (until the formation of the Arbitral Tribunal) shall be the language or prevailing language of the Arbitration Agreement, unless the parties have agreed in writing otherwise.

17.2 In the event that the Arbitration Agreement is written in more than one language of equal standing, the LCIA Court may, unless the Arbitration Agreement provides that the arbitration proceedings shall be conducted from the outset in more than one language, determine which of those languages shall be the initial language of the arbitration.

17.3 A non-participating or defaulting party shall have no cause for complaint if communications to and from the LCIA Court and Registrar are conducted in the initial language(s) of the arbitration or of the arbitral seat.

17.4 Following the formation of the Arbitral Tribunal, unless the parties have agreed upon the language or languages of the arbitration, the Arbitral Tribunal shall decide upon the language(s) of the arbitration after giving the parties a reasonable opportunity to make written comments and taking into account the initial language(s) of the arbitration and any other matter it may consider appropriate in the circumstances.

17.5 If any document is expressed in a language other than the language(s) of the arbitration and no translation of such document is submitted by the party relying upon the document, the Arbitral Tribunal may order or (if the Arbitral Tribunal has not been formed) the Registrar may request that party to submit a translation of all or any part of that document in any language(s) of the arbitration or of the arbitral seat.

Article 18 Authorised Representatives of a Party

18.1 Any party may be represented in the arbitration by one or more authorised representatives appearing by name before the Arbitral Tribunal.

18.2 Until the Arbitral Tribunal's formation, the Registrar may request from any party: (i) written proof of the authority granted by that party to any authorised representative designated in its Request or Response; and (ii) written confirmation of the names, email and postal addresses of all such party's authorised representatives in the arbitration. After its formation, at any time, the Arbitral Tribunal may order any party to provide similar proof or confirmation in any form it considers appropriate.

18.3 Following the Arbitral Tribunal's formation, any intended change or addition by a party to its authorised representatives shall be notified promptly in writing to all other parties, the Arbitral Tribunal, the tribunal secretary (if any) and the Registrar; and any such intended change or addition shall only take effect in the arbitration subject to the approval of the Arbitral Tribunal.

18.4 The Arbitral Tribunal may withhold approval of any intended change or addition to a party's authorised representatives where such change or addition could compromise the composition of the Arbitral Tribunal or the finality of any award (on the grounds of possible conflict of interest or other like impediment). In deciding whether to grant or withhold such approval, the Arbitral Tribunal shall have regard to the circumstances, including: the general principle that a party may be represented by an authorised representative chosen by that party, the stage which the arbitration has reached, the efficiency resulting from maintaining the composition of the Arbitral Tribunal (as constituted throughout the arbitration) and any likely wasted costs or loss of time resulting from such change or addition.

18.5 Each party shall ensure that all its authorised representatives appearing by name before the Arbitral Tribunal have agreed to comply with the general guidelines contained in the Annex to the LCIA Rules, as a condition of such representation. In permitting any authorised representative so to appear, a party shall thereby represent that the authorised representative has agreed to such compliance.

18.6 In the event of a complaint by one party against another party's authorised representative appearing by name before the Arbitral Tribunal (or of such complaint by the Arbitral Tribunal upon its own initiative), the Arbitral Tribunal may decide, after consulting the parties and granting that authorised representative a reasonable opportunity to answer the complaint, whether or not the authorised representative has violated the general guidelines. If such violation is found by the Arbitral Tribunal, the Arbitral Tribunal may order any or all of the following sanctions against the authorised representative: (i) a written reprimand; (ii) a written caution as to future conduct in the arbitration; and (iii) any other measure necessary to fulfil within the arbitration the general duties required of the Arbitral Tribunal under Articles 14.1(i) and (ii).

Article 19 Hearing(s)

19.1 Any party has the right to a hearing before the Arbitral Tribunal prior to any ruling of the Arbitral Tribunal on its jurisdiction and authority (pursuant to Article 23) or any award on the merits. The Arbitral Tribunal may itself decide that a hearing should be held at any stage, unless the parties have agreed in writing upon a documents-only arbitration. For these purposes, a hearing may consist of several part-hearings (as decided by the Arbitral Tribunal).

19.2 The Arbitral Tribunal shall organise the conduct of any hearing in advance, in consultation with the parties. The Arbitral Tribunal shall have the fullest authority under the Arbitration Agreement to establish the conduct of a hearing, including its date, duration, form, content, procedure, time-limits and geographical place (if applicable). As to form, a hearing may take place in person, or virtually by conference call, videoconference or using other communications technology with participants in one or more geographical places (or in a combined form). As to content, the Arbitral Tribunal may require the parties to address specific questions or issues arising from the parties' dispute. The Arbitral Tribunal may also limit the extent to which questions or issues are to be addressed.

19.3 The Arbitral Tribunal shall give to the parties reasonable notice in writing of any hearing.

19.4 All hearings shall be held in private, unless the parties agree otherwise in writing.

Article 20 Witnesses

20.1 The provisions of this Article 20 shall apply to any fact or expert witness on whose evidence a party relies.

20.2 Before any hearing, the Arbitral Tribunal may order any party to give written notice of the identity of each witness that party wishes to call (including rebuttal witnesses), as well as the subject matter of that witness's testimony, its content and its relevance to the issues in the arbitration.

20.3 Subject to any order otherwise by the Arbitral Tribunal, the testimony of a witness may be presented by a party in written form, either as a signed statement or like document.

20.4 The Arbitral Tribunal may decide the time, manner and form in which these written materials shall be exchanged between the parties and presented to the Arbitral Tribunal; and it may allow, refuse or limit the written and oral testimony of witnesses.

20.5 The Arbitral Tribunal and any party may request that a witness, on whose written testimony another party relies, should attend for oral questioning at a hearing before the Arbitral Tribunal. If the Arbitral Tribunal orders that other party to secure the attendance of that witness and the witness refuses or fails to attend the hearing without good cause, the Arbitral Tribunal may place such weight on the written testimony or exclude all or any part thereof altogether as it considers appropriate in the circumstances.

20.6 Subject to the mandatory provisions of any applicable law, rules of law and any order of the Arbitral Tribunal otherwise, it shall not be improper for any party or its authorised representatives to interview any potential witness for the purpose of presenting his or her testimony in written form to the Arbitral Tribunal or producing such person as an oral witness at any hearing.

20.7 Subject to any order by the Arbitral Tribunal otherwise, any individual intending to testify to the Arbitral Tribunal may be treated as a witness notwithstanding that the individual is a party to the arbitration or was, remains or has become an officer, employee, owner or shareholder of any party or is otherwise identified with any party.

20.8 Subject to the mandatory provisions of any applicable law, the Arbitral Tribunal shall be entitled (but not required) to administer any appropriate oath or affirmation to any witness at any hearing, prior to the oral testimony of that witness.

20.9 Any witness who gives oral testimony at a hearing before the Arbitral Tribunal may be questioned by each of the parties under the control of the Arbitral Tribunal. The Arbitral Tribunal may put questions at any stage of such testimony.

Article 21 Expert to Arbitral Tribunal

21.1 The Arbitral Tribunal, after consultation with the parties, may appoint one or more experts to report in writing to the Arbitral Tribunal and the parties on specific issues in the arbitration, as identified by the Arbitral Tribunal.

21.2 Any such expert shall be and remain impartial and independent of the parties; and he or she shall sign a written declaration to such effect, delivered to the Arbitral Tribunal and copied to all parties.

21.3 The Arbitral Tribunal may require any party at any time to give to such expert any relevant information or to provide access to any relevant documents, goods, samples, property, site or thing for inspection under that party's control on such terms as the Arbitral Tribunal thinks appropriate in the circumstances.

21.4 If any party so requests or the Arbitral Tribunal considers it necessary, the Arbitral Tribunal may order the expert, after delivery of the expert's written report, to attend a hearing at which the parties shall have a reasonable opportunity to question the expert on the report and to present witnesses in order to testify on relevant issues arising from the report. Articles 20.8 and 20.9 of the LCIA Rules shall apply, with necessary changes, to any expert to the Arbitral Tribunal.

21.5 The fees and expenses of any expert appointed by the Arbitral Tribunal under this Article 21 may be paid out of the Advance Payment for Costs payable by the parties under Article 24 and shall form part of the Arbitration Costs under Article 28.1.

Article 22 Additional Powers

22.1 The Arbitral Tribunal shall have the power, upon the application of any party or (save for sub-paragraph (x) below) upon its own initiative, but in either case only after giving the parties a reasonable opportunity to state their views and upon such terms (as to costs and otherwise) as the Arbitral Tribunal may decide:

(i) to allow a party to supplement, modify or amend any claim, defence, counterclaim, cross-claim, defence to counterclaim, defence to cross-claim and reply, including a Request, Response and any other written statement, submitted by such party;

(ii) to abridge or extend (even where the period of time has expired) any period of time prescribed under the Arbitration Agreement, any other agreement of the parties or any order made by the Arbitral Tribunal;

(iii) to conduct such enquiries as may appear to the Arbitral Tribunal to be necessary or expedient, including whether and to what extent the Arbitral Tribunal should itself take the initiative in identifying relevant issues and ascertaining relevant facts and the law(s) or rules of law applicable to the Arbitration Agreement, the arbitration and the merits of the parties' dispute;

(iv) to order any party to make any documents, goods, samples, property, site or thing under its control available for inspection by the Arbitral Tribunal, any other party, any expert to such party and any expert to the Tribunal;

(v) to order any party to produce to the Arbitral Tribunal and to other parties documents or copies of documents in their possession, custody or power which the Arbitral Tribunal decides to be relevant;

(vi) to decide whether or not to apply any strict rules of evidence (or any other rules) as to the admissibility, relevance or weight of any material tendered by a party on any issue of fact or expert opinion; and to decide the time, manner and form in which such material should be exchanged between the parties and presented to the Arbitral Tribunal;

(vii) to decide the stage of the arbitration at which any issue or issues shall be determined, in what order, and the procedure to be adopted at each stage in accordance with Article 14 above;

(viii) to determine that any claim, defence, counterclaim, cross-claim, defence to counterclaim or defence to cross-claim is manifestly outside the jurisdiction of the Arbitral Tribunal, or is inadmissible or manifestly without merit; and where appropriate to issue an order or award to that effect (an "Early Determination");

(ix) to order compliance with any legal obligation or payment of compensation for breach of any legal obligation or specific performance of any agreement (including any arbitration agreement or any contract relating to land);

(x) to allow one or more third persons to be joined in the arbitration as a party provided any such third person and the applicant party have consented expressly to such joinder in writing following the Commencement Date or (if earlier) in the Arbitration Agreement; and thereafter to make a single final award, or separate awards, in respect of all parties so implicated in the arbitration; and

(xi) to order the discontinuance of the arbitration if it appears to the Arbitral Tribunal that the arbitration has been abandoned by the parties or all claims and any counterclaims or cross-claims have been withdrawn by the parties, after giving the parties a reasonable opportunity to state their views.

22.2 By agreeing to arbitration under the Arbitration Agreement, the parties shall be treated as having agreed not to apply to any state court or other legal authority for any order available from the Arbitral Tribunal (if formed) under Article 22.1, except with the agreement in writing of all parties.

22.3 The Arbitral Tribunal shall decide the parties' dispute in accordance with the law(s) or rules of law chosen by the parties as applicable to the merits of their dispute. If and to the extent that the Arbitral Tribunal decides that the parties have made no such choice, the Arbitral Tribunal shall apply the law(s) or rules of law which it considers appropriate.

22.4 The Arbitral Tribunal shall only apply to the merits of the dispute principles deriving from "ex aequo et bono", "amiable composition" or "honourable engagement" where the parties have so agreed in writing.

22.5 Subject to any order of the Arbitral Tribunal under Article 22.1(ii), the LCIA Court may also set, abridge or extend any period of time under the Arbitration Agreement or other agreement of the parties (even where the period of time has expired).

22.6 Without prejudice to Article 22.1(xi), the LCIA Court may determine, after giving the parties a reasonable opportunity to state their views, that the arbitration shall be discontinued if it appears to the LCIA Court that the arbitration has been abandoned by the parties or all claims and any counterclaims or cross-claims have been withdrawn by the parties.

Article 22A Power to Order Consolidation/Concurrent Conduct of Arbitrations

22.7 The Arbitral Tribunal shall have the power to order with the approval of the LCIA Court, upon the application of any party, after giving all affected parties a reasonable opportunity to state their views and upon such terms (as to costs and otherwise) as the Arbitral Tribunal may decide:

(i) the consolidation of the arbitration with one or more other arbitrations into a single arbitration subject to the LCIA Rules where all the parties to the arbitrations to be consolidated so agree in writing;

(ii) the consolidation of the arbitration with one or more other arbitrations subject to the LCIA Rules and commenced under the same arbitration agreement or any compatible arbitration agreement(s) and either between the same disputing parties or arising out of the same transaction or series of related transactions, provided that no arbitral tribunal has yet been formed by the LCIA Court for such other arbitration(s) or, if already formed, that such arbitral tribunal(s) is(are) composed of the same arbitrators; and

(iii) that two or more arbitrations, subject to the LCIA Rules and commenced under the same arbitration agreement or any compatible arbitration agreement(s) and either between the same disputing parties or arising out of the same transaction or series of related transactions, shall be conducted concurrently where the same arbitral tribunal is constituted in respect of each arbitration.

22.8 Without prejudice to the generality of Article 22.7, the LCIA Court may:

(i) consolidate an arbitration with one or more other arbitrations into a single arbitration subject to the LCIA Rules where all the parties to the arbitrations to be consolidated so agree in writing; and

(ii) determine, after giving the parties a reasonable opportunity to state their views, that two or more arbitrations, subject to the LCIA Rules and commenced under the same arbitration agreement or any compatible arbitration agreement(s) and either between the same disputing parties or arising out of the same transaction or series of related transactions, shall be consolidated to form one single arbitration subject to the LCIA Rules, provided that no arbitral tribunal has yet been formed by the LCIA Court for any of the arbitrations to be consolidated.

Article 23 Jurisdiction and Authority

23.1 The Arbitral Tribunal shall have the power to rule upon its own jurisdiction and authority, including any objection to the initial or continuing existence, validity, effectiveness or scope of the Arbitration Agreement.

23.2 For that purpose, an arbitration clause which forms or was intended to form part of another agreement shall be treated as an arbitration agreement independent of that other agreement. A decision by the Arbitral Tribunal that such other agreement is non-existent, invalid or ineffective shall not entail (of itself) the non-existence, invalidity or ineffectiveness of the arbitration clause.

23.3 An objection by a Respondent that the Arbitral Tribunal does not have jurisdiction shall be raised as soon as possible but not later than the time for its Statement of Defence; and a like objection by any party responding to a counterclaim or cross-claim shall be raised as soon as possible but not later than the time for its Statement of Defence to Counterclaim or Cross-Claim. An objection that the Arbitral Tribunal is exceeding the scope of its authority shall be raised promptly after the Arbitral Tribunal has indicated its intention to act upon the matter alleged to lie beyond its authority. The Arbitral Tribunal may nevertheless admit an untimely objection as to its jurisdiction or authority if it considers the delay justified in the circumstances.

23.4 The Arbitral Tribunal may decide the objection to its jurisdiction or authority in an award as to jurisdiction or authority or later in an award on the merits, as it considers appropriate in the circumstances.

23.5 By agreeing to arbitration under the Arbitration Agreement, after the formation of the Arbitral Tribunal the parties shall be treated as having agreed not to apply to any state court or other legal authority for any relief regarding the Arbitral Tribunal's jurisdiction or authority, except (i) with the prior agreement in writing of all parties to the arbitration, or (ii) the prior authorisation of the Arbitral Tribunal, or (iii) following the latter's award on the objection to its jurisdiction or authority.

Article 24 Advance Payment for Costs

24.1 The LCIA Court may direct the parties, in such proportions and at such times as it thinks appropriate, to make one or more payments to the LCIA (the "Advance Payment for Costs") in order to secure payment of the Arbitration Costs under Article 28.1. Such payments by the parties may be applied by the LCIA to pay any item of such Arbitration Costs (including the LCIA's own fees and expenses) in accordance with the LCIA Rules.

24.2 The Advance Payment for Costs shall be the property of the LCIA, to be disbursed or otherwise applied by the LCIA in accordance with the LCIA Rules and invested having regard to the interests of the LCIA. The parties agree that the LCIA shall not act as trustee and its sole duty to the parties in respect of the Advance Payment for Costs shall be to act pursuant to these LCIA Rules.

24.3 In the event that, at the conclusion of the arbitration, the Advance Payment for Costs exceeds the total amount of the Arbitration Costs under Article 28.1, the excess amount shall be transferred by the LCIA to the parties in such proportions as the parties may agree in writing or, failing such agreement, in the same proportions and to the same parties as the Advance Payment for Costs was paid to the LCIA, subject to any order of the Arbitral Tribunal.

24.4 The LCIA will make reasonable attempts to contact the parties in order to arrange for the transfer of the excess amount, using the contact details provided to the LCIA during the proceedings. If a response is not received from a party so contacted within 30 days, the LCIA will provide that party with written notice of its intention to retain the excess amount. If no response is received within a further 60 days, the party will be deemed irrevocably to have waived any right to claim and/or receive the excess amount.

24.5 Save for exceptional circumstances, the Arbitral Tribunal should not proceed with the arbitration without having ascertained from the Registrar that the LCIA is or will be in requisite funds as regards outstanding and future Arbitration Costs.

24.6 In the event that a party fails or refuses to make any payment on account of the Arbitration Costs as directed by the LCIA Court, the LCIA Court may direct the other party or parties to effect a further Advance Payment for Costs in an equivalent amount to allow the arbitration to proceed (subject to any order or award on Arbitration Costs).

24.7 In such circumstances, the party effecting the further Advance Payment for Costs may request the Arbitral Tribunal to make an order or award in order to recover that amount as a debt immediately due and payable to that party by the defaulting party, together with any interest.

24.8 Failure by a claiming, counterclaiming or cross claiming party to make promptly and in full any required payment may be treated by the LCIA Court or the Arbitral Tribunal as a withdrawal from the arbitration of the claim, counterclaim or cross-claim respectively, thereby removing such claim, counterclaim or cross-claim (as the case may be) from the scope of the Arbitral Tribunal's jurisdiction under the Arbitration Agreement, subject to any terms decided by the LCIA Court or the Arbitral Tribunal as to the reinstatement of the claim, counterclaim or cross-claim in the event of subsequent payment by the claiming, counterclaiming or cross-claiming party. Such a withdrawal shall not preclude the claiming, counterclaiming or cross-claiming party from defending as a respondent any claim, counterclaim or cross-claim made by another party.

Article 24A Compliance

24.9 Any dealings between a party and the LCIA will be subject to any requirements applicable to that party or the LCIA relating to bribery, corruption, terrorist financing, fraud, tax evasion, money laundering and/or economic or trade sanctions ("Prohibited Activity"), and the LCIA will deal with any party on the understanding that it is complying with all such requirements.

24.10 The LCIA may refuse to act on any instruction and/or accept or make any payment if the LCIA determines (in its sole discretion and without the need to state any reasons) that doing so may involve Prohibited Activity, or breach any law, regulation, or other legal duty which applies to it, or that doing so might otherwise expose the LCIA to enforcement action or censure from any regulator or law enforcement agency.

24.11 The parties agree to provide the LCIA with any information and/or documents reasonably requested by the LCIA for the purpose of compliance with laws relating to Prohibited Activity. The LCIA may take any action it considers appropriate to comply with any applicable obligations relating to Prohibited Activity, including disclosure of any information and documents to courts, law enforcement agencies or regulatory authorities.

Article 25 Interim and Conservatory Measures

25.1 The Arbitral Tribunal shall have the power upon the application of any party, after giving all other parties a reasonable opportunity to respond to such application and upon such terms as the Arbitral Tribunal considers appropriate in the circumstances:

(i) to order any respondent party to a claim, counterclaim or cross-claim to provide security for all or part of the amount in dispute, by way of deposit or bank guarantee or in any other manner;

(ii) to order the preservation, storage, sale or other disposal of any monies, documents, goods, samples, property, site or thing under the control of any party and relating to the subject-matter of the arbitration; and

(iii) to order on a provisional basis, subject to a final decision in an award, any relief which the Arbitral Tribunal would have power to grant in an award, including the payment of money or the disposition of property as between any parties.

Such terms may include the provision by the applicant party of a cross-indemnity, secured in such manner as the Arbitral Tribunal considers appropriate, for any costs or losses incurred by the respondent party in complying with the Arbitral Tribunal's order. Any amount payable under such cross-indemnity and any consequential relief may be decided by the Arbitral Tribunal by one or more awards in the arbitration.

25.2 The Arbitral Tribunal shall have the power upon the application of a party, after giving all other parties a reasonable opportunity to respond to such application, to order any claiming, counterclaiming or cross-claiming party to provide or procure security for Legal Costs and Arbitration Costs by way of deposit or bank guarantee or in any other manner and upon such terms as the Arbitral Tribunal considers appropriate in the circumstances. Such terms may include the provision by the applicant of a cross-indemnity, itself secured in such manner as the Arbitral Tribunal considers appropriate, for any costs and losses incurred by such claimant, counterclaimant or cross-claimant in complying with the Arbitral Tribunal's order. Any amount payable under such cross-indemnity and any consequential relief may be decided by the Arbitral Tribunal by one or more awards in the arbitration. In the event that a claiming, counterclaiming or cross-claiming party does not comply with any order to provide security, the Arbitral Tribunal may stay that party's claims, counterclaims or cross-claims or dismiss them by an award.

25.3 A party may apply to a competent state court or other legal authority for interim or conservatory measures that the Arbitral Tribunal would have power to order under Article 25.1: (i) before the formation of the Arbitral Tribunal; and (ii) after the formation of the Arbitral Tribunal, in exceptional cases and with the Arbitral Tribunal's authorisation, until the final award. After the Commencement Date, any application and any order for such measures before the formation of the Arbitral Tribunal shall be communicated promptly in writing by the applicant party to the Registrar; after its formation, also to the Arbitral Tribunal; and in both cases also to all other parties.

25.4 By agreeing to arbitration under the Arbitration Agreement, the parties shall be taken to have agreed not to apply to any state court or other legal authority for any order for security for Legal Costs or Arbitration Costs.

Article 26 Award(s)

26.1 The Arbitral Tribunal may make separate awards on different issues at different times, including interim payments on account of any claim, counterclaim or cross-claim (including Legal and Arbitration Costs under Article 28). Such awards shall have the same status as any other award made by the Arbitral Tribunal.

26.2 The Arbitral Tribunal shall make any award in writing and, unless all parties agree in writing otherwise, shall state the reasons upon which such award is based. The award shall also state the date when the award is made and the seat of the arbitration; and it shall be signed by the Arbitral Tribunal or those of its members assenting to it. Unless the parties agree otherwise, or the Arbitral Tribunal or LCIA Court directs otherwise, any award may be signed electronically and/or in counterparts and assembled into a single instrument.

26.3 An award may be expressed in any currency, unless the parties have agreed otherwise.

26.4 Unless the parties have agreed otherwise, the Arbitral Tribunal may order that simple or compound interest shall be paid by any party on any sum awarded at such rates as the Arbitral Tribunal decides to be appropriate (without being bound by rates of interest practised by any state court or other legal authority) in respect of any period which the Arbitral Tribunal decides to be appropriate ending not later than the date upon which the award is complied with.

26.5 Where there is more than one arbitrator and the Arbitral Tribunal fails to agree on any issue, the arbitrators shall decide that issue by a majority. Failing a majority decision on any issue, the presiding arbitrator shall decide that issue.

26.6 If any arbitrator refuses or fails to sign an award, the signatures of the majority or (failing a majority) of the presiding arbitrator shall be sufficient, provided that the reason for any omitted signature is stated in the award by the majority or by the presiding arbitrator.

26.7 The sole or presiding arbitrator shall be responsible for delivering the award to the LCIA Court, which shall transmit to the parties the award authenticated by the Registrar as an LCIA award, provided that all Arbitration Costs have been paid in full to the LCIA in accordance with Articles 24 and 28. Such transmission may be made by any electronic means, and (if so requested by any party or if transmission by electronic means to a party is not possible) in paper form. In the event of any disparity between electronic and paper forms, the electronic form shall prevail.

26.8 Every award (including reasons for such award) shall be final and binding on the parties. The parties undertake to carry out any award immediately and without any delay (subject only to Article 27); and the parties also waive irrevocably their right to any form of appeal, review or recourse to any state court or other legal authority, insofar as such waiver shall not be prohibited under any applicable law.

26.9 In the event of any final settlement of the parties' dispute, the Arbitral Tribunal may decide to make an award recording the settlement if the parties jointly so request in writing (a "Consent Award"), provided always that such Consent Award shall contain an express statement on its face that it is an award made at the parties' joint request and with their consent. A Consent Award need not contain reasons or a determination in relation to the Arbitration Costs or Legal Costs. If the parties do not jointly request a Consent Award, on written confirmation by the parties to the LCIA Court that a final settlement has been reached, the Arbitral Tribunal shall be discharged and the arbitration proceedings concluded by the LCIA Court, subject to payment by the parties of any outstanding Arbitration Costs in accordance with Articles 24 and 28.

Article 27 Correction of Award(s) and Additional Award(s)

27.1 Within 28 days of receipt of any award, a party may by written notice to the Registrar (copied to all other parties) request the Arbitral Tribunal to correct in the award any error in computation, any clerical or typographical error, any ambiguity or any mistake of a similar nature. If, after consulting the parties, the Arbitral Tribunal considers the request to be justified, it shall make the correction by recording it in an addendum to the award within 28 days of receipt of the request. If, after consulting the parties, the Arbitral Tribunal does not consider the request to be justified it may nevertheless issue an addendum to the award dealing with the request, including any Arbitration Costs and Legal Costs related thereto.

27.2 The Arbitral Tribunal may also correct any error (including any error in computation, any clerical or typographical error, any ambiguity or any mistake of a similar nature) upon its own initiative in the form of an addendum to the award within 28 days of the date of the award, after consulting the parties.

27.3 Within 28 days of receipt of the final award, a party may by written notice to the Registrar (copied to all other parties), request the Arbitral Tribunal to make an additional award as to any claim, counterclaim or cross-claim presented in the arbitration but not decided in any award. If, after consulting the parties, the Arbitral Tribunal considers the request to be justified, it shall make the additional award within 56 days of receipt of the request. If, after consulting the parties, the Arbitral Tribunal does not consider the request to be justified it may nevertheless issue an addendum to the award dealing with the request, including any Arbitration Costs and Legal Costs related thereto.

27.4 As to any claim, counterclaim or cross-claim presented in the arbitration but not decided in any award, the Arbitral Tribunal may also make an additional award upon its own initiative within 28 days of the date of the award, after consulting the parties.

27.5 The provisions of Article 26.2 to 26.7 shall apply to any addendum to an award or additional award made hereunder. An addendum to an award shall be treated as part of the award.

Article 28 Arbitration Costs and Legal Costs

28.1 The costs of the arbitration other than the legal or other expenses incurred by the parties themselves (the "Arbitration Costs") shall be determined by the LCIA Court in accordance with the Schedule of Costs. The parties shall be jointly and severally liable to the LCIA and the Arbitral Tribunal for such Arbitration Costs.

28.2 The Arbitral Tribunal shall specify by an order or award the amount of the Arbitration Costs determined by the LCIA Court. The Arbitral Tribunal shall decide the proportions in which the parties shall bear such Arbitration Costs (in the absence of a final settlement of the parties' dispute regarding liability for such costs). If the Arbitral Tribunal has decided that all or any part of the Arbitration Costs shall be borne by a party other than a party which has already covered such costs by way of a payment to the LCIA under Article 24, the latter party shall have the right to recover the appropriate amount of Arbitration Costs from the former party.

28.3 The Arbitral Tribunal shall also have the power to decide by an order or award that all or part of the legal or other expenses incurred by a party (the "Legal Costs") be paid by another party. The Arbitral Tribunal shall decide the amount of such Legal Costs on such reasonable basis as it thinks appropriate. The Arbitral Tribunal shall not be required to apply the rates or procedures for assessing such costs practised by any state court or other legal authority.

28.4 The Arbitral Tribunal shall make its decisions on both Arbitration Costs and Legal Costs on the general principle that costs should reflect the parties' relative success and failure in the award or arbitration or under different issues, except where it appears to the Arbitral Tribunal that in the circumstances the application of such a general principle would be inappropriate under the Arbitration Agreement or otherwise. The Arbitral Tribunal may also take into account the conduct of the parties and that of their authorised representatives in the arbitration, including any cooperation in facilitating the proceedings as to time and cost and any non-cooperation resulting in undue delay and unnecessary expense. Any decision on costs by the Arbitral Tribunal shall be made with reasons in the order or award containing such decision (unless it is a Consent Award).

28.5 In the event that the parties have howsoever agreed before their dispute that one or more parties shall pay the whole or any part of the Arbitration Costs or Legal Costs whatever the result of any dispute, arbitration or award, such agreement (in order to be effective) shall be confirmed by the parties in writing after the Commencement Date.

28.6 If the arbitration is abandoned, suspended, withdrawn or concluded, by agreement or otherwise, before the final award is made, the parties shall remain jointly and severally liable to pay to the LCIA and the Arbitral Tribunal the Arbitration Costs determined by the LCIA Court.

Article 29 Determinations and Decisions by LCIA Court

29.1 The determinations of the LCIA Court with respect to all matters relating to the arbitration shall be conclusive and binding upon the parties and the Arbitral Tribunal, unless otherwise directed by the LCIA Court. Save for reasoned decisions on arbitral challenges under Article 10, such determinations are to be treated as administrative in nature; and the LCIA Court shall not be required to give reasons for any such determination.

29.2 To the extent permitted by any applicable law, the parties shall be taken to have waived any right of appeal or review in respect of any determination and decision of the LCIA Court to any state court or other legal authority. If such appeal or review takes place due to mandatory provisions of any applicable law or otherwise, the LCIA Court may determine whether or not the arbitration should continue, notwithstanding such appeal or review.

Article 30 Confidentiality

30.1 The parties undertake as a general principle to keep confidential all awards in the arbitration, together with all materials in the arbitration created for the purpose of the arbitration and all other documents produced by another party in the proceedings not otherwise in the public domain, save and to the extent that disclosure may be required of a party by legal duty, to protect or pursue a legal right, or to enforce or challenge an award in legal proceedings before a state court or other legal authority. The parties shall seek the same undertaking of confidentiality from all those that it involves in the arbitration, including but not limited to any authorised representative, witness of fact, expert or service provider.

30.2 Article 30.1 of the LCIA Rules shall also apply, with necessary changes, to the Arbitral Tribunal, any tribunal secretary and any expert to the Arbitral Tribunal. Notwithstanding any other provision of the LCIA Rules, the deliberations of the Arbitral Tribunal shall remain confidential to its members and if appropriate any tribunal secretary, save as required by any applicable law and to the extent that disclosure of an arbitrator's refusal to participate in the arbitration is required of the other members of the Arbitral Tribunal under Articles 10, 12, 26.6 and 27.5.

30.3 The LCIA does not publish any award or any part of an award without the prior written consent of all parties and the Arbitral Tribunal.

Article 30A Data Protection

30.4 Any processing of personal data by the LCIA is subject to applicable data protection legislation, and the LCIA's data protection notice can be found on the LCIA website.

30.5 In accordance with its duties under Article 14.1, at an early stage of the arbitration the Arbitral Tribunal shall, in consultation with the parties and where appropriate the LCIA, consider whether it is appropriate to adopt:

(i) any specific information security measures to protect the physical and electronic information shared in the arbitration; and

(ii) any means to address the processing of personal data produced or exchanged in the arbitration in light of applicable data protection or equivalent legislation.

30.6 The LCIA and the Arbitral Tribunal may issue directions addressing information security or data protection, which shall be binding on the parties, and in the case of those issued by the LCIA, also on the members of the Arbitral Tribunal, subject to the mandatory provisions of any applicable law or rules of law.

Article 31 Limitation of Liability and Jurisdiction Clause

31.1 None of the LCIA (including its officers, members and employees), the LCIA Court (including its President, Vice Presidents, Honorary Vice Presidents, former Vice Presidents and members), the LCIA Board (including any board member), the Registrar (including any deputy Registrar), any arbitrator, any Emergency Arbitrator, any tribunal secretary and any expert to the Arbitral Tribunal shall be liable to any party howsoever for any act or omission in connection with any arbitration, save: (i) where the act or omission is shown by that party to constitute conscious and deliberate wrongdoing committed by the body or person alleged to be liable to that party; or (ii) to the extent that any part of this provision is shown to be prohibited by any applicable law.

31.2 After the award has been made and all possibilities of any addendum to the award or additional award under Article 27 have lapsed or been exhausted, none of the LCIA (including its officers, members and employees), the LCIA Court (including its President, Vice Presidents, Honorary Vice Presidents, former Vice Presidents and members), the LCIA Board (including any board member), the Registrar (including any deputy Registrar), any arbitrator, any Emergency Arbitrator, any tribunal secretary and any expert to the Arbitral Tribunal shall be under any legal obligation to make any statement to any person about any matter concerning the arbitration; nor shall any party seek to make any of these bodies or persons a witness in any legal or other proceedings arising out of the arbitration.

31.3 Any party agreeing to arbitration under or in accordance with the LCIA Rules irrevocably agrees that the courts of England and Wales shall have exclusive jurisdiction to hear and decide any action, suit or proceedings between that party and the LCIA (including its officers, members and employees), the LCIA Court (including its President, Vice Presidents, Honorary Vice Presidents, former Vice Presidents and members), the LCIA Board (including any board member), the Registrar (including any deputy Registrar) any arbitrator, any Emergency Arbitrator, any tribunal secretary and/or any expert to the Arbitral Tribunal which may arise out of or in connection with any such arbitration and, for these purposes, each party irrevocably submits to the jurisdiction of the courts of England and Wales.

Article 32 General Rules

32.1 A party who knows that any provision of the Arbitration Agreement has not been complied with and yet proceeds with the arbitration without promptly stating its objection as to such non-compliance to the Registrar (before the formation of the Arbitral Tribunal) or the Arbitral Tribunal (after its formation), shall be treated as having irrevocably waived its right to object for all purposes.

32.2 For all matters not expressly provided in the Arbitration Agreement, the LCIA, the LCIA Court, the Registrar, the Arbitral Tribunal, any tribunal secretary and each of the parties shall act at all times in good faith, respecting the spirit of the Arbitration Agreement, and shall make every reasonable effort to ensure that any award is legally recognised and enforceable at the arbitral seat.

32.3 If and to the extent that any part of the Arbitration Agreement is decided by the Arbitral Tribunal, the Emergency Arbitrator, or any court or other legal authority of competent jurisdiction to be invalid, ineffective or unenforceable, such decision shall not, of itself, adversely affect any order or award by the Arbitral Tribunal or the Emergency Arbitrator or any other part of the Arbitration Agreement which shall remain in full force and effect, unless prohibited by any applicable law.

Index (in alphabetical order)

Advance Payment for Costs:	see Article 24.1;
Arbitral Tribunal:	see Article 5.2;
Arbitration Agreement:	see Preamble;
Arbitration Costs:	see Articles 9.10 & 28.1;
Authorised Representative(s):	see Articles 1.1(i), 2.1(i), 18.1, 18.3, 18.4 & Annex;
Claimant:	see Articles 1.1 & 1.6;
Commencement Date:	see Article 1.4;
Consent Award:	see Article 26.9;
Consolidation:	see Article 22A;

Data Protection:	see Article 30A;
Early Determination:	see Articles 14.6(vi) & 22.1(viii);
Emergency Arbitrator:	see Article 9.4;
LCIA Court:	see Article 3.1;
LCIA Rules:	see Preamble;
Legal Costs:	see Articles 9.10 & 28.3;
Prohibited Activity:	see Article 24.9;
Registrar:	see Articles 1.1 & 3.2;
Request:	see Article 1.1;
Respondent:	see Articles 1.1(iii) & 2.6;
Response:	see Article 2.1;
Special Fee:	see Article 9.5;
Statement of Case:	see Article 15.2;
Statement of Defence:	see Article 15.3;
Statement of Counterclaim:	see Article 15.3;
Statement of Reply:	see Article 15.4;
Statement of Defence to Counterclaim:	see Article 15.4; and
Tribunal Secretary:	see Article 14A.

(N.B. This Index comprises both defined and other undefined terms. All references to any person or party include both masculine and feminine).

ANNEX TO THE LCIA RULES

General Guidelines for the Authorised Representatives of the Parties (Articles 18.5 and 18.6 of the LCIA Rules)

Paragraph 1: These general guidelines are intended to promote the good and equal conduct of the authorised representatives of the parties appearing by name within the arbitration. Nothing in these guidelines is intended to derogate from the Arbitration Agreement or to undermine any authorised representative's primary duty of loyalty to the party represented in the arbitration or the obligation to present that party's case effectively to the Arbitral Tribunal. Nor shall these guidelines derogate from any mandatory laws, rules of law, professional rules or codes of conduct if and to the extent that any are shown to apply to an authorised representative appearing in the arbitration.

Paragraph 2: An authorised representative should not engage in activities intended unfairly to obstruct the arbitration or to jeopardise the finality of any award, including repeated challenges to an arbitrator's appointment or to the jurisdiction or authority of the Arbitral Tribunal where such challenges are known to be unfounded by that authorised representative.

Paragraph 3: An authorised representative should not knowingly make any false statement to the Arbitral Tribunal or the LCIA Court.

Paragraph 4: An authorised representative should not knowingly procure or assist in the preparation of or rely upon any false evidence presented to the Arbitral Tribunal or the LCIA Court.

Paragraph 5: An authorised representative should not knowingly conceal or assist in the concealment of any document (or any part thereof) which is ordered to be produced by the Arbitral Tribunal.

Paragraph 6: During the arbitration proceedings, an authorised representative should not deliberately initiate or attempt to initiate any unilateral contact relating to the arbitration or the parties' dispute with any member of the LCIA Court exercising any function in regard to the arbitration or, from the Arbitral Tribunal's formation onwards, any member of the Arbitral Tribunal or the tribunal secretary (if any), which has not been disclosed in writing prior to or shortly after the time of such contact to all other parties, all members of the Arbitral Tribunal and the Registrar in accordance with

Article 13.4. An authorised representative may, however, have unilateral contact with the Registrar regarding administrative matters.

Paragraph 7: In accordance with Articles 18.5 and 18.6, the Arbitral Tribunal may decide whether an authorised representative has violated these general guidelines and, if so, how to exercise its discretion to impose any or all of the sanctions listed in Article 18.6.

9.4.5 Netherlands Arbitration Institute Arbitration Rules ('NAI') (2015)[1]

In force as of 1 January 2015

SECTION ONE – GENERAL

Article 1 - Definitions

In these Rules, the following terms and expressions shall have the following meanings:

a) "administrator": the director of the NAI as provided for in the NAI's articles of association and, in the director's absence, the member of the executive board designated by the executive board to that end, or an acting administrator appointed as such by the executive board;
b) "documents": procedural and other documents, including data on a data carrier as well as data presented by electronic means;
c) "Executive Board": the executive board of the NAI;
d) "Committee": the committee appointed by the NAI Executive Board that decides on challenge requests as referred to in Article 19;
e) "claimant": one or more claimants;
f) "NAI": the Netherlands Arbitration Institute (Stichting Nederlands Arbitrage Instituut);
g) "arbitration agreement": an agreement by which the parties bind themselves to subject to arbitration any disputes that have arisen or may arise between them from a particular legal relationship, ensuing from an agreement or otherwise, and/or the determination only of the quality or condition of goods, and/or the determination only of the quantum of damages or monetary debt, and/or the filling of gaps or modification of the aforementioned legal relationship;
h) "Rules": the arbitration rules of the NAI;
i) "arbitral tribunal": an arbitral tribunal consisting of one or more arbitrators that has been composed in accordance with the provisions of these Rules or according to the applicable rules of arbitration law;
j) "respondent": one or more respondents; and
k) "chair": the chair of the arbitral tribunal appointed in accordance with Articles 13, 14 or 39 and, in the event of an arbitral tribunal consisting of one arbitrator, the arbitrator where permitted by the context of the provision.

Article 2 - Scope

These Rules shall apply if the parties have referred to arbitration by or before the NAI or in accordance with the Rules of the NAI.

Article 3 - Communications

1. Requests and communications shall be made or confirmed in writing in the manner provided for in this article.
2. Unless the sender is unable to do so, all requests, communications and other documents to the administrator, the Committee, the third person as referred to in Article 39 and/or the NAI shall only

1 The Netherlands Arbitration Institute Arbitration Rules (2015) are reproduced by kind permission of the Netherlands Arbitration Institute and are available at: www.nai-nl.org.

be sent electronically by e-mail to the address secretariaat@nai-nl.org or to any other address to be specified by the NAI.
3. The time at which a request or communication is received electronically by the administrator, the Committee, the third person as referred to in Article 39 and/or the NAI shall be the time at which the request or communication has reached a data processing system for which the NAI is responsible.
4. The NAI shall send a request or communication addressed to one or more addressees electronically by e-mail if the addressee, by providing its e-mail address, has communicated that it may be reached for these purposes by such means.
5. After sending the arbitration file to the arbitral tribunal, the parties shall send their requests, communications and other documents directly to the arbitral tribunal while at the same time sending a copy to all parties. A copy of each request, communication or other document shall be sent to the administrator at the same time. The same applies to requests, communications or documents from the arbitral tribunal to the parties and between the parties, it being understood that, in the latter event, a copy must also be sent to the arbitral tribunal.
6. Unless the arbitral tribunal decides otherwise, all requests, communications or other instruments in writing between the parties and the arbitral tribunal shall be sent in electronic form by e-mail if the parties, by providing their e-mail addresses, have communicated that they may be reached for these purposes by such means.
7. The time at which a request, communication or other document is received electronically by the arbitral tribunal shall be the time at which the request, the communication and/or the other document has reached a data processing system for which one of the members of the arbitral tribunal is responsible.
8. The time at which a request, communication or other document is sent electronically by the arbitral tribunal, the administrator, the Committee, the third person as referred to in Article 39 and/or the NAI shall be the time at which the message has reached a data processing system for which the arbitrator or arbitrators, or the NAI, is/are not responsible.

Article 4 – Time limits

1. For the purposes of these Rules, a time limit shall commence on the day a request or communication is sent or, if not sent in electronic form as provided for in Article 3, on the day of receipt of a request or communication, unless explicitly provided otherwise in these Rules or by the arbitral tribunal.
2. In special events, the administrator shall be authorised to extend or to shorten the time limits mentioned in Articles 8(4), 12(3), 13(1), 13(2), 13(3), 13(5), 13(6), 14(2), 36(11), 53(5) and 55(6) at the request of a party or of his own motion.
3. In special events, the arbitral tribunal shall be authorised to extend a time limit set by it or agreed by the parties at the request of a party or of its own motion.

Article 5 – Language

1. The proceedings shall be conducted in the language or languages agreed by the parties or, in the absence of such agreement, in the language or languages determined by the arbitral tribunal.
2. Until such time that the arbitral tribunal has determined the language or languages as referred to in the first paragraph, at the request of the other party or of his own motion, the administrator may require a party to submit a translation of the requests, communications and other documents it has submitted in a language in which the other party is proficient, and in a form and within a time limit as determined by the administrator.
3. Without prejudice to the provisions of paragraph 1 and paragraph 2, if any request, communication or other document is written in a language in which the administrator or the arbitral tribunal is not proficient, the administrator and, after acceptance of the mandate, the arbitral tribunal may require the party making the request or the communication or submitting the document to provide a translation in a language, in a form and within a time limit determined by the administrator or the arbitral tribunal.

Article 6 – Confidentiality
Arbitration is confidential and all persons involved either directly or indirectly shall be bound to secrecy, except and insofar as disclosure ensues from the law or the parties' agreement.

SECTION TWO – COMMENCEMENT OF ARBITRATION

Article 7 – Request for arbitration
1. Arbitration shall be commenced by submitting a request for arbitration to the administrator. Arbitration shall be deemed to have been commenced on the day of receipt of the request for arbitration by the administrator.
2. The request for arbitration shall contain the following particulars:
  a) the name, the address, the place of residence, the telephone number, the e-mail address and, as applicable, the VAT number of each of the parties;
  b) the name, the address, the place of residence, the telephone number and the e-mail address of the person or persons representing the claimant in the arbitration;
  c) the e-mail address at which the claimant may be reached for electronic communication for the duration of the arbitral proceedings;
  d) a brief description of the dispute;
  e) a clear specification of the claim along with, if possible, a specification of the monetary interest of each of the claims;
  f) a reference to the arbitration agreement and any other agreement(s) to which the arbitration relates, along with copies of the relevant agreements;
  g) insofar as already appointed, the name, the address, the place of residence, the telephone number and the e-mail address of the arbitrator or arbitrators appointed by the claimant or the parties;
  h) the method of appointment of the arbitrator or arbitrators if the parties have agreed a method of appointment that deviates from Article 13, paragraphs 1 to 4, inclusive;
  i) the arrangements between the parties, or the claimant's preference, in respect of the number of arbitrators, the qualifications of arbitrators, the place of arbitration and the language of the arbitration; and
  j) insofar as applicable, any other particulars concerning the arbitral procedure.
3. The request for arbitration shall be submitted in the manner provided for in Article 3(2). If the claimant is unable to do so, the request for arbitration may be submitted in another manner. The administrator shall be authorised to suspend handling the request as long as it does not satisfy the requirements mentioned in paragraph 2. Suspension shall not prejudice the provisions of paragraph 1.
4. The administrator shall confirm receipt of the request for arbitration to the claimant, stating the date of receipt.

Article 8 – Short answer
1. The administrator shall send a copy of the request for arbitration to the respondent, stating the date of receipt, and shall invite the respondent to submit a short written answer in response.
2. The short answer shall contain the following information:
  a) the name, the address, the place of residence, the telephone number, the e-mail address and, as applicable, the VAT number of the respondent;
  b) the name, the address, the place of residence, the telephone number and the e-mail address of the person or persons representing the respondent in the arbitration;
  c) the e-mail address at which the respondent can be reached for electronic communication for the duration of the arbitral proceedings;
  d) a reply to the information referred to in Article 7(2)(e), (f), (g) insofar as an appointment by the parties is concerned, (h) and

e) and, insofar as applicable, the respondent's preference in respect of the number of arbitrators, the qualifications of arbitrators, the place of arbitration, and the language of the arbitration;
f) insofar as applicable, the name, the address, the place of residence, the telephone number and the e-mail address of the arbitrator appointed by the respondent; and
g) insofar as applicable, any other particulars concerning the arbitral procedure.

3. The respondent may present a counterclaim against the claimant in the short answer, with due observance of the provisions of Article 24(2). The requirements mentioned in Articles 7(2)(d), and (f) shall apply mutatis mutandis to the counterclaim.
4. The short answer shall be submitted within fourteen days of the invitation referred to in paragraph 1 in the manner provided for in Article 3(2), a copy of which shall be sent to the claimant at the same time. If it is not possible for the respondent to send the short answer electronically, it may be submitted in another manner within this time limit, while sending a copy to the claimant at the same time. The administrator shall confirm receipt of the short answer to the parties.

Article 9 – Purport of the request for arbitration and the short answer
1. The request for arbitration and the short answer do not prejudice the parties' right to present a statement of claim and a statement of defence, respectively, with due observance of the provisions of Article 23.
2. Insofar as the administrator is involved in the determination of the number of arbitrators and/or the appointment of the arbitrator or the arbitrators, the administrator shall derive the necessary information from the request for arbitration and the short answer.

Article 10 – Plea as to the non-existence of an arbitration agreement
1. By cooperating in the appointment of the arbitrator or arbitrators in the manner provided for in Section Three, the parties shall not forfeit the right to challenge the jurisdiction of the arbitral tribunal on the ground of non-existence of a valid arbitration agreement.
2. A respondent that has appeared in the arbitral proceedings and that wishes to raise a plea that the arbitral tribunal does not have jurisdiction on the ground of non-existence of a valid arbitration agreement must do so before submitting any defence, specifically in the statement of defence or, in the absence thereof, by the first written or oral defence after acceptance of the mandate by the arbitral tribunal at the latest.
3. If a respondent has failed to raise a plea in accordance with the provisions of the previous paragraph, its right to rely on this later, in the arbitral proceedings or before the court, shall be forfeited, unless this plea is made on the ground that the dispute is not capable of settlement by arbitration.
4. The arbitral tribunal shall rule on its lack of jurisdiction. If the arbitral tribunal declares that it has no jurisdiction, the declaration of no jurisdiction shall constitute an arbitral award to which the provisions of Sections Five and Six are applicable.
5. An arbitration agreement shall be considered and decided upon as a separate agreement. The arbitral tribunal shall have the power to decide on the existence and the validity of the main contract of which the arbitration agreement forms part or to which it is related.
6. A plea that the arbitral tribunal does not have jurisdiction shall not prevent the NAI from administering the case.

SECTION THREE – THE ARBITRAL TRIBUNAL

Article 11 – The arbitrator
1. Any natural person of legal capacity may be appointed as arbitrator. Subject to the provisions of Articles 13(4) and 14(4), no person shall be precluded from appointment by reason of their nationality.

2. An arbitrator shall perform his mandate independently, impartially and to the best of his knowledge and ability.
3. A person approached to be engaged as arbitrator who has reason to suspect that there could be justifiable doubts as to his impartiality or independence shall communicate the same in writing to the person who approached him, stating the suspected reason(s).
4. A person who intends to accept his mandate shall, prior to the confirmation of appointment as provided for in Article 16(1), sign a statement confirming his independence and impartiality, availability and acceptance of the mandate on condition of confirmation by the administrator and send this statement to the administrator. Any communication as referred to in paragraph 3 that has been sent shall be included in the statement. The administrator shall send a copy of the statement to the parties and, if the arbitral tribunal consists of multiple arbitrators, to the co-arbitrators.
5. An arbitrator who, during the arbitral proceedings, suspects that there could be justifiable doubts as to his impartiality or independence shall communicate the same in writing to the administrator, the parties and, if the arbitral tribunal consists of multiple arbitrators, to the co-arbitrators in writing, stating the suspected reason(s).

Article 12 – Number of arbitrators
1. The proceedings shall be conducted before an uneven number of arbitrators.
2. If the parties have not agreed the number of arbitrators, or if the agreed method of determining that number is not carried out and the parties cannot reach agreement on the number, the administrator shall set the number at one or three, taking account of the parties' preference, the scope of the dispute, the complexity of the case and the parties' interest in efficient proceedings.
3. If the parties have agreed an even number of arbitrators, the arbitrators shall appoint an additional arbitrator who shall act as the chair of the arbitral tribunal. If the arbitrators fail to reach agreement in respect of the appointment of the additional arbitrator within fourteen days of accepting their mandate, such arbitrator shall be appointed at the request of the most diligent party in accordance with the provisions of Article 14.

Article 13 – Appointment of the arbitral tribunal
1. If an arbitral tribunal consisting of one arbitrator must be appointed, the parties, if no joint appointment has become evident by the short answer at the latest, shall notify the administrator of the name, the address, the place of residence, the telephone number and the e-mail address of the arbitrator jointly appointed by them within fourteen days after a request from the administrator to that end. If such a notice is not received within this period, the arbitrator shall be appointed in accordance with the provisions of Article 14.
2. If an arbitral tribunal consisting of three arbitrators must be appointed, the claimant and the respondent shall each appoint an arbitrator. Any party that has not yet appointed an arbitrator shall appoint an arbitrator, stating the name, the address, the place of residence, the telephone number and the e-mail address of the arbitrator appointed, within fourteen days after a request from the administrator to that end. If no notice of such an appointment is received within this period, the arbitrator shall be appointed in accordance with the provisions of Article 14, it being understood that the list shall only be sent to the party that did not appoint an arbitrator on time.
3. If an arbitral tribunal consisting of three arbitrators must be appointed, the two arbitrators appointed in accordance with Article 13(2) shall jointly, if applicable with due observance of the wish referred to in paragraph 4, appoint a chair of the arbitral tribunal, stating the name, the address, the place of residence, the telephone number and the e-mail address of the chair, within fourteen days after a request from the administrator to that end. If no notice of such an appointment is received within this period, the chair shall be appointed in accordance with the provisions of Article 14.

4. If an arbitral tribunal consisting of three arbitrators must be appointed in arbitration proceedings between parties that do not have the same nationality, each of the parties may require that the chair shall not have the same nationality as any of the parties by giving notice to the administrator in the request for arbitration or the short answer, respectively. The administrator shall state this wish in the request referred to in paragraph 3.
5. The appointment of the arbitrator or the arbitrators in accordance with the procedures provided for in this Article 13 or in Article 14 shall take place within three months after the arbitration has been commenced.
6. If the parties have agreed a method of appointment of the arbitrator or arbitrators that deviates from the procedures provided for in this Article 13 or in Article 14, the appointment shall take place in the manner as agreed by the parties. If this method of appointment is not, or not entirely, performed within the time limit agreed by the parties or, in the absence of such time limit, within four weeks after the arbitration has been commenced, the appointment of the arbitrator or arbitrators shall take place in accordance with paragraphs 1 to 4, inclusive, of this article.

Article 14 – List procedure
1. In derogation of the method of appointment provided for in Article 13, the parties may agree that the arbitrator or arbitrators shall be appointed in accordance with the list procedure provided for in this Article 14. In that event, the administrator shall send the list referred to in paragraph 2 as soon as possible after receipt of the short answer or, in the absence thereof, after expiry of the time limit for submitting the short answer.
2. The administrator shall send each of the parties an identical list of persons' names. This list shall contain at least three names in the event that one arbitrator is to be appointed and at least nine names, three of which being prospective chairmen, in the event that three arbitrators are to be appointed. A party may delete from the list the names of persons against whom this party has strong objections, and may number the remaining names in its order of preference. If the administrator has not received a list back from a party within fourteen days, it shall be assumed that all of the persons named on the list are equally acceptable to that party as arbitrator.
3. With due observance of the preferences and/or objections expressed by the parties, the administrator shall invite persons named on the list to serve as arbitrators. If the returned lists show that there are an insufficient number of persons on those lists who are acceptable as arbitrators to each of the parties, or a person will not or cannot accept the administrator's invitation to serve as arbitrator or proves unable to serve as arbitrator for any other reasons and an insufficient number of persons remain on the returned lists that are acceptable as arbitrators to each of the parties, the administrator shall be authorised to directly appoint one or several other persons as arbitrators.
4. If an arbitral tribunal must be appointed in arbitration proceedings between parties that do not have the same nationality in accordance with this article, each of the parties may require that, in the event of an arbitral tribunal consisting of one arbitrator, this arbitrator and, in the event of an arbitral tribunal consisting of three arbitrators, the chair will not have the same nationality as any of the parties by giving notice to the administrator in the request for arbitration or the short answer, respectively.

Article 15 – Appointment in the event of multiple claimants and/or respondents
1. If there are multiple claimants and/or respondents and the appointment of the arbitral tribunal shall take place in the manner provided for in Article 13, each of the joint claimants and the joint respondents shall appoint an arbitrator if an arbitral tribunal consisting of three arbitrators must be appointed.
2. If the joint claimants or the joint respondents fail to appoint an arbitrator within the time limit set in Article 13(2), the entire arbitral tribunal shall be appointed in the manner provided for in Article 14.

Article 16 – Confirmation of appointment
1. The appointment of an arbitrator under the provisions of this section and Article 36(4) shall be confirmed by the administrator after receipt of the statement referred to in Article 11(4), unless the arbitrator, in the administrator's opinion, offers insufficient safeguards for sound arbitration.
2. If the administrator does not confirm an appointment, he shall request the party that was entitled to appoint the arbitrator or the arbitrators appointed by the parties to appoint a different arbitrator or chair or, if the parties have so agreed, to appoint a different arbitrator or chair in accordance with the list procedure provided for in Article 14 within fourteen days. If the administrator refuses to confirm the appointment of the new arbitrator, the right of appointment shall lapse and the administrator shall directly appoint the relevant arbitrator.

Article 17 – Release from mandate
1. An arbitrator who has accepted his mandate may, at his own request, be released from his mandate either with the consent of the parties or by the administrator.
2. An arbitrator who has accepted his mandate may be released from his mandate by the parties jointly. The parties shall immediately notify the arbitrator and the administrator of the release.
3. An arbitrator who has accepted his mandate and who has become unable de jure or de facto to perform his mandate may, at the request of any party, be released from his mandate by the administrator.
4. An arbitrator who has accepted his mandate may be released from his mandate by the administrator of his own motion if he (i) has become unable de jure or de facto to perform his mandate, or (ii) does not perform his mandate in accordance with these Rules.
5. An arbitral tribunal that has accepted its mandate may, at the request of any of the parties, be released from its mandate by the administrator if, taking account of all the circumstances, it performs its mandate in an unacceptably slow manner despite reminders.
6. In the events mentioned in paragraphs 1, 3, 4 and 5, the administrator shall not proceed to release from the mandate until the parties have been given the opportunity to make their views known to him.

Article 18 – Replacement of an arbitrator
1. Unless the parties have agreed another manner of replacement, an arbitrator who has been released from his mandate or an arbitral tribunal that has been released from its mandate for any reason whatsoever shall be replaced pursuant to the rules applicable to the original appointment. The same shall apply in the event of the death of an arbitrator.
2. The proceedings shall be suspended by operation of law for the duration of the replacement. After replacement, the proceedings shall continue from the stage they had reached, unless the arbitral tribunal wishes to handle the case again in full or in part.

Article 19 – Challenge
1. An arbitrator may be challenged by a party in accordance with the provisions of this article if there are justifiable doubts as to his impartiality or independence.

A party may only challenge an arbitrator appointed by that party for reasons of which that party became aware after the appointment was made. A party may not challenge an arbitrator appointed in accordance with Article 13(3) or Article 14 if it has acquiesced in this appointment, unless that party only became aware of the ground for the challenge afterwards.
2. The challenging party shall give written notice of the challenge, stating reasons, to the arbitrator concerned, the other party, the administrator and, if the arbitral tribunal consists of multiple arbitrators, the co-arbitrators. The notice shall be given within fourteen days of the communication referred to in Articles 11(3), 11(4) or 11(5) or, in other events, within fourteen days after the reason for the challenge becomes known to the challenging party.

3. The arbitral tribunal may suspend the arbitral proceedings from the day of receipt of the notice, as referred to in paragraph 3, or afterwards, pending the challenge procedure, from the moment that the arbitral tribunal considers appropriate.
4. If a challenged arbitrator does not resign within fourteen days after the day of receipt of a timely notice as referred to in paragraph 3, the Committee shall, at the request of the most diligent party, decide whether the challenge is well founded as soon as possible. The Committee may give the arbitrator who has been challenged and the parties the opportunity to be heard. The decision shall be sent by the administrator to the parties, the arbitrator and, if the arbitral tribunal consists of multiple arbitrators, the co-arbitrators.
5. If the challenged arbitrator resigns or if the Committee finds the challenge to be well founded, the challenged arbitrator shall be replaced in accordance with Article 18(1).
6. If a challenged arbitrator resigns, this does not imply acceptance that the reasons for the challenge are well founded.
7. A party that has reasons to challenge an arbitrator shall base a challenge request in accordance with the provisions of this article on these reasons, on pain of forfeiture of the right to invoke them later in the arbitral proceedings or in court.

Article 20 – Secretary
At the request of the arbitral tribunal, the administrator may appoint a lawyer as the arbitral tribunal's secretary. The provisions of Articles 11, 16 and 19 shall apply mutatis mutandis.

SECTION FOUR – THE PROCEDURE (GENERAL)

Article 21 – Procedure in general
1. Without prejudice to the provisions of applicable mandatory arbitration law, the arbitral tribunal shall determine the manner in which and the time limits within which the proceedings will be conducted, with due observance of any arrangements between the parties in that regard and the provisions of these Rules and having regard to the circumstances of the arbitration.
2. The arbitral tribunal shall treat the parties equally. The arbitral tribunal shall give the parties the opportunity mutually to set out and explain their positions and to comment on each other's positions and on all documents and other information brought to the attention of the arbitral tribunal during the proceedings.
3. The arbitral tribunal shall guard against unreasonable delay of the proceedings and, if necessary, at the request of a party or of its own motion, take measures.
4. At any stage of the proceedings, at the request of a party or of its own motion, the arbitral tribunal may hold a meeting with the parties to discuss the course of the proceedings and/or further determine the disputed points of fact and law.
5. If a party fails to wholly or partially satisfy any provision mentioned in Section Four or any order, decision or measure of the arbitral tribunal under the provisions of Section Four, the arbitral tribunal may draw any conclusions from such failure that it considers appropriate.
6. Each party may appear in the proceedings in person, or be represented by a practising lawyer or by a representative expressly authorised in writing for this purpose. Each party may be assisted by any persons of its choice.
7. If the parties have not determined the place of arbitration by agreement, such place shall, as soon as possible, be determined by the arbitral tribunal and communicated to the parties and to the administrator.
8. The arbitral tribunal may hold hearings, deliberate and hear witnesses and experts at any place, within or outside the Netherlands, it considers appropriate. Except in the events provided for in Articles 26(2) and 31, hearings shall be held in the presence of the full arbitral tribunal.

9. If the arbitral tribunal consists of multiple arbitrators, procedural matters of minor importance may be decided by the chair of the arbitral tribunal.
10. Instead of a personal appearance of a witness, an expert or a party, the arbitral tribunal may determine that the relevant person have direct contact with the arbitral tribunal and, insofar as applicable, with others by electronic means. The arbitral tribunal shall determine, in consultation with those concerned, which electronic means shall be used to this end and in which manner this shall occur.

Article 22 – File dispatch and determination of rules of procedure
1. After the appointment of all members of the arbitral tribunal has been confirmed, the administrator shall send the arbitration file to the arbitral tribunal.
2. As soon as possible after receipt of the arbitration file, the arbitral tribunal shall determine the rules of procedure following consultation with the parties, including a (provisional) schedule for the further course of the arbitration.

Article 23 – Exchange of statements
1. Unless the parties have agreed otherwise, the arbitral tribunal shall give the claimant and the respondent the opportunity to present a statement of claim and a statement of defence, respectively.
2. Unless the parties have agreed otherwise, the arbitral tribunal shall be free to determine whether any further statements may be presented.

Article 24 – Counterclaim
1. A counterclaim shall be admissible if it is subject to the same arbitration agreement as the one on which the claim is based or if that same arbitration agreement has been expressly or tacitly declared applicable by the parties.
2. A counterclaim that is not presented at the latest with the statement of defence or, in the absence thereof, with the first written or oral defence after the arbitral tribunal has accepted its mandate cannot be presented afterwards in the same arbitration except in special circumstances at the arbitral tribunal's discretion.
3. Articles 10, 23, 32 and 34 shall apply mutatis mutandis to the counterclaim.

Article 25 – Hearing
1. The arbitral tribunal shall give the parties the opportunity to explain their case at an oral hearing, unless the parties waive that opportunity.
2. The arbitral tribunal shall determine the time and place of the hearing.
3. In addition to the parties and persons mentioned in Articles 20, 21(6), 28 and 29, the arbitral tribunal may admit other persons to the hearing after it has heard the parties in that regard.

Article 26 – Evidence in general
1. The arbitral tribunal shall be free to determine the rules of evidence, the admissibility of evidence, the division of the burden of proof and the assessment of evidence, unless the parties have agreed otherwise.
2. Having heard the parties, the arbitral tribunal may designate its chair to hear witnesses or experts or to conduct an on-site examination or viewing, unless the parties have agreed otherwise.

Article 27 – Production of documents
1. Unless the parties have agreed otherwise, the statements referred to in Article 23 shall, insofar as possible, be accompanied by the documents relied upon by the parties.

2. The arbitral tribunal may, at the request of any of the parties or of its own motion, order the inspection of a copy of or an extract from specific documents that the arbitral tribunal deems relevant for the dispute from the party which has these documents at its disposal, unless the parties have agreed otherwise. The arbitral tribunal shall determine the conditions under which and the manner in which inspection of a copy of or an extract from documents are provided.

Article 28 – Witnesses and experts

1. The arbitral tribunal may allow the parties to furnish evidence by hearing witnesses and experts or, at the request of any of the parties or of its own motion, order the parties to furnish evidence by hearing witnesses and experts.
2. The arbitral tribunal may determine the form in which statements of witnesses and experts are given. A party shall be free to submit written witness statements or expert advice it has obtained along with the statements referred to in Article 23. If a party so requests or if the arbitral tribunal so determines, the party submitting the advice shall call the expert to provide a further explanation at the hearing.
3. If an oral examination of witnesses or experts takes place, the arbitral tribunal shall determine the time, place and order for the oral examination and the manner in which the examination will be conducted.
4. The names of the witnesses or experts that a party wishes to have heard shall be communicated to the arbitral tribunal and the other party in a timely manner.
5. If the arbitral tribunal considers it necessary, it shall hear the witnesses after they have sworn or affirmed that they will tell the whole truth and nothing but the truth.
6. The arbitral tribunal shall decide whether and in what form a report of the examination will be drafted. If the chair of the arbitral tribunal hears the witnesses or experts in accordance with Article 26(2), a report of the examination shall in any event be drafted.

Article 29 – Assistance to the arbitral tribunal

1. The arbitral tribunal may appoint one or more experts to give written advice. The arbitral tribunal shall consult the parties regarding the terms of reference to be issued to the experts. The arbitral tribunal shall send the parties a copy of the appointment and the terms of reference of the experts as soon as possible.
2. If a party does not provide the expert with the information he requires or render the cooperation he needs, the expert may request that the arbitral tribunal order the relevant party to do so.
3. After receipt of the expert's report, the arbitral tribunal shall send a copy thereof to the parties as soon as possible.
4. At the request of any of the parties, the experts shall be heard at a hearing of the arbitral tribunal. If a party wishes to make such a request, it shall so notify the arbitral tribunal and the other party as soon as possible. At the hearing, the arbitral tribunal shall give the parties the opportunity to ask the experts questions and to present their own experts.
5. Without prejudice to the provisions in paragraph 4, the arbitral tribunal shall give the parties the opportunity to be heard regarding the advice of the experts appointed by the arbitral tribunal.
6. The arbitral tribunal may call in technical assistance in the arbitral proceedings and make arrangements for the presence of an interpreter at the hearing.

Article 30 – On-site inspection

The arbitral tribunal may, at the request of any of the parties or of its own motion, examine a local situation or conduct a viewing, within or outside the Netherlands. The arbitral tribunal shall give the parties the opportunity to be present at the on-site examination or viewing.

Article 31 – Personal appearance of the parties
At any stage of the proceedings, the arbitral tribunal may order the parties to appear at a hearing in person for the purpose of providing information or attempting to arrive at a settlement. Having heard the parties, the arbitral tribunal may designate its chair to hold the hearing, unless the parties have agreed otherwise.

Article 32 – Amendment of claim
1. A party may amend or increase its claim or the grounds thereof until the beginning of the last hearing or, if no hearing is held, in the last admissible statement at the latest. This shall not be permitted afterwards, except in special events at the arbitral tribunal's discretion. A party may reduce its claim at any time.
2. The other party is authorised to object to an amendment or increase if it will be unreasonably hindered in its defence or the proceedings will be unreasonably delayed as a result. Having heard the parties, the arbitral tribunal shall decide on the other party's objection as soon as possible.
3. In the event of a party's non-appearance as referred to in Article 34, the arbitral tribunal shall give this party the opportunity to comment on an amendment or increase.

Article 33 – Withdrawal of a request for arbitration
1. The claimant may withdraw its request for arbitration as long as the respondent has not presented a statement of defence as referred to in Article 23 or, if there is no written treatment, as long as no hearing has been held.
2. Afterwards, the request for arbitration may only be withdrawn with the respondent's permission, without prejudice to the provisions of Articles 53(5) and 55(6).
3. The administrator and, after acceptance of its mandate, the arbitral tribunal shall confirm the withdrawal through the intervention of the administrator.

Article 34 – Default of a party
1. If the claimant fails to present a statement of claim as referred to in Article 23 within the time limit determined by the arbitral tribunal or to reasonably explain its claim within a time limit determined by the arbitral tribunal in accordance with an order of the arbitral tribunal, without asserting well founded reasons, the arbitral tribunal may, by award, or in another manner it considers appropriate, bring an end to the arbitral proceedings.
2. If the respondent fails to present a statement of defence as referred to in Article 23 within the time limit determined by the arbitral tribunal, without asserting well founded reasons, the arbitral tribunal may immediately make an award.
3. In the award referred to in the second paragraph, the claim shall be wholly or partially awarded, unless it appears to the arbitral tribunal to be unlawful or unfounded. The arbitral tribunal may, before making its award, require proof from the claimant of one or more of its assertions.
4. If a party, although reasonably having been called, fails to appear at the hearing without asserting well founded reasons, the arbitral tribunal may continue the arbitral proceedings and make an award.

SECTION FOUR A – PROVISIONAL RELIEF

Article 35 – Provisional relief in general
1. During pending arbitral proceedings on the merits, the arbitral tribunal may, at the request of any of the parties and with due observance of the provisions of this article, grant provisional relief related to the claim or counterclaim as presented.
2. If the place of arbitration is located within the Netherlands for the arbitral proceedings on the merits, all urgent cases that require immediately enforceable provisional relief in view of the parties' interests,

regardless of whether arbitral proceedings on the merits are pending, an arbitral tribunal appointed to that end in accordance with Article 36 may, at the request of any of the parties, grant provisional relief in summary arbitral proceedings with due observance of the provisions of this Section Four A. If the place of arbitration has not been determined for the arbitral proceedings on the merits, Rotterdam shall be the place of arbitration for the summary arbitral proceedings.
3. The arbitral tribunal referred to in paragraph 1 and paragraph 2 may, in conjunction with the provisional relief, require any party to provide sufficient security, including the provision of security for the claim or counterclaim in the main action and the costs of the arbitral proceedings on the merits.
4. The decision on the provisional relief may be taken in the form of an order by the arbitral tribunal or in the form of an arbitral award, to which the provisions of Sections Five and Six are applicable. At the request of a party, the arbitral tribunal, having heard the other party or parties, may convert an order by the arbitral tribunal into an arbitral award, in which it shall state the request.
5. The decision on the provisional relief shall not in any way prejudice the arbitral tribunal's ultimate ruling in the arbitral proceedings on the merits.
6. The arbitral tribunal referred to in paragraph 1 and paragraph 2 may, at the unanimous request of the parties, instead of taking a decision on provisional relief, immediately take a decision on the merits, in which it shall state the request. Such a decision on the merits shall constitute an arbitral award to which the provisions of, inter alia, Sections Five and Six shall be applicable. If such a decision is taken by the arbitral tribunal as referred to in paragraph 2 in the form of a final award on the merits, the determination of and order to pay the arbitration costs as referred to in Article 44(1)(f) shall also comprise the costs of the arbitral proceedings on the merits. Without prejudice to the provisions of Articles 47, 48 and 49 in respect of the arbitral tribunal referred to in paragraph 1, this final award shall end the arbitral tribunal's mandate in the arbitral proceedings on the merits.
7. The arbitral tribunal may, at the unanimous request of the parties, convert an arbitral award as referred to in paragraph 4 into an arbitral award as referred to in paragraph 6, in which it shall state the request.

Article 36 – Summary arbitral proceedings
1. The provisions of Sections One, Five and Seven shall apply in full to the summary arbitral proceedings referred to in Article 35(2). The provisions of Sections Two to Four, inclusive, shall only apply insofar as reference is made to them in this section.
2. Summary arbitral proceedings shall be commenced by submitting a request for summary arbitral proceedings to the administrator. They shall be deemed to have been commenced on the day of receipt of the request for summary arbitral proceedings by the administrator. The request shall contain the particulars mentioned in Article 7(2)(a), (b), (c), (d), (e) and (f), the agreed place of arbitration, language and a description of the grounds of the claim and of the grounds on which the urgent interest as required in Article 35(2) is based. Articles 7(3) and 7(4) shall apply mutatis mutandis.
3. The claimant shall immediately and properly bring a copy of the request, along with any documents, to the attention of every respondent. Proof that notice has been given to every respondent shall be submitted to the proceedings at the hearing mentioned in paragraph 5 at the latest.
4. As soon as possible after receipt of the request, the administrator shall appoint the arbitral tribunal, consisting of one arbitrator, which, as arbitral tribunal, shall take a decision in summary arbitral proceedings. If the parties have agreed a method of appointment of the arbitral tribunal and/or a multiple number of arbitrators, that agreement shall not be applied with regard to the appointment and composition of the arbitral tribunal referred to in the previous sentence, unless the parties, in so many words, have provided for a method of appointment of an arbitral tribunal in summary proceedings. No person shall be precluded from appointment as arbitrator in summary arbitral proceedings by reason of their nationality. Articles 11(2), 11(3), 11(4), 11(5), 16, 17, 18(2), 19 and 20 shall apply in full. In the

events as referred to in Article 18(1), a new arbitrator shall be appointed by the method provided in the first sentence.
5. The arbitral tribunal shall determine the date, time and place of the hearing at which the request will be handled in summary arbitral proceedings and shall immediately communicate this information to the parties. Statements shall only be presented if the arbitral tribunal so determines, without prejudice to the provisions of paragraph 6 and paragraph 7. Article 25(3) shall apply mutatis mutandis.
6. If the respondent wishes to raise a plea that the arbitral tribunal does not have jurisdiction on the ground of non-existence of a valid arbitration agreement, it shall raise such a plea before submitting a defence, at the hearing mentioned in paragraph 5 at the latest or, if a statement is presented prior to that hearing, in that statement at the latest. Article 10 shall apply mutatis mutandis.
7. The respondent is entitled to present a counterclaim in summary arbitral proceedings. A counterclaim shall be presented by a statement to be presented to the arbitral tribunal at the beginning of the hearing referred to in paragraph 5 at the latest, with simultaneous dispatch or handing of copies to the claimant and dispatch to the administrator.
8. The provisions of Articles 21(2), 21(3), 21(5), 26 to 34, inclusive, 37 and 38 shall apply mutatis mutandis to the summary arbitral proceedings.
9. If the arbitral tribunal finds that the case is insufficiently urgent or too complicated to be decided in summary arbitral proceedings, it may deny all or part of the claim for that reason while referring the parties to arbitration on the merits. If no arbitral proceedings on the merits are pending they shall be commenced under Article 7.
10. The provisions of Section Six shall apply to the summary arbitral proceedings, it being understood that the administration costs and the deposit must be paid and deposited, respectively, prior to the hearing referred to in paragraph 5 and, in the event that a counterclaim is presented at the hearing, as soon as possible after that hearing.
11. The arbitral tribunal is authorised to suspend the hearing or stay its decision if any of the parties have failed to satisfy their payment obligations pursuant to paragraph 10. If, after a single reminder from the administrator, a party fails to satisfy its payment obligation pursuant to paragraph 10 within the time limit specified by the administrator, it shall be deemed to have withdrawn its claim or counterclaim.

SECTION FOUR B – THE PROCEDURE AND THIRD PERSONS

Article 37 – Joinder and intervention

1. At the written request of a third person who has an interest in arbitral proceedings to which these Rules apply, the arbitral tribunal may allow that person to join or intervene in the proceedings, provided that the same arbitration agreement as between the original parties applies or enters into force between the parties and the third person. By the allowance of the joinder or intervention, the third person shall become a party to the arbitral proceedings.
2. The request shall be submitted to the administrator. The administrator shall send a copy of the request to the parties and to the arbitral tribunal as soon as possible.
3. The arbitral tribunal shall give the parties the opportunity to make their opinions on the request known. The arbitral tribunal may give the third person the opportunity to make its opinion on the request known.
4. The arbitral tribunal may suspend the proceedings after receipt of a request as referred to in paragraph 1. After the lifting of the suspension or allowance of a joinder or an intervention, the arbitral tribunal shall arrange the further course of the proceedings, unless the parties have made provision for this by agreement.
5. Regardless of whether the same arbitration agreement as between the original parties applies or enters into force between the parties and the third person, by submitting the request for joinder or intervention, the third person agrees that the provisions of Section Six and Article 61 shall apply.

Article 38 – Impleader

1. At the request of a party, the arbitral tribunal may allow that party to implead a third person, provided that the same arbitration agreement as between the original parties applies or enters into force between the interested party and the third person.
2. The arbitral tribunal shall give the parties and the third person the opportunity to make their opinions on the request known.
3. The arbitral tribunal shall not allow the impleader if the arbitral tribunal finds it implausible, in advance, that the third person will be required to bear the adverse consequences of a possible award against the interested party or is of the opinion that impleader proceedings are likely to cause unreasonable or unnecessary delay of the proceedings.
4. After allowance of an impleader, the interested party shall send the notice of impleader to the arbitral tribunal, the administrator and the other party as soon as possible.
5. Article 37(4) shall apply mutatis mutandis.

Article 39 – Consolidation

1. In respect of arbitral proceedings pending in the Netherlands to which these Rules apply, a party may request that a third person to be appointed in accordance with paragraph 3 order consolidation with other arbitral proceedings pending within or outside the Netherlands to which these Rules apply, unless the parties have agreed otherwise.
2. The request shall be submitted to the administrator. The administrator shall send a copy of the request to all parties and, if appointed, to the arbitrators as soon as possible. Each of the pending arbitral proceedings may be suspended by the arbitral tribunal from the day of receipt of the request.
3. he third person shall be appointed as follows:
   (a) the administrator invites the parties to jointly appoint a third person within fourteen days;
   (b) if the parties have not appointed a third person within this time limit, the administrator shall appoint a third person directly;
   (c) unless all parties have agreed otherwise, none of the arbitrators appointed in the arbitral proceedings whose consolidation is requested shall be appointed as a third person; and
   (d) Articles 11, 17, 18, 19 and 20 shall apply mutatis mutandis to the appointment of the third person.
4. Consolidation may be ordered insofar as it does not cause unreasonable delay in the pending proceedings, also in view of the stage they have reached, and the two arbitral proceedings are so closely connected that good administration of justice renders it expedient to hear and determine them together to avoid the risk of irreconcilable decisions resulting from separate proceedings.
5. The third person may grant or refuse the request, after such person has given all parties and, if appointed, the arbitrators an opportunity to make their opinions known. The administrator shall communicate the decision to all parties and the arbitral tribunals concerned.
6. If the third person orders consolidation, the parties shall, in mutual consultation, appoint the arbitrator or arbitrators, in an uneven number, to the consolidated proceedings. If the parties fail to reach agreement in this regard within four weeks of the order for consolidation, the third person shall, at the request of the most diligent party, appoint the arbitrator or arbitrators. Articles 11(3), 11(4) and 16 shall apply mutatis mutandis. These Rules shall continue to apply to the consolidated arbitral proceedings.
7. The mandate of the arbitrator or arbitrators who are not appointed again shall terminate upon the appointment of the arbitrator or arbitrators to the consolidated proceedings. The third person shall, if necessary, determine the remuneration for the work already carried out by the arbitrator or arbitrators with due observance of the provisions of Article 54.
8. The provisions of Section Six shall apply mutatis mutandis to the request for consolidation.

SECTION FIVE – THE AWARD

Article 40 – Time limit

1. At the end of the hearing as referred to in Articles 25 and 36(5), the arbitral tribunal shall communicate to the parties at which time the arbitral tribunal will make its award. If the parties decided not to hold a hearing as referred to in Article 25, the notice shall be sent after presentation of the last statement. The arbitral tribunal shall be authorised to extend the time limit one or more times if necessary. In any event the arbitral tribunal shall decide expeditiously.
2. The mandate to the arbitral tribunal shall continue until its last final award is sent to the parties or, in the event referred to in Article 45(1)(b), upon the deposit of the last final award with the registry of the district court, without prejudice to the provisions of Articles 47 to 49, inclusive.

Article 41 – Types of award

The arbitral tribunal may make a final award, a partial final award or an interim award.

Article 42 – Measure for decision-making

1. The arbitral tribunal shall decide in accordance with the rules of law.
2. If a choice of law has been made by the parties, the arbitral tribunal shall decide in accordance with the rules of law designated by the parties. Failing such designation of law, the arbitral tribunal shall decide in accordance with the rules of law which it considers appropriate.
3. The arbitral tribunal shall decide as *amiable compositeur* if the parties, by agreement, have authorised it to do so.
4. In any event, in its decision the arbitral tribunal shall take into account any applicable trade usages.

Article 43 – Decision and signing

1. If the arbitral tribunal consists of multiple arbitrators, it shall decide by a majority of votes.
2. The award containing the decision shall be drawn up in quadruplicate in writing and signed by the arbitrator or arbitrators.
3. If a minority of the arbitrators refuses to sign, this shall be stated by the other arbitrators in the award signed by them. A similar statement shall be made if a minority is incapable of signing and it is unlikely that the impediment will cease to exist shortly.
4. The award shall not state a minority opinion. However, a minority may express its opinion to the co-arbitrators and the parties in a separate written document. This document shall not be considered to be a part of the award.

Article 44 – Contents of the award

1. The award shall in any event contain:
   - (a) the name and place of residence of the arbitrator or each of the arbitrators;
   - (b) the name and place of residence of each of the parties;
   - (c) a brief summary of the proceedings;
   - (d) a description of the claim and, if submitted, of the counterclaim;
   - (e) the reasons for the decision given in the award;
   - (f) the determination and order to pay the arbitration costs as referred to in Article 57;
   - (g) the decision;
   - (h) the place where the award is made, as determined by the parties or by the arbitral tribunal, with the determination of the place of arbitration in accordance with Article 21(7); and
   - (i) the date on which the award is made.

2. If the award is a decision to grant provisional relief, a partial final award or an interim award, the determination of and the order to pay the arbitration costs mentioned in paragraph 1(f) may be stayed until a later point in the proceedings.
3. In derogation of the provisions of paragraph 1(e), the award shall contain no grounds for the decision given if, after the arbitration has been commenced, the parties agree in writing that no grounds shall be given for the decision.

Article 45 – Sending and deposit of the award
1. The administrator shall ensure on behalf of the arbitral tribunal that, as soon as possible:
   (a) an original of the award, or a copy thereof certified by an arbitrator or by the administrator as the designated third person, is sent to the parties; and
   (b) if the parties have so requested from the administrator before the award is made, an original of a final or partial final award made in the Netherlands is deposited with the registry of the district court within whose district the place of arbitration is located, after which the administrator shall notify the parties and arbitral tribunal of the date of deposit as soon as possible.
2. An original of the award shall remain in the NAI archives for a period of ten years. During that period, each of the parties may request the administrator to provide a certified copy of the award at cost.

Article 46 – Binding effect of the award
An arbitral award shall be binding upon the parties with effect from the day on which it is made. By agreeing arbitration before or by the NAI or according to the Rules of the NAI, the parties shall be deemed to have accepted the obligation to comply with the award as soon as possible.

Article 47 – Rectification of the award
1. A party may, within two months after the date of the award, request that the arbitral tribunal correct a manifest computing error, clerical error or other error that lends itself to simple rectification in the award.
2. If the particulars referred to in Article 44(1)(a), (b), (h) and (i) are stated incorrectly or are partially or wholly absent from the award, a party may, within two months after the date of the award, request that the arbitral tribunal correct such particulars.
3. The request shall be submitted to the administrator. The administrator shall send a copy of the request to the arbitral tribunal and the other party as soon as possible.
4. The arbitral tribunal may, within two months after the date of the award, also of its own motion, proceed to the correction referred to in paragraph 1 and paragraph 2.
5. Before the arbitral tribunal decides on the request referred to in paragraph 1 or paragraph 2, or decides of its own motion to proceed to the correction as referred to in paragraph 4, it shall give the parties the opportunity to comment on the matter.
6. If the arbitral tribunal proceeds to the correction, it shall be mentioned by the arbitral tribunal in a separate document, which document shall be considered to be a part of the award. The document shall be drawn up in quadruplicate and shall contain:
   (a) the particulars stated in Article 44(1) (a) and (b);
   (b) a reference to the award to which the rectification relates;
   (c) the correction;
   (d) the date of the correction, it being understood that the date of the award to which the correction relates remains decisive; and
   (e) a signature to which the provisions of Article 43 apply.
7. The administrator shall ensure that the document referred to in paragraph 6 will be sent to the parties as soon as possible; the provisions of Article 45(1) shall apply mutatis mutandis.

8. If the arbitral tribunal denies the request for the correction, it shall so notify the parties by intervention of the administrator.

Article 48 – Additional award

1. Within two months after the date of the award, any party may request the arbitral tribunal to make an additional award as to any one or more claims or counterclaims presented to the arbitral tribunal but not decided by it.
2. The request shall be submitted to the administrator. The administrator shall send a copy of the request to the arbitral tribunal and the other party as soon as possible.
3. Before the arbitral tribunal decides on the request, it shall give the parties the opportunity to comment on the matter.
4. An additional award shall constitute an arbitral award to which the provisions of this section shall be applicable.
5. If the arbitral tribunal denies a request for an additional award, it shall so notify the parties by intervention of the administrator. If the award regarding which an additional award was requested is deposited with the registry of the district court in accordance with the provisions of Article 45(1)(b), the administrator shall ensure deposit, on behalf of the arbitral tribunal, of a copy of this notice, signed by an arbitrator or the secretary of the arbitral tribunal, with the registry in the same manner.

Article 49 – Remission during setting aside proceedings

1. If, during setting aside proceedings against an arbitral award made with due observance of the provisions of this section, the competent court enables the arbitral tribunal by remission to reverse the ground for setting aside, the arbitral tribunal's mandate shall revive at the time referred to in paragraph 2 in the sense that it shall be expected to reverse the ground for setting aside indicated by the competent court if possible, by reopening the arbitral proceedings or by taking any other measure considered appropriate by the arbitral tribunal.
2. The most diligent party shall notify the administrator as soon as possible of the decision by the competent court, submitting a copy of the decision and sending a copy to the other party at the same time. The administrator shall ensure that the notice is sent to the arbitral tribunal. The further mandate of the arbitral tribunal referred to in paragraph 1 shall commence on the day of receipt of the notice by the arbitral tribunal.
3. In the event of remission, the arbitral tribunal, having heard the parties, shall decide on the further rules of procedure. The provisions of Section Four shall only apply insofar as the arbitral tribunal so determines. In addition to Articles 55(1) and 55(4), the administrator shall be authorised to require a deposit for the fees and disbursements of the arbitrator or arbitrators from the party that he deems to be the most diligent party.
4. Before the arbitral tribunal decides, it shall give the parties the opportunity to be heard.
5. If the arbitral tribunal finds that the ground for setting aside is capable of being reversed, it shall make a corresponding arbitral award that replaces the award in respect of which the claim for setting aside was presented.

Article 50 – Arbitral award on agreed terms

1. If the parties reach a settlement during the proceedings, the parties may jointly request the arbitral tribunal to record its contents in an arbitral award.
2. The award on agreed terms referred to in paragraph 1 shall be regarded as an arbitral award to which the provisions of this section shall be applicable, it being understood that the award, in derogation of the provisions of Article 44(1)(e), need not contain any grounds for the decision rendered.

Article 51 – Publication of the award

The NAI shall be authorised to have the award published without stating the names of the parties and leaving out all other information that might reveal the parties' identities, unless a party objects to such publication with the administrator within two months of the date of the award.

SECTION SIX – COSTS

Article 52 – Costs of the arbitration

The costs of the arbitration shall be understood to mean the costs mentioned in Articles 53, 54 and 56 and the other costs necessarily incurred in the arbitration in the opinion of the arbitral tribunal.

Article 53 – Administration costs

1. Upon commencing the arbitration, the claimant shall owe the NAI administration costs in accordance with the provisions of paragraph 2. The administrator shall notify the claimant of this amount as soon as possible after receipt of the request for arbitration.
2. The administration costs shall be calculated on the basis of the total monetary interest of the claims, including contingent claims, using the scale determined by the Executive Board as included in Appendix A to these Rules. The Executive Board may make interim changes to this scale in accordance with the provisions of Article 62. In the event that the administration costs cannot be calculated on the basis of the scale, the administrator shall decide.
3. In the event that a counterclaim, including a contingent counterclaim, is submitted, the respondent shall also be charged administration costs according to the provisions of paragraph 2. The administrator shall notify the respondent of this amount as soon as possible after the counterclaim has been presented.
4. In the event of an increase of claim or counterclaim or if it emerges during the proceedings that the total monetary interest is higher than assumed by the administrator at the time notice was given as referred to in paragraph 1 or paragraph 3, the claimant and the respondent, respectively, shall owe a supplemental amount of administration costs according to the provisions of paragraph 2.
5. The administrator shall see to the collection of the administration costs owed. If, after a second reminder from the administrator, the administration costs owed by a party are not received by the NAI within fourteen days, this party shall be deemed to have withdrawn its claim or counterclaim.
6. If a claimant withdraws its request for arbitration before the arbitration file is sent to the arbitral tribunal, it shall receive back half of the administration costs it has paid. The same applies if a respondent withdraws its counterclaim before the arbitration file is sent. In other events, the administration costs shall not be reimbursed.

Article 54 – Arbitrator fees and disbursements

1. The fees and disbursements of the arbitrator or arbitrators shall be reasonably determined by the administrator after consulting with the arbitrator or arbitrators.
2. If an arbitrator is released from his mandate before the last final award, such arbitrator may claim reasonable compensation, to be determined by the administrator, for fees and disbursements, except in special circumstances at the administrator's discretion.
3. If the arbitral tribunal's mandate is terminated before the last final award, the arbitrator or arbitrators may also claim reasonable compensation, to be determined by the administrator, for fees and disbursements, unless termination is effected pursuant to Article 17(5).
4. In determining the fee, the time that the arbitrator or arbitrators devoted to the proceedings, the monetary interest of the claims and counterclaims and the complexity of the proceedings shall be taken into account.

Article 55 – Deposit

1. The administrator shall require a deposit from the claimant from which, insofar as possible, the fees and disbursements of the arbitrator or arbitrators shall be paid. If the respondent has submitted a counterclaim, including a contingent counterclaim, the administrator may also require a deposit from the respondent for the same.
2. The costs of the secretary, the expert appointed by the arbitral tribunal, technical assistance and an interpreter shall also be paid from the deposit, if and insofar as these costs were incurred by the arbitral tribunal. If the parties have agreed to deposit the award with the court registry, the deposit shall also be used to pay the associated costs.
3. As soon as possible after the arbitration file has been sent, the arbitrator or the chair shall consult with the administrator regarding the scope of work expected from him, in order to determine the amount of the deposit.
4. The administrator may require the claimant and/or the respondent to increase the deposit until fourteen days after the last hearing at the latest or, in the absence of a hearing, until fourteen days after receipt by the arbitral tribunal of the last permitted statement at the latest.
5. The administrator shall notify the arbitral tribunal of the deposit.
6. The arbitral tribunal shall be authorised to suspend the arbitration in respect of the claim or the counterclaim as long as he relevant party has not made the deposit required. If the NAI does not receive the deposit required from a party within fourteen days after a second reminder from the administrator, that party shall be deemed to have withdrawn its claim or counterclaim.
7. The NAI shall not be held to pay any costs that are not covered by a deposit. The costs referred to in paragraph 2 shall first be paid from the deposit. No interest shall be paid on the amount of the deposit made.

Article 56 – Costs of legal assistance

The arbitral tribunal may order the unsuccessful party to pay reasonable compensation for the successful party's legal assistance, if and insofar as these costs were necessary in the arbitral tribunal's opinion.

Article 57 – Determination of arbitration costs and order

1. The arbitral tribunal shall determine the costs of the arbitration with due observance of the provisions of Article 54.
2. The unsuccessful party shall be ordered to pay the costs of the arbitration, except in special events at the arbitral tribunal's discretion. If each of the parties is partially unsuccessful, the arbitral tribunal may divide all or part of the costs of the arbitration.
3. In ordering a party to pay the costs, the arbitral tribunal shall take account of the deposit made under Article 55. Insofar as the deposit made by a party is used to pay costs that the other party is ordered to pay in accordance with the previous paragraph, the latter party shall be ordered to reimburse the former party for such amount.
4. Payment of the costs of the arbitration may also be ordered if a party did not expressly seek such payment.
5. If the mandate of an arbitrator or arbitrators is terminated before the last final award, the compensation for fees and disbursements determined in accordance with Article 54 and the costs referred to in Article 55(2) shall be borne by the parties in proportion to their contribution to the deposit. The administrator may, insofar as necessary in derogation of Article 55(4), require the claimant and/or the respondent to supplement the deposit to the full amount of said compensation and costs.

SECTION SEVEN – FINAL PROVISIONS

Article 58 – Timely objection
A party that has appeared in the proceedings shall make objection to the arbitral tribunal without unreasonable delay, sending a copy thereof to the other party and the administrator as soon as it knows or reasonably should know of any act contrary to, or failure to act in accordance with, any provision of these Rules, the arbitration agreement or any order, decision or measure of the arbitral tribunal. If a party fails to do so, then the right to rely on this later, in the arbitral proceedings or before the ordinary court, shall be forfeited.

Article 59 – Competent provisional relief judge
If the place of arbitration is located in the Netherlands, the provisional relief judge of the Rotterdam district court shall have jurisdiction for the cases as referred to in Article 1027(3) (appointment of the arbitrator or arbitrators), Article 1028 (privileged position of a party with regard to the appointment of the arbitrator or arbitrators) and Article 1041a (hearing an unwilling witness) of the Dutch Code of Civil Procedure.

Article 60 – Contingencies
Without prejudice to the provisions of Article 21(1), in all events not provided for in these Rules, action shall be taken in accordance with the spirit of these Rules.

Article 61 – Limitation of liability
The NAI, its board members and personnel, the members of its Advisory & Supervisory Board, the members of the Committee, the arbitrator or arbitrators and any secretary that may have been appointed, the third person as referred to in Article 39 and any other persons involved in the case by any or all of them shall not be liable either by contract or otherwise for any damage caused by their own or any other person's acts or omissions or caused by the use of any aids in or involving arbitration, all this unless and insofar as mandatory Dutch law precludes exoneration. The NAI, its board members and personnel shall not be liable for payment of any amount that is not covered by the deposit.

Article 62 – Amendment of the Rules
1. The Executive Board may amend these Rules at any time. The amendments shall have no effect on arbitral proceedings already pending.
2. The Rules shall apply in the form they have at the time at which the arbitration is commenced.
3. In derogation of paragraph 2, Articles 39, 42(1) and 42(3) shall only apply to arbitration agreements concluded on or after 1 January 2015 in which the parties have referred to arbitration by or before the NAI or according to the Rules of the NAI, unless the parties have agreed otherwise. With such arbitration agreements concluded before 1 January 2015, Article 45 and, in that connection, Article 1(g) of the Rules applicable until 1 January 2015 shall continue to apply.

1. The NAI

1.1 The Netherlands Arbitration Institute (Stichting Nederlands Arbitrage Instituut; "NAI") was founded in 1949. The NAI Executive Board consists of people from the business community, the legal profession and science who have extensive experience in the fields of arbitration, binding advice and mediation.

1.2 The Institute's mission is to promote arbitration, binding advice and other legal means for the prevention, limitation and resolution of disputes. Since its establishment, the NAI has pursued this aim by providing trade and industry with a soundly regulated arbitral procedure. These Arbitration

Rules form the basis of that procedure. In addition, the NAI may be designated as an appointing authority for the appointment of arbitrators, also if the parties have not agreed to applicability of these Arbitration Rules. Besides arbitration, the NAI also offers binding advice and mediation as types of alternative dispute resolution, for which it has drafted separate rules. The NAI secretariat provides the administration required in these types of dispute resolution under the direction of the administrator.

2. The NAI Arbitration Rules

2.1 A new Dutch Arbitration Act (Articles 1020-1076 of the Dutch Code of Civil Procedure) entered into force on 1 January 2015. A revised version of the Arbitration Rules entered into force on the same date.

Article 62(2) provides that the Arbitration Rules apply in the form they have at the time at which the arbitration is commenced. Consequently, this version of the Arbitration Rules applies to arbitration commenced on or after 1 January 2015, regardless of the date on which the arbitration agreement was concluded. The provisions on consolidation (Article 39) and the measure for decision-making to be used by arbitrators (Articles 42(1) and 42(3)) form an exception to this. Those articles apply only if (i) the arbitration agreement was concluded after 1 January 2015 or (ii) the parties have agreed otherwise (Article 62(3)).

Please refer to the NAI website, www.nai-nl.org, for relevant literature on the Dutch Arbitration Act and the NAI Arbitration Rules.

3. Format and contents of an agreement for NAI arbitration

3.1 Arbitration requires an agreement. The Act uses the general term "arbitration agreement". Such an agreement may consist of a clause in an agreement stipulating that any future disputes will be submitted to arbitration (the arbitration clause). For existing disputes, an arbitration agreement is concluded in the form of a submission agreement.

3.2 The Act requires that every arbitration agreement be proven by an instrument in writing. This means that an oral arbitration agreement or customary practice is insufficient to prove the existence of an arbitration agreement.

3.3 Arbitration in accordance with the NAI Arbitration Rules also requires that the parties have agreed the applicability of these Rules. In the event of an arbitration clause, the clause recommended by the NAI may be used (see p. 6). The parties may also elect to word their arbitration clause differently. However, the wording provided by the NAI has proven in practice to cause the least amount of difficulties.

3.4 If the parties have not agreed an arbitration clause, they may still submit any disputes that have arisen between them to NAI arbitration by entering into a submission agreement. To that end, a document accepted by the parties in writing will suffice if it contains: (a) the names of the parties, (b) an indication of the disputes the parties are submitting to arbitration (preferably broadly worded), and (c) the provision that these disputes are to be resolved in accordance with the NAI Arbitration Rules.

3.5 In drafting the arbitration agreement, the parties may provide for various matters, such as the number of arbitrators, the method of appointment, the place of arbitration, the language of the arbitration, and the measure for decision-making (see the notes to the model clause). The place of arbitration determines the applicable arbitration law. If, for instance, a place of arbitration in the Netherlands is elected, Dutch arbitration law applies. That does not mean, however, that hearings are to be held in this place as well. The parties may also elect to rule out the option of consolidation of the arbitral proceedings with other arbitral proceedings (see also point 12 below).

4. Commencement of arbitration

4.1 Both in the event of an arbitration clause and in the event of a submission agreement, NAI arbitration is commenced by submitting a request for arbitration to the NAI administrator by e-mail (Articles 3(2) and 7(3)). If the claimant is unable to submit the request by e-mail, it may be submitted in another manner (Article 7(3)). The request is not tied to a specific format. If desired, the request form available on the NAI website may be used.

4.2 The request must contain the particulars mentioned in (a) to (j), inclusive, of Article 7(2). The administrator is authorised to suspend handling the request as long as it does not satisfy the requirements mentioned in Article 7(2).

4.3 The administrator will send a copy to the respondent. The respondent will then have fourteen days to submit a short answer in response (Article 8). It may simultaneously present a (conditional or unconditional) counterclaim (Article 8(3)). Although any counterclaim should preferably be known at the earliest possible stage of the proceedings (in particular with a view to the arbitrator or arbitrators to be appointed), the respondent may also present a counterclaim later. It must do so at the latest with the statement of defence or, if no statement of defence is presented, with its first written or oral defence after the arbitrators have accepted their mandate (Article 24(2)).

4.4 The request for arbitration and the short answer may be summary. They are intended primarily to (i) provide the NAI secretariat with the information required for the administration of the arbitration and (ii) provide insight into the nature and circumstances of the dispute in connection with any determination of the number of arbitrators and any appointment of the arbitrator or arbitrators. After the arbitrators have been appointed, the parties will be given ample opportunity to present their arguments. The short answer is not considered to be a 'first defence' within the meaning of, for example, Article 10. The request for arbitration and the short answer are not a statement of claim and statement of defence, either; these can only be presented after the arbitrators have been appointed (Articles 9 and 23).

4.5 The commencement of summary arbitral proceedings in cases in which arbitration on the merits is not yet pending between the same parties and no arbitral tribunal has as yet been appointed is regulated in Article 35(2) and Article 36. Please refer to point 9 of this Explanation for an explanation of summary arbitral proceedings in general and the manner in which the Arbitration Rules provide for such proceedings.

5. Plea as to the non-existence of an arbitration agreement

5.1 The administrator does not assess whether the parties have agreed to arbitration and have declared the Arbitration Rules applicable. The arbitral tribunal will assess any objection by the respondent that no (NAI) arbitration has been agreed (Article 10).

5.2 A respondent wishing to raise a plea as to the non-existence of a valid (NAI) arbitration agreement must do so in a timely manner, i.e. at the latest in the statement of defence or, in the absence thereof, prior to the first written or oral defence. If the respondent has failed to raise such a plea in a timely manner, there will be no opportunity later, in the arbitral proceedings or before the court, to complain about the non-existence of an (NAI) arbitration agreement (unless it makes the plea on the ground that the dispute is not capable of settlement by arbitration). Similar rules apply to summary arbitral proceedings (Article 36(6)).

6. Appointment of arbitrators

6.1 Arbitral proceedings are conducted before one or more arbitrators, always being an uneven number (Article 12(1)). If the parties have agreed an even number of arbitrators, an additional arbitrator will be appointed as chair of the arbitral tribunal in order to arrive at an uneven number (Article 12(3)).

6.2 If the parties have not agreed the number of arbitrators, or if they have agreed a method of determining arbitrators but cannot jointly reach agreement in this respect, the administrator will set the number of arbitrators at one or three. In doing so, the administrator will take account of the parties' preference, the scope of the dispute, the complexity of the case and the parties' interest in efficient proceedings (Article 12(2)). As a rule, one arbitrator will be appointed for arbitration involving a financial interest of less than EUR 500,000.

Appointment by the parties

6.3 Unless the parties have agreed otherwise, the arbitral tribunal will be appointed in accordance with the procedure set out in Article 13:

(i) If the arbitral tribunal consists of one arbitrator, the parties will jointly appoint an arbitrator when submitting the request for arbitration or the short answer (or at least within fourteen days after the administrator has asked them to do so). If they fail to do so within this time-limit, the arbitrator will be appointed in accordance with the list procedure of Article 14.

(ii) If the arbitral tribunal consists of three arbitrators, the claimant and the respondent will each appoint an arbitrator in the request for arbitration and the short answer, respectively (or at least within fourteen days after the administrator has asked them to do so). If any party fails to do so within this time-limit, the administrator will send that party or those parties a list of possible arbitrators and the relevant arbitrator will be appointed in accordance with the list procedure of Article 14. Subsequently, within fourteen days after the administrator has asked them to do so, the two arbitrators thus appointed will appoint the third arbitrator, who will also act as the chair of the arbitral tribunal. If they fail to do so within this time-limit, the third arbitrator will be appointed in accordance with the list procedure of Article 14.

List procedure

6.4 In derogation of Article 13, the parties may agree that the arbitrator or arbitrators will be appointed in accordance with the list procedure set out in Article 14. Under the list procedure, the administrator compiles a list of the names of possible arbitrators after receipt of the short answer. This list contains at least three names if one arbitrator is to be appointed and at least nine names (including the prospective chairmen) if three arbitrators are to be appointed. The list is sent to both parties. Each party then has fourteen days to deliberate, delete the names of those persons against whom it has strong objections and number the remaining names in its order of preference. Based on a comparison of the returned lists, the administrator subsequently appoints the arbitrator or arbitrators. The administrator is not required to provide the parties with new lists if there is an insufficient number of persons on the returned lists who are acceptable as arbitrators to each of the parties. The same applies if a sufficient number of persons appear on the returned lists but they cannot or will not accept their appointment. In such events, the administrator may directly proceed to appoint other arbitrators.

6.5 Please refer to point 9 below for the appointment of the arbitral tribunal in summary arbitral proceedings.

6.6 The appointment of an arbitrator will be confirmed by the administrator, unless the arbitrator, in the administrator's opinion, offers insufficient safeguards for sound arbitration (Article 16(1)). As and when necessary, the administrator may also take account of the required availability of the arbitrator and the parties' interest in expeditious proceedings. The confirmation of an appointment by the administrator does not affect the option of challenging an arbitrator; the ultimate decision on a challenge request is reserved to the Committee (see point 11 below).

7. The procedure

7.1 After the arbitrator or arbitrators have been appointed, the actual arbitral proceedings commence. Unless the parties have made other arrangements, the course of the proceedings will be determined by the arbitral tribunal in consultation with the parties and generally take the following form. First the claimant and respondent are given the opportunity to submit a statement of claim and a statement of defence, respectively. This may be followed by a second exchange of statements (a statement of reply and a statement of rejoinder). Then a hearing is held, in which the parties and/or their counsel may each further set out their arguments. Any witnesses or experts may also be heard at this hearing, or at a separate hearing. After the hearing, the arbitral tribunal deliberates (if it consists of more than one arbitrator) and the award is written. The award is drafted in four copies and signed by the arbitrator or arbitrators, after which the administrator, on behalf of the arbitral tribunal, sends a certified copy of the award to the parties.

7.2 The above is a concise version of the proceedings in average arbitration. All the rules can be found in Section Four of the Arbitration Rules (Articles 21-39). The parties are free to agree a different procedure. Apart from such an agreement, the arbitral tribunal is also authorised to determine a different procedure depending on the nature and circumstances of the dispute.

7.3 The Arbitration Rules provide that the arbitral tribunal must guard against unreasonable delay of the proceedings and, if necessary, take measures at the request of a party or of its own motion (Article 21(3)).

7.4 At the end of the hearing, the arbitral tribunal communicates to the parties at which time it will make its award. If the parties have waived a hearing as referred to in Article 25, the arbitral tribunal will communicate this after the last statement has been presented. The arbitral tribunal is authorised to extend the time-limit one or more times if necessary. In any event, however, the arbitral tribunal will decide expeditiously (Article 40(1)).

7.5 Article 17(4) gives the administrator the authority to release an arbitrator from his mandate of his own motion (but if he does so, this does not automatically release the entire arbitral tribunal). Failure to perform the mandate given to an arbitrator (as referred to in Article 17(4)) also includes the provision in Article 21(3) in respect of guarding against any delay of the arbitral proceedings.

8. The costs

8.1 The arbitrator fees are determined on the basis of the time that the arbitrator or arbitrators devoted to the proceedings, the monetary interest of the claims and counterclaims and the complexity of the proceedings (Article 54(4)). A party presenting a (conditional or unconditional) claim or counterclaim must pay a deposit to the NAI for the fees and other costs of the arbitrators (Article 55). The NAI has adopted guidelines for determining the hourly rate for arbitrators, which are available on the NAI website.

8.2 Upon commencing the arbitration, administration costs are owed to the NAI (Article 53). These costs are calculated on the basis of the scale included in the Appendix to the Arbitration Rules (see Appendix) and have been determined such that the NAI – a non-profit foundation – can cover the costs of its organisation. Administration costs are also due for a counterclaim or conditional (counter) claim.

8.3 Arbitration may involve other costs as well, for example costs for witnesses, experts and the arbitral tribunal's secretary. These costs are not incurred in every arbitration, however, and depend on the nature and circumstances of the dispute.

8.4 As soon as possible after the arbitration file has been sent, the arbitrator or, if there are multiple arbitrators, the chair of the arbitral tribunal will consult with the administrator regarding the work expected and the amount of the deposit (Article 55(3)). This amount may be increased during the proceedings. In that event, the administrator may require the claimant and/or respondent to supplement the deposit. This may be done at the latest on the fourteenth day after the last hearing or, in the absence of a hearing, on the fourteenth day after receipt by the arbitral tribunal of the last permitted statement (Article 55(4)).

8.5 In principle, the unsuccessful party will be ordered to pay the costs of the arbitration. If both parties are partially successful, the arbitral tribunal may divide all or part of the costs of the arbitration (Article 57(2)).

9. Provisional relief - the summary arbitral proceedings

9.1 The Arbitration Rules provide for the option of provisional relief:

(i) if arbitral proceedings on the merits are already pending, the arbitral tribunal appointed in that case may, at the request of any of the parties, grant provisional relief related to the claim or counterclaim as presented (Article 35(1));

(ii) provided that the place of arbitration is located within the Netherlands, in all urgent cases that require immediately relief in view of the parties' interests, an arbitral tribunal appointed to that end may also, at the request of a party, grant provisional relief in summary arbitral proceedings. This option is open regardless of whether arbitral proceedings on the merits are already pending (Article 35(2)).

9.2 This means that even if arbitral proceedings on the merits are already pending and the place of arbitration in those proceedings is located within the Netherlands, a party that wishes to present a claim for granting provisional relief may present this claim, in its discretion, to the existing arbitral tribunal pursuant to Article 35(1) or to an arbitral tribunal to be appointed especially to that end pursuant to Article 35(2). In the latter event, however, the claiming party should bear in mind that the arbitral tribunal in summary proceedings will apply a stricter urgency test and, in the absence of a (sufficiently) urgent interest, will deny the provisional relief sought and will rule that the claim for granting provisional relief must be submitted to the arbitral tribunal in the arbitral proceedings on the merits.

9.3 In the event of summary arbitral proceedings as referred to in Article 35(2), the arbitral tribunal consists of one arbitrator, who will be appointed to that end by the administrator. If the parties have agreed a method of appointment of the arbitral tribunal and/or a multiple number of arbitrators, this will not be applied with regard to the appointment of the arbitral tribunal in summary arbitral proceedings, unless the parties have provided for this in so many words (Article 36(4)). The further course of the proceedings will be in accordance with the provisions of Article 36.

9.4 The arbitral tribunal may, in conjunction with the provisional relief, require any party to provide sufficient security, both for the provisional relief sought and for the claim or counterclaim in the main action and the costs of the arbitral proceedings on the merits (Article 35(3)). This power is vested in both the arbitral tribunal on the merits referred to in Article 35(1) and the arbitral tribunal in summary arbitral proceedings referred to in Article 35(2).

9.5 The decision on the provisional relief does not in any way prejudice the ultimate ruling in the arbitral proceedings on the merits (Article 35(5)). The decision may be taken in the form of an order by the arbitral tribunal or in the form of an arbitral award (Article 35(4)). An arbitral tribunal as referred to in Article 35(1) or Article 35(2) may, at the unanimous request of the parties, instead of taking a decision on provisional relief, take a decision on the merits in the form of an arbitral award (Article 35(6)), or convert an arbitral award on provisional relief into an arbitral award on the merits (Article 35(7)).

9.6 Summary arbitral proceedings are distinct from accelerated proceedings. Proceedings of this type – called "expedited proceedings" in arbitration – do result in a decision regarding the dispute itself, albeit within a short period of time. In urgent cases, a party may ask the arbitral tribunal to establish appropriate rules of procedure. The parties may also agree reduced time-limits themselves. As summary arbitral proceedings significantly and predominantly accommodate the need for an expedited decision or relief, the Arbitration Rules have no separate provisions governing "expedited arbitration".

10. Impartiality and independence

10.1 The fundamental principle of the impartiality and independence of arbitrators is laid down in Article 11(2). These requirements of impartiality and independence entail that an arbitrator may not have any close personal or business ties with any of the parties or with any of his co-arbitrators, nor may he have any direct personal or business interest in the outcome of the proceedings. If a person who cannot satisfy these requirements is approached to be engaged as arbitrator, he must decline the invitation to act as arbitrator.

Before the appointment

10.2 Before being appointed, a proposed arbitrator may be in contact with a party – or its representative or attorney – with regard to the case, provided that (i) the contact is limited to the availability and qualifications of the arbitrator himself or potential candidates for the role of chair of the arbitral tribunal, and (ii) the substantive or procedural aspects of the case are not discussed, save to the extent that this is necessary to inform the proposed arbitrator of the background of the case. The proposed arbitrator may not communicate his opinion on the case to any of the parties prior to his appointment.

10.3 If the proposed arbitrator has reason to suspect that there could be justifiable doubts as to his impartiality and independence, he will communicate the same in writing to the person who approached him (Article 11(3)). The suspected reason(s) for these justifiable doubts will also be stated.

10.4 Prior to the confirmation of appointment (Article 16(1)), each arbitrator must sign a statement confirming his independence and impartiality and send this statement to the administrator (Article 11(4)).

During the proceedings

10.5 During the proceedings, the arbitrator may not have any contact with any of the parties about matters relating to the proceedings, unless the other parties and (if the tribunal consists of multiple arbitrators) his co-arbitrators have given their consent.

10.6 If an arbitrator, during the arbitral proceedings, suspects that there could be justifiable doubts as to his impartiality and independence, he will communicate the same in writing to the administrator, the parties and, if the arbitral tribunal consists of multiple arbitrators, to the co-arbitrators (Article 11(5)). The suspected reason(s) for these justifiable doubts will also be stated.

Challenge

10.7 If a party wishes to challenge an arbitrator in response to the communications mentioned in points 10.3 and 10.6, it must do so within fourteen days of receipt of the relevant communication (see point 11.2 below).

11. Challenge

11.1 If there are justifiable doubts as to the independence or impartiality of an arbitrator, that arbitrator may be challenged by a party (Article 19(1)). A party may only challenge an arbitrator appointed by that party for reasons of which that party became aware only after the appointment was made. A chair of the arbitral tribunal appointed in accordance with Article 13(3) or an arbitrator appointed in accordance with the list procedure of Article 14 may only be challenged by a party if that party became aware of the reasons for challenge only after the appointment of that arbitrator (Article 19(2)).

11.2 If an arbitrator, in accordance with Article 11(3), 11(4) or 11(5), communicates circumstances or reasons that may give rise to justifiable doubts as to his independence or impartiality and a party wishes to challenge this arbitrator for that reason, that party must give written notice to the arbitrator concerned, the other party and, if the arbitral tribunal consists of multiple arbitrators, the co-arbitrators within fourteen days of receipt of this communication. In all other events, such notice must be given within fourteen days after the party that wishes to challenge an arbitrator has become aware of the reason for the challenge (Article 19(3)).

11.3 The challenged arbitrator may resign of his own motion within fourteen days of receipt of a timely notice of challenge, without thereby accepting that the reason for the challenge is well-founded (Articles 19(5) and 19(7)). If the challenged arbitrator does not do so, (members of) the Committee appointed by the NAI Executive Board will decide on the challenge request. The Committee may give the challenged arbitrator and the parties the opportunity to be heard before it takes a decision.

11.4 If an arbitrator resigns of his own motion in response to a challenge request or if the Committee finds the challenge request to be well-founded, the relevant arbitrator will be replaced according to the rules applicable to the original appointment, unless the parties have agreed otherwise (Articles 19(6) and 18(1)).

12. Consolidation

12.1 A party may submit a request to the administrator for consolidation of arbitral proceedings pending in the Netherlands with other arbitral proceedings pending within or outside the Netherlands, provided that the NAI Arbitration Rules apply to both arbitral proceedings (Article 39(1)). Such consolidation may be ordered insofar as it does not cause unreasonable delay in the pending proceedings (Article 39(4)).

12.2 The administrator will send a copy of the request for consolidation to all parties and, insofar as already appointed, the arbitrators, and will invite the parties to jointly appoint a third person within fourteen days, which third person will decide on the request for consolidation (Articles 39(2) and 39(3)(a)). The pending arbitral proceedings may be suspended by the arbitral tribunal from the day of receipt of the request for consolidation (Article 39(2)). If the parties fail to reach agreement, the administrator will directly appoint the third person (Article 39(3)(b)). In principle, the arbitrators appointed in the arbitral proceedings whose consolidation is requested will not be appointed as a third person to decide on the request for consolidation, unless the parties have agreed otherwise (Article 39(3)(c)).

12.3 Before deciding on the request for consolidation, the third person will give the parties and, insofar as already appointed, the arbitrators an opportunity to make their opinions known (Article 39(5)).

12.4 If the third person orders consolidation, the parties, in mutual consultation, will have four weeks to appoint the arbitrator or arbitrators (in an uneven number) to the consolidated proceedings. If the parties are unable to reach agreement in this regard within this time-limit, the third person will, at the request of the most diligent party, appoint the arbitrator or arbitrators (Article 39(6)).

12.5 The mandate of the arbitrator or arbitrators appointed to the proceedings that were separately commenced will terminate if they are not appointed again to the consolidated proceedings. Insofar as necessary, the third person will determine the remuneration for the work carried out by such arbitrator(s) (Article 39(7)).

13. Confidentiality and secrecy

13.1 Article 6 provides that NAI arbitration is confidential and that all persons involved either directly or indirectly are bound to secrecy, except – and insofar as – disclosure ensues from the law or an agreement between the parties.

13.2 The NAI is authorised to publish the award in anonymous form. If, however, a party objects to publication of the award with the administrator within two months of the date of the award, the award will not be published (Article 51). In the event of any publication of an arbitral award, the NAI will anonymise the award with the utmost care.

14. International arbitration

14.1 In line with the Dutch Arbitration Act, the Arbitration Rules do not distinguish between national and international arbitration. The Arbitration Rules may also be applied regardless of whether the place of arbitration is located within or outside the Netherlands. It should be noted, however, that if the place of arbitration is located outside the Netherlands, the Dutch Arbitration Act does not apply (see Article 1073 of this Act).

14.2 Summary arbitral proceedings may also be conducted in international arbitration, but only if the place of arbitration is located in the Netherlands, as noted in point 9.1(ii) above.

14.3 For arbitration with foreign parties, a translation of the Arbitration Rules is available in English on the NAI website.

15. UNCITRAL Arbitration Rules

15.1 The NAI is willing to act as Appointing Authority under the Arbitration Rules of the United Nations Commission on International Trade Law (UNCITRAL) if the parties have so agreed. In that event, the arbitration clause as recommended by UNCITRAL may read:

> *Any dispute, controversy or claim arising out of or relating to this contract, or the breach, termination or invalidity thereof, shall be settled by arbitration in accordance with the UNCITRAL Arbitration Rules.*
> *The appointing authority shall be the Netherlands Arbitration Institute, Rotterdam.*
> *The number of arbitrators shall be [one or three].*
> *The place of arbitration shall be [town or country].*
> *The language(s) to be used in the arbitral proceedings shall be [language].*

15.2 If such an arbitration agreement has been concluded, the NAI Arbitration Rules do not apply and the NAI will appoint arbitrators in accordance with the UNCITRAL Rules. If desired, the NAI secretariat may be asked to provide technical assistance (meeting rooms, secretarial work, etc.) in international arbitration of this type as well.

15.3 The administration costs payable when the NAI acts as Appointing Authority are specified in the Appendix to the Arbitration Rules (see Appendix).

16. Exclusion of liability

Article 61 provides for the limitation of liability.

9.4.6 ICSID Convention Arbitration Rules (2022)

INTRODUCTORY NOTE

The ICSID Arbitration Rules were adopted by the Administrative Council of the Centre pursuant to Article 6(1)(c) of the ICSID Convention.
The ICSID Arbitration Rules are supplemented by the ICSID Administrative and Financial Regulations.
The ICSID Arbitration Rules apply from the date of registration of a Request for arbitration until an Award is rendered and to any post-Award remedy proceedings.

CHAPTER I: GENERAL PROVISIONS

Rule 1: Application of Rules
(1) These Rules shall apply to any arbitration proceeding conducted under the Convention on the Settlement of Investment Disputes between States and Nationals of Other States ("Convention") in accordance with Article 44 of the Convention.
(2) The Tribunal shall apply any agreement of the parties on procedural matters to the extent that it does not conflict with the Convention or the ICSID Administrative and Financial Regulations.

Rule 2: Party and Party Representative
(1) For the purposes of these Rules, "party" includes all parties acting as claimant or as respondent.
(2) Each party may be represented or assisted by agents, counsel, advocates or other advisors, whose names and proof of authority to act shall be promptly notified by that party to the Secretary-General ("representative(s)").

Rule 3: General Duties
(1) The Tribunal and the parties shall conduct the proceeding in good faith and in an expeditious and cost-effective manner.
(2) The Tribunal shall treat the parties equally and provide each party with a reasonable opportunity to present its case.

Rule 4: Method of Filing
(1) A document to be filed in the proceeding shall be filed with the Secretary-General, who shall acknowledge its receipt.
(2) Documents shall be filed electronically. In special circumstances, the Tribunal may order that documents also be filed in a different format.

Rule 5: Supporting Documents
(1) Supporting documents, including witness statements, expert reports, exhibits and legal authorities, shall be filed together with the request, written submission, observations or communication to which they relate.
(2) An extract of a document may be filed as a supporting document if the extract is not misleading. The Tribunal or a party may require a fuller extract or a complete version of the document.
(3) If the authenticity of a supporting document is disputed, the Tribunal may order a party to provide a certified copy or to make the original available for examination.

Rule 6: Routing of Documents

The Secretary-General shall transmit a document filed in the proceeding to:

(a) the other party, unless the parties communicate directly with each other;

(b) the Tribunal, unless the parties communicate directly with the Tribunal on request of the Tribunal or by agreement of the parties; and

(c) the Chairman of the Administrative Council ("Chair") if applicable.

Rule 7: Procedural Languages, Translation and Interpretation

(1) The parties may agree to use one or two procedural languages in the proceeding. The parties shall consult with the Tribunal and the Secretary-General regarding the use of a language that is not an official language of the Centre. If the parties do not agree on the procedural language(s), each party may select one of the official languages of the Centre.

(2) In a proceeding with one procedural language:

(a) documents shall be filed and hearings shall be conducted in that procedural language;

(b) documents in another language shall be accompanied by a translation into that procedural language; and

(c) testimony in another language shall be interpreted into that procedural language.

(3) In a proceeding with two procedural languages:

(a) documents may be filed and hearings may be conducted in either procedural language, unless the Tribunal orders that a document be filed in both procedural languages or that a hearing be conducted with interpretation into both procedural languages;

(b) documents in another language shall be accompanied by a translation into either procedural language, unless the Tribunal orders translation into both procedural languages;

(c) testimony in another language shall be interpreted into either procedural language, unless the Tribunal orders interpretation into both procedural languages;

(d) the Tribunal and the Secretary-General may communicate in either procedural language; and

(e) all orders, decisions and the Award shall be rendered in both procedural languages, unless the parties agree otherwise.

(4) Translation of only the relevant part of a supporting document is sufficient, unless the Tribunal orders a party to provide a fuller or a complete translation. If the translation is disputed, the Tribunal may order a party to provide a certified translation.

Rule 8: Correction of Errors

A party may correct an accidental error in a document promptly upon discovery and before the Award is rendered. The parties may refer any dispute regarding a correction to the Tribunal for determination.

Rule 9: Calculation of Time Limits

(1) References to time shall be determined based on the time at the seat of the Centre on the relevant date.

(2) Any time limit expressed as a period of time shall be calculated from the day after the date on which:

(a) the Tribunal, or the Secretary-General if applicable, announces the period; or

(b) the procedural step starting the period is taken.

(3) A time limit shall be satisfied if a procedural step is taken or a document is received by the Secretary-General on the relevant date, or on the subsequent business day if the date falls on a Saturday or Sunday.

Rule 10: Fixing Time Limits

(1) The Tribunal, or the Secretary-General if applicable, shall fix time limits for the completion of each procedural step in the proceeding, other than time limits prescribed by the Convention or these Rules.

(2) In fixing time limits pursuant to paragraph (1), the Tribunal, or the Secretary-General if applicable, shall consult with the parties as far as possible.
(3) The Tribunal may delegate the power to fix time limits to its President.

Rule 11: Extension of Time Limits Applicable to Parties
(1) The time limits in Articles 49, 51 and 52 of the Convention cannot be extended. An application or request filed after the expiry of such time limits shall be disregarded.
(2) A time limit prescribed by the Convention or these Rules, other than those referred to in paragraph (1), may only be extended by agreement of the parties. A procedural step taken or document received after the expiry of such time limit shall be disregarded, unless the parties agree otherwise or the Tribunal decides that there are special circumstances justifying the failure to meet the time limit.
(3) A time limit fixed by the Tribunal or the Secretary-General may be extended by agreement of the parties or the Tribunal, or the Secretary-General if applicable, upon reasoned application by either party made prior to its expiry. A procedural step taken or document received after the expiry of such time limit shall be disregarded, unless the parties agree otherwise or the Tribunal, or the Secretary-General if applicable, decides that there are special circumstances justifying the failure to meet the time limit.
(4) The Tribunal may delegate the power to extend time limits to its President.

Rule 12: Time Limits Applicable to the Tribunal
(1) The Tribunal shall use best efforts to meet time limits to render orders, decisions and the Award.
(2) If the Tribunal cannot comply with an applicable time limit, it shall advise the parties of the special circumstances justifying the delay and the date when it anticipates rendering the order, decision or Award.

CHAPTER II: ESTABLISHMENT OF THE TRIBUNAL

Rule 13: General Provisions Regarding the Establishment of the Tribunal
(1) The Tribunal shall be constituted without delay after registration of the Request for arbitration.
(2) The majority of the arbitrators on a Tribunal shall be nationals of States other than the State party to the dispute and the State whose national is a party to the dispute, unless the Sole Arbitrator or each individual member of the Tribunal is appointed by agreement of the parties.
(3) A party may not appoint an arbitrator who is a national of the State party to the dispute or the State whose national is a party to the dispute without agreement of the other party.
(4) A person previously involved in the resolution of the dispute as a conciliator, judge, mediator or in a similar capacity may be appointed as an arbitrator only by agreement of the parties.

Rule 14: Notice of Third-Party Funding
(1) A party shall file a written notice disclosing the name and address of any non-party from which the party, directly or indirectly, has received funds for the pursuit or defense of the proceeding through a donation or grant, or in return for remuneration dependent on the outcome of the proceeding ("third-party funding"). If the non-party providing funding is a juridical person, the notice shall include the names of the persons and entities that own and control that juridical person.
(2) A party shall file the notice referred to in paragraph (1) with the Secretary-General upon registration of the Request for arbitration, or immediately upon concluding a third-party funding arrangement after registration. The party shall immediately notify the Secretary-General of any changes to the information in the notice.
(3) The Secretary-General shall transmit the notice of third-party funding and any notification of changes to the information in such notice to the parties and to any arbitrator proposed for appointment

or appointed in a proceeding for purposes of completing the arbitrator declaration required by Rule 19(3)(b).
(4) The Tribunal may order disclosure of further information regarding the funding agreement and the non-party providing funding pursuant to Rule 36(3).

Rule 15: Method of Constituting the Tribunal
(1) The number of arbitrators and the method of their appointment must be determined before the Secretary-General can act on any appointment proposed by a party.
(2) The parties shall endeavor to agree on any uneven number of arbitrators and the method of their appointment. If the parties do not advise the Secretary-General of an agreement within 45 days after the date of registration, the Tribunal shall be constituted in accordance with Article 37(2)(b) of the Convention.

Rule 16: Appointment of Arbitrators to a Tribunal Constituted in Accordance with Article 37(2)(b) of the Convention
If the Tribunal is to be constituted in accordance with Article 37(2)(b) of the Convention, each party shall appoint an arbitrator and the parties shall jointly appoint the President of the Tribunal.

Rule 17: Assistance of the Secretary-General with Appointment
The parties may jointly request that the Secretary-General assist with the appointment of the President of the Tribunal or a Sole Arbitrator.

Rule 18: Appointment of Arbitrators by the Chair in Accordance with Article 38 of the Convention
(1) If the Tribunal has not been constituted within 90 days after the date of registration, or such other period as the parties may agree, either party may request that the Chair appoint the arbitrator(s) who have not yet been appointed pursuant to Article 38 of the Convention.
(2) The Chair shall appoint the President of the Tribunal after appointing any members who have not yet been appointed.
(3) The Chair shall consult with the parties as far as possible before appointing an arbitrator and shall use best efforts to appoint any arbitrator(s) within 30 days after receipt of the request to appoint.

Rule 19: Acceptance of Appointment
(1) A party appointing an arbitrator shall notify the Secretary-General of the appointment and provide the appointee's name, nationality and contact information.
(2) Upon receipt of a notification pursuant to paragraph (1), the Secretary-General shall request an acceptance from the appointee and shall transmit to the appointee the information received from the parties relevant to completion of the declaration referred to in paragraph (3)(b).
(3) Within 20 days after receipt of the request for acceptance of an appointment, the appointee shall:
- (a) accept the appointment; and
- (b) provide a signed declaration in the form published by the Centre, addressing matters including the arbitrator's independence, impartiality, availability and commitment to maintain the confidentiality of the proceeding.

(4) The Secretary-General shall notify the parties of the acceptance of appointment by each arbitrator and transmit the signed declaration to them.
(5) The Secretary-General shall notify the parties if an arbitrator fails to accept the appointment or provide a signed declaration within the time limit referred to in paragraph (3), and another person shall be appointed as arbitrator in accordance with the method followed for the previous appointment.
(6) Each arbitrator shall have a continuing obligation promptly to disclose any change of circumstances relevant to the declaration referred to in paragraph (3)(b).

Rule 20: Replacement of Arbitrators Prior to Constitution of the Tribunal

(1) At any time before the Tribunal is constituted:

(a) an arbitrator may withdraw an acceptance;

(b) a party may replace an arbitrator whom it appointed; or

(c) the parties may agree to replace any arbitrator.

(2) A replacement arbitrator shall be appointed as soon as possible, in accordance with the method by which the withdrawing or replaced arbitrator was appointed.

Rule 21: Constitution of the Tribunal

(1) The Tribunal shall be deemed to be constituted on the date the Secretary-General notifies the parties that all the arbitrators have accepted their appointments and signed the declaration required by Rule 19(3)(b).

(2) As soon as the Tribunal is constituted, the Secretary-General shall transmit the Request for arbitration, the supporting documents, the notice of registration and communications with the parties to each member.

CHAPTER III: DISQUALIFICATION OF ARBITRATORS AND VACANCIES

Rule 22: Proposal for Disqualification of Arbitrators

(1) A party may file a proposal to disqualify one or more arbitrators ("proposal") in accordance with the following procedure:

(a) the proposal shall be filed after the constitution of the Tribunal and within 21 days after the later of:

(i) the constitution of the Tribunal; or

(ii) the date on which the party proposing the disqualification first knew or first should have known of the facts on which the proposal is based;

(b) the proposal shall include the grounds on which it is based, a statement of the relevant facts, law and arguments, and any supporting documents;

(c) the other party shall file its response and any supporting documents within 21 days after receipt of the proposal;

(d) the arbitrator to whom the proposal relates may file a statement that is limited to factual information relevant to the proposal. The statement shall be filed within five days after the earlier of receipt of the response or expiry of the time limit referred to in paragraph (1)(c); and

(e) each party may file a final written submission on the proposal within seven days after the earlier of receipt of the statement or expiry of the time limit referred to in paragraph (1)(d).

(2) The proceeding shall be suspended upon the filing of the proposal until a decision on the proposal has been made, except to the extent that the parties agree to continue the proceeding.

Rule 23: Decision on the Proposal for Disqualification

(1) The decision on a proposal shall be made by the arbitrators not subject to the proposal or by the Chair in accordance with Article 58 of the Convention.

(2) For the purposes of Article 58 of the Convention:

(a) if the arbitrators not subject to a proposal are unable to decide the proposal for any reason, they shall notify the Secretary-General and they shall be considered equally divided;

(b) if a subsequent proposal is filed while the decision on a prior proposal is pending, both proposals shall be decided by the Chair as if they were a proposal to disqualify a majority of the Tribunal.

(3) The arbitrators not subject to the proposal and the Chair shall use best efforts to decide any proposal within 30 days after the later of the expiry of the time limit referred to in Rule 22(1)(e) or the notice in Rule 23(2)(a).

Rule 24: Incapacity or Failure to Perform Duties
If an arbitrator becomes incapacitated or fails to perform the duties required of an arbitrator, the procedure in Rules 22 and 23 shall apply.

Rule 25: Resignation
(1) An arbitrator may resign by notifying the Secretary-General and the other members of the Tribunal and providing reasons for the resignation.
(2) If the arbitrator was appointed by a party, the other members of the Tribunal shall promptly notify the Secretary-General whether they consent to the arbitrator's resignation for the purposes of Rule 26(3)(a).

Rule 26: Vacancy on the Tribunal
(1) The Secretary-General shall notify the parties of any vacancy on the Tribunal.
(2) The proceeding shall be suspended from the date of notice of the vacancy until the vacancy is filled.
(3) A vacancy on the Tribunal shall be filled by the method used to make the original appointment, except that the Chair shall fill the following vacancies from the Panel of Arbitrators:
- (a) a vacancy caused by the resignation of a party-appointed arbitrator without the consent of the other members of the Tribunal; or
- (b) a vacancy that has not been filled within 45 days after the notice of vacancy.

(4) Once a vacancy has been filled and the Tribunal has been reconstituted, the proceeding shall continue from the point it had reached at the time the vacancy was notified. Any portion of a hearing shall be recommenced if the newly appointed arbitrator considers it necessary to decide a pending matter.

CHAPTER IV: CONDUCT OF THE PROCEEDING

Rule 27: Orders and Decisions
(1) The Tribunal shall make the orders and decisions required for the conduct of the proceeding.
(2) Orders and decisions may be made by any appropriate means of communication, shall indicate the reasons upon which they are made, and may be signed by the President on behalf of the Tribunal.
(3) The Tribunal shall consult with the parties prior to making an order or decision it is authorized by these Rules to make on its own initiative.

Rule 28: Waiver
Subject to Article 45 of the Convention, if a party knows or should have known that an applicable rule, agreement of the parties, or any order or decision of the Tribunal or the Secretary-General has not been complied with, and does not object promptly, then that party shall be deemed to have waived its right to object to that non-compliance, unless the Tribunal decides that there are special circumstances justifying the failure to object promptly.

Rule 29: First Session
(1) The Tribunal shall hold a first session to address the procedure, including the matters listed in paragraph (4).
(2) The first session may be held in person or remotely, by any means that the Tribunal deems appropriate. The agenda, method and date of the first session shall be determined by the President of the Tribunal after consulting with the other members and the parties.
(3) The first session shall be held within 60 days after the constitution of the Tribunal or such other period as the parties may agree. If the President of the Tribunal determines that it is not possible to convene the parties and the other members within this period, the Tribunal shall decide whether to

hold the first session solely between the President of the Tribunal and the parties, or solely among the Tribunal members based on the parties' written submissions.

(4) Before the first session, the Tribunal shall invite the parties' views on procedural matters, including:

(a) the applicable arbitration rules;

(b) the division of advances payable pursuant to ICSID Administrative and Financial Regulation 15;

(c) the procedural language(s), translation and interpretation;

(d) the method of filing and routing of documents;

(e) the number, length, type and format of written submissions;

(f) the place of hearings and whether a hearing will be held in person or remotely;

(g) whether there will be requests for production of documents as between the parties and, if so, the scope, timing and procedure for such requests;

(h) the procedural calendar;

(i) the manner of making recordings and transcripts of hearings;

(j) the publication of documents and recordings;

(k) the treatment of confidential or protected information; and

(l) any other procedural matter raised by either party or the Tribunal.

(5) The Tribunal shall issue an order recording the parties' agreements and any Tribunal decisions on the procedure within 15 days after the later of the first session or the last written submission on procedural matters addressed at the first session.

Rule 30: Written Submissions

(1) The parties shall file the following written submissions:

(a) a memorial by the requesting party;

(b) a counter-memorial by the other party;

and, unless the parties agree otherwise:

(c) a reply by the requesting party; and

(d) a rejoinder by the other party.

(2) A memorial shall contain a statement of the relevant facts, law and arguments, and the request for relief. A counter-memorial shall contain a statement of the relevant facts, including an admission or denial of facts stated in the memorial, and any necessary additional facts, a statement of law in reply to the memorial, arguments and the request for relief. A reply and rejoinder shall be limited to responding to the previous written submission and addressing any relevant facts that are new or could not have been known prior to filing the reply or rejoinder.

(3) A party may file unscheduled written submissions, observations or supporting documents only after obtaining leave of the Tribunal, unless the filing of such documents is provided for by the Convention or these Rules. The Tribunal may grant such leave upon a timely and reasoned application if it finds such written submissions, observations or supporting documents are necessary in view of all relevant circumstances.

Rule 31: Case Management Conferences

With a view to conducting an expeditious and cost-effective proceeding, the Tribunal shall convene one or more case management conferences with the parties at any time after the first session to:

(a) identify uncontested facts;

(b) clarify and narrow the issues in dispute; or

(c) address any other procedural or substantive issue related to the resolution of the dispute.

Rule 32: Hearings

(1) The Tribunal shall hold one or more hearings, unless the parties agree otherwise.

(2) The President of the Tribunal shall determine the date, time and method of holding a hearing after consulting with the other members of the Tribunal and the parties.

(3) A hearing in person may be held at any place agreed to by the parties after consulting with the Tribunal and the Secretary-General. If the parties do not agree on the place of a hearing, it shall be held at the seat of the Centre pursuant to Article 62 of the Convention.
(4) Any member of the Tribunal may put questions to the parties and ask for explanations at any time during a hearing.

Rule 33: Quorum
The participation of a majority of the members of the Tribunal by any appropriate means of communication shall be required at the first session, case management conferences, hearings and deliberations, except as provided in these Rules or unless the parties agree otherwise.

Rule 34: Deliberations
(1) The deliberations of the Tribunal shall take place in private and remain confidential.
(2) The Tribunal may deliberate at any place and by any means it considers appropriate.
(3) The Tribunal may be assisted by the Secretary of the Tribunal at its deliberations. No other person shall assist the Tribunal at its deliberations, unless the Tribunal decides otherwise and notifies the parties.
(4) The Tribunal shall deliberate on any matter for decision immediately after the last submission on that matter.

Rule 35: Decisions Made by Majority Vote
The Tribunal shall make decisions by a majority of the votes of all its members. Abstention shall count as a negative vote.

CHAPTER V: EVIDENCE

Rule 36: Evidence: General Principles
(1) The Tribunal shall determine the admissibility and probative value of the evidence adduced.
(2) Each party has the burden of proving the facts relied on to support its claim or defense.
(3) The Tribunal may call upon a party to produce documents or other evidence if it deems it necessary at any stage of the proceeding.

Rule 37: Disputes Arising from Requests for Production of Documents
In deciding a dispute arising out of a party's objection to the other party's request for production of documents, the Tribunal shall consider all relevant circumstances, including:
(a) the scope and timeliness of the request;
(b) the relevance and materiality of the documents requested;
(c) the burden of production; and
(d) the basis of the objection.

Rule 38: Witnesses and Experts
(1) A party intending to rely on evidence given by a witness shall file a written statement by that witness. The statement shall identify the witness, contain the evidence of the witness, and be signed and dated.
(2) A witness who has filed a written statement may be called for examination at a hearing.
(3) The Tribunal shall determine the manner in which the examination is conducted.
(4) A witness shall be examined before the Tribunal, by the parties, and under the control of the President. Any member of the Tribunal may put questions to the witness.
(5) A witness shall be examined in person unless the Tribunal determines that another means of examination is appropriate in the circumstances.

(6) Each witness shall make the following declaration before giving evidence:

"I solemnly declare upon my honor and conscience that I shall speak the truth, the whole truth, and nothing but the truth."

(7) Paragraphs (1)-(5) shall apply, with necessary modifications, to evidence given by an expert.

(8) Each expert shall make the following declaration before giving evidence:

"I solemnly declare upon my honor and conscience that my statement will be in accordance with my sincere belief."

Rule 39: Tribunal-Appointed Experts

(1) Unless the parties agree otherwise, the Tribunal may appoint one or more independent experts to report to it on specific matters within the scope of the dispute.

(2) The Tribunal shall consult with the parties on the appointment of an expert, including on the terms of reference and fees of the expert.

(3) Upon accepting an appointment by the Tribunal, an expert shall provide a signed declaration in the form published by the Centre.

(4) The parties shall provide the Tribunal-appointed expert with any information, document or other evidence that the expert may require. The Tribunal shall decide any dispute regarding the evidence required by the Tribunal-appointed expert.

(5) The parties shall have the right to make submissions on the report of the Tribunal-appointed expert.

(6) Rule 38 shall apply, with necessary modifications, to the Tribunal-appointed expert.

Rule 40: Visits and Inquiries

(1) The Tribunal may order a visit to any place connected with the dispute, on its own initiative or upon a party's request, if it deems the visit necessary, and may conduct inquiries there as appropriate.

(2) The order shall define the scope of the visit and the subject of any inquiry, the procedure to be followed, the applicable time limits and other relevant terms.

(3) The parties shall have the right to participate in any visit or inquiry.

CHAPTER VI: SPECIAL PROCEDURES

Rule 41: Manifest Lack of Legal Merit

(1) A party may object that a claim is manifestly without legal merit. The objection may relate to the substance of the claim, the jurisdiction of the Centre, or the competence of the Tribunal.

(2) The following procedure shall apply:

- (a) a party shall file a written submission no later than 45 days after the constitution of the Tribunal;
- (b) the written submission shall specify the grounds on which the objection is based and contain a statement of the relevant facts, law and arguments;
- (c) the Tribunal shall fix time limits for submissions on the objection;
- (d) if a party files the objection before the constitution of the Tribunal, the Secretary-General shall fix time limits for written submissions on the objection, so that the Tribunal may consider the objection promptly upon its constitution; and
- (e) the Tribunal shall render its decision or Award on the objection within 60 days after the later of the constitution of the Tribunal or the last submission on the objection.

(3) If the Tribunal decides that all claims are manifestly without legal merit, it shall render an Award to that effect. Otherwise, the Tribunal shall issue a decision on the objection and fix any time limit necessary for the further conduct of the proceeding.

(4) A decision that a claim is not manifestly without legal merit shall be without prejudice to the right of a party to file a preliminary objection pursuant to Rule 43 or to argue subsequently in the proceeding that a claim is without legal merit.

Rule 42: Bifurcation

(1) A party may request that a question be addressed in a separate phase of the proceeding ("request for bifurcation").

(2) If a request for bifurcation relates to a preliminary objection, Rule 44 shall apply.

(3) The following procedure shall apply to a request for bifurcation other than a request referred to in Rule 44:

(a) the request for bifurcation shall be filed as soon as possible;

(b) the request for bifurcation shall state the questions to be bifurcated;

(c) the Tribunal shall fix time limits for submissions on the request for bifurcation;

(d) the Tribunal shall issue its decision on the request for bifurcation within 30 days after the last submission on the request; and

(e) the Tribunal shall fix any time limit necessary for the further conduct of the proceeding.

(4) In determining whether to bifurcate, the Tribunal shall consider all relevant circumstances, including whether:

(a) bifurcation would materially reduce the time and cost of the proceeding;

(b) determination of the questions to be bifurcated would dispose of all or a substantial portion of the dispute; and

(c) the questions to be addressed in separate phases of the proceeding are so intertwined as to make bifurcation impractical.

(5) If the Tribunal orders bifurcation pursuant to this Rule, it shall suspend the proceeding with respect to any questions to be addressed at a later phase, unless the parties agree otherwise.

(6) The Tribunal may at any time on its own initiative decide whether a question should be addressed in a separate phase of the proceeding.

Rule 43: Preliminary Objections

(1) A party may file a preliminary objection that the dispute or any ancillary claim is not within the jurisdiction of the Centre or for other reasons is not within the competence of the Tribunal ("preliminary objection").

(2) A party shall notify the Tribunal and the other party of its intent to file a preliminary objection as soon as possible.

(3) The Tribunal may at any time on its own initiative consider whether a dispute or an ancillary claim is within the jurisdiction of the Centre or within its own competence.

(4) The Tribunal may address a preliminary objection in a separate phase of the proceeding or join the objection to the merits. It may do so upon request of a party pursuant to Rule 44 or at any time on its own initiative, in accordance with the procedure in Rule 44(2)-(4).

Rule 44: Preliminary Objections with a Request for Bifurcation

(1) The following procedure shall apply with respect to a request for bifurcation relating to a preliminary objection:

(a) unless the parties agree otherwise, the request for bifurcation shall be filed:

(i) within 45 days after filing the memorial on the merits;

(ii) within 45 days after filing the written submission containing the ancillary claim, if the objection relates to the ancillary claim; or

(iii) as soon as possible after the facts on which the preliminary objection is based become known to a party, if those facts were unknown to that party on the dates referred to in paragraph (1)(a)(i) and (ii);

(b) the request for bifurcation shall state the preliminary objection to which it relates;

(c) unless the parties agree otherwise, the proceeding on the merits shall be suspended until the Tribunal decides whether to bifurcate;

(d) the Tribunal shall fix time limits for submissions on the request for bifurcation; and
(e) the Tribunal shall issue its decision on a request for bifurcation within 30 days after the last submission on the request.

(2) In determining whether to bifurcate, the Tribunal shall consider all relevant circumstances, including whether:
(a) bifurcation would materially reduce the time and cost of the proceeding;
(b) determination of the preliminary objection would dispose of all or a substantial portion of the dispute; and
(c) the preliminary objection and the merits are so intertwined as to make bifurcation impractical.

(3) If the Tribunal decides to address the preliminary objection in a separate phase of the proceeding, it shall:
(a) suspend the proceeding on the merits, unless the parties agree otherwise;
(b) fix time limits for submissions on the preliminary objection;
(c) render its decision or Award on the preliminary objection within 180 days after the last submission, in accordance with Rule 58(1)(b); and
(d) fix any time limit necessary for the further conduct of the proceeding if the Tribunal does not render an Award.

(4) If the Tribunal decides to join the preliminary objection to the merits, it shall:
(a) fix time limits for submissions on the preliminary objection;
(b) modify any time limits for submissions on the merits, as required; and
(c) render its Award within 240 days after the last submission in the proceeding, in accordance with Rule 58(1)(c).

Rule 45: Preliminary Objections without a Request for Bifurcation

If a party does not request bifurcation of a preliminary objection within the time limits referred to in Rule 44(1)(a) or the parties confirm that they will not request bifurcation, the preliminary objection shall be joined to the merits and the following procedure shall apply:
(a) the Tribunal shall fix time limits for submissions on the preliminary objection;
(b) the memorial on the preliminary objection shall be filed:
(i) by the date to file the counter-memorial on the merits;
(ii) by the date to file the next written submission after an ancillary claim, if the objection relates to the ancillary claim; or
(iii) as soon as possible after the facts on which the objection is based become known to a party, if those facts were unknown to that party on the dates referred to in paragraph (b)(i) and (ii);
(c) the party filing the memorial on preliminary objections shall also file its counter-memorial on the merits, or, if the objection relates to an ancillary claim, file its next written submission after the ancillary claim; and
(d) the Tribunal shall render its Award within 240 days after the last submission in the proceeding, in accordance with Rule 58(1)(c).

Rule 46: Consolidation or Coordination of Arbitrations

(1) Parties to two or more pending arbitrations administered by the Centre may agree to consolidate or coordinate these arbitrations.

(2) Consolidation joins all aspects of the arbitrations sought to be consolidated and results in one Award. To be consolidated pursuant to this Rule, the arbitrations shall have been registered in accordance with the Convention and shall involve the same Contracting State (or constituent subdivision or agency of the Contracting State).

(3) Coordination aligns specific procedural aspects of two or more pending arbitrations, but the arbitrations remain separate proceedings and result in separate Awards.

(4) The parties referred to in paragraph (1) shall jointly provide the Secretary-General with proposed terms for the conduct of the consolidated or coordinated arbitrations and consult with the Secretary-General to ensure that the proposed terms are capable of being implemented.
(5) After the consultation referred to in paragraph (4), the Secretary-General shall communicate the proposed terms agreed by the parties to the Tribunals constituted in the arbitrations. Such Tribunals shall make any order or decision required to implement these terms.

Rule 47: Provisional Measures

(1) A party may at any time request that the Tribunal recommend provisional measures to preserve that party's rights, including measures to:
 (a) prevent action that is likely to cause current or imminent harm to that party or prejudice to the arbitral process;
 (b) maintain or restore the status quo pending determination of the dispute; or
 (c) preserve evidence that may be relevant to the resolution of the dispute.
(2) The following procedure shall apply:
 (a) the request shall specify the rights to be preserved, the measures requested, and the circumstances that require such measures;
 (b) the Tribunal shall fix time limits for submissions on the request;
 (c) if a party requests provisional measures before the constitution of the Tribunal, the Secretary-General shall fix time limits for written submissions on the request so that the Tribunal may consider the request promptly upon its constitution; and
 (d) the Tribunal shall issue its decision on the request within 30 days after the later of the constitution of the Tribunal or the last submission on the request.
(3) In deciding whether to recommend provisional measures, the Tribunal shall consider all relevant circumstances, including:
 (a) whether the measures are urgent and necessary; and
 (b) the effect that the measures may have on each party.
(4) The Tribunal may recommend provisional measures on its own initiative. The Tribunal may also recommend provisional measures different from those requested by a party.
(5) A party shall promptly disclose any material change in the circumstances upon which the Tribunal recommended provisional measures.
(6) The Tribunal may at any time modify or revoke the provisional measures, on its own initiative or upon a party's request.
(7) A party may request any judicial or other authority to order provisional measures if such recourse is permitted by the instrument recording the parties' consent to arbitration.

Rule 48: Ancillary Claims

(1) Unless the parties agree otherwise, a party may file an incidental or additional claim or a counterclaim ("ancillary claim") arising directly out of the subject-matter of the dispute, provided that such ancillary claim is within the scope of the consent of the parties and the jurisdiction of the Centre.
(2) An incidental or additional claim shall be presented no later than in the reply, and a counterclaim shall be presented no later than in the counter-memorial, unless the Tribunal decides otherwise.
(3) The Tribunal shall fix time limits for submissions on the ancillary claim.

Rule 49: Default

(1) A party is in default if it fails to appear or present its case or indicates that it will not appear or present its case.
(2) If a party is in default at any stage of the proceeding, the other party may request that the Tribunal address the questions submitted to it and render an Award.

(3) Upon receipt of the request referred to in paragraph (2), the Tribunal shall notify the defaulting party of the request and grant a grace period to cure the default, unless it is satisfied that the defaulting party does not intend to appear or present its case. The grace period shall not exceed 60 days without the consent of the other party.
(4) If the request in paragraph (2) relates to a failure to appear at a hearing, the Tribunal may:
(a) reschedule the hearing to a date within 60 days after the original date;
(b) proceed with the hearing in the absence of the defaulting party and fix a time limit for the defaulting party to file a written submission within 60 days after the hearing; or
(c) cancel the hearing and fix a time limit for the parties to file written submissions within 60 days after the original date of the hearing.
(5) If the default relates to a scheduled procedural step other than a hearing, the Tribunal may set the grace period to cure the default by fixing a new time limit for the defaulting party to complete that step within 60 days after the date of the notice of default referred to in paragraph (3).
(6) If the defaulting party fails to act within the grace period or if no such period is granted, the Tribunal shall resume consideration of the dispute and render an Award. For this purpose:
(a) a party's default shall not be deemed an admission of the assertions made by the other party;
(b) the Tribunal may invite the party that is not in default to make submissions and produce evidence; and
(c) the Tribunal shall examine the jurisdiction of the Centre and its own competence and, if it is satisfied, decide whether the submissions made are well-founded.

CHAPTER VII: COSTS

Rule 50: Costs of the Proceeding

The costs of the proceeding are all costs incurred by the parties in connection with the proceeding, including:
(a) the legal fees and expenses of the parties;
(b) the fees and expenses of the Tribunal, Tribunal assistants approved by the parties and Tribunal-appointed experts; and
(c) the administrative charges and direct costs of the Centre.

Rule 51: Statement of and Submission on Costs

The Tribunal shall request that each party file a statement of its costs and a written submission on the allocation of costs before allocating the costs between the parties.

Rule 52: Decisions on Costs

(1) In allocating the costs of the proceeding, the Tribunal shall consider all relevant circumstances, including:
(a) the outcome of the proceeding or any part of it;
(b) the conduct of the parties during the proceeding, including the extent to which they acted in an expeditious and cost-effective manner and complied with these Rules and the orders and decisions of the Tribunal;
(c) the complexity of the issues; and
(d) the reasonableness of the costs claimed.
(2) If the Tribunal renders an Award pursuant to Rule 41(3), it shall award the prevailing party its reasonable costs, unless the Tribunal determines that there are special circumstances justifying a different allocation of costs.
(3) The Tribunal may make an interim decision on costs at any time, on its own initiative or upon a party's request.
(4) The Tribunal shall ensure that all decisions on costs are reasoned and form part of the Award.

Rule 53: Security for Costs

(1) Upon request of a party, the Tribunal may order any party asserting a claim or counterclaim to provide security for costs.

(2) The following procedure shall apply:

(a) the request shall include a statement of the relevant circumstances and the supporting documents;

(b) the Tribunal shall fix time limits for submissions on the request;

(c) if a party requests security for costs before the constitution of the Tribunal, the Secretary-General shall fix time limits for written submissions on the request so that the Tribunal may consider the request promptly upon its constitution; and

(d) the Tribunal shall issue its decision on the request within 30 days after the later of the constitution of the Tribunal or the last submission on the request.

(3) In determining whether to order a party to provide security for costs, the Tribunal shall consider all relevant circumstances, including:

(a) that party's ability to comply with an adverse decision on costs;

(b) that party's willingness to comply with an adverse decision on costs;

(c) the effect that providing security for costs may have on that party's ability to pursue its claim or counterclaim; and

(d) the conduct of the parties.

(4) The Tribunal shall consider all evidence adduced in relation to the circumstances in paragraph (3), including the existence of third-party funding.

(5) The Tribunal shall specify any relevant terms in an order to provide security for costs and shall fix a time limit for compliance with the order.

(6) If a party fails to comply with an order to provide security for costs, the Tribunal may suspend the proceeding. If the proceeding is suspended for more than 90 days, the Tribunal may, after consulting with the parties, order the discontinuance of the proceeding.

(7) A party shall promptly disclose any material change in the circumstances upon which the Tribunal ordered security for costs.

(8) The Tribunal may at any time modify or revoke its order on security for costs, on its own initiative or upon a party's request.

CHAPTER VIII: SUSPENSION, SETTLEMENT AND DISCONTINUANCE

Rule 54: Suspension of the Proceeding

(1) The Tribunal shall suspend the proceeding by agreement of the parties.

(2) The Tribunal may suspend the proceeding upon the request of either party or on its own initiative, except as otherwise provided in the ICSID Administrative and Financial Regulations or these Rules.

(3) The Tribunal shall give the parties the opportunity to make observations before ordering a suspension pursuant to paragraph (2).

(4) In its order suspending the proceeding, the Tribunal shall specify:

(a) the period of the suspension;

(b) any relevant terms; and

(c) a modified procedural calendar to take effect on resumption of the proceeding, if necessary.

(5) The Tribunal shall extend the period of a suspension prior to its expiry by agreement of the parties.

(6) The Tribunal may extend the period of a suspension prior to its expiry, on its own initiative or upon a party's request, after giving the parties an opportunity to make observations.

(7) The Secretary-General shall suspend the proceeding pursuant to paragraph (1) or extend the suspension pursuant to paragraph (5) if the Tribunal has not yet been constituted or if there is a vacancy on the Tribunal. The parties shall inform the Secretary-General of the period of the suspension and any terms agreed to by the parties.

Rule 55: Settlement and Discontinuance by Agreement of the Parties

(1) If the parties notify the Tribunal that they have agreed to discontinue the proceeding, the Tribunal shall issue an order taking note of the discontinuance.

(2) If the parties agree on a settlement of the dispute before the Award is rendered, the Tribunal:

(a) shall issue an order taking note of the discontinuance of the proceeding, if the parties so request; or

(b) may record the settlement in the form of an Award, if the parties file the complete and signed text of their settlement and request that the Tribunal embody such settlement in an Award.

(3) The Secretary-General shall issue the order referred to in paragraphs (1) and (2)(a) if the Tribunal has not yet been constituted or if there is a vacancy on the Tribunal.

Rule 56: Discontinuance at Request of a Party

(1) If a party requests the discontinuance of the proceeding, the Tribunal shall fix a time limit within which the other party may oppose the discontinuance. If no objection in writing is made within the time limit, the other party shall be deemed to have acquiesced in the discontinuance and the Tribunal shall issue an order taking note of the discontinuance of the proceeding. If any objection in writing is made within the time limit, the proceeding shall continue.

(2) The Secretary-General shall fix the time limit and issue the order referred to in paragraph (1) if the Tribunal has not yet been constituted or if there is a vacancy on the Tribunal.

Rule 57: Discontinuance for Failure of Parties to Act

(1) If the parties fail to take any steps in the proceeding for more than 150 consecutive days, the Tribunal shall notify them of the time elapsed since the last step taken in the proceeding.

(2) If the parties fail to take a step within 30 days after the notice referred to in paragraph (1), they shall be deemed to have discontinued the proceeding and the Tribunal shall issue an order taking note of the discontinuance.

(3) If either party takes a step within 30 days after the notice referred to in paragraph (1), the proceeding shall continue.

(4) The Secretary-General shall issue the notice and the order referred to in paragraphs (1) and (2) if the Tribunal has not yet been constituted or if there is a vacancy on the Tribunal.

CHAPTER IX: THE AWARD

Rule 58: Timing of the Award

(1) The Tribunal shall render the Award as soon as possible, and in any event no later than:

(a) 60 days after the later of the Tribunal constitution or the last submission, if the Award is rendered pursuant to Rule 41(3);

(b) 180 days after the last submission if the Award is rendered pursuant to Rule 44(3)(c); or

(c) 240 days after the last submission in all other cases.

(2) A statement of costs and submission on costs filed pursuant to Rule 51 shall not be considered a submission for the purposes of paragraph (1).

Rule 59: Contents of the Award

(1) The Award shall be in writing and shall contain:

(a) a precise designation of each party;

(b) the names of the representatives of the parties;

(c) a statement that the Tribunal was established in accordance with the Convention and a description of the method of its constitution;

(d) the name of each member of the Tribunal and the appointing authority of each;

(e) the date and place of the first session, case management conferences and hearings;
(f) a brief summary of the proceeding;
(g) a statement of the relevant facts as found by the Tribunal;
(h) a brief summary of the submissions of the parties, including the relief sought;
(i) the decision of the Tribunal on every question submitted to it, and the reasons on which the Award is based; and
(j) a statement of the costs of the proceeding, including the fees and expenses of each member of the Tribunal, and a reasoned decision on costs.

(2) The Award shall be signed by the members of the Tribunal who voted for it. It may be signed by electronic means if the parties agree.
(3) Any member of the Tribunal may attach an individual opinion or a statement of dissent to the Award before the Award is rendered.

Rule 60: Rendering of the Award
(1) Once the Award has been signed by the members of the Tribunal who voted for it, the Secretary-General shall promptly:
(a) dispatch a certified copy of the Award to each party, together with any individual opinion and statement of dissent, indicating the date of dispatch on the Award; and
(b) deposit the Award in the archives of the Centre, together with any individual opinion and statement of dissent.

(2) The Award shall be deemed to have been rendered on the date of dispatch of certified copies of the Award.
(3) The Secretary-General shall provide additional certified copies of the Award to a party upon request.

Rule 61: Supplementary Decision and Rectification
(1) A party requesting a supplementary decision on, or the rectification of, an Award pursuant to Article 49(2) of the Convention shall file the request with the Secretary-General and pay the lodging fee published in the schedule of fees within 45 days after the Award was rendered.
(2) The request referred to in paragraph (1) shall:
(a) identify the Award to which it relates;
(b) be signed by each requesting party or its representative and be dated;
(c) specify:
(i) with respect to a request for a supplementary decision, any question which the Tribunal omitted to decide in the Award;
(ii) with respect to a request for rectification, any clerical, arithmetical or similar error in the Award; and
(d) attach proof of payment of the lodging fee.

(3) Upon receipt of the request and the lodging fee, the Secretary-General shall promptly:
(a) transmit the request to the other party;
(b) register the request, or refuse registration if the request is not filed or the fee is not paid within the time limit referred to in paragraph (1); and
(c) notify the parties of the registration or refusal to register.

(4) As soon as the request is registered, the Secretary-General shall transmit the request and the notice of registration to each member of the Tribunal.
(5) The President of the Tribunal shall determine the procedure to consider the request, after consulting with the other members of the Tribunal and the parties.
(6) Rules 59-60 shall apply to any decision of the Tribunal pursuant to this Rule.
(7) The Tribunal shall issue a decision on the request for supplementary decision or rectification within 60 days after the last submission on the request.

(8) The date of dispatch of certified copies of the supplementary decision or rectification shall be the relevant date for the purposes of calculating the time limits in Articles 51(2) and 52(2) of the Convention.
(9) A supplementary decision or rectification under this Rule shall become part of the Award and shall be reflected on all certified copies of the Award.

CHAPTER X: PUBLICATION, ACCESS TO PROCEEDINGS AND NON-DISPUTING PARTY SUBMISSIONS

Rule 62: Publication of Awards and Decisions on Annulment

(1) With consent of the parties, the Centre shall publish every Award, supplementary decision on an Award, rectification, interpretation, and revision of an Award, and decision on annulment.
(2) The parties may consent to publication of the full text or to a jointly redacted text of the documents referred to in paragraph (1).
(3) Consent to publish the documents referred to in paragraph (1) shall be deemed to have been given if no party objects in writing to such publication within 60 days after the dispatch of the document.
(4) Absent consent of the parties pursuant to paragraphs (1)-(3), the Centre shall publish excerpts of the documents referred to in paragraph (1). The following procedure shall apply to publication of excerpts:
- (a) the Secretary-General shall propose excerpts to the parties within 60 days after the date upon which either party objects to publication or notifies the Secretary-General that the parties disagree on redaction of the document;
- (b) the parties may send comments on the proposed excerpts to the Secretary-General within 60 days after their receipt, including whether any information in the proposed excerpts is confidential or protected as defined in Rule 66; and
- (c) the Secretary-General shall consider any comments received on the proposed excerpts and publish such excerpts within 30 days after the expiry of the time limit referred to in paragraph (4)(b).

Rule 63: Publication of Orders and Decisions

(1) The Centre shall publish orders and decisions, with any redactions agreed to by the parties and jointly notified to the Secretary-General within 60 days after the order or decision is issued.
(2) If either party notifies the Secretary-General within the 60-day period referred to in paragraph (1) that the parties disagree on any proposed redactions, the Secretary-General shall refer the order or decision to the Tribunal to decide any disputed redactions. The Centre shall publish the order or decision in accordance with the decision of the Tribunal.
(3) In deciding a dispute pursuant to paragraph (2), the Tribunal shall ensure that publication does not disclose any confidential or protected information as defined in Rule 66.

Rule 64: Publication of Documents Filed in the Proceeding

(1) With consent of the parties, the Centre shall publish any written submission or supporting document filed by a party in the proceeding, with any redactions agreed to by the parties and jointly notified to the Secretary-General.
(2) Absent consent of the parties pursuant to paragraph (1), a party may refer to the Tribunal a dispute regarding the redaction of a written submission, excluding supporting documents, that it filed in the proceeding. The Tribunal shall decide any disputed redactions and the Centre shall publish the written submission in accordance with the decision of the Tribunal.
(3) In deciding a dispute pursuant to paragraph (2), the Tribunal shall ensure that publication does not disclose any confidential or protected information as defined in Rule 66.

Rule 65: Observation of Hearings

(1) The Tribunal shall allow persons in addition to the parties, their representatives, witnesses and experts during their testimony, and persons assisting the Tribunal, to observe hearings, unless either party objects.

(2) The Tribunal shall establish procedures to prevent the disclosure of confidential or protected information as defined in Rule 66 to persons observing the hearings.

(3) Upon request of a party, the Centre shall publish recordings or transcripts of hearings, unless the other party objects.

Rule 66: Confidential or Protected Information

For the purposes of Rules 62-65, confidential or protected information is information which is protected from public disclosure:

(a) by the instrument of consent to arbitration;

(b) by the applicable law or applicable rules;

(c) in the case of information of a State party to the dispute, by the law of that State;

(d) in accordance with the orders and decisions of the Tribunal;

(e) by agreement of the parties;

(f) because it constitutes confidential business information or protected personal information;

(g) because public disclosure would impede law enforcement;

(h) because a State party to the dispute considers that public disclosure would be contrary to its essential security interests;

(i) because public disclosure would aggravate the dispute between the parties; or

(j) because public disclosure would undermine the integrity of the arbitral process.

Rule 67: Submission of Non-Disputing Parties

(1) Any person or entity that is not a party to the dispute ("non-disputing party") may apply for permission to file a written submission in the proceeding. The application shall be made in the procedural language(s) used in the proceeding.

(2) In determining whether to permit a non-disputing party submission, the Tribunal shall consider all relevant circumstances, including:

- (a) whether the submission would address a matter within the scope of the dispute;
- (b) how the submission would assist the Tribunal to determine a factual or legal issue related to the proceeding by bringing a perspective, particular knowledge or insight that is different from that of the parties;
- (c) whether the non-disputing party has a significant interest in the proceeding;
- (d) the identity, activities, organization and ownership of the non-disputing party, including any direct or indirect affiliation between the non-disputing party, a party or a non-disputing Treaty Party; and
- (e) whether any person or entity will provide the non-disputing party with financial or other assistance to file the submission.

(3) The parties shall have the right to make observations on whether a non-disputing party should be permitted to file a written submission in the proceeding and on any conditions for filing such a submission.

(4) The Tribunal shall ensure that non-disputing party participation does not disrupt the proceeding or unduly burden or unfairly prejudice either party. To this end, the Tribunal may impose conditions on the non-disputing party, including with respect to the format, length, scope or publication of the written submission and the time limit to file the submission.

(5) The Tribunal shall issue a reasoned decision on whether to permit a non-disputing party submission within 30 days after the last written submission on the application.

(6) The Tribunal shall provide the non-disputing party with relevant documents filed in the proceeding, unless either party objects.
(7) If the Tribunal permits a non-disputing party to file a written submission, the parties shall have the right to make observations on the submission.

Rule 68: Participation of Non-Disputing Treaty Party
(1) The Tribunal shall permit a Party to a treaty that is not a party to the dispute ("non-disputing Treaty Party") to make a submission on the interpretation of the treaty at issue in the dispute and upon which consent to arbitration is based. The Tribunal may, after consulting with the parties, invite a non-disputing Treaty Party to make such a submission.
(2) The Tribunal shall ensure that non-disputing Treaty Party participation does not disrupt the proceeding or unduly burden or unfairly prejudice either party. To this end, the Tribunal may impose conditions on the making of the submission by the non-disputing Treaty Party, including with respect to the format, length, scope or publication of the submission, and the time limit to file the submission.
(3) The Tribunal shall provide the non-disputing Treaty Party with relevant documents filed in the proceeding, unless either party objects.
(4) The parties shall have the right to make observations on the submission of the non-disputing Treaty Party.

CHAPTER XI: INTERPRETATION, REVISION AND ANNULMENT OF THE AWARD

Rule 69: The Application
(1) A party applying for interpretation, revision or annulment of an Award shall file the application with the Secretary-General, together with any supporting documents, and pay the lodging fee published in the schedule of fees.
(2) The application shall:
- (a) identify the Award to which it relates;
- (b) be in a language in which the Award was rendered or if the Award was not rendered in an official language of the Centre, be in an official language;
- (c) be signed by each applicant or its representative and be dated;
- (d) attach proof of any representative's authority to act; and
- (e) attach proof of payment of the lodging fee.

(3) An application for interpretation pursuant to Article 50(1) of the Convention may be filed at any time after the Award is rendered and shall specify the points in dispute concerning the meaning or scope of the Award.
(4) An application for revision pursuant to Article 51(1) of the Convention shall be filed within 90 days after the discovery of a fact of such a nature as decisively to affect the Award, and in any event within three years after the Award (or any supplementary decision on or rectification of the Award) was rendered. The application shall specify:
- (a) the change sought in the Award;
- (b) the newly discovered fact that decisively affects the Award; and
- (c) that the fact was unknown to the Tribunal and to the applicant when the Award was rendered, and that the applicant's ignorance of that fact was not due to negligence.

(5) An application for annulment pursuant to Article 52(1) of the Convention shall:
- (a) be filed within 120 days after the Award (or any supplementary decision on or rectification of the Award) was rendered if the application is based on any of the grounds in Article 52(1)(a), (b), (d) or (e) of the Convention; or
- (b) be filed within 120 days after the discovery of corruption on the part of a member of the Tribunal and in any event within three years after the Award (or any supplementary decision on or

rectification of the Award) was rendered, if the application is based on Article 52(1)(c) of the Convention; and
(c) specify the grounds on which it is based, limited to the grounds in Article 52(1)(a)-(e) of the Convention, and the reasons in support of each ground.

(6) Upon receipt of an application and the lodging fee, the Secretary-General shall promptly:
(a) transmit the application and the supporting documents to the other party;
(b) register the application, or refuse registration if the application is not filed or the fee is not paid within the time limits referred to in paragraphs (4) or (5); and
(c) notify the parties of the registration or refusal to register.

(7) At any time before registration, an applicant may notify the Secretary-General in writing of the withdrawal of the application or, if there is more than one applicant, that it is withdrawing from the application. The Secretary-General shall promptly notify the parties of the withdrawal, unless the application has not yet been transmitted to the other party pursuant to paragraph (6)(a).

Rule 70: Interpretation or Revision: Reconstitution of the Tribunal

(1) As soon as an application for the interpretation or revision of an Award is registered, the Secretary-General shall:
(a) transmit the notice of registration, the application and any supporting documents to each member of the original Tribunal; and
(b) request each member of the Tribunal to inform the Secretary-General within 10 days whether that member can take part in the consideration of the application.

(2) If all members of the Tribunal can take part in the consideration of the application, the Secretary-General shall notify the Tribunal and the parties of the reconstitution of the Tribunal.

(3) If the Tribunal cannot be reconstituted in accordance with paragraph (2), the Secretary-General shall invite the parties to constitute a new Tribunal without delay. The new Tribunal shall have the same number of arbitrators and be appointed by the same method as the original Tribunal.

Rule 71: Annulment: Appointment of the ad hoc Committee

(1) As soon as an application for annulment of an Award is registered, the Chair shall appoint an ad hoc Committee in accordance with Article 52(3) of the Convention.

(2) Each member of the Committee shall provide a signed declaration in accordance with Rule 19(3).

(3) The Committee shall be deemed to be constituted on the date the Secretary-General notifies the parties that all members have accepted their appointments.

Rule 72: Procedure Applicable to Interpretation, Revision and Annulment

(1) Except as provided below, these Rules shall apply, with necessary modifications, to any procedure relating to the interpretation, revision or annulment of an Award and to the decision of the Tribunal or Committee.

(2) The procedural agreements and orders on matters addressed at the first session of the original Tribunal shall continue to apply to an interpretation, revision or annulment proceeding, with necessary modifications, unless the parties agree or the Tribunal or Committee orders otherwise.

(3) In addition to the application, the written procedure shall consist of one round of written submissions in an interpretation or revision proceeding, and two rounds of written submissions in an annulment proceeding, unless the parties agree or the Tribunal or Committee orders otherwise.

(4) A hearing shall be held upon the request of either party, or if ordered by the Tribunal or Committee.

(5) The Tribunal or Committee shall issue its decision within 120 days after the last submission on the application.

Rule 73: Stay of Enforcement of the Award

(1) A party to an interpretation, revision or annulment proceeding may request a stay of enforcement of all or part of the Award at any time before the final decision on the application.

(2) If the stay is requested in the application for revision or annulment of an Award, enforcement shall be stayed provisionally until the Tribunal or Committee decides on the request.

(3) The following procedure shall apply:

(a) the request shall specify the circumstances that require the stay;

(b) the Tribunal or Committee shall fix time limits for submissions on the request;

(c) if a party files the request before the constitution of the Tribunal or Committee, the Secretary-General shall fix time limits for written submissions on the request so that the Tribunal or Committee may consider the request promptly upon its constitution; and

(d) the Tribunal or Committee shall issue its decision on the request within 30 days after the later of the constitution of the Tribunal or Committee or the last submission on the request.

(4) If a Tribunal or Committee decides to stay enforcement of the Award, it may impose conditions for the stay, or for lifting the stay, in view of all relevant circumstances.

(5) A party shall promptly disclose to the Tribunal or Committee any change in the circumstances upon which the enforcement was stayed.

(6) The Tribunal or Committee may at any time modify or terminate a stay of enforcement, on its own initiative or upon a party's request.

(7) A stay of enforcement shall terminate on the date of dispatch of the decision on the application for interpretation, revision or annulment, or on the date of discontinuance of the proceeding.

Rule 74: Resubmission of Dispute after an Annulment

(1) If a Committee annuls all or part of an Award, either party may file with the Secretary-General a request to resubmit the dispute to a new Tribunal, together with any supporting documents, and pay the lodging fee published in the schedule of fees.

(2) The request shall:

(a) identify the Award to which it relates;

(b) be in an official language of the Centre;

(c) be signed by each requesting party or its representative and be dated;

(d) attach proof of any representative's authority to act; and

(e) specify which aspect(s) of the dispute is resubmitted to the new Tribunal.

(3) Upon receipt of a request for resubmission and the lodging fee, the Secretary-General shall promptly:

(a) transmit the request and the supporting documents to the other party;

(b) register the request;

(c) notify the parties of the registration; and

(d) invite the parties to constitute a new Tribunal without delay, which shall have the same number of arbitrators, and be appointed by the same method as the original Tribunal, unless the parties agree otherwise.

(4) If the original Award was annulled in part, the new Tribunal shall not reconsider any portion of the Award that was not annulled.

(5) Except as otherwise provided in paragraphs (1)-(4), these Rules shall apply to the resubmission proceeding.

(6) The procedural agreements and orders on matters addressed at the first session of the original Tribunal shall not apply to the resubmission proceeding, unless the parties agree otherwise.

CHAPTER XII: EXPEDITED ARBITRATION

Rule 75: Consent of Parties to Expedited Arbitration

(1) At any time, the parties to an arbitration conducted under the Convention may consent to expedite the arbitration in accordance with this Chapter ("expedited arbitration") by jointly notifying the Secretary-General in writing of their consent.

(2) Chapters I-XI of the Arbitration Rules apply to an expedited arbitration except that:

(a) Rules 15, 16, 18, 39, 40, 41, 42, 44 and 46 do not apply in an expedited arbitration; and

(b) Rules 19, 29, 37, 43, 49, 58, 61 and 72, as modified by Rules 76-84, apply in an expedited arbitration.

(3) If the parties consent to expedited arbitration after the constitution of the Tribunal pursuant to Chapter II, Rules 76-78 shall not apply, and the expedited arbitration shall proceed subject to all members of the Tribunal confirming their availability pursuant to Rule 79(2). If an arbitrator is unavailable to proceed on an expedited basis, the arbitrator may offer to resign.

Rule 76: Number of Arbitrators and Method of Constituting the Tribunal for Expedited Arbitration

(1) The Tribunal in an expedited arbitration shall consist of a Sole Arbitrator appointed pursuant to Rule 77 or a three-member Tribunal appointed pursuant to Rule 78.

(2) The parties shall jointly notify the Secretary-General in writing of their election of a Sole Arbitrator or a three-member Tribunal within 30 days after the date of the notice of consent referred to in Rule 75(1).

(3) If the parties do not notify the Secretary-General of their election within the time limit referred to in paragraph (2), the Tribunal shall consist of a Sole Arbitrator to be appointed pursuant to Rule 77.

(4) An appointment pursuant to Rule 77 or 78 is an appointment in accordance with the method agreed by the parties pursuant to Article 37(2)(a) of the Convention.

Rule 77: Appointment of Sole Arbitrator for Expedited Arbitration

(1) The parties shall jointly appoint the Sole Arbitrator within 20 days after the notice referred to in Rule 76(2).

(2) The Secretary-General shall appoint the Sole Arbitrator if:

(a) the parties do not appoint the Sole Arbitrator within the time limit referred to in paragraph (1);

(b) the parties notify the Secretary-General that they are unable to agree on the Sole Arbitrator; or

(c) the appointee declines the appointment or does not comply with Rule 79(1).

(3) The following procedure shall apply to an appointment by the Secretary-General of the Sole Arbitrator pursuant to paragraph (2):

(a) the Secretary-General shall transmit a list of five candidates for appointment as Sole Arbitrator to the parties within 10 days after the relevant event referred to in paragraph (2);

(b) each party may strike one name from the list and shall rank the remaining candidates in order of preference and transmit such ranking to the Secretary-General within 10 days after receipt of the list;

(c) the Secretary-General shall inform the parties of the result of the rankings on the next business day after receipt of the rankings and shall appoint the candidate with the best ranking. If two or more candidates share the best ranking, the Secretary-General shall select one of them; and

(d) if the selected candidate declines the appointment or does not comply with Rule 79(1), the Secretary-General shall select the next highest-ranked candidate.

Rule 78: Appointment of Three-Member Tribunal for Expedited Arbitration

(1) A three-member Tribunal shall be appointed in accordance with the following procedure:
  (a) each party shall appoint an arbitrator ("co-arbitrator") within 20 days after the notice referred to in Rule 76(2); and
  (b) the parties shall jointly appoint the President of the Tribunal within 20 days after the receipt of the acceptances from both co-arbitrators.

(2) The Secretary-General shall appoint the arbitrators not yet appointed if:
  (a) an appointment is not made within the applicable time limit referred to in paragraph (1);
  (b) the parties notify the Secretary-General that they are unable to agree on the President of the Tribunal; or
  (c) an appointee declines the appointment or does not comply with Rule 79(1).

(3) The following procedure shall apply to the appointment by the Secretary-General of any arbitrators pursuant to paragraph (2):
  (a) the Secretary-General shall first appoint the co-arbitrator(s) not yet appointed. The Secretary-General shall consult with the parties as far as possible and use best efforts to appoint the co-arbitrator(s) within 15 days after the relevant event in paragraph (2);
  (b) within 10 days after the later of the date on which both co-arbitrators have accepted their appointments or the relevant event referred to in paragraph (2), the Secretary-General shall transmit a list of five candidates for appointment as President of the Tribunal to the parties;
  (c) each party may strike one name from the list and shall rank the remaining candidates in order of preference and transmit such ranking to the Secretary-General within 10 days after receipt of the list;
  (d) the Secretary-General shall inform the parties of the result of the rankings on the next business day after receipt of the rankings and shall appoint the candidate with the best ranking. If two or more candidates share the best ranking, the Secretary-General shall select one of them; and
  (e) if the selected candidate declines the appointment or does not comply with Rule 79(1), the Secretary-General shall select the next highest-ranked candidate.

Rule 79: Acceptance of Appointment in Expedited Arbitration

(1) An arbitrator appointed pursuant to Rule 77 or 78 shall accept the appointment and provide a declaration pursuant to Rule 19(3) within 10 days after receipt of the request for acceptance.

(2) An arbitrator appointed to a Tribunal constituted pursuant to Chapter II shall confirm being available to conduct an expedited arbitration within 10 days after receipt of the notice of consent pursuant to Rule 75(3).

Rule 80: First Session in Expedited Arbitration

(1) The Tribunal shall hold a first session pursuant to Rule 29 within 30 days after the constitution of the Tribunal.

(2) The first session shall be held remotely, unless both parties and the Tribunal agree it shall be held in person.

Rule 81: Procedural Schedule in Expedited Arbitration

(1) The following schedule for written submissions and the hearing shall apply in an expedited arbitration:
  (a) the claimant shall file a memorial within 60 days after the first session;
  (b) the respondent shall file a counter-memorial within 60 days after the date of filing the memorial;
  (c) the memorial and counter-memorial referred to in paragraph (1) (a) and (b) shall be no longer than 200 pages;

(d) the claimant shall file a reply within 40 days after the date of filing the counter-memorial;
(e) the respondent shall file a rejoinder within 40 days after the date of filing the reply;
(f) the reply and rejoinder referred to in paragraph (1)(d) and (e) shall be no longer than 100 pages;
(g) the hearing shall be held within 60 days after the last written submission is filed;
(h) the parties shall file statements of their costs and written submissions on costs within 10 days after the last day of the hearing referred to in paragraph (1)(g); and
(i) the Tribunal shall render the Award as soon as possible, and in any event no later than 120 days after the hearing referred to in paragraph (1)(g).

(2) Any preliminary objection, counterclaim, incidental or additional claim shall be joined to the schedule referred to in paragraph (1). The Tribunal shall adjust the schedule if a party raises any such matter, taking into account the expedited nature of the process.
(3) The Tribunal may extend the time limits referred to in paragraph (1) by up to 30 days to decide a dispute arising from requests to produce documents pursuant to Rule 37. The Tribunal shall decide such requests based on written submissions and without an in-person hearing.
(4) Any schedule for submissions other than those referred to in paragraphs (1)-(3) shall run in parallel with the schedule referred to in paragraph (1), unless the proceeding is suspended or the Tribunal decides that there are special circumstances justifying the suspension of the schedule. In fixing time limits for such submissions, the Tribunal shall take into account the expedited nature of the process.

Rule 82: Default in Expedited Arbitration
A Tribunal may grant a party in default a grace period not to exceed 30 days pursuant to Rule 49.

Rule 83: Procedural Schedule for Supplementary Decision and Rectification in Expedited Arbitration
The Tribunal shall issue a supplementary decision or rectification pursuant to Rule 61 within 30 days after the last submission on the request.

Rule 84: Procedural Schedule for Interpretation, Revision or Annulment in Expedited Arbitration
(1) The following schedule for written submissions and the hearing shall apply to the procedure relating to an interpretation, revision or annulment of an Award rendered in an expedited arbitration:
(a) the applicant shall file a memorial on interpretation, revision or annulment within 30 days after the first session;
(b) the other party shall file a counter-memorial on interpretation, revision or annulment within 30 days after the memorial;
(c) the memorial and counter-memorial referred to in paragraph (1) (a) and (b) shall be no longer than 100 pages;
(d) a hearing shall be held within 45 days after the date for filing the counter-memorial;
(e) the parties shall file statements of their costs and written submissions on costs within 5 days after the last day of the hearing referred to in paragraph (1)(d); and
(f) the Tribunal or Committee shall issue the decision on interpretation, revision or annulment as soon as possible, and in any event no later than 60 days after the hearing referred to in paragraph (1)(d).

(2) Any schedule for submissions other than those referred to in paragraph (1) shall run in parallel with the schedule referred to in paragraph (1), unless the proceeding is suspended or the Tribunal or Committee decides that there are special circumstances justifying the suspension of the schedule. In fixing time limits for such submissions, the Tribunal or Committee shall take into account the expedited nature of the process.

Rule 85: Resubmission of a Dispute after Annulment in Expedited Arbitration
The consent of the parties to expedited arbitration pursuant to Rule 75 shall not apply to resubmission of the dispute.

Rule 86: Opting Out of Expedited Arbitration
(1) The parties may opt out of an expedited arbitration at any time by jointly notifying the Tribunal and Secretary-General in writing of their agreement.
(2) Upon request of a party, the Tribunal may decide that an arbitration should no longer be expedited. In deciding the request, the Tribunal shall consider the complexity of the issues, the stage of the proceeding and all other relevant circumstances.
(3) The Tribunal, or the Secretary-General if a Tribunal has not been constituted, shall determine the further procedure pursuant to Chapters I-XI and fix any time limit necessary for the conduct of the proceeding.

9.5 *Soft Law*

9.5.1 IBA Rules on the Taking of Evidence in International Arbitration (2020)[1]

Adopted by a resolution of the IBA Council 29 May 2010 International Bar Association

About the Arbitration Committee

Established as the Committee in the International Bar Association's Legal Practice Division which focuses on the laws, practice and procedures relating to the arbitration of transnational disputes, the Arbitration Committee currently has over 2,300 members from over 90 countries, and membership is increasing steadily.

Through its publications and conferences, the Committee seeks to share information about international arbitration, promote its use and improve its effectiveness. The Committee maintains standing subcommittees and, as appropriate, establishes Task Forces to address specific issues. At the time of issuance of these revised Rules, the Committee has four subcommittees, namely the Rules of Evidence Subcommittee, the Investment Treaty Arbitration Subcommittee, the Conflicts of Interest Subcommittee, and the Recognition and Enforcement of Arbitral Awards Subcommittee; and two task forces: the Task Force on Attorney Ethics in Arbitration and the Task Force on Arbitration Agreements.

Foreword

These IBA Rules on the Taking of Evidence in International Arbitration ('IBA Rules of Evidence') are a revised version of the IBA Rules on the Taking of Evidence in International Commercial Arbitration, prepared by a Working Party of the Arbitration Committee whose members are listed on pages i and ii.

The IBA issued these Rules as a resource to parties and to arbitrators to provide an efficient, economical and fair process for the taking of evidence in international arbitration. The Rules provide mechanisms for the presentation of documents, witnesses of fact and expert witnesses, inspections, as well as the conduct of evidentiary hearings. The Rules are designed to be used in conjunction with, and adopted together with, institutional, ad hoc or other rules or procedures governing international arbitrations. The IBA Rules of Evidence reflect procedures in use in many different legal systems, and they may be particularly useful when the parties come from different legal cultures.

Since their issuance in 1999, the IBA Rules on the Taking of Evidence in International Commercial Arbitration have gained wide acceptance within the international arbitral community. In 2008, a review process was initiated at the instance of Sally Harpole and Pierre Bienvenu, the then Co-Chairs of the Arbitration Committee. The revised version of the IBA Rules of Evidence was developed by

1 IBA Rules on the Taking of Evidence in International Arbitration (2020) is reproduced by kind permission of the International Bar Association, London, UK, and is available at: www.ibanet.org/Publications/publications_IBA_guides_and_free_materials.aspx.© International Bar Association.

the members of the IBA Rules of Evidence Review Subcommittee, assisted by members of the 1999 Working Party. These revised Rules replace the IBA Rules on the Taking of Evidence in International Commercial Arbitration, which themselves replaced the IBA Supplementary Rules Governing the Presentation and Reception of Evidence in International Commercial Arbitration, issued in 1983.

If parties wish to adopt the IBA Rules of Evidence in their arbitration clause, it is recommended that they add the following language to the clause, selecting one of the alternatives therein provided:

'[In addition to the institutional, ad hoc or other rules chosen by the parties,] [t]he parties agree that the arbitration shall be conducted according to the IBA Rules of Evidence as current on the date of [this agreement/the commencement of the arbitration].'

In addition, parties and Arbitral Tribunals may adopt the IBA Rules of Evidence, in whole or in part, at the commencement of the arbitration, or at any time thereafter. They may also vary them or use them as guidelines in developing their own procedures.

The IBA Rules of Evidence were adopted by resolution of the IBA Council on 29 May 2010. The IBA Rules of Evidence are available in English, and translations in other languages are planned. Copies of the IBA Rules of Evidence may be ordered from the IBA, and the Rules are available to download at The Rules

Preamble

1. These IBA Rules on the Taking of Evidence in International Arbitration are intended to provide an efficient, economical and fair process for the taking of evidence in international arbitrations, particularly those between Parties from different legal traditions. They are designed to supplement the legal provisions and the institutional, ad hoc or other rules that apply to the conduct of the arbitration.
2. Parties and Arbitral Tribunals may adopt the IBA Rules of Evidence, in whole or in part, to govern arbitration proceedings, or they may vary them or use them as guidelines in developing their own procedures. The Rules are not intended to limit the flexibility that is inherent in, and an advantage of, international arbitration, and Parties and Arbitral Tribunals are free to adapt them to the particular circumstances of each arbitration.
3. The taking of evidence shall be conducted on the principles that each Party shall act in good faith and be entitled to know, reasonably in advance of any Evidentiary Hearing or any fact or merits determination, the evidence on which the other Parties rely.

Definitions

In the IBA Rules of Evidence:

'Arbitral Tribunal' means a sole arbitrator or a panel of arbitrators;

'Claimant' means the Party or Parties who commenced the arbitration and any Party who, through joinder or otherwise, becomes aligned with such Party or Parties;

'Document' means a writing, communication, picture, drawing, program or data of any kind, whether recorded or maintained on paper or by electronic, audio, visual or any other means;

'Evidentiary Hearing' means any hearing, whether or not held on consecutive days, at which the Arbitral Tribunal, whether in person, by teleconference, videoconference or other method, receives oral or other evidence;

'Expert Report' means a written statement by a Tribunal-Appointed Expert or a Party-Appointed Expert;

'General Rules' mean the institutional, ad hoc or other rules that apply to the conduct of the arbitration;

'IBA Rules of Evidence' or *'Rules'* means these IBA Rules on the Taking of Evidence in International Arbitration, as they may be revised or amended from time to time;

'Party' means a party to the arbitration;

'Party-Appointed Expert' means a person or organisation appointed by a Party in order to report on specific issues determined by the Party;

'Request to Produce' means a written request by a Party that another Party produce Documents;

'Respondent' means the Party or Parties against whom the Claimant made its claim, and any Party who, through joinder or otherwise, becomes aligned with such Party or Parties, and includes a Respondent making a counter-claim;

'Tribunal-Appointed Expert' means a person or organisation appointed by the Arbitral Tribunal in order to report to it on specific issues determined by the Arbitral Tribunal; and

'Witness Statement' means a written statement of testimony by a witness of fact.

Article 1 Scope of Application

1. Whenever the Parties have agreed or the Arbitral Tribunal has determined to apply the IBA Rules of Evidence, the Rules shall govern the taking of evidence, except to the extent that any specific provision of them may be found to be in conflict with any mandatory provision of law determined to be applicable to the case by the Parties or by the Arbitral Tribunal.
2. Where the Parties have agreed to apply the IBA Rules of Evidence, they shall be deemed to have agreed, in the absence of a contrary indication, to the version as current on the date of such agreement.
3. In case of conflict between any provisions of the IBA Rules of Evidence and the General Rules, the Arbitral Tribunal shall apply the IBA Rules of Evidence in the manner that it determines best in order to accomplish the purposes of both the General Rules and the IBA Rules of Evidence, unless the Parties agree to the contrary.
4. In the event of any dispute regarding the meaning of the IBA Rules of Evidence, the Arbitral Tribunal shall interpret them according to their purpose and in the manner most appropriate for the particular arbitration.
5. Insofar as the IBA Rules of Evidence and the General Rules are silent on any matter concerning the taking of evidence and the Parties have not agreed otherwise, the Arbitral Tribunal shall conduct the taking of evidence as it deems appropriate, in accordance with the general principles of the IBA Rules of Evidence.

Article 2 Consultation on Evidentiary Issues

1. The Arbitral Tribunal shall consult the Parties at the earliest appropriate time in the proceedings and invite them to consult each other with a view to agreeing on an efficient, economical and fair process for the taking of evidence.
2. The consultation on evidentiary issues may address the scope, timing and manner of the taking of evidence, including:
   (a) the preparation and submission of Witness Statements and Expert Reports;
   (b) the taking of oral testimony at any Evidentiary Hearing;
   (c) the requirements, procedure and format applicable to the production of Documents;
   (d) the level of confidentiality protection to be afforded to evidence in the arbitration; and
   (e) the promotion of efficiency, economy and conservation of resources in connection with the taking of evidence.

3. The Arbitral Tribunal is encouraged to identify to the Parties, as soon as it considers it to be appropriate, any issues:

(a) that the Arbitral Tribunal may regard as relevant to the case and material to its outcome; and/or

(b) for which a preliminary determination may be appropriate.

Article 3 Documents

1. Within the time ordered by the Arbitral Tribunal, each Party shall submit to the Arbitral Tribunal and to the other Parties all Documents available to it on which it relies, including public Documents and those in the public domain, except for any Documents that have already been submitted by another Party.

2. Within the time ordered by the Arbitral Tribunal, any Party may submit to the Arbitral Tribunal and to the other Parties a Request to Produce.

3. A Request to Produce shall contain:

(a) *(i)* a description of each requested Document sufficient to identify it, or

(ii) a description in sufficient detail (including subject matter) of a narrow and specific requested category of Documents that are reasonably believed to exist; in the case of Documents maintained in electronic form, the requesting Party may, or the Arbitral Tribunal may order that it shall be required to, identify specific files, search terms, individuals or other means of searching for such Documents in an efficient and economical manner;

(b) a statement as to how the Documents requested are relevant to the case and material to its outcome; and

(c) *(i)* a statement that the Documents requested are not in the possession, custody or control of the requesting Party or a statement of the reasons why it would be unreasonably burdensome for the requesting Party to produce such Documents, and

(ii) a statement of the reasons why the requesting Party assumes the Documents requested are in the possession, custody or control of another Party.

4. Within the time ordered by the Arbitral Tribunal, the Party to whom the Request to Produce is addressed shall produce to the other Parties and, if the Arbitral Tribunal so orders, to it, all the Documents requested in its possession, custody or control as to which it makes no objection.

5. If the Party to whom the Request to Produce is addressed has an objection to some or all of the Documents requested, it shall state the objection in writing to the Arbitral Tribunal and the other Parties within the time ordered by the Arbitral Tribunal. The reasons for such objection shall be any of those set forth in Article 9.2 or a failure to satisfy any of the requirements of Article 3.3.

6. Upon receipt of any such objection, the Arbitral Tribunal may invite the relevant Parties to consult with each other with a view to resolving the objection.

7. Either Party may, within the time ordered by the Arbitral Tribunal, request the Arbitral Tribunal to rule on the objection. The Arbitral Tribunal shall then, in consultation with the Parties and in timely fashion, consider the Request to Produce and the objection. The Arbitral Tribunal may order the Party to whom such Request is addressed to produce any requested Document in its possession, custody or control as to which the Arbitral Tribunal determines that *(i)* the issues that the requesting Party wishes to prove are relevant to the case and material to its outcome; *(ii)* none of the reasons for objection set forth in Article 9.2 applies; and *(iii)* the requirements of Article 3.3 have been satisfied. Any such Document shall be produced to the other Parties and, if the Arbitral Tribunal so orders, to it.

8. In exceptional circumstances, if the propriety of an objection can be determined only by review of the Document, the Arbitral Tribunal may determine that it should not review the Document. In that event, the Arbitral Tribunal may, after consultation with the Parties, appoint an independent and impartial expert, bound to confidentiality, to review any such Document and to report on the objection. To the extent that the objection is upheld by the Arbitral Tribunal, the expert shall not disclose to the Arbitral Tribunal and to the other Parties the contents of the Document reviewed.

9. If a Party wishes to obtain the production of Documents from a person or organisation who is not a Party to the arbitration and from whom the Party cannot obtain the Documents on its own, the Party may, within the time ordered by the Arbitral Tribunal, ask it to take whatever steps are legally available to obtain the requested Documents, or seek leave from the Arbitral Tribunal to take such steps itself. The Party shall submit such request to the Arbitral Tribunal and to the other Parties in writing, and the request shall contain the particulars set forth in Article 3.3, as applicable. The Arbitral Tribunal shall decide on this request and shall take, authorize the requesting Party to take, or order any other Party to take, such steps as the Arbitral Tribunal considers appropriate if, in its discretion, it determines that *(i)* the Documents would be relevant to the case and material to its outcome, *(ii)* the requirements of Article 3.3, as applicable, have been satisfied and *(iii)* none of the reasons for objection set forth in Article 9.2 applies.
10. At any time before the arbitration is concluded, the Arbitral Tribunal may *(i)* request any Party to produce Documents, *(ii)* request any Party to use its best efforts to take or *(iii)* itself take, any step that it considers appropriate to obtain Documents from any person or organisation. A Party to whom such a request for Documents is addressed may object to the request for any of the reasons set forth in Article 9.2. In such cases, Article 3.4 to Article 3.8 shall apply correspondingly.
11. Within the time ordered by the Arbitral Tribunal, the Parties may submit to the Arbitral Tribunal and to the other Parties any additional Documents on which they intend to rely or which they believe have become relevant to the case and material to its outcome as a consequence of the issues raised in Documents, Witness Statements or Expert Reports submitted or produced, or in other submissions of the Parties.
12. With respect to the form of submission or production of Documents:
   (a) copies of Documents shall conform to the originals and, at the request of the Arbitral Tribunal, any original shall be presented for inspection;
   (b) Documents that a Party maintains in electronic form shall be submitted or produced in the form most convenient or economical to it that is reasonably usable by the recipients, unless the Parties agree otherwise or, in the absence of such agreement, the Arbitral Tribunal decides otherwise;
   (c) a Party is not obligated to produce multiple copies of Documents which are essentially identical unless the Arbitral Tribunal decides otherwise; and
   (d) translations of Documents shall be submitted
   together with the originals and marked as translations with the original language identified.
13. Any Document submitted or produced by a Party or non-Party in the arbitration and not otherwise in the public domain shall be kept confidential by the Arbitral Tribunal and the other Parties, and shall be used only in connection with the arbitration. This requirement shall apply except and to the extent that disclosure may be required of a Party to fulfil a legal duty, protect or pursue a legal right, or enforce or challenge an award in bona fide legal proceedings before a state court or other judicial authority. The Arbitral Tribunal may issue orders to set forth the terms of this confidentiality. This requirement shall be without prejudice to all other obligations of confidentiality in the arbitration.
14. If the arbitration is organised into separate issues or phases (such as jurisdiction, preliminary determinations, liability or damages), the Arbitral Tribunal may, after consultation with the Parties, schedule the submission of Documents and Requests to Produce separately for each issue or phase.

Article 4 Witnesses of Fact
1. Within the time ordered by the Arbitral Tribunal, each Party shall identify the witnesses on whose testimony it intends to rely and the subject matter of that testimony.
2. Any person may present evidence as a witness, including a Party or a Party's officer, employee or other representative.
3. It shall not be improper for a Party, its officers, employees, legal advisors or other representatives to interview its witnesses or potential witnesses and to discuss their prospective testimony with them.

4. The Arbitral Tribunal may order each Party to submit within a specified time to the Arbitral Tribunal and to the other Parties Witness Statements by each witness on whose testimony it intends to rely, except for those witnesses whose testimony is sought pursuant to Articles 4.9 or 4.10. If Evidentiary Hearings are organised into separate issues or phases (such as jurisdiction, preliminary determinations, liability or damages), the Arbitral Tribunal or the Parties by agreement may schedule the submission of Witness Statements separately for each issue or phase.
5. Each Witness Statement shall contain:
  (a) the full name and address of the witness, a statement regarding his or her present and past relationship (if any) with any of the Parties, and a description of his or her background, qualifications, training and experience, if such a description may be relevant to the dispute or to the contents of the statement;
  (b) a full and detailed description of the facts, and the source of the witness's information as to those facts, sufficient to serve as that witness's evidence in the matter in dispute. Documents on which the witness relies that have not already been submitted shall be provided;
  (c) a statement as to the language in which the Witness Statement was originally prepared and the language in which the witness anticipates giving testimony at the Evidentiary Hearing;
  (d) an affirmation of the truth of the Witness Statement; and
  (e) the signature of the witness and its date and place.
6. If Witness Statements are submitted, any Party may, within the time ordered by the Arbitral Tribunal, submit to the Arbitral Tribunal and to the other Parties revised or additional Witness Statements, including statements from persons not previously named as witnesses, so long as any such revisions or additions respond only to matters contained in another Party's Witness Statements, Expert Reports or other submissions that have not been previously presented in the arbitration.
7. If a witness whose appearance has been requested pursuant to Article 8.1 fails without a valid reason to appear for testimony at an Evidentiary Hearing, the Arbitral Tribunal shall disregard any Witness Statement related to that Evidentiary Hearing by that witness unless, in exceptional circumstances, the Arbitral Tribunal decides otherwise.
8. If the appearance of a witness has not been requested pursuant to Article 8.1, none of the other Parties shall be deemed to have agreed to the correctness of the content of the Witness Statement.
9. If a Party wishes to present evidence from a person who will not appear voluntarily at its request, the Party may, within the time ordered by the Arbitral Tribunal, ask it to take whatever steps are legally available to obtain the testimony of that person, or seek leave from the Arbitral Tribunal to take such steps itself. In the case of a request to the Arbitral Tribunal, the Party shall identify the intended witness, shall describe the subjects on which the witness's testimony is sought and shall state why such subjects are relevant to the case and material to its outcome. The Arbitral Tribunal shall decide on this request and shall take, authorize the requesting Party to take or order any other Party to take, such steps as the Arbitral Tribunal considers appropriate if, in its discretion, it determines that the testimony of that witness would be relevant to the case and material to its outcome.
10. At any time before the arbitration is concluded, the Arbitral Tribunal may order any Party to provide for, or to use its best efforts to provide for, the appearance for testimony at an Evidentiary Hearing of any person, including one whose testimony has not yet been offered. A Party to whom such a request is addressed may object for any of the reasons set forth in Article 9.2.

Article 5 Party-Appointed Experts
1. A Party may rely on a Party-Appointed Expert as a means of evidence on specific issues. Within the time ordered by the Arbitral Tribunal, (i) each Party shall identify any Party-Appointed Expert on whose testimony it intends to rely and the subject-matter of such testimony; and (ii) the Party-Appointed Expert shall submit an Expert Report.

2. The Expert Report shall contain:
   (a) the full name and address of the Party-Appointed Expert, a statement regarding his or her present and past relationship (if any) with any of the Parties, their legal advisors and the Arbitral Tribunal, and a description of his or her background, qualifications, training and experience;
   (b) a description of the instructions pursuant to which he or she is providing his or her opinions and conclusions;
   (c) a statement of his or her independence from the Parties, their legal advisors and the Arbitral Tribunal;
   (d) a statement of the facts on which he or she is basing his or her expert opinions and conclusions;
   (e) his or her expert opinions and conclusions, including a description of the methods, evidence and information used in arriving at the conclusions. Documents on which the Party-Appointed Expert relies that have not already been submitted shall be provided;
   (f) if the Expert Report has been translated, a statement as to the language in which it was originally prepared, and the language in which the Party-Appointed Expert anticipates giving testimony at the Evidentiary Hearing;
   (g) an affirmation of his or her genuine belief in the opinions expressed in the Expert Report;
   (h) the signature of the Party-Appointed Expert and its date and place; and
   (i) if the Expert Report has been signed by more than one person, an attribution of the entirety or specific parts of the Expert Report to each author.

3. If Expert Reports are submitted, any Party may, within the time ordered by the Arbitral Tribunal, submit to the Arbitral Tribunal and to the other Parties revised or additional Expert Reports, including reports or statements from persons not previously identified as Party Appointed Experts, so long as any such revisions or additions respond only to matters contained in another Party's Witness Statements, Expert Reports or other submissions that have not been previously presented in the arbitration.

4. The Arbitral Tribunal in its discretion may order that any Party-Appointed Experts who will submit or who have submitted Expert Reports on the same or related issues meet and confer on such issues. At such meeting, the Party-Appointed Experts shall attempt to reach agreement on the issues within the scope of their Expert Reports, and they shall record in writing any such issues on which they reach agreement, any remaining areas of disagreement and the reasons therefore.

5. If a Party-Appointed Expert whose appearance has been requested pursuant to Article 8.1 fails without a valid reason to appear for testimony at an Evidentiary Hearing, the Arbitral Tribunal shall disregard any Expert Report by that Party-Appointed Expert related to that Evidentiary Hearing unless, in exceptional circumstances, the Arbitral Tribunal decides otherwise.

6. If the appearance of a Party-Appointed Expert has not been requested pursuant to Article 8.1, none of the other Parties shall be deemed to have agreed to the correctness of the content of the Expert Report.

Article 6 Tribunal-Appointed Experts

1. The Arbitral Tribunal, after consulting with the Parties, may appoint one or more independent Tribunal-Appointed Experts to report to it on specific issues designated by the Arbitral Tribunal. The Arbitral Tribunal shall establish the terms of reference for any Tribunal-Appointed Expert Report after consulting with the Parties. A copy of the final terms of reference shall be sent by the Arbitral Tribunal to the Parties.

2. The Tribunal-Appointed Expert shall, before accepting appointment, submit to the Arbitral Tribunal and to the Parties a description of his or her qualifications and a statement of his or her independence from the Parties, their legal advisors and the Arbitral Tribunal. Within the time ordered by the Arbitral Tribunal, the Parties shall inform the Arbitral Tribunal whether they have any objections as to the Tribunal-Appointed Expert's qualifications and independence. The Arbitral Tribunal shall decide promptly whether to accept any such objection. After the appointment of a Tribunal-Appointed

Expert, a Party may object to the expert's qualifications or independence only if the objection is for reasons of which the Party becomes aware after the appointment has been made. The Arbitral Tribunal shall decide promptly what, if any, action to take.

3. Subject to the provisions of Article 9.2, the Tribunal-Appointed Expert may request a Party to provide any information or to provide access to any Documents, goods, samples, property, machinery, systems, processes or site for inspection, to the extent relevant to the case and material to its outcome. The authority of a Tribunal-Appointed Expert to request such information or access shall be the same as the authority of the Arbitral Tribunal. The Parties and their representatives shall have the right to receive any such information and to attend any such inspection. Any disagreement between a Tribunal-Appointed Expert and a Party as to the relevance, materiality or appropriateness of such a request shall be decided by the Arbitral Tribunal, in the manner provided in Articles 3.5 through 3.8. The Tribunal-Appointed Expert shall record in the Expert Report any non-compliance by a Party with an appropriate request or decision by the Arbitral Tribunal and shall describe its effects on the determination of the specific issue.

4. The Tribunal-Appointed Expert shall report in writing to the Arbitral Tribunal in an Expert Report. The Expert Report shall contain:

(a) the full name and address of the Tribunal-Appointed Expert, and a description of his or her background, qualifications, training and experience;
(b) statement of the facts on which he or she is basing his or her expert opinions and conclusions;
(c) his or her expert opinions and conclusions, including a description of the methods, evidence and information used in arriving at the conclusions. Documents on which the Tribunal-Appointed Expert relies that have not already been submitted shall be provided;
(d) if the Expert Report has been translated, a statement as to the language in which it was originally prepared, and the language in which the Tribunal-Appointed Expert anticipates giving testimony at the Evidentiary Hearing;
(e) an affirmation of his or her genuine belief in the opinions expressed in the Expert Report;
(f) the signature of the Tribunal-Appointed Expert and its date and place; and
(g) if the Expert Report has been signed by more than one person, an attribution of the entirety or specific parts of the Expert Report to each author.

5. The Arbitral Tribunal shall send a copy of such Expert Report to the Parties. The Parties may examine any information, Documents, goods, samples, property, machinery, systems, processes or site for inspection that the Tribunal-Appointed Expert has examined and any correspondence between the Arbitral Tribunal and the Tribunal-Appointed Expert. Within the time ordered by the Arbitral Tribunal, any Party shall have the opportunity to respond to the Expert Report in a submission by the Party or through a Witness Statement or an Expert Report by a Party-Appointed Expert. The Arbitral Tribunal shall send the submission, Witness Statement or Expert Report to the Tribunal-Appointed Expert and to the other Parties.

6. At the request of a Party or of the Arbitral Tribunal, the Tribunal-Appointed Expert shall be present at an Evidentiary Hearing. The Arbitral Tribunal may question the Tribunal-Appointed Expert, and he or she may be questioned by the Parties or by any Party-Appointed Expert on issues raised in his or her Expert Report, the Parties' submissions or Witness Statement or the Expert Reports made by the Party-Appointed Experts pursuant to Article 6.5.

7. Any Expert Report made by a Tribunal-Appointed Expert and its conclusions shall be assessed by the Arbitral Tribunal with due regard to all circumstances of the case.

8. The fees and expenses of a Tribunal-Appointed Expert, to be funded in a manner determined by the Arbitral Tribunal, shall form part of the costs of the arbitration.

Article 7 Inspection

Subject to the provisions of Article 9.2, the Arbitral Tribunal may, at the request of a Party or on its own motion, inspect or require the inspection by a Tribunal- Appointed Expert or a Party-Appointed Expert of any site, property, machinery or any other goods, samples, systems, processes or Documents, as it deems appropriate. The Arbitral Tribunal shall, in consultation with the Parties, determine the timing and arrangement for the inspection. The Parties and their representatives shall have the right to attend any such inspection.

Article 8 Evidentiary Hearing

1. Within the time ordered by the Arbitral Tribunal, each Party shall inform the Arbitral Tribunal and the other Parties of the witnesses whose appearance it requests. Each witness (which term includes, for the purposes of this Article, witnesses of fact and any experts) shall, subject to Article 8.2, appear for testimony at the Evidentiary Hearing if such person's appearance has been requested by any Party or by the Arbitral Tribunal. Each witness shall appear in person unless the Arbitral Tribunal allows the use of videoconference or similar technology with respect to a particular witness.
2. The Arbitral Tribunal shall at all times have complete control over the Evidentiary Hearing. The Arbitral Tribunal may limit or exclude any question to, answer by or appearance of a witness, if it considers such question, answer or appearance to be irrelevant, immaterial, unreasonably burdensome, duplicative or otherwise covered by a reason for objection set forth in Article 9.2. Questions to a witness during direct and re-direct testimony may not be unreasonably leading.
3. With respect to oral testimony at an Evidentiary Hearing:
   (a) the Claimant shall ordinarily first present the testimony of its witnesses, followed by the Respondent presenting the testimony of its witnesses;
   (b) following direct testimony, any other Party may question such witness, in an order to be determined by the Arbitral Tribunal. The Party who initially presented the witness shall subsequently have the opportunity to ask additional questions on the matters raised in the other Parties' questioning;
   (c) thereafter, the Claimant shall ordinarily first present the testimony of its Party-Appointed Experts, followed by the Respondent presenting the testimony of its Party-Appointed Experts. The Party who initially presented the Party-Appointed Expert shall subsequently have the opportunity to ask additional questions on the matters raised in the other Parties' questioning;
   (d) the Arbitral Tribunal may question a Tribunal-Appointed Expert, and he or she may be questioned by the Parties or by any Party-Appointed Expert, on issues raised in the Tribunal-Appointed Expert Report, in the Parties' submissions or in the Expert Reports made by the Party-Appointed Experts;
   (e) if the arbitration is organised into separate issues or phases (such as jurisdiction, preliminary determinations, liability and damages), the Parties may agree or the Arbitral Tribunal may order the scheduling of testimony separately for each issue or phase;
   (f) the Arbitral Tribunal, upon request of a Party or on its own motion, may vary this order of proceeding, including the arrangement of testimony by particular issues or in such a manner that witnesses be questioned at the same time and in confrontation with each other (witness conferencing);
   (g) the Arbitral Tribunal may ask questions to a witness at any time.
4. A witness of fact providing testimony shall first affirm, in a manner determined appropriate by the Arbitral Tribunal, that he or she commits to tell the truth or, in the case of an expert witness, his or her genuine belief in the opinions to be expressed at the Evidentiary Hearing. If the witness has submitted a Witness Statement or an Expert Report, the witness shall confirm it. The Parties may agree or the Arbitral Tribunal may order that the Witness Statement or Expert Report shall serve as that witness's direct testimony.

5. Subject to the provisions of Article 9.2, the Arbitral Tribunal may request any person to give oral or written evidence on any issue that the Arbitral Tribunal considers to be relevant to the case and material to its outcome. Any witness called and questioned by the Arbitral Tribunal may also be questioned by the Parties.

Article 9 Admissibility and Assessment of Evidence

1. The Arbitral Tribunal shall determine the admissibility, relevance, materiality and weight of evidence.

2. The Arbitral Tribunal shall, at the request of a Party or on its own motion, exclude from evidence or production any Document, statement, oral testimony or inspection for any of the following reasons:

   (a) lack of sufficient relevance to the case or materiality to its outcome;

   (b) legal impediment or privilege under the legal or ethical rules determined by the Arbitral Tribunal to be applicable;

   (c) unreasonable burden to produce the requested evidence;

   (d) loss or destruction of the Document that has been shown with reasonable likelihood to have occurred;

   (e) grounds of commercial or technical confidentiality that the Arbitral Tribunal determines to be compelling;

   (f) grounds of special political or institutional sensitivity (including evidence that has been classified as secret by a government or a public international institution) that the Arbitral Tribunal determines to be compelling; or

   (g) considerations of procedural economy, proportionality, fairness or equality of the Parties that the Arbitral Tribunal determines to be compelling.

3. In considering issues of legal impediment or privilege under Article 9.2(b), and insofar as permitted by any mandatory legal or ethical rules that are determined by it to be applicable, the Arbitral Tribunal may take into account:

   (a) any need to protect the confidentiality of a Document created or statement or oral communication made in connection with and for the purpose of providing or obtaining legal advice;

   (b) any need to protect the confidentiality of a Document created or statement or oral communication made in connection with and for the purpose of settlement negotiations;

   (c) the expectations of the Parties and their advisors at the time the legal impediment or privilege is said to have arisen;

   (d) any possible waiver of any applicable legal impediment or privilege by virtue of consent, earlier disclosure, affirmative use of the Document, statement, oral communication or advice contained therein, or otherwise; and

   (e) the need to maintain fairness and equality as between the Parties, particularly if they are subject to different legal or ethical rules.

4. The Arbitral Tribunal may, where appropriate, make necessary arrangements to permit evidence to be presented or considered subject to suitable confidentiality protection.

5. If a Party fails without satisfactory explanation to produce any Document requested in a Request to Produce to which it has not objected in due time or fails to produce any Document ordered to be produced by the Arbitral Tribunal, the Arbitral Tribunal may infer that such document would be adverse to the interests of that Party.

6. If a Party fails without satisfactory explanation to make available any other relevant evidence, including testimony, sought by one Party to which the Party to whom the request was addressed has not objected in due time or fails to make available any evidence, including testimony, ordered by the Arbitral Tribunal to be produced, the Arbitral Tribunal may infer that such evidence would be adverse to the interests of that Party.

7. If the Arbitral Tribunal determines that a Party has failed to conduct itself in good faith in the taking of evidence, the Arbitral Tribunal may, in addition to any other measures available under these Rules, take such failure into account in its assignment of the costs of the arbitration, including costs arising out of or in connection with the taking of evidence.

9.5.2 IBA Guidelines on Conflicts of Interest in International Arbitration (2014)[1]

Adopted by resolution of the IBA Council on Thursday 23 October 2014 Updated, 10 August 2015

Since their issuance in 2004, the *IBA Guidelines on Conflicts of Interest in International Arbitration* (the 'Guidelines') have gained wide acceptance within the international arbitration community. Arbitrators commonly use the Guidelines when making decisions about prospective appointments and disclosures. Likewise, parties and their counsel frequently consider the Guidelines in assessing the impartiality and independence of arbitrators, and arbitral institutions and courts also often consult the Guidelines in considering challenges to arbitrators. As contemplated when the Guidelines were first adopted, on the eve of their tenth anniversary it was considered appropriate to reflect on the accumulated experience of using them and to identify areas of possible clarification or improvement. Accordingly, in 2012, the IBA Arbitration Committee initiated a review of the Guidelines, which was conducted by an expanded Conflicts of Interest Subcommittee (the 'Subcommittee'), representing diverse legal cultures and a range of perspectives, including counsel, arbitrators and arbitration users. The Subcommittee was chaired by David Arias, later co-chaired by Julie Bédard, and the review process was conducted under the leadership of Pierre Bienvenu and Bernard Hanotiau.

While the Guidelines were originally intended to apply to both commercial and investment arbitration, it was found in the course of the review process that uncertainty lingered as to their application to investment arbitration. Similarly, despite a comment in the original version of the Guidelines that their application extended to non-legal professionals serving as arbitrator, there appeared to remain uncertainty in this regard as well. A consensus emerged in favour of a general affirmation that the Guidelines apply to both commercial and investment arbitration, and to both legal and non-legal professionals serving as arbitrator.

The Subcommittee has carefully considered a number of issues that have received attention in international arbitration practice since 2004, such as the effects of so-called 'advance waivers', whether the fact of acting concurrently as counsel and arbitrator in unrelated cases raising similar legal issues warrants disclosure, 'issue' conflicts, the independence and impartiality of arbitral or administrative secretaries and third-party funding. The revised Guidelines reflect the Subcommittee's conclusions on these issues.

The Subcommittee has also considered, in view of the evolution of the global practice of international arbitration, whether the revised Guidelines should impose stricter standards in regard to arbitrator disclosure. The revised Guidelines reflect the conclusion that, while the basic approach of the 2004 Guidelines should not be altered, disclosure should be required in certain circumstances not contemplated in the 2004 Guidelines. It is also essential to reaffirm that the fact of requiring disclosure – or of an arbitrator making a disclosure – does not imply the existence of doubts as to the impartiality or independence of the arbitrator. Indeed, the standard for disclosure differs from the standard for

1 IBA Guidelines on Conflict of Interest in International Arbitration (2014) is reproduced by kind permission of the International Bar Association, London, UK, and is available at: www.ibanet.org/Publications/publications_IBA_guides_and_free_materials.aspx.© International Bar Association.

challenge. Similarly, the revised Guidelines are not in any way intended to discourage the service as arbitrators of lawyers practising in large firms or legal associations.

The Guidelines were adopted by resolution of the IBA Council on Thursday 23 October 2014. The Guidelines are available for download at: www.ibanet. org/Publications/publications_IBA_guides_ and_ free_materials.aspx.

Introduction

1. Arbitrators and party representatives are often unsure about the scope of their disclosure obligations. The growth of international business, including larger corporate groups and international law firms, has generated more disclosures and resulted in increased complexity in the analysis of disclosure and conflict of interest issues. Parties have more opportunities to use

challenges of arbitrators to delay arbitrations, or to deny the opposing party the arbitrator of its choice. Disclosure of any relationship, no matter how minor or serious, may lead to unwarranted or frivolous challenges. At the same time, it is important that more information be made available to the parties, so as to protect awards against challenges based upon alleged failures to disclose, and to promote a level playing field among parties and among counsel engaged in international arbitration.

2. Parties, arbitrators, institutions and courts face complex decisions about the information that arbitrators should disclose and the standards to apply to disclosure. In addition, institutions and courts face difficult decisions when an objection or a challenge is made after a disclosure. There is a tension between, on the one hand, the parties' right to disclosure of circumstances that may call into question an arbitrator's impartiality or independence in order to protect the parties' right to a fair hearing, and, on the other hand, the need to avoid unnecessary challenges against arbitrators in order to protect the parties' ability to select arbitrators of their choosing.

3. It is in the interest of the international arbitration community that arbitration proceedings are not hindered by ill-founded challenges against arbitrators and that the legitimacy of the process is not affected by uncertainty and a lack of uniformity in the applicable standards for disclosures, objections and challenges. The 2004 Guidelines reflected the view that the standards existing at the time lacked sufficient clarity and uniformity in their application. The Guidelines, therefore, set forth some 'General Standards and Explanatory Notes on the Standards'. Moreover, in order to promote greater consistency and to avoid unnecessary challenges and arbitrator withdrawals and removals, the Guidelines list specific situations indicating whether they warrant disclosure or disqualification of an arbitrator. Such lists, designated 'Red', 'Orange' and 'Green' (the 'Application Lists'), have been updated and appear at the end of these revised Guidelines.

4. The Guidelines reflect the understanding of the IBA Arbitration Committee as to the best current international practice, firmly rooted in the principles expressed in the General Standards below. The General Standards and the Application Lists are based upon statutes and case law in a cross-section of jurisdictions, and upon the judgement and experience of practitioners involved in international arbitration. In reviewing the 2004 Guidelines, the IBA Arbitration Committee updated its analysis of the laws and practices in a number of jurisdictions. The Guidelines seek to balance the various interests of parties, representatives, arbitrators and arbitration institutions, all of whom have a responsibility for ensuring the integrity, reputation and efficiency of international arbitration. Both the 2004 Working Group and the Subcommittee in 2012/2014 have sought and considered the views of leading arbitration institutions, corporate counsel and other persons involved in international arbitration through public consultations at IBA annual meetings, and at meetings with arbitrators and practitioners. The comments received were reviewed in detail and many were adopted. The IBA Arbitration Committee is grateful for the serious consideration given to its proposals by so many institutions and individuals.

5. The Guidelines apply to international commercial arbitration and investment arbitration, whether the representation of the parties is carried out by lawyers or non-lawyers, and irrespective of whether or not non-legal professionals serve as arbitrators.
6. These Guidelines are not legal provisions and do not override any applicable national law or arbitral rules chosen by the parties. However, it is hoped that, as was the case for the 2004 Guidelines and other sets of rules and guidelines of the IBA Arbitration Committee, the revised Guidelines will find broad acceptance within the international arbitration community, and that they will assist parties, practitioners, arbitrators, institutions and courts in dealing with these important questions of impartiality and independence. The IBA Arbitration Committee trusts that the Guidelines will be applied with robust common sense and without unduly formalistic interpretation.
7. The Application Lists cover many of the varied situations that commonly arise in practice, but they do not purport to be exhaustive, nor could they be. Nevertheless, the IBA Arbitration Committee is confident that the Application Lists provide concrete guidance that is useful in applying the General Standards. The IBA Arbitration Committee will continue to study the actual use of the Guidelines with a view to furthering their improvement.
8. In 1987, the IBA published *Rules of Ethics for International Arbitrators*. Those Rules cover more topics than these Guidelines, and they remain in effect as to subjects that are not discussed in the Guidelines. The Guidelines supersede the *Rules of Ethics* as to the matters treated here.

PART I: GENERAL STANDARDS REGARDING IMPARTIALITY, INDEPENDENCE AND DISCLOSURE

(1) General Principle

Every arbitrator shall be impartial and independent of the parties at the time of accepting an appointment to serve and shall remain so until the final award has been rendered or the proceedings have otherwise finally terminated.

Explanation to General Standard 1:

A fundamental principle underlying these Guidelines is that each arbitrator must be impartial and independent of the parties at the time he or she accepts an appointment to act as arbitrator, and must remain so during the entire course of the arbitration proceeding, including the time period for the correction or interpretation of a final award under the relevant rules, assuming such time period is known or readily ascertainable.

The question has arisen as to whether this obligation should extend to the period during which the award may be challenged before the relevant courts. The decision taken is that this obligation should not extend in this manner, unless the final award may be referred back to the original Arbitral Tribunal under the relevant applicable law or relevant institutional rules. Thus, the arbitrator's obligation in this regard ends when the Arbitral Tribunal has rendered the final award, and any correction or interpretation as may be permitted under the relevant rules has been issued, or the time for seeking the same has elapsed, the proceedings have been finally terminated (for example, because of a settlement), or the arbitrator otherwise no longer has jurisdiction. If, after setting aside or other proceedings, the dispute is referred back to the same Arbitral Tribunal, a fresh round of disclosure and review of potential conflicts of interests may be necessary.

(2) Conflicts of Interest

a) An arbitrator shall decline to accept an appointment or, if the arbitration has already been commenced, refuse to continue to act as an arbitrator, if he or she has any doubt as to his or her ability to be impartial or independent.
b) The same principle applies if facts or circumstances exist, or have arisen since the appointment, which, from the point of view of a reasonable third person having knowledge of the relevant facts and circumstances, would give rise to justifiable doubts as to the arbitrator's impartiality or independence, unless the parties have accepted the arbitrator in accordance with the requirements set out in General Standard 4.
c) Doubts are justifiable if a reasonable third person, having knowledge of the relevant facts and circumstances, would reach the conclusion that there is a likelihood that the arbitrator may be influenced by factors other than the merits of the case as presented by the parties in reaching his or her decision.
d) Justifiable doubts necessarily exist as to the arbitrator's impartiality or independence in any of the situations described in the Non-Waivable Red List.

Explanation to General Standard 2:

(a) If the arbitrator has doubts as to his or her ability to be impartial and independent, the arbitrator must decline the appointment. This standard should apply regardless of the stage of the proceedings. This is a basic principle that is spelled out in these Guidelines in order to avoid confusion and to foster confidence in the arbitral process.
(b) In order for standards to be applied as consistently as possible, the test for disqualification is an objective one.
The wording 'impartiality or independence' derives from the widely adopted Article 12 of the United Nations Commission on International Trade Law (UNCITRAL) Model Law, and the use of an appearance test based on justifiable doubts as to the impartiality or independence of the arbitrator, as provided in Article 12(2) of the UNCITRAL Model Law, is to be applied objectively (a 'reasonable third person test'). Again, as described in the Explanation to General Standard 3(e), this standard applies regardless of the stage of the proceedings.
(c) Laws and rules that rely on the standard of justifiable doubts often do not define that standard. This General Standard is intended to provide some context for making this determination.
(d) The Non-Waivable Red List describes circumstances that necessarily raise justifiable doubts as to the arbitrator's impartiality or independence. For example, because no one is allowed to be his or her own judge, there cannot be identity between an arbitrator and a party. The parties, therefore, cannot waive the conflict of interest arising in such a situation.

(3) Disclosure by the Arbitrator

a) If facts or circumstances exist that may, in the eyes of the parties, give rise to doubts as to the arbitrator's impartiality or independence, the arbitrator shall disclose such facts or circumstances to the parties, the arbitration institution or other appointing authority (if any, and if so required by the applicable institutional rules) and the co-arbitrators, if any, prior to accepting his or her appointment or, if thereafter, as soon as he or she learns of them.
b) An advance declaration or waiver in relation to possible conflicts of interest arising from facts and circumstances that may arise in the future does not discharge the arbitrator's ongoing duty of disclosure under General Standard 3(a).

c) It follows from General Standards 1 and 2(a) that an arbitrator who has made a disclosure considers himself or herself to be impartial and independent of the parties, despite the disclosed facts, and, therefore, capable of performing his or her duties as arbitrator. Otherwise, he or she would have declined the nomination or appointment at the outset, or resigned.
d) Any doubt as to whether an arbitrator should disclose certain facts or circumstances should be resolved in favour of disclosure.
e) When considering whether facts or circumstances exist that should be disclosed, the arbitrator shall not take into account whether the arbitration is at the beginning or at a later stage.

Explanation to General Standard 3:

a) The arbitrator's duty to disclose under General Standard 3(a) rests on the principle that the parties have an interest in being fully informed of any facts or circumstances that may be relevant in their view. Accordingly, General Standard 3(d) provides that any doubt as to whether certain facts or circumstances should be disclosed should be resolved in favour of disclosure. However, situations that, such as those set out in the Green List, could never lead to disqualification under the objective test set out in General Standard 2, need not be disclosed. As reflected in General Standard 3(c), a disclosure does not imply that the disclosed facts are such as to disqualify the arbitrator under General Standard 2. The duty of disclosure under General Standard 3(a) is ongoing in nature.
b) The IBA Arbitration Committee has considered the increasing use by prospective arbitrators of declarations in respect of facts or circumstances that may arise in the future, and the possible conflicts of interest that may result, sometimes referred to as 'advance waivers'. Such declarations do not discharge the arbitrator's ongoing duty of disclosure under General Standard 3(a). The Guidelines, however, do not otherwise take a position as to the validity and effect of advance declarations or waivers, because the validity and effect of any advance declaration or waiver must be assessed in view of the specific text of the advance declaration or waiver, the particular circumstances at hand and the applicable law.
c) A disclosure does not imply the existence of a conflict of interest. An arbitrator who has made a disclosure to the parties considers himself or herself to be impartial and independent of the parties, despite the disclosed facts, or else he or she would have declined the nomination, or resigned. An arbitrator making a disclosure thus feels capable of performing his or her duties. It is the purpose of disclosure to allow the parties to judge whether they agree with the evaluation of the arbitrator and, if they so wish, to explore the situation further. It is hoped that the promulgation of this General Standard will eliminate the misconception that disclosure itself implies doubts sufficient to disqualify the arbitrator, or even creates a presumption in favour of disqualification. Instead, any challenge should only be successful if an objective test, as set forth in General Standard 2 above, is met. Under Comment 5 of the Practical Application of the General Standards, a failure to disclose certain facts and circumstances that may, in the eyes of the parties, give rise to doubts as to the arbitrator's impartiality or independence, does not necessarily mean that a conflict of interest exists, or that a disqualification should ensue.
d) In determining which facts should be disclosed, an arbitrator should take into account all circumstances known to him or her. If the arbitrator finds that he or she should make a disclosure, but that professional secrecy rules or other rules of practice or professional conduct prevent such disclosure, he or she should not accept the appointment, or should resign.
e) Disclosure or disqualification (as set out in General Standards 2 and 3) should not depend on the particular stage of the arbitration. In order to determine whether the arbitrator should disclose, decline the appointment or refuse to continue to act, the facts and circumstances alone are relevant, not the current stage of the proceedings, or the consequences of the withdrawal. As a practical matter, arbitration institutions may make a distinction depending on the stage of the arbitration.

Courts may likewise apply different standards. Nevertheless, no distinction is made by these Guidelines depending on the stage of the arbitral proceedings. While there are practical concerns, if an arbitrator must withdraw after the arbitration has commenced, a distinction based on the stage of the arbitration would be inconsistent with the General Standards.

(4) Waiver by the Parties

a) If, within 30 days after the receipt of any disclosure by the arbitrator, or after a party otherwise learns of facts or circumstances that could constitute a potential conflict of interest for an arbitrator, a party does not raise an express objection with regard to that arbitrator, subject to paragraphs (b) and (c) of this General Standard, the party is deemed to have waived any potential conflict of interest in respect of the arbitrator based on such facts or circumstances and may not raise any objection based on such facts or circumstances at a later stage.
b) However, if facts or circumstances exist as described in the Non-Waivable Red List, any waiver by a party (including any declaration or advance waiver, such as that contemplated in General Standard 3(b)), or any agreement by the parties to have such a person serve as arbitrator, shall be regarded as invalid.
c) A person should not serve as an arbitrator when a conflict of interest, such as those exemplified in the Waivable Red List, exists. Nevertheless, such a person may accept appointment as arbitrator, or continue to act as an arbitrator, if the following conditions are met:
   (i) all parties, all arbitrators and the arbitration institution, or other appointing authority (if any), have full knowledge of the conflict of interest; and
   (ii) all parties expressly agree that such a person may serve as arbitrator, despite the conflict of interest.
d) An arbitrator may assist the parties in reaching a settlement of the dispute, through conciliation, mediation or otherwise, at any stage of the proceedings. However, before doing so, the arbitrator should receive an express agreement by the parties that acting in such a manner shall not disqualify the arbitrator from continuing to serve as arbitrator. Such express agreement shall be considered to be an effective waiver of any potential conflict of interest that may arise from the arbitrator's participation in such a process, or from information that the arbitrator may learn in the process. If the assistance by the arbitrator does not lead to the final settlement of the case, the parties remain bound by their waiver. However, consistent with General Standard 2(a) and notwithstanding such agreement, the arbitrator shall resign if, as a consequence of his or her involvement in the settlement process, the arbitrator develops doubts as to his or her ability to remain impartial or independent in the future course of the arbitration.

Explanation to General Standard 4:

a) Under General Standard 4(a), a party is deemed to have waived any potential conflict of interest, if such party has not raised an objection in respect of such conflict of interest within 30 days. This time limit should run from the date on which the party learns of the relevant facts or circumstances, including through the disclosure process.
b) General Standard 4(b) serves to exclude from the scope of General Standard 4(a) the facts and circumstances described in the Non-Waivable Red List. Some arbitrators make declarations that seek waivers from the parties with respect to facts or circumstances that may arise in the future. Irrespective of any such waiver sought by the arbitrator, as provided in General Standard 3(b), facts and circumstances arising in the course of the arbitration should be disclosed to the parties by virtue of the arbitrator's ongoing duty of disclosure.

c) Notwithstanding a serious conflict of interest, such as those that are described by way of example in the Waivable Red List, the parties may wish to engage such a person as an arbitrator. Here, party autonomy and the desire to have only impartial and independent arbitrators must be balanced. Persons with a serious conflict of interest, such as those that are described by way of example in the Waivable Red List, may serve as arbitrators only if the parties make fully informed, explicit waivers.
d) The concept of the Arbitral Tribunal assisting the parties in reaching a settlement of their dispute in the course of the arbitration proceedings is well-established in some jurisdictions, but not in others. Informed consent by the parties to such a process prior to its beginning should be regarded as an effective waiver of a potential conflict of interest. Certain jurisdictions may require such consent to be in writing and signed by the parties. Subject to any requirements of applicable law, express consent may be sufficient and may be given at a hearing and reflected in the minutes or transcript of the proceeding. In addition, in order to avoid parties using an arbitrator as mediator as a means of disqualifying the arbitrator, the General Standard makes clear that the waiver should remain effective, if the mediation is unsuccessful. In giving their express consent, the parties should realise the consequences of the arbitrator assisting them in a settlement process, including the risk of the resignation of the arbitrator.

(5) Scope

(a) These Guidelines apply equally to tribunal chairs, sole arbitrators and co-arbitrators, howsoever appointed.
(b) Arbitral or administrative secretaries and assistants, to an individual arbitrator or the Arbitral Tribunal, are bound by the same duty of independence and impartiality as arbitrators, and it is the responsibility of the Arbitral Tribunal to ensure that such duty is respected at all stages of the arbitration.

Explanation to General Standard 5:

a) Because each member of an Arbitral Tribunal has an obligation to be impartial and independent, the General Standards do not distinguish between sole arbitrators, tribunal chairs, party-appointed arbitrators or arbitrators appointed by an institution.
b) Some arbitration institutions require arbitral or administrative secretaries and assistants to sign a declaration of independence and impartiality. Whether or not such a requirement exists, arbitral or administrative secretaries and assistants to the Arbitral Tribunal are bound by the same duty of independence and impartiality (including the duty of disclosure) as arbitrators, and it is the responsibility of the Arbitral Tribunal to ensure that such duty is respected at all stages of the arbitration. Furthermore, this duty applies to arbitral or administrative secretaries and assistants to either the Arbitral Tribunal or individual members of the Arbitral Tribunal.

(6) Relationships

(a) The arbitrator is in principle considered to bear the identity of his or her law firm, but when considering the relevance of facts or circumstances to determine whether a potential conflict of interest exists, or whether disclosure should be made, the activities of an arbitrator's law firm, if any, and the relationship of the arbitrator with the law firm, should be considered in each individual case. The fact that the activities of the arbitrator's firm involve one of the parties shall not necessarily constitute a source of such conflict, or a reason for disclosure. Similarly, if one of the parties is a member of a group with which the arbitrator's firm has a relationship, such fact should be considered in each individual case, but shall not necessarily constitute by itself a source of a conflict of interest, or a reason for disclosure.

(b) If one of the parties is a legal entity, any legal or physical person having a controlling influence on the legal entity, or a direct economic interest in, or a duty to indemnify a party for, the award to be rendered in the arbitration, may be considered to bear the identity of such party.

Explanation to General Standard 6:

a) The growing size of law firms should be taken into account as part of today's reality in international arbitration. There is a need to balance the interests of a party to appoint the arbitrator of its choice, who may be a partner at a large law firm, and the importance of maintaining confidence in the impartiality and independence of international arbitrators. The arbitrator must, in principle, be considered to bear the identity of his or her law firm, but the activities of the arbitrator's firm should not automatically create a conflict of interest. The relevance of the activities of the arbitrator's firm, such as the nature, timing and scope of the work by the law firm, and the relationship of the arbitrator with the law firm, should be considered in each case. General Standard 6(a) uses the term 'involve' rather than 'acting for' because the relevant connections with a party may include activities other than representation on a legal matter. Although barristers' chambers should not be equated with law firms for the purposes of conflicts, and no general standard is proffered for barristers' chambers, disclosure may be warranted in view of the relationships among barristers, parties or counsel. When a party to an arbitration is a member of a group of companies, special questions regarding conflicts of interest arise. Because individual corporate structure arrangements vary widely, a catch-all rule is not appropriate. Instead, the particular circumstances of an affiliation with another entity within the same group of companies, and the relationship of that entity with the arbitrator's law firm, should be considered in each individual case.

b) When a party in international arbitration is a legal entity, other legal and physical persons may have a controlling influence on this legal entity, or a direct economic interest in, or a duty to indemnify a party for, the award to be rendered in the arbitration. Each situation should be assessed individually, and General Standard 6(b) clarifies that such legal persons and individuals may be considered effectively to be that party. Third-party funders and insurers in relation to the dispute may have a direct economic interest in the award, and as such may be considered to be the equivalent of the party. For these purposes, the terms 'third-party funder' and 'insurer' refer to any person or entity that is contributing funds, or other material support, to the prosecution or defence of the case and that has a direct economic interest in, or a duty to indemnify a party for, the award to be rendered in the arbitration.

(7) Duty of the Parties and the Arbitrator

a) A party shall inform an arbitrator, the Arbitral Tribunal, the other parties and the arbitration institution or other appointing authority (if any) of any relationship, direct or indirect, between the arbitrator and the party (or another company of the same group of companies, or an individual having a controlling influence on the party in the arbitration), or between the arbitrator and any person or entity with a direct economic interest in, or a duty to indemnify a party for, the award to be rendered in the arbitration. The party shall do so on its own initiative at the earliest opportunity.

(b) A party shall inform an arbitrator, the Arbitral Tribunal, the other parties and the arbitration institution or other appointing authority (if any) of the identity of its counsel appearing in the arbitration, as well as of any relationship, including membership of the same barristers' chambers, between its counsel and the arbitrator. The party shall do so on its own initiative at the earliest opportunity, and upon any change in its counsel team.

(c) In order to comply with General Standard 7(a), a party shall perform reasonable enquiries and provide any relevant information available to it.
(d) An arbitrator is under a duty to make reasonable enquiries to identify any conflict of interest, as well as any facts or circumstances that may reasonably give rise to doubts as to his or her impartiality or independence. Failure to disclose a conflict is not excused by lack of knowledge, if the arbitrator does not perform such reasonable enquiries.

Explanation to General Standard 7:

(a) The parties are required to disclose any relationship with the arbitrator. Disclosure of such relationships should reduce the risk of an unmeritorious challenge of an arbitrator's impartiality or independence based on information learned after the appointment. The parties' duty of disclosure of any relationship, direct or indirect, between the arbitrator and the party (or another company of the same group of companies, or an individual having a controlling influence on the party in the arbitration) has been extended to relationships with persons or entities having a direct economic interest in the award to be rendered in the arbitration, such as an entity providing funding for the arbitration, or having a duty to indemnify a party for the award.
(b) Counsel appearing in the arbitration, namely the persons involved in the representation of the parties in the arbitration, must be identified by the parties at the earliest opportunity. A party's duty to disclose the identity of counsel appearing in the arbitration extends to all members of that party's counsel team and arises from the outset of the proceedings.
(c) In order to satisfy their duty of disclosure, the parties are required to investigate any relevant information that is reasonably available to them. In addition, any party to an arbitration is required, at the outset and on an ongoing basis during the entirety of the proceedings, to make a reasonable effort to ascertain and to disclose available information that, applying the general standard, might affect the arbitrator's impartiality or independence.
(d) In order to satisfy their duty of disclosure under the Guidelines, arbitrators are required to investigate any relevant information that is reasonably available to them.

PART II: PRACTICAL APPLICATION OF THE GENERAL STANDARDS

1. If the Guidelines are to have an important practical influence, they should address situations that are likely to occur in today's arbitration practice and should provide specific guidance to arbitrators, parties, institutions and courts as to which situations do or do not constitute conflicts of interest, or should or should not be disclosed. For this purpose, the Guidelines categorise situations that may occur in the following Application Lists. These lists cannot cover every situation. In all cases, the General Standards should control the outcome.

2. The Red List consists of two parts: 'a Non-Waivable Red List' (see General Standards 2(d) and 4(b)); and 'a Waivable Red List' (see General Standard 4(c)). These lists are non-exhaustive and detail specific situations that, depending on the facts of a given case, give rise to justifiable doubts as to the arbitrator's impartiality and independence. That is, in these circumstances, an objective conflict of interest exists from the point of view of a reasonable third person having knowledge of the relevant facts and circumstances (see General Standard 2(b)). The Non-Waivable Red List includes situations deriving from the overriding principle that no person can be his or her own judge. Therefore, acceptance of such a situation cannot cure the conflict. The Waivable Red List covers situations that are serious but not as severe. Because of their seriousness, unlike circumstances described in the Orange List, these situations should be considered waivable, but only if and when the parties, being aware of the conflict

of interest situation, expressly state their willingness to have such a person act as arbitrator, as set forth in General Standard 4(c).

3. The Orange List is a non-exhaustive list of specific situations that, depending on the facts of a given case, may, in the eyes of the parties, give rise to doubts as to the arbitrator's impartiality or independence. The Orange List thus reflects situations that would fall under General Standard 3(a), with the consequence that the arbitrator has a duty to disclose such situations. In all these situations, the parties are deemed to have accepted the arbitrator if, after disclosure, no timely objection is made, as established in General Standard 4(a).

4. Disclosure does not imply the existence of a conflict of interest; nor should it by itself result either in a disqualification of the arbitrator, or in a presumption regarding disqualification. The purpose of the disclosure is to inform the parties of a situation that they may wish to explore further in order to determine whether objectively – that is, from the point of view of a reasonable third person having knowledge of the relevant facts and circumstances – there are justifiable doubts as to the arbitrator's impartiality or independence. If the conclusion is that there are no justifiable doubts, the arbitrator can act. Apart from the situations covered by the Non-Waivable Red List, he or she can also act if there is no timely objection by the parties or, in situations covered by the Waivable Red List, if there is a specific acceptance by the parties in accordance with General Standard 4(c). If a party challenges the arbitrator, he or she can nevertheless act, if the authority that rules on the challenge decides that the challenge does not meet the objective test for disqualification.

5. A later challenge based on the fact that an arbitrator did not disclose such facts or circumstances should not result automatically in non-appointment, later disqualification or a successful challenge to any award. Nondisclosure cannot by itself make an arbitrator partial or lacking independence: only the facts or circumstances that he or she failed to disclose can do so.

6. Situations not listed in the Orange List or falling outside the time limits used in some of the Orange List situations are generally not subject to disclosure. However, an arbitrator needs to assess on a case-by-case basis whether a given situation, even though not mentioned in the Orange List, is nevertheless such as to give rise to justifiable doubts as to his or her impartiality or independence. Because the Orange List is a non-exhaustive list of examples, there may be situations not mentioned, which, depending on the circumstances, may need to be disclosed by an arbitrator. Such may be the case, for example, in the event of repeat past appointments by the same party or the same counsel beyond the three-year period provided for in the Orange List, or when an arbitrator concurrently acts as counsel in an unrelated case in which similar issues of law are raised. Likewise, an appointment made by the same party or the same counsel appearing before an arbitrator, while the case is ongoing, may also have to be disclosed, depending on the circumstances. While the Guidelines do not require disclosure of the fact that an arbitrator concurrently serves, or has in the past served, on the same Arbitral Tribunal with another member of the tribunal, or with one of the counsel in the current proceedings, an arbitrator should assess on a case-by-case basis whether the fact of having frequently served as counsel with, or as an arbitrator on, Arbitral Tribunals with another member of the tribunal may create a perceived imbalance within the tribunal. If the conclusion is 'yes', the arbitrator should consider a disclosure.

7. The Green List is a non-exhaustive list of specific situations where no appearance and no actual conflict of interest exists from an objective point of view. Thus, the arbitrator has no duty to disclose situations falling within the Green List. As stated in the Explanation to General Standard 3(a), there should be a limit to disclosure, based on reasonableness; in some situations, an objective test should prevail over the purely subjective test of 'the eyes' of the parties.

8. The borderline between the categories that comprise the Lists can be thin. It can be debated whether a certain situation should be on one List instead of another. Also, the Lists contain, for various situations, general terms such as 'significant' and 'relevant'. The Lists reflect international principles and best practices to the extent possible. Further definition of the norms, which are to be interpreted reasonably in light of the facts and circumstances in each case, would be counterproductive.

1. Non-Waivable Red List

1.1 There is an identity between a party and the arbitrator, or the arbitrator is a legal representative or employee of an entity that is a party in the arbitration.
1.2 The arbitrator is a manager, director or member of the supervisory board, or has a controlling influence on one of the parties or an entity that has a direct economic interest in the award to be rendered in the arbitration.
1.3 The arbitrator has a significant financial or personal interest in one of the parties, or the outcome of the case.
1.4 The arbitrator or his or her firm regularly advises the party, or an affiliate of the party, and the arbitrator or his or her firm derives significant financial income therefrom.

2. Waivable Red List

2.1 Relationship of the arbitrator to the dispute
2.1.1 The arbitrator has given legal advice, or provided an expert opinion, on the dispute to a party or an affiliate of one of the parties.
2.1.2 The arbitrator had a prior involvement in the dispute.
2.2 Arbitrator's direct or indirect interest in the dispute
2.2.1 The arbitrator holds shares, either directly or indirectly, in one of the parties, or an affiliate of one of the parties, this party or an affiliate being privately held.
2.2.2 A close family member3 of the arbitrator has a significant financial interest in the outcome of the dispute.
2.2.3 The arbitrator, or a close family member of the arbitrator, has a close relationship with a non-party who may be liable to recourse on the part of the unsuccessful party in the dispute.
2.3 Arbitrator's relationship with the parties or counsel
2.3.1 The arbitrator currently represents or advises one of the parties, or an affiliate of one of the parties.
2.3.2 The arbitrator currently represents or advises the lawyer or law firm acting as counsel for one of the parties.
2.3.3 The arbitrator is a lawyer in the same law firm as the counsel to one of the parties.
2.3.4 The arbitrator is a manager, director or member of the supervisory board, or has a controlling influence in an affiliate4 of one of the parties, if the affiliate is directly involved in the matters in dispute in the arbitration.
2.3.5 The arbitrator's law firm had a previous but terminated involvement in the case without the arbitrator being involved himself or herself.
2.3.6 The arbitrator's law firm currently has a significant commercial relationship with one of the parties, or an affiliate of one of the parties.
2.3.7 The arbitrator regularly advises one of the parties, or an affiliate of one of the parties, but neither the arbitrator nor his or her firm derives a significant financial income therefrom.
2.3.8 The arbitrator has a close family relationship with one of the parties, or with a manager, director or member of the supervisory board, or any person having a controlling influence in one of the parties, or an affiliate of one of the parties, or with a counsel representing a party.

2.3.9 A close family member of the arbitrator has a significant financial or personal interest in one of the parties, or an affiliate of one of the parties.

3. Orange List

3.1 Previous services for one of the parties or other involvement in the case

3.1.1 The arbitrator has, within the past three years, served as counsel for one of the parties, or an affiliate of one of the parties, or has previously advised or been consulted by the party, or an affiliate of the party, making the appointment in an unrelated matter, but the arbitrator and the party, or the affiliate of the party, have no ongoing relationship.

3.1.2 The arbitrator has, within the past three years, served as counsel against one of the parties, or an affiliate of one of the parties, in an unrelated matter.

3.1.3 The arbitrator has, within the past three years, been appointed as arbitrator on two or more occasions by one of the parties, or an affiliate of one of the parties.

3.1.4 The arbitrator's law firm has, within the past three years, acted for or against one of the parties, or an affiliate of one of the parties, in an unrelated matter without the involvement of the arbitrator.

3.1.5 The arbitrator currently serves, or has served within the past three years, as arbitrator in another arbitration on a related issue involving one of the parties, or an affiliate of one of the parties.

3.2 Current services for one of the parties

3.2.1 The arbitrator's law firm is currently rendering services to one of the parties, or to an affiliate of one of the parties, without creating a significant commercial relationship for the law firm and without the involvement of the arbitrator.

3.2.2 A law firm or other legal organisation that shares significant fees or other revenues with the arbitrator's law firm renders services to one of the parties, or an affiliate of one of the parties, before the Arbitral Tribunal.

3.2.3 The arbitrator or his or her firm represents a party, or an affiliate of one of the parties to the arbitration, on a regular basis, but such representation does not concern the current dispute.

3.3 Relationship between an arbitrator and another arbitrator or counsel

3.3.1 The arbitrator and another arbitrator are lawyers in the same law firm.

3.3.2 The arbitrator and another arbitrator, or the counsel for one of the parties, are members of the same barristers' chambers.

3.3.3 The arbitrator was, within the past three years, a partner of, or otherwise affiliated with, another arbitrator or any of the counsel in the arbitration.

3.3.4 A lawyer in the arbitrator's law firm is an arbitrator in another dispute involving the same party or parties, or an affiliate of one of the parties.

3.3.5 A close family member of the arbitrator is a partner or employee of the law firm representing one of the parties, but is not assisting with the dispute.

3.3.6 A close personal friendship exists between an arbitrator and a counsel of a party.

3.3.7 Enmity exists between an arbitrator and counsel appearing in the arbitration.

3.3.8 The arbitrator has, within the past three years, been appointed on more than three occasions by the same counsel, or the same law firm.

3.3.9 The arbitrator and another arbitrator, or counsel for one of the parties in the arbitration, currently act or have acted together within the past three years as co-counsel.

3.4 Relationship between arbitrator and party and others involved in the arbitration

3.4.1 The arbitrator's law firm is currently acting adversely to one of the parties, or an affiliate of one of the parties.

3.4.2 The arbitrator has been associated with a party, or an affiliate of one of the parties, in a professional capacity, such as a former employee or partner.

3.4.3 A close personal friendship exists between an arbitrator and a manager or director or a member of the supervisory board of: a party; an entity that has a direct economic interest in the award to be rendered in the arbitration; or any person having a controlling influence, such as a controlling shareholder interest, on one of the parties or an affiliate of one of the parties or a witness or expert.

3.4.4 Enmity exists between an arbitrator and a manager or director or a member of the supervisory board of: a party; an entity that has a direct economic interest in the award; or any person having a controlling influence in one of the parties or an affiliate of one of the parties or a witness or expert.

3.4.5 If the arbitrator is a former judge, he or she has, within the past three years, heard a significant case involving one of the parties, or an affiliate of one of the parties.

3.5 Other circumstances

3.5.1 The arbitrator holds shares, either directly or indirectly, that by reason of number or denomination constitute a material holding in one of the parties, or an affiliate of one of the parties, this party or affiliate being publicly listed.

3.5.2 The arbitrator has publicly advocated a position on the case, whether in a published paper, or speech, or otherwise.

3.5.3 The arbitrator holds a position with the appointing authority with respect to the dispute.

3.5.4 The arbitrator is a manager, director or member of the supervisory board, or has a controlling influence on an affiliate of one of the parties, where the affiliate is not directly involved in the matters in dispute in the arbitration.

4. Green List

4.1 Previously expressed legal opinions

4.1.1 The arbitrator has previously expressed a legal opinion (such as in a law review article or public lecture) concerning an issue that also arises in the arbitration (but this opinion is not focused on the case).

4.2 Current services for one of the parties

4.2.1 A firm, in association or in alliance with the arbitrator's law firm, but that does not share significant fees or other revenues with the arbitrator's law firm, renders services to one of the parties, or an affiliate of one of the parties, in an unrelated matter.

4.3 Contacts with another arbitrator, or with counsel for one of the parties

4.3.1 The arbitrator has a relationship with another arbitrator, or with the counsel for one of the parties, through membership in the same professional association, or social or charitable organisation, or through a social media network.

4.3.2 The arbitrator and counsel for one of the parties have previously served together as arbitrators.

4.3.3 The arbitrator teaches in the same faculty or school as another arbitrator or counsel to one of the parties, or serves as an officer of a professional association or social or charitable organisation with another arbitrator or counsel for one of the parties.

4.3.4 The arbitrator was a speaker, moderator or organiser in one or more conferences, or participated in seminars or working parties of a professional, social or charitable organisation, with another arbitrator or counsel to the parties.

4.4 Contacts between the arbitrator and one of the parties

4.4.1 The arbitrator has had an initial contact with a party, or an affiliate of a party (or their counsel) prior to appointment, if this contact is limited to the arbitrator's availability and qualifications to serve, or to the names of possible candidates for a chairperson, and did not address the merits or procedural aspects of the dispute, other than to provide the arbitrator with a basic understanding of the case.

4.4.2 The arbitrator holds an insignificant amount of shares in one of the parties, or an affiliate of one of the parties, which is publicly listed.

4.4.3 The arbitrator and a manager, director or member of the supervisory board, or any person having a controlling influence on one of the parties, or an affiliate of one of the parties, have worked together as joint experts, or in another professional capacity, including as arbitrators in the same case.

4.4.4 The arbitrator has a relationship with one of the parties or its affiliates through a social media network.

Part X
Public International Law and International Investment Law

10.1 Conventions

10.1.1 Convention On The Settlement Of Investment Disputes Between States And Nationals Of Other States (ICSID Convention) (1966)

International Centre For Settlement Of Investment Disputes Submitted to Governments by the Executive Directors of the International Bank for Reconstruction and Development, Submitted: March 18, 1965, Washington Entered into Force: October 14, 1966

PREAMBLE

The Contracting States

Considering the need for international cooperation for economic development, and the role of private international investment therein;

Bearing in mind the possibility that from time to time disputes may arise in connection with such investment between Contracting States and nationals of other Contracting States; *Recognizing* that while such disputes would usually be subject to national legal processes, international methods of settlement may be appropriate in certain cases;

Attaching particular importance to the availability of facilities for international conciliation or arbitration to which Contracting States and nationals of other Contracting States may submit such disputes if they so desire;

Desiring to establish such facilities under the auspices of the International Bank for Reconstruction and Development;

Recognizing that mutual consent by the parties to submit such disputes to conciliation or to arbitration through such facilities constitutes a binding agreement which requires in particular that due consideration be given to any recommendation of conciliators, and that any arbitral award be complied with; and

Declaring that no Contracting State shall by the mere fact of its ratification, acceptance or approval of this Convention and without its consent be deemed to be under any obligation to submit any particular dispute to conciliation or arbitration,

Have agreed as follows:

CHAPTER I INTERNATIONAL CENTRE FOR SETTLEMENT OF INVESTMENT DISPUTES

SECTION 1: ESTABLISHMENT AND ORGANIZATION

Article 1

1. There is hereby established the International Centre for Settlement of Investment Disputes (hereinafter called the Centre).

2. The purpose of the Centre shall be to provide facilities for conciliation and arbitration of investment disputes between Contracting States and nationals of other Contracting States in accordance with the provisions of this Convention.

Article 2
The seat of the Centre shall be at the principal office for the International Bank for Re-construction and Development (hereinafter called the Bank). The seat may be moved to another place by decision of the Administrative Council adopted by a majority of two-thirds of its members.

Article 3
The Centre shall have an Administrative Council and a Secretariat and shall maintain a Panel of Conciliators and a Panel of Arbitrators

SECTION 2: THE ADMINISTRATIVE COUNCIL

Article 4
The Administrative Council shall be composed of one representative of each Contract-ing State. An alternate may act as representative in case of his principal's absence from a meeting or inability to act.

In the absence of a contrary designation, each governor and alternate of the Bank appointed by a Contracting State shall be ex officio its representative and its alternate respectively.

Article 5
The President of the Bank shall be ex officio Chairman of the Administrative Council (hereinafter called the Chairman) but shall have no vote. During his absence or inability to act and during any vacancy in the office of President of the Bank, the person for the time being acting as President shall act as Chairman of the Administrative Council.

Article 6
1. Without prejudice to the powers and functions vested in it by other provisions of this Convention, the Administrative Council shall

(a) adopt the administrative and Financial regulations of the Centre;
(b) adopt the rules of procedure for the institution of conciliation and arbitration proceedings;
(c) adopt the rules of procedure for conciliation and arbitration proceedings (hereinafter called the Conciliation Rules and the Arbitration Rules);
(d) approve arrangements with the Bank for the use of the Bank's administrative facilities and services
(e) determine the conditions of service of the Secretary-General and of any Deputy Secretary-General.;
(f) adopt the annual budget of revenues and expenditures of the Centre;
(g) approve the annual report on the operation of the Centre.

The decisions referred to in sub-paragraphs (a), (b), (c) and (0 above shall be adopted by a majority of two-thirds of the members of the Administrative Council.

2. The Administrative Council may appoint such committees as it considers necessary.

3. The Administrative Council shall also exercise such other powers and perform such other functions as it shall determine to be necessary for the implementation of the pro-visions of the Convention.

Article 7

1. The Administrative Council shall hold an annual meeting and such other meetings as may be determined by the Council, or convened by the Chairman, or convened by the Secretary-General at the request of not less than five members of the Council.
2. Each member of the Administrative Council shall have one vote and, except as otherwise herein provided, all matters before the Council shall be decided by a majority of the votes cast.
3. A quorum for any meeting of the Administrative Council shall be a majority of its members.
4. The Administrative Council may establish, by a majority of two-thirds of its members, a procedure whereby the Chairman may seek a vote of the Council without convening a meeting of the Council. The vote shall be considered valid only if the majority of the members of the Council cast their votes within the time limit fixed by the said procedure.

Article 8

Members of the Administrative Council and the Chairman shall serve without remuneration from the Centre.

SECTION 3: THE SECRETARIAT

Article 9

The Secretariat shall consist of a Secretary-General, one or more Deputy Secretaries-General and staff,

Article 10

1. The Secretary-General and any Deputy Secretary-General shall be elected by the Administrative Council by a majority of two-thirds of its members upon the nomination of the Chairman for a term of service not exceeding six years and shall be eligible for re-election. After consulting the members of the Administrative Council, the Chairman shall propose one or more candidates for each such office.
2. The offices of Secretary-General and Deputy Secretary-General shall be incompatible with the exercise of any political function. Neither the Secretary-General nor any Deputy Secretary-General may hold any other employment or engage in any other occupation except with the approval of the Administrative Council.
3. During the Secretary General's absence or inability to act, and during any vacancy of the office of Secretary-General, the Deputy Secretary-General shall act as Secretary-General. If there shall be more than one Deputy Secretary-General, the Administrative Council shall determine in advance the order in which they shall act as Secretary-General.

Article 11

The Secretary-General shall be the legal representative and the principal officer of the Centre and shall be responsible for its administration, including the appointment of staff, in accordance with the provisions of this Convention and the rules adopted by the Administrative Council. He shall perform the function of registrar and shall have the power to authenticate arbitral awards rendered pursuant to this Convention, and to certify copies thereof.

SECTION 4: THE PANELS

Article 12

The Panel of Conciliators and the Panel of Arbitrators shall each consist of qualified persons, designated as hereinafter provided, who are willing to serve thereon.

Article 13
1. Each Contracting State may designate to each Panel four persons who may but need not be its nationals.
2. The Chairman may designate ten persons to each Panel: The persons so designated to a Panel shall each have a, different nationality.

Article 14
1. Persons designated to serve on the Panels shall be persons of high moral character and recognized competence in the Fields of law, commerce, industry or finance, who may be relied upon to exercise independent judgement. Competence in the Field of law shall be of particular importance in the case of persons on the Panel or Arbitrators.
2. The Chairman, in designating persons to serve on the Panels, shall in addition pay due regard to the importance of assuring representation on the Panels of the principal legal systems of the world and of the main forms of economic activity.

Article 15
1. Panel members shall serve for renewable periods of six years.
2. In case of death or resignation of a member of a Panel, the authority which designated the member shall have the right to designate another person to serve for the remainder of that member's term.
3. Panel members shall continue in office until their successors have been designated.

Article 16
1. A person may serve on both Panels.
2. If a person shall have been designated to serve on the same Panel by more than one Contracting State, or by one or more Contracting States and the Chairman, he shall be deemed to have been designated by the authority which First designated him or, if one such authority is the State or which he is a national, by that State.
3. All designations shall be notified to the Secretary-General and shall take effect from the date on which the notification is received.

SECTION 5: FINANCING THE CENTRE

Article 17
If the expenditure of the Centre cannot be met out of charges for the use of its facilities, or out of other receipts, the excess shall be borne by Contracting States which are members of the Bank in proportion to their respective subscriptions to the capital stock of the Bank, and by Contracting States which are not members of the Bank in accordance with rules adopted by the Administrative Council.

SECTION 6: STATUS, IMMUNITIES AND PRIVILEGES

The Centre shall have full international legal personality. The legal capacity of the Centre shall include the capacity
(a) to contract;
(b) to acquire and dispose of movable and immovable property;
(c) to institute legal proceedings

Article 19
To enable the Centre to fulfil its functions, it shall enjoy in the territories of each Contracting State the immunities and privileges set forth in this Section.

Article 20

The Centre, its property and assets shall enjoy immunity from all legal process, except when the Centre waives this immunity.

Article 21

The Chairman, the members of the Administrative Council, persons acting as conciliators or arbitrators or members of a Committee appointed pursuant to paragraph (3) of Article 52, and the officers and employees of the Secretariat.

(a) shall enjoy immunity from legal process with respect to acts performed by them in the exercise of their functions, except when the Centre waives this immunity;

(b) not being local nationals, shall enjoy the same immunities from immigration restrictions, alien registration requirements and national service obligations, the same facilities as regards exchange restrictions and the same treatment in respect of travelling facilities as are accorded by Contracting States to the representatives, officials and employees of comparable rank of other Contracting States.

Article 22

The provisions of Article 21 shall apply to persons appearing in proceedings under this Convention as parties, agents, counsel, advocates, witnesses or experts; provided, however, that sub-paragraph (b) thereof shall apply only in connection with their travel to and from, and their stay at, the place where the proceedings are held.

Article 23

1. The archives of the Centre shall be inviolable, wherever they may be.
2. With regard to its official communications, the Centre shall be accorded by each Contracting State treatment not less favorable than that accorded to other international organizations.

Article 24

1. The Centre, its assets, property and income, and its operations and transactions authorized by this Convention shall be exempt from all taxation and customs duties. The Centre shall also be exempt from liability for the collection or payment of any taxes or customs duties.
2. Except in the case of local nationals, no tax shall be levied on or in respect of expense allowances paid by the Centre to the Chairman or members of the Administrative Council, or on or in respect of salaries, expense allowances or other emoluments paid by the Centre to officials or employees of the Secretariat.
3. No tax shall be levied on or in respect of fees or expense allowances received by persons acting as conciliators, or arbitrators, or members of a Committee appointed pursuant to paragraph (3) of Article 52, in proceedings under this Convention, if the sole jurisdictional basis for such tax is the location of the Centre or the place where such proceedings are conducted or the place where such fees or allowances are paid.

CHAPTER II – JURISDICTION OF THE CENTRE

Article 25

1. The jurisdiction of the Centre shall extend to any legal dispute arising directly out of an investment, between a Contracting State (or any constituent subdivision or agency of a Contracting State designated to the Centre by that State) and a national of another Contracting State, which the parties to the dispute consent in writing to submit to the Centre. When the parties have given their consent, no party may withdraw its consent unilaterally.

2. "National of another Contracting State" means:

(a) any natural person who had the nationality of a Contracting State other than the State party to the dispute on the date on which the parties consented to submit such dispute to conciliation or arbitration as well as on the date on which the request was registered pursuant to paragraph (3) of Article 28 or paragraph (3) of Article 36, but does not include any person who on either date also had the nationality of the Contracting State party to the dispute; and

(b) any juridical person which had the nationality of a Contracting State other than the State party to the dispute on the date on which the parties consented to submit such dispute to conciliation or arbitration and any juridical person which had the nationality of the Contracting State party to the dispute on that date and which, because of foreign control, the parties have agreed should be treated as a national of another Contracting State for the purposes of this Convention.

3. Consent by a constituent subdivision or agency of a Contracting State shall require the approval of that State unless that State notifies the Centre that no such approval is required.

4. Any Contracting State may, at the time of ratification, acceptance or approval of this Convention or at any time thereafter, notify the Centre of the class or classes of disputes which it would or would not consider submitting to the jurisdiction of the Centre. The Secretary-General shall forthwith transmit such notification to all Contracting States. Such notification shall not constitute the consent required by paragraph (1).

Article 26

Consent of the parties to arbitration under this Convention shall, unless otherwise stated, be deemed consent to such arbitration to the exclusion of any other remedy. A Contracting State may require the exhaustion of local administrative or judicial remedies as a condition of its consent to arbitration under this Convention.

Article 27

1. No Contracting State shall give diplomatic protection, or bring an international claim, in respect of a dispute which one of its nationals and another Contracting State shall have consented to submit or shall have submitted to arbitration under this Convention, unless such other Contracting State shall have failed to abide by and comply with the award rendered in such dispute.

2. Diplomatic protection, for the purposes of paragraph (1), shall not include informal diplomatic exchanges for the sole purpose of facilitating a settlement of the dispute.

CHAPTER III – CONCILIATION

SECTION 1: REQUEST FOR CONCILIATION

Article 28

1. Any Contracting State or any national of a Contracting State wishing to institute conciliation proceedings shall address a request to that effect in writing to the Secretary-General who shall send a copy of the request to the other party.

2. The request shall contain information concerning the issues in dispute, the identity of the parties and their consent to conciliation in accordance with the rules of procedure for the institution of conciliation and arbitration proceedings.

3. The Secretary-General shall register the request unless he finds, on the basis of the information contained in the request, that the dispute is manifestly outside the jurisdiction of the Centre. He shall forthwith notify the parties of registration or refusal to register.

SECTION 2: CONSTITUTION OF THE CONCILIATION COMMISSION

Article 29

1. The Conciliation Commission (hereinafter called the Commission) shall be constituted as soon as possible after registration of a request pursuant to Article 28.
2. (a) The Commission shall consist of a sole conciliator or any uneven number of conciliators appointed as the parties shall agree.
   (b) Where the parties do not agree upon the number of conciliators and the method of their appointment, the Commission shall consist of three conciliators, one conciliator appointed by each party and the third, who shall be the president of the Commission, appointed by agreement of the parties.

Article 30

If the Commission shall not have been constituted within 90 days after notice of registration of the request has been dispatched by the Secretary-General in accordance with paragraph (3) of Article 28, or such other period as the parties may agree, the Chairman shall, at the request of either party and after consulting both parties as far as possible, appoint the conciliator or conciliators not yet appointed.

Article 31

1. Conciliators may be appointed from outside the Panel of Conciliators, except in the case of appointments by the Chairman pursuant to Article 30.
2. Conciliators appointed from outside the Panel of Conciliators shall possess the qualities stated in paragraph (1) of Article 14.

SECTION 3: CONCILIATION PROCEEDINGS

Article 32

1. The Commission shall be the judge of its own competence.
2. Any objection by a party to the dispute that the dispute is not within the jurisdiction of the Centre, or for other reasons is not within the competence of the Commission, shall be considered by the Commission which shall determine whether to deal with it as a preliminary question or to join it to the merits of the dispute.

Article 33

Any conciliation proceeding shall be conducted in accordance with the provisions of this Section and, except as parties otherwise agree, in accordance with the Conciliation Rules in effect on the date on which the parties consented to conciliation. If any question of procedure arises which is not covered by this Section or the Conciliation Rules or any rules agreed by the parties, the Commission shall decide the question.

Article 34

1. It shall be the duty of the Commission to clarify the issues in dispute between the parties and to endeavor to bring about agreement between them upon mutually accept-able terms. To that end, the Commission may at any stage of the proceedings and from time to time recommend terms of settlement to the parties. The parties shall cooperate in good faith with the Commission in order to enable the Commission to carry out its functions, and shall give their most serious consideration to its recommendations.

If the parties reach agreement, the Commission shall draw up a report noting the issues 136 in dispute and recording that the parties have reached agreement. If, at any stage of the proceedings, it appears to the Commission that there is no likelihood of agreement between the parties, it shall close the proceedings and shall draw up a report noting the submission of the dispute and recording the failure of the parties to reach agreement. If one party fails to appear or participate in the proceedings, the Commission shall close the proceedings and shall draw up a report noting that party's failure to appear or participate.

Article 35
Except as the parties to the dispute shall otherwise agree, neither party to a conciliation proceeding shall be entitled in any other proceeding, whether before arbitrators or in a court of law or otherwise, to invoke or rely on any views expressed or statements or ad-missions or offers of settlement made by the other party in the conciliation proceedings, or the report or any recommendations made by the Commission.

CHAPTER IV – ARBITRATION

SECTION 1: REQUEST FOR ARBITRATION

Article 36
1. Any Contracting State or any national of a Contracting State wishing to institute arbitration proceedings shall address a request to that effect in writing to the Secretary-General who shall send a copy of the request to the other party
2. The request shall contain information concerning the issues in dispute, the identity of the parties and their consent to arbitration in accordance with the rules of procedure for the institution of conciliation and arbitration proceedings.
3. The Secretary-General shall register the request unless he finds, on the basis of the information contained in the request, that the dispute is manifestly outside the jurisdiction of the Centre. He shall forthwith notify the parties of registration or refusal to register.

SECTION 2; CONSTITUTION OF THE TRIBUNAL

Article 37
1. The Arbitral Tribunal (hereinafter called the Tribunal) shall be constituted as soon as possible after registration of a request pursuant to Article 36.
2. (a) The Tribunal shall consist of a sole arbitrator or any uneven number of arbitrators appointed as the parties shall agree.
   (b) Where the parties do not agree upon the number of arbitrators and the method of their appointment, the Tribunal shall consist of three arbitrators, one arbitrator appointed by each party and the third, who shall be the president of the Tribunal, appointed by agreement of the parties.

Article 38
If the Tribunal shall not have been constituted within 90 days after notice of registration of the request has been dispatched by the Secretary-General in accordance with para-graph (3) of Article 36, or such other period as the parties may agree, the Chairman shall, at the request of either party and after consulting both parties as far as possible, appoint the arbitrator or arbitrators not yet appointed. Arbitrators appointed by the Chairman pursuant to this Article shall not be nationals of the Contracting State party to the dispute or of the Contracting State whose national is a party to the dispute.

Article 39

The majority of the arbitrators shall be nationals of States other than the Contracting State party to the dispute and the Contracting State whose national is a party to the dispute; provided, however, that the foregoing provisions of this Article shall not apply if the sole arbitrator or each individual member of the Tribunal has been appointed by agreement of the parties.

Article 40

1. Arbitrators may be appointed from outside the Panel of Arbitrators, except in the case of appointments by the Chairman pursuant to Article 38.
2. Arbitrators appointed from outside the Panel of Arbitrators shall possess the qualities stated in paragraph (1) of Article 14.

SECTION 3: POWERS AND FUNCTIONS OF THE TRIBUNAL

Article 41

1. The Tribunal shall be the judge of its own competence.
2. Any objection by a party to the dispute that that dispute is not within the jurisdiction of the Centre, or for other reasons is not within the competence of the Tribunal, shall be considered by the Tribunal which shall determine whether to deal with it as a preliminary question or to join it to the merits of the dispute.

Article 42

1. The Tribunal shall decide a dispute in accordance with such rules of law as may be agreed by the parties. In the absence of such agreement, the Tribunal shall apply the law of the Contracting State party to the dispute (including its rules on the conflict of laws) and such rules of international law as may be applicable.
2. The Tribunal may not bring in a Finding of non liquet on the ground of silence or obscurity of the law.
3. The provisions of paragraphs (1) and (2) shall not prejudice the power of the Tribunal to decide a dispute *ex aequo et bono* if the parties so agree.

Article 43

1. Except as the parties otherwise agree, the Tribunal may, if it deems it necessary at any stage of the proceedings;
   (a) call upon the parties to produce documents or other evidence, and
   (b) visit the scene connected with the dispute, and conduct such inquiries there as it may deem appropriate.

Article 44

Any arbitration proceeding shall be conducted in accordance with the provisions of this Section and, except as the parties otherwise agree, in accordance with the Arbitration Rules in effect on the date on which the parties consented to arbitration. If any question of procedure arises which is not covered by this Section or the Arbitration Rules or any rules agreed by the parties, the Tribunal shall decide the question.

Article 45

1. Failure of a party to appear or to present his case shall not be deemed an admission of the other party's assertions.

2. If a party fails to appear or to present his case at any stage of the proceedings the other party may request the Tribunal to deal with the questions submitted to it and to render an award. Before rendering an award, the Tribunal shall notify, and grant a period of grace to, the party failing to appear or to present its case, unless it is satisfied that that party does not intend to do so.

Article 46
Except as the parties otherwise agree, the Tribunal shall, if requested by a party, determine any incidental or additional claims or counter-claims arising directly out of the subject-matter of the dispute provided that they are within the scope of the consent of the parties and are otherwise within the jurisdiction of the Centre.

Article 47
Except as the parties otherwise agree, the Tribunal may, if it considers that the circum-stances so require, recommend any provisional measures which should be taken to preserve the respective rights of either party.

SECTION 4: THE AWARD

Article 48
1. The Tribunal shall decide questions by a majority of the votes of all its members.
2. The award of the Tribunal shall be in writing and shall be signed by the members of the Tribunal who voted for it.
3. The award shall deal with every question submitted to the Tribunal, and shall state the reasons upon which it is based.
4. Any member of the Tribunal may attach his individual opinion to the award, whether he dissents from the majority or not, or a statement of his dissent.
5. The Centre shall not publish the award without the consent of the parties.

Article 49
1. The Secretary-General shall promptly dispatch certified copies of the award to the parties. The award shall be deemed to have been rendered on the date on which the certified copies were dispatched.
2. The Tribunal upon the request of a party made within 45 days after the date on which 188 the award was rendered may after notice to the other party decide any question which it had omitted to decide in the award, and shall rectify any clerical, arithmetical or similar error in the award. Its decision shall become part of the award and shall be notified to the parties in the same manner as the award. The periods of time provided for under paragraph (2) of Article 51 and paragraph (2) of Article $2 shall run from the date on which the decision was rendered.

SECTION 5: INTERPRETATION, REVISION AND ANNULMENT OF THE AWARD

Article 50
1. If any dispute shall arise between the parties as to the meaning or scope of an award, either party may request interpretation of the award by an application in writing addressed to the Secretary-General.
2. The request shall, if possible, be submitted to the Tribunal which rendered the award. 192 If this shall not be possible, a new Tribunal shall be constituted in accordance with Section 2 of this Chapter. The Tribunal may, if it considers that the circumstances so require, stay enforcement of the award pending its decision.

Article 51

1. Either party may request revision of the award by an application in writing addressed to the Secretary-General on the ground of discovery of some fact of such a nature as decisively to affect the award, provided that when the award was rendered that fact was unknown to the Tribunal and to the applicant and that the applicant's ignorance of that fact was not due to negligence.
2. The application shall be made within 90 days after the discovery of such fact and in any event within three years after the date on which the award was rendered.

The request shall, if possible, be submitted to the Tribunal which rendered the award. If this shall not be possible, a new Tribunal shall be constituted in accordance with Section 2 of this Chapter.

4. The Tribunal may, if it considers that the circumstances so require, stay enforcement of the award pending its decision. If the applicant requests a stay of enforcement of the award in his application, enforcement shall be stayed provisionally until the Tribunal rules on such request.

Article 52

1. Either party may request annulment of the award by an application in writing ad-dressed to the Secretary-General on one or more of the following grounds:
   (a) that the Tribunal was not properly constituted;
   (b) that the Tribunal has manifestly exceeded its powers;
   (c) that there was corruption on the part of a member of the Tribunal;
   (d) that there has been a serious departure from a fundamental rule of procedure; or
   (e) that the award has failed to state the reasons on which it is based.
2. The application shall be made within 120 days after the date on which the award was rendered except that when annulment is requested on the ground of corruption such application shall be made within 120 days after discovery of the corruption and in any event within three years after the date on which the award was rendered.
3. On receipt of the request the Chairman shall forthwith appoint from the Panel of Arbitrators an ad hoc Committee of three persons. None of the members of the Committee shall have been a member of the Tribunal which rendered the award, shall be of the same nationality as any such member, shall be a national of the State party to the dispute or of the State whose national is a party to the dispute, shall have been designated to the Panel of Arbitrators by either of those States, or shall have acted as a conciliator in the same dispute. The Committee shall have the authority to annul the award or any part thereof on any of the grounds set forth in paragraph (1).
4. The provisions of Articles 41-45, 48, 49, 53 and 54, and of Chapters VI and VII shall apply mutatis mutandis to proceedings before the Committee.
5. The Committee may, if it considers that the circumstances so require, stay enforcement of the award pending its decision. If the applicant requests a stay of enforcement of the award in his application, enforcement shall be stayed provisionally until the Committee rules on such request.
6. If the award is annulled the dispute shall, at the request of either party, be submitted to a new Tribunal constituted in accordance with Section 2 of this Chapter.

SECTION 6: RECOGNITION AND ENFORCEMENT OF THE AWARD

Article 53

1. The award shall be binding on the parties and shall not be subject to any appeal or to any other remedy except those provided for in this Convention. Each party shall abide by and comply with the terms of the award except to the extent that enforcement shall have been stayed pursuant to the relevant provisions of this Convention.
2. For the purposes of this Section, "award" shall include any decision interpreting, revising or annulling such award pursuant to Articles 50, 51 or 52.

Article 54
1. Each Contracting State shall recognize an award rendered pursuant to this Convention as binding and enforce the pecuniary obligations imposed by that award within its territories as if it were a final judgment of a court in that State. A Contracting State with a federal constitution may enforce such an award in or through its federal courts and may provide that such courts shall treat the award as if it were a final judgement of the courts of a constituent state.
2. A party seeking recognition or enforcement in the territories of a Contracting State shall furnish to a competent court or other authority which such State shall have designated for this purpose a copy of the award certified by the Secretary-General. Each Contracting State shall notify the Secretary-General of the designation of the competent court or other authority for this purpose and of any subsequent change in such designation.
3. Execution of the award shall be governed by the laws concerning the execution of judgments in force in the State in whose territories such execution is sought.

Article 55
Nothing in Article 54 shall be construed as derogating from the law in force in any Contracting State relating to immunity of that State or of any foreign State from execution.

CHAPTER V – REPLACEMENT AND DISQUALIFICATION OF CONCILIATORS AND ARBITRATORS

Article 56
1. After a Commission or a Tribunal has been constituted and proceedings have begun, its composition shall remain unchanged; provided, however, that if a conciliator or an arbitrator should die, become incapacitated, or resign, the resulting vacancy shall be filled in accordance with the provisions of Section 2 of Chapter III or Section 2 of Chapter IV.
2. A member of a Commission or Tribunal shall continue to serve in that capacity notwithstanding that he shall have ceased to be a member of the Panel.
3. If a conciliator or arbitrator appointed by a party shall have resigned without the consent of the Commission or Tribunal of which he was a member, the Chairman shall appoint a person from the appropriate Panel to fill the resulting vacancy.

Article 57
A party may propose to a Commission or Tribunal the disqualification of any of its mem-bers on account of any fact indicating a manifest lack of the qualities required by para-graph (1) of Article 14. A party to arbitration proceedings may, in addition, propose the disqualification of an arbitrator on the ground that he was ineligible for appointment to the Tribunal under Section 2 of Chapter IV.

Article 58
The decision on any proposal to disqualify a conciliator or arbitrator shall be taken by the other members of the Commission or Tribunal as the case may be, provided that where those members are equally divided, or in the case of a proposal to disqualify a sole conciliator or arbitrator, or a majority of the conciliators or arbitrators, the Chairman shall take that decision. If it is decided that the proposal well-founded the conciliator or arbitrator to whom the decision relates shall be replaced in accordance with the provisions of Section 2 of Chapter III or Section 2 of Chapter IV.

CHAPTER VI – COST OF PROCEEDINGS

Article 59
The charges payable by the parties for the use of the facilities of the Centre shall be determined by the Secretary-General in accordance with the regulations adopted by the Administrative Council.

Article 60
1. Each Commission and each Tribunal shall determine the fees and expenses of its members within limits established from time to time by the Administrative Council and after consultation with the Secretary-General.
2. Nothing in paragraph (1) of this Article shall preclude the parties from agreeing in advance with the Commission or Tribunal concerned upon the fees and expenses of its members.

Article 61
1. In the case of conciliation proceedings the fees and expenses of members of the Commission as well as the charges for the use of the facilities of the Centre, shall be borne equally by the parties. Each party shall bear any other expenses it incurs in connection with the proceedings.
2. In the case of arbitration proceedings the Tribunal shall, except as the parties otherwise agree, assess the expenses incurred by the parties in connection with the proceedings, and shall decide how and by whom those expenses, the fees and expenses of the members of the Tribunal and the charges for the use of the facilities of the Centre shall be paid. Such decision shall form part of the award.

CHAPTER VII – PLACE OF PROCEEDINGS

Article 62
Conciliation and arbitration proceedings shall be held at the seat of the Centre except as hereinafter provided.

Article 63
Conciliation and arbitration proceedings may be held, if the parties so agree,
(a) at the seat of the Permanent Court of Arbitration or of any other appropriate institution, whether private or public, with which the Centre may make arrangements for that purpose; or
(b) at any other place approved by the Commission or Tribunal after consultation with the Secretary-General.

CHAPTERV VIII – DISPUTES BETWEEN CONTRACTING STATES

Article 64
Any dispute arising between Contracting States concerning the interpretation or application of this Convention which is not settled by negotiation shall be referred to the International Court of Justice by the application of any party to such dispute, unless the States concerned agree to another method of settlement.

CHAPTER IX – AMENDMENT

Article 65
Any Contracting State may propose amendment of this Convention. The text of a pro-posed amendment shall be communicated to the Secretary-General not less than 90 days prior to the meeting

of the Administrative Council at which such amendment is to be considered and shall forthwith be transmitted by him to all the members of the Administrative Council.

Article 66
If the Administrative Council shall so decide by a majority of two-thirds of its members, the proposed amendment shall be Circulated to all Contracting States for ratification, acceptance or approval. Each amendment shall enter into force 30 days after dispatch by the depository of the Convention of a notification to Contracting States that all Contracting States have ratified, accepted or approved the amendment.

CHAPTER X FINAL PROVISIONS

Article 67
This Convention shall be open for signature on behalf of States members of the Bank. It shall also be open for signature on behalf of any other State which is a party to the Statute of the International Court of Justice and which the Administrative Council, by a vote of two-thirds of its members, shall have invited to sign the Convention.

Article 68
1. This Convention shall be subject to ratification, acceptance or approval by the signatory States in accordance with their respective constitutional procedures.
2. This Convention shall enter into force 30 days after the date of deposit of the twentieth instrument of ratification, acceptance or approval. It shall enter into force for each State which subsequently deposits its instrument of ratification, acceptance or approval 30 days after the date of such deposit.

Article 69
Each Contracting State shall take such legislative or other measures as may be necessary for making the provisions of this Convention effective in its territories.

Article 70
This Convention shall apply to all territories for whose international relations a Contracting State is responsible, except those which are excluded by such State by written notice to the depository of this Convention either at the time of ratification, acceptance or approval or subsequently.

Article 71
Any Contracting State may denounce this Convention by written notice to the depositary of this Convention. The denunciation shall take effect six months after receipt of such notice.

Article 72
Notice by Contracting State pursuant to Articles 70 or 71 shall not affect the rights or obligations under this Convention of that State or of any of its constituent subdivisions or agencies or of any national of that State arising out of consent to the jurisdiction of the Centre given by one of them before such notice was received by the depositary.

Article 73
Instruments of ratification, acceptance or approval of this Convention and of amendments thereto shall be deposited with the Bank which shall act as the depositary of this Convention. The depositary shall transmit certified copies of this Convention to States members of the Bank and to any other State invited to sign the Convention.

[Article 74]

The depositary shall register this Convention with the Secretariat of the United Nations in accordance with Article 102 of the Charter of the United Nations and the Regulations thereunder adopted by the General Assembly.

Article 74 [Article 75]

The depositary shall notify all signatory States of the following:

(a) signatures in accordance with Article 67;

(b) deposits of instruments of ratification, acceptance and approval in accordance with Article 73;

(c) the date on which this Convention enters into force in accordance with Article 68;

(d) exclusions from territorial application pursuant to Article 70;

(e) the date on which any amendment of this Convention enters into force in accordance with Article 66; and

(f) denunciations in accordance with Article 71.

[Post Provisions]

[Post Clauses (If any: Signed; Witnessed; Done; Authentic Texts; & Deposited Clauses)]

DONE at Washington, in the English, French and Spanish languages, all three texts being equally authentic, in a single copy which shall remain deposited in the archives of the International Bank for Reconstruction and Development, which has indicated by its signature below its agreement to fulfil the functions with which it is charged under this Convention.

10.1.2 The Energy Charter Treaty (1998)

(Annex 1 to the Final Act of the European Energy Charter Conference, signed 17 December 1994, entered into force 16 April 1998)

PREAMBLE

The Contracting Parties to this Treaty,
Having regard to the Charter of Paris for a New Europe signed on 21 November 1990;
Having regard to the European Energy Charter adopted in the Concluding Document of the Hague Conference on the European Energy Charter signed at The Hague on 17 December 1991;

Recalling that all signatories to the Concluding Document of the Hague Conference undertook to pursue the objectives and principles of the European Energy Charter and implement and broaden their cooperation as soon as possible by negotiating in good faith an Energy Charter Treaty and Protocols, and desiring to place the commitments contained in that Charter on a secure and binding international legal basis;

Desiring also to establish the structural framework required to implement the principles enunciated in the European Energy Charter;

Wishing to implement the basic concept of the European Energy Charter initiative which is to catalyse economic growth by means of measures to liberalise investment and trade in energy;

Affirming that Contracting Parties attach the utmost importance to the effective implementation of full national treatment and most favoured nation treatment, and that these commitments will be applied to the Making of Investments pursuant to a supplementary treaty;

Having regard to the objective of progressive liberalisation of international trade and to the principle of avoidance of discrimination in international trade as enunciated in the Agreement *Establishing* the World Trade Organization and as otherwise provided for in this Treaty;

Determined progressively to remove technical, administrative and other barriers to trade in Energy Materials and Products and Energy-Related Equipment, technologies and services;

Looking to the eventual membership in the World Trade Organization of those Contracting Parties which are not currently members thereof and concerned to provide interim trade arrangements which will assist those Contracting Parties and not impede their preparation for such membership;

Mindful of the rights and obligations of certain Contracting Parties which are also members of the World Trade Organization;

Having regard to competition rules concerning mergers, monopolies, anti- competitive practices and abuse of dominant position;

Having regard also to the Treaty on the Non-Proliferation of Nuclear Weapons, the Nuclear Suppliers Guidelines and other international nuclear non- proliferation obligations or understandings;

Recognising the necessity for the most efficient exploration, production, conversion, storage, transport, distribution and use of energy;

Recalling the United Nations Framework Convention on Climate Change, the Convention on Long-Range Transboundary Air Pollution and its protocols, and other international environmental agreements with energy-related aspects; and

Recognising the increasingly urgent need for measures to protect the environment, including the decommissioning of energy installations and waste disposal, and for internationally-agreed objectives and criteria for these purposes,

HAVE AGREED AS FOLLOWS:

Part I: Definitions and Purpose

Article 1: Definitions

As used in this Treaty:

(1) "Charter" means the European Energy Charter adopted in the Concluding Document of the Hague Conference on the European Energy Charter signed at The Hague on 17 December 1991; signature of the Concluding Document is considered to be signature of the Charter.

(2) "Contracting Party" means a state or Regional Economic Integration Organisation which has consented to be bound by this Treaty and for which the Treaty is in force.

(3) "Regional Economic Integration Organisation" means an organisation constituted by states to which they have transferred competence over certain matters a number of which are governed by this Treaty, including the authority to take decisions binding on them in respect of those matters.

(4) "Energy Materials and Products", based on the Harmonised System of the World Customs Organization and the Combined Nomenclature of the European Communities, means the items included in Annexes EM I or EM II.

(4bis) "Energy-Related Equipment", based on the Harmonised System of the World Customs Organization, means the items included in Annexes EQ I or EQ II.

(5) "Economic Activity in the Energy Sector" means an economic activity concerning the exploration, extraction, refining, production, storage, land transport, transmission, distribution, trade, marketing, or sale of Energy Materials and Products except those included in Annex NI, or concerning the distribution of heat to multiple premises.

(6) "Investment" means every kind of asset, owned or controlled directly or indirectly by an Investor and includes:

- (a) tangible and intangible, and movable and immovable, property, and any property rights such as leases, mortgages, liens, and pledges;
- (b) a company or business enterprise, or shares, stock, or other forms of equity participation in a company or business enterprise, and bonds and other debt of a company or business enterprise;
- (c) claims to money and claims to performance pursuant to contract having an economic value and associated with an Investment;
- (d) Intellectual Property;
- (e) Returns;
- (f) any right conferred by law or contract or by virtue of any licences and permits granted pursuant to law to undertake any Economic Activity in the Energy Sector.

A change in the form in which assets are invested does not affect their character as investments and the term "Investment" includes all investments, whether existing at or made after the later of the date of entry into force of this Treaty for the Contracting Party of the Investor making the investment and that for the Contracting Party in the Area of which the investment is made (hereinafter referred to as the "Effective Date") provided that the Treaty shall only apply to matters affecting such investments after the Effective Date.

"Investment" refers to any investment associated with an Economic Activity in the Energy Sector and to investments or classes of investments designated by a Contracting Party in its Area as "Charter efficiency projects" and so notified to the Secretariat.

(7) "Investor" means:

- (a) with respect to a Contracting Party:
  - (i) a natural person having the citizenship or nationality of or who is permanently residing in that Contracting Party in accordance with its applicable law;

(ii) a company or other organisation organised in accordance with the law applicable in that Contracting Party;

(b) with respect to a "third state", a natural person, company or other organisation which fulfils, mutatis mutandis, the conditions specified in subparagraph (a) for a Contracting Party.

(8) "Make Investments" or "Making of Investments" means establishing new Investments, acquiring all or part of existing Investments or moving into different fields of Investment activity.

(9) "Returns" means the amounts derived from or associated with an Investment, irrespective of the form in which they are paid, including profits, dividends, interest, capital gains, royalty payments, management, technical assistance or other fees and payments in kind.

(10) "Area" means with respect to a state that is a Contracting Party:

(a) the territory under its sovereignty, it being understood that territory includes land, internal waters and the territorial sea; and

(b) subject to and in accordance with the international law of the sea: the sea, sea-bed and its subsoil with regard to which that Contracting Party exercises sovereign rights and jurisdiction.

With respect to a Regional Economic Integration Organisation which is a Contracting Party, Area means the Areas of the member states of such Organisation, under the provisions contained in the agreement establishing that Organisation.

(11) (a) WTO" means the World Trade Organization established by the Agreement Establishing the World Trade Organization.

(b) "WTO Agreement" means the Agreement Establishing the World Trade Organization, its Annexes and the decisions, declarations and understandings related thereto, as subsequently rectified, amended and modified from time to time.

(c) "GATT 1994" means the General Agreement on Tariffs and Trade as specified in Annex 1A to the Agreement Establishing the World Trade Organization, as subsequently rectified, amended or modified from time to time.

(12) "Intellectual Property" includes copyrights and related rights, trademarks, geographical indications, industrial designs, patents, layout designs of integrated circuits and the protection of undisclosed information.

(13) (a) "Energy Charter Protocol" or "Protocol" means a treaty, the negotiation of which is authorised and the text of which is adopted by the Charter Conference, which is entered into by two or more Contracting Parties in order to complement, supplement, extend or amplify the provisions of this Treaty with respect to any specific sector or category of activity within the scope of this Treaty, or to areas of cooperation pursuant to Title III of the Charter.

(b) "Energy Charter Declaration" or "Declaration" means a non- binding instrument, the negotiation of which is authorised and the text of which is approved by the Charter Conference, which is entered into by two or more Contracting Parties to complement or supplement the provisions of this Treaty.

(14) "Freely Convertible Currency" means a currency which is widely traded in international foreign exchange markets and widely used in international transactions.

Article 2: Purpose of the Treaty

This Treaty establishes a legal framework in order to promote long-term cooperation in the energy field, based on complementarities and mutual benefits, in accordance with the objectives and principles of the Charter.

PART II: COMMERCE

Article 3: International Markets

The Contracting Parties shall work to promote access to international markets on commercial terms, and generally to develop an open and competitive market, for Energy Materials and Products and Energy-Related Equipment.

Article 4: Non-Derogation from WTO Agreement

Nothing in this Treaty shall derogate, as between particular Contracting Parties which are members of the WTO, from the provisions of the WTO Agreement as they are applied between those Contracting Parties.

Article 5: Trade-Related Investment Measures

(1) A Contracting Party shall not apply any trade-related investment measure that is inconsistent with the provisions of article III or XI of the GATT 1994; this shall be without prejudice to the Contracting Party's rights and obligations under the WTO Agreement and Article 29.

(2) Such measures include any investment measure which is mandatory or enforceable under domestic law or under any administrative ruling, or compliance with which is necessary to obtain an advantage, and which requires:

(a) the purchase or use by an enterprise of products of domestic origin or from any domestic source, whether specified in terms of particular products, in terms of volume or value of products, or in terms of a proportion of volume or value of its local production; or

(b) that an enterprise's purchase or use of imported products be limited to an amount related to the volume or value of local products that it exports;

or which restricts:

(c) the importation by an enterprise of products used in or related to its local production, generally or to an amount related to the volume or value of local production that it exports;

(d) the importation by an enterprise of products used in or related to its local production by restricting its access to foreign exchange to an amount related to the foreign exchange inflows attributable to the enterprise; or

(e) the exportation or sale for export by an enterprise of products, whether specified in terms of particular products, in terms of volume or value of products, or in terms of a proportion of volume or value of its local production.

(3) Nothing in paragraph (1) shall be construed to prevent a Contracting Party from applying the trade-related investment measures described in subparagraphs (2)(a) and (c) as a condition of eligibility for export promotion, foreign aid, government procurement or preferential tariff or quota programmes.

(4) Notwithstanding paragraph (1), a Contracting Party may temporarily continue to maintain trade-related investment measures which were in effect more than 180 days before its signature of this Treaty, subject to the notification and phase-out provisions set out in Annex TRM.

Article 6: Competition

(1) Each Contracting Party shall work to alleviate market distortions and barriers to competition in Economic Activity in the Energy Sector.

(2) Each Contracting Party shall ensure that within its jurisdiction it has and enforces such laws as are necessary and appropriate to address unilateral and concerted anti-competitive conduct in Economic Activity in the Energy Sector.

(3) Contracting Parties with experience in applying competition rules shall give full consideration to providing, upon request and within available resources, technical assistance on the development and implementation of competition rules to other Contracting Parties.

(4) Contracting Parties may cooperate in the enforcement of their competition rules by consulting and exchanging information.
(5) If a Contracting Party considers that any specified anti-competitive conduct carried out within the Area of another Contracting Party is adversely affecting an important interest relevant to the purposes identified in this Article, the Contracting Party may notify the other Contracting Party and may request that its competition authorities initiate appropriate enforcement action. The notifying Contracting Party shall include in such notification sufficient information to permit the notified Contracting Party to identify the anti-competitive conduct that is the subject of the notification and shall include an offer of such further information and cooperation as the notifying Contracting Party is able to provide. The notified Contracting Party or, as the case may be, the relevant competition authorities may consult with the competition authorities of the notifying Contracting Party and shall accord full consideration to the request of the notifying Contracting Party in deciding whether or not to initiate enforcement action with respect to the alleged anti-competitive conduct identified in the notification. The notified Contracting Party shall inform the notifying Contracting Party of its decision or the decision of the relevant competition authorities and may if it wishes inform the notifying Contracting Party of the grounds for the decision. If enforcement action is initiated, the notified Contracting Party shall advise the notifying Contracting Party of its outcome and, to the extent possible, of any significant interim development.
(6) Nothing in this Article shall require the provision of information by a Contracting Party contrary to its laws regarding disclosure of information, confidentiality or business secrecy.
(7) The procedures set forth in paragraph (5) and Article 27(1) shall be the exclusive means within this Treaty of resolving any disputes that may arise over the implementation or interpretation of this Article.

Article 7: Transit
(1) Each Contracting Party shall take the necessary measures to facilitate the Transit of Energy Materials and Products consistent with the principle of freedom of transit and without distinction as to the origin, destination or ownership of such Energy Materials and Products or discrimination as to pricing on the basis of such distinctions, and without imposing any unreasonable delays, restrictions or charges.
(2) Contracting Parties shall encourage relevant entities to cooperate in:

- (a) modernising Energy Transport Facilities necessary to the Transit of Energy Materials and Products;
- (b) the development and operation of Energy Transport Facilities serving the Areas of more than one Contracting Party;
- (c) measures to mitigate the effects of interruptions in the supply of Energy Materials and Products;
- (d) facilitating the interconnection of Energy Transport Facilities.

(3) Each Contracting Party undertakes that its provisions relating to transport of Energy Materials and Products and the use of Energy Transport Facilities shall treat Energy Materials and Products in Transit in no less favourable a manner than its provisions treat such materials and products originating in or destined for its own Area, unless an existing international agreement provides otherwise.
(4) In the event that Transit of Energy Materials and Products cannot be achieved on commercial terms by means of Energy Transport Facilities the Contracting Parties shall not place obstacles in the way of new capacity being established, except as may be otherwise provided in applicable legislation which is consistent with paragraph (1).
(5) A Contracting Party through whose Area Energy Materials and Products may transit shall not be obliged to

- (a) permit the construction or modification of Energy Transport Facilities; or
- (b) permit new or additional Transit through existing Energy Transport Facilities,

which it demonstrates to the other Contracting Parties concerned would endanger the security or efficiency of its energy systems, including the security of supply.

Contracting Parties shall, subject to paragraphs (6) and (7), secure established flows of Energy Materials and Products to, from or between the Areas of other Contracting Parties.

(6) A Contracting Party through whose Area Energy Materials and Products transit shall not, in the event of a dispute over any matter arising from that Transit, interrupt or reduce, permit any entity subject to its control to interrupt or reduce, or require any entity subject to its jurisdiction to interrupt or reduce the existing flow of Energy Materials and Products prior to the conclusion of the dispute resolution procedures set out in paragraph (7), except where this is specifically provided for in a contract or other agreement governing such Transit or permitted in accordance with the conciliator's decision.

(7) The following provisions shall apply to a dispute described in paragraph (6), but only following the exhaustion of all relevant contractual or other dispute resolution remedies previously agreed between the Contracting Parties party to the dispute or between any entity referred to in paragraph (6) and an entity of another Contracting Party party to the dispute:

(a) A Contracting Party party to the dispute may refer it to the Secretary General by a notification summarising the matters in dispute. The Secretary General shall notify all Contracting Parties of any such referral.

(b) Within 30 days of receipt of such a notification, the Secretary General, in consultation with the parties to the dispute and the other Contracting Parties concerned, shall appoint a conciliator. Such a conciliator shall have experience in the matters subject to dispute and shall not be a national or citizen of or permanently resident in a party to the dispute or one of the other Contracting Parties concerned.

(c) The conciliator shall seek the agreement of the parties to the dispute to a resolution thereof or upon a procedure to achieve such resolution. If within 90 days of his appointment he has failed to secure such agreement, he shall recommend a resolution to the dispute or a procedure to achieve such resolution and shall decide the interim tariffs and other terms and conditions to be observed for Transit from a date which he shall specify until the dispute is resolved.

(d) The Contracting Parties undertake to observe and ensure that the entities under their control or jurisdiction observe any interim decision under subparagraph (c) on tariffs, terms and conditions for 12 months following the conciliator's decision or until resolution of the dispute, whichever is earlier.

(e) Notwithstanding subparagraph (b) the Secretary General may elect not to appoint a conciliator if in his judgement the dispute concerns Transit that is or has been the subject of the dispute resolution procedures set out in subparagraphs (a) to (d) and those proceedings have not resulted in a resolution of the dispute.

(f) The Charter Conference shall adopt standard provisions concerning the conduct of conciliation and the compensation of conciliators.

(8) Nothing in this Article shall derogate from a Contracting Party's rights and obligations under international law including customary international law, existing bilateral or multilateral agreements, including rules concerning submarine cables and pipelines.

(9) This Article shall not be so interpreted as to oblige any Contracting Party which does not have a certain type of Energy Transport Facilities used for Transit to take any measure under this Article with respect to that type of Energy Transport Facilities. Such a Contracting Party is, however, obliged to comply with paragraph (4).

(10) For the purposes of this Article:

(a) "Transit" means

(i) the carriage through the Area of a Contracting Party, or to or from port facilities in its Area for loading or unloading, of Energy Materials and Products originating in the Area of another state and destined for the Area of a third state, so long as either the other state or the third state is a Contracting Party; or

(ii) the carriage through the Area of a Contracting Party of Energy Materials and Products originating in the Area of another Contracting Party and destined for the Area of that other Contracting Party, unless the two Contracting Parties concerned decide otherwise and record their decision by a joint entry in Annex N. The two Contracting Parties may delete their listing in Annex N by delivering a joint written notification of their intentions to the Secretariat, which shall transmit that notification to all other Contracting Parties. The deletion shall take effect four weeks after such former notification.

(b) "Energy Transport Facilities" consist of high-pressure gas transmission pipelines, high-voltage electricity transmission grids and lines, crude oil transmission pipelines, coal slurry pipelines, oil product pipelines, and other fixed facilities specifically for handling Energy Materials and Products.

Article 8: Transfer of Technology

(1) The Contracting Parties agree to promote access to and transfer of energy technology on a commercial and non-discriminatory basis to assist effective trade in Energy Materials and Products and Investment and to implement the objectives of the Charter subject to their laws and regulations, and to the protection of Intellectual Property rights.

(2) Accordingly, to the extent necessary to give effect to paragraph (1) the Contracting Parties shall eliminate existing and create no new obstacles to the transfer of technology in the field of Energy Materials and Products and related equipment and services, subject to non-proliferation and other international obligations.

Article 9: Access to Capital

(1) The Contracting Parties acknowledge the importance of open capital markets in encouraging the flow of capital to finance trade in Energy Materials and Products and for the making of and assisting with regard to Investments in Economic Activity in the Energy Sector in the Areas of other Contracting Parties, particularly those with economies in transition. Each Contracting Party shall accordingly endeavour to promote conditions for access to its capital market by companies and nationals of other Contracting Parties, for the purpose of financing trade in Energy Materials and Products and for the purpose of Investment in Economic Activity in the Energy Sector in the Areas of those other Contracting Parties, on a basis no less favourable than that which it accords in like circumstances to its own companies and nationals or companies and nationals of any other Contracting Party or any third state, whichever is the most favourable.

(2) A Contracting Party may adopt and maintain programmes providing for access to public loans, grants, guarantees or insurance for facilitating trade or Investment abroad. It shall make such facilities available, consistent with the objectives, constraints and criteria of such programmes (including any objectives, constraints or criteria relating to the place of business of an applicant for any such facility or the place of delivery of goods or services supplied with the support of any such facility) for Investments in the Economic Activity in the Energy Sector of other Contracting Parties or for financing trade in Energy Materials and Products with other Contracting Parties.

(3) Contracting Parties shall, in implementing programmes in Economic Activity in the Energy Sector to improve the economic stability and investment climates of the Contracting Parties, seek as appropriate to encourage the operations and take advantage of the expertise of relevant international financial institutions.

(4) Nothing in this Article shall prevent:

(a) financial institutions from applying their own lending or underwriting practices based on market principles and prudential considerations; or

(b) a Contracting Party from taking measures:

(i) for prudential reasons, including the protection of Investors, consumers, depositors, policy-holders or persons to whom a fiduciary duty is owed by a financial service supplier; or

(ii) to ensure the integrity and stability of its financial system and capital markets.

PART III: INVESTMENT PROMOTION AND PROTECTION

Article 10: Promotion, Protection and Treatment of Investments

(1) Each Contracting Party shall, in accordance with the provisions of this Treaty, encourage and create stable, equitable, favourable and transparent conditions for Investors of other Contracting Parties to make Investments in its Area. Such conditions shall include a commitment to accord at all times to Investments of Investors of other Contracting Parties fair and equitable treatment. Such Investments shall also enjoy the most constant protection and security and no Contracting Party shall in any way impair by unreasonable or discriminatory measures their management, maintenance, use, enjoyment or disposal. In no case shall such Investments be accorded treatment less favourable than that required by international law, including treaty obligations. Each Contracting Party shall observe any obligations it has entered into with an Investor or an Investment of an Investor of any other Contracting Party.

(2) Each Contracting Party shall endeavour to accord to Investors of other Contracting Parties, as regards the Making of Investments in its Area, the Treatment described in paragraph (3).

(3) For the purposes of this Article, "Treatment" means treatment accorded by a Contracting Party which is no less favourable than that which it accords to its own Investors or to Investors of any other Contracting Party or any third state, whichever is the most favourable.

(4) A supplementary treaty shall, subject to conditions to be laid down therein, oblige each party thereto to accord to Investors of other parties, as regards the Making of Investments in its Area, the Treatment described in paragraph (3). That treaty shall be open for signature by the states and Regional Economic Integration Organisations which have signed or acceded to this Treaty. Negotiations towards the supplementary treaty shall commence not later than 1 January 1995, with a view to concluding it by 1 January 1998.

(5) Each Contracting Party shall, as regards the Making of Investments in its Area, endeavour to:

(a) limit to the minimum the exceptions to the Treatment described in paragraph (3);

(b) progressively remove existing restrictions affecting Investors of other Contracting Parties.

(6) (a) A Contracting Party may, as regards the Making of Investments in its Area, at any time declare voluntarily to the Charter Conference, through the Secretariat, its intention not to introduce new exceptions to the Treatment described in paragraph (3).

(b) A Contracting Party may, furthermore, at any time make a voluntary commitment to accord to Investors of other Contracting Parties, as regards the Making of Investments in some or all Economic Activities in the Energy Sector in its Area, the Treatment described in paragraph (3). Such commitments shall be notified to the Secretariat and listed in Annex VC and shall be binding under this Treaty.

(7) Each Contracting Party shall accord to Investments in its Area of Investors of other Contracting Parties, and their related activities including management, maintenance, use, enjoyment or disposal, treatment no less favourable than that which it accords to Investments of its own Investors or of the Investors of any other Contracting Party or any third state and their related activities including management, maintenance, use, enjoyment or disposal, whichever is the most favourable.

(8) The modalities of application of paragraph (7) in relation to programmes under which a Contracting Party provides grants or other financial assistance, or enters into contracts, for energy technology research and development, shall be reserved for the supplementary treaty described in paragraph (4). Each Contracting Party shall through the Secretariat keep the Charter Conference informed of the modalities it applies to the programmes described in this paragraph.

(9) Each state or Regional Economic Integration Organisation which signs or accedes to this Treaty shall, on the date it signs the Treaty or deposits its instrument of accession, submit to the Secretariat a report summarising all laws, regulations or other measures relevant to:

(a) exceptions to paragraph (2); or

(b) the programmes referred to in paragraph (8).

A Contracting Party shall keep its report up to date by promptly submitting amendments to the Secretariat. The Charter Conference shall review these reports periodically.

In respect of subparagraph (a) the report may designate parts of the energy sector in which a Contracting Party accords to Investors of other Contracting Parties the Treatment described in paragraph (3).

In respect of subparagraph (b) the review by the Charter Conference may consider the effects of such programmes on competition and Investments.

(10) Notwithstanding any other provision of this Article, the treatment described in paragraphs (3) and (7) shall not apply to the protection of Intellectual Property; instead, the treatment shall be as specified in the corresponding provisions of the applicable international agreements for the protection of Intellectual Property rights to which the respective Contracting Parties are parties.

(11) For the purposes of Article 26, the application by a Contracting Party of a trade-related investment measure as described in Article 5(1) and (2) to an Investment of an Investor of another Contracting Party existing at the time of such application shall, subject to Article 5(3) and (4), be considered a breach of an obligation of the former Contracting Party under this Part.

(12) Each Contracting Party shall ensure that its domestic law provides effective means for the assertion of claims and the enforcement of rights with respect to Investments, investment agreements, and investment authorisations.

Article 11: Key Personnel

(1) A Contracting Party shall, subject to its laws and regulations relating to the entry, stay and work of natural persons, examine in good faith requests by Investors of another Contracting Party, and key personnel who are employed by such Investors or by Investments of such Investors, to enter and remain temporarily in its Area to engage in activities connected with the making or the development, management, maintenance, use, enjoyment or disposal of relevant Investments, including the provision of advice or key technical services.

(2) A Contracting Party shall permit Investors of another Contracting Party which have Investments in its Area, and Investments of such Investors, to employ any key person of the Investor's or the Investment's choice regardless of nationality and citizenship provided that such key person has been permitted to enter, stay and work in the Area of the former Contracting Party and that the employment concerned conforms to the terms, conditions and time limits of the permission granted to such key person.

Article 12: Compensation for Losses

(1) Except where Article 13 applies, an Investor of any Contracting Party which suffers a loss with respect to any Investment in the Area of another Contracting Party owing to war or other armed conflict, state of national emergency, civil disturbance, or other similar event in that Area, shall be accorded by the latter Contracting Party, as regards restitution, indemnification, compensation or other settlement, treatment which is the most favourable of that which that Contracting Party accords to any other Investor, whether its own Investor, the Investor of any other Contracting Party, or the Investor of any third state.

(2) Without prejudice to paragraph (1), an Investor of a Contracting Party which, in any of the situations referred to in that paragraph, suffers a loss in the Area of another Contracting Party resulting from

(a) requisitioning of its Investment or part thereof by the latter's forces or authorities; or

(b) destruction of its Investment or part thereof by the latter's forces or authorities, which was not required by the necessity of the situation,

shall be accorded restitution or compensation which in either case shall be prompt, adequate and effective.

Article 13: Expropriation

(1) Investments of Investors of a Contracting Party in the Area of any other Contracting Party shall not be nationalised, expropriated or subjected to a measure or measures having effect equivalent to nationalisation or expropriation (hereinafter referred to as "Expropriation") except where such Expropriation is:

(a) for a purpose which is in the public interest;
(b) not discriminatory;
(c) carried out under due process of law; and
(d) accompanied by the payment of prompt, adequate and effective compensation.

Such compensation shall amount to the fair market value of the Investment expropriated at the time immediately before the Expropriation or impending Expropriation became known in such a way as to affect the value of the Investment (hereinafter referred to as the "Valuation Date").

Such fair market value shall at the request of the Investor be expressed in a Freely Convertible Currency on the basis of the market rate of exchange existing for that currency on the Valuation Date. Compensation shall also include interest at a commercial rate established on a market basis from the date of Expropriation until the date of payment.

(2) The Investor affected shall have a right to prompt review, under the law of the Contracting Party making the Expropriation, by a judicial or other competent and independent authority of that Contracting Party, of its case, of the valuation of its Investment, and of the payment of compensation, in accordance with the principles set out in paragraph (1).

(3) For the avoidance of doubt, Expropriation shall include situations where a Contracting Party expropriates the assets of a company or enterprise in its Area in which an Investor of any other Contracting Party has an Investment, including through the ownership of shares.

Article 14: Transfers Related to Investments

(1) Each Contracting Party shall with respect to Investments in its Area of Investors of any other Contracting Party guarantee the freedom of transfer into and out of its Area, including the transfer of:

(a) the initial capital plus any additional capital for the maintenance and development of an Investment;
(b) Returns;
(c) payments under a contract, including amortisation of principal and accrued interest payments pursuant to a loan agreement;
(d) unspent earnings and other remuneration of personnel engaged from abroad in connection with that Investment;
(e) proceeds from the sale or liquidation of all or any part of an Investment;
(f) payments arising out of the settlement of a dispute;
(g) payments of compensation pursuant to Articles 12 and 13.

(2) Transfers under paragraph (1) shall be effected without delay and (except in case of a Return in kind) in a Freely Convertible Currency.

(3) Transfers shall be made at the market rate of exchange existing on the date of transfer with respect to spot transactions in the currency to be transferred. In the absence of a market for foreign exchange, the rate to be used will be the most recent rate applied to inward investments or the most recent exchange rate for conversion of currencies into Special Drawing Rights, whichever is more favourable to the Investor.

(4) Notwithstanding paragraphs (1) to (3), a Contracting Party may protect the rights of creditors, or ensure compliance with laws on the issuing, trading and dealing in securities and the satisfaction of judgements in civil, administrative and criminal adjudicatory proceedings, through the equitable, non-discriminatory, and good faith application of its laws and regulations.
(5) Notwithstanding paragraph (2), Contracting Parties which are states that were constituent parts of the former Union of Soviet Socialist Republics may provide in agreements concluded between them that transfers of payments shall be made in the currencies of such Contracting Parties, provided that such agreements do not treat Investments in their Areas of Investors of other Contracting Parties less favourably than either Investments of Investors of the Contracting Parties which have entered into such agreements or Investments of Investors of any third state.
(6) Notwithstanding subparagraph (1)(b), a Contracting Party may restrict the transfer of a Return in kind in circumstances where the Contracting Party is permitted under Article 29(2)(a) or the WTO Agreement56 to restrict or prohibit the exportation or the sale for export of the product constituting the Return in kind; provided that a Contracting Party shall permit transfers of Returns in kind to be effected as authorised or specified in an investment agreement, investment authorisation, or other written agreement between the Contracting Party and either an Investor of another Contracting Party or its Investment.

Article 15: Subrogation
(1) If a Contracting Party or its designated agency (hereinafter referred to as the "Indemnifying Party") makes a payment under an indemnity or guarantee given in respect of an Investment of an Investor (hereinafter referred to as the "Party Indemnified") in the Area of another Contracting Party (hereinafter referred to as the "Host Party"), the Host Party shall recognise:

(a) the assignment to the Indemnifying Party of all the rights and claims in respect of such Investment; and
(b) the right of the Indemnifying Party to exercise all such rights and enforce such claims by virtue of subrogation.

(2) The Indemnifying Party shall be entitled in all circumstances to:

(a) the same treatment in respect of the rights and claims acquired by it by virtue of the assignment referred to in paragraph (1); and
(b) the same payments due pursuant to those rights and claims,

as the Party Indemnified was entitled to receive by virtue of this Treaty in respect of the Investment concerned.
(3) In any proceeding under Article 26, a Contracting Party shall not assert as a defence, counterclaim, right of set-off or for any other reason, that indemnification or other compensation for all or part of the alleged damages has been received or will be received pursuant to an insurance or guarantee contract.

Article 16: Relation to Other Agreements
(1) nothing in Part III or V of this Treaty shall be construed to derogate from any provision of such terms of the other agreement or from any right to dispute resolution with respect thereto under that agreement; and
(2) nothing in such terms of the other agreement shall be construed to derogate from any provision of Part III or V of this Treaty or from any right to dispute resolution with respect thereto under this Treaty,

where any such provision is more favourable to the Investor or Investment.

Article 17: Non-Application of Part III in Certain Circumstances
Each Contracting Party reserves the right to deny the advantages of this Part to:

(1) a legal entity if citizens or nationals of a third state own or control such entity and if that entity has no substantial business activities in the Area of the Contracting Party in which it is organised; or
(2) an Investment, if the denying Contracting Party establishes that such Investment is an Investment of an Investor of a third state with or as to which the denying Contracting Party:
(a) does not maintain a diplomatic relationship; or
(b) adopts or maintains measures that:
(i) prohibit transactions with Investors of that state; or
(ii) would be violated or circumvented if the benefits of this Part were accorded to Investors of that state or to their Investments.

PART IV: MISCELLANEOUS PROVISIONS

Article 18: Sovereignty over Energy Resources
(1) The Contracting Parties recognise state sovereignty and sovereign rights over energy resources. They reaffirm that these must be exercised in accordance with and subject to the rules of international law.
(2) Without affecting the objectives of promoting access to energy resources, and exploration and development thereof on a commercial basis, the Treaty shall in no way prejudice the rules in Contracting Parties governing the system of property ownership of energy resources.
(3) Each state continues to hold in particular the rights to decide the geographical areas within its Area to be made available for exploration and development of its energy resources, the optimisation of their recovery and the rate at which they may be depleted or otherwise exploited, to specify and enjoy any taxes, royalties or other financial payments payable by virtue of such exploration and exploitation, and to regulate the environmental and safety aspects of such exploration, development and reclamation within its Area, and to participate in such exploration and exploitation, inter alia, through direct participation by the government or through state enterprises.
(4) The Contracting Parties undertake to facilitate access to energy resources, inter alia, by allocating in a non-discriminatory manner on the basis of published criteria authorisations, licences, concessions and contracts to prospect and explore for or to exploit or extract energy resources.

Article 19: Environmental Aspects
(1) In pursuit of sustainable development and taking into account its obligations under those international agreements concerning the environment to which it is party, each Contracting Party shall strive to minimise in an economically efficient manner harmful Environmental Impacts occurring either within or outside its Area from all operations within the Energy Cycle in its Area, taking proper account of safety. In doing so each Contracting Party shall act in a Cost-Effective manner. In its policies and actions each Contracting Party shall strive to take precautionary measures to prevent or minimise environmental degradation. The Contracting Parties agree that the polluter in the Areas of Contracting Parties, should, in principle, bear the cost of pollution, including transboundary pollution, with due regard to the public interest and without distorting Investment in the Energy Cycle or international trade. Contracting Parties shall accordingly:
(a) take account of environmental considerations throughout the formulation and implementation of their energy policies;
(b) promote market-oriented price formation and a fuller reflection of environmental costs and benefits throughout the Energy Cycle;
(c) having regard to Article 34(4), encourage cooperation in the attainment of the environmental objectives of the Charter and cooperation in the field of international environmental standards for the Energy Cycle, taking into account differences in adverse effects and abatement costs between Contracting Parties;

(d) have particular regard to Improving Energy Efficiency, to developing and using renewable energy sources, to promoting the use of cleaner fuels and to employing technologies and technological means that reduce pollution;
(e) promote the collection and sharing among Contracting Parties of information on environmentally sound and economically efficient energy policies and Cost-Effective practices and technologies;
(f) promote public awareness of the Environmental Impacts of energy systems, of the scope for the prevention or abatement of their adverse Environmental Impacts, and of the costs associated with various prevention or abatement measures;
(g) promote and cooperate in the research, development and application of energy efficient and environmentally sound technologies, practices and processes which will minimise harmful Environmental Impacts of all aspects of the Energy Cycle in an economically efficient manner;
(h) encourage favourable conditions for the transfer and dissemination of such technologies consistent with the adequate and effective protection of Intellectual Property rights;
(i) promote the transparent assessment at an early stage and prior to decision, and subsequent monitoring, of Environmental Impacts of environmentally significant energy investment projects;
(j) promote international awareness and information exchange on Contracting Parties' relevant environmental programmes and standards and on the implementation of those programmes and standards;
(k) participate, upon request, and within their available resources, in the development and implementation of appropriate environmental programmes in the Contracting Parties.

(2) At the request of one or more Contracting Parties, disputes concerning the application or interpretation of provisions of this Article shall, to the extent that arrangements for the consideration of such disputes do not exist in other appropriate international fora, be reviewed by the Charter Conference aiming at a solution.

(3) For the purposes of this Article:

"Energy Cycle" means the entire energy chain, including activities related to prospecting for, exploration, production, conversion, storage, transport, distribution and consumption of the various forms of energy, and the treatment and disposal of wastes, as well as the decommissioning, cessation or closure of these activities, minimising harmful Environmental Impacts;

(a) "Environmental Impact" means any effect caused by a given activity on the environment, including human health and safety, flora, fauna, soil, air, water, climate, landscape and historical monuments or other physical structures or the interactions among these factors; it also includes effects on cultural heritage or socio-economic conditions resulting from alterations to those factors;
(b) "Improving Energy Efficiency" means acting to maintain the same unit of output (of a good or service) without reducing the quality or performance of the output, while reducing the amount of energy required to produce that output;
(c) "Cost-Effective" means to achieve a defined objective at the lowest cost or to achieve the greatest benefit at a given cost.

Article 20: Transparency

(1) Laws, regulations, judicial decisions and administrative rulings of general application which affect trade in Energy Materials and Products or Energy Related Equipment are, in accordance with Article 29(2)(a), among the measures subject to the transparency disciplines of the WTO Agreement.

(2) Laws, regulations, judicial decisions and administrative rulings of general application made effective by any Contracting Party, and agreements in force between Contracting Parties, which affect other matters covered by this Treaty shall also be published promptly in such a manner as to enable Contracting Parties and Investors to become acquainted with them. The provisions of this paragraph

shall not require any Contracting Party to disclose confidential information which would impede law enforcement or otherwise be contrary to the public interest or would prejudice the legitimate commercial interests of any Investor.

(3) Each Contracting Party shall designate one or more enquiry points to which requests for information about the above mentioned laws, regulations, judicial decisions and administrative rulings may be addressed and shall communicate promptly such designation to the Secretariat which shall make it available on request.

Article 21: Taxation

(1) Except as otherwise provided in this Article, nothing in this Treaty shall create rights or impose obligations with respect to Taxation Measures of the Contracting Parties. In the event of any inconsistency between this Article and any other provision of the Treaty, this Article shall prevail to the extent of the inconsistency.

(2) Article 7(3) shall apply to Taxation Measures other than those on income or on capital, except that such provision shall not apply to:

- (a) an advantage accorded by a Contracting Party pursuant to the tax provisions of any convention, agreement or arrangement described in subparagraph (7)(a)(ii); or
- (b) any Taxation Measure aimed at ensuring the effective collection of taxes, except where the measure of a Contracting Party arbitrarily discriminates against Energy Materials and Products originating in, or destined for the Area of another Contracting Party or arbitrarily restricts benefits accorded under Article 7(3).

(3) Article 10(2) and (7) shall apply to Taxation Measures of the Contracting Parties other than those on income or on capital, except that such provisions shall not apply to:

- (a) impose most favoured nation obligations with respect to advantages accorded by a Contracting Party pursuant to the tax provisions of any convention, agreement or arrangement described in subparagraph (7)(a)(ii) or resulting from membership of any Regional Economic Integration Organisation; or
- (b) any Taxation Measure aimed at ensuring the effective collection of taxes, except where the measure arbitrarily discriminates against an Investor of another Contracting Party or arbitrarily restricts benefits accorded under the Investment provisions of this Treaty.

Article 29(2) to (8)63 shall apply to Taxation Measures other than those on income or on capital.

(4) (a) Article 13 shall apply to taxes.

- (b) Whenever an issue arises under Article 13, to the extent it pertains to whether a tax constitutes an expropriation or whether a tax alleged to constitute an expropriation is discriminatory, the following provisions shall apply:
  - (i) The Investor or the Contracting Party alleging expropriation shall refer the issue of whether the tax is an expropriation or whether the tax is discriminatory to the relevant Competent Tax Authority. Failing such referral by the Investor or the Contracting Party, bodies called upon to settle disputes pursuant to Article 26(2)(c) or 27(2) shall make a referral to the relevant Competent Tax Authorities;
  - (ii) The Competent Tax Authorities shall, within a period of six months of such referral, strive to resolve the issues so referred. Where non-discrimination issues are concerned, the Competent Tax Authorities shall apply the non-discrimination provisions of the relevant tax convention or, if there is no non-discrimination provision in the relevant tax convention applicable to the tax or no such tax convention is in force between the Contracting Parties concerned, they shall apply the non-discrimination principles under the Model Tax Convention on Income and Capital of the Organisation for Economic Cooperation and Development;

(iii) Bodies called upon to settle disputes pursuant to Article 26(2)(c) or 27(2) may take into account any conclusions arrived at by the Competent Tax Authorities regarding whether the tax is an expropriation. Such bodies shall take into account any conclusions arrived at within the six-month period prescribed in subparagraph (b)(ii) by the Competent Tax Authorities regarding whether the tax is discriminatory. Such bodies may also take into account any conclusions arrived at by the Competent Tax Authorities after the expiry of the six-month period;

(iv) Under no circumstances shall involvement of the Competent Tax Authorities, beyond the end of the six-month period referred to in subparagraph (b)(ii), lead to a delay of proceedings under Articles 26 and 27.

(5) For the avoidance of doubt, Article 14 shall not limit the right of a Contracting Party to impose or collect a tax by withholding or other means.

(6) For the purposes of this Article:

(a) The term "Taxation Measure" includes:

(i) any provision relating to taxes of the domestic law of the Contracting Party or of a political subdivision thereof or a local authority therein; and

(ii) any provision relating to taxes of any convention for the avoidance of double taxation or of any other international agreement or arrangement by which the Contracting Party is bound.

(b) There shall be regarded as taxes on income or on capital all taxes imposed on total income, on total capital or on elements of income or of capital, including taxes on gains from the alienation of property, taxes on estates, inheritances and gifts, or substantially similar taxes, taxes on the total amounts of wages or salaries paid by enterprises, as well as taxes on capital appreciation.

(c) A "Competent Tax Authority" means the competent authority pursuant to a double taxation agreement in force between the Contracting Parties or, when no such agreement is in force, the minister or ministry responsible for taxes or their authorised representatives.

(d) For the avoidance of doubt, the terms "tax provisions" and "taxes" do not include customs duties.

Article 22: State and Privileged Enterprises

Each Contracting Party shall ensure that any state enterprise which it maintains or establishes shall conduct its activities in relation to the sale or provision of goods and services in its Area in a manner consistent with the Contracting Party's obligations under Part III of this Treaty.

(1) No Contracting Party shall encourage or require such a state enterprise to conduct its activities in its Area in a manner inconsistent with the Contracting Party's obligations under other provisions of this Treaty.

(2) Each Contracting Party shall ensure that if it establishes or maintains an entity and entrusts the entity with regulatory, administrative or other governmental authority, such entity shall exercise that authority in a manner consistent with the Contracting Party's obligations under this Treaty.

(3) No Contracting Party shall encourage or require any entity to which it grants exclusive or special privileges to conduct its activities in its Area in a manner inconsistent with the Contracting Party's obligations under this Treaty.

(4) For the purposes of this Article, "entity" includes any enterprise, agency or other organisation or individual.

Article 23: Observance by Sub-National Authorities

(1) Each Contracting Party is fully responsible under this Treaty for the observance of all provisions of the Treaty, and shall take such reasonable measures as may be available to it to ensure such observance by regional and local governments and authorities within its Area.

(2) The dispute settlement provisions in Parts II, IV and V of this Treaty may be invoked in respect of measures affecting the observance of the Treaty by a Contracting Party which have been taken by regional or local governments or authorities within the Area of the Contracting Party.

Article 24: Exceptions

(1) This Article shall not apply to Articles 12, 13 and 29.

(2) The provisions of this Treaty other than

(a) those referred to in paragraph (1); and

(b) with respect to subparagraph (i), Part III of the Treaty

shall not preclude any Contracting Party from adopting or enforcing any measure

(i) necessary to protect human, animal or plant life or health;

(ii) essential to the acquisition or distribution of Energy Materials and Products in conditions of short supply arising from causes outside the control of that Contracting Party, provided that any such measure shall be consistent with the principles that

(A) all other Contracting Parties are entitled to an equitable share of the international supply of such Energy Materials and Products; and

(B) any such measure that is inconsistent with this Treaty shall be discontinued as soon as the conditions giving rise to it have ceased to exist; or

(iii) designed to benefit Investors who are aboriginal people or socially or economically disadvantaged individuals or groups or their Investments and notified to the Secretariat as such, provided that such measure

(A) has no significant impact on that Contracting Party's economy; and

(B) does not discriminate between Investors of any other Contracting Party and Investors of that Contracting Party not included among those for whom the measure is intended, provided that no such measure shall constitute a disguised restriction on Economic Activity in the Energy Sector, or arbitrary or unjustifiable discrimination between Contracting Parties or between Investors or other interested persons of Contracting Parties. Such measures shall be duly motivated and shall not nullify or impair any benefit one or more other Contracting Parties may reasonably expect under this Treaty to an extent greater than is strictly necessary to the stated end.

(3) The provisions of this Treaty other than those referred to in paragraph (1) shall not be construed to prevent any Contracting Party from taking any measure which it considers necessary:

(i) for the protection of its essential security interests including those relating to the supply of Energy Materials and Products to a military establishment; or

(ii) taken in time of war, armed conflict or other emergency in international relations;

(b) relating to the implementation of national policies respecting the non-proliferation of nuclear weapons or other nuclear explosive devices or needed to fulfil its obligations under the Treaty on the Non-Proliferation of Nuclear Weapons, the Nuclear Suppliers Guidelines, and other international nuclear non-proliferation obligations or understandings; or

(c) for the maintenance of public order.

Such measure shall not constitute a disguised restriction on Transit.

(4) The provisions of this Treaty which accord most favoured nation treatment shall not oblige any Contracting Party to extend to the Investors of any other Contracting Party any preferential treatment:

(a) resulting from its membership of a free-trade area or customs union; or

(b) which is accorded by a bilateral or multilateral agreement concerning economic cooperation between states that were constituent parts of the former Union of Soviet Socialist Republics pending the establishment of their mutual economic relations on a definitive basis.

Article 25: Economic Integration Agreements

The provisions of this Treaty shall not be so construed as to oblige a Contracting Party which is party to an Economic Integration Agreement (hereinafter referred to as "EIA") to extend, by means of most favoured nation treatment, to another Contracting Party which is not a party to that EIA, any preferential treatment applicable between the parties to that EIA as a result of their being parties thereto.

(1) For the purposes of paragraph (1), "EIA" means an agreement substantially liberalising, inter alia, trade and investment, by providing for the absence or elimination of substantially all discrimination between or among parties thereto through the elimination of existing discriminatory measures and/ or the prohibition of new or more discriminatory measures, either at the entry into force of that agreement or on the basis of a reasonable time frame.

(2) This Article shall not affect the application of the WTO Agreement according to Article 29.

PART V: DISPUTE SETTLEMENT

Article 26: Settlement of Disputes between an Investor and a Contracting Party

(1) Disputes between a Contracting Party and an Investor of another Contracting Party relating to an Investment of the latter in the Area of the former, which concern an alleged breach of an obligation of the former under Part III shall, if possible, be settled amicably.

(2) If such disputes cannot be settled according to the provisions of paragraph (1) within a period of three months from the date on which either party to the dispute requested amicable settlement, the Investor party to the dispute may choose to submit it for resolution:

- (a) to the courts or administrative tribunals of the Contracting Party party to the dispute;
- (b) in accordance with any applicable, previously agreed dispute settlement procedure; or
- (c) in accordance with the following paragraphs of this Article.

(3) (a) Subject only to subparagraphs (b) and (c), each Contracting Party hereby gives its unconditional consent to the submission of a dispute to international arbitration or conciliation in accordance with the provisions of this Article.

- (b) (i) The Contracting Parties listed in Annex ID do not give such unconditional consent where the Investor has previously submitted the dispute under subparagraph (2)(a) or (b).
  - (ii) For the sake of transparency, each Contracting Party that is listed in Annex ID shall provide a written statement of its policies, practices and conditions in this regard to the Secretariat no later than the date of the deposit of its instrument of ratification, acceptance or approval in accordance with Article 39 or the deposit of its instrument of accession in accordance with Article 41.
- (c) A Contracting Party listed in Annex IA does not give such unconditional consent with respect to a dispute arising under the last sentence of Article 10(1).

(4) In the event that an Investor chooses to submit the dispute for resolution under subparagraph (2)(c), the Investor shall further provide its consent in writing for the dispute to be submitted to:

- (a) (i) The International Centre for Settlement of Investment Disputes, established pursuant to the Convention on the Settlement of Investment Disputes between States and Nationals of other States opened for signature at Washington, 18 March 1965 (hereinafter referred to as the "ICSID Convention"), if the Contracting Party of the Investor and the Contracting Party party to the dispute are both parties to the ICSID Convention; or
  - (ii) The International Centre for Settlement of Investment Disputes, established pursuant to the Convention referred to in subparagraph (a)(i), under the rules governing the Additional Facility for the Administration of Proceedings by the Secretariat of the Centre (hereinafter referred to as the "Additional Facility Rules"), if the Contracting Party of the Investor or the Contracting Party party to the dispute, but not both, is a party to the ICSID Convention;

(b) a sole arbitrator or ad hoc arbitration tribunal established under the Arbitration Rules of the United Nations Commission on International Trade Law (hereinafter referred to as "UNCITRAL"); or

(c) an arbitral proceeding under the Arbitration Institute of the Stockholm Chamber of Commerce.

(5) (a) The consent given in paragraph (3) together with the written consent of the Investor given pursuant to paragraph (4) shall be considered to satisfy the requirement for:

(i) written consent of the parties to a dispute for purposes of Chapter II of the ICSID Convention and for purposes of the Additional Facility Rules;

(ii) an "agreement in writing" for purposes of article II of the United Nations Convention on the Recognition and Enforcement of Foreign Arbitral Awards, done at New York, 10 June 1958 (hereinafter referred to as the "New York Convention"); and

(iii) "the parties to a contract [to] have agreed in writing" for the purposes of article 1 of the UNCITRAL Arbitration Rules.

(b) Any arbitration under this Article shall at the request of any party to the dispute be held in a state that is a party to the New York Convention. Claims submitted to arbitration hereunder shall be considered to arise out of a commercial relationship or transaction for the purposes of article I of that Convention.

(6) A tribunal established under paragraph (4) shall decide the issues in dispute in accordance with this Treaty and applicable rules and principles of international law.

(7) An Investor other than a natural person which has the nationality of a Contracting Party party to the dispute on the date of the consent in writing referred to in paragraph (4) and which, before a dispute between it and that Contracting Party arises, is controlled by Investors of another Contracting Party, shall for the purpose of article 25(2)(b) of the ICSID Convention be treated as a "national of another Contracting State" and shall for the purpose of article 1(6) of the Additional Facility Rules be treated as a "national of another State".

(8) The awards of arbitration, which may include an award of interest, shall be final and binding upon the parties to the dispute. An award of arbitration concerning a measure of a sub-national government or authority of the disputing Contracting Party shall provide that the Contracting Party may pay monetary damages in lieu of any other remedy granted. Each Contracting Party shall carry out without delay any such award and shall make provision for the effective enforcement in its Area of such awards.

Article 27: Settlement of Disputes between Contracting Parties

(1) Contracting Parties shall endeavour to settle disputes concerning the application or interpretation of this Treaty through diplomatic channels.

(2) If a dispute has not been settled in accordance with paragraph (1) within a reasonable period of time, either party thereto may, except as otherwise provided in this Treaty or agreed in writing by the Contracting Parties, and except as concerns the application or interpretation of Article 6 or Article 19 or, for Contracting Parties listed in Annex IA, the last sentence of Article 10(1), upon written notice to the other party to the dispute submit the matter to an ad hoc tribunal under this Article.

(3) Such an ad hoc arbitral tribunal shall be constituted as follows:

(a) The Contracting Party instituting the proceedings shall appoint one member of the tribunal and inform the other Contracting Party to the dispute of its appointment within 30 days of receipt of the notice referred to in paragraph (2) by the other Contracting Party;

(b) Within 60 days of the receipt of the written notice referred to in paragraph (2), the other Contracting Party party to the dispute shall appoint one member. If the appointment is not made within the time limit prescribed, the Contracting Party having instituted the proceedings may, within 90 days of the receipt of the written notice referred to in paragraph (2), request that the appointment be made in accordance with subparagraph (d);

(c) A third member, who may not be a national or citizen of a Contracting Party party to the dispute, shall be appointed by the Contracting Parties parties to the dispute. That member shall be the President of the tribunal. If, within 150 days of the receipt of the notice referred to in paragraph (2), the Contracting Parties are unable to agree on the appointment of a third member, that appointment shall be made, in accordance with subparagraph (d), at the request of either Contracting Party submitted within 180 days of the receipt of that notice;
(d) Appointments requested to be made in accordance with this paragraph shall be made by the Secretary General of the Permanent Court of International Arbitration within 30 days of the receipt of a request to do so. If the Secretary General is prevented from discharging this task, the appointments shall be made by the First Secretary of the Bureau. If the latter, in turn, is prevented from discharging this task, the appointments shall be made by the most senior Deputy;
(e) Appointments made in accordance with subparagraphs (a) to (d) shall be made with regard to the qualifications and experience, particularly in matters covered by this Treaty, of the members to be appointed;
(f) In the absence of an agreement to the contrary between the Contracting Parties, the Arbitration Rules of UNCITRAL shall govern, except to the extent modified by the Contracting Parties parties to the dispute or by the arbitrators. The tribunal shall take its decisions by a majority vote of its members;
(g) The tribunal shall decide the dispute in accordance with this Treaty and applicable rules and principles of international law;
(h) The arbitral award shall be final and binding upon the Contracting Parties parties to the dispute;
(i) Where, in making an award, a tribunal finds that a measure of a regional or local government or authority within the Area of a Contracting Party listed in Part I of Annex P is not in conformity with this Treaty, either party to the dispute may invoke the provisions of Part II of Annex P;
(j) The expenses of the tribunal, including the remuneration of its members, shall be borne in equal shares by the Contracting Parties parties to the dispute. The tribunal may, however, at its discretion direct that a higher proportion of the costs be paid by one of the Contracting Parties parties to the dispute;
(k) Unless the Contracting Parties parties to the dispute agree otherwise, the tribunal shall sit in The Hague, and use the premises and facilities of the Permanent Court of Arbitration;
(l) A copy of the award shall be deposited with the Secretariat which shall make it generally available.

Article 28: Non-Application of Article 27 to Certain Disputes
A dispute between Contracting Parties with respect to the application or interpretation of Article 5 or 29 shall not be settled under Article 27 unless the Contracting Parties parties to the dispute so agree.

PART VI: TRANSITIONAL PROVISIONS

Article 29: Interim Provisions on Trade-Related Matters
(1) The provisions of this Article shall apply to trade in Energy Materials and Products and Energy-Related Equipment while any Contracting Party is not a member of the WTO.
(2) (a) Trade in Energy Materials and Products and Energy-Related Equipment between Contracting Parties at least one of which is not a member of the WTO shall be governed, subject to subparagraph
(b) and to the exceptions and rules provided for in Annex W, by the provisions of the WTO Agreement, as applied and practised with regard to Energy Materials and Products and Energy-Related Equipment by members of the WTO among themselves, as if all Contracting Parties were members of the WTO.

(b) Such trade of a Contracting Party which is a state that was a constituent part of the former Union of Soviet Socialist Republics may instead be governed, subject to the provisions of Annex TFU, by an agreement between two or more such states, until 1 December 1999 or the admission of that Contracting Party to the WTO, whichever is the earlier.

(3) (a) Each signatory to this Treaty, and each state or Regional Economic Integration Organisation acceding to this Treaty before 24 April 1998, shall on the date of its signature or of its deposit of its instrument of accession provide to the Secretariat a list of all customs duties and charges of any kind imposed on or in connection with importation or exportation of Energy Materials and Products, notifying the level of such customs duties and charges applied on such date of signature or deposit. Each signatory to this Treaty, and each state or Regional Economic Integration Organisation acceding to this Treaty before 24 April 1998, shall on that date provide to the Secretariat a list of all customs duties and charges of any kind imposed on or in connection with importation or exportation of Energy-Related Equipment, notifying the level of such customs duties and charges applied on that date.

(b) Each state or Regional Economic Integration Organisation acceding to this Treaty on or after 24 April 1998, shall, on the date of its deposit of its instrument of accession, provide to the Secretariat a list of all customs duties and charges of any kind imposed on or in connection with importation or exportation of Energy Materials and Products and Energy-Related Equipment, notifying the level of such customs duties and charges applied on such date of deposit.

Any changes to such customs duties or charges of any kind imposed on or in connection with importation or exportation shall be notified to the Secretariat, which shall inform the Contracting Parties of such changes.

(4) Each Contracting Party shall endeavour not to increase any customs duty or charge of any kind imposed on or in connection with importation or exportation:

(a) in the case of the importation of Energy Materials and Products listed in Annex EM I or Energy-Related Equipment listed in Annex EQ I and described in Part I of the Schedule relating to the Contracting Party referred to in article II of the GATT 1994, above the level set forth in that Schedule, if the Contracting Party is a member of the WTO;

(b) in the case of the exportation of Energy Materials and Products listed in Annex EM I or Energy-Related Equipment listed in Annex EQ I, and that of their importation if the Contracting Party is not a member of the WTO, above the level most recently notified to the Secretariat, except as permitted by the provisions made applicable by subparagraph (2)(a).

(5) A Contracting Party may increase such customs duty or other charge above the level referred to in paragraph (4) only if:

(a) in case of a customs duty or other charge imposed on or in connection with importation, such action is not inconsistent with the applicable provisions of the WTO Agreement, other than those provisions of the WTO Agreement listed in Annex W; or

(b) it has, to the fullest extent practicable under its legislative procedures, notified the Secretariat of its proposal for such an increase, given other interested Contracting Parties reasonable opportunity for consultation with respect to its proposal, and accorded consideration to any representations from such Contracting Parties.

(6) In respect of trade between Contracting Parties at least one of which is not a member of the WTO, no such Contracting Party shall increase any customs duty or charge of any kind imposed on or in connection with importation or exportation of Energy Materials and Products listed in Annex EM II or Energy-Related Equipment listed in Annex EQ II above the lowest of the levels applied on the date of the decision by the Charter Conference to list the particular item in the relevant Annex.

A Contracting Party may increase such customs duty or other charge above that level only if:

(a) in case of a customs duty or other charge imposed on or in connection with importation, such action is not inconsistent with the applicable provisions of the WTO Agreement, other than those provisions of the WTO Agreement listed in Annex W; or
(b) in exceptional circumstances not elsewhere provided for in this Treaty, the Charter Conference decides to waive the obligation otherwise imposed on a Contracting Party by this paragraph, consenting to an increase in a customs duty, subject to any conditions the Charter Conference may impose.

(7) Notwithstanding paragraph (6), in the case of trade referred to in that paragraph, Contracting Parties listed in Annex BR in respect of Energy Materials and Products listed in Annex EM II, or in Annex BRQ in respect of Energy-Related Equipment listed in Annex EQ II, shall not increase any customs duty or other charge above the level resulting from their commitments or any provisions applicable to them under the WTO Agreement.

(8) Other duties and charges imposed on or in connection with importation or exportation of Energy Materials and Products or Energy-Related Equipment shall be subject to the provisions of the Understanding on the Interpretation of Article II: 1(b) of the GATT 1994 as modified according to Annex W.

(9) Annex D shall apply:
(a) to disputes regarding compliance with provisions applicable to trade under this Article;
(b) to disputes regarding the application by a Contracting Party of any measure, whether or not it conflicts with the provisions of this Article, which is considered by another Contracting Party to nullify or impair any benefit accruing to it directly or indirectly under this Article; and
(c) unless the Contracting Parties parties to the dispute agree otherwise, to disputes regarding compliance with Article 5 between Contracting Parties at least one of which is not a member of the WTO,

Except that Annex D shall not apply to any dispute between Contracting Parties, the substance of which arises under an agreement that:
(i) has been notified in accordance with and meets the other requirements of sub-paragraph (2)(b) and Annex TFU; or
(ii) establishes a free-trade area or a customs union as described in article XXIV of the GATT 1994.

Article 30: Developments in International Trading Arrangements
Contracting Parties undertake that in the light of the results of the Uruguay Round of Multilateral Trade Negotiations embodied principally in the Final Act thereof done at Marrakesh, 15 April 1994, they will commence consideration not later than 1 July 1995 or the entry into force of this Treaty, whichever is the later, of appropriate amendments to this Treaty with a view to the adoption of any such amendments by the Charter Conference.

Article 31: Energy-Related Equipment
The provisional Charter Conference shall at its first meeting commence examination of the inclusion of energy-related equipment in the trade provisions of this Treaty.

Article 32: Transitional Arrangements
(1) In recognition of the need for time to adapt to the requirements of a market economy, a Contracting Party listed in Annex T may temporarily suspend full compliance with its obligations under one or more of the following provisions of this Treaty, subject to the conditions in paragraphs (3) to (6):
Article 6(2) and (5)
Article 7(4)
Article 9(1)
Article 10(7) specific measures

Article 14(1)(d) related only to transfer of unspent earnings Article 20(3)
Article 22(1) and (3)

(2) Other Contracting Parties shall assist any Contracting Party which has suspended full compliance under paragraph (1) to achieve the conditions under which such suspension can be terminated. This assistance may be given in whatever form the other Contracting Parties consider most effective to respond to the needs notified under subparagraph (4)(c) including, where appropriate, through bilateral or multilateral arrangements.

(3) The applicable provisions, the stages towards full implementation of each, the measures to be taken and the date or, exceptionally, contingent event, by which each stage shall be completed and measure taken are listed in Annex T for each Contracting Party claiming transitional arrangements. Each such Contracting Party shall take the measure listed by the date indicated for the relevant provision and stage as set out in Annex T. Contracting Parties which have temporarily suspended full compliance under paragraph (1) undertake to comply fully with the relevant obligations by 1 July 2001. Should a Contracting Party find it necessary, due to exceptional circumstances, to request that the period of such temporary suspension be extended or that any further temporary suspension not previously listed in Annex T be introduced, the decision on a request to amend Annex T shall be made by the Charter Conference.

(4) A Contracting Party which has invoked transitional arrangements shall notify the Secretariat no less often than once every 12 months:

(a) of the implementation of any measures listed in its Annex T and of its general progress to full compliance;

(b) of the progress it expects to make during the next 12 months towards full compliance with its obligations, of any problem it foresees and of its proposals for dealing with that problem;

(c) of the need for technical assistance to facilitate completion of the stages set out in Annex T as necessary for the full implementation of this Treaty, or to deal with any problem notified pursuant to subparagraph (b) as well as to promote other necessary market- oriented reforms and modernisation of its energy sector;

(d) of any possible need to make a request of the kind referred to in paragraph (3).

(5) The Secretariat shall:

(a) circulate to all Contracting Parties the notifications referred to in paragraph (4);

(b) circulate and actively promote, relying where appropriate on arrangements existing within other international organisations, the matching of needs for and offers of technical assistance referred to in paragraph (2) and subparagraph (4)(c);

(c) circulate to all Contracting Parties at the end of each six month period a summary of any notifications made under subparagraph (4)(a) or (d).

(6) The Charter Conference shall annually review the progress by Contracting Parties towards implementation of the provisions of this Article and the matching of needs and offers of technical assistance referred to in paragraph (2) and subparagraph (4)(c). In the course of that review it may decide to take appropriate action.

PART VII: STRUCTURE AND INSTITUTIONS

Article 33: Energy Charter Protocols and Declarations

(1) The Charter Conference may authorise the negotiation of a number of Energy Charter Protocols or Declarations in order to pursue the objectives and principles of the Charter.

(2) Any signatory to the Charter may participate in such negotiation.

(3) A state or Regional Economic Integration Organisation shall not become a party to a Protocol or Declaration unless it is, or becomes at the same time, a signatory to the Charter and a Contracting Party to this Treaty.

(4) Subject to paragraph (3) and subparagraph (6)(a), final provisions applying to a Protocol shall be defined in that Protocol.

(5) A Protocol shall apply only to the Contracting Parties which consent to be bound by it, and shall not derogate from the rights and obligations of those Contracting Parties not party to the Protocol.

(6) (a) A Protocol may assign duties to the Charter Conference and functions to the Secretariat, provided that no such assignment may be made by an amendment to a Protocol unless that amendment is approved by the Charter Conference, whose approval shall not be subject to any provisions of the Protocol which are authorised by subparagraph (b).

(b) A Protocol which provides for decisions thereunder to be taken by the Charter Conference may, subject to subparagraph (a), provide with respect to such decisions:

(i) for voting rules other than those contained in Article 36;

(ii) that only parties to the Protocol shall be considered to be Contracting Parties for the purposes of Article 36 or eligible to vote under the rules provided for in the Protocol.

Article 34: Energy Charter Conference

(1) The Contracting Parties shall meet periodically in the Energy Charter Conference (referred to herein as the "Charter Conference") at which each Contracting Party shall be entitled to have one representative. Ordinary meetings shall be held at intervals determined by the Charter Conference.

(2) Extraordinary meetings of the Charter Conference may be held at such times as may be determined by the Charter Conference, or at the written request of any Contracting Party, provided that, within six weeks of the request being communicated to the Contracting Parties by the Secretariat, it is supported by at least one-third of the Contracting Parties.

(3) The functions of the Charter Conference shall be to:

(a) carry out the duties assigned to it by this Treaty and any Protocols;

(b) keep under review and facilitate the implementation of the principles of the Charter and of the provisions of this Treaty and the Protocols;

(c) facilitate in accordance with this Treaty and the Protocols the coordination of appropriate general measures to carry out the principles of the Charter;

(d) consider and adopt programmes of work to be carried out by the Secretariat;

(e) consider and approve the annual accounts and budget of the Secretariat;

consider and approve or adopt the terms of any headquarters or other agreement, including privileges and immunities considered necessary for the Charter Conference and the Secretariat;

(f) encourage cooperative efforts aimed at facilitating and promoting market-oriented reforms and modernisation of energy sectors in those countries of Central and Eastern Europe and the former Union of Soviet Socialist Republics undergoing economic transition;

(g) authorise and approve the terms of reference for the negotiation of Protocols, and consider and adopt the texts thereof and of amendments thereto;

(h) authorise the negotiation of Declarations, and approve their issuance;

(i) decide on accessions to this Treaty;

(j) authorise the negotiation of and consider and approve or adopt association agreements;

(k) consider and adopt texts of amendments to this Treaty;

(l) consider and approve modifications of and technical changes to the Annexes to this Treaty;

(m) consider and approve the listing of signatories in Annexes BR or BRQ or in both these Annexes;

(n) consider and approve the addition of items to Annex EM II from Annex EM I with the corresponding deletion of those items from Annex EM I and consider and approve the addition of items to Annex EQ II from Annex EQ I with the corresponding deletion of those items from Annex EQ I;

(o) appoint the Secretary General and take all decisions necessary for the establishment and functioning of the Secretariat including the structure, staff levels and standard terms of employment of officials and employees.

(4) In the performance of its duties, the Charter Conference, through the Secretariat, shall cooperate with and make as full a use as possible, consistently with economy and efficiency, of the services and programmes of other institutions and organisations with established competence in matters related to the objectives of this Treaty.

(5) The Charter Conference may establish such subsidiary bodies as it considers appropriate for the performance of its duties.

(6) The Charter Conference shall consider and adopt rules of procedure and financial rules.

(7) In 1999 and thereafter at intervals (of not more than five years) to be determined by the Charter Conference, the Charter Conference shall thoroughly review the functions provided for in this Treaty in the light of the extent to which the provisions of the Treaty and Protocols have been implemented. At the conclusion of each review the Charter Conference may amend or abolish the functions specified in paragraph (3) and may discharge the Secretariat.

Article 35: Secretariat

(1) In carrying out its duties, the Charter Conference shall have a Secretariat which shall be composed of a Secretary General and such staff as are the minimum consistent with efficient performance.

(2) The Secretary General shall be appointed by the Charter Conference. |The first such appointment shall be for a maximum period of five years.

(3) In the performance of its duties the Secretariat shall be responsible to and report to the Charter Conference.

(4) The Secretariat shall provide the Charter Conference with all necessary assistance for the performance of its duties and shall carry out the functions assigned to it in this Treaty or in any Protocol and any other functions assigned to it by the Charter Conference.

(5) The Secretariat may enter into such administrative and contractual arrangements as may be required for the effective discharge of its functions.

Article 36: Voting

(1) Unanimity of the Contracting Parties Present and Voting at the meeting of the Charter Conference where such matters fall to be decided shall be required for decisions by the Charter Conference to:

(a) adopt amendments to this Treaty other than amendments to Articles 34 and 35 and Annex T;

(b) approve accessions to this Treaty under Article 41 by states or Regional Economic Integration Organisations which were not signatories to the Charter as of 16 June 1995;

(c) authorise the negotiation of and approve or adopt the text of association agreements;

(d) approve modifications to Annexes EM, NI, W and B;

(e) approve technical changes to the Annexes to this Treaty; and

(f) approve the Secretary General's nominations of panelists under Annex D, paragraph (7).

(g) approve the addition of items to Annex EM II from Annex EM I with the corresponding deletion of those items from Annex EM I and approve the addition of items to Annex EQ II from Annex EQ I with the corresponding deletion of those items from Annex EQ I.

The Contracting Parties shall make every effort to reach agreement by consensus on any other matter requiring their decision under this Treaty. If agreement cannot be reached by consensus, paragraphs (2) to (5) shall apply.

(2) Decisions on budgetary matters referred to in Article 34(3)(e) shall be taken by a qualified majority of Contracting Parties whose assessed contributions as specified in Annex B represent, in combination, at least three-fourths of the total assessed contributions specified therein.

(3) Decisions on matters referred to in Article 34(7) shall be taken by a three- fourths majority of the Contracting Parties.
(4) Except in cases specified in subparagraphs (1)(a) to (g), paragraphs (2) and (3), and subject to paragraph (6), decisions provided for in this Treaty shall be taken by a three-fourths majority of the Contracting Parties Present and Voting at the meeting of the Charter Conference at which such matters fall to be decided.
(5) For purposes of this Article, "Contracting Parties Present and Voting" means Contracting Parties present and casting affirmative or negative votes, provided that the Charter Conference may decide upon rules of procedure to enable such decisions to be taken by Contracting Parties by correspondence.
(6) Except as provided in paragraph (2), no decision referred to in this Article shall be valid unless it has the support of a simple majority of the Contracting Parties.
(7) A Regional Economic Integration Organisation shall, when voting, have a number of votes equal to the number of its member states which are Contracting Parties to this Treaty; provided that such an Organisation
shall not exercise its right to vote if its member states exercise theirs, and vice versa.
(8) In the event of persistent arrears in a Contracting Party's discharge of financial obligations under this Treaty, the Charter Conference may suspend that Contracting Party's voting rights in whole or in part.

Article 37: Funding Principles
(1) Each Contracting Party shall bear its own costs of representation at meetings of the Charter Conference and any subsidiary bodies.
(2) The cost of meetings of the Charter Conference and any subsidiary bodies shall be regarded as a cost of the Secretariat.
(3) The costs of the Secretariat shall be met by the Contracting Parties assessed according to their capacity to pay, determined as specified in Annex B, the provisions of which may be modified in accordance with Article 36(1)(d).
(4) A Protocol shall contain provisions to assure that any costs of the Secretariat arising from that Protocol are borne by the parties thereto.
(5) The Charter Conference may in addition accept voluntary contributions from one or more Contracting Parties or from other sources. Costs met from such contributions shall not be considered costs of the Secretariat for the purposes of paragraph (3).

PART VIII: FINAL PROVISIONS

Article 38: Signature
This Treaty shall be open for signature at Lisbon from 17 December 1994 to 16 June 1995 by the states and Regional Economic Integration Organisations which have signed the Charter.

Article 39: Ratification, Acceptance or Approval
This Treaty shall be subject to ratification, acceptance or approval by signatories. Instruments of ratification, acceptance or approval shall be deposited with the Depositary.

Article 40: Application to Territories
(1) Any state or Regional Economic Integration Organisation may at the time of signature, ratification, acceptance, approval or accession, by a declaration deposited with the Depositary, declare that the Treaty shall be binding upon it with respect to all the territories for the international relations of which it is responsible, or to one or more of them. Such declaration shall take effect at the time the Treaty enters into force for that Contracting Party.

(2) Any Contracting Party may at a later date, by a declaration deposited with the Depositary, bind itself under this Treaty with respect to other territory specified in the declaration. In respect of such territory the Treaty shall enter into force on the ninetieth day following the receipt by the Depositary of such declaration.
(3) Any declaration made under the two preceding paragraphs may, in respect of any territory specified in such declaration, be withdrawn by a notification to the Depositary. The withdrawal shall, subject to the applicability of Article 47(3), become effective upon the expiry of one year after the date of receipt of such notification by the Depositary.
(4) The definition of "Area" in Article 1(10) shall be construed having regard to any declaration deposited under this Article.

Article 41: Accession
This Treaty shall be open for accession, from the date on which the Treaty is closed for signature, by states and Regional Economic Integration Organisations which have signed the Charter, on terms to be approved by the Charter Conference. The instruments of accession shall be deposited with the Depositary.

Article 42: Amendments
(1) Any Contracting Party may propose amendments to this Treaty.
(2) The text of any proposed amendment to this Treaty shall be communicated to the Contracting Parties by the Secretariat at least three months before the date on which it is proposed for adoption by the Charter Conference.
(3) Amendments to this Treaty, texts of which have been adopted by the Charter Conference, shall be communicated by the Secretariat to the Depositary which shall submit them to all Contracting Parties for ratification, acceptance or approval.
(4) Instruments of ratification, acceptance or approval of amendments to this Treaty shall be deposited with the Depositary. Amendments shall enter into force between Contracting Parties having ratified, accepted or approved them on the ninetieth day after deposit with the Depositary of instruments of ratification, acceptance or approval by at least three- fourths of the Contracting Parties. Thereafter the amendments shall enter into force for any other Contracting Party on the ninetieth day after that Contracting Party deposits its instrument of ratification, acceptance or approval of the amendments.

Article 43: Association Agreements
(1) The Charter Conference may authorise the negotiation of association agreements with states or Regional Economic Integration Organisations, or with international organisations, in order to pursue the objectives and principles of the Charter and the provisions of this Treaty or one or more Protocols.
(2) The relationship established with and the rights enjoyed and obligations incurred by an associating state, Regional Economic Integration Organisation, or international organisation shall be appropriate to the particular circumstances of the association, and in each case shall be set out in the association agreement.

Article 44: Entry into Force
(1) This Treaty shall enter into force on the ninetieth day after the date of deposit of the thirtieth instrument of ratification, acceptance or approval thereof, or of accession thereto, by a state or Regional Economic Integration Organisation which is a signatory to the Charter as of 16 June 1995.
(2) For each state or Regional Economic Integration Organisation which ratifies, accepts or approves this Treaty or accedes thereto after the deposit of the thirtieth instrument of ratification, acceptance or approval, it shall enter into force on the ninetieth day after the date of deposit by such state or Regional Economic Integration Organisation of its instrument of ratification, acceptance, approval or accession.

(3) For the purposes of paragraph (1), any instrument deposited by a Regional Economic Integration Organisation shall not be counted as additional to those deposited by member states of such Organisation.

Article 45: Provisional Application

(1) Each signatory agrees to apply this Treaty provisionally pending its entry into force for such signatory in accordance with Article 44, to the extent that such provisional application is not inconsistent with its constitution, laws or regulations.

(2) (a) Notwithstanding paragraph (1) any signatory may, when signing, deliver to the Depository a declaration that it is not able to accept provisional application. The obligation contained in paragraph (1) shall not apply to a signatory making such a declaration. Any such signatory may at any time withdraw that declaration by written notification to the Depository.

(b) Neither a signatory which makes a declaration in accordance with subparagraph (a) nor Investors of that signatory may claim the benefits of provisional application under paragraph (1).

(c) Notwithstanding subparagraph (a), any signatory making a declaration referred to in subparagraph (a) shall apply Part VII provisionally pending the entry into force of the Treaty for such signatory in accordance with Article 44, to the extent that such provisional application is not inconsistent with its laws or regulations.

(3) (a) Any signatory may terminate its provisional application of this Treaty by written notification to the Depository of its intention not to become a Contracting Party to the Treaty. Termination of provisional application for any signatory shall take effect upon the expiration of 60 days from the date on which such signatory's written notification is received by the Depository.

(b) In the event that a signatory terminates provisional application under subparagraph (a), the obligation of the signatory under paragraph (1) to apply Parts III and V with respect to any Investments made in its Area during such provisional application by Investors of other signatories shall nevertheless remain in effect with respect to those Investments for twenty years following the effective date of termination, except as otherwise provided in subparagraph (c).

(c) Subparagraph (b) shall not apply to any signatory listed in Annex PA. A signatory shall be removed from the list in Annex PA effective upon delivery to the Depository of its request therefor.

(4) Pending the entry into force of this Treaty the signatories shall meet periodically in the provisional Charter Conference, the first meeting of which shall be convened by the provisional Secretariat referred to in paragraph (5) not later than 180 days after the opening date for signature of the Treaty as specified in Article 38.

(5) The functions of the Secretariat shall be carried out on an interim basis by a provisional Secretariat until the entry into force of this Treaty pursuant to Article 44 and the establishment of a Secretariat.

(6) The signatories shall, in accordance with and subject to the provisions of paragraph (1) or subparagraph (2)(c) as appropriate, contribute to the costs of the provisional Secretariat as if the signatories were Contracting Parties under Article 37(3). Any modifications made to Annex B by the signatories shall terminate upon the entry into force of this Treaty.

(7) A state or Regional Economic Integration Organisation which, prior to this Treaty's entry into force, accedes to the Treaty in accordance with Article 41 shall, pending the Treaty's entry into force, have the rights and assume the obligations of a signatory under this Article.

Article 46: Reservations

No reservations may be made to this Treaty.

Article 47: Withdrawal

(1) At any time after five years from the date on which this Treaty has entered into force for a Contracting Party, that Contracting Party may give written notification to the Depositary of its withdrawal from the Treaty.

(2) Any such withdrawal shall take effect upon the expiry of one year after the date of the receipt of the notification by the Depositary, or on such later date as may be specified in the notification of withdrawal.

(3) The provisions of this Treaty shall continue to apply to Investments made in the Area of a Contracting Party by Investors of other Contracting Parties or in the Area of other Contracting Parties by Investors of that Contracting Party as of the date when that Contracting Party's withdrawal from the Treaty takes effect for a period of 20 years from such date.

(4) All Protocols to which a Contracting Party is party shall cease to be in force for that Contracting Party on the effective date of its withdrawal from this Treaty.

Article 48: Status of Annexes and Decisions

The Annexes to this Treaty and the Decisions set out in Annex 2 to the Final Act of the European Energy Charter Conference signed at Lisbon on 17 December 1994, as well as the Decisions adopted in connection with the adoption of the Amendment to the Trade-Related Provisions of the Energy Charter Treaty are an integral part of the Energy Charter Treaty.

Article 49: Depositary

The Government of the Portuguese Republic shall be the Depositary of this Treaty.

Article 50: Authentic Texts

In witness whereof the undersigned, being duly authorised to that effect, have signed this Treaty in English, French, German, Italian, Russian and Spanish, of which every text is equally authentic, in one original, which will be deposited with the Government of the Portuguese Republic.

Done at Lisbon on the seventeenth day of December in the year one thousand nine hundred and ninety-four.

10.1.3 Reciprocal Investment Promotion and Protection Agreement Between the Government of the Kingdom of Morocco and the Government of the Federal Republic of Nigeria (2013)

Signed 10 December 2019, entered into force 1 July 2020.

PREAMBLE

The Government of the Kingdom of Morocco; and the Government of the Federal Republic of Nigeria hereinafter referred to as the "Parties"

DESIRING to strengthen the bonds of friendship and cooperation between the State Parties;

Recognizing the important contribution investment can make to the sustainable development of the state parties, including the reduction of poverty, increase of productive capacity, economic growth, the transfer of technology, and the furtherance of human rights and human development;

Seeking to promote, encourage and increase investment opportunities that enhance sustainable development within the territories of the state parties;

Understanding that sustainable development requires the fulfillment of the economic, social and environmental pillars that are embedded within the concept;

Reaffirming the right of the State Parties to regulate and to introduce new measures relating to investments in their territories in order to meet national policy objectives and taking into account any asymmetries with respect to the measures in place, the particular need of developing countries to exercise this right;

Seeking an overall balance of the rights and obligations among the State Parties, the investors, and the investments under this Agreement;

HAVE AGREED as follows:

Article 1. Definitions

For the purpose of this agreement and unless stated otherwise the following words and terms shall have this meanings:

"Investor" refers to:

1) Any individual who is a natural person or a permanent resident of a Party, according to its laws, that makes an investment in the territory of the other Party.
2) Any legal entity including companies, corporations, commercial associations provided that legal entity is
   (a) Established or constituted or organized in accordance with the laws of a Party
   (b) Having its headquarters and the center of its economic activity or principal place of business in the territory of that Party
   (c) That invests in the territory of the other Party S d) Legal entities which not constituted under the law of that Party shall be but a controlled, directly or indirectly by a natural person as defined in 1) or by legal entities as defined in 2).
3) This Agreement shall not apply to investments by natural persons who are nationals of both Parties and who are permanent resident of a Host Party.

"Investment" Investment means an enterprise within the territory of one State established, acquired, expanded or operated, in good faith, by an investor of the other State in accordance with law of the Party in whose territory the investment is made taken together with the asset of the enterprise which contribute sustainable development of that Party and has the characteristics of an investment involving a commitment of capital or other similar resources, pending profit, risk-taking and certain duration. An enterprise will possess the following assets:

(a) Shares, stocks, debentures and other instruments of the enterprise or another enterprise;
(b) A debt security of another enterprise;
(c) Loans to an enterprise;
(d) Movable or immovable property and other property rights such as mortgages, liens or pledges;
(e) Claims to money or to any performance under contract having a financial value;
(f) Copyrights and intellectual property rights such as patents, trademarks, industrial designs and trade names, to the extent they are recognized under the law of the Host State;
(g) Rights conferred by law or under contract, including licenses to cultivate, extract or exploit natural resources;

For greater certainty, Investment does not include:

(a) Debt securities issued by a government or loans to a government
(b) Portfolio investments
(c) Claims to money that arise solely from commercial contracts for the sale of goods or services by a national or enterprise in the territory of another party, or the extension of credit in connection with a commercial transaction, or a any claims to money that do not involve interest set out in sub paragraphs (a) and (g) above.
(d) letters of bank credit; and
(e) claims to money with maturities less than three years.

"Party" means individually as a Party and collectively as Parties.

"Returns" means output, net of tax, from an investment and money yielded by an investment and includes, in particular although not exclusively, profits, dividends, interest, capital gains, royalties and fees;

"Freely usable currency" means a currency widely used to make payments for international transactions subject to parties laws and investment policies applicable from time to time.

"Environmental Impact Assessment" means the process used to predict the environmental consequences (positive or negative) of a plan, policy, program or project prior to move forward with the proposed action.

"Social Impact Assessment" means the process of assessing or estimating in advance the social consequences that are likely to follow from specific actions project development, particularly in the context of appropriate national, state or provincial environment policy legislation.

"Territory" means;

(a) The land territory, internal waters and territorial sea, including the air space above the areas of the Party;
(b) The exclusive economic zone of the Party as determined by its domestic law, consistent with the Part V of the united Nations Convention of Law of the Sea;
(c) The Continental shelf of the Party as determined by its domestic law, consistent with the Part VI of the United Nations Convention of Law of the Sea.

"Host Party" means the Party in whose territory the investment is located.

Article 2. Objective of the Agreement

The objective of this Agreement is to promote and protect co-operation between the Parties in order to facilitate and encourage mutual investment. This objective shall be achieved through institutional governance as defined in this Agreement, by the establishment of an agenda on investment co-operation, facilitation and by the development of mechanisms or on mitigation, prevention an resolution of disputes, among other instruments mutually agreed by the Parties.

Article 3. Scope of the Agreement
This Agreement shall apply to all Investors and Investments made by investors of either Party in the territory of the other Party, accepted or admitted as such in accordance with its laws and regulations, whether made before or after the coming into force of this Agreement, but shall not apply to any dispute raised before the entry into force of this Agreement.

Article 4. Institutional Governance
1. For the purpose of this agreement, the Parties hereby establish a Joint Committee for the administration of this Agreement (hereinafter referred to as "Joint Committee").
2. The Joint Committee shall be composed of representatives as designated by both Parties.
3. The Joint Committee shall meet at such times, in such places and though such
means as the Parties may agree. Meetings shall be held, whenever it is necessary, with alternating Chair between the Parties.
4. The joint Committee shall have the following responsibilities:
   (a) Monitor the implementation and execution of this Agreement;
   (b) Debate and share opportunities for the expansion of mutual Investment;
   (c) Request and welcome the participation of the private sector and civil society, when applicable, on specific issues related to the work of the Joint Committee;
   and
   (d) Seek to resolve any issues or disputes concerning Parties' investment in an amicable manner.
5. The joint Committee shall not replace or impair in any way, any other agreement- or the diplomatic channels existing between the Parties.

Article 5. Exchange of Investment Information
1. The Parties shall exchange information concerning investment, particularly through the Joint Committee. Whenever possible, the information shall, reveal, in advance, useful data on procedures and special requirements for investment, business opportunities and expectations for major parties projects.
2. For this purpose, the Party shall provide, when requested, with clarity and respect for the level of protection granted, information, related, in particular, to the following items:
   (a) Regulatory conditions for investment.
   (b) Specific incentives and legal landmarks that may affect investment;
   (c) Public policies and legal landmarks that may affect investment;
   (d) Legal framework for investment, including legislation on the establishment
   of companies and joint ventures;
   (e) Related international treaties.
   f) Trade procedures and tax regimes;
   (g) Statistical information on the market for goods and services;
   (h) Available infrastructure and public services;
   (i) Social and labor requirements;
   (j) Information on specific economic sectors or segments previously identified
   by the Parties; and
   (k) State and Local government's projects and understandings on investment.
3. The Parties shall also discuss initiatives to strengthen the role of investors in Public-Private Partnerships (PPPs), especially though greater transparency and early access to regulatory information.

4. The Parties shall fully respect the level of protection granted to such ·information as required by the submitting Party.
5. The Parties shall encourage the involvement of the private sector, as a key player directly interested in the best results derived from this Agreement.
6. The Parties shall disseminate among the relevant business sectors, general information on investment, regulatory frameworks and business opportunities in the territory of the other Party.

Article 6. National Treatment and the Most Favoured Nation Provisions
1. Each Party, as far as possible, shall encourage and create favorable conditions for investors of the other Party to make investments in its territory, and admit such investments in accordance with its laws and regulations in force.
2. Each Party shall allow investors of the other Party to invest and contract business in conditions no less favourable than that accorded, in like circumstances, to investments of its own investors in accordance with its laws and regulations.
3. For greater certainty-, references to "like circumstances" in paragraph 2 requires an overall examination on a case-by-case basis of all the circumstances of an investment including, but not limited to:
(a) its effects on third person and the local community;
(b) its effects on the local, regional or national environment, including the cumulative effects of all investments within a jurisdiction on the environment;
(c) the sector in which the investor is in;
(d) the aim of the measure concerned;
(f) the regulatory process generally applied in relation to the measure concerned; The examination referred to in this paragraph shall not be limited to or be biased toward anyone factor.
4. Each Party shall allow investors of the other Party to make an investment and conduct business in conditions no less favourable than that accorded, in like circumstances, to investors of another third state.
5. The treatment granted under 1,2,3 and 4 of this article shall not be construed as to preclude national security-, public security- or public order nor oblige one Party to extend to the investors of the other Party and their investment the benefit of any treatment, preference or privilege resulting from:
(a) its membership of, or association with, any existing or future free trade areas, customs union, economic union, common market or monetary union, or
(b) an existing or future free trade agreement
(c) any international agreement or any domestic legislation relating wholly or mainly to taxation.
(d) other Agreement for the avoidance of double taxation or by virtue of its participation in customs union and free trade areas, or on basis of reciprocity with a third country.
6. As soon as practicable after a party adopts a measure under this Article that Party shall inform the Other party of the justification for the measures adopted, as well as the scope and relevance of such measures.

Article 7. Minimum Standard of Treatment
1. Each Party shall accord to investments treatment in accordance with customary international law, including fair and equitable treatment and full protection and security.
2. For greater certainty, paragraph 1 prescribes the customary international law minimum standard of treatment of aliens as the minimum standard of treatment to be afforded to covered investments. The concepts of "fair and equitable treatment" and "full protection and security" does not require treatment in addition to or beyond that which is required by that standard, and does not create additional substantive rights. The obligation in paragraph 1 to provide:

(a) "fair and equitable treatment" includes the obligation not to deny justice in criminal, civil or administrative adjudicatory proceedings in accordance with the principle of due process embodied in the principal legal systems of a Party.

(b) "full protection and security" requires each Party to provide the level of police protection required under customary international law.

3. A determination that there has been a breach of another provision of this Agreement, or of a separate international agreement, does not establish that there has been a breach of this Article.

4. For greater clarity, the Parties confirm their shared understanding that 'customary international Law' generally and as specifically referred in this Agreement results from a general and consistent practice of States that they follow from a sense of legal obligation. The Parties also confirm that the customary international law minimum standard of treatment of aliens refers to all customary international law principles that protect the economic rights and interest of aliens.

Article 8. Expropriation and Compensation

1. A Party shall not nationalize or expropriate an investment directly or indirectly through measures having an effect equivalent to nationalization or expropriation except:

(a) for a public purpose;

(b) in a non discrimination manner;

(c) on payment of prompt, adequate, and effective compensation; and

(d) in accordance with due process of law

2. For the purpose of this Agreement,

(a) Indirect expropriation results from a series of measures of a Party having an equivalent effect of direct expropriation without formal transfer of title or outright seizure

(b) the determination of whether a measure or series of measures of a Party constitute indirect expropriation requites a case-to-case, fact based inquiry into various factors including, but not limited to the scope of the measures or series of measures and their interference with the reasonable and distinguishable concerning the investment:

3. The compensation referred to in paragraph 1 shall be equivalent to the fair market value of the expropriated investment immediately before the expropriation took place and must not reflect a change in value occurring because the intended expropriation had become known earlier.

4. Compensation shall be paid without delay and shall be fully realizable and freely transferable

5. If the fair market value is denominated in a freely convertible currency, the compensation referred to in paragraph 3 shall be no less than the fair market value on the date of expropriation, plus interest at a commercially reasonable rate for that currency, accrued from the date of expropriation until the date of payment.

6. If the fair market value is denominated in a currency that is not freely usable, the compensation referred to in paragraph 3 – converted into the currency of payment at the market rate of exchange prevailing on the date of payment, shall be no less than;

(a) The fair market value on the date of expropriation, converted into freely usable currency at the market rate of exchange prevailing on that date, plus b) Interest, at a commercially reasonable rate for that freely usable currency, occurred from the date of expropriation until the date of payment.

7. The affected investor shall have a right under the law of the expropriating party to a review of its case and the valuation of its investment by a judicial or other independent authority of that party in accordance with the principles set out in this article.

8. This Article does not apply to the issuance of a compulsory licence granted in relation to intellectual property rights or to the revocation, limitation or creation of an intellectual property right, to the extent that the issuance, revocation, limitation or creation is consistent with the WTO Agreement.

Article 9. Compensation for Damages and Loss

1. Investors of one Party whose investments in the territory of the other Party suffer losses due to war, armed conflict, revolution, state of national emergency, insurrection, civil disturbances or other similar events, shall be accorded by the latter Party treatment, as regards restitution, indemnification, compensation or other settlement, no less favourable treatment than that which the latter Party accords to its own investors or to investors of a third State.
2. Without prejudice to paragraph 1 of this Article, investors of one Party who, in any of the situations referred to in that paragraph suffer losses in the territory of the other Contracting Party resulting from:
   (a) requisitioning of their property by its forces or authorities; or
   (b) destruction of their property by its forces or authorities, which was not caused in combat action or was not required by the necessity of the situation; shall be accorded restitution or adequate compensation.

Article 10. Transparency

1. In line with the principles of this Agreement, each Party shall ensure that all measures that affect investment are administered in a reasonable, objective and impartial manner, in accordance with its legal system.
2. Each Party shall, wherever possible, ensure that its laws, regulations and administrative rulings of general application with respect to matters covered by this Agreement, are published in the shortest possible time and be accessible, if possible, by electronic means, so as to enable interested people and the other Party to become acquainted.
3. The Parties shall give due publicity of this Agreement to their respective and private financial agents, responsible for technical evaluation of risks and the approval of loans, credits, guarantees and related insurances for investment in the territory of the other Party.
4. The Parries agree to consult periodically on ways to improve the transparency practices set out in this Article, publication of laws and decisions relating to investment.
5. The Parries agree that in the event of resort to arbitration, the arbitral proceedings shall be transparent. For greater clarity, the notice of arbitration, the pleadings memorials, brief submitted to the tribunal, written submissions, minutes of transcripts of hearings, orders, awards and decisions of the tribunal shall be available to the public. The tribunal shall conduct hearings open to the public provided that any protected information that is submitted to the tribunal shall be protected in accordance with the applicable law.

Article 11. Transfers

1. Each Party shall in accordance with legal system and its international obligations, allow the free transfer of funds related to an investment, namely;
   (a) capital and additional capital amounts used to maintain and increase investment;
   (b) profits, dividends, interest, capital, gains, royalty payments, management fees, technical assistance and other fees, returns in kind;
   (c) repayments of any loan including interest thereon, relating directly to the investment.
   (d) Proceeds from sales of their shares;
   (e) Proceeds received by investors in case of sale or partial sale or liquidation;
   (f) Payments arising from an investment dispute/ award;
   (g) The amount of compensation in case of expropriation;
   (h) salaries and other remuneration going to nationals of one Contracting Party who have been allowed to work in the territory of the other Contracting Party in connection with an investment.
2. Each Party may prevent or delay a transfer through the equitable, non- discriminatory and good faith application of its laws and regulations relating to:
   (a) Bankruptcy, insolvency, or the protection of rights of creditors;

(b) Issuing, trading, or dealing in securities, features, options or derivatives;
(c) Criminal or penal offences;
(d) Financial reporting or record keeping or transfers when necessary to assist law enforcement or financial regulatory authorities; or
(e) Ensuring compliance with orders or judgments in judicial or administrative proceedings.

3. Each Party shall permit transfers relating to a covered investment to be made in a freely usable currency at the market rate of exchange prevailing at the time of transfer.

4. It is understood that this Agreement does not prevent a Party from requiring, prior to transfers relating to an investment, from investors to fulfill their tax obligations related to the investment in question.

Article 12. Temporary Sefeguard Measure

1. A Party may adopt or maintain restrictions on payments or transfers related to investments:
(a) In the event of serious balance of payments and external financial difficulties or threat thereof,
(b) Ensuring the integrity of a party's financial system It is recognized that particular pressures on the balance of payments of a Party in the process of economic development may necessitate the use of restrictions to ensure, inter alia, the maintenance of a level of financial reserves adequate for the implementation of its program of economic development.

2. The restrictions referred to in paragraph 1 shall:
(a) Not exceed those necessary to deal with the circumstances described in paragraph 1;
(b) be temporary and be phased out progressively as the situation specified in paragraph 1 improves;
(c) be applied on a non-discriminatory basis such that the other Party is treated no less favorably than non-Party.

3. Any restrictions adopted or maintained under therein shall be promptly notified to the other Party, paragraph 1 or any changes

4. The Party adopting any restrictions under paragraph 1 shall commence consultations with the other Party in order to review the restrictions adopted by it.

Article 13. Investment and Environment

1. The Parties recognize that their respective environmental laws policies and multilateral environmental agreements to which they are both party, play an important role in protecting the environment.

2. The Parties recognize that each Party retains the right to exercise discretion with respect to regulatory, compliance, investigatory, and prosecutorial matters and to make decisions regarding the allocation of resources to enforcement with respect to other environmental matters determined to have higher priorities.

3. The Parties recognize that each Parry undertakes to respect and observe the social responsibility owed to the other Party.

4. Nothing in this Agreement shall be constructed to prevent a Party from adopting maintaining, or enforcing, in a non-discriminatory manner, any measure otherwise consistent with this Agreement that it considers appropriate to ensure that investment activity in its territory is undertaken in a manner sensitive to environmental and social concerns.

Article 14. Impact Assessment

1. Investors or the investment shall comply with environmental assessment screening and assessment processes applicable to their proposed investments prior to their establishment, as required by the laws of the host state for such an investment or the laws of the home state for such an investment, whichever is more rigorous in relation to the investment in question.

2. Investors or the investment shall conduct a social impact assessment of the potential investment. The Parties shall adopt standards for this purpose at the meeting of the Joint Committee.

3)Investors, their investment and host state authorities shall apply the precautionary principle to their environmental impact assessment and to decisions taken in relation to a proposed investment, including any necessary mitigation or alternative approaches of the precautionary principle by investors and investments shall be described in the environmental impact assessment they undertake.

Article 15. Investment, Labour and Human Rights Protection

1. The Parties reaffirm their respective obligations as members of the International Labour Organization (ILO) and their commitments under the ILO Declaration on Fundamental Principles and Rights at Work and its Follow-up.

2. The parties recognize that it is inappropriate to encourage investment by weakening or reducing the protection accorded in domestic labour laws.

Accordingly, each Party shall ensure that it does not waive or otherwise derogate from or offer to waive or otherwise derogate from its labour laws where the waiver or derogation would be inconsistent with the labour rights conferred by domestic laws and international labour instruments in which both are parties are signatories, or fail to effectively enforce its labour laws through a sustained or recurring course of action or inaction.

3. The Parties recognize that it is inappropriate to encourage investment by relaxing domestic labour, public health or safety. They shall not waive or otherwise derogate from, or offer to waive or otherwise derogate from, such measures as an encouragement for the establishment, acquisition, expansion, or retention in their territories, of an investment.

5. Each Party shall ensure that its laws and regulations provide for high levels of labour and human rights protection appropriate to its economic and social situation, and shall strive to continue to improve these law and regulations.

6. All parties shall ensure that their laws, policies and actions are consistent with the international human rights agreements to which they are a Party.

Article 16. Subrogation

1. Where one Party or its designated agency has guaranteed any indemnity against non-commercial risks in respect of an investment by any of its investors in the territory of the other Party and has made payment to such investors in respect of their claims under this agreement, the other Party agrees that the first Party or its designated agency is entitled by virtue of subrogation to exercise the rights and assert the claims of those investors. The subrogated rights or claims shall not exceed the original rights or claims of such investors.

2. In case of subrogation as defined in paragraph 1 of this Article, the investor shall not be entitled to require a claim, unless he is authorized to do so by the Party or its designated agency.

Article 17. Anti-Corruption

1. Each Contracting Party shall ensure that measures and efforts are undertaken to prevent and combat corruption regarding matters covered by this Agreement in accordance with its laws and regulations.

2. Investors and their Investments shall not, prior to the establishment of an Investment or afterwards, offer, promise or give any undue pecuniary or other advantage, whether directly or through intermediaries, to a public official of the Host State, or a member of an official's family or business associate or other person in close proximity to an official, for that official or for a third party, in order that the official or third party act or refrain from acting in relation to the performance of official duties, in order to achieve any favour in relation to a proposed investment or any licences, permits, contracts or other rights in relations to an investment.

3. Investors and their Investments shall not be complicit in any act described in Paragraph 1 above, including incitement, aiding and abetting, and conspiracy to commit Of authorization of such acts.

4. A breach of this article by an investor or an investment is deemed to constitute a breach of the domestic law of the Host State Party concerning the establishment and operation of an investment.
5. The States Parties to this Agreement, consistent with their applicable law, shall prosecute and where convicted penalize persons that have breached the applicable law implementing this obligation.

Article 18. Post-Establishment Obligations
1. Investments shall, in keeping with good practice requirements relating to the size and nature of the investment, maintain an environmental management system. Companies in areas of resource exploitation and high-risk industrial enterprises shall maintain a current certification to ISO 14001 or an equivalent environmental management standard.
2. Investors and Investments shall uphold human rights in the host state.
3. Investors and investments shall act in accordance with core labour standards as required by the ILO Declaration on Fundamental Principles and Rights of Work, 1998.
4. Investors and investments shall not manage or operate the investments in a manner that circumvents international environmental, labour and human rights obligations to which the host state and/or home state are Parties.

Article 19. Corporate Governance and Practices
1. In accordance with the size and nature of an investment,
   (a) Investments shall meet or exceed national and internationally accepted standards of corporate governance for the sector involved, in particular for transparency and accounting practices.
   (b) Investments shall establish and maintain, where appropriate, local community liaison processes, in accordance with internationally accepted standards when available.
   (c) Where relevant internationally accepted standards of the type described in this Article are not available or have been developed without the participation of developing countries, the Joint Committees may establish such standards.

Article 20. Investor Liablity
Investors shall be subject to civil actions for liability in the judicial process of their home state for the acts or decisions made in relation to the investment where such acts or decisions lead to significant damage, personal injuries or loss of life in the host state.

Article 21. Access to Investor Information
1. Host States have the right to seek information from a potential Investor or its home state about its corporate governance history and its practices as an Investor, including in its home state.
2. Host States shall protect confidential business information they receive in this regard.
3. Host States may make the information provided available to the public in the community where the investment may be located, subject to the protection of confidential business information and to other applicable domestic laws.

Article 22. Denial of Benefits
1. A Party may deny the benefits of this Agreement to an Investor of another Party that is an Investment of such Party and to Investments of such investor if investors of a non-Party own or control the Investment and the denying Party:
   (a) Does not maintain diplomatic relations with the non-Party; or
   (b) Adopts or maintains measures with respect to the non-Party that prohibit transactions with the investment or that would be violated or circumvented if the benefits of this Agreement were accorded to the Investment or to its Investments.

2. A Party may deny the benefits of this Agreement to an Investor of another Party that is an investment of such other Party and to Investments of that Investor if the Investment has no substantial business activities in the territory of the other Party and persons of non-Party, or of the denying Party, own or control the Investment.

Artcile 23. Right of State to Regulate
1. In accordance with customary international law and other general principles of international law, the Host State has the right to take regulatory or other measures to ensure that development in its territory is consistent with the goals and principles of sustainable development, and with other legitimate social and economic policy objectives.
2. Except where the rights of Host State are expressly stated as an exception to the obligation of this Agreement, a Host State's pursuit of its rights to regulate shall be understood as embodied within a balance of the rights and obligations of Investors and Investments and Host States, as set out in the Agreement.
3. For greater certainly, non-discriminatory measures taken by a State Party to comply with its international obligations under other treaties shall not constitute a breach of this Agreement.

Article 24. Corporate Social Responsibility
1. In addition to the obligation to comply with all applicable laws and regulations of the Host State and the obligations in this Agreement, and in accordance with the size, capacities and nature of an investments, and taking into account the development plans and priorities of the Host State and the Sustainable Development Goals of the United Nations, investors and their investments should strive to make the maximum feasible contributions to the sustainable development of the Host State and local community through high levels of socially responsible practices.
2. Investors should apply the LO Tripartite Declaration on Multinational Investments and Social Policy as well as specific or sectorial standards of responsible practice where these exist.
3. Where standards of corporate social responsibility increase, investors should strive to apply and achieve the higher level standards.

Article 25. Assistance and Facilitation for Foreign Investment
1. The Home State should assist the Host State in the promotion and facilitation of foreign investment in particular by their own investors. Such assistance shall be consistent with the development goals and priorities of the Host State. Such assistance may include, inter alia :

(a) Capacity building with respect to Host State agencies and programs on investment promotion and facilitation;
(b) Insurance programs based on commercial principles;
(c) Technology transfer; and
(d) Periodic trade missions, support for joint business councils and other cooperative efforts to promote sustainable investments.
(e) The Home State shall inform the Host State of the form and extent of available assistance as appropriate for the type and size of different Investments.

Article 26. Disputes Prevention
1. Before initiating an eventual arbitration procedure, any dispute between the Parties shall be assessed through consultations and negotiations by the Joint Committee.
2. A Party may submit a specific question of interest of an investor to the Joint Committee:

(a) To initiate the procedure, the Party of the interested investor shall submit, in writing, its request to the Joint Committee, specifying the name of the interested investor and the encountered challenges and difficulties;

(b) The joint Committee shall have 90 days, extendable by mutual agreement by 60 additional days, upon justification, to submit relevant information about the presented case;
(c) In order to facilitate the search for a solution between the Parties, whenever possible, the following shall participate in the bilateral meeting:
- Representatives of the Investor;
- Representatives of the Parties or non-party entities involved in the measure or situation under consultation.

(d) The procedure for dialogue and bilateral consultation ends by the initiative of any Party upon presentation of summarized report in the subsequent Joint Committee meeting, that shall include:
- Identification of the Party;
- Identification of the Investors;
- Description of the measure under consultation; and
- Position of the Parties concerning the measure.

3. The Joint Committee shall, whenever possible, call for special meetings to review the submitted matters.
4. The meeting of the Joint Committee and all documentation, as well as steps taken in the context of the mechanism established in this Article, shall remain confidential, except for the submitted reports.
5. If the dispute cannot be resolved within six (6) months from the date of the written request for consultations and negotiations, the investor may, after the international arbitration mechanisms.

Article 27. Settlement of Disputes Between a Party and Investor of the Other Party
1. If disputes cannot be settled according to the provisions of article 26, the Investor concerned may submit at his preference the dispute settlement to :
(a) The International Center for the settlement disputes established under the Convention on the settlement of investment disputes between states and Nationals of other States of March 18, 1965 done in Washington, D.C, if this Convention is applicable to the Parties;
(b) an arbitral ad hoc tribunal established under the Arbitration Rules of the United Nations Commission on International Trade Law (UNCITRAL).
(c) any other arbitral institutions or any arbitration rules, if the disputing parties agree.
2. The Arbitral Tribunal shall be established as follows:
(a) each Party to the dispute shall appoint one arbitrator, and the two arbitrators thus appointed, shall select by mutual agreement a third arbitrator, who must be a citizen of a third country, and who shall act as Chairman of the Tribunal. All the arbitrators must be appointed within two months from the date of notification by one Party to the other Party of its intention to submit the dispute to arbitration.
(b) if the periods specified in paragraph (2) (a) herein above have not been respected, either Party, in the absence of any other agreement, shall invite the Secretary General, or Vice-Secretary General of the permanent Court of Arbitration at The Hague to make the necessary appointments.
(c) the Arbitral Tribunal shall reach its decisions by a majority of vote. These decisions shall be final and legally binding upon the parties and shall be enforced. The decisions shall be taken in conformity within the provisions of this Agreement, the national law of the Host Party and the applicable rules of international law.
(d) Each party to the dispute shall bear the cost of its representation in the arbitral proceedings; the cost of arbitrators and the remaining costs shall be borne in equal parts by the parties to the dispute.
(e) No measures of constraint before or after a final award, such as attachment, garnishment or execution, can be taken against the goods of the Party complained against, in particular:

(i) property, including bank accounts, used or intended for use in the exercise of the functions of the diplomatic mission of the Host Party or its consular posts, its special missions, its missions to international organizations, or its delegations in international organizations organs or to international conferences;
(ii) military property or property used or intended to be used in the performance of military functions;
(iii) central bank property or other monetary authority of the Host Party;
(iv) property forming part of the cultural heritage of the Host Party or its archives which are not put or intended to be sold;
(v) property forming part of an exhibition of objects of scientific, cultural and historical value that are not put or intended to be sold.

(t) the Tribunal shall interpret its award and give reasons and bases of its decision at the request of either Party. Unless otherwise agreed by the Parties, the venue of arbitration shall be at the seat of the Permanent Court of Arbitration at the Hague (the Netherlands).

Article 28. Settlement of Disputes Between the Parties

1. The Parties shall strive with good faith and mutual cooperation to reach a fair and quick settlement of any dispute arising between them concerning interpretation or execution of this Agreement in accordance to the provisions of Article 19. In the event the dispute has not been settled, it may be submitted at the request of either Party to an Arbitral Tribunal composed of three members.
2. Within a period of two months from the date of receiving the said request each Party shall appoint one arbitrator, and the two arbitrators so appointed shall appoint, within a period of two months and with the approval of both Parties a national of a third country as Chairman of the Tribunal.
3)within the periods specified in paragraph (2) of this Article the necessary appointments have not been made, either Party may, in the absence of any other agreement, invites the President of the International Court of Justice to make any necessary appointments. If the President is a national of either Party or otherwise prevented from discharging the said function, the Vice-President shall be invited to I make the necessary appointments. If the Vice-President is a national of either Party or if the too is prevented from discharging the said function, the member of the International Court of Justice next in seniority who is not a national of either Party shall be invited to make the necessary appointments.
4. The Arbitral Tribunal shall reach its decisions by a majority of votes. Such decisions shall be final and binding on both Parties. Each Party shall bear the cost of its own member of the Tribunal and of its representation in the arbitral proceedings; the cost of the Chairman and the remaining costs shall be borne in equal parts by the Parties. The Tribunal may, however, decide that a higher proportion of costs shall be borne by one of the two Parties and this award shall be binding on both Parties. The tribunal shall determine its own procedures.
5. Unless agreed otherwise by the Parties, the venue of Arbitration shall be the seat of the Permanent Court of Arbitration at The Hague (Ibe Netherlands).
6. All claims shall be submitted and all hearing session shall be completed within a period of six months from the date the third member is appointed, unless otherwise agreed. The Tribunal shall issue its decision within two months from the date of submitting the final claims or the date of closing the general sessions, whichever is later.
7. It shall not be permitted to submit a dispute to an Arbitral Tribunal pursuant to the provisions of this Article, if the same dispute was submitted to another Arbitral Tribunal which is still under hearing by that Tribunal save where there is consolidation.

Article 29. Consolidation

1. Where two or more claims have been submitted separately to arbitration under Articles 27 and 28 respectively and the claims have a question of law or fact in common and arise out of the same events or circumstances, any disputing party may seek a consolidation order in accordance with this Agreement of all the disputing Parties sought to be covered by the order.
2. The Parties at the Joint Committee shall agree on the procedure for consolidation and who shall be the appointing authority.

Article 30. Amendment

This Agreement may be amended at any time at the request of either Party giving the other Party six (6) months' notice in writing and such amendment shall enter into force upon notification through Diplomatic Channel by Parries that their respective constitutional requirements for its entry into force have been fulfilled.

Article 31. Entry Into Force

This Agreement, or any amendments thereof, shall enter into force on the latter date on which either Party notifies the other that its internal juridical requirements for the entry into force of this Agreement or its amendments have been fulfilled.

Article 32. Duration

This Agreement shall remain in force for a period of ten (10) years, and may be renewed for a further period as may be agreed by the parries. Either party may give notice in writing in the ninth (9) year of its intention to renew the Agreement.

Article 33. Periodic Review This Agreement

1. The State Parries shall meet every five years after the entry into force of this Agreement to review its operation and effectiveness, including the levels of investment between the Parties.
2. The State Parries may adopt joint measures in order to improve the effectiveness of this Agreement.

Article 34. Termination

At any time, either of the parries' may terminate this Agreement by providing written notice of termination to the other party. The termination shall take effect on a date the parties agree on, or, if the parries are unable to reach an agreement, 6 months after the date on which the termination notice is delivered.

IN WITNESS WHEREOF, the undersigned, duly authorized by their respective Governments, have signed this Agreement in two languages, English and Arabic. Both texts being equally authentic. In case of difference of interpretation, the English text shall prevail.
Done at Ahuja, on 3 December 2016.

10.1.4 United States-Mexico-Canada Agreement ('USCMA') (2020) (selected articles)

Signed 10 December 2019, entered into force 1 July 2020.

CHAPTER 14 INVESTMENT

Article 14.1: Definitions

For the purposes of this Chapter:

covered investment means, with respect to a Party, an investment in its territory of an investor of another Party in existence as of the date of entry into force of this Agreement or established, acquired, or expanded thereafter;

enterprise means an enterprise as defined in Article 1.5 (General Definitions), and a branch of an enterprise;

enterprise of a Party means an enterprise constituted or organized under the law of a Party, or a branch located in the territory of a Party and carrying out business activities there;

freely usable currency means "freely usable currency" as determined by the International Monetary Fund under its Articles of Agreement;

investment means every asset that an investor owns or controls, directly or indirectly, that has the characteristics of an investment, including such characteristics as the commitment of capital or other resources, the expectation of gain or profit, or the assumption of risk. An investment may include:

(a) an enterprise;
(b) shares, stock and other forms of equity participation in an enterprise;
(c) bonds, debentures, other debt instruments, and loans;
(d) futures, options, and other derivatives;
(e) turnkey, construction, management, production, concession, revenue-sharing, and other similar contracts;
(f) intellectual property rights;
(g) licenses, authorizations, permits, and similar rights conferred pursuant to a Party's law; and
(h) other tangible or intangible, movable or immovable property, and related property rights, such as liens, mortgages, pledges, and leases,

but investment does not mean:

(i) an order or judgment entered in a judicial or administrative action;
(j) claims to money that arise solely from:
   (i) commercial contracts for the sale of goods or services by a natural person or enterprise in the territory of a Party to an enterprise in the territory of another Party, or
   (ii) the extension of credit in connection with a commercial contract referred to in subparagraph (j)(i);

investor of a non-Party means, with respect to a Party, an investor that attempts to make, is making, or has made an investment in the territory of that Party, that is not an investor of a Party; and

investor of a Party means a Party, or a national or an enterprise of a Party, that attempts to make, is making, or has made an investment in the territory of another Party, provided however that:

(a) a natural person who is a dual citizen is deemed to be exclusively a national of the State of his or her dominant and effective citizenship; and
(b) a natural person who is a citizen of a Party and a permanent resident of another Party is deemed to be exclusively a national of the Party of which that natural person is a citizen.

Article 14.2: Scope

1. This Chapter applies to measures adopted or maintained by a Party relating to:
   (a) investors of another Party;
   (b) covered investments; and
   (c) with respect to Article 14.10 (Performance Requirements) and Article 14.16 (Investment and Environmental, Health, Safety, and other Regulatory Objectives), all investments in the territory of that Party.
2. A Party's obligations under this Chapter apply to measures adopted or maintained by:
   (a) the central, regional, or local governments or authorities of that Party; and
   (b) a person, including a state enterprise or another body, when it exercises any governmental authority delegated to it by central, regional, or local governments or authorities of that Party.
3. For greater certainty, this Chapter, except as provided for in Annex 14-C (Legacy Investment Claims and Pending Claims) does not bind a Party in relation to an act or fact that took place or a situation that ceased to exist before the date of entry into force of this Agreement.
4. For greater certainty, an investor may only submit a claim to arbitration under this Chapter as provided under Annex 14-C (Legacy Investment Claims and Pending Claims), Annex 14-D (Mexico-United States Investment Disputes), or Annex 14-E (Mexico-United States Investment Disputes Related to Covered Government Contracts).

Article 14.3: Relation to Other Chapters

1. In the event of any inconsistency between this Chapter and another Chapter of this Agreement, the other Chapter shall prevail to the extent of the inconsistency.
2. This Chapter does not apply to measures adopted or maintained by a Party to the extent that they are covered by Chapter 17 (Financial Services).
3. A requirement of a Party that a service supplier of another Party post a bond or other form of financial security as a condition for the cross-border supply of a service does not of itself make this Chapter applicable to measures adopted or maintained by the Party relating to the cross-border supply of the service. This Chapter applies to measures adopted or maintained by the Party relating to the posted bond or financial security, to the extent that the bond or financial security is a covered investment.
4. For greater certainty, consistent with Article 15.2.2(a) (Scope), Article 15.5 (Market Access), and Article 15.8 (Development and Administration of Measures) apply to measures adopted or maintained by a Party relating to the supply of a service in its territory by a covered investment.

Article 14.4: National Treatment

1. Each Party shall accord to investors of another Party treatment no less favorable than that it accords, in like circumstances, to its own investors with respect to the establishment, acquisition, expansion, management, conduct, operation, and sale or other disposition of investments in its territory.
2. Each Party shall accord to covered investments treatment no less favorable than that it accords, in like circumstances, to investments in its territory of its own investors with respect to the establishment, acquisition, expansion, management, conduct, operation, and sale or other disposition of investments.
3. The treatment accorded by a Party under paragraphs 1 and 2 means, with respect to a government other than at the central level, treatment no less favorable than the most favorable treatment accorded, in like circumstances, by that government to investors, and to investments of investors, of the Party of which it forms a part.
4. For greater certainty, whether treatment is accorded in "like circumstances" under this Article depends on the totality of the circumstances, including whether the relevant treatment distinguishes between investors or investments on the basis of legitimate public welfare objectives.

Article 14.5: Most-Favored-Nation Treatment

1. Each Party shall accord to investors of another Party treatment no less favorable than the treatment it accords, in like circumstances, to investors of any other Party or of any non-Party with respect to the establishment, acquisition, expansion, management, conduct, operation, and sale or other disposition of investments in its territory.
2. Each Party shall accord to covered investments treatment no less favorable than that it accords, in like circumstances, to investments in its territory of investors of any other Party or of any non-Party with respect to the establishment, acquisition, expansion, management, conduct, operation, and sale or other disposition of investments.
3. The treatment accorded by a Party under paragraphs 1 and 2 means, with respect to a government other than at the central level, treatment no less favorable than the most favorable treatment accorded, in like circumstances, by that government to investors in its territory, and to investments of those investors, of any other Party or of any non-Party.
4. For greater certainty, whether treatment is accorded in "like circumstances" under this Article depends on the totality of the circumstances, including whether the relevant treatment distinguishes between investors or investments on the basis of legitimate public welfare objectives.

Article 14.6: Minimum Standard of Treatment

1. Each Party shall accord to covered investments treatment in accordance with customary international law, including fair and equitable treatment and full protection and security.
2. For greater certainty, paragraph 1 prescribes the customary international law minimum standard of treatment of aliens as the standard of treatment to be afforded to covered investments. The concepts of "fair and equitable treatment" and "full protection and security" do not require treatment in addition to or beyond that which is required by that standard, and do not create additional substantive rights. The obligations in paragraph 1 to provide:
   (a) "fair and equitable treatment" includes the obligation not to deny justice in criminal, civil, or administrative adjudicatory proceedings in accordance with the principle of due process embodied in the principal legal systems of the world; and
   (b) "full protection and security" requires each Party to provide the level of police protection required under customary international law.
3. A determination that there has been a breach of another provision of this Agreement, or of a separate international agreement, does not establish that there has been a breach of this Article.
4. For greater certainty, the mere fact that a Party takes or fails to take an action that may be inconsistent with an investor's expectations does not constitute a breach of this Article, even if there is loss or damage to the covered investment as a result.

Article 14.7: Treatment in Case of Armed Conflict or Civil Strife

1. Notwithstanding Article 14.12.5(b) (Non-Conforming Measures), each Party shall accord to investors of another Party and to covered investments non-discriminatory treatment with respect to measures it adopts or maintains relating to losses suffered by investments in its territory owing to armed conflict or civil strife.
2. Notwithstanding paragraph 1, if an investor of a Party, in a situation referred to in paragraph 1, suffers a loss in the territory of another Party resulting from:
   (a) requisitioning of its covered investment or part thereof by the latter's forces or authorities; or
   (b) destruction of its covered investment or part thereof by the latter's forces or authorities, which was not required by the necessity of the situation,

   the latter Party shall provide the investor restitution, compensation, or both, as appropriate, for that loss.

3. Paragraph 1 does not apply to existing measures relating to subsidies or grants that would be inconsistent with Article 14.4 (National Treatment) but for Article 14.12.5(b) (Non-Conforming Measures).

Article 14.8: Expropriation and Compensation

1. No Party shall expropriate or nationalize a covered investment either directly or indirectly through measures equivalent to expropriation or nationalization (expropriation), except:
   (a) for a public purpose;
   (b) in a non-discriminatory manner;
   (c) on payment of prompt, adequate, and effective compensation in accordance with paragraphs 2, 3, and 4; and
   (d) in accordance with due process of law.
2. Compensation shall:
   (a) be paid without delay;
   (b) be equivalent to the fair market value of the expropriated investment immediately before the expropriation took place (the date of expropriation);
   (c) not reflect any change in value occurring because the intended expropriation had become known earlier; and
   (d) be fully realizable and freely transferable.
3. If the fair market value is denominated in a freely usable currency, the compensation paid shall be no less than the fair market value on the date of expropriation, plus interest at a commercially reasonable rate for that currency, accrued from the date of expropriation until the date of payment.
4. If the fair market value is denominated in a currency that is not freely usable, the compensation paid – converted into the currency of payment at the market rate of exchange prevailing on the date of payment – shall be no less than:
   (a) the fair market value on the date of expropriation, converted into a freely usable currency at the market rate of exchange prevailing on that date; plus
   (b) interest, at a commercially reasonable rate for that freely usable currency, accrued from the date of expropriation until the date of payment.
5. For greater certainty, whether an action or series of actions by a Party constitutes an expropriation shall be determined in accordance with paragraph 1 of this Article and Annex 14-B (Expropriation).
6. This Article does not apply to the issuance of compulsory licenses granted in relation to intellectual property rights in accordance with the TRIPS Agreement, or to the revocation, limitation, or creation of intellectual property rights, to the extent that the issuance, revocation, limitation, or creation is consistent with Chapter 20 (Intellectual Property) and the TRIPS Agreement.

Article 14.9: Transfers

1. Each Party shall permit all transfers relating to a covered investment to be made freely and without delay into and out of its territory. These transfers include:
   (a) contributions to capital;
   (b) profits, dividends, interest, capital gains, royalty payments, management fees, technical assistance, and other fees;
   (c) proceeds from the sale of all or any part of the covered investment or from the partial or complete liquidation of the covered investment;
   (d) payments made under a contract entered into by the investor, or the covered investment, including payments made pursuant to a loan agreement or employment contract; and
   (e) payments made pursuant to Article 14.7 (Treatment in Case of Armed Conflict or Civil Strife) and Article 14.8 (Expropriation and Compensation).

2. Each Party shall permit transfers relating to a covered investment to be made in a freely usable currency at the market rate of exchange prevailing at the time of transfer.
3. A Party shall not require its investors to transfer, or penalize its investors that fail to transfer, the income, earnings, profits, or other amounts derived from, or attributable to, investments in the territory of another Party.
4. Each Party shall permit returns in kind relating to a covered investment to be made as authorized or specified in a written agreement between the Party and a covered investment or an investor of another Party.
5. Notwithstanding paragraphs 1, 2, and 4, a Party may prevent or delay a transfer through the equitable, non-discriminatory, and good faith application of its laws relating to:
   (a) bankruptcy, insolvency, or the protection of the rights of creditors;
   (b) issuing, trading, or dealing in securities or derivatives;
   (c) criminal or penal offenses;
   (d) financial reporting or record keeping of transfers when necessary to assist law enforcement or financial regulatory authorities; or
   (e) ensuring compliance with orders or judgments in judicial or administrative proceedings.
6. Notwithstanding paragraph 4, a Party may restrict transfers of returns in kind in circumstances where it could otherwise restrict those transfers under this Agreement, including as set out in paragraph 5.

Article 14.10: Performance Requirements
1. No Party shall, in connection with the establishment, acquisition, expansion, management, conduct, operation, or sale or other disposition of an investment of an investor of a Party or of a non-Party in its territory, impose or enforce any requirement, or enforce any commitment or undertaking:
   (a) to export a given level or percentage of goods or services;
   (b) to achieve a given level or percentage of domestic content;
   (c) to purchase, use, or accord a preference to a good produced or a service supplied in its territory, or to purchase a good or a service from a person in its territory;
   (d) to relate in any way the volume or value of imports to the volume or value of exports or to the amount of foreign exchange inflows associated with the investment;
   (e) to restrict sales of a good or a service in its territory that the investment produces or supplies by relating those sales in any way to the volume or value of its exports or foreign exchange earnings;
   (f) to transfer a technology, a production process, or other proprietary knowledge to a person in its territory;
   (g) to supply exclusively from the territory of the Party a good that the investment produces or a service that it supplies to a specific regional market or to the world market;
   (h) (i) to purchase, use, or accord a preference to, in its territory, technology of the Party or of a person of the Party, or
      (ii) that prevents the purchase or use of, or the according of a preference to, in its territory, a technology; or
   (i) to adopt:
      (i) a given rate or amount of royalty under a license contract, or
      (ii) a given duration of the term of a license contract,

   in regard to any license contract in existence at the time the requirement is imposed or enforced, or any commitment or undertaking is enforced, or any future license contract freely entered into between the investor and a person in its territory, provided that the requirement is imposed or the commitment or undertaking is enforced in a manner that constitutes direct interference with that license contract by an exercise of non-judicial governmental authority of a Party. For greater certainty, paragraph 1(i) does not apply when the license contract is concluded between the investor and a Party.

2. No Party shall condition the receipt or continued receipt of an advantage, in connection with the establishment, acquisition, expansion, management, conduct, operation, or sale or other disposition of an investment of an investor of a Party or of a non-Party in its territory, on compliance with any requirement:

(a) to achieve a given level or percentage of domestic content;

(b) to purchase, use, or accord a preference to a good produced in its territory, or to purchase a good from a person in its territory;

(c) to relate in any way the volume or value of imports to the volume or value of exports or to the amount of foreign exchange inflows associated with the investment;

(d) to restrict sales of goods or services in its territory that the investment produces or supplies by relating those sales in any way to the volume or value of its exports or foreign exchange earnings; or

(e) (i) to purchase, use or accord a preference to, in its territory, technology of the Party or of a person of the Party, or

(ii) that prevents the purchase or use of, or the according of a preference to, in its territory, a technology.

3. In relation to paragraphs 1 and 2:

(a) Nothing in paragraph 2 shall be construed to prevent a Party from conditioning the receipt or continued receipt of an advantage, in connection with an investment of an investor of a Party or of a non-Party in its territory, on compliance with a requirement to locate production, supply a service, train or employ workers, construct or expand particular facilities, or carry out research and development, in its territory.

(b) Paragraphs 1(f), 1(h), 1(i), and 2(e) do not apply:

(i) if a Party authorizes use of an intellectual property right in accordance with Article 31 of the TRIPS Agreement, or to a measure requiring the disclosure of proprietary information that fall within the scope of, and is consistent with, Article 39 of the TRIPS Agreement, or

(ii) if the requirement is imposed or the commitment or undertaking is enforced by a court, administrative tribunal, or competition authority, after judicial or administrative process, to remedy an alleged violation of competition laws.

(c) Provided that such measures are not applied in an arbitrary or unjustifiable manner, or do not constitute a disguised restriction on international trade or investment, paragraphs 1(b), 1(c), 1(f), 2(a), and 2(b) shall not be construed to prevent a Party from adopting or maintaining measures:

(i) necessary to secure compliance with laws and regulations that are not inconsistent with this Agreement,

(ii) necessary to protect human, animal or plant life or health, or

(iii) related to the conservation of living or non-living exhaustible natural resources.

(d) Paragraphs 1(a), 1(b), 1(c), 2(a), and 2(b) do not apply to qualification requirements for a good or a service with respect to export promotion and foreign aid programs.

(e) Paragraphs 1(b), 1(c), 1(f), 1(g), 1(h), 1(i), 2(a), 2(b), and 2(e) do not apply to government procurement.

(f) Paragraphs 2(a) and 2(b) do not apply to requirements imposed by an importing Party relating to the content of a good necessary to qualify for preferential tariffs or preferential quotas.

(g) Paragraphs 1(h), 1(i), and 2(e) shall not be construed to prevent a Party from adopting or maintaining measures to protect legitimate public welfare objectives, provided that such measures are not applied in an arbitrary or unjustifiable manner, or in a manner that constitutes a disguised restriction on international trade or investment.

4. For greater certainty, paragraphs 1 and 2 do not apply to any commitment, undertaking, or requirement other than those set out in those paragraphs.

5. This Article does not preclude enforcement of any commitment, undertaking, or requirement between private parties, if a Party did not impose or require the commitment, undertaking, or requirement.

Article 14.11: Senior Management and Boards of Directors
1. No Party shall require that an enterprise of that Party that is a covered investment appoint to senior management positions a natural person of a particular nationality.
2. A Party may require that a majority of the board of directors, or any committee thereof, of an enterprise of that Party that is a covered investment, be of a particular nationality, or resident in the territory of the Party, provided that the requirement does not materially impair the ability of the investor to exercise control over its investment.

Article 14.12: Non-Conforming Measures
1. Article 14.4 (National Treatment), Article 14.5 (Most-Favored-Nation Treatment), Article 14.10 (Performance Requirements), and Article 14.11 (Senior Management and Boards of Directors) do not apply to:
   (a) any existing non-conforming measure that is maintained by a Party at:
      (i) the central level of government, as set out by that Party in its Schedule to Annex I,
      (ii) a regional level of government, as set out by that Party in its Schedule to Annex I, or
      (iii) a local level of government;
   (b) the continuation or prompt renewal of any non-conforming measure referred to in subparagraph (a); or
   (c) an amendment to any non-conforming measure referred to in subparagraph (a) to the extent that the amendment does not decrease the conformity of the measure, as it existed immediately before the amendment, with Article 14.4 (National Treatment), Article 14.5 (Most-Favored-Nation Treatment), Article 14.10 (Performance Requirements), or Article 14.11 (Senior Management and Boards of Directors).
2. Article 14.4 (National Treatment), Article 14.5 (Most-Favored-Nation Treatment), Article 14.10 (Performance Requirements), and Article 14.11 (Senior Management and Boards of Directors) do not apply to any measure that a Party adopts or maintains with respect to sectors, sub-sectors, or activities, as set out by that Party in its Schedule to Annex II.
3. No Party shall, under any measure adopted after the date of entry into force of this Agreement and covered by its Schedule to Annex II, require an investor of another Party, by reason of its nationality, to sell or otherwise dispose of an investment existing at the time the measure becomes effective.
4. (a) Article 14.4 (National Treatment) does not apply to any measure that falls within an exception to, or derogation from, the obligations imposed by:
      (i) Article 20.8 (National Treatment), or
      (ii) Article 3 of the TRIPS Agreement, if the exception or derogation relates to matters not addressed by Chapter 20 (Intellectual Property Rights);
   (b) Article 14.5 (Most-Favored-Nation Treatment) does not apply to any measure that falls within Article 5 of the TRIPS Agreement, or an exception to, or derogation from, an obligation imposed by:
      (i) Article 20.8 (National Treatment), or
      (ii) Article 4 of the TRIPS Agreement.
5. Article 14.4 (National Treatment), Article 14.5 (Most-Favored-Nation Treatment), and Article 14.11 (Senior Management and Boards of Directors) do not apply to:
   (a) government procurement; or
   (b) subsidies or grants provided by a Party, including government-supported loans, guarantees, and insurance.

Article 14.13: Special Formalities and Information Requirements

1. Nothing in Article 14.4 (National Treatment) shall be construed to prevent a Party from adopting or maintaining a measure that prescribes special formalities in connection with covered investments, such as a requirement that investors be residents of the Party or that covered investments be legally constituted under the laws or regulations of the Party, provided that these formalities do not materially impair the protections afforded by the Party to investors of another Party and covered investments pursuant to this Chapter.

2. Notwithstanding Article 14.4 (National Treatment) and Article 14.5 (Most-Favored-Nation Treatment), a Party may require an investor of another Party or its covered investment to provide information concerning that investment solely for informational or statistical purposes. The Party shall protect such information that is confidential from any disclosure that would prejudice the competitive position of the investor or its covered investment. Nothing in this paragraph shall be construed to prevent a Party from otherwise obtaining or disclosing information in connection with the equitable and good faith application of its law.

Article 14.14: Denial of Benefits

1. A Party may deny the benefits of this Chapter to an investor of another Party that is an enterprise of that other Party and to investments of that investor if the enterprise:

   (a) is owned or controlled by a person of a non-Party or of the denying Party; and

   (b) has no substantial business activities in the territory of any Party other than the denying Party.

2. A Party may deny the benefits of this Chapter to an investor of another Party that is an enterprise of that other Party and to investments of that investor if persons of a non-Party own or control the enterprise and the denying Party adopts or maintains measures with respect to the non- Party or a person of the non-Party that prohibit transactions with the enterprise or that would be violated or circumvented if the benefits of this Chapter were accorded to the enterprise or to its investments.

Article 14.15: Subrogation

If a Party, or an agency of a Party, makes a payment to an investor of the Party under a guarantee, a contract of insurance, or other form of indemnity that it has entered into with respect to a covered investment, the other Party in whose territory the covered investment was made shall recognize the subrogation or transfer of any right the investor would have possessed with respect to the covered investment but for the subrogation, and the investor shall be precluded from pursuing that right to the extent of the subrogation, unless a Party or an agency of a Party authorizes the investor to act on its behalf.

Article 14.16: Investment and Environmental, Health, Safety, and other Regulatory Objectives

Nothing in this Chapter shall be construed to prevent a Party from adopting, maintaining, or enforcing any measure otherwise consistent with this Chapter that it considers appropriate to ensure that investment activity in its territory is undertaken in a manner sensitive to environmental, health, safety, or other regulatory objectives.

Article 14.17: Corporate Social Responsibility

The Parties reaffirm the importance of each Party encouraging enterprises operating within its territory or subject to its jurisdiction to voluntarily incorporate into their internal policies those internationally recognized standards, guidelines, and principles of corporate social responsibility that have been endorsed or are supported by that Party, which may include the OECD Guidelines for Multinational Enterprises. These standards, guidelines, and principles may address areas such as labor, environment, gender equality, human rights, indigenous and aboriginal peoples' rights, and corruption.

ANNEX 14-A CUSTOMARY INTERNATIONAL LAW

The Parties confirm their shared understanding that "customary international law" generally and as specifically referenced in Article 14.6 (Minimum Standard of Treatment) results from a general and consistent practice of States that they follow from a sense of legal obligation. The customary international law minimum standard of treatment of aliens refers to all customary international law principles that protect the investments of aliens.

ANNEX 14-B EXPROPRIATION

The Parties confirm their shared understanding that:
1. An action or a series of actions by a Party cannot constitute an expropriation unless it interferes with a tangible or intangible property right or property interest in an investment.
2. Article 14.8.1 (Expropriation and Compensation) addresses two situations. The first is direct expropriation, in which an investment is nationalized or otherwise directly expropriated through formal transfer of title or outright seizure.
3. The second situation addressed by Article 14.8.1 (Expropriation and Compensation) is indirect expropriation, in which an action or series of actions by a Party has an effect equivalent to direct expropriation without formal transfer of title or outright seizure.
   (a) The determination of whether an action or series of actions by a Party, in a specific fact situation, constitutes an indirect expropriation, requires a case-by-case, fact- based inquiry that considers, among other factors:
      (i) the economic impact of the government action, although the fact that an action or series of actions by a Party has an adverse effect on the economic value of an investment, standing alone, does not establish that an indirect expropriation has occurred,
      (ii) the extent to which the government action interferes with distinct, reasonable investment-backed expectations, and
      (iii) the character of the government action, including its object, context, and intent.
   (b) Non-discriminatory regulatory actions by a Party that are designed and applied to protect legitimate public welfare objectives, such as health, safety and the environment, do not constitute indirect expropriations, except in rare circumstances.

ANNEX 14-C LEGACY INVESTMENT CLAIMS AND PENDING CLAIMS
1. Each Party consents, with respect to a legacy investment, to the submission of a claim to arbitration in accordance with Section B of Chapter 11 (Investment) of NAFTA 1994 and this Annex alleging breach of an obligation under:
   (a) Section A of Chapter 11 (Investment) of NAFTA 1994;
   (b) Article 1503(2) (State Enterprises) of NAFTA 1994; and
   (c) Article 1502(3)(a) (Monopolies and State Enterprises) of NAFTA 1994 where the monopoly has acted in a manner inconsistent with the Party's obligations under Section A of Chapter 11 (Investment) of NAFTA 1994.
2. The consent under paragraph 1 and the submission of a claim to arbitration in accordance with Section B of Chapter 11 (Investment) of NAFTA 1994 and this Annex shall satisfy the requirements of:
   (a) Chapter II of the ICSID Convention (Jurisdiction of the Centre) and the ICSID Additional Facility Rules for written consent of the parties to the dispute;
   (b) Article II of the New York Convention for an "agreement in writing"; and
   (c) Article I of the Inter-American Convention for an "agreement".
3. A Party's consent under paragraph 1 shall expire three years after the termination of NAFTA 1994.

4. For greater certainty, an arbitration initiated pursuant to the submission of a claim under paragraph 1 may proceed to its conclusion in accordance with Section B of Chapter 11 (Investment) of NAFTA 1994, the Tribunal's jurisdiction with respect to such a claim is not affected by the expiration of consent referenced in paragraph 3, and Article 1136 (Finality and Enforcement of an Award) of NAFTA 1994 (excluding paragraph 5) applies with respect to any award made by the Tribunal.
5. For greater certainty, an arbitration initiated pursuant to the submission of a claim under Section B of Chapter 11 (Investment) of NAFTA 1994 while NAFTA 1994 is in force may proceed to its conclusion in accordance with Section B of Chapter 11 (Investment) of NAFTA 1994, the Tribunal's jurisdiction with respect to such a claim is not affected by the termination of NAFTA 1994, and Article 1136 of NAFTA 1994 (excluding paragraph 5) applies with respect to any award made by the Tribunal.
6. For the purposes of this Annex:
  (a) "legacy investment" means an investment of an investor of another Party in the territory of the Party established or acquired between January 1, 1994, and the date of termination of NAFTA 1994, and in existence on the date of entry into force of this Agreement;
  (b) "investment", "investor", and "Tribunal" have the meanings accorded in Chapter 11 (Investment) of NAFTA 1994; and
  (c) "ICSID Convention", "ICSID Additional Facility Rules", "New York Convention", and "Inter-American Convention" have the meanings accorded in Article 14.D.1 (Definitions).

ANNEX 14-D MEXICO-UNITED STATES INVESTMENT DISPUTES

Article 14.D.1: Definitions

For the purposes of this Annex:

Annex Party means Mexico or the United States;

Centre means the International Centre for Settlement of Investment Disputes (ICSID) established by the ICSID Convention;

claimant means an investor of an Annex Party that is a party to a qualifying investment dispute, excluding an investor that is owned or controlled by a person of a non-Annex Party that, on the date of signature of this Agreement, the other Annex Party has determined to be a non-market economy for purposes of its trade remedy laws and with which no Party has a free trade agreement;

disputing parties means the claimant and the respondent;

disputing party means either the claimant or the respondent;

ICSID Additional Facility Rules means the Rules Governing the Additional Facility for the Administration of Proceedings by the Secretariat of the International Centre for Settlement of Investment Disputes;

ICSID Convention means the Convention on the Settlement of Investment Disputes between States and Nationals of other States, done at Washington, March 18, 1965;

Inter-American Convention means the *Inter-American Convention on International Commercial Arbitration*, done at Panama, January 30, 1975;

New York Convention means the Convention on the Recognition and Enforcement of Foreign Arbitral Awards, done at New York, June 10, 1958;

non-disputing Annex Party means the Annex Party that is not a party to a qualifying investment dispute;

protected information means confidential business information or information that is privileged or otherwise protected from disclosure under a Party's law, including classified government information;

qualifying investment dispute means an investment dispute between an investor of an Annex Party and the other Annex Party;

respondent means the Annex Party that is a party to a qualifying investment dispute;

Secretary-General means the Secretary-General of ICSID; and

UNCITRAL Arbitration Rules means the arbitration rules of the United Nations Commission on International Trade Law.

Article 14.D.2: Consultation and Negotiation

1. In the event of a qualifying investment dispute, the claimant and the respondent should initially seek to resolve the dispute through consultation and negotiation, which may include the use of non-binding, third party procedures, such as good offices, conciliation, or mediation.
2. For greater certainty, the initiation of consultations and negotiations shall not be construed as recognition of the jurisdiction of the tribunal.

Article 14.D.3: Submission of a Claim to Arbitration

1. In the event that a disputing party considers that a qualifying investment dispute cannot be settled by consultation and negotiation:
   (a) the claimant, on its own behalf, may submit to arbitration under this Annex a claim:
      (i) that the respondent has breached:
         (A) Article 14.4 (National Treatment) or Article 14.5 (Most-Favored-Nation Treatment), except with respect to the establishment or acquisition of an investment, or
         (B) Article 14.8 (Expropriation and Compensation), except with respect to indirect expropriation, and
      (ii) that the claimant has incurred loss or damage by reason of, or arising out of, that breach; and
   (b) the claimant, on behalf of an enterprise of the respondent that is a juridical person that the claimant owns or controls directly or indirectly, may submit to arbitration under this Annex a claim:
      (i) that the respondent has breached:
         (A) Article 14.4 (National Treatment) or Article 14.5 (Most-Favored-Nation Treatment), except with respect to the establishment or acquisition of an investment, or
         (B) Article 14.8 (Expropriation and Compensation), except with respect to indirect expropriation, and
      (ii) that the enterprise has incurred loss or damage by reason of, or arising out of, that breach.
2. At least 90 days before submitting any claim to arbitration under this Annex, the claimant shall deliver to the respondent a written notice of its intention to submit a claim to arbitration (notice of intent). The notice shall specify:
   (a) the name and address of the claimant and, if a claim is submitted on behalf of an enterprise, the name, address, and place of incorporation of the enterprise;
   (b) for each claim, the provision of this Agreement alleged to have been breached and any other relevant provisions;
   (c) the legal and factual basis for each claim; and
   (d) the relief sought and the approximate amount of damages claimed.
3. The claimant may submit a claim referred to in paragraph 1 under one of the following alternatives:
   (a) the ICSID Convention and the ICSID Rules of Procedure for Arbitration Proceedings, provided that both the respondent and the Party of the claimant are parties to the ICSID Convention;
   (b) the ICSID Additional Facility Rules, provided that either the respondent or the Party of the claimant is a party to the ICSID Convention;
   (c) the UNCITRAL Arbitration Rules; or
   (d) if the claimant and respondent agree, any other arbitral institution or any other arbitration rules.
4. A claim shall be deemed submitted to arbitration under this Annex when the claimant's notice of or request for arbitration (notice of arbitration):
   (a) referred to in the ICSID Convention is received by the Secretary-General;

(b) referred to in the ICSID Additional Facility Rules is received by the Secretary- General;
(c) referred to in the UNCITRAL Arbitration Rules, together with the statement of claim referred to therein, are received by the respondent; or
(d) referred to under any arbitral institution or arbitration rules selected under paragraph 3(d) is received by the respondent.

A claim asserted by the claimant for the first time after such notice of arbitration is submitted shall be deemed submitted to arbitration under this Annex on the date of its receipt under the applicable arbitration rules.

5. The arbitration rules applicable under paragraph 3 that are in effect on the date the claim or claims were submitted to arbitration under this Annex shall govern the arbitration except to the extent modified by this Agreement.

6. The claimant shall provide with the notice of arbitration:
(a) the name of the arbitrator that the claimant appoints; or
(b) the claimant's written consent for the Secretary-General to appoint that arbitrator.

Article 14.D.4: Consent to Arbitration

1. Each Annex Party consents to the submission of a claim to arbitration under this Annex in accordance with this Agreement.

2. The consent under paragraph 1 and the submission of a claim to arbitration under this Annex shall be deemed to satisfy the requirements of:
(a) Chapter II of the ICSID Convention (Jurisdiction of the Centre) and the ICSID Additional Facility Rules for written consent of the parties to the dispute;
(b) Article II of the New York Convention for an "agreement in writing"; and
(c) Article I of the Inter-American Convention for an "agreement".

Article 14.D.5: Conditions and Limitations on Consent

1. No claim shall be submitted to arbitration under this Annex unless:
(a) the claimant (for claims brought under Article 14.D.3.1(a) (Submission of a Claim to Arbitration)) and the claimant or the enterprise (for claims brought under Article 14.D.3.1(b)) first initiated a proceeding before a competent court or administrative tribunal of the respondent with respect to the measures alleged to constitute a breach referred to in Article 14.D.3;
(b) the claimant or the enterprise obtained a final decision from a court of last resort of the respondent or 30 months have elapsed from the date the proceeding in subparagraph (a) was initiated;
(c) no more than four years have elapsed from the date on which the claimant first acquired, or should have first acquired, knowledge of the breach alleged under Article 14.D.3.1 (Submission of a Claim to Arbitration) and knowledge that the claimant (for claims brought under Article 14.D.3.1(a)) or the enterprise (for claims brought under Article 14.D.3.1(b)) has incurred loss or damage;
(d) the claimant consents in writing to arbitration in accordance with the procedures set out in this Agreement; and
(e) the notice of arbitration is accompanied:
  (i) for claims submitted to arbitration under Article 14.D.3.1(a) (Submission of a Claim to Arbitration), by the claimant's written waiver, and
  (ii) for claims submitted to arbitration under Article 14.D.3.1(b) (Submission of a Claim to Arbitration), by the claimant's and the enterprise's written waivers,

of any right to initiate or continue before any court or administrative tribunal under the law of an Annex Party, or any other dispute settlement procedures, any proceeding with respect to any measure alleged to constitute a breach referred to in Article 14.D.3 (Submission of a Claim to Arbitration).

2. Notwithstanding paragraph 1(e), the claimant (for claims brought under Article 14.D.3.1(a) (Submission of a Claim to Arbitration)) and the claimant or the enterprise (for claims brought under Article 14.D.3.1(b)) may initiate or continue an action that seeks interim injunctive relief and does not involve the payment of monetary damages before a judicial or administrative tribunal of the respondent, provided that the action is brought for the sole purpose of preserving the claimant's or the enterprise's rights and interests during the pendency of the arbitration.

Article 14.D.6: Selection of Arbitrators

1. Unless the disputing parties agree otherwise, the tribunal shall comprise three arbitrators, one arbitrator appointed by each of the disputing parties and the third, who shall be the presiding arbitrator, appointed by agreement of the disputing parties.
2. The Secretary-General shall serve as appointing authority for an arbitration under this Annex.
3. If a tribunal has not been constituted within a period of 75 days after the date that a claim is submitted to arbitration under this Annex, the Secretary-General, on the request of a disputing party, shall appoint, in his or her discretion, the arbitrator or arbitrators not yet appointed. The Secretary-General shall not appoint a national of either the respondent or the Party of the claimant as the presiding arbitrator unless the disputing parties agree otherwise.
4. For the purposes of Article 39 of the ICSID Convention and Article 7 of Schedule C to the ICSID Additional Facility Rules, and without prejudice to an objection to an arbitrator on a ground other than nationality:
   (a) the respondent agrees to the appointment of each individual member of a tribunal established under the ICSID Convention or the ICSID Additional Facility Rules;
   (b) a claimant referred to in Article 14.D.3.1(a) (Submission of a Claim to Arbitration) may submit a claim to arbitration under this Annex, or continue a claim, under the ICSID Convention or the ICSID Additional Facility Rules, only on condition that the claimant agrees in writing to the appointment of each individual member of the tribunal; and
   (c) a claimant referred to in Article 14.D.3.1(b) (Submission of a Claim to Arbitration) may submit a claim to arbitration under this Annex, or continue a claim, under the ICSID Convention or the ICSID Additional Facility Rules, only on condition that the claimant and the enterprise agree in writing to the appointment of each individual member of the tribunal.
5. Arbitrators appointed to a tribunal for claims submitted under Article 14.D.3.1 shall:
   (a) comply with the International Bar Association Guidelines on Conflicts of Interest in International Arbitration, including guidelines regarding direct or indirect conflicts of interest, or any supplemental guidelines or rules adopted by the Annex Parties;
   (b) not take instructions from any organization or government regarding the dispute; and
   (c) not, for the duration of the proceedings, act as counsel or as party-appointed expert or witness in any pending arbitration under the annexes to this Chapter.
6. Challenges to arbitrators shall be governed by the procedures in the UNCITRAL Arbitration Rules.

Article 14.D.7: Conduct of the Arbitration

1. The disputing parties may agree on the legal place of any arbitration under the arbitration rules applicable under Article 14.D.3.3 (Submission of a Claim to Arbitration). If the disputing parties fail to reach agreement, the tribunal shall determine the place in accordance with the applicable arbitration rules, provided that the place shall be in the territory of a State that is a party to the New York Convention.
2. The non-disputing Annex Party may make oral and written submissions to the tribunal regarding the interpretation of this Agreement.
3. After consultation with the disputing parties, the tribunal may accept and consider written amicus curiae submissions regarding a matter of fact or law within the scope of the dispute that may assist the

tribunal in evaluating the submissions and arguments of the disputing parties from a person or entity that is not a disputing party but has a significant interest in the arbitral proceedings. Each submission shall identify the author; disclose any affiliation, direct or indirect, with any disputing party; and identify any person, government, or other entity that has provided, or will provide, any financial or other assistance in preparing the submission. Each submission shall be in a language of the arbitration and comply with any page limits and deadlines set by the tribunal. The tribunal shall provide the disputing parties with an opportunity to respond to such submissions. The tribunal shall ensure that the submissions do not disrupt or unduly burden the arbitral proceedings, or unfairly prejudice any disputing party.

4. Without prejudice to a tribunal's authority to address other objections as a preliminary question, such as an objection that a dispute is not within the competence of the tribunal, including an objection to the tribunal's jurisdiction, a tribunal shall address and decide as a preliminary question any objection by the respondent that, as a matter of law, a claim submitted is not a claim for which an award in favor of the claimant may be made under Article 14.D.13 (Awards) or that a claim is manifestly without legal merit.

(a) An objection under this paragraph shall be submitted to the tribunal as soon as possible after the tribunal is constituted, and in no event later than the date the tribunal fixes for the respondent to submit its counter-memorial or, in the case of an amendment to the notice of arbitration, the date the tribunal fixes for the respondent to submit its response to the amendment.

(b) On receipt of an objection under this paragraph, the tribunal shall suspend any proceedings on the merits, establish a schedule for considering the objection consistent with any schedule it has established for considering any other preliminary question, and issue a decision or award on the objection, stating the grounds therefor.

(c) In deciding an objection under this paragraph that a claim submitted is not a claim for which an award in favor of the claimant may be made under Article 14.D.13 (Awards), the tribunal shall assume to be true the claimant's factual allegations in support of any claim in the notice of arbitration (or any amendment thereof) and, in disputes brought under the UNCITRAL Arbitration Rules, the statement of claim referred to in the relevant article of the UNCITRAL Arbitration Rules. The tribunal may also consider any relevant facts not in dispute.

(d) The respondent does not waive any objection as to competence, including an objection to jurisdiction, or any argument on the merits merely because the respondent did or did not raise an objection under this paragraph or make use of the expedited procedure set out in paragraph 5.

5. In the event that the respondent so requests within 45 days after the tribunal is constituted, the tribunal shall decide on an expedited basis an objection under paragraph 4 or any objection that the dispute is not within the tribunal's competence, including an objection that the dispute is not within the tribunal's jurisdiction. The tribunal shall suspend any proceedings on the merits and issue a decision or award on the objection, stating the grounds therefor, no later than 150 days after the date of the request. However, if a disputing party requests a hearing, the tribunal may take an additional 30 days to issue the decision or award. Regardless of whether a hearing is requested, a tribunal may, on a showing of extraordinary cause, delay issuing its decision or award by an additional brief period, which may not exceed 30 days.

6. When the tribunal decides a respondent's objection under paragraph 4 or 5, it may, if warranted, award to the prevailing disputing party reasonable costs and attorney's fees incurred in submitting or opposing the objection. In determining whether such an award is warranted, the tribunal shall consider whether either the claimant's claim or the respondent's objection was frivolous, and shall provide the disputing parties a reasonable opportunity to comment.

7. For greater certainty, if an investor of an Annex Party submits a claim under this Annex, the investor has the burden of proving all elements of its claims, consistent with general principles of international law applicable to international arbitration.

8. A respondent may not assert as a defense, counterclaim, right of set-off, or for any other reason, that the claimant has received or will receive indemnification or other compensation for all or part of the alleged damages pursuant to an insurance or guarantee contract.
9. A tribunal may order an interim measure of protection to preserve the rights of a disputing party, or to ensure that the tribunal's jurisdiction is made fully effective, including an order to preserve evidence in the possession or control of a disputing party or to protect the tribunal's jurisdiction. A tribunal may not order attachment or enjoin the application of a measure alleged to constitute a breach referred to in Article 14.D.3 (Submission of a Claim to Arbitration). For the purposes of this paragraph, an order includes a recommendation.
10. The tribunal and the disputing parties shall endeavor to conduct the arbitration in an expeditious and cost-effective manner.
11. Following the submission of a claim to arbitration under this Annex, if the disputing parties fail to take any steps in the proceedings for more than 150 days, or such period as they may agree with the approval of the tribunal, the tribunal shall notify the disputing parties that they shall be deemed to have discontinued the proceedings if the parties fail to take any steps within 30 days after the notice is received. If the parties fail to take any steps within that time period, the tribunal shall take note of the discontinuance in an order. If a tribunal has not yet been constituted, the Secretary-General shall assume these responsibilities.
12. In any arbitration conducted under this Annex, at the request of a disputing party, a tribunal shall, before issuing a decision or award on liability, transmit its proposed decision or award to the disputing parties. Within 60 days after the tribunal transmits its proposed decision or award, the disputing parties may submit written comments to the tribunal concerning any aspect of its proposed decision or award. The tribunal shall consider any comments and issue its decision or award no later than 45 days after the expiration of the 60 day comment period.

Article 14.D.8: Transparency of Arbitral Proceedings
1. Subject to paragraphs 2 and 4, the respondent shall, after receiving the following documents, promptly transmit them to the non-disputing Annex Party and make them available to the public:
- (a) the notice of intent;
- (b) the notice of arbitration;
- (c) pleadings, memorials, and briefs submitted to the tribunal by a disputing party and any written submissions submitted pursuant to Article 14.D.7.2 and 14.D.7.3 (Conduct of the Arbitration), and Article 14.D.12 (Consolidation);
- (d) minutes or transcripts of hearings of the tribunal, if available; and
- (e) orders, awards, and decisions of the tribunal.

2. The tribunal shall conduct hearings open to the public and shall determine, in consultation with the disputing parties, the appropriate logistical arrangements. If a disputing party intends to use information in a hearing that is designated as protected information or otherwise subject to paragraph 3 it shall so advise the tribunal. The tribunal shall make appropriate arrangements to protect such information from disclosure which may include closing the hearing for the duration of the discussion of that information.
3. Nothing in this Annex, including paragraph 4(d), requires a respondent to make available to the public or otherwise disclose during or after the arbitral proceedings, including the hearing, protected information, or to furnish or allow access to information that it may withhold in accordance with Article 32.2 (Essential Security) or Article 32.7 (Disclosure of Information).
4. Any protected information that is submitted to the tribunal shall be protected from disclosure in accordance with the following procedures:

(a) subject to subparagraph (d), neither the disputing parties nor the tribunal shall disclose to the non-disputing Annex Party or to the public any protected information if the disputing party that provided the information clearly designates it in accordance with subparagraph (b);
(b) any disputing party claiming that certain information constitutes protected information shall clearly designate the information according to any schedule set by the tribunal;
(c) a disputing party shall, according to any schedule set by the tribunal, submit a redacted version of the document that does not contain the protected information. Only the redacted version shall be disclosed in accordance with paragraph 1; and
(d) the tribunal, subject to paragraph 3, shall decide any objection regarding the designation of information claimed to be protected information. If the tribunal determines that the information was not properly designated, the disputing party that submitted the information may:
   (i) withdraw all or part of its submission containing that information, or
   (ii) agree to resubmit complete and redacted documents with corrected designations in accordance with the tribunal's determination and subparagraph (c).

In either case, the other disputing party shall, whenever necessary, resubmit complete and redacted documents which either remove the information withdrawn under subparagraph (d)(i) by the disputing party that first submitted the information or redesignate the information consistent with the designation under subparagraph (d)(ii) of the disputing party that first submitted the information.
5. Nothing in this Annex requires a respondent to withhold from the public information required to be disclosed by its laws. The respondent should endeavor to apply those laws in a manner sensitive to protecting from disclosure information that has been designated as protected information.

Article 14.D.9: Governing Law

1. Subject to paragraph 2, when a claim is submitted under Article 14.D.3.1 (Submission of a Claim to Arbitration), the tribunal shall decide the issues in dispute in accordance with this Agreement and applicable rules of international law.
2. A decision of the Commission on the interpretation of a provision of this Agreement under Article 30.2 (Functions of the Commission) shall be binding on a tribunal, and any decision or award issued by a tribunal must be consistent with that decision.

Article 14.D.10: Interpretation of Annexes

1. If a respondent asserts as a defense that the measure alleged to be a breach is within the scope of a non-conforming measure set out in Annex I or Annex II, the tribunal shall, on request of the respondent, request the interpretation of the Commission on the issue. The Commission shall submit in writing any decision on its interpretation under Article 30.2 (Functions of the Commission) to the tribunal within 90 days of delivery of the request.
2. A decision issued by the Commission under paragraph 1 shall be binding on the tribunal, and any decision or award issued by the tribunal must be consistent with that decision. If the Commission fails to issue such a decision within 90 days, the tribunal shall decide the issue.

Article 14.D.11: Expert Reports

Without prejudice to the appointment of other kinds of experts when authorized by the applicable arbitration rules, a tribunal, on request of a disputing party or, unless the disputing parties disapprove, on its own initiative, may appoint one or more experts to report to it in writing on any factual issue concerning scientific matters raised by a disputing party in a proceeding, subject to any terms and conditions that the disputing parties may agree.

Article 14.D.12: Consolidation

1. If two or more claims have been submitted separately to arbitration under Article 14.D.3.1 (Submission of a Claim to Arbitration) and the claims have a question of law or fact in common and arise out of the same events or circumstances, any disputing party may seek a consolidation order in accordance with the agreement of all the disputing parties sought to be covered by the order or the terms of paragraphs 2 through 10.

2. A disputing party that seeks a consolidation order under this Article shall deliver, in writing, a request to the Secretary-General and to all the disputing parties sought to be covered by the order and shall specify in the request:

(a) the names and addresses of all the disputing parties sought to be covered by the order;
(b) the nature of the order sought; and
(c) the grounds on which the order is sought.

3. Unless the Secretary-General finds within a period of 30 days after the date of receiving a request under paragraph 2 that the request is manifestly unfounded, a tribunal shall be established under this Article.

4. Unless all the disputing parties sought to be covered by the order agree otherwise, a tribunal established under this Article shall comprise three arbitrators:

(a) one arbitrator appointed by agreement of the claimants;
(b) one arbitrator appointed by the respondent; and
(c) the presiding arbitrator appointed by the Secretary-General, provided that the presiding arbitrator is not a national of the respondent or of the Party of the claimants.

5. If, within a period of 60 days after the date when the Secretary-General receives a request made under paragraph 2, the respondent fails or the claimants fail to appoint an arbitrator in accordance with paragraph 4, the Secretary-General, on request of any disputing party sought to be covered by the order, shall appoint, in his or her discretion, the arbitrator or arbitrators not yet appointed.

6. If a tribunal established under this Article is satisfied that two or more claims that have been submitted to arbitration under Article 14.D.3.1 (Submission of a Claim to Arbitration) have a question of law or fact in common, and arise out of the same events or circumstances, the tribunal may, in the interest of fair and efficient resolution of the claims, and after hearing the disputing parties, by order:

(a) assume jurisdiction over, and hear and determine together, all or part of the claims;
(b) assume jurisdiction over, and hear and determine one or more of the claims, the determination of which it believes would assist in the resolution of the others; or
(c) instruct a tribunal previously established under Article 14.D.6 (Selection of Arbitrators) to assume jurisdiction over, and hear and determine together, all or part of the claims, provided that:
  (i) that tribunal, on request of a claimant that was not previously a disputing party before that tribunal, shall be reconstituted with its original members, except that the arbitrator for the claimants shall be appointed pursuant to paragraphs 4(a) and 5, and
  (ii) that tribunal shall decide whether a prior hearing shall be repeated.

7. If a tribunal has been established under this Article, a claimant that has submitted a claim to arbitration under Article 14.D.3.1 (Submission of a Claim to Arbitration) and that has not been named in a request made under paragraph 2 may make a written request to the tribunal that it be included in any order made under paragraph 6. The request shall specify:

(a) the name and address of the claimant;
(b) the nature of the order sought; and
(c) the grounds on which the order is sought.

The claimant shall deliver a copy of its request to the Secretary-General.

8. A tribunal established under this Article shall conduct its proceedings in accordance with the UNCITRAL Arbitration Rules, except as modified by this Annex.

9. A tribunal established under Article 14.D.6 (Selection of Arbitrators) shall not have jurisdiction to decide a claim, or a part of a claim, over which a tribunal established or instructed under this Article has assumed jurisdiction.
10. On the application of a disputing party, a tribunal established under this Article, pending its decision under paragraph 6, may order that the proceedings of a tribunal established under Article 14.D.6 (Selection of Arbitrators) be stayed, unless the latter tribunal has already adjourned its proceedings.

Article 14.D.13: Awards
1. When a tribunal makes a final award, the tribunal may award, separately or in combination, only:
   (a) monetary damages and any applicable interest; and
   (b) restitution of property, in which case the award shall provide that the respondent may pay monetary damages and any applicable interest in lieu of restitution.
2. For greater certainty, if an investor of an Annex Party submits a claim to arbitration under Article 14.D.3.1 (Submission of a Claim to Arbitration), it may recover only for loss or damage that is established on the basis of satisfactory evidence and that is not inherently speculative.
3. For greater certainty, if an investor of an Annex Party submits a claim to arbitration under Article 14.D.3.1(a) (Submission of a Claim to Arbitration), it may recover only for loss or damage incurred in its capacity as an investor of an Annex Party.
4. A tribunal may also award costs and attorney's fees incurred by the disputing parties in connection with the arbitral proceedings, and shall determine how and by whom those costs and attorney's fees shall be paid, in accordance with this Annex and the applicable arbitration rules.
5. Subject to paragraph 1, if a claim is submitted to arbitration under Article 14.D.3.1(b) (Submission of a Claim to Arbitration) and an award is made in favor of the enterprise:
   (a) an award of restitution of property shall provide that restitution be made to the enterprise;
   (b) an award of monetary damages and any applicable interest shall provide that the sum be paid to the enterprise; and
   (c) the award shall provide that it is made without prejudice to any right that any person may have under applicable domestic law with respect to the relief provided in the award.
6. A tribunal shall not award punitive damages.
7. An award made by a tribunal has no binding force except between the disputing parties and in respect of the particular case.
8. Subject to paragraph 9 and the applicable review procedure for an interim award, a disputing party shall abide by and comply with an award without delay.
9. A disputing party shall not seek enforcement of a final award until:
   (a) in the case of a final award made under the ICSID Convention:
      (i) 120 days have elapsed from the date the award was rendered and no disputing party has requested revision or annulment of the award, or
      (ii) revision or annulment proceedings have been completed; and
   (b) in the case of a final award under the ICSID Additional Facility Rules, the UNCITRAL Arbitration Rules, or the rules selected pursuant to Article 14.D.3.3(d) (Submission of a Claim to Arbitration):
      (i) 90 days have elapsed from the date the award was rendered and no disputing party has commenced a proceeding to revise, set aside or annul the award, or
      (ii) a court has dismissed or allowed an application to revise, set aside or annul the award and there is no further appeal.
10. Each Annex Party shall provide for the enforcement of an award in its territory.
11. If the respondent fails to abide by or comply with a final award, on delivery of a request by the Party of the claimant, a panel shall be established under Article 31.6 (Establishment of a Panel). The requesting Party may seek in those proceedings:

(a) a determination that the failure to abide by or comply with the final award is inconsistent with the obligations of this Agreement; and
(b) in accordance with Article 31.17 (Panel Report), a recommendation that the respondent abide by or comply with the final award.

12. A disputing party may seek enforcement of an arbitration award under the ICSID Convention, the New York Convention, or the Inter-American Convention regardless of whether proceedings have been taken under paragraph 11.
13. A claim that is submitted to arbitration under this Annex shall be considered to arise out of a commercial relationship or transaction for the purposes of Article I of the New York Convention and Article I of the Inter-American Convention.

Article 14.D.14: Service of Documents
Delivery of notice and other documents to an Annex Party shall be made to the place named for that Annex Party in Appendix 1 (Service of Documents on an Annex Party). An Annex Party shall promptly make publicly available and notify the other Annex Party of any change to the place referred to in that Appendix.

APPENDIX 1 SERVICE OF DOCUMENTS ON AN ANNEX PARTY

Mexico

Notices and other documents in disputes under this Annex shall be served on Mexico by delivery to:
Dirección General de Consultoría Jurídica de Comercio Internacional Secretaría de Economía
Pachuca #189, piso 19 Col. Condesa
Demarcación Territorial Cuauhtémoc Ciudad de México
C.P. 06140

United States

Notices and other documents in disputes under this Annex shall be served on the United States by delivery to:
Executive Director (L/H-EX)
Office of the Legal Adviser & Bureau of Legislative Affairs
U.S. Department of State 600 19th Street, NW Washington, D.C. 20552

APPENDIX 2 PUBLIC DEBT

1. For greater certainty, no award shall be made in favor of a claimant for a claim under Article 14.D.3.1 (Submission of a Claim to Arbitration) with respect to default or non-payment of debt issued by a Party unless the claimant meets its burden of proving that such default or non- payment constitutes a breach of a relevant obligation in the Chapter.
2. No claim that a restructuring of debt issued by a Party, standing alone, breaches an obligation in this Chapter shall be submitted to arbitration under Article 14.D.3.1 (Submission of a Claim to Arbitration), provided that the restructuring is effected as provided for under the debt instrument's terms, including the debt instrument's governing law.

APPENDIX 3 SUBMISSION OF A CLAIM TO ARBITRATION

An investor of the United States may not submit to arbitration a claim that Mexico has breached an obligation under this Chapter either:

(a) on its own behalf under Article 14.D.3.1(a) (Submission of a Claim to Arbitration); or

(b) on behalf of an enterprise of Mexico that is a juridical person that the investor owns or controls directly or indirectly under Article 14.D.3.1(b) (Submission of a Claim to Arbitration),

if the investor or the enterprise, respectively, has alleged that breach of an obligation under this Chapter, as distinguished from breach of other obligations under Mexican law, in proceedings before a court or administrative tribunal of Mexico.

ANNEX 14-E MEXICO-UNITED STATES INVESTMENT DISPUTES RELATED TO COVERED GOVERNMENT CONTRACTS

1. Annex 14-D (Mexico-United States Investment Disputes) applies as modified by this Annex to the settlement of a qualifying investment dispute under this Chapter in the circumstances set out in paragraph 2.

2. In the event that a disputing party considers that a qualifying investment dispute cannot be settled by consultation and negotiation:

(a) the claimant, on its own behalf, may submit to arbitration under Annex 14-D (Mexico-United States Investment Disputes) a claim:

(i) that the respondent has breached any obligation under this Chapter, provided that:

(A) the claimant is:

(1) a party to a covered government contract, or

(2) engaged in activities in the same covered sector in the territory of the respondent as an enterprise of the respondent that the claimant owns or controls directly or indirectly and that is a party to a covered government contract, and

(B) the respondent is a party to another international trade or investment agreement that permits investors to initiate dispute settlement procedures to resolve an investment dispute with a government, and

(ii) that the claimant has incurred loss or damage by reason of, or arising out of, that breach;

(b) the claimant, on behalf of an enterprise of the respondent that is a juridical person that the claimant owns or controls directly or indirectly, may submit to arbitration under Annex 14-D (Mexico-United States Investment Disputes) a claim:

(i) that the respondent has breached any obligation under this Chapter, provided that:

(A) the enterprise is:

(1) a party to a covered government contract,

(2) engaged in activities in the same covered sector in the territory of the respondent as the claimant and the claimant is a party to a covered government contract, or

(3) engaged in activities in the same covered sector in the territory of the respondent as another enterprise of the respondent that the claimant owns or controls directly or indirectly and that is a party to a covered government contract, and

(B) the respondent is a party to another international trade or investment agreement that permits investors to initiate dispute settlement procedures to resolve an investment dispute with a government, and

(ii) that the enterprise has incurred loss or damage by reason of, or arising out of, that breach.

3. For the purposes of paragraph 2, if a covered government contract is terminated in a manner inconsistent with an obligation under this Chapter, the claimant or enterprise that was previously a

party to the contract shall be deemed to remain a party for the duration of the contract, as if it had not been terminated.

4. No claim shall be submitted to arbitration under paragraph 2 if:
   (a) less than six months have elapsed from the events giving rise to the claim; and
   (b) more than three years have elapsed from the date on which the claimant first acquired, or should have first acquired, knowledge of the breach alleged under paragraph 2 and knowledge that the claimant (for claims brought under paragraph 2(a)) or the enterprise (for claims brought under paragraph 2(b)) has incurred loss or damage.
5. For greater certainty, the Annex Parties may agree to modify or eliminate this Annex.
6. For the purposes of this Annex:
   (a) "covered government contract" means a written agreement between a national authority of an Annex Party and a covered investment or investor of the other Annex Party, on which the covered investment or investor relies in establishing or acquiring a covered investment other than the written agreement itself, that grants rights to the covered investment or investor in a covered sector;
   (b) "covered sector" means:
      (i) activities with respect to oil and natural gas that a national authority of an Annex Party controls, such as exploration, extraction, refining, transportation, distribution, or sale,
      (ii) the supply of power generation services to the public on behalf of an Annex Party,
      (iii) the supply of telecommunications services to the public on behalf of an Annex Party,
      (iv) the supply of transportation services to the public on behalf of an Annex Party, or
      (v) the ownership or management of roads, railways, bridges, or canals that are not for the exclusive or predominant use and benefit of the government of an Annex Party;
   (c) "national authority" means an authority at the central level of government; and
   (d) "written agreement" means an agreement in writing, negotiated, and executed by two or more parties, whether in a single instrument or in multiple instruments.

10.1.5 Comprehensive and Progressive Agreement for Trans-Pacific Partnership ('CPTPP') (2018)

Signed 8 March 2018 entered into force 30 December 2018.

PREAMBLE

The Parties to this Agreement, resolving to:

Reaffirm the matters embodied in the preamble to the Trans-Pacific Partnership Agreement, done at Auckland on 4 February 2016 (hereinafter referred to as "the TPP");

Realise expeditiously the benefits of the TPP through this Agreement and their strategic and economic significance;

Contribute to maintaining open markets, increasing world trade, and creating new economic opportunities for people of all incomes and economic backgrounds;

Promote further regional economic integration and cooperation between them;

Enhance opportunities for the acceleration of regional trade liberalisation and investment;

Reaffirm the importance of promoting corporate social responsibility, cultural identity and diversity, environmental protection and conservation, gender equality, indigenous rights, labour rights, inclusive trade, sustainable development and traditional knowledge, as well as the importance of preserving their right to regulate in the public interest; and

Welcome the accession of other States or separate customs territories to this Agreement,

HAVE AGREED as follows:

Article 1: Incorporation of the Trans-Pacific Partnership Agreement

1. The Parties hereby agree that, under the terms of this Agreement, the provisions of the Trans-Pacific Partnership Agreement, done at Auckland on 4 February 2016 ("the TPP") are incorporated, by reference, into and made part of this Agreement mutatis mutandis, except for Article 30.4 (Accession), Article 30.5 (Entry into Force), Article 30.6 (Withdrawal) and Article 30.8 (Authentic Texts).
2. For the purposes of this Agreement, references to the date of signature in the TPP shall mean the date of signature of this Agreement.
3. In the event of any inconsistency between this Agreement and the TPP, when the latter is in force, this Agreement shall prevail to the extent of the inconsistency.

Article 2: Suspension of the Application of Certain Provisions

Upon the date of entry into force of this Agreement, the Parties shall suspend the application of the provisions set out in the Annex to this Agreement, until the Parties agree to end suspension of one or more of these provisions.

Article 3: Entry into Force

1. This Agreement shall enter into force 60 days after the date on which at least six or at least 50 per cent of the number of signatories to this Agreement, whichever is smaller, have notified the Depositary in writing of the completion of their applicable legal procedures.

2. For any signatory to this Agreement for which this Agreement has not entered into force under paragraph 1, this Agreement shall enter into force 60 days after the date on which that signatory has notified the Depositary in writing of the completion of its applicable legal procedures.

Article 4: Withdrawal
1. Any Party may withdraw from this Agreement by providing written notice of withdrawal to the Depositary. A withdrawing Party shall simultaneously notify the other Parties of its withdrawal through the overall contact points designated under Article 27.5 (Contact Points) of the TPP.
2. A withdrawal shall take effect six months after a Party provides written notice to the Depositary under paragraph 1, unless the Parties agree on a different period. If a Party withdraws, this Agreement shall remain in force for the remaining Parties.

Article 5: Accession
After the date of entry into force of this Agreement, any State or separate customs territory may accede to this Agreement, subject to such terms and conditions as may be agreed between the Parties and that State or separate customs territory.

Article 6: Review of the Comprehensive and Progressive Agreement for Trans-Pacific Partnership
Further to Article 27.2 (Functions of the Commission) of the TPP, if the entry into force of the TPP is imminent or if the TPP is unlikely to enter into force, the Parties shall, on request of a Party, review the operation of this Agreement so as to consider any amendment to this Agreement and any related matters.

Article 7: Authentic Texts
The English, Spanish and French texts of this Agreement are equally authentic. In the event of any divergence between those texts, the English text shall prevail.

In witness whereof the undersigned, being duly authorised by their respective Governments, have signed this Agreement.

DONE at Santiago the eighth day of March, two thousand and eighteen, in the English, French and Spanish languages.

ANNEX[1]

1. Chapter 5 (Customs Administration and Trade Facilitation)
   Article 5.7 (Express Shipments) – paragraph 1 – subparagraph (f): second sentence
2. Chapter 9 (Investment)
   (a) Article 9.1 (Definitions):
      (i) definition of investment agreement including footnotes 5 through 9;
      (ii) definition of investment authorisation including footnotes 10 and 11;
   (b) Article 9.19 (Submission of a Claim to Arbitration)
      (i) paragraph 1:
         (A) subparagraph (a)(i)(B) including footnote 31;
         (B) subparagraph (a)(i)(C);
         (C) subparagraph (b)(i)(B);

1 To assist with the understanding of this Annex, the Parties have used a colon to indicate the specific portion(s) of a provision that has been suspended.

(D) subparagraph (b)(i)(C);

(E) the chaussette "provided that a claimant may submit pursuant to subparagraph (a)(i)(C) or (b)(i)(C) a claim for breach of an investment agreement only if the subject matter of the claim and the claimed damages directly relate to the covered investment that was established or acquired, or sought to be established or acquired, in reliance on the relevant investment agreement.";

(ii) paragraph 2: all of this paragraph including footnote 32;

(iii) paragraph 3 – subparagraph (b): the phrase "investment authorisation or investment agreement";

(c) Article 9.22 (Selection of Arbitrators): paragraph 5;

(d) Article 9.25 (Governing Law): paragraph 2 including footnote 35;

(e) Annex 9-L (Investment Agreements): all of this Annex

3. Chapter 10 (Cross-Border Trade in Services) Annex 10-B (Express Delivery Services):

(a) paragraph 5 including footnote 13;

(b) paragraph 6 including footnote 14

4. Chapter 11 (Financial Services)

(a) Article 11.2 (Scope) – paragraph 2 – subparagraph (b): the phrase "Article 9.6 (Minimum Standard of Treatment)" including footnote 3;

(b) Annex 11-E: all of this Annex

5. Chapter 13 (Telecommunications)

Article 13.21 (Resolution of Telecommunications Disputes) – paragraph 1: subparagraph (d) including the heading "Reconsideration" and footnote 22

6. Chapter 15 (Government Procurement)

(a) Article 15.8 (Conditions for Participation): paragraph 5 including footnote 1;

(b) Article 15.24 (Further Negotiations) – paragraph 2: the phrase "No later than three years after the date of entry into force of this Agreement"[2]

7. Chapter 18 (Intellectual Property)

(a) Article 18.8 (National Treatment): the last two sentences of footnote 4;

(b) Article 18.37 (Patentable Subject Matter)

(i) paragraph 2: all of this paragraph;

(ii) paragraph 4: the last sentence;

(c) Article 18.46 (Patent Term Adjustment for Unreasonable Granting Authority Delays): all of this Article including footnotes 36 through 39;

(d) Article 18.48 (Patent Term Adjustment for Unreasonable Curtailment): all of this Article including footnotes 45 through 48;

(e) Article 18.50 (Protection of Undisclosed Test or Other Data): all of this Article including footnotes 50 through 57;

(f) Article 18.51 (Biologics): all of this Article including footnotes 58 through 60;

(g) Article 18.63 (Term of Protection for Copyright and Related Rights): all of this Article including footnotes 74 through 77;

(h) Article 18.68 (Technological Protection Measures (TPMs)): all of this Article including footnotes 82 through 95;

(i) Article 18.69 (Rights Management Information (RMI)): all of this Article including footnotes 96 through 99;

---

2 The Parties agree that negotiations referred to in paragraph 2 of Article 15.24 (Further Negotiations) shall commence no earlier than five years after entry into force of this Agreement, unless the Parties agree otherwise. Such negotiations shall commence at the request of a Party.

(j) Article 18.79 (Protection of Encrypted Program-Carrying Satellite and Cable Signals): all of this Article including footnotes 139 through 146;
(k) Article 18.82 (Legal Remedies and Safe Harbours): all of this Article including footnotes 149 through 159;
(l) Annex 18-E (Annex to Section J): all of this Annex;
(m) Annex 18-F (Annex to Section J): all of this Annex

8. Chapter 20 (Environment)

Article 20.17 (Conservation and Trade) - paragraph 5: the phrase "or another applicable law" including footnote 26

9. Chapter 26 (Transparency and Anti-Corruption)

Annex 26-A (Transparency and Procedural Fairness for Pharmaceutical Products and Medical Devices): Article 3 (Procedural Fairness) including footnotes 11 through 16

10. Annex II

Schedule of Brunei Darussalam – 14 – paragraph 3: the phrase "after the signature of this Agreement"

11. Annex IV

Schedule of Malaysia – 3 and 4 – Scope of Non-Conforming Activities (hereinafter referred to as the "Scope"): all references to the phrase "after signature of this Agreement"

CHAPTER 9 INVESTMENT

SECTION A

Article 9.1: Definitions

For the purposes of this Chapter:

Centre means the International Centre for Settlement of Investment Disputes (ICSID) established by the ICSID Convention;

claimant means an investor of a Party that is a party to an investment dispute with another Party. If that investor is a natural person, who is a permanent resident of a Party and a national of another Party, that natural person may not submit a claim to arbitration against that latter Party;

covered investment means, with respect to a Party, an investment in its territory of an investor of another Party in existence as of the date of entry into force of this Agreement for those Parties or established, acquired, or expanded thereafter;

disputing parties means the claimant and the respondent;

disputing party means either the claimant or the respondent;

enterprise means an enterprise as defined in Article 1.3 (General Definitions), and a branch of an enterprise;

enterprise of a Party means an enterprise constituted or organised under the law of a Party, or a branch located in the territory of a Party and carrying out business activities there;

freely usable currency means "freely usable currency" as determined by the International Monetary Fund under its Articles of Agreement;

ICC Arbitration Rules means the arbitration rules of the International Chamber of Commerce;

ICSID Additional Facility Rules means the Rules Governing the Additional Facility for the Administration of Proceedings by the Secretariat of the International Centre for Settlement of Investment Disputes;

ICSID Convention means the Convention on the Settlement of Investment Disputes between States and Nationals of other States, done at Washington, March 18, 1965;

Inter-American Convention means the Inter-American Convention on International Commercial Arbitration, done at Panama, January 30, 1975;

investment means every asset that an investor owns or controls, directly or indirectly, that has the characteristics of an investment, including such characteristics as the commitment of capital or other resources, the expectation of gain or profit, or the assumption of risk. Forms that an investment may take include:

(a) an enterprise;
(b) shares, stock and other forms of equity participation in an enterprise;
(c) bonds, debentures, other debt instruments and loans;
(d) futures, options and other derivatives;
(e) turnkey, construction, management, production, concession, revenue-sharing and other similar contracts;
(f) intellectual property rights;
(g) licences, authorisations, permits and similar rights conferred pursuant to the Party's law; and
(h) other tangible or intangible, movable or immovable property, and related property rights, such as leases, mortgages, liens and pledges,

but investment does not mean an order or judgment entered in a judicial or administrative action.

investment agreement means a written agreement that is concluded and takes effect after the date of entry into force of this Agreement between an authority at the central level of government of a Party and a covered investment or an investor of another Party and that creates an exchange of rights and obligations, binding on both parties under the law applicable under Article 9.25.2 (Governing Law), on which the covered investment or the investor relies in establishing or acquiring a covered investment other than the written agreement itself, and that grants rights to the covered investment or investor:

(a) with respect to natural resources that a national authority controls, such as oil, natural gas, rare earth minerals, timber, gold, iron ore and other similar resources, including for their exploration, extraction, refining, transportation, distribution or sale;
(b) to supply services on behalf of the Party for consumption by the general public for: power generation or distribution, water treatment or distribution, telecommunications, or other similar services supplied on behalf of the Party for consumption by the general public; or
(c) to undertake infrastructure projects, such as the construction of roads, bridges, canals, dams or pipelines or other similar projects; provided, however, that the infrastructure is not for the exclusive or predominant use and benefit of the government;

investment authorisation means an authorisation that the foreign investment authority of a Party grants to a covered investment or an investor of another Party;

investor of a non-Party means, with respect to a Party, an investor that attempts to make, is making, or has made an investment in the territory of that Party, that is not an investor of a Party;

investor of a Party means a Party, or a national or an enterprise of a Party, that attempts to make, is making, or has made an investment in the territory of another Party;

LCIA Arbitration Rules means the arbitration rules of the London Court of International Arbitration;

negotiated restructuring means the restructuring or rescheduling of a debt instrument that has been effected through (a) a modification or amendment of that debt instrument, as provided for under its terms, or (b) a comprehensive debt exchange or other similar process in which the holders of no less than 75 per cent of the aggregate principal amount of the outstanding debt under that debt instrument have consented to the debt exchange or other process;

New York Convention means the Convention on the Recognition and Enforcement of Foreign Arbitral Awards, done at New York, June 10, 1958;

non-disputing Party means a Party that is not a party to an investment dispute;

protected information means confidential business information or information that is privileged or otherwise protected from disclosure under a Party's law, including classified government information;

respondent means the Party that is a party to an investment dispute;

Secretary-General means the Secretary-General of ICSID; and

UNCITRAL Arbitration Rules means the arbitration rules of the United Nations Commission on International Trade Law.

Article 9.2: Scope

1. This Chapter shall apply to measures adopted or maintained by a Party relating to:
   (a) investors of another Party;
   (b) covered investments; and
   (c) with respect to Article 9.10 (Performance Requirements) and Article 9.16 (Investment and Environmental, Health and other Regulatory Objectives), all investments in the territory of that Party.
2. A Party's obligations under this Chapter shall apply to measures adopted or maintained by:
   (a) the central, regional or local governments or authorities of that Party; and
   (b) any person, including a state enterprise or any other body, when it exercises any governmental authority delegated to it by central, regional or local governments or authorities of that Party.
3. For greater certainty, this Chapter shall not bind a Party in relation to an act or fact that took place or a situation that ceased to exist before the date of entry into force of this Agreement for that Party.

Article 9.3: Relation to Other Chapters

1. In the event of any inconsistency between this Chapter and another Chapter of this Agreement, the other Chapter shall prevail to the extent of the inconsistency.
2. A requirement of a Party that a service supplier of another Party post a bond or other form of financial security as a condition for the cross-border supply of a service does not of itself make this Chapter applicable to measures adopted or maintained by the Party relating to such cross-border supply of the service. This Chapter shall apply to measures adopted or maintained by the Party relating to the posted bond or financial security, to the extent that the bond or financial security is a covered investment.
3. This Chapter shall not apply to measures adopted or maintained by a Party to the extent that they are covered by Chapter 11 (Financial Services).

Article 9.4: National Treatment

1. Each Party shall accord to investors of another Party treatment no less favourable than that it accords, in like circumstances, to its own investors with respect to the establishment, acquisition, expansion, management, conduct, operation, and sale or other disposition of investments in its territory.
2. Each Party shall accord to covered investments treatment no less favourable than that it accords, in like circumstances, to investments in its territory of its own investors with respect to the establishment, acquisition, expansion, management, conduct, operation, and sale or other disposition of investments.
3. For greater certainty, the treatment to be accorded by a Party under paragraphs 1 and 2 means, with respect to a regional level of government, treatment no less favourable than the most favourable treatment accorded, in like circumstances, by that regional level of government to investors, and to investments of investors, of the Party of which it forms a part.

Article 9.5: Most-Favoured-Nation Treatment

1. Each Party shall accord to investors of another Party treatment no less favourable than that it accords, in like circumstances, to investors of any other Party or of any non-Party with respect to the establishment, acquisition, expansion, management, conduct, operation, and sale or other disposition of investments in its territory.
2. Each Party shall accord to covered investments treatment no less favourable than that it accords, in like circumstances, to investments in its territory of investors of any other Party or of any non-Party

with respect to the establishment, acquisition, expansion, management, conduct, operation, and sale or other disposition of investments.
3. For greater certainty, the treatment referred to in this Article does not encompass international dispute resolution procedures or mechanisms, such as those included in Section B (Investor-State Dispute Settlement).

Article 9.6: Minimum Standard of Treatment
1. Each Party shall accord to covered investments treatment in accordance with applicable customary international law principles, including fair and equitable treatment and full protection and security.
2. For greater certainty, paragraph 1 prescribes the customary international law minimum standard of treatment of aliens as the standard of treatment to be afforded to covered investments. The concepts of "fair and equitable treatment" and "full protection and security" do not require treatment in addition to or beyond that which is required by that standard, and do not create additional substantive rights. The obligations in paragraph 1 to provide:
(a) "fair and equitable treatment" includes the obligation not to deny justice in criminal, civil or administrative adjudicatory proceedings in accordance with the principle of due process embodied in the principal legal systems of the world; and
(b) "full protection and security" requires each Party to provide the level of police protection required under customary international law.
3. A determination that there has been a breach of another provision of this Agreement, or of a separate international agreement, does not establish that there has been a breach of this Article.
4. For greater certainty, the mere fact that a Party takes or fails to take an action that may be inconsistent with an investor's expectations does not constitute a breach of this Article, even if there is loss or damage to the covered investment as a result.
5. For greater certainty, the mere fact that a subsidy or grant has not been issued, renewed or maintained, or has been modified or reduced, by a Party, does not constitute a breach of this Article, even if there is loss or damage to the covered investment as a result.

Article 9.7: Treatment in Case of Armed Conflict or Civil Strife
1. Notwithstanding Article 9.12.6(b) (Non-Conforming Measures), each Party shall accord to investors of another Party and to covered investments non- discriminatory treatment with respect to measures it adopts or maintains relating to losses suffered by investments in its territory owing to armed conflict or civil strife.
2. Notwithstanding paragraph 1, if an investor of a Party, in a situation referred to in paragraph 1, suffers a loss in the territory of another Party resulting from:
(a) requisitioning of its covered investment or part thereof by the latter's forces or authorities; or
(b) destruction of its covered investment or part thereof by the latter's forces or authorities, which was not required by the necessity of the situation,

the latter Party shall provide the investor restitution, compensation or both, as appropriate, for that loss.
3. Paragraph 1 shall not apply to existing measures relating to subsidies or grants that would be inconsistent with Article 9.4 (National Treatment) but for Article 9.12.6(b) (Non-Conforming Measures).

Article 9.8: Expropriation and Compensation
1. No Party shall expropriate or nationalise a covered investment either directly or indirectly through measures equivalent to expropriation or nationalisation (expropriation), except:
(a) for a public purpose;
(b) in a non-discriminatory manner;

(c) on payment of prompt, adequate and effective compensation in accordance with paragraphs 2, 3 and 4; and
(d) in accordance with due process of law.

2. Compensation shall:
(a) be paid without delay;
(b) be equivalent to the fair market value of the expropriated investment immediately before the expropriation took place (the date of expropriation);
(c) not reflect any change in value occurring because the intended expropriation had become known earlier; and
(d) be fully realisable and freely transferable.

3. If the fair market value is denominated in a freely usable currency, the compensation paid shall be no less than the fair market value on the date of expropriation, plus interest at a commercially reasonable rate for that currency, accrued from the date of expropriation until the date of payment.

4. If the fair market value is denominated in a currency that is not freely usable, the compensation paid, converted into the currency of payment at the market rate of exchange prevailing on the date of payment, shall be no less than:
(a) the fair market value on the date of expropriation, converted into a freely usable currency at the market rate of exchange prevailing on that date; plus
(b) interest, at a commercially reasonable rate for that freely usable currency, accrued from the date of expropriation until the date of payment.

5. This Article shall not apply to the issuance of compulsory licences granted in relation to intellectual property rights in accordance with the TRIPS Agreement, or to the revocation, limitation or creation of intellectual property rights, to the extent that the issuance, revocation, limitation or creation is consistent with Chapter 18 (Intellectual Property) and the TRIPS Agreement.

6. For greater certainty, a Party's decision not to issue, renew or maintain a subsidy or grant, or decision to modify or reduce a subsidy or grant,
(a) in the absence of any specific commitment under law or contract to issue, renew or maintain that subsidy or grant; or
(b) in accordance with any terms or conditions attached to the issuance, renewal, modification, reduction and maintenance of that subsidy or grant,

standing alone, does not constitute an expropriation.

Article 9.9: Transfers

1. Each Party shall permit all transfers relating to a covered investment to be made freely and without delay into and out of its territory. Such transfers include:
(a) contributions to capital;
(b) profits, dividends, interest, capital gains, royalty payments, management fees, technical assistance fees and other fees;
(c) proceeds from the sale of all or any part of the covered investment or from the partial or complete liquidation of the covered investment;
(d) payments made under a contract, including a loan agreement;
(e) payments made pursuant to Article 9.7 (Treatment in Case of Armed Conflict or Civil Strife) and Article 9.8 (Expropriation and Compensation); and
(f) payments arising out of a dispute.

2. Each Party shall permit transfers relating to a covered investment to be made in a freely usable currency at the market rate of exchange prevailing at the time of transfer.

3. Each Party shall permit returns in kind relating to a covered investment to be made as authorised or specified in a written agreement between the Party and a covered investment or an investor of another Party.

4. Notwithstanding paragraphs 1, 2 and 3, a Party may prevent or delay a transfer through the equitable, non-discriminatory and good faith application of its laws relating to:
(a) bankruptcy, insolvency or the protection of the rights of creditors;
(b) issuing, trading or dealing in securities, futures, options or derivatives;
(c) criminal or penal offences;
(d) financial reporting or record keeping of transfers when necessary to assist law enforcement or financial regulatory authorities; or
(e) ensuring compliance with orders or judgments in judicial or administrative proceedings.
5. Notwithstanding paragraph 3, a Party may restrict transfers of returns in kind in circumstances where it could otherwise restrict such transfers under this Agreement, including as set out in paragraph 4.

Article 9.10: Performance Requirements
1. No Party shall, in connection with the establishment, acquisition, expansion, management, conduct, operation, or sale or other disposition of an investment of an investor of a Party or of a non-Party in its territory, impose or enforce any requirement, or enforce any commitment or undertaking:
(a) to export a given level or percentage of goods or services;
(b) to achieve a given level or percentage of domestic content;
(c) to purchase, use or accord a preference to goods produced in its territory, or to purchase goods from persons in its territory;
(d) to relate in any way the volume or value of imports to the volume or value of exports or to the amount of foreign exchange inflows associated with the investment;
(e) to restrict sales of goods or services in its territory that the investment produces or supplies by relating those sales in any way to the volume or value of its exports or foreign exchange earnings;
(f) to transfer a particular technology, a production process or other proprietary knowledge to a person in its territory;
(g) to supply exclusively from the territory of the Party the goods that the investment produces or the services that it supplies to a specific regional market or to the world market;
(h) (i) to purchase, use or accord a preference to, in its territory, technology of the Party or of a person of the Party; or
(ii) that prevents the purchase or use of, or the according of a preference to, in its territory, a particular technology; or
(i) to adopt:
(i) a given rate or amount of royalty under a licence contract; or
(ii) a given duration of the term of a licence contract,
in regard to any licence contract in existence at the time the requirement is imposed or enforced, or any commitment or undertaking is enforced, or any future licence contract freely entered into between the investor and a person in its territory, provided that the requirement is imposed or the commitment or undertaking is enforced in a manner that constitutes direct interference with that licence contract by an exercise of non- judicial governmental authority of a Party. For greater certainty, paragraph 1(i) does not apply when the licence contract is concluded between the investor and a Party.
2. No Party shall condition the receipt or continued receipt of an advantage, in connection with the establishment, acquisition, expansion, management, conduct, operation, or sale or other disposition of an investment of an investor of a Party or of a non-Party in its territory, on compliance with any requirement:
(a) to achieve a given level or percentage of domestic content;
(b) to purchase, use or accord a preference to goods produced in its territory, or to purchase goods from persons in its territory;

(c) to relate in any way the volume or value of imports to the volume or value of exports or to the amount of foreign exchange inflows associated with the investment; or
(d) to restrict sales of goods or services in its territory that the investment produces or supplies by relating those sales in any way to the volume or value of its exports or foreign exchange earnings.

3. (a) Nothing in paragraph 2 shall be construed to prevent a Party from conditioning the receipt or continued receipt of an advantage, in connection with an investment of an investor of a Party or of a non-Party in its territory, on compliance with a requirement to locate production, supply a service, train or employ workers, construct or expand particular facilities, or carry out research and development, in its territory.
(b) Paragraphs 1(f), 1(h) and 1(i) shall not apply:
(i) if a Party authorises use of an intellectual property right in accordance with Article 31 of the TRIPS Agreement, or to measures requiring the disclosure of proprietary information that fall within the scope of, and are consistent with, Article 39 of the TRIPS Agreement; or
(ii) if the requirement is imposed or the commitment or undertaking is enforced by a court, administrative tribunal or competition authority to remedy a practice determined after judicial or administrative process to be anticompetitive under the Party's competition laws.
(c) Paragraph 1(i) shall not apply if the requirement is imposed or the commitment or undertaking is enforced by a tribunal as equitable remuneration under the Party's copyright laws.
(d) Provided that such measures are not applied in an arbitrary or unjustifiable manner, or do not constitute a disguised restriction on international trade or investment, paragraphs 1(b), 1(c), 1(f), 2(a) and 2(b) shall not be construed to prevent a Party from adopting or maintaining measures, including environmental measures:
(i) necessary to secure compliance with laws and regulations that are not inconsistent with this Agreement;
(ii) necessary to protect human, animal or plant life or health; or
(iii) related to the conservation of living or non-living exhaustible natural resources.
(e) Paragraphs 1(a), 1(b), 1(c), 2(a) and 2(b) shall not apply to qualification requirements for goods or services with respect to export promotion and foreign aid programs.
(f) Paragraphs 1(b), 1(c), 1(f), 1(g), 1(h), 1(i), 2(a) and 2(b) shall not apply to government procurement.
(g) Paragraphs 2(a) and 2(b) shall not apply to requirements imposed by an importing Party relating to the content of goods necessary to qualify for preferential tariffs or preferential quotas.
(h) Paragraphs (1)(h) and (1)(i) shall not be construed to prevent a Party from adopting or maintaining measures to protect legitimate public welfare objectives, provided that such measures are not applied in an arbitrary or unjustifiable manner, or in a manner that constitutes a disguised restriction on international trade or investment.

4. For greater certainty, nothing in paragraph 1 shall be construed to prevent a Party, in connection with the establishment, acquisition, expansion, management, conduct, operation, or sale or other disposition of an investment of an investor of a Party or of a non-Party in its territory, from imposing or enforcing a requirement, or enforcing a commitment or undertaking, to employ or train workers in its territory provided that the employment or training does not require the transfer of a particular technology, production process or other proprietary knowledge to a person in its territory.

5. For greater certainty, paragraphs 1 and 2 shall not apply to any commitment, undertaking or requirement other than those set out in those paragraphs.

6. This Article does not preclude enforcement of any commitment, undertaking or requirement between private parties, if a Party did not impose or require the commitment, undertaking or requirement.

Article 9.11: Senior Management and Boards of Directors

1. No Party shall require that an enterprise of that Party that is a covered investment appoint to a senior management position a natural person of any particular nationality.

2. A Party may require that a majority of the board of directors, or any committee thereof, of an enterprise of that Party that is a covered investment, be of a particular nationality or resident in the territory of the Party, provided that the requirement does not materially impair the ability of the investor to exercise control over its investment.

Article 9.12: Non-Conforming Measures

1. Article 9.4 (National Treatment), Article 9.5 (Most-Favoured-Nation Treatment), Article 9.10 (Performance Requirements) and Article 9.11 (Senior Management and Boards of Directors) shall not apply to:

(a) any existing non-conforming measure that is maintained by a Party at:

(i) the central level of government, as set out by that Party in its Schedule to Annex I;

(ii) a regional level of government, as set out by that Party in its Schedule to Annex I; or

(iii) a local level of government;

(b) the continuation or prompt renewal of any non-conforming measure referred to in subparagraph (a); or

(c) an amendment to any non-conforming measure referred to in subparagraph (a), to the extent that the amendment does not decrease the conformity of the measure, as it existed immediately before the amendment, with Article 9.4 (National Treatment), Article 9.5 (Most-Favoured-Nation Treatment), Article 9.10 (Performance Requirements) or Article 9.11 (Senior Management and Boards of Directors).

2. Article 9.4 (National Treatment), Article 9.5 (Most-Favoured-Nation Treatment), Article 9.10 (Performance Requirements) and Article 9.11 (Senior Management and Boards of Directors) shall not apply to any measure that a Party adopts or maintains with respect to sectors, subsectors or activities, as set out by that Party in its Schedule to Annex II.

3. If a Party considers that a non-conforming measure applied by a regional level of government of another Party, as referred to in paragraph 1(a)(ii), creates a material impediment to investment in relation to the former Party, it may request consultations with regard to that measure. These Parties shall enter into consultations with a view to exchanging information on the operation of the measure and to considering whether further steps are necessary and appropriate.

4. No Party shall, under any measure adopted after the date of entry into force of this Agreement for that Party and covered by its Schedule to Annex II, require an investor of another Party, by reason of its nationality, to sell or otherwise dispose of an investment existing at the time the measure becomes effective.

5. (a) Article 9.4 (National Treatment) shall not apply to any measure that falls within an exception to, or derogation from, the obligations which are imposed by:

(i) Article 18.8 (National Treatment); or

(ii) Article 3 of the TRIPS Agreement, if the exception or derogation relates to matters not addressed by Chapter 18 (Intellectual Property).

(b) Article 9.5 (Most-Favoured-Nation Treatment) shall not apply to any measure that falls within Article 5 of the TRIPS Agreement, or an exception to, or derogation from, the obligations which are imposed by:

(i) Article 18.8 (National Treatment); or

(ii) Article 4 of the TRIPS Agreement.

6. Article 9.4 (National Treatment), Article 9.5 (Most-Favoured-Nation Treatment) and Article 9.11 (Senior Management and Boards of Directors) shall not apply to:

(a) government procurement; or

(b) subsidies or grants provided by a Party, including government- supported loans, guarantees and insurance.

7. For greater certainty, any amendments or modifications to a Party's Schedules to Annex I or Annex II, pursuant to this Article, shall be made in accordance with Article 30.2 (Amendments).

Article 9.13: Subrogation

If a Party, or any agency, institution, statutory body or corporation designated by the Party, makes a payment to an investor of the Party under a guarantee, a contract of insurance or other form of indemnity that it has entered into with respect to a covered investment, the other Party in whose territory the covered investment was made shall recognise the subrogation or transfer of any rights the investor would have possessed under this Chapter with respect to the covered investment but for the subrogation, and the investor shall be precluded from pursuing these rights to the extent of the subrogation.

1. Nothing in Article 9.4 (National Treatment) shall be construed to prevent a Party from adopting or maintaining a measure that prescribes special formalities in connection with a covered investment, such as a residency requirement for registration or a requirement that a covered investment be legally constituted under the laws or regulations of the Party, provided that these formalities do not materially impair the protections afforded by the Party to investors of another Party and covered investments pursuant to this Chapter.

2. Notwithstanding Article 9.4 (National Treatment) and Article 9.5 (Most- Favoured-Nation Treatment), a Party may require an investor of another Party or its covered investment to provide information concerning that investment solely for informational or statistical purposes. The Party shall protect such information that is confidential from any disclosure that would prejudice the competitive position of the investor or the covered investment. Nothing in this paragraph shall be construed to prevent a Party from otherwise obtaining or disclosing information in connection with the equitable and good faith application of its law.

Article 9.15: Denial of Benefits

1. A Party may deny the benefits of this Chapter to an investor of another Party that is an enterprise of that other Party and to investments of that investor if the enterprise:

(a) is owned or controlled by a person of a non-Party or of the denying Party; and

(b) has no substantial business activities in the territory of any Party other than the denying Party.

2. A Party may deny the benefits of this Chapter to an investor of another Party that is an enterprise of that other Party and to investments of that investor if persons of a non-Party own or control the enterprise and the denying Party adopts or maintains measures with respect to the non-Party or a person of the non-Party that prohibit transactions with the enterprise or that would be violated or circumvented if the benefits of this Chapter were accorded to the enterprise or to its investments.

Article 9.16: Investment and Environmental, Health and other Regulatory Objectives

Nothing in this Chapter shall be construed to prevent a Party from adopting, maintaining or enforcing any measure otherwise consistent with this Chapter that it considers appropriate to ensure that investment activity in its territory is undertaken in a manner sensitive to environmental, health or other regulatory objectives.

Article 9.17: Corporate Social Responsibility

The Parties reaffirm the importance of each Party encouraging enterprises operating within its territory or subject to its jurisdiction to voluntarily incorporate into their internal policies those internationally recognised standards, guidelines and principles of corporate social responsibility that have been endorsed or are supported by that Party.

SECTION B: INVESTOR-STATE DISPUTE SETTLEMENT ARTICLE 9.18: CONSULTATION AND NEGOTIATION

1. In the event of an investment dispute, the claimant and the respondent should initially seek to resolve the dispute through consultation and negotiation, which may include the use of non-binding, third party procedures, such as good offices, conciliation or mediation.
2. The claimant shall deliver to the respondent a written request for consultations setting out a brief description of facts regarding the measure or measures at issue.
3. For greater certainty, the initiation of consultations and negotiations shall not be construed as recognition of the jurisdiction of the tribunal.

Article 9.19: Submission of a Claim to Arbitration

1. If an investment dispute has not been resolved within six months of the receipt by the respondent of a written request for consultations pursuant to Article
   9.18.2 (Consultation and Negotiation):
   (a) the claimant, on its own behalf, may submit to arbitration under this Section a claim:
      (i) that the respondent has breached:
         (A) an obligation under Section A;
         (B) an investment authorisation; or
         (C) an investment agreement; and
      (ii) that the claimant has incurred loss or damage by reason of, or arising out of, that breach; and
   (b) the claimant, on behalf of an enterprise of the respondent that is a juridical person that the claimant owns or controls directly or indirectly, may submit to arbitration under this Section a claim:
      (i) that the respondent has breached:
         (A) an obligation under Section A;
         (B) an investment authorisation; or
         (C) an investment agreement; and
      (ii) that the enterprise has incurred loss or damage by reason of, or arising out of, that breach,

   provided that a claimant may submit pursuant to subparagraph (a)(i)(C) or (b)(i)(C) a claim for breach of an investment agreement only if the subject matter of the claim and the claimed damages directly relate to the covered investment that was established or acquired, or sought to be established or acquired, in reliance on the relevant investment agreement.
2. When the claimant submits a claim pursuant to paragraph 1(a)(i)(B), 1(a)(i)(C), 1(b)(i)(B) or 1(b)(i)(C), the respondent may make a counterclaim in connection with the factual and legal basis of the claim or rely on a claim for the purpose of a set off against the claimant.
3. At least 90 days before submitting any claim to arbitration under this Section, the claimant shall deliver to the respondent a written notice of its
   intention to submit a claim to arbitration (notice of intent). The notice shall specify:
   (a) the name and address of the claimant and, if a claim is submitted on behalf of an enterprise, the name, address and place of incorporation of the enterprise;
   (b) for each claim, the provision of this Agreement, investment authorisation or investment agreement alleged to have been breached and any other relevant provisions;
   (c) the legal and factual basis for each claim; and
   (d) the relief sought and the approximate amount of damages claimed.
4. The claimant may submit a claim referred to in paragraph 1 under one of the following alternatives:
   (a) the ICSID Convention and the ICSID Rules of Procedure for Arbitration Proceedings, provided that both the respondent and the Party of the claimant are parties to the ICSID Convention;

(b) the ICSID Additional Facility Rules, provided that either the respondent or the Party of the claimant is a party to the ICSID Convention;
(c) the UNCITRAL Arbitration Rules; or
(d) if the claimant and respondent agree, any other arbitral institution or any other arbitration rules.

5. A claim shall be deemed submitted to arbitration under this Section when the claimant's notice of or request for arbitration (notice of arbitration):
(a) referred to in the ICSID Convention is received by the Secretary- General;
(b) referred to in the ICSID Additional Facility Rules is received by the Secretary-General;
(c) referred to in the UNCITRAL Arbitration Rules, together with the statement of claim referred to therein, are received by the respondent; or
(d) referred to under any arbitral institution or arbitration rules selected under paragraph 4(d) is received by the respondent.

A claim asserted by the claimant for the first time after such notice of arbitration is submitted shall be deemed submitted to arbitration under this Section on the date of its receipt under the applicable arbitration rules.

6. The arbitration rules applicable under paragraph 4 that are in effect on the date the claim or claims were submitted to arbitration under this Section shall govern the arbitration except to the extent modified by this Agreement.

7. The claimant shall provide with the notice of arbitration:
(a) the name of the arbitrator that the claimant appoints; or
(b) the claimant's written consent for the Secretary-General to appoint that arbitrator.

Article 9.20: Consent of Each Party to Arbitration

1. Each Party consents to the submission of a claim to arbitration under this Section in accordance with this Agreement.

2. The consent under paragraph 1 and the submission of a claim to arbitration under this Section shall be deemed to satisfy the requirements of:
(a) Chapter II of the ICSID Convention (Jurisdiction of the Centre) and the ICSID Additional Facility Rules for written consent of the parties to the dispute;
(b) Article II of the New York Convention for an "agreement in writing"; and
(c) Article I of the Inter-American Convention for an "agreement".

Article 9.21: Conditions and Limitations on Consent of Each Party

1. No claim shall be submitted to arbitration under this Section if more than three years and six months have elapsed from the date on which the claimant first acquired, or should have first acquired, knowledge of the breach alleged under Article 9.19.1 (Submission of a Claim to Arbitration) and knowledge that the claimant (for claims brought under Article 9.19.1(a)) or the enterprise (for claims brought under Article 9.19.1(b)) has incurred loss or damage.

2. No claim shall be submitted to arbitration under this Section unless:
(a) the claimant consents in writing to arbitration in accordance with the procedures set out in this Agreement; and
(b) the notice of arbitration is accompanied:
(i) for claims submitted to arbitration under Article 9.19.1(a) (Submission of a Claim to Arbitration), by the claimant's written waiver; and
(ii) for claims submitted to arbitration under Article 9.19.1(b) (Submission of a Claim to Arbitration), by the claimant's and the enterprise's written waivers,

of any right to initiate or continue before any court or administrative tribunal under the law of a Party, or any other dispute settlement procedures, any proceeding with respect to any measure alleged to constitute a breach referred to in Article 9.19 (Submission of a Claim to Arbitration).

3. Notwithstanding paragraph 2(b), the claimant (for claims brought under Article 9.19.1(a) (Submission of a Claim to Arbitration)) and the claimant or the enterprise (for claims brought under Article 9.19.1(b)) may initiate or continue an action that seeks interim injunctive relief and does not involve the payment of monetary damages before a judicial or administrative tribunal of the respondent, provided that the action is brought for the sole purpose of preserving the claimant's or the enterprise's rights and interests during the pendency of the arbitration.

Article 9.22: Selection of Arbitrators

1. Unless the disputing parties agree otherwise, the tribunal shall comprise three arbitrators, one arbitrator appointed by each of the disputing parties and the third, who shall be the presiding arbitrator, appointed by agreement of the disputing parties.

2. The Secretary-General shall serve as appointing authority for an arbitration under this Section.

3. If a tribunal has not been constituted within a period of 75 days after the date that a claim is submitted to arbitration under this Section, the Secretary- General, on the request of a disputing party, shall appoint, in his or her discretion, the arbitrator or arbitrators not yet appointed. The Secretary-General shall not appoint a national of either the respondent or the Party of the claimant as the presiding arbitrator unless the disputing parties agree otherwise.

4. For the purposes of Article 39 of the ICSID Convention and Article 7 of Schedule C to the ICSID Additional Facility Rules, and without prejudice to an objection to an arbitrator on a ground other than nationality:

(a) the respondent agrees to the appointment of each individual member of a tribunal established under the ICSID Convention or the ICSID Additional Facility Rules;

(b) a claimant referred to in Article 9.19.1(a) (Submission of a Claim to Arbitration) may submit a claim to arbitration under this Section, or continue a claim, under the ICSID Convention or the ICSID Additional Facility Rules, only on condition that the claimant agrees in writing to the appointment of each individual member of the tribunal; and

(c) a claimant referred to in Article 9.19.1(b) (Submission of a Claim to Arbitration) may submit a claim to arbitration under this Section, or continue a claim, under the ICSID Convention or the ICSID Additional Facility Rules, only on condition that the claimant and the enterprise agree in writing to the appointment of each individual member of the tribunal.

5. In the appointment of arbitrators to a tribunal for claims submitted under Article 9.19.1(a)(i)(B) (Submission of a Claim to Arbitration), Article 9.19.1(b)(i)(B), Article 9.19.1(a)(i)(C) or Article 9.19.1(b)(i)(C), each disputing party shall take into account the expertise or relevant experience of particular candidates with respect to the relevant governing law under Article 9.25.2 (Governing Law). If the parties fail to agree on the appointment of the presiding arbitrator, the Secretary-General shall also take into account the expertise or relevant experience of particular candidates with respect to the relevant governing law under Article 9.25.2.

6. The Parties shall, prior to the entry into force of this Agreement, provide guidance on the application of the Code of Conduct for Dispute Settlement Proceedings under Chapter 28 (Dispute Settlement) to arbitrators selected to serve on investor-State dispute settlement tribunals pursuant to this Article, including any necessary modifications to the Code of Conduct to conform to the context of investor-State dispute settlement. The Parties shall also provide guidance on the application of other relevant rules or guidelines on conflicts of interest in international arbitration. Arbitrators shall comply with that guidance in addition to the applicable arbitral rules regarding independence and impartiality of arbitrators.

Article 9.23: Conduct of the Arbitration

1. The disputing parties may agree on the legal place of any arbitration under the arbitration rules applicable under Article 9.19.4 (Submission of a Claim to Arbitration). If the disputing parties fail to reach agreement, the tribunal shall determine the place in accordance with the applicable arbitration rules, provided that the place shall be in the territory of a State that is a party to the New York Convention.

2. A non-disputing Party may make oral and written submissions to the tribunal regarding the interpretation of this Agreement.

3. After consultation with the disputing parties, the tribunal may accept and consider written amicus curiae submissions regarding a matter of fact or law within the scope of the dispute that may assist the tribunal in evaluating the submissions and arguments of the disputing parties from a person or entity that is not a disputing party but has a significant interest in the arbitral proceedings. Each submission shall identify the author; disclose any affiliation, direct or indirect, with any disputing party; and identify any person, government or other entity that has provided, or will provide, any financial or other assistance in preparing the submission. Each submission shall be in a language of the arbitration and comply with any page limits and deadlines set by the tribunal. The tribunal shall provide the disputing parties with an opportunity to respond to such submissions. The tribunal shall ensure that the submissions do not disrupt or unduly burden the arbitral proceedings, or unfairly prejudice any disputing party.

4. Without prejudice to a tribunal's authority to address other objections as a preliminary question, such as an objection that a dispute is not within the competence of the tribunal, including an objection to the tribunal's jurisdiction, a tribunal shall address and decide as a preliminary question any objection by the respondent that, as a matter of law, a claim submitted is not a claim for which an award in favour of the claimant may be made under Article 9.29 (Awards) or that a claim is manifestly without legal merit.

(a) An objection under this paragraph shall be submitted to the tribunal as soon as possible after the tribunal is constituted, and in no event later than the date the tribunal fixes for the respondent to submit its counter-memorial or, in the case of an amendment to the notice of arbitration, the date the tribunal fixes for the respondent to submit its response to the amendment.

(b) On receipt of an objection under this paragraph, the tribunal shall suspend any proceedings on the merits, establish a schedule for considering the objection consistent with any schedule it has established for considering any other preliminary question, and issue a decision or award on the objection, stating the grounds therefor.

(c) In deciding an objection under this paragraph that a claim submitted is not a claim for which an award in favour of the claimant may be made under Article 9.29 (Awards), the tribunal shall assume to be true the claimant's factual allegations in support of any claim in the notice of arbitration (or any amendment thereof) and, in disputes brought under the UNCITRAL Arbitration Rules, the statement of claim referred to in the relevant article of the UNCITRAL Arbitration Rules. The tribunal may also consider any relevant facts not in dispute.

(d) The respondent does not waive any objection as to competence, including an objection to jurisdiction, or any argument on the merits merely because the respondent did or did not raise an objection under this paragraph or make use of the expedited procedure set out in paragraph 5.

5. In the event that the respondent so requests within 45 days after the tribunal is constituted, the tribunal shall decide on an expedited basis an objection under paragraph 4 or any objection that the dispute is not within the tribunal's competence, including an objection that the dispute is not within the tribunal's jurisdiction. The tribunal shall suspend any proceedings on the merits and issue a decision or award on the objection, stating the grounds therefor, no later than 150 days after the date of the request. However, if a disputing party requests a hearing, the tribunal may take an additional 30 days to issue the decision or award. Regardless of whether a hearing is requested, a tribunal may,

on a showing of extraordinary cause, delay issuing its decision or award by an additional brief period, which may not exceed 30 days.
6. When the tribunal decides a respondent's objection under paragraph 4 or 5, it may, if warranted, award to the prevailing disputing party reasonable costs and attorney's fees incurred in submitting or opposing the objection. In determining whether such an award is warranted, the tribunal shall consider whether either the claimant's claim or the respondent's objection was frivolous, and shall provide the disputing parties a reasonable opportunity to comment.
7. For greater certainty, if an investor of a Party submits a claim under this Section, including a claim alleging that a Party breached Article 9.6 (Minimum Standard of Treatment), the investor has the burden of proving all elements of its claims, consistent with general principles of international law applicable to international arbitration.
8. A respondent may not assert as a defence, counterclaim, right of set-off or for any other reason, that the claimant has received or will receive indemnification or other compensation for all or part of the alleged damages pursuant to an insurance or guarantee contract.
9. A tribunal may order an interim measure of protection to preserve the rights of a disputing party, or to ensure that the tribunal's jurisdiction is made fully effective, including an order to preserve evidence in the possession or control of a disputing party or to protect the tribunal's jurisdiction. A tribunal may not order attachment or enjoin the application of a measure alleged to constitute a breach referred to in Article 9.19 (Submission of a Claim to Arbitration). For the purposes of this paragraph, an order includes a recommendation.
10. In any arbitration conducted under this Section, at the request of a disputing party, a tribunal shall, before issuing a decision or award on liability, transmit its proposed decision or award to the disputing parties. Within 60 days after the tribunal transmits its proposed decision or award, the disputing parties may submit written comments to the tribunal concerning any aspect of its proposed decision or award. The tribunal shall consider any comments and issue its decision or award no later than 45 days after the expiration of the 60 day comment period.
11. In the event that an appellate mechanism for reviewing awards rendered by investor-State dispute settlement tribunals is developed in the future under other institutional arrangements, the Parties shall consider whether awards rendered under Article 9.29 (Awards) should be subject to that appellate mechanism. The Parties shall strive to ensure that any such appellate mechanism they consider adopting provides for transparency of proceedings similar to the transparency provisions established in Article 9.24 (Transparency of Arbitral Proceedings).

Article 9.24: Transparency of Arbitral Proceedings
1. Subject to paragraphs 2 and 4, the respondent shall, after receiving the following documents, promptly transmit them to the non-disputing Parties and make them available to the public:
  (a) the notice of intent;
  (b) the notice of arbitration;
  (c) pleadings, memorials and briefs submitted to the tribunal by a disputing party and any written submissions submitted pursuant to Article 9.23.2 (Conduct of the Arbitration) and Article 9.23.3 and Article 9.28 (Consolidation);
  (d) minutes or transcripts of hearings of the tribunal, if available; and
  (e) orders, awards and decisions of the tribunal.
2. The tribunal shall conduct hearings open to the public and shall determine, in consultation with the disputing parties, the appropriate logistical arrangements. If a disputing party intends to use information in a hearing that is designated as protected information or otherwise subject to paragraph 3 it shall so advise the tribunal. The tribunal shall make appropriate arrangements to protect such information from disclosure which may include closing the hearing for the duration of the discussion of that information.

3. Nothing in this Section, including paragraph 4(d), requires a respondent to make available to the public or otherwise disclose during or after the arbitral proceedings, including the hearing, protected information, or to furnish or allow access to information that it may withhold in accordance with Article 29.2 (Security Exceptions) or Article 29.7 (Disclosure of Information).
4. Any protected information that is submitted to the tribunal shall be protected from disclosure in accordance with the following procedures:

(a) subject to subparagraph (d), neither the disputing parties nor the tribunal shall disclose to any non-disputing Party or to the public any protected information if the disputing party that provided the information clearly designates it in accordance with subparagraph (b);

(b) any disputing party claiming that certain information constitutes protected information shall clearly designate the information according to any schedule set by the tribunal;

(c) a disputing party shall, according to any schedule set by the tribunal, submit a redacted version of the document that does not contain the protected information. Only the redacted version shall be disclosed in accordance with paragraph 1; and

(d) the tribunal, subject to paragraph 3, shall decide any objection regarding the designation of information claimed to be protected information. If the tribunal determines that the information was not properly designated, the disputing party that submitted the information may:

  (i) withdraw all or part of its submission containing that information; or

  (ii) agree to resubmit complete and redacted documents with corrected designations in accordance with the tribunal's determination and subparagraph (c).

In either case, the other disputing party shall, whenever necessary, resubmit complete and redacted documents which either remove the information withdrawn under subparagraph (d)(i) by the disputing party that first submitted the information or redesignate the information consistent with the designation under subparagraph (d)(ii) of the disputing party that first submitted the information.
5. Nothing in this Section requires a respondent to withhold from the public information required to be disclosed by its laws. The respondent should endeavour to apply those laws in a manner sensitive to protecting from disclosure information that has been designated as protected information.

Article 9.25: Governing Law
1. Subject to paragraph 3, when a claim is submitted under Article 9.19.1(a)(i)(A) (Submission of a Claim to Arbitration) or Article 9.19.1(b)(i)(A), the tribunal shall decide the issues in dispute in accordance with this Agreement and applicable rules of international law.
2. Subject to paragraph 3 and the other provisions of this Section, when a claim is submitted under Article 9.19.1(a)(i)(B) (Submission of a Claim to Arbitration), Article 9.19.1(a)(i)(C), Article 9.19.1(b)(i)(B) or Article 9.19.1(b)(i)(C), the tribunal shall apply:

(a) the rules of law applicable to the pertinent investment authorisation or specified in the pertinent investment authorisation or investment agreement, or as the disputing parties may agree otherwise; or

(b) if, in the pertinent investment agreement the rules of law have not been specified or otherwise agreed:

  (i) the law of the respondent, including its rules on the conflict of laws; and

  (ii) such rules of international law as may be applicable.

3. A decision of the Commission on the interpretation of a provision of this Agreement under Article 27.2.2(f) (Functions of the Commission) shall be binding on a tribunal, and any decision or award issued by a tribunal must be consistent with that decision.

Article 9.26: Interpretation of Annexes

1. If a respondent asserts as a defence that the measure alleged to be a breach is within the scope of a non-conforming measure set out in Annex I or Annex II, the tribunal shall, on request of the respondent, request the interpretation of the Commission on the issue. The Commission shall submit in writing any decision on its interpretation under Article 27.2.2(f) (Functions of the Commission) to the tribunal within 90 days of delivery of the request.
2. A decision issued by the Commission under paragraph 1 shall be binding on the tribunal, and any decision or award issued by the tribunal must be consistent with that decision. If the Commission fails to issue such a decision within 90 days, the tribunal shall decide the issue.

Article 9.27: Expert Reports

Without prejudice to the appointment of other kinds of experts when authorised by the applicable arbitration rules, a tribunal, on request of a disputing party or, unless the disputing parties disapprove, on its own initiative, may appoint one or more experts to report to it in writing on any factual issue concerning scientific matters raised by a disputing party in a proceeding, subject to any terms and conditions that the disputing parties may agree.

Article 9.28: Consolidation

1. If two or more claims have been submitted separately to arbitration under Article 9.19.1 (Submission of a Claim to Arbitration) and the claims have a question of law or fact in common and arise out of the same events or circumstances, any disputing party may seek a consolidation order in accordance with the agreement of all the disputing parties sought to be covered by the order or the terms of paragraphs 2 through 10.
2. A disputing party that seeks a consolidation order under this Article shall deliver, in writing, a request to the Secretary-General and to all the disputing parties sought to be covered by the order and shall specify in the request:
   (a) the names and addresses of all the disputing parties sought to be covered by the order;
   (b) the nature of the order sought; and
   (c) the grounds on which the order is sought.
3. Unless the Secretary-General finds within a period of 30 days after the date of receiving a request under paragraph 2 that the request is manifestly unfounded, a tribunal shall be established under this Article.
4. Unless all the disputing parties sought to be covered by the order agree otherwise, a tribunal established under this Article shall comprise three arbitrators:
   (a) one arbitrator appointed by agreement of the claimants;
   (b) one arbitrator appointed by the respondent; and
   (c) the presiding arbitrator appointed by the Secretary-General, provided that the presiding arbitrator is not a national of the respondent or of a Party of any claimant.
5. If, within a period of 60 days after the date when the Secretary-General receives a request made under paragraph 2, the respondent fails or the claimants fail to appoint an arbitrator in accordance with paragraph 4, the Secretary- General, on request of any disputing party sought to be covered by the order, shall appoint, in his or her discretion, the arbitrator or arbitrators not yet appointed.
6. If a tribunal established under this Article is satisfied that two or more claims that have been submitted to arbitration under Article 9.19.1 (Submission of a Claim to Arbitration) have a question of law or fact in common, and arise out of the same events or circumstances, the tribunal may, in the interest of fair and efficient resolution of the claims, and after hearing the disputing parties, by order:
   (a) assume jurisdiction over, and hear and determine together, all or part of the claims;

(b) assume jurisdiction over, and hear and determine one or more of the claims, the determination of which it believes would assist in the resolution of the others; or
(c) instruct a tribunal previously established under Article 9.22 (Selection of Arbitrators) to assume jurisdiction over, and hear and determine together, all or part of the claims, provided that:
(i) that tribunal, on request of a claimant that was not previously a disputing party before that tribunal, shall be reconstituted with its original members, except that the arbitrator for the claimants shall be appointed pursuant to paragraphs 4(a) and 5; and
(ii) that tribunal shall decide whether a prior hearing shall be repeated.

7. If a tribunal has been established under this Article, a claimant that has submitted a claim to arbitration under Article 9.19.1 (Submission of a Claim to Arbitration) and that has not been named in a request made under paragraph 2 may make a written request to the tribunal that it be included in any order made under paragraph 6. The request shall specify:
(a) the name and address of the claimant;
(b) the nature of the order sought; and
(c) the grounds on which the order is sought.

The claimant shall deliver a copy of its request to the Secretary-General.

8. A tribunal established under this Article shall conduct its proceedings in accordance with the UNCITRAL Arbitration Rules, except as modified by this Section.

9. A tribunal established under Article 9.22 (Selection of Arbitrators) shall not have jurisdiction to decide a claim, or a part of a claim, over which a tribunal established or instructed under this Article has assumed jurisdiction.

10. On the application of a disputing party, a tribunal established under this Article, pending its decision under paragraph 6, may order that the proceedings of a tribunal established under Article 9.22 (Selection of Arbitrators) be stayed, unless the latter tribunal has already adjourned its proceedings.

Article 9.29: Awards

1. When a tribunal makes a final award, the tribunal may award, separately or in combination, only:
(a) monetary damages and any applicable interest; and
(b) restitution of property, in which case the award shall provide that the respondent may pay monetary damages and any applicable interest in lieu of restitution.

2. For greater certainty, if an investor of a Party submits a claim to arbitration under Article 9.19.1(a) (Submission of a Claim to Arbitration), it may recover only for loss or damage that it has incurred in its capacity as an investor of a Party.

3. A tribunal may also award costs and attorney's fees incurred by the disputing parties in connection with the arbitral proceeding, and shall determine how and by whom those costs and attorney's fees shall be paid, in accordance with this Section and the applicable arbitration rules.

4. For greater certainty, for claims alleging the breach of an obligation under Section A with respect to an attempt to make an investment, when an award is made in favour of the claimant, the only damages that may be awarded are those that the claimant has proven were sustained in the attempt to make the investment, provided that the claimant also proves that the breach was the proximate cause of those damages. If the tribunal determines such claims to be frivolous, the tribunal may award to the respondent reasonable costs and attorney's fees.

5. Subject to paragraph 1, if a claim is submitted to arbitration under Article 9.19.1(b) (Submission of a Claim to Arbitration) and an award is made in favour of the enterprise:
(a) an award of restitution of property shall provide that restitution be made to the enterprise;
(b) an award of monetary damages and any applicable interest shall provide that the sum be paid to the enterprise; and
(c) the award shall provide that it is made without prejudice to any right that any person may have under applicable domestic law with respect to the relief provided in the award.

6. A tribunal shall not award punitive damages.
7. An award made by a tribunal shall have no binding force except between the disputing parties and in respect of the particular case.
8. Subject to paragraph 9 and the applicable review procedure for an interim award, a disputing party shall abide by and comply with an award without delay.
9. A disputing party shall not seek enforcement of a final award until:
   (a) in the case of a final award made under the ICSID Convention:
      (i) 120 days have elapsed from the date the award was rendered and no disputing party has requested revision or annulment of the award; or
      (ii) revision or annulment proceedings have been completed; and
   (b) in the case of a final award under the ICSID Additional Facility Rules, the UNCITRAL Arbitration Rules, or the rules selected pursuant to Article 9.19.4(d) (Submission of a Claim to Arbitration):
      (i) 90 days have elapsed from the date the award was rendered and no disputing party has commenced a proceeding to revise, set aside or annul the award; or
      (ii) a court has dismissed or allowed an application to revise, set aside or annul the award and there is no further appeal.
10. Each Party shall provide for the enforcement of an award in its territory.
11. If the respondent fails to abide by or comply with a final award, on delivery of a request by the Party of the claimant, a panel shall be established under Article 28.7 (Establishment of a Panel). The requesting Party may seek in those proceedings:
   (a) a determination that the failure to abide by or comply with the final award is inconsistent with the obligations of this Agreement; and
   (b) in accordance with Article 28.17 (Initial Report), a recommendation that the respondent abide by or comply with the final award.
12. A disputing party may seek enforcement of an arbitration award under the ICSID Convention, the New York Convention or the Inter-American Convention regardless of whether proceedings have been taken under paragraph 11.
13. A claim that is submitted to arbitration under this Section shall be considered to arise out of a commercial relationship or transaction for the purposes of Article I of the New York Convention and Article I of the Inter- American Convention.

Article 9.30: Service of Documents
Delivery of notice and other documents to a Party shall be made to the place named for that Party in Annex 9-D (Service of Documents on a Party Under Section B). A Party shall promptly make publicly available and notify the other Parties of any change to the place referred to in that Annex.

ANNEX 9-A CUSTOMARY INTERNATIONAL LAW

The Parties confirm their shared understanding that "customary international law" generally and as specifically referenced in Article 9.6 (Minimum Standard of Treatment) results from a general and consistent practice of States that they follow from a sense of legal obligation. The customary international law minimum standard of treatment of aliens refers to all customary international law principles that protect the investments of aliens.

ANNEX 9-B EXPROPRIATION

The Parties confirm their shared understanding that:
1. An action or a series of actions by a Party cannot constitute an expropriation unless it interferes with a tangible or intangible property right or property interest in an investment.
2. Article 9.8.1 (Expropriation and Compensation) addresses two situations. The first is direct expropriation, in which an investment is nationalised or otherwise directly expropriated through formal transfer of title or outright seizure.
3. The second situation addressed by Article 9.8.1 (Expropriation and Compensation) is indirect expropriation, in which an action or series of actions by a Party has an effect equivalent to direct expropriation without formal transfer of title or outright seizure.

(a) The determination of whether an action or series of actions by a Party, in a specific fact situation, constitutes an indirect expropriation, requires a case-by-case, fact-based inquiry that considers, among other factors:
  (i) the economic impact of the government action, although the fact that an action or series of actions by a Party has an adverse effect on the economic value of an investment, standing alone, does not establish that an indirect expropriation has occurred;
  (ii) the extent to which the government action interferes with distinct, reasonable investment-backed expectations; and
  (iii) the character of the government action.

(b) Non-discriminatory regulatory actions by a Party that are designed and applied to protect legitimate public welfare objectives, such as public health, safety and the environment, do not constitute indirect expropriations, except in rare circumstances.

ANNEX 9-C EXPROPRIATION RELATING TO LAND

1. Notwithstanding the obligations under Article 9.8 (Expropriation and Compensation), where Singapore is the expropriating Party, any measure of direct expropriation relating to land shall be for a purpose and upon payment of compensation at market value, in accordance with the applicable domestic legislation and any subsequent amendments thereto relating to the amount of compensation where such amendments provide for the method of determination of the compensation which is no less favourable to the investor for its expropriated investment than such method of determination in the applicable domestic legislation as at the time of entry into force of this Agreement for Singapore.
2. Notwithstanding the obligations under Article 9.8 (Expropriation and Compensation), where Viet Nam is the expropriating Party, any measure of direct expropriation relating to land shall be: (i) for a purpose in accordance with the applicable domestic legislation; and (ii) upon payment of compensation equivalent to the market value, while recognising the applicable domestic legislation.

ANNEX 9-D SERVICE OF DOCUMENTS ON A PARTY UNDER SECTION B (INVESTOR-STATE DISPUTE SETTLEMENT)

Australia

Notices and other documents in disputes under Section B (Investor-State Dispute Settlement) shall be served on Australia by delivery to:

Department of Foreign Affairs and Trade
R.G. Casey Building John McEwen Crescent Barton ACT 0221 Australia

Brunei Darussalam

Notices and other documents in disputes under Section B (Investor-State Dispute Settlement) shall be served on Brunei Darussalam by delivery to:

The Permanent Secretary (Trade) Ministry of Foreign Affairs and Trade Jalan Subok
Bandar Seri Begawan, BD 2710 Brunei Darussalam

Canada

Notices and other documents in disputes under Section B (Investor-State Dispute Settlement) shall be served on Canada by delivery to:
Office of the Deputy Attorney General of Canada Justice Building
239 Wellington Street Ottawa, Ontario
K1A 0H8
Canada

Chile

Notices and other documents in disputes under Section B (Investor-State Dispute Settlement) shall be served on Chile by delivery to:

Dirección de Asuntos Jurídicos del Ministerio de Relaciones Exteriores de la República de Chile
Teatinos 180 Santiago Chile

Japan

Notices and other documents in disputes under Section B (Investor-State Dispute Settlement) shall be served on Japan by delivery to:

Economic Affairs Bureau Ministry of Foreign Affairs
2-2-1 Kasumigaseki, Chiyoda-ku Tokyo
Japan

Malaysia

Notices and other documents in disputes under Section B (Investor-State Dispute Settlement) shall be served on Malaysia by delivery to:

Attorney General's Chambers Level 16, No. 45 Persiaran Perdana
Precint 4
Federal Government Administrative Centre 62100 Putrajaya
Malaysia

Mexico

Notices and other documents in disputes under Section B (Investor-State Dispute Settlement) shall be served on Mexico by delivery to:

Dirección General de Consultoría Jurídica de Comercio Internacional Secretaría de Economía
Alfonso Reyes #30, piso 17 Col. Hipódromo Condesa Del. Cuauhtémoc
México D.F.
C.P. 06140

New Zealand

Notices and other documents in disputes under Section B (Investor-State Dispute Settlement) shall be served on New Zealand by delivery to:

The Secretary
Ministry of Foreign Affairs and Trade 195 Lambton Quay
Wellington 6011 New Zealand

Peru

Notices and other documents in disputes under Section B (Investor-State Dispute Settlement) shall be served on Peru by delivery to:

Dirección General de Asuntos de Economía Internacional, Competencia y Productividad
Ministerio de Economía y Finanzas Jirón Lampa 277, piso 5
Lima, Perú

Singapore

Notices and other documents in disputes under Section B (Investor-State Dispute Settlement) shall be served on Singapore by delivery to:

Permanent Secretary Ministry of Trade & Industry 100 High Street #09-01
Singapore 179434 Singapore

United States

Notices and other documents in disputes under Section B (Investor-State Dispute Settlement) shall be served on the United States by delivery to:

Executive Director (L/EX) Office of the Legal Adviser Department of State Washington, D.C.20520
United States of America

Viet Nam

Notices and other documents in disputes under Section B (Investor-State Dispute Settlement) shall be served on Viet Nam by delivery to:

General Director
Department of International Law Ministry of Justice
60 Tran Phu Street Ba Dinh District Ha Noi
Viet Nam

ANNEX 9-E TRANSFERS

Chile

1. Notwithstanding Article 9.9 (Transfers), Chile reserves the right of the Central Bank of Chile (Banco Central de Chile) to maintain or adopt measures in conformity with Law 18.840, Constitutional Organic Law of the Central Bank of Chile (Ley 18.840, Ley Orgánica Constitucional del Banco Central de Chile), and Decreto con Fuerza de Ley No3 de 1997, Ley General de Bancos (General Banking Act) and Ley 18.045, Ley de Mercado de Valores (Securities Market Law), in order to ensure currency stability and the normal operation of domestic and foreign payments. Such measures include, inter alia, the establishment of restrictions or limitations on current payments and transfers (capital movements) to or from Chile, as well as transactions related to them, such as requiring that deposits, investments or credits from or to a foreign country, be subject to a reserve requirement (encaje).
2. Notwithstanding paragraph 1, the reserve requirements that the Central Bank of Chile can apply pursuant to Article 49 No. 2 of Law 18.840, shall not exceed 30 per cent of the amount transferred and shall not be imposed for a period which exceeds two years.

ANNEX 9-F DL 600

Chile

1. The obligations and commitments contained in this Chapter do not apply to Decree Law 600, Foreign Investment Statute (Decreto Ley 600, Estatuto de la Inversión Extranjera) (hereinafter referred to in this Annex as "DL 600"), or its successors, and to Law 18.657, Foreign Capital Investment Fund Law (Ley 18.657, Ley de Fondos de Inversión de Capital Extranjero), with respect to:

   (a) The right of the Foreign Investment Committee of Chile (Comité de Inversiones Extranjeras) or its successor to accept or reject applications to invest through an investment contract under DL 600 and the right to regulate the terms and conditions of foreign investment under DL 600 and Law 18.657.

   (b) The right to maintain existing requirements that transfers from Chile of proceeds from the sale of all or any part of an investment of an investor of a Party or from the partial or complete liquidation of the investment which may not take place until a period not to exceed:

      (i) in the case of an investment made pursuant to DL 600, one year from the date of transfer to Chile; or

      (ii) in the case of an investment made pursuant to Law 18.657, five years from the date of transfer to Chile.

   (c) The right to adopt measures, consistent with this Annex, establishing future special voluntary investment programmes in addition to the general regime for foreign investment in Chile, except that any such measures may restrict transfers from Chile of proceeds from the sale of all or any part of an investment of an investor of another Party or from the partial or complete liquidation of the investment for a period not to exceed five years from the date of transfer to Chile.

2. For greater certainty, except to the extent that paragraph 1(b) or (c) provides an exception to Article 9.9 (Transfers), the investment entered through an investment contract under DL 600, through Law 18.657 or through any future special voluntary investment programme, will be subject to the obligations and commitments of this Chapter, to the extent that the investment is a covered investment under Chapter 9 (Investment).

ANNEX 9-G PUBLIC DEBT

1. The Parties recognise that the purchase of debt issued by a Party entails commercial risk. For greater certainty, no award shall be made in favour of a claimant for a claim under Article 9.19.1(a)(i)(A) (Submission of a Claim to Arbitration) or Article 9.19.1(b)(i)(A) with respect to default or non-payment of debt issued by a Party unless the claimant meets its burden of proving that such default or non-payment constitutes a breach of an obligation under Section A, including an uncompensated expropriation pursuant to Article 9.8 (Expropriation and Compensation).
2. No claim that a restructuring of debt issued by a Party breaches an obligation under Section A shall be submitted to, or if already submitted continue in, arbitration under Section B (Investor-State Dispute Settlement) if the restructuring is a negotiated restructuring at the time of submission, or becomes a negotiated restructuring after that submission, except for a claim that the restructuring violates Article 9.4 (National Treatment) or Article 9.5 (Most- Favoured-Nation Treatment).
3. Notwithstanding Article 9.19.4 (Submission of a Claim to Arbitration), and subject to paragraph 2, an investor of another Party shall not submit a claim under Section B (Investor-State Dispute Settlement) that a restructuring of debt issued by a Party breaches an obligation under Section A, other than Article 9.4 (National Treatment) or Article 9.5 (Most-Favoured-Nation Treatment), unless 270 days have elapsed from the date of receipt by the respondent of the written request for consultations pursuant to Article 9.18.2 (Consultation and Negotiation).

ANNEX 9-H

1. A decision under Australia's foreign investment policy, which consists of the Foreign Acquisitions and Takeovers Act 1975, Foreign Acquisitions and Takeovers Regulations 1989, Financial Sector (Shareholdings) Act 1998 and associated Ministerial Statements by the Treasurer of the Commonwealth of Australia or a minister acting on his or her behalf, on whether or not to approve a foreign investment proposal, shall not be subject to the dispute settlement provisions under Section B (Investor-State Dispute Settlement) or Chapter 28 (Dispute Settlement).
2. A decision by Canada following a review under the Investment Canada Act (R.S.C. 1985, c.28 (1st Supp.)), with respect to whether or not to permit an investment that is subject to review, shall not be subject to the dispute settlement provisions under Section B (Investor-State Dispute Settlement) or Chapter 28 (Dispute Settlement).
3. A decision by the National Commission on Foreign Investment (Comisión Nacional de Inversiones Extranjeras) following a review pursuant to the entry at Annex I – Mexico – 6 with respect to whether or not to permit an acquisition that is subject to review, shall not be subject to the dispute settlement provisions of Section B (Investor-State Dispute Settlement) or Chapter 28 (Dispute Settlement).
4. A decision under New Zealand's Overseas Investment Act 2005 to grant consent, or to decline to grant consent, to an overseas investment transaction that requires prior consent under that Act shall not be subject to the dispute settlement provisions under Section B (Investor-State Dispute Settlement) or Chapter 28 (Dispute Settlement).

ANNEX 9-I NON-CONFORMING MEASURES RATCHET MECHANISM

Notwithstanding Article 9.12.1(c) (Non-Conforming Measures), for Viet Nam for three years after the date of entry into force of this Agreement for it:

(a) Article 9.4 (National Treatment), Article 9.5 (Most-Favoured- Nation Treatment), Article 9.10 (Performance Requirements) and Article 9.11 (Senior Management and Boards of Directors) shall not apply to an amendment to any non-conforming measure referred to in Article 9.12.1(a) (Non-

Conforming Measures) to the extent that the amendment does not decrease the conformity of the measure, as it existed at the date of entry into force of this Agreement for Viet Nam, with Article 9.4 (National Treatment), Article 9.5 (Most-Favoured-Nation Treatment), Article 9.10 (Performance Requirements) or Article 9.11 (Senior Management and Boards of Directors);

(b) Viet Nam shall not withdraw a right or benefit from an investor or covered investment of another Party, in reliance on which the investor or covered investment has taken any concrete action, through an amendment to any non-conforming measure referred to in Article 9.12.1(a) (Non-Conforming Measures) that decreases the conformity of the measure as it existed immediately before the amendment; and

(c) Viet Nam shall provide to the other Parties the details of any amendment to a non-conforming measure referred to in Article 9.12.1(a) (Non-Conforming Measures) that would decrease the conformity of the measure, as it existed immediately before the amendment, at least 90 days before making the amendment.

ANNEX 9-J SUBMISSION OF A CLAIM TO ARBITRATION

1. An investor of a Party may not submit to arbitration under Section B (Investor-State Dispute Settlement) a claim that Chile, Mexico, Peru or Viet Nam has breached an obligation under Section A either:

(a) on its own behalf under Article 9.19.1(a) (Submission of a Claim to Arbitration); or

(b) on behalf of an enterprise of Chile, Mexico, Peru, or Viet Nam, that is a juridical person that the investor owns or controls directly or indirectly under 9.19.1(b) (Submission of a Claim to Arbitration),

if the investor or the enterprise, respectively, has alleged that breach of an obligation under Section A in proceedings before a court or administrative tribunal of Chile, Mexico, Peru or Viet Nam.

2. For greater certainty, if an investor of a Party elects to submit a claim of the type described in paragraph 1 to a court or administrative tribunal of Chile, Mexico, Peru or Viet Nam, that election shall be definitive and exclusive, and the investor may not thereafter submit the claim to arbitration under Section B (Investor-State Dispute Settlement).

ANNEX 9-K SUBMISSION OF CERTAIN CLAIMS FOR THREE YEARS AFTER ENTRY INTO FORCE

Malaysia

Without prejudice to a claimant's right to submit other claims to arbitration pursuant to Article 9.19 (Submission of a Claim to Arbitration), Malaysia does not consent to the submission of a claim that Malaysia has breached a government procurement contract with a covered investment, below the specified contract value, for a period of three years after the date of entry into force of this Agreement for Malaysia. The specified contract values are: (a) for goods, SDR 1,500,000; (b) for services, SDR 2,000,000; and (c) for construction, SDR 63,000,000.

ANNEX 9-L INVESTMENT AGREEMENTS

A. Agreements with selected international arbitration clauses

1. An investor of a Party may not submit to arbitration a claim for breach of an investment agreement under Article 9.19.1(a)(i)(C) (Submission of a Claim to Arbitration) or Article 9.19.1(b)(i)(C) if the

investment agreement provides the respondent's consent for the investor to arbitrate the alleged breach of the investment agreement and further provides that:

(a) a claim may be submitted for breach of the investment agreement under at least one of the following alternatives:
   (i) the ICSID Convention and the ICSID Rules of Procedure for Arbitration Proceedings, provided that both the respondent and the Party of the investor are parties to the ICSID Convention;
   (ii) the ICSID Additional Facility Rules, provided that either the respondent or the Party of the investor is a party to the ICSID Convention;
   (iii) the UNCITRAL Arbitration Rules;
   (iv) the ICC Arbitration Rules; or
   (v) the LCIA Arbitration Rules; and
(b) in the case of arbitration not under the ICSID Convention, the legal place of the arbitration shall be:
   (i) in the territory of a State that is party to the New York Convention; and
   (ii) outside the territory of the respondent.

2. Notwithstanding Article 9.21.2(b) (Conditions and Limitations on Consent of Each Party), if a claimant submits to arbitration a claim that the respondent has breached:

(a) an obligation under Section A pursuant to Article 9.19.1(a)(i)(A) (Submission of a Claim to Arbitration) or Article 9.19.1(b)(i)(A); or
(b) an investment authorisation pursuant to Article 9.19.1(a)(i)(B) (Submission of a Claim to Arbitration) or Article 9.19.1(b)(i)(B),

the claimant's submission of a written waiver shall not preclude its right to initiate or continue an arbitration under an investment agreement, if that investment agreement meets the criteria in paragraph 1, with respect to any measure alleged to constitute a breach referred to in Article 9.19 (Submission of a Claim to Arbitration).

3. If a claimant:

(a) submits to arbitration a claim that the respondent has breached an obligation under Section A pursuant to Article 9.19.1(a)(i)(A) (Submission of a Claim to Arbitration) or Article 9.19.1(b)(i)(A) or an investment authorisation pursuant to Article 9.19.1(a)(i)(B) or Article 9.19.1(b)(i)(B); and
(b) submits a claim to arbitration under an investment agreement that meets the criteria in paragraph 1, and the claims have a question of law or fact in common and arise out of the same events or circumstances,

any disputing party may seek a consolidation order in accordance with the agreement of all the disputing parties sought to be covered by the order or the terms of paragraphs 2 through 10 of Article 9.28 (Consolidation).

B. Certain agreements between Peru and covered investments or investors

1. Pursuant to Legislative Decrees 662 and 757, Peru may enter into agreements known as "stability agreements" with covered investments or investors of another Party.
2. As part of a stability agreement referred to in paragraph 1, Peru accords certain benefits to the covered investment or the investor that is a party to the agreement. These benefits typically include a commitment to maintain the existing income tax regime applicable to such covered investment or investor during a specified period of time.
3. A stability agreement referred to in paragraph 1 may constitute one of multiple written instruments that make up an "investment agreement", as defined in Article 9.1 (Definitions). If that is the case, a

breach of such a stability agreement by Peru may constitute a breach of the investment agreement of which it is a part.
4. If a stability agreement does not constitute one of multiple instruments that make up an "investment agreement", as defined in Article 9.1 (Definitions), a breach of such a stability agreement by Peru shall not constitute a breach of an investment agreement.

C. Limitation of Mexico's consent to arbitration

1. Without prejudice to a claimant's right to submit other claims pursuant to Article 9.19 (Submission of a Claim to Arbitration), Mexico does not consent to the submission of any claim to arbitration under Article 9.19.1(a)(i)(C) or 9.19.1(b)(i)(C) if the submission to arbitration of that claim would be inconsistent with the following laws with respect to the relevant acts of authority:

(a) Hydrocarbons Law, Articles 20 and 21;
(b) Law on Public Works and Related Services, Article 98, paragraph 2;
(c) Public Private Partnerships Law, Article 139, paragraph 3;
(d) Law on Roads, Bridges, and Federal Motor Carriers, Article 80;
(e) Ports Law, Article 3, paragraph 2;
(f) Airports Law, Article 3, paragraph 2;
(g) Regulatory Law of the Railway Service, Article 4, paragraph 2;
(h) Commercial and Navigation Maritimes Law, Article 264, paragraph 2;
(i) Civil Aviation Law, Article 3, paragraph 2; and
(j) Political Constitution of the United Mexican States, Article 28, paragraph 20, subparagraph VII, and Federal Telecommunications and Broadcasting Law, Article 312,

provided, however, that the application of the provisions referred to in subparagraphs (a) through (i) shall not be used as a disguised means to repudiate or breach the investment agreement.
2. If any law referred to in paragraph 1 is amended to permit the submission to arbitration of such a claim after the entry into force of this Agreement for Mexico, the limitation of Mexico's consent specified in paragraph 1 shall not apply with respect to that law.

D. Specific Canadian entities under subpart (c) of definition

For Canada, authority at the central level of government includes entities listed under Schedule III of the Financial Administration Act (R.S.C. 1985, c. F- 11), and port or bridge authorities, that have concluded an investment agreement under subpart (c) of the definition of "investment agreement" only if the government directs or controls the day to day operations or activities of the entity or authority in carrying out its obligations under the investment agreement.

10.1.6 Comprehensive Economic and Trade Agreement ('CETA') (2017) (selected articles)

Signed 30 October 2016, entered into force provisionally on 21 September 2017.

CHAPTER EIGHT – INVESTMENT

SECTION A DEFINITIONS AND SCOPE

Article 8.1 Definitions

For the purposes of this Chapter:

activities carried out in the exercise of governmental authority means activities carried out neither on a commercial basis nor in competition with one or more economic operators;

aircraft repair and maintenance services means activities undertaken on an aircraft or a part of an aircraft while it is withdrawn from service and do not include so-called line maintenance;

airport operation services means the operation or management, on a fee or contract basis, of airport infrastructure, including terminals, runways, taxiways and aprons, parking facilities, and intra-airport transportation systems. For greater certainty, airport operation services do not include the ownership of, or investment in, airports or airport lands, or any of the functions carried out by a board of directors. Airport operation services do not include air navigation services;

attachment means the seizure of property of a disputing party to secure or ensure the satisfaction of an award;

computer reservation system services means the supply of a service by computerised systems that contain information about air carriers' schedules, availability, fares and fare rules, through which reservations can be made or tickets may be issued;

confidential or protected information means:

(a) confidential business information; or

(b) information which is protected against disclosure to the public;

(i) in the case of information of the respondent, under the law of the respondent;

(ii) in the case of other information, under a law or rules that the Tribunal determines to be applicable to the disclosure of such information;

covered investment means, with respect to a Party, an investment:

(a) in its territory;

(b) made in accordance with the applicable law at the time the investment is made;

(c) directly or indirectly owned or controlled by an investor of the other Party; and

(d) existing on the date of entry into force of this Agreement, or made or acquired thereafter;

disputing party means the investor that initiates proceedings pursuant to Section F or the respondent. For the purposes of Section F and without prejudice to Article 8.14, an investor does not include a Party;

disputing parties means both the investor and the respondent;

enjoin means an order to prohibit or restrain an action;

enterprise means an enterprise as defined in Article 1.1 (Definitions of general application) and a branch or representative office of an enterprise;

ground handling services means the supply of a service on a fee or contract basis for: ground administration and supervision, including load control and communications; passenger handling; baggage handling; cargo and mail handling; ramp handling and aircraft services; fuel and oil handling;

aircraft line maintenance, flight operations and crew administration; surface transport; or catering services. Ground handling services do not include security services or the operation or management of centralised airport infrastructure, such as baggage handling systems, de-icing facilities, fuel distribution systems, or intra-airport transport systems;

ICSID means the International Centre for Settlement of Investment Disputes;

ICSID Additional Facility Rules means the Rules Governing the Additional Facility for the Administration of Proceedings by the Secretariat of the International Centre for Settlement of Investment Disputes;

ICSID Convention means the Convention on the Settlement of Investment Disputes between States and Nationals of other States, done at Washington on 18 March 1965;

intellectual property rights means copyright and related rights, trademark rights, rights in geographical indications, rights in industrial designs, patent rights, rights in layout designs of integrated circuits, rights in relation to protection of undisclosed information, and plant breeders' rights; and, if such rights are provided by a Party's law, utility model rights. The CETA Joint Committee may, by decision, add other categories of intellectual property to this definition;

investment means every kind of asset that an investor owns or controls, directly or indirectly, that has the characteristics of an investment, which includes a certain duration and other characteristics such as the commitment of capital or other resources, the expectation of gain or profit, or the assumption of risk. Forms that an investment may take include:

(a) an enterprise;
(b) shares, stocks and other forms of equity participation in an enterprise;
(c) bonds, debentures and other debt instruments of an enterprise;
(d) a loan to an enterprise;
(e) any other kind of interest in an enterprise;
(f) an interest arising from:
    (i) a concession conferred pursuant to the law of a Party or under a contract, including to search for, cultivate, extract or exploit natural resources,
    (ii) a turnkey, construction, production or revenue-sharing contract; or
    (iii) other similar contracts;
(g) intellectual property rights;
(h) other moveable property, tangible or intangible, or immovable property and related rights;
(i) claims to money or claims to performance under a contract.

For greater certainty, **claims to money** does not include:

(a) claims to money that arise solely from commercial contracts for the sale of goods or services by a natural person or enterprise in the territory of a Party to a natural person or enterprise in the territory of the other Party.
(b) the domestic financing of such contracts; or
(c) any order, judgment, or arbitral award related to sub-subparagraph (a) or (b).

Returns that are invested shall be treated as investments. Any alteration of the form in which assets are invested or reinvested does not affect their qualification as investment;

investor means a Party, a natural person or an enterprise of a Party, other than a branch or a representative office, that seeks to make, is making or has made an investment in the territory of the other Party;

For the purposes of this definition, an **enterprise of a Party** is:

(a) an enterprise that is constituted or organised under the laws of that Party and has substantial business activities in the territory of that Party; or
(b) an enterprise that is constituted or organised under the laws of that Party and is directly or indirectly owned or controlled by a natural person of that Party or by an enterprise mentioned under paragraph (a) ;

locally established enterprise means a juridical person that is constituted or organised under the laws of the respondent and that an investor of the other Party owns or controls directly or indirectly;

natural person means:

(a) in the case of Canada, a natural person who is a citizen or permanent resident of Canada; and

(b) in the case of the EU Party, a natural person having the nationality of one of the Member States of the European Union according to their respective laws, and, for Latvia, also a natural person permanently residing in the Republic of Latvia who is not a citizen of the Republic of Latvia or any other state but who is entitled, under laws and regulations of the Republic of Latvia, to receive a non-citizen's passport.

A natural person who is a citizen of Canada and has the nationality of one of the Member States of the European Union is deemed to be exclusively a natural person of the Party of his or her dominant and effective nationality.

A natural person who has the nationality of one of the Member States of the European Union or is a citizen of Canada, and is also a permanent resident of the other Party, is deemed to be exclusively a natural person of the Party of his or her nationality or citizenship, as applicable;

New York Convention means the United Nations Convention on the Recognition and Enforcement of Foreign Arbitral Awards, done at New York on 10 June 1958;

non-disputing Party means Canada, if the European Union or a Member State of the European Union is the respondent, or the European Union, if Canada is the respondent;

respondent means Canada or, in the case of the European Union, either the Member State of the European Union or the European Union pursuant to Article 8.21;

returns means all amounts yielded by an investment or reinvestment, including profits, royalties and interest or other fees and payments in kind;

selling and marketing of air transport services means opportunities for the air carrier concerned to sell and market freely its air transport services including all aspects of marketing such as market research, advertising and distribution, but does not include the pricing of air transport services or the applicable conditions;

third party funding means any funding provided by a natural or legal person who is not a disputing party but who enters into an agreement with a disputing party in order to finance part or all of the cost of the proceedings either through a donation or grant, or in return for remuneration dependent on the outcome of the dispute;

Tribunal means the tribunal established under Article 8.27;

UNCITRAL Arbitration Rules means the arbitration rules of the United Nations Commission on International Trade Law; and

UNCITRAL Transparency Rules means the UNCITRAL Rules on Transparency in Treaty-based Investor-State Arbitration;

Article 8.2 Scope

1. This Chapter applies to a measure adopted or maintained by a Party in its territory (5) relating to:

(a) an investor of the other Party;

(b) a covered investment; and

(c) with respect to Article 8.5, any investments in its territory.

2. With respect to the establishment or acquisition of a covered investment (6), Sections B and C do not apply to a measure relating to:

(a) air services, or related services in support of air services and other services supplied by means of air transport (7), other than:

(i) aircraft repair and maintenance services;

(ii) the selling and marketing of air transport services;

(iii) computer reservation system (CRS) services;

(iv) ground handling services;
(v) airport operation services; or
(b) activities carried out in the exercise of governmental authority.

3. For the EU Party, Sections B and C do not apply to a measure with respect to audio-visual services. For Canada, Sections B and C do not apply to a measure with respect to cultural industries.

4. Claims may be submitted by an investor under this Chapter only in accordance with Article 8.18, and in compliance with the procedures set out in Section F. Claims in respect of an obligation set out in Section B are excluded from the scope of Section F. Claims under Section C with respect to the establishment or acquisition of a covered investment are excluded from the scope of Section F. Section D applies only to a covered investment and to investors in respect of their covered investment.

5. This Chapter does not affect the rights and obligations of the Parties under the Agreement on Air Transport between Canada and the European Community and its Member States, done at Brussels on 17 December 2009 and Ottawa on 18 December 2009.

Article 8.3 Relation to other chapters

1. This Chapter does not apply to measures adopted or maintained by a Party to the extent that the measures apply to investors or to their investments covered by Chapter Thirteen (Financial Services).

2. A requirement by a Party that a service supplier of the other Party post a bond or other form of financial security as a condition for supplying a service in its territory does not of itself make this Chapter applicable to measures adopted or maintained by the Party relating to the supply of that cross-border service. This Chapter applies to measures adopted or maintained by the Party relating to the posted bond or financial security to the extent that such bond or financial security is a covered investment.

SECTION B ESTABLISHMENT OF INVESTMENTS

Article 8.4 Market access

1. A Party shall not adopt or maintain with respect to market access through establishment by an investor of the other Party, on the basis of its entire territory or on the basis of the territory of a national, provincial, territorial, regional or local level of government, a measure that:

(a) imposes limitations on:
(i) the number of enterprises that may carry out a specific economic activity whether in the form of numerical quotas, monopolies, exclusive suppliers or the requirement of an economic needs test;
(ii) the total value of transactions or assets in the form of numerical quotas or the requirement of an economic needs test;
(iii) the total number of operations or the total quantity of output expressed in terms of designated numerical units in the form of quotas or the requirement of an economic needs test (8) ;
(iv) the participation of foreign capital in terms of maximum percentage limit on foreign shareholding or the total value of individual or aggregate foreign investment; or
(v) the total number of natural persons that may be employed in a particular sector or that an enterprise may employ and who are necessary for, and directly related to, the performance of economic activity in the form of numerical quotas or the requirement of an economic needs test; or
(b) restricts or requires specific types of legal entity or joint venture through which an enterprise may carry out an economic activity.

2. For greater certainty, the following are consistent with paragraph 1:
(a) a measure concerning zoning and planning regulations affecting the development or use of land, or another analogous measure;

(b) a measure requiring the separation of the ownership of infrastructure from the ownership of the goods or services provided through that infrastructure to ensure fair competition, for example in the fields of energy, transportation and telecommunications;
(c) a measure restricting the concentration of ownership to ensure fair competition;
(d) a measure seeking to ensure the conservation and protection of natural resources and the environment, including a limitation on the availability, number and scope of concessions granted, and the imposition of a moratorium or ban;
(e) a measure limiting the number of authorisations granted because of technical or physical constraints, for example telecommunications spectrum and frequencies; or
(f) a measure requiring that a certain percentage of the shareholders, owners, partners, or directors of an enterprise be qualified or practice a certain profession such as lawyers or accountants.

Article 8.5 Performance requirements

1. A Party shall not impose, or enforce the following requirements, or enforce a commitment or undertaking, in connection with the establishment, acquisition, expansion, conduct, operation, and management of any investments in its territory to:
(a) export a given level or percentage of a good or service;
(b) achieve a given level or percentage of domestic content;
(c) purchase, use or accord a preference to a good produced or service provided in its territory, or to purchase a good or service from natural persons or enterprises in its territory;
(d) relate the volume or value of imports to the volume or value of exports or to the amount of foreign exchange inflows associated with that investment;
(e) restrict sales of a good or service in its territory that the investment produces or provides by relating those sales to the volume or value of its exports or foreign exchange earnings;
(f) transfer technology, a production process or other proprietary knowledge to a natural person or enterprise in its territory; or
(g) supply exclusively from the territory of the Party a good produced or a service provided by the investment to a specific regional or world market.

2. A Party shall not condition the receipt or continued receipt of an advantage, in connection with the establishment, acquisition, expansion, management, conduct or operation of any investments in its territory, on compliance with any of the following requirements:
(a) to achieve a given level or percentage of domestic content;
(b) to purchase, use or accord a preference to a good produced in its territory, or to purchase a good from a producer in its territory;
(c) to relate the volume or value of imports to the volume or value of exports or to the amount of foreign exchange inflows associated with that investment; or
(d) to restrict sales of a good or service in its territory that the investment produces or provides by relating those sales to the volume or value of its exports or foreign exchange earnings.

3. Paragraph 2 does not prevent a Party from conditioning the receipt or continued receipt of an advantage, in connection with an investment in its territory, on compliance with a requirement to locate production, provide a service, train or employ workers, construct or expand particular facilities, or carry out research and development in its territory.

4. Subparagraph 1(f) does not apply if the requirement is imposed or the commitment or undertaking is enforced by a court, administrative tribunal or competition authority to remedy a violation of competition laws.

5. The provisions of:
(a) subparagraphs 1(a), (b) and (c), and 2(a) and (b), do not apply to qualification requirements for a good or service with respect to participation in export promotion and foreign aid programs;

(b) this Article does not apply to procurement by a Party of a good or service purchased for governmental purposes and not with a view to commercial resale or with a view to use in the supply of a good or service for commercial sale, whether or not that procurement is 'covered procurement' within the meaning of Article 19.2 (Scope and coverage).

6. For greater certainty, subparagraphs 2(a) and (b) do not apply to requirements imposed by an importing Party relating to the content of a good necessary to qualify for preferential tariffs or preferential quotas.

7. This Article is without prejudice to World Trade Organization commitments of a Party.

SECTION C NON-DISCRIMINATORY TREATMENT

Article 8.6 National treatment

1. Each Party shall accord to an investor of the other Party and to a covered investment, treatment no less favourable than the treatment it accords, in like situations to its own investors and to their investments with respect to the establishment, acquisition, expansion, conduct, operation, management, maintenance, use, enjoyment and sale or disposal of their investments in its territory.

2. The treatment accorded by a Party under paragraph 1 means, with respect to a government in Canada other than at the federal level, treatment no less favourable than the most favourable treatment accorded, in like situations, by that government to investors of Canada in its territory and to investments of such investors.

3. The treatment accorded by a Party under paragraph 1 means, with respect to a government of or in a Member State of the European Union, treatment no less favourable than the most favourable treatment accorded, in like situations, by that government to investors of the EU in its territory and to investments of such investors.

Article 8.7 Most-favoured-nation treatment

1. Each Party shall accord to an investor of the other Party and to a covered investment, treatment no less favourable than the treatment it accords in like situations, to investors of a third country and to their investments with respect to the establishment, acquisition, expansion, conduct, operation, management, maintenance, use, enjoyment and sale or disposal of their investments in its territory.

2. For greater certainty, the treatment accorded by a Party under paragraph 1 means, with respect to a government in Canada other than at the federal level, or, with respect to a government of or in a Member State of the European Union, treatment accorded, in like situations, by that government to investors in its territory, and to investments of such investors, of a third country.

3 Paragraph 1 does not apply to treatment accorded by a Party providing for recognition, including through an arrangement or agreement with a third country that recognises the accreditation of testing and analysis services and service suppliers, the accreditation of repair and maintenance services and service suppliers, as well as the certification of the qualifications of or the results of or work done by those accredited services and service suppliers.

4. For greater certainty, the 'treatment' referred to in paragraphs 1 and 2 does not include procedures for the resolution of investment disputes between investors and states provided for in other international investment treaties and other trade agreements. Substantive obligations in other international investment treaties and other trade agreements do not in themselves constitute 'treatment', and thus cannot give rise to a breach of this Article, absent measures adopted or maintained by a Party pursuant to those obligations.

Article 8.8 Senior management and boards of directors

A Party shall not require that an enterprise of that Party, that is also a covered investment, appoint to senior management or board of director positions, natural persons of any particular nationality.

SECTION D INVESTMENT PROTECTION

Article 8.9 Investment and regulatory measures

1. For the purpose of this Chapter, the Parties reaffirm their right to regulate within their territories to achieve legitimate policy objectives, such as the protection of public health, safety, the environment or public morals, social or consumer protection or the promotion and protection of cultural diversity.
2. For greater certainty, the mere fact that a Party regulates, including through a modification to its laws, in a manner which negatively affects an investment or interferes with an investor's expectations, including its expectations of profits, does not amount to a breach of an obligation under this Section.
3. For greater certainty, a Party's decision not to issue, renew or maintain a subsidy:
   (a) in the absence of any specific commitment under law or contract to issue, renew, or maintain that subsidy; or
   (b) in accordance with any terms or conditions attached to the issuance, renewal or maintenance of the subsidy,

   does not constitute a breach of the provisions of this Section.
4. For greater certainty, nothing in this Section shall be construed as preventing a Party from discontinuing the granting of a subsidy (9) or requesting its reimbursement where such measure is necessary in order to comply with international obligations between the Parties or has been ordered by a competent court, administrative tribunal or other competent authority (10), or requiring that Party to compensate the investor therefor.

Article 8.10 Treatment of investors and of covered investments

1. Each Party shall accord in its territory to covered investments of the other Party and to investors with respect to their covered investments fair and equitable treatment and full protection and security in accordance with paragraphs 2 through 7.
2. A Party breaches the obligation of fair and equitable treatment referenced in paragraph 1 if a measure or series of measures constitutes:
   (a) denial of justice in criminal, civil or administrative proceedings;
   (b) fundamental breach of due process, including a fundamental breach of transparency, in judicial and administrative proceedings;
   (c) manifest arbitrariness;
   (d) targeted discrimination on manifestly wrongful grounds, such as gender, race or religious belief;
   (e) abusive treatment of investors, such as coercion, duress and harassment; or
   (f) a breach of any further elements of the fair and equitable treatment obligation adopted by the Parties in accordance with paragraph 3 of this Article.
3. The Parties shall regularly, or upon request of a Party, review the content of the obligation to provide fair and equitable treatment. The Committee on Services and Investment, established under Article 26.2.1(b) (Specialised committees), may develop recommendations in this regard and submit them to the CETA Joint Committee for decision.
4. When applying the above fair and equitable treatment obligation, the Tribunal may take into account whether a Party made a specific representation to an investor to induce a covered investment, that created a legitimate expectation, and upon which the investor relied in deciding to make or maintain the covered investment, but that the Party subsequently frustrated.
5. For greater certainty, 'full protection and security' refers to the Party's obligations relating to the physical security of investors and covered investments.
6. For greater certainty, a breach of another provision of this Agreement, or of a separate international agreement does not establish a breach of this Article.

7. For greater certainty, the fact that a measure breaches domestic law does not, in and of itself, establish a breach of this Article. In order to ascertain whether the measure breaches this Article, the Tribunal must consider whether a Party has acted inconsistently with the obligations in paragraph 1.

Article 8.11 Compensation for losses
Notwithstanding Article 8.15.5(b), each Party shall accord to investors of the other Party, whose covered investments suffer losses owing to armed conflict, civil strife, a state of emergency or natural disaster in its territory, treatment no less favourable than that it accords to its own investors or to the investors of a third country, whichever is more favourable to the investor concerned, as regards restitution, indemnification, compensation or other settlement.

Article 8.12 Expropriation
1. A Party shall not nationalise or expropriate a covered investment either directly, or indirectly through measures having an effect equivalent to nationalisation or expropriation ('expropriation'), except:
(a) for a public purpose;
(b) under due process of law;
(c) in a non-discriminatory manner; and
(d) on payment of prompt, adequate and effective compensation.
For greater certainty, this paragraph shall be interpreted in accordance with Annex 8-A.
2. The compensation referred to in paragraph 1 shall amount to the fair market value of the investment at the time immediately before the expropriation or the impending expropriation became known, whichever is earlier. Valuation criteria shall include going concern value, asset value including the declared tax value of tangible property, and other criteria, as appropriate, to determine fair market value.
3. The compensation shall also include interest at a normal commercial rate from the date of expropriation until the date of payment and shall, in order to be effective for the investor, be paid and made transferable, without delay, to the country designated by the investor and in the currency of the country of which the investor is a national or in any freely convertible currency accepted by the investor.
4. The affected investor shall have the right, under the law of the expropriating Party, to a prompt review of its claim and of the valuation of its investment, by a judicial or other independent authority of that Party, in accordance with the principles set out in this Article.
5. This Article does not apply to the issuance of compulsory licences granted in relation to intellectual property rights, to the extent that such issuance is consistent with the TRIPS Agreement.
6. For greater certainty, the revocation, limitation or creation of intellectual property rights, to the extent that these measures are consistent with the TRIPS Agreement and Chapter Twenty (Intellectual Property), do not constitute expropriation. Moreover, a determination that these measures are inconsistent with the TRIPS Agreement or Chapter Twenty (Intellectual Property) does not establish an expropriation.

Article 8.13 Transfers
1. Each Party shall permit all transfers relating to a covered investment to be made without restriction or delay in a freely convertible currency and at the market rate of exchange applicable on the date of transfer. Such transfers include:
(a) contributions to capital, such as principal and additional funds to maintain, develop or increase the investment;

(b) profits, dividends, interest, capital gains, royalty payments, management fees, technical assistance and other fees, or other forms of returns or amounts derived from the covered investment;
(c) proceeds from the sale or liquidation of the whole or a part of the covered investment;
(d) payments made under a contract entered into by the investor or the covered investment, including payments made pursuant to a loan agreement;
(e) payments made pursuant to Articles 8.11 and 8.12;
(f) earnings and other remuneration of foreign personnel working in connection with an investment; and
(g) payments of damages pursuant to an award issued under Section F.

2. A Party shall not require its investors to transfer, or penalise its investors for failing to transfer, the income, earnings, profits or other amounts derived from, or attributable to, investments in the territory of the other Party.

3. Nothing in this Article shall be construed to prevent a Party from applying in an equitable and non-discriminatory manner and not in a way that would constitute a disguised restriction on transfers, its laws relating to:
(a) bankruptcy, insolvency or the protection of the rights of creditors;
(b) issuing, trading or dealing in securities;
(c) criminal or penal offences;
(d) financial reporting or record keeping of transfers when necessary to assist law enforcement or financial regulatory authorities; and
(e) the satisfaction of judgments in adjudicatory proceedings.

Article 8.14 Subrogation

If a Party, or an agency of a Party, makes a payment under an indemnity, guarantee or contract of insurance that it has entered into in respect of an investment made by one of its investors in the territory of the other Party, the other Party shall recognise that the Party or its agency shall be entitled in all circumstances to the same rights as those of the investor in respect of the investment. These rights may be exercised by the Party or an agency of the Party, or by the investor if the Party or an agency of the Party so authorises.

1. Articles 8.4 through 8.8 do not apply to:
(a) an existing non-conforming measure that is maintained by a Party at the level of:
(i) the European Union, as set out in its Schedule to Annex I;
(ii) a national government, as set out by that Party in its Schedule to Annex I;
(iii) a provincial, territorial, or regional government, as set out by that Party in its Schedule to Annex I; or
(iv) a local government;
(b) the continuation or prompt renewal of a non-conforming measure referred to in subparagraph (a) ; or
(c) an amendment to a non-conforming measure referred to in subparagraph (a) to the extent that the amendment does not decrease the conformity of the measure, as it existed immediately before the amendment, with Articles 8.4 through 8.8.

2. Articles 8.4 through 8.8 do not apply to a measure that a Party adopts or maintains with respect to a sector, subsector or activity, as set out in its Schedule to Annex II.

3. Without prejudice to Articles 8.10 and 8.12, a Party shall not adopt a measure or series of measures after the date of entry into force of this Agreement and covered by its Schedule to Annex II, that require, directly or indirectly an investor of the other Party, by reason of nationality, to sell or otherwise dispose of an investment existing at the time the measure or series of measures become effective.

4. In respect of intellectual property rights, a Party may derogate from Articles 8.5.1(f), 8.6, and 8.7 if permitted by the TRIPS Agreement, including any amendments to the TRIPS Agreement in force for both Parties, and waivers to the TRIPS Agreement adopted pursuant to Article IX of the WTO Agreement.
5. Articles 8.4, 8.6, 8.7 and 8.8 do not apply to:
(a) procurement by a Party of a good or service purchased for governmental purposes and not with a view to commercial resale or with a view to use in the supply of a good or service for commercial sale, whether or not that procurement is 'covered procurement' within the meaning of Article 19.2 (Scope and coverage) ; or
(b) subsidies, or government support relating to trade in services, provided by a Party.

Article 8.16 Denial of benefits
A Party may deny the benefits of this Chapter to an investor of the other Party that is an enterprise of that Party and to investments of that investor if:
(a) an investor of a third country owns or controls the enterprise; and
(b) the denying Party adopts or maintains a measure with respect to the third country that:
(i) relates to the maintenance of international peace and security; and
(ii) prohibits transactions with the enterprise or would be violated or circumvented if the benefits of this Chapter were accorded to the enterprise or to its investments.

Article 8.17 Formal requirements
Notwithstanding Articles 8.6 and 8.7, a Party may require an investor of the other Party, or its covered investment, to provide routine information concerning that investment solely for informational or statistical purposes, provided that those requests are reasonable and not unduly burdensome. The Party shall protect confidential or protected information from any disclosure that would prejudice the competitive position of the investor or the covered investment. This paragraph does not prevent a Party from otherwise obtaining or disclosing information in connection with the equitable and good faith application of its laws.

SECTION F RESOLUTION OF INVESTMENT DISPUTES BETWEEN INVESTORS AND STATES

Article 8.18 Scope
1. Without prejudice to the rights and obligations of the Parties under Chapter Twenty-Nine (Dispute Settlement), an investor of a Party may submit to the Tribunal constituted under this Section a claim that the other Party has breached an obligation under:
(a) Section C, with respect to the expansion, conduct, operation, management, maintenance, use, enjoyment and sale or disposal of its covered investment, or
(b) Section D,
where the investor claims to have suffered loss or damage as a result of the alleged breach.
2. Claims under subparagraph 1(a) with respect to the expansion of a covered investment may be submitted only to the extent the measure relates to the existing business operations of a covered investment and the investor has, as a result, incurred loss or damage with respect to the covered investment.
3. For greater certainty, an investor may not submit a claim under this Section if the investment has been made through fraudulent misrepresentation, concealment, corruption, or conduct amounting to an abuse of process.
4. A claim with respect to restructuring of debt issued by a Party may only be submitted under this Section in accordance with Annex 8-B.

5. The Tribunal constituted under this Section shall not decide claims that fall outside of the scope of this Article.

Article 8.19 Consultations
1. A dispute should as far as possible be settled amicably. Such a settlement may be agreed at any time, including after the claim has been submitted pursuant to Article 8.23. Unless the disputing parties agree to a longer period, consultations shall be held within 60 days of the submission of the request for consultations pursuant to paragraph 4.
2. Unless the disputing parties agree otherwise, the place of consultation shall be:
   (a) Ottawa, if the measures challenged are measures of Canada;
   (b) Brussels, if the measures challenged include a measure of the European Union; or
   (c) the capital of the Member State of the European Union, if the measures challenged are exclusively measures of that Member State.
3. The disputing parties may hold the consultations through videoconference or other means where appropriate, such as in the case where the investor is a small or medium-sized enterprise.
4. The investor shall submit to the other Party a request for consultations setting out:
   (a) the name and address of the investor and, if such request is submitted on behalf of a locally established enterprise, the name, address and place of incorporation of the locally established enterprise;
   (b) if there is more than one investor, the name and address of each investor and, if there is more than one locally established enterprise, the name, address and place of incorporation of each locally established enterprise;
   (c) the provisions of this Agreement alleged to have been breached;
   (d) the legal and the factual basis for the claim, including the measures at issue; and
   (e) the relief sought and the estimated amount of damages claimed.

The request for consultations shall contain evidence establishing that the investor is an investor of the other Party and that it owns or controls the investment including, if applicable, that it owns or controls the locally established enterprise on whose behalf the request is submitted.
5. The requirements of the request for consultations set out in paragraph 4 shall be met with sufficient specificity to allow the respondent to effectively engage in consultations and to prepare its defence.
6. A request for consultations must be submitted within:
   (a) three years after the date on which the investor or, as applicable, the locally established enterprise, first acquired or should have first acquired, knowledge of the alleged breach and knowledge that the investor or, as applicable, the locally established enterprise, has incurred loss or damage thereby; or
   (b) two years after an investor or, as applicable, the locally established enterprise, ceases to pursue claims or proceedings before a tribunal or court under the law of a Party, or when such proceedings have otherwise ended and, in any event, no later than 10 years after the date on which the investor or, as applicable, the locally established enterprise, first acquired or should have first acquired knowledge of the alleged breach and knowledge that the investor has incurred loss or damage thereby.
7. A request for consultations concerning an alleged breach by the European Union or a Member State of the European Union shall be sent to the European Union.
8. In the event that the investor has not submitted a claim pursuant to Article 8.23 within 18 months of submitting the request for consultations, the investor is deemed to have withdrawn its request for consultations and, if applicable, its notice requesting a determination of the respondent, and shall not submit a claim under this Section with respect to the same measures. This period may be extended by agreement of the disputing parties.

Article 8.20 Mediation

1. The disputing parties may at any time agree to have recourse to mediation.
2. Recourse to mediation is without prejudice to the legal position or rights of either disputing party under this Chapter and is governed by the rules agreed to by the disputing parties including, if available, the rules for mediation adopted by the Committee on Services and Investment pursuant to Article 8.44.3(c).
3. The mediator is appointed by agreement of the disputing parties. The disputing parties may also request that the Secretary General of ICSID appoint the mediator.
4. The disputing parties shall endeavour to reach a resolution of the dispute within 60 days from the appointment of the mediator.
5. If the disputing parties agree to have recourse to mediation, Articles 8.19.6 and 8.19.8 shall not apply from the date on which the disputing parties agreed to have recourse to mediation to the date on which either disputing party decides to terminate the mediation. A decision by a disputing party to terminate the mediation shall be transmitted by way of a letter to the mediator and the other disputing party.

Article 8.21 Determination of the respondent for disputes with the European Union or its Member States

1. If the dispute cannot be settled within 90 days of the submission of the request for consultations, the request concerns an alleged breach of this Agreement by the European Union or a Member State of the European Union and the investor intends to submit a claim pursuant to Article 8.23, the investor shall deliver to the European Union a notice requesting a determination of the respondent.
2. The notice under paragraph 1 shall identify the measures in respect of which the investor intends to submit a claim.
3. The European Union shall, after having made a determination, inform the investor as to whether the European Union or a Member State of the European Union shall be the respondent.
4. In the event that the investor has not been informed of the determination within 50 days of delivering its notice requesting such determination:
   (a) if the measures identified in the notice are exclusively measures of a Member State of the European Union, the Member State shall be the respondent;
   (b) if the measures identified in the notice include measures of the European Union, the European Union shall be the respondent.
5. The investor may submit a claim pursuant to Article 8.23 on the basis of the determination made pursuant to paragraph 3, and, if no such determination has been communicated to the investor, on the basis of the application of paragraph 4.
6. If the European Union or a Member State of the European Union is the respondent, pursuant to paragraph 3 or 4, neither the European Union, nor the Member State of the European Union may assert the inadmissibility of the claim, lack of jurisdiction of the Tribunal or otherwise object to the claim or award on the ground that the respondent was not properly determined pursuant to paragraph 3 or identified on the basis of the application of paragraph 4.
7. The Tribunal shall be bound by the determination made pursuant to paragraph 3 and, if no such determination has been communicated to the investor, the application of paragraph 4.

Article 8.22 Procedural and other requirements for the submission of a claim to the Tribunal

1. An investor may only submit a claim pursuant to Article 8.23 if the investor:
   (a) delivers to the respondent, with the submission of a claim, its consent to the settlement of the dispute by the Tribunal in accordance with the procedures set out in this Section;
   (b) allows at least 180 days to elapse from the submission of the request for consultations and, if applicable, at least 90 days to elapse from the submission of the notice requesting a determination of the respondent;

(c) has fulfilled the requirements of the notice requesting a determination of the respondent;
(d) has fulfilled the requirements related to the request for consultations;
(e) does not identify a measure in its claim that was not identified in its request for consultations;
(f) withdraws or discontinues any existing proceeding before a tribunal or court under domestic or international law with respect to a measure alleged to constitute a breach referred to in its claim; and
(g) waives its right to initiate any claim or proceeding before a tribunal or court under domestic or international law with respect to a measure alleged to constitute a breach referred to in its claim.

2. If the claim submitted pursuant to Article 8.23 is for loss or damage to a locally established enterprise or to an interest in a locally established enterprise that the investor owns or controls directly or indirectly, the requirements in subparagraphs 1(f) and (g) apply both to the investor and the locally established enterprise.
3. The requirements of subparagraphs 1(f) and (g) and paragraph 2 do not apply in respect of a locally established enterprise if the respondent or the investor's host state has deprived the investor of control of the locally established enterprise, or has otherwise prevented the locally established enterprise from fulfilling those requirements.
4. Upon request of the respondent, the Tribunal shall decline jurisdiction if the investor or, as applicable, the locally established enterprise fails to fulfil any of the requirements of paragraphs 1 and 2.
5. The waiver provided pursuant to subparagraph 1(g) or paragraph 2 as applicable shall cease to apply:
(a) if the Tribunal rejects the claim on the basis of a failure to meet the requirements of paragraph 1 or 2 or on any other procedural or jurisdictional grounds;
(b) if the Tribunal dismisses the claim pursuant to Article 8.32 or Article 8.33; or
(c) if the investor withdraws its claim, in conformity with the applicable rules under Article 8.23.2, within 12 months of the constitution of the division of the Tribunal.

Article 8.23Submission of a claim to the Tribunal

1. If a dispute has not been resolved through consultations, a claim may be submitted under this Section by:
(a) an investor of a Party on its own behalf; or
(b) an investor of a Party, on behalf of a locally established enterprise which it owns or controls directly or indirectly.
2. A claim may be submitted under the following rules:
(a) the ICSID Convention and Rules of Procedure for Arbitration Proceedings;
(b) the ICSID Additional Facility Rules if the conditions for proceedings pursuant to paragraph (a) do not apply;
(c) the UNCITRAL Arbitration Rules; or
(d) any other rules on agreement of the disputing parties.
3. In the event that the investor proposes rules pursuant to subparagraph 2(d), the respondent shall reply to the investor's proposal within 20 days of receipt. If the disputing parties have not agreed on such rules within 30 days of receipt, the investor may submit a claim under the rules provided for in subparagraph 2(a), (b) or (c).
4. For greater certainty, a claim submitted under subparagraph 1(b) shall satisfy the requirements of Article 25(1) of the ICSID Convention.
5. The investor may, when submitting its claim, propose that a sole Member of the Tribunal should hear the claim. The respondent shall give sympathetic consideration to that request, in particular if the investor is a small or medium-sized enterprise or the compensation or damages claimed are relatively low.

6. The rules applicable under paragraph 2 are those that are in effect on the date that the claim or claims are submitted to the Tribunal under this Section, subject to the specific rules set out in this Section and supplemented by rules adopted pursuant to Article 8.44.3(b).
7. A claim is submitted for dispute settlement under this Section when:
(a) the request under Article 36(1) of the ICSID Convention is received by the Secretary-General of ICSID;
(b) the request under Article 2 of Schedule C of the ICSID Additional Facility Rules is received by the Secretariat of ICSID;
(c) the notice under Article 3 of the UNCITRAL Arbitration Rules is received by the respondent; or
(d) the request or notice initiating proceedings is received by the respondent in accordance with the rules agreed upon pursuant to subparagraph 2(d).
8. Each Party shall notify the other Party of the place of delivery of notices and other documents by the investors pursuant to this Section. Each Party shall ensure this information is made publicly available.

Article 8.24 Proceedings under another international agreement
Where a claim is brought pursuant to this Section and another international agreement and:
(a) there is a potential for overlapping compensation; or
(b) the other international claim could have a significant impact on the resolution of the claim brought pursuant to this Section,

the Tribunal shall, as soon as possible after hearing the disputing parties, stay its proceedings or otherwise ensure that proceedings brought pursuant to another international agreement are taken into account in its decision, order or award.

Article 8.25 Consent to the settlement of the dispute by the Tribunal
1. The respondent consents to the settlement of the dispute by the Tribunal in accordance with the procedures set out in this Section.
2. The consent under paragraph 1 and the submission of a claim to the Tribunal under this Section shall satisfy the requirements of:
(a) Article 25 of the ICSID Convention and Chapter II of Schedule C of the ICSID Additional Facility Rules regarding written consent of the disputing parties; and,
(b) Article II of the New York Convention for an agreement in writing.

Article 8.26 Third party funding
1. Where there is third party funding, the disputing party benefiting from it shall disclose to the other disputing party and to the Tribunal the name and address of the third party funder.
2. The disclosure shall be made at the time of the submission of a claim, or, if the financing agreement is concluded or the donation or grant is made after the submission of a claim, without delay as soon as the agreement is concluded or the donation or grant is made.

Article 8.27 Constitution of the Tribunal
1. The Tribunal established under this Section shall decide claims submitted pursuant to Article 8.23.
2. The CETA Joint Committee shall, upon the entry into force of this Agreement, appoint fifteen Members of the Tribunal. Five of the Members of the Tribunal shall be nationals of a Member State of the European Union, five shall be nationals of Canada (11) and five shall be nationals of third countries.
3. The CETA Joint Committee may decide to increase or to decrease the number of the Members of the Tribunal by multiples of three. Additional appointments shall be made on the same basis as provided for in paragraph 2.
4. The Members of the Tribunal shall possess the qualifications required in their respective countries for appointment to judicial office, or be jurists of recognised competence. They shall have

demonstrated expertise in public international law. It is desirable that they have expertise in particular, in international investment law, in international trade law and the resolution of disputes arising under international investment or international trade agreements.

5. The Members of the Tribunal appointed pursuant to this Section shall be appointed for a five-year term, renewable once. However, the terms of seven of the 15 persons appointed immediately after the entry into force of this Agreement, to be determined by lot, shall extend to six years. Vacancies shall be filled as they arise. A person appointed to replace a Member of the Tribunal whose term of office has not expired shall hold office for the remainder of the predecessor's term. In principle, a Member of the Tribunal serving on a division of the Tribunal when his or her term expires may continue to serve on the division until a final award is issued.

6. The Tribunal shall hear cases in divisions consisting of three Members of the Tribunal, of whom one shall be a national of a Member State of the European Union, one a national of Canada and one a national of a third country. The division shall be chaired by the Member of the Tribunal who is a national of a third country.

7. Within 90 days of the submission of a claim pursuant to Article 8.23, the President of the Tribunal shall appoint the Members of the Tribunal composing the division of the Tribunal hearing the case on a rotation basis, ensuring that the composition of the divisions is random and unpredictable, while giving equal opportunity to all Members of the Tribunal to serve.

8. The President and Vice-President of the Tribunal shall be responsible for organisational issues and shall be appointed for a two-year term and shall be drawn by lot from among the Members of the Tribunal who are nationals of third countries. They shall serve on the basis of a rotation drawn by lot by the Chair of the CETA Joint Committee. The Vice-President shall replace the President when the President is unavailable.

9. Notwithstanding paragraph 6, the disputing parties may agree that a case be heard by a sole Member of the Tribunal to be appointed at random from the third country nationals. The respondent shall give sympathetic consideration to a request from the claimant to have the case heard by a sole Member of the Tribunal, in particular where the claimant is a small or medium-sized enterprise or the compensation or damages claimed are relatively low. Such a request shall be made before the constitution of the division of the Tribunal.

10. The Tribunal may draw up its own working procedures.

11. The Members of the Tribunal shall ensure that they are available and able to perform the functions set out under this Section.

12. In order to ensure their availability, the Members of the Tribunal shall be paid a monthly retainer fee to be determined by the CETA Joint Committee.

13. The fees referred to in paragraph 12 shall be paid equally by both Parties into an account managed by the ICSID Secretariat. In the event that one Party fails to pay the retainer fee the other Party may elect to pay. Any such arrears by a Party shall remain payable, with appropriate interest.

14. Unless the CETA Joint Committee adopts a decision pursuant to paragraph 15, the amount of the fees and expenses of the Members of the Tribunal on a division constituted to hear a claim, other than the fees referred to in paragraph 12, shall be those determined pursuant to Regulation 14(1) of the Administrative and Financial Regulations of the ICSID Convention in force on the date of the submission of the claim and allocated by the Tribunal among the disputing parties in accordance with Article 8.39.5.

15. The CETA Joint Committee may, by decision, transform the retainer fee and other fees and expenses into a regular salary, and decide applicable modalities and conditions.

16. The ICSID Secretariat shall act as Secretariat for the Tribunal and provide it with appropriate support.

17. If the CETA Joint Committee has not made the appointments pursuant to paragraph 2 within 90 days from the date that a claim is submitted for dispute settlement, the Secretary General of ICSID

shall, at the request of either disputing party appoint a division consisting of three Members of the Tribunal, unless the disputing parties have agreed that the case is to be heard by a sole Member of the Tribunal. The Secretary General of ICSID shall make the appointment by random selection from the existing nominations. The Secretary-General of ICSID may not appoint as chair a national of either Canada or a Member State of the European Union unless the disputing parties agree otherwise.

Article 8.28 Appellate Tribunal

1. An Appellate Tribunal is hereby established to review awards rendered under this Section.
2. The Appellate Tribunal may uphold, modify or reverse the Tribunal's award based on:
   (a) errors in the application or interpretation of applicable law;
   (b) manifest errors in the appreciation of the facts, including the appreciation of relevant domestic law;
   (c) the grounds set out in Article 52(1) (a) through (e) of the ICSID Convention, in so far as they are not covered by paragraphs (a) and (b).
3. The Members of the Appellate Tribunal shall be appointed by a decision of the CETA Joint Committee at the same time as the decision referred to in paragraph 7.
4. The Members of the Appellate Tribunal shall meet the requirements of Article 8.27.4 and comply with Article 8.30.
5. The division of the Appellate Tribunal constituted to hear the appeal shall consist of three randomly appointed Members of the Appellate Tribunal.
6. Articles 8.36 and 8.38 shall apply to the proceedings before the Appellate Tribunal.
7. The CETA Joint Committee shall promptly adopt a decision setting out the following administrative and organisational matters regarding the functioning of the Appellate Tribunal:
   (a) administrative support;
   (b) procedures for the initiation and the conduct of appeals, and procedures for referring issues back to the Tribunal for adjustment of the award, as appropriate;
   (c) procedures for filling a vacancy on the Appellate Tribunal and on a division of the Appellate Tribunal constituted to hear a case;
   (d) remuneration of the Members of the Appellate Tribunal;
   (e) provisions related to the costs of appeals;
   (f) the number of Members of the Appellate Tribunal; and
   (g) any other elements it determines to be necessary for the effective functioning of the Appellate Tribunal.
8. The Committee on Services and Investment shall periodically review the functioning of the Appellate Tribunal and may make recommendations to the CETA Joint Committee. The CETA Joint Committee may revise the decision referred to in paragraph 7, if necessary.
9. Upon adoption of the decision referred to in paragraph 7:
   (a) a disputing party may appeal an award rendered pursuant to this Section to the Appellate Tribunal within 90 days after its issuance;
   (b) a disputing party shall not seek to review, set aside, annul, revise or initiate any other similar procedure as regards an award under this Section;
   (c) an award rendered pursuant to Article 8.39 shall not be considered final and no action for enforcement of an award may be brought until either:
      (i) 90 days from the issuance of the award by the Tribunal has elapsed and no appeal has been initiated;
      (ii) an initiated appeal has been rejected or withdrawn; or
      (iii) 90 days have elapsed from an award by the Appellate Tribunal and the Appellate Tribunal has not referred the matter back to the Tribunal;

(d) a final award by the Appellate Tribunal shall be considered as a final award for the purposes of Article 8.41; and
(e) Article 8.41.3 shall not apply.

Article 8.29 Establishment of a multilateral investment tribunal and appellate mechanism
The Parties shall pursue with other trading partners the establishment of a multilateral investment tribunal and appellate mechanism for the resolution of investment disputes. Upon establishment of such a multilateral mechanism, the CETA Joint Committee shall adopt a decision providing that investment disputes under this Section will be decided pursuant to the multilateral mechanism and make appropriate transitional arrangements.

Article 8.30 Ethics
1. The Members of the Tribunal shall be independent. They shall not be affiliated with any government (12). They shall not take instructions from any organisation, or government with regard to matters related to the dispute. They shall not participate in the consideration of any disputes that would create a direct or indirect conflict of interest. They shall comply with the International Bar Association Guidelines on Conflicts of Interest in International Arbitration or any supplemental rules adopted pursuant to Article 8.44.2. In addition, upon appointment, they shall refrain from acting as counsel or as party-appointed expert or witness in any pending or new investment dispute under this or any other international agreement.
2. If a disputing party considers that a Member of the Tribunal has a conflict of interest, it may invite the President of the International Court of Justice to issue a decision on the challenge to the appointment of such Member. Any notice of challenge shall be sent to the President of the International Court of Justice within 15 days of the date on which the composition of the division of the Tribunal has been communicated to the disputing party, or within 15 days of the date on which the relevant facts came to its knowledge, if they could not have reasonably been known at the time of composition of the division. The notice of challenge shall state the grounds for the challenge.
3. If, within 15 days from the date of the notice of challenge, the challenged Member of the Tribunal has elected not to resign from the division, the President of the International Court of Justice may, after receiving submissions from the disputing parties and after providing the Member of the Tribunal an opportunity to submit any observations, issue a decision on the challenge. The President of the International Court of Justice shall endeavour to issue the decision and to notify the disputing parties and the other Members of the division within 45 days of receipt of the notice of challenge. A vacancy resulting from the disqualification or resignation of a Member of the Tribunal shall be filled promptly.
4. Upon a reasoned recommendation from the President of the Tribunal, or on their joint initiative, the Parties, by decision of the CETA Joint Committee, may remove a Member from the Tribunal where his or her behaviour is inconsistent with the obligations set out in paragraph 1 and incompatible with his or her continued membership of the Tribunal.

Article 8.31 Applicable law and interpretation
1. When rendering its decision, the Tribunal established under this Section shall apply this Agreement as interpreted in accordance with the Vienna Convention on the Law of Treaties, and other rules and principles of international law applicable between the Parties.
2. The Tribunal shall not have jurisdiction to determine the legality of a measure, alleged to constitute a breach of this Agreement, under the domestic law of a Party. For greater certainty, in determining the consistency of a measure with this Agreement, the Tribunal may consider, as appropriate, the domestic law of a Party as a matter of fact. In doing so, the Tribunal shall follow the prevailing interpretation given to the domestic law by the courts or authorities of that Party and any meaning given to domestic law by the Tribunal shall not be binding upon the courts or the authorities of that Party.

3. Where serious concerns arise as regards matters of interpretation that may affect investment, the Committee on Services and Investment may, pursuant to Article 8.44.3(a), recommend to the CETA Joint Committee the adoption of interpretations of this Agreement. An interpretation adopted by the CETA Joint Committee shall be binding on the Tribunal established under this Section. The CETA Joint Committee may decide that an interpretation shall have binding effect from a specific date.

Article 8.32 Claims manifestly without legal merit
1. The respondent may, no later than 30 days after the constitution of the division of the Tribunal, and in any event before its first session, file an objection that a claim is manifestly without legal merit.
2. An objection shall not be submitted under paragraph 1 if the respondent has filed an objection pursuant to Article 8.33.
3. The respondent shall specify as precisely as possible the basis for the objection.
4. On receipt of an objection pursuant to this Article, the Tribunal shall suspend the proceedings on the merits and establish a schedule for considering such an objection consistent with its schedule for considering any other preliminary question.
5. The Tribunal, after giving the disputing parties an opportunity to present their observations, shall at its first session or promptly thereafter, issue a decision or award stating the grounds therefor. In doing so, the Tribunal shall assume the alleged facts to be true.
6. This Article shall be without prejudice to the Tribunal's authority to address other objections as a preliminary question or to the right of the respondent to object, in the course of the proceeding, that a claim lacks legal merit.

Article 8.33 Claims unfounded as a matter of law
1. Without prejudice to the Tribunal's authority to address other objections as a preliminary question or to a respondent's right to raise any such objections at an appropriate time, the Tribunal shall address and decide as a preliminary question any objection by the respondent that, as a matter of law, a claim, or any part thereof, submitted pursuant to Article 8.23 is not a claim for which an award in favour of the claimant may be made under this Section, even if the facts alleged were assumed to be true.
2. An objection under paragraph 1 shall be submitted to the Tribunal no later than the date the Tribunal fixes for the respondent to submit its counter-memorial.3. If an objection has been submitted pursuant to Article 8.32, the Tribunal may, taking into account the circumstances of that objection, decline to address, under the procedures set out in this Article, an objection submitted pursuant to paragraph 1.
4. On receipt of an objection under paragraph 1, and, if appropriate, after rendering a decision pursuant to paragraph 3, the Tribunal shall suspend any proceedings on the merits, establish a schedule for considering the objection consistent with any schedule it has established for considering any other preliminary question, and issue a decision or award on the objection stating the grounds therefor.

Article 8.34 Interim measures of protection
The Tribunal may order an interim measure of protection to preserve the rights of a disputing party or to ensure that the Tribunal's jurisdiction is made fully effective, including an order to preserve evidence in the possession or control of a disputing party or to protect the Tribunal's jurisdiction. The Tribunal shall not order attachment or enjoin the application of the measure alleged to constitute a breach referred to in Article 8.23. For the purposes of this Article, an order includes a recommendation.

Article 8.35 Discontinuance
If, following the submission of a claim under this Section, the investor fails to take any steps in the proceeding during 180 consecutive days or such period as the disputing parties may agree, the investor is deemed to have withdrawn its claim and to have discontinued the proceeding. The Tribunal shall,

at the request of the respondent, and after notice to the disputing parties, in an order take note of the discontinuance. After the order has been rendered the authority of the Tribunal shall lapse.

Article 8.36 Transparency of proceedings

1. The UNCITRAL Transparency Rules, as modified by this Chapter, shall apply in connection with proceedings under this Section.
2. The request for consultations, the notice requesting a determination of the respondent, the notice of determination of the respondent, the agreement to mediate, the notice of intent to challenge a Member of the Tribunal, the decision on challenge to a Member of the Tribunal and the request for consolidation shall be included in the list of documents to be made available to the public under Article 3(1) of the UNCITRAL Transparency Rules.
3. Exhibits shall be included in the list of documents to be made available to the public under Article 3(2) of the UNCITRAL Transparency Rules.
4. Notwithstanding Article 2 of the UNCITRAL Transparency Rules, prior to the constitution of the Tribunal, Canada or the European Union as the case may be shall make publicly available in a timely manner relevant documents pursuant to paragraph 2, subject to the redaction of confidential or protected information. Such documents may be made publicly available by communication to the repository.
5. Hearings shall be open to the public. The Tribunal shall determine, in consultation with the disputing parties, the appropriate logistical arrangements to facilitate public access to such hearings. If the Tribunal determines that there is a need to protect confidential or protected information, it shall make the appropriate arrangements to hold in private that part of the hearing requiring such protection.
6. Nothing in this Chapter requires a respondent to withhold from the public information required to be disclosed by its laws. The respondent should apply those laws in a manner sensitive to protecting from disclosure information that has been designated as confidential or protected information.

Article 8.37 Information sharing

1. A disputing party may disclose to other persons in connection with the proceedings, including witnesses and experts, such unredacted documents as it considers necessary in the course of proceedings under this Section. However, the disputing party shall ensure that those persons protect the confidential or protected information contained in those documents.
2. This Agreement does not prevent a respondent from disclosing to officials of, as applicable, the European Union, Member States of the European Union and sub-national governments, such unredacted documents as it considers necessary in the course of proceedings under this Section. However, the respondent shall ensure that those officials protect the confidential or protected information contained in those documents.

Article 8.38 Non-disputing Party

1. The respondent shall, within 30 days after receipt or promptly after any dispute concerning confidential or protected information has been resolved, deliver to the non-disputing Party:
   (a) a request for consultations, a notice requesting a determination of the respondent, a notice of determination of the respondent, a claim submitted pursuant to Article 8.23, a request for consolidation, and any other documents that are appended to such documents;
   (b) on request:
      (i) pleadings, memorials, briefs, requests and other submissions made to the Tribunal by a disputing party;
      (ii) written submissions made to the Tribunal pursuant to Article 4 of the UNCITRAL Transparency Rules;

(iii) minutes or transcripts of hearings of the Tribunal, if available; and
(iv) orders, awards and decisions of the Tribunal; and
(c) on request and at the cost of the non-disputing Party, all or part of the evidence that has been tendered to the Tribunal, unless the requested evidence is publicly available.

2. The Tribunal shall accept or, after consultation with the disputing parties, may invite, oral or written submissions from the non-disputing Party regarding the interpretation of this Agreement. The non-disputing Party may attend a hearing held under this Section.
3. The Tribunal shall not draw any inference from the absence of a submission pursuant to paragraph 2.
4. The Tribunal shall ensure that the disputing parties are given a reasonable opportunity to present their observations on a submission by the non-disputing Party to this Agreement.

Article 8.39 Final award

1. If the Tribunal makes a final award against the respondent, the Tribunal may only award, separately or in combination:
(a) monetary damages and any applicable interest;
(b) restitution of property, in which case the award shall provide that the respondent may pay monetary damages representing the fair market value of the property at the time immediately before the expropriation, or impending expropriation became known, whichever is earlier, and any applicable interest in lieu of restitution, determined in a manner consistent with Article 8.12.

2. Subject to paragraphs 1 and 5, if a claim is made under Article 8.23.1(b) :
(a) an award of monetary damages and any applicable interest shall provide that the sum be paid to the locally established enterprise;
(b) an award of restitution of property shall provide that restitution be made to the locally established enterprise;
(c) an award of costs in favour of the investor shall provide that it is to be made to the investor; and
(d) the award shall provide that it is made without prejudice to a right that a person, other than a person which has provided a waiver pursuant to Article 8.22, may have in monetary damages or property awarded under a Party's law.

3. Monetary damages shall not be greater than the loss suffered by the investor or, as applicable, the locally established enterprise, reduced by any prior damages or compensation already provided. For the calculation of monetary damages, the Tribunal shall also reduce the damages to take into account any restitution of property or repeal or modification of the measure.
4. The Tribunal shall not award punitive damages.5. The Tribunal shall order that the costs of the proceedings be borne by the unsuccessful disputing party. In exceptional circumstances, the Tribunal may apportion costs between the disputing parties if it determines that apportionment is appropriate in the circumstances of the claim. Other reasonable costs, including costs of legal representation and assistance, shall be borne by the unsuccessful disputing party, unless the Tribunal determines that such apportionment is unreasonable in the circumstances of the claim. If only parts of the claims have been successful the costs shall be adjusted, proportionately, to the number or extent of the successful parts of the claims.
6. The CETA Joint Committee shall consider supplemental rules aimed at reducing the financial burden on claimants who are natural persons or small and medium-sized enterprises. Such supplemental rules may, in particular, take into account the financial resources of such claimants and the amount of compensation sought.
7. The Tribunal and the disputing parties shall make every effort to ensure the dispute settlement process is carried out in a timely manner. The Tribunal shall issue its final award within 24 months of the date the claim is submitted pursuant to Article 8.23. If the Tribunal requires additional time to issue its final award, it shall provide the disputing parties the reasons for the delay.

Article 8.40 Indemnification or other compensation

A respondent shall not assert, and the Tribunal shall not accept a defence, counterclaim, right of setoff, or similar assertion, that an investor or, as applicable, a locally established enterprise, has received or will receive indemnification or other compensation pursuant to an insurance or guarantee contract in respect of all or part of the compensation sought in a dispute initiated pursuant to this Section.

Article 8.41 Enforcement of awards

1. An award issued pursuant to this Section shall be binding between the disputing parties and in respect of that particular case.
2. Subject to paragraph 3, a disputing party shall recognise and comply with an award without delay.
3. A disputing party shall not seek enforcement of a final award until:
   (a) in the case of a final award issued under the ICSID Convention:
      (i) 120 days have elapsed from the date the award was rendered and no disputing party has requested revision or annulment of the award; or
      (ii) enforcement of the award has been stayed and revision or annulment proceedings have been completed;
   (b) in the case of a final award under the ICSID Additional Facility Rules, the UNCITRAL Arbitration Rules, or any other rules applicable pursuant to Article 8. 23.2(d) :
      (i) 90 days have elapsed from the date the award was rendered and no disputing party has commenced a proceeding to revise, set aside or annul the award; or
      (ii) enforcement of the award has been stayed and a court has dismissed or allowed an application to revise, set aside or annul the award and there is no further appeal.
4. Execution of the award shall be governed by the laws concerning the execution of judgments or awards in force where the execution is sought.
5. A final award issued pursuant to this Section is an arbitral award that is deemed to relate to claims arising out of a commercial relationship or transaction for the purposes of Article 1 of the New York Convention.
6. For greater certainty, if a claim has been submitted pursuant to Article 8.23.2(a), a final award issued pursuant to this Section shall qualify as an award under Chapter IV, Section 6 of the ICSID Convention.

Article 8.42 Role of the Parties

1. A Party shall not bring an international claim, in respect of a claim submitted pursuant to Article 8.23, unless the other Party has failed to abide by and comply with the award rendered in that dispute.
2. Paragraph 1 shall not exclude the possibility of dispute settlement under Chapter Twenty-Nine (Dispute Settlement) in respect of a measure of general application even if that measure is alleged to have breached this Agreement as regards a specific investment in respect of which a claim has been submitted pursuant to Article 8.23 and is without prejudice to Article 8.38.
3. Paragraph 1 does not preclude informal exchanges for the sole purpose of facilitating a settlement of the dispute.

Article 8.43 Consolidation

1. When two or more claims that have been submitted separately pursuant to Article 8.23 have a question of law or fact in common and arise out of the same events or circumstances, a disputing party or the disputing parties, jointly, may seek the establishment of a separate division of the Tribunal pursuant to this Article and request that such division issue a consolidation order ('request for consolidation').
2. The disputing party seeking a consolidation order shall first deliver a notice to the disputing parties it seeks to be covered by this order.

3. If the disputing parties notified pursuant to paragraph 2 have reached an agreement on the consolidation order to be sought, they may make a joint request for the establishment of a separate division of the Tribunal and a consolidation order pursuant to this Article. If the disputing parties notified pursuant to paragraph 2 have not reached agreement on the consolidation order to be sought within 30 days of the notice, a disputing party may make a request for the establishment of a separate division of the Tribunal and a consolidation order pursuant to this Article.
4. The request shall be delivered, in writing, to the President of the Tribunal and to all the disputing parties sought to be covered by the order, and shall specify:
   (a) the names and addresses of the disputing parties sought to be covered by the order;
   (b) the claims, or parts thereof, sought to be covered by the order; and
   (c) the grounds for the order sought.
5. A request for consolidation involving more than one respondent shall require the agreement of all such respondents.
6. The rules applicable to the proceedings under this Article are determined as follows:
   (a) if all of the claims for which a consolidation order is sought have been submitted to dispute settlement under the same rules pursuant to Article 8.23, these rules shall apply;
   (b) if the claims for which a consolidation order is sought have not been submitted to dispute settlement under the same rules:
      (i) the investors may collectively agree on the rules pursuant to Article 8.23.2; or
      (ii) if the investors cannot agree on the applicable rules within 30 days of the President of the Tribunal receiving the request for consolidation, the UNCITRAL Arbitration Rules shall apply.
7. The President of the Tribunal shall, after receipt of a consolidation request and in accordance with the requirements of Article 8.27.7 constitute a new division ('consolidating division') of the Tribunal which shall have jurisdiction over some or all of the claims, in whole or in part, which are the subject of the joint consolidation request.
8. If, after hearing the disputing parties, a consolidating division is satisfied that claims submitted pursuant to Article 8.23 have a question of law or fact in common and arise out of the same events or circumstances, and consolidation would best serve the interests of fair and efficient resolution of the claims including the interest of consistency of awards, the consolidating division of the Tribunal may, by order, assume jurisdiction over some or all of the claims, in whole or in part.
9. If a consolidating division of the Tribunal has assumed jurisdiction pursuant to paragraph 8, an investor that has submitted a claim pursuant to Article 8.23 and whose claim has not been consolidated may make a written request to the Tribunal that it be included in such order provided that the request complies with the requirements set out in paragraph 4. The consolidating division of the Tribunal shall grant such order where it is satisfied that the conditions of paragraph 8 are met and that granting such a request would not unduly burden or unfairly prejudice the disputing parties or unduly disrupt the proceedings. Before consolidating division of the Tribunal issues that order, it shall consult with the disputing parties.
10. On application of a disputing party, a consolidating division of the Tribunal established under this Article, pending its decision under paragraph 8, may order that the proceedings of the division of the Tribunal appointed under Article 8.27.7 be stayed unless the latter Tribunal has already adjourned its proceedings.
11. The division of the Tribunal appointed under Article 8.27.7 shall cede jurisdiction in relation to the claims, or parts thereof, over which a consolidating division of the Tribunal established under this Article has assumed jurisdiction.
12. The award of a consolidating division of the Tribunal established under this Article in relation to those claims, or parts thereof, over which it has assumed jurisdiction is binding on the division of the Tribunal appointed under Article 8.27.7 as regards those claims, or parts thereof.

13. An investor may withdraw a claim under this Section that is subject to consolidation and such claim shall not be resubmitted pursuant to Article 8.23. If it does so no later than 15 days after receipt of the notice of consolidation, its earlier submission of the claim shall not prevent the investor's recourse to dispute settlement other than under this Section.
14. At the request of an investor, a consolidating division of the Tribunal may take such measures as it sees fit in order to preserve the confidential or protected information of that investor in relation to other investors. Those measures may include the submission of redacted versions of documents containing confidential or protected information to the other investors or arrangements to hold parts of the hearing in private.

Article 8.44 Committee on Services and Investment
1. The Committee on Services and Investment shall provide a forum for the Parties to consult on issues related to this Chapter, including:
(a) difficulties which may arise in the implementation of this Chapter;
(b) possible improvements of this Chapter, in particular in the light of experience and developments in other international fora and under the Parties' other agreements.
2. The Committee on Services and Investment shall, on agreement of the Parties, and after completion of their respective internal requirements and procedures, adopt a code of conduct for the Members of the Tribunal to be applied in disputes arising out of this Chapter, which may replace or supplement the rules in application, and may address topics including:
(a) disclosure obligations;
(b) the independence and impartiality of the Members of the Tribunal; and
(c) confidentiality.
The Parties shall make best efforts to ensure that the code of conduct is adopted no later than the first day of the provisional application or entry into force of this Agreement, as the case may be, and in any event no later than two years after such date.
3. The Committee Services and Investment may, on agreement of the Parties, and after completion of their respective internal requirements and procedures:
(a) recommend to the CETA Joint Committee the adoption of interpretations of this Agreement pursuant to Article 8.31.3;
(b) adopt and amend rules supplementing the applicable dispute settlement rules, and amend the applicable rules on transparency. These rules and amendments are binding on the Tribunal established under this Section;
(c) adopt rules for mediation for use by disputing parties as referred to in Article 8.20;
(d) recommend to the CETA Joint Committee the adoption of any further elements of the fair and equitable treatment obligation pursuant to Article 8.10.3; and
(e) make recommendations to the CETA Joint Committee on the functioning of the Appellate Tribunal pursuant to Article 8.28.8.

Article 8.45 Exclusion
The dispute settlement provisions of this Section and of Chapter Twenty-Nine (Dispute Settlement) do not apply to the matters referred to in Annex 8-C.

CHAPTER TWENTY-TWO – TRADE AND SUSTAINABLE DEVELOPMENT

Article 22.1 Context and objectives
1. The Parties recall the Rio Declaration on Environment and Development of 1992, the Agenda 21 on Environment and Development of 1992, the Johannesburg Declaration on Sustainable Development of 2002 and the Plan of Implementation of the World Summit on Sustainable Development of 2002,

the Ministerial Declaration of the United Nations Economic and Social Council on Creating an environment at the national and international levels conducive to generating full and productive employment and decent work for all, and its impact on sustainable development of 2006, and the ILO Declaration on Social Justice for a Fair Globalisation of 2008. The Parties recognise that economic development, social development and environmental protection are interdependent and mutually reinforcing components of sustainable development, and reaffirm their commitment to promoting the development of international trade in such a way as to contribute to the objective of sustainable development, for the welfare of present and future generations.
2. The Parties underline the benefit of considering trade-related labour and environmental issues as part of a global approach to trade and sustainable development. Accordingly, the Parties agree that the rights and obligations under Chapters Twenty-Three (Trade and Labour) and Twenty-Four (Trade and Environment) are to be considered in the context of this Agreement.
3. In this regard, through the implementation of Chapters Twenty-Three (Trade and Labour) and Twenty-Four (Trade and Environment), the Parties aim to:
(a) promote sustainable development through the enhanced coordination and integration of their respective labour, environmental and trade policies and measures;
(b) promote dialogue and cooperation between the Parties with a view to developing their trade and economic relations in a manner that supports their respective labour and environmental protection measures and standards, and to upholding their environmental and labour protection objectives in a context of trade relations that are free, open and transparent;
(c) enhance enforcement of their respective labour and environmental law and respect for labour and environmental international agreements;
(d) promote the full use of instruments, such as impact assessment and stakeholder consultations, in the regulation of trade, labour and environmental issues and encourage businesses, civil society organisations and citizens to develop and implement practices that contribute to the achievement of sustainable development goals; and(e) promote public consultation and participation in the discussion of sustainable development issues that arise under this Agreement and in the development of relevant law and policies.

Article 22.2 Transparency
The Parties stress the importance of ensuring transparency as a necessary element to promote public participation and making information public within the context of this Chapter, in accordance with the provisions of this Chapter and Chapter Twenty-Seven (Transparency) as well as Articles 23.6 (Public information and awareness) and 24.7 (Public information and awareness).

Article 22.3 Cooperation and promotion of trade supporting sustainable development
1. The Parties recognise the value of international cooperation to achieve the goal of sustainable development and the integration at the international level of economic, social and environmental development and protection initiatives, actions and measures. Therefore, the Parties agree to dialogue and consult with each other with regard to trade-related sustainable development issues of common interest.
2. The Parties affirm that trade should promote sustainable development. Accordingly, each Party shall strive to promote trade and economic flows and practices that contribute to enhancing decent work and environmental protection, including by:
(a) encouraging the development and use of voluntary schemes relating to the sustainable production of goods and services, such as eco-labelling and fair trade schemes;
(b) encouraging the development and use of voluntary best practices of corporate social responsibility by enterprises, such as those in the OECD Guidelines for Multinational Enterprises, to strengthen coherence between economic, social and environmental objectives;

(c) encouraging the integration of sustainability considerations in private and public consumption decisions; and

(d) promoting the development, the establishment, the maintenance or the improvement of environmental performance goals and standards.

3. The Parties recognise the importance of addressing specific sustainable development issues by assessing the potential economic, social and environmental impacts of possible actions, taking account of the views of stakeholders. Therefore, each Party commits to review, monitor and assess the impact of the implementation of this Agreement on sustainable development in its territory in order to identify any need for action that may arise in connection with this Agreement. The Parties may carry out joint assessments. These assessments will be conducted in a manner that is adapted to the practices and conditions of each Party, through the respective participative processes of the Parties, as well as those processes set up under this Agreement.

Article 22.4 Institutional mechanisms

1. The Committee on Trade and Sustainable Development, established under Article 26.2.1(g) (Specialised committees), shall be comprised of high level representatives of the Parties responsible for matters covered by this Chapter and Chapters Twenty-Three (Trade and Labour) and Twenty-Four (Trade and Environment). The Committee on Trade and Sustainable Development shall oversee the implementation of those Chapters, including cooperative activities and the review of the impact of this Agreement on sustainable development, and address in an integrated manner any matter of common interest to the Parties in relation to the interface between economic development, social development and environmental protection. With regard to Chapters Twenty-Three (Trade and Labour) and Twenty-Four (Trade and Environment), the Committee on Trade and Sustainable Development can also carry out its duties through dedicated sessions comprising participants responsible for any matter covered, respectively, under these Chapters.

2. The Committee on Trade and Sustainable Development shall meet within the first year of the entry into force of this Agreement, and thereafter as often as the Parties consider necessary. The contact points referred to in Articles 23.8 (Institutional mechanisms) and 24.13 (Institutional mechanisms) are responsible for the communication between the Parties regarding the scheduling and the organisation of those meetings or dedicated sessions.

. Each regular meeting or dedicated session of the Committee on Trade and Sustainable Development includes a session with the public to discuss matters relating to the implementation of the relevant Chapters, unless the Parties decide otherwise.

4. The Committee on Trade and Sustainable Development shall promote transparency and public participation. To this end:

(a) any decision or report of the Committee on Trade and Sustainable Development shall be made public, unless it decides otherwise;

(b) the Committee on Trade and Sustainable Development shall present updates on any matter related to this Chapter, including its implementation, to the Civil Society Forum referred to in Article 22.5. Any view or opinion of the Civil Society Forum shall be presented to the Parties directly, or through the consultative mechanisms referred to in Articles 23.8.3 (Institutional mechanisms) and 24.13 (Institutional mechanisms). The Committee on Trade and Sustainable Development shall report annually on the follow-up to those communications;

(c) the Committee on Trade and Sustainable Development shall report annually on any matter that it addresses pursuant to Article 24.7.3 (Public information and awareness) or Article 23.8.4 (Institutional mechanisms).

Article 22.5 Civil Society Forum

1. The Parties shall facilitate a joint Civil Society Forum composed of representatives of civil society organisations established in their territories, including participants in the consultative mechanisms referred to in Articles 23.8.3 (Institutional mechanisms) and 24.13 (Institutional mechanisms), in order to conduct a dialogue on the sustainable development aspects of this Agreement.
2. The Civil Society Forum shall be convened once a year unless otherwise agreed by the Parties. The Parties shall promote a balanced representation of relevant interests, including independent representative employers, unions, labour and business organisations, environmental groups, as well as other relevant civil society organisations as appropriate. The Parties may also facilitate participation by virtual means.

CHAPTER TWENTY-FOUR – TRADE AND ENVIRONMENT

Article 24.1 Definition

For the purposes of this Chapter:

environmental law means a law, including a statutory or regulatory provision, or other **legally binding** measure of a Party, the purpose of which is the protection of the environment, including the prevention of a danger to human life or health from environmental impacts, such as those that aim at:

(a) the prevention, abatement or control of the release, discharge, or emission of pollutants or environmental contaminants,
(b) the management of chemicals and waste or the dissemination of information related thereto, or
(c) the conservation and protection of wild flora or fauna, including endangered species and their habitats, as well as protected areas,

but does not include a measure of a Party solely related to worker health and safety, which is subject to Chapter Twenty-Three (Trade and Labour), or a measure of a Party the purpose of which is to manage the subsistence or aboriginal harvesting of natural resources.

Article 24.2 Context and objectives

The Parties recognise that the environment is a fundamental pillar of sustainable development and recognise the contribution that trade could make to sustainable development. The Parties stress that enhanced cooperation to protect and conserve the environment brings benefits that will:

(a) promote sustainable development;
(b) strengthen the environmental governance of the Parties;
(c) build upon international environmental agreements to which they are party; and
(d) complement the objectives of this Agreement.

Article 24.3 Right to regulate and levels of protection

The Parties recognise the right of each Party to set its environmental priorities, to establish its levels of environmental protection, and to adopt or modify its laws and policies accordingly and in a manner consistent with the multilateral environmental agreements to which it is party and with this Agreement. Each Party shall seek to ensure that those laws and policies provide for and encourage high levels of environmental protection, and shall strive to continue to improve such laws and policies and their underlying levels of protection.

Article 24.4 Multilateral environmental agreements

1. The Parties recognise the value of international environmental governance and agreements as a response of the international community to global or regional environmental problems and stress the need to enhance the mutual supportiveness between trade and environment policies, rules, and measures.

2. Each Party reaffirms its commitment to effectively implement in its law and practices, in its whole territory, the multilateral environmental agreements to which it is party.
3. The Parties commit to consult and cooperate as appropriate with respect to environmental issues of mutual interest related to multilateral environmental agreements, and in particular, trade-related issues. This commitment includes exchanging information on:
(a) the implementation of multilateral environmental agreements, to which a Party is party;
(b) on-going negotiations of new multilateral environmental agreements; and
(c) each Party's respective views on becoming a party to additional multilateral environmental agreements.
4. The Parties acknowledge their right to use Article 28.3 (General exceptions) in relation to environmental measures, including those taken pursuant to multilateral environmental agreements to which they are party.

Article 24.5 Upholding levels of protection
1. The Parties recognise that it is inappropriate to encourage trade or investment by weakening or reducing the levels of protection afforded in their environmental law.
2. A Party shall not waive or otherwise derogate from, or offer to waive or otherwise derogate from, its environmental law, to encourage trade or the establishment, acquisition, expansion or retention of an investment in its territory.
3. A Party shall not, through a sustained or recurring course of action or inaction, fail to effectively enforce its environmental law to encourage trade or investment.

Article 24.6 Access to remedies and procedural guarantees
1. Pursuant to the obligations in Article 24.5:
(a) each Party shall, in accordance with its law, ensure that its authorities competent to enforce environmental law give due consideration to alleged violations of environmental law brought to its attention by any interested persons residing or established in its territory; and
(b) each Party shall ensure that administrative or judicial proceedings are available to persons with a legally recognised interest in a particular matter or who maintain that a right is infringed under its law, in order to permit effective action against infringements of its environmental law, including appropriate remedies for violations of such law.
2. Each Party shall, in accordance with its domestic law, ensure that the proceedings referred to in subparagraph 1(b) are not unnecessarily complicated or prohibitively costly, do not entail unreasonable time limits or unwarranted delays, provide injunctive relief if appropriate, and are fair, equitable and transparent, including by:
(a) providing defendants with reasonable notice when a proceeding is initiated, including a description of the nature of the proceeding and the basis of the claim;
(b) providing the parties to the proceeding with a reasonable opportunity to support or defend their respective positions, including by presenting information or evidence, prior to a final decision;
(c) providing that final decisions are made in writing and give reasons as appropriate to the case and based on information or evidence in respect of which the parties to the proceeding were offered the opportunity to be heard; and
(d) allowing the parties to administrative proceedings an opportunity for review and, if warranted, correction of final administrative decisions within a reasonable period of time by a tribunal established by law, with appropriate guarantees of tribunal independence and impartiality.

Article 24.7 Public information and awareness
1. In addition to Article 27.1 (Publication), each Party shall encourage public debate with and among non-state actors as regards the development and definition of policies that may lead to the adoption of environmental law by its public authorities.
2. Each Party shall promote public awareness of its environmental law, as well as enforcement and compliance procedures, by ensuring the availability of information to stakeholders.
3. Each Party shall be open to receive and shall give due consideration to submissions from the public on matters related to this Chapter, including communications on implementation concerns. Each Party shall inform its respective civil society organisations of those communications through the consultative mechanisms referred to in Article 24.13.5.

Article 24.8 Scientific and technical information
1. When preparing and implementing measures aimed at environmental protection that may affect trade or investment between the Parties, each Party shall take into account relevant scientific and technical information and related international standards, guidelines, or recommendations.
2. The Parties acknowledge that where there are threats of serious or irreversible damage, the lack of full scientific certainty shall not be used as a reason for postponing cost-effective measures to prevent environmental degradation.

Article 24.9 Trade favouring environmental protection
1. The Parties are resolved to make efforts to facilitate and promote trade and investment in environmental goods and services, including through addressing the reduction of non-tariff barriers related to these goods and services.
2. The Parties shall, consistent with their international obligations, pay special attention to facilitating the removal of obstacles to trade or investment in goods and services of particular relevance for climate change mitigation and in particular trade or investment in renewable energy goods and related services.

Article 24.10 Trade in forest products
1. The Parties recognise the importance of the conservation and sustainable management of forests for providing environmental functions and economic and social opportunities for present and future generations, and of market access for forest products harvested in accordance with the law of the country of harvest and from sustainably managed forests.
2. To this end, and in a manner consistent with their international obligations, the Parties undertake to:

(a) encourage trade in forest products from sustainably managed forests and harvested in accordance with the law of the country of harvest;
(b) exchange information, and if appropriate, cooperate on initiatives to promote sustainable forest management, including initiatives designed to combat illegal logging and related trade;
(c) promote the effective use of the Convention on International Trade in Endangered Species of Wild Fauna and Flora, done at Washington on 3 March 1973, with regard to timber species considered at risk; and
(d) sustainable management of forests.

3. The Parties shall discuss the subjects referred to in paragraph 2, in the Committee on Trade and Sustainable Development or in the Bilateral Dialogue on Forest Products referred to in Chapter Twenty-Five (Bilateral Dialogues and Cooperation), in accordance with their respective spheres of competence.

Article 24.11 Trade in fisheries and aquaculture products

1. The Parties recognise the importance of the conservation and the sustainable and responsible management of fisheries and aquaculture and their contribution to providing environmental, economic and social opportunities for present and future generations.

2. To this end, and in a manner consistent with their international obligations, the Parties undertake to:

(a) adopt or maintain effective monitoring, control and surveillance measures, such as observer schemes, vessel monitoring schemes, transhipment control, inspections at sea, port state control, and associated sanctions, aimed at the conservation of fish stocks and the prevention of overfishing;

(b) adopt or maintain actions and cooperate to combat illegal, unreported and unregulated ('IUU') fishing, including, where appropriate, the exchange of information on IUU activities in their waters and the implementation of policies and measures to exclude IUU products from trade flows and fish farming operations;

(c) cooperate with, and where appropriate in, regional fisheries management organisations in which the Parties are either members, observers, or cooperating non-contracting parties, with the aim of achieving good governance, including by advocating for science-based decisions and for compliance with those decisions in these organisations; and

(d) promote the development of an environmentally responsible and economically competitive aquaculture industry.

Article 24.12 Cooperation on environment issues

1. The Parties recognise that enhanced cooperation is an important element to advance the objectives of this Chapter, and commit to cooperate on trade-related environmental issues of common interest, in areas such as:

(a) the potential impact of this Agreement on the environment and ways to enhance, prevent, or mitigate such impact, taking into account any impact assessment carried out by the Parties;

(b) activity in international fora dealing with issues relevant for both trade and environmental policies, including in particular the WTO, the OECD, the United Nations Environment Programme, and multilateral environmental agreements;

(c) the environmental dimension of corporate social responsibility and accountability, including the implementation and follow-up of internationally recognised guidelines;

(d) the trade impact of environmental regulations and standards as well as the environmental impact of trade and investment rules including on the development of environmental regulations and policy;

(e) trade-related aspects of the current and future international climate change regime, as well as domestic climate policies and programmes relating to mitigation and adaptation, including issues relating to carbon markets, ways to address adverse effects of trade on climate, as well as means to promote energy efficiency and the development and deployment of low-carbon and other climate-friendly technologies;

(f) trade and investment in environmental goods and services, including environmental and green technologies and practices; renewable energy; energy efficiency; and water use, conservation and treatment;

(g) cooperation on trade-related aspects of the conservation and sustainable use of biological diversity;

(h) promotion of life-cycle management of goods, including carbon accounting and end-of-life management, extended producer-responsibility, recycling and reduction of waste, and other best practices;

(i) improved understanding of the effects of economic activity and market forces on the environment; and
(j) exchange of views on the relationship between multilateral environmental agreements and international trade rules.

2. Cooperation further to paragraph 1 shall take place through actions and instruments that may include technical exchanges, exchanges of information and best practices, research projects, studies, reports, conferences and workshops.

3. The Parties will consider views or input from the public and interested stakeholders for the definition and implementation of their cooperation activities, and they may involve such stakeholders further in those activities, as appropriate.

Article 24.13 Institutional mechanisms

1. Each Party shall designate an office to serve as contact point with the other Party for the implementation of this Chapter, including with regard to:
(a) cooperative programmes and activities in accordance with Article 24.12;
(b) the receipt of submissions and communications under Article 24.7.3; and
(c) information to be provided to the other Party, the Panel of Experts, and the public.

2. Each Party shall inform the other Party, in writing, of the contact point referred to in paragraph 1.

3. The Committee on Trade and Sustainable Development established under Article 26.2.1(g) (Specialised committees) shall, through its regular meetings or dedicated sessions comprising participants responsible for matters covered under this Chapter:
(a) oversee the implementation of this Chapter and review the progress achieved under it;
(b) discuss matters of common interest; and
(c) discuss any other matter within the scope of this Chapter as the Parties jointly decide.

4. The Parties shall take into account the activities of relevant multilateral environmental organisations or bodies so as to promote greater cooperation and coherence between the work of the Parties and these organisations or bodies.

5. Each Party shall make use of existing, or establish new, consultative mechanisms, such as domestic advisory groups, to seek views and advice on issues relating to this Chapter. These consultative mechanisms shall comprise independent representative organisations of civil society in a balanced representation of environmental groups, business organisations, as well as other relevant stakeholders as appropriate. Through such consultative mechanisms, stakeholders may submit opinions and make recommendations on any matter related to this Chapter on their own initiative.

Article 24.14 Consultations

1. A Party may request consultations with the other Party regarding any matter arising under this Chapter by delivering a written request to the contact point of the other Party. The Party shall present the matter clearly in the request, identify the questions at issue, and provide a brief summary of any claims under this Chapter. Consultations must commence promptly after a Party delivers a request for consultations.

2. During consultations, each Party shall provide the other Party with sufficient information in its possession to allow a full examination of the matters raised, subject to its law regarding the protection of confidential or proprietary information.

3. If relevant, and if both Parties consent, the Parties shall seek the information or views of any person, organisation, or body, including the relevant international organisation or body, that may contribute to the examination of the matter at issue.

4. If a Party considers that further discussion of the matter is required, that Party may request that the Committee on Trade and Sustainable Development be convened to consider the matter by delivering a written request to the contact point of the other Party. The Committee on Trade and Sustainable

Development shall convene promptly and endeavour to resolve the matter. If appropriate, it shall seek the advice of the Parties' civil society organisations through the consultative mechanisms referred to in Article 24.13.5.
5. Each Party shall make publicly available any solution or decision on a matter discussed under this Article.

Article 24.15 Panel of Experts
1. For any matter that is not satisfactorily addressed through consultations under Article 24.14, a Party may, 90 days after the receipt of the request for consultations under Article 24.14.1, request that a Panel of Experts be convened to examine that matter, by delivering a written request to the contact point of the other Party.
2. Subject to the provisions of this Chapter, the Parties shall apply the Rules of Procedure and Code of Conduct set out in Annexes 29-A and 29-B, unless the Parties decide otherwise.
3. The Panel of Experts is composed of three panellists.
4. The Parties shall consult with a view to reaching an agreement on the composition of the Panel of Experts within 10 working days of the receipt by the responding Party of a request for the establishment of a Panel of Experts. Due attention shall be paid to ensuring that proposed panellists meet the requirements set out in paragraph 7 and have the expertise appropriate to the particular matter.
5. If the Parties are unable to decide on the composition of the Panel of Experts within the period of time specified in paragraph 4, the selection procedure set out in paragraphs 3 through 7 of Article 29.7 (Composition of the arbitration panel) applies in respect of the list established in paragraph 6.
6. The Committee on Trade and Sustainable Development shall, at its first meeting after the entry into force of this Agreement, establish a list of at least nine individuals chosen for their objectivity, reliability, and sound judgment, who are willing and able to serve as panellists. Each Party shall name at least three individuals to the list to serve as panellists. The Parties shall also name at least three individuals who are not nationals of either Party and who are willing and able to serve as chairperson of a Panel of Experts. The Committee on Trade and Sustainable Development shall ensure that the list is always maintained at this level.
7. The experts proposed as panellists must have specialised knowledge or expertise in environmental law, issues addressed in this Chapter, or in the resolution of disputes arising under international agreements. They must be independent, serve in their individual capacities and not take instructions from any organisation or government with regard to the matter in issue. They must not be affiliated with the governments of either Party, and must comply with the Code of Conduct referred to in paragraph 2.
8. Unless the Parties otherwise decide, within five working days of the date of the selection of the panellists, the terms of reference of the Panel of Experts are as follows:

'to examine, in the light of the relevant provisions of Chapter Twenty-Four (Trade and Environment), the matter referred to in the request for the establishment of the Panel of Experts, and to deliver a report in accordance with Article 24.15 (Panel of Experts) of Chapter Twenty-Four (Trade and Environment), that makes recommendations for the resolution of the matter'.

9. In respect of matters related to multilateral environmental agreements as set out in Article 24.4, the Panel of Experts should seek views and information from relevant bodies established under these agreements, including any pertinent available interpretative guidance, findings, or decisions adopted by those bodies (32).
10. The Panel of Experts shall issue to the Parties an interim report and a final report setting out the findings of fact, its determinations on the matter, including as to whether the responding Party has conformed with its obligations under this Chapter and the rationale behind any findings, determinations and recommendations that it makes. The Panel of Experts shall deliver to the Parties the interim report within 120 days after the last panellist is selected, or as otherwise decided by the

Parties. The Parties may provide comments to the Panel of Experts on the interim report within 45 days of its delivery. After considering these comments, the Panel of Experts may reconsider its report or carry out any further examination that it considers appropriate. The Panel of Experts shall deliver the final report to the Parties within 60 days of the submission of the interim report. Each Party shall make the final report publicly available within 30 days of its delivery.

11. If the final report of the Panel of Experts determines that a Party has not conformed with its obligations under this Chapter, the Parties shall engage in discussions and shall endeavour, within three months of the delivery of the final report, to identify an appropriate measure or, if appropriate, to decide upon a mutually satisfactory action plan. In these discussions, the Parties shall take into account the final report. The responding Party shall inform, in a timely manner, its civil society organisations, through the consultative mechanisms referred to in Article 24.13.5, and the requesting Party of its decision on any action or measure to be implemented. The Committee on Trade and Sustainable Development shall monitor the follow-up to the final report and the recommendations of the Panel of Experts. The civil society organisations, through the consultative mechanisms referred to in Article 24.13.5, and the Civil Society Forum may submit observations to the Committee on Trade and Sustainable Development in this regard.

12. If the Parties reach a mutually agreed solution to the matter following the establishment of a Panel of Experts, they shall notify the Committee on Trade and Sustainable Development and the Panel of Experts of that solution. Upon that notification, the panel procedure shall be terminated.

Article 24.16 Dispute resolution

1. For any dispute that arises under this Chapter, the Parties shall only have recourse to the rules and procedures provided for in this Chapter.

2. The Parties shall make every attempt to arrive at a mutually satisfactory resolution of a dispute. At any time, the Parties may have recourse to good offices, conciliation, or mediation to resolve that dispute.

CHAPTER TWENTY-EIGHT – EXCEPTIONS

Article 28.1 Definitions

For the purposes of this Chapter:

residence means residence for tax purposes;

tax convention means a convention for the avoidance of double taxation or other international taxation agreement or arrangement; and

tax and **taxation measure** includes an excise duty, but does not include:

(a) a customs duty as defined in Article 1.1 (General definitions), and

(b) a measure listed in exceptions (b) or (c) in the definition of 'customs duty' in Article 1.1 (General definitions).

Article 28.2 Party-specific definitions

For the purposes of this Chapter:

competition authority means:

(a) for Canada, the Commissioner of Competition or a successor notified to the other Party through the CETA contact points; and

(b) for the European Union, the Commission of the European Union with respect to its responsibilities pursuant to the competition laws of the European Union;

competition laws means:

(a) for Canada, the Competition Act, R.S.C. 1985, c. C-34; and

(b) for the European Union, Articles 101, 102 and 106 of the Treaty on the Functioning of the European Union, of 13 December 2007, Council Regulation (EC) No. 139/2004 of 20 January 2004 on the control of concentrations between undertakings, and their implementing regulations or amendments; and

information protected under its competition laws means:

(a) for Canada, information within the scope of Section 29 of the Competition Act, R.S.C. 1985, c. C-34; and

(b) for the European Union, information within the scope of Article 28 of Council Regulation (EC) No. 1/2003 of 16 December 2002 on the implementation of the rules on competition laid down in Articles 81 and 82 of the Treaty or Article 17 of Council Regulation (EC) No. 139/2004 of 20 January 2004 on the control of concentrations between undertakings.

Article 28.3 General exceptions

1. For the purposes of Article 30.8.5 (Termination, suspension or incorporation of other existing agreements), Chapters Two (National Treatment and Market Access for Goods), Five (Sanitary and Phytosanitary Measures), and Six (Customs and Trade Facilitation), the Protocol on rules of origin and origin procedures and Sections B (Establishment of investment) and C (Non-discriminatory treatment) of Chapter Eight (Investment), Article XX of the GATT 1994 is incorporated into and made part of this Agreement. The Parties understand that the measures referred to in Article XX (b) of the GATT 1994 include environmental measures necessary to protect human, animal or plant life or health. The Parties understand that Article XX(g) of the GATT 1994 applies to measures for the conservation of living and non-living exhaustible natural resources.

2. For the purposes of Chapters Nine (Cross-Border Trade in Services), Ten (Temporary Entry and Stay of Natural Persons for Business Purposes), Twelve (Domestic Regulation), Thirteen (Financial Services), Fourteen (International Maritime Transport Services), Fifteen (Telecommunications), Sixteen (Electronic Commerce), and Sections B (Establishment of investments) and C (Non-discriminatory treatment) of Chapter Eight (Investment), subject to the requirement that such measures are not applied in a manner which would constitute a means of arbitrary or unjustifiable discrimination between the Parties where like conditions prevail, or a disguised restriction on trade in services, nothing in this Agreement shall be construed to prevent the adoption or enforcement by a Party of measures necessary:

(a) to protect public security or public morals or to maintain public order (33) ;

(b) to protect human, animal or plant life or health (34) ; or

(c) to secure compliance with laws or regulations which are not inconsistent with the provisions of this Agreement including those relating to:

(i) the prevention of deceptive and fraudulent practices or to deal with the effects of a default on contracts;

(ii) the protection of the privacy of individuals in relation to the processing and dissemination of personal data and the protection of confidentiality of individual records and accounts; or

(iii) safety.

Article 28.4 Temporary safeguard measures with regard to capital movements and payments

1. Where, in exceptional circumstances, capital movements and payments, including transfers, cause or threaten to cause serious difficulties for the operation of the economic and monetary union of the European Union, the European Union may impose safeguard measures that are strictly necessary to address such difficulties for a period not to exceed 180 days.

2. Measures imposed by the European Union pursuant to paragraph 1 shall not constitute a means of arbitrary or unjustifiable discrimination in respect of Canada or its investors compared to a third

country or its investors. The European Union shall inform Canada forthwith and present, as soon as possible, a schedule for the removal of such measures.

Article 28.5 Restrictions in case of serious balance of payments and external financial difficulties
1. Where Canada or a Member State of the European Union that is not a member of the European Monetary Union experiences serious balance-of-payments or external financial difficulties, or threat thereof, it may adopt or maintain restrictive measures with regard to capital movements or payments, including transfers.
2. Measures referred to in paragraph 1 shall:
(a) not treat a Party less favourably than a third country in like situations;
(b) be consistent with the Articles of Agreement of the International Monetary Fund, done at Bretton Woods on 22 July 1944, as applicable;
(c) avoid unnecessary damage to the commercial, economic and financial interests of a Party;
(d) be temporary and phased out progressively as the situation specified in paragraph 1 improves and shall not exceed 180 days. If extremely exceptional circumstances arise such that a Party seeks to extend such measures beyond a period of 180 days, it will consult in advance with the other Party regarding the implementation of any proposed extension.
3. In the case of trade in goods, a Party may adopt restrictive measures in order to safeguard its balance-of-payments or external financial position. Such measures shall be in accordance with the GATT 1994 and the Understanding on the Balance-of-Payments Provisions of the General Agreement on Tariffs and Trade 1994, contained in Annex 1A to the WTO Agreement.
4. In the case of trade in services, a Party may adopt restrictive measures in order to safeguard its balance-of-payments or external financial position. Such measures shall be in accordance with the GATS.
5. A Party that adopts or maintains a measure referred to in paragraph 1 shall promptly notify the other Party and provide, as soon as possible, a schedule for its removal.
6. Where the restrictions are adopted or maintained under this Article, consultations between the Parties shall be held promptly in the CETA Joint Committee, if such consultations are not otherwise taking place in a forum outside of this Agreement. The consultations held under this paragraph shall assess the balance-of-payments or external financial difficulty that led to the respective measures, taking into account, among other things, such factors as:
(a) the nature and extent of the difficulties;
(b) the external economic and trading environment; or
(c) the availability of alternative corrective measures.
7. The consultations pursuant to paragraph 6 shall address the compliance of any restrictive measures with paragraphs 1 through 4. The Parties shall accept all findings of statistical and other facts presented by the International Monetary Fund ('IMF') relating to foreign exchange, monetary reserves, balance-of-payments, and their conclusions shall be based on the assessment by the IMF of the balance-of-payments and the external financial situation of the Party concerned.

Article 28.6 National security
Nothing in this Agreement shall be construed:
(a) to require a Party to furnish or allow access to information if that Party determines that the disclosure of this information would be contrary to its essential security interests; or
(b) to prevent a Party from taking an action that it considers necessary to protect its essential security interests:
(i) connected to the production of or traffic in arms, ammunition and implements of war and to such traffic and transactions in other goods and materials, services and technology

undertaken, and to economic activities, carried out directly or indirectly for the purpose of supplying a military or other security establishment (35) ;
(ii) taken in time of war or other emergency in international relations; or
(iii) relating to fissionable and fusionable materials or the materials from which they are derived; or
(c) prevent a Party from taking any action in order to carry out its international obligations for the purpose of maintaining international peace and security.

Article 28.7 Taxation
1. Nothing in this Agreement shall be construed to prevent a Party from adopting or maintaining any taxation measure that distinguishes between persons who are not in the same situation, in particular with regard to their place of residence or with regard to the place where their capital is invested.
2. Nothing in this Agreement shall be construed to prevent a Party from adopting or maintaining any taxation measure aimed at preventing the avoidance or evasion of taxes pursuant to its tax laws or tax conventions.
3. This Agreement does not affect the rights and obligations of a Party under a tax convention. In the event of inconsistency between this Agreement and a tax convention, that convention prevails to the extent of the inconsistency.
4. Nothing in this Agreement or in any arrangement adopted under this Agreement shall apply:
(a) to a taxation measure of a Party that provides a more favourable tax treatment to a corporation, or to a shareholder of a corporation, on the basis that the corporation is wholly or partly owned or controlled, directly or indirectly, by one or more investors who are residents of that Party;
(b) to a taxation measure of a Party that provides an advantage relating to the contributions made to, or income of, an arrangement providing for the deferral of, or exemption from, tax for pension, retirement, savings, education, health, disability or other similar purposes, conditional on a requirement that that Party maintains continuous jurisdiction over such arrangement;
(c) to a taxation measure of a Party that provides an advantage relating to the purchase or consumption of a particular service, conditional on a requirement that the service be provided in the territory of that Party;
(d) to a taxation measure of a Party that is aimed at ensuring the equitable and effective imposition or collection of taxes, including a measure that is taken by a Party in order to ensure compliance with the Party's taxation system;
(e) to a taxation measure that provides an advantage to a government, a part of a government, or a person that is directly or indirectly owned, controlled or established by a government;
(f) to an existing non-conforming taxation measure not otherwise covered in paragraphs 1, 2 and 4(a) through (e), to the continuation or prompt renewal of such a measure, or an amendment of such a measure, provided that the amendment does not decrease its conformity with the provisions of this Agreement as it existed immediately before the amendment.
5. For greater certainty, the fact that a taxation measure constitutes a significant amendment to an existing taxation measure, takes immediate effect as of its announcement, clarifies the intended application of an existing taxation measure, or has an unexpected impact on an investor or covered investment, does not, in and of itself, constitute a violation of Article 8.10 (Treatment of investors and of covered investments).
6. Articles 8.7 (Most-favoured-nation treatment), 9.5 (Most-favoured-nation treatment) and 13.4 (Most-favoured-nation treatment) do not apply to an advantage accorded by a Party pursuant to a tax convention.
7. (a) Where an investor submits a request for consultations pursuant to Article 8.19 (Consultations) claiming that a taxation measure breaches an obligation under Sections C (Non-discriminatory

treatment) or D (Investment protection) of Chapter Eight (Investment), the respondent may refer the matter for consultation and joint determination by the Parties as to whether:

(i) the measure is a taxation measure;

(ii) the measure, if it is found to be a taxation measure, breaches an obligation under Sections C (Non-discriminatory treatment) or D (Investment protection) of Chapter Eight (Investment) ; or

(iii) there is an inconsistency between the obligations in this Agreement that are alleged to have been breached and those of a tax convention.

(b) A referral pursuant to subparagraph (a) cannot be made later than the date the Tribunal fixes for the respondent to submit its counter-memorial. Where the respondent makes such a referral the time periods or proceedings specified in Section F (Resolution of investment disputes between investors and states) of Chapter Eight (Investment) shall be suspended. If within 180 days from the referral the Parties do not agree to consider the issue, or fail to make a joint determination, the suspension of the time periods or proceedings shall no longer apply and the investor may proceed with its claim.

(c) A joint determination by the Parties pursuant to subparagraph (a) shall be binding on the Tribunal.

(d) Each Party shall ensure that its delegation for the consultations to be conducted pursuant to subparagraph (a) shall include persons with relevant expertise on the issues covered by this Article, including representatives from the relevant tax authorities of each Party. For Canada, this means officials from the Department of Finance Canada.

8. For greater certainty,

(a) taxation measure of a Party means a taxation measure adopted at any level of government of a Party; and

(b) for measures of a sub-national government, resident of a Party, means either resident of that sub-national jurisdiction or resident of the Party of which it forms a part.

Article 28.8 Disclosure of information

1. This Agreement does not require a Party to furnish or allow access to information which, if disclosed, would impede law enforcement or the disclosure of which is prohibited or restricted under its law.

2. In the course of a dispute settlement procedure under this Agreement,

(a) a Party is not required to furnish or allow access to information protected under its competition laws; and

(b) a competition authority of a Party is not required to furnish or allow access to information that is privileged or otherwise protected from disclosure.

Article 28.9 Exceptions applicable to culture

The Parties recall the exceptions applicable to culture as set out in the relevant provisions of Chapters Seven (Subsidies), Eight (Investment), Nine (Cross-Border Trade in Services), Twelve (Domestic Regulation) and Nineteen (Government Procurement).

Article 28.10 WTO waivers

Parties agree that a measure in conformity with a waiver decision adopted by the WTO pursuant to Article IX of the WTO Agreement is deemed to be also in conformity with the duplicated provision in this Agreement.

10.1.7 General Agreement on Tariffs and Trade ('GATT') (1994) (selected articles)

Formerly GATT 1947, signed 15 April 1994, entered into force 1 January 1995.

PREFACE

The General Agreement on Tariffs and Trade came into force on 1 January 1948. This booklet contains the complete text of the General Agreement together with all amendments which have become effective since its entry into force. The text is identical to that published, since 1969, as Volume IV in the series Basic Instruments and Selected Documents. A guide to the legal sources of the provisions of the Agreement is provided in an appendix. An Analytical Index, containing notes on the drafting, interpretation and application of the articles of the Agreement has been prepared and published by the secretariat. A second publication, complementary to this one, contains the text of the agreements reached as a result of the Tokyo Round of Multilateral Trade Negotiations (1973-1979).

The General Agreement is applied "provisionally" by all contracting parties. The original contracting parties, and also those former territories of Belgium, France, the Netherlands and the United Kingdom which, after attaining independence, acceded to the General Agreement under Article XXVI:5(c), apply the GATT under the Protocol of Provisional Application, the text of which is reproduced in this volume. Chile applies the General Agreement under a Special Protocol of September 1948. The contracting parties which have acceded since 1948 apply the General Agreement under their respective Protocols of Accession.

For the convenience of the reader, **asterisks** mark the portions of the text which should be read in conjunction with notes and supplementary provisions in Annex I to the Agreement. In accordance with Article XXXIV, Annexes A to I are an integral part of the Agreement. The Schedules of tariff concessions annexed to the General Agreement (not here reproduced) are also, in accordance with Article II:7, an integral part of the Agreement.

By the Decision of 23 March 1965, the CONTRACTING PARTIES changed the title of the head of the GATT secretariat from "Executive Secretary" to "Director-General". However, in the absence of an amendment to the General Agreement to take account of this change, the title "Executive Secretary" has been retained in the text of Articles XVIII:12(e), XXIII:2 and XXVI:4, 5 and 6. The Decision of 23 March 1965 provides that the duties and powers conferred upon the Executive Secretary by the General Agreement "shall be exercised by the person holding the position of Director-General, who shall, for this purpose, also hold the position of Executive Secretary".

THE GENERAL AGREEMENT ON TARIFFS AND TRADE

The Governments of the COMMONWEALTH OF AUSTRALIA, the KKINGDOM OF BELGIUM, the UNITED STATES OF BRAZIL, BURMA, CANADA, CEYLON, the REPUBLIC OF CHILE, the REPUBLIC OF CHINA, the REPUBLIC OF CUBA, the CZECHOSLOVAK REPUBLIC, the FRENCH REPUBLIC, INDIA, LEBANON, the GRAND-DUCHY OF LUXEMBURG, the KINGDOM OF THE NETHERLANDS, NEW ZEALAND, the KINGDOM OF NORWAY, PAKISTAN, SOUTHERN

RHODESIA, SYRIA, the UNION OF SOUTH AFRICA, the UNITED KINGDOM OF GREAT BRITAIN AND NORTHERN IRELAND, and the UNITED STATES OF AMERICA:

Recognizing that their relations in the field of trade and economic endeavour should be conducted with a view to raising standards of living, ensuring full employment and a large and steadily growing volume of real income and effective demand, developing the full use of the resources of the world and expanding the production and exchange of goods,

Being desirous of contributing to these objectives by entering into reciprocal and mutually advantageous arrangements directed to the substantial reduction of tariffs and other barriers to trade and to the elimination of discriminatory treatment in international commerce,

Have through their Representatives agreed as follows:

PART I

Article I General Most-Favoured-Nation Treatment

1. With respect to customs duties and charges of any kind imposed on or in connection with importation or exportation or imposed on the international transfer of payments for imports or exports, and with respect to the method of levying such duties and charges, and with respect to all rules and formalities in connection with importation and exportation, and with respect to all matters referred to in paragraphs 2 and 4 of Article III,* any advantage, favour, privilege or immunity granted by any contracting party to any product originating in or destined for any other country shall be accorded immediately and unconditionally to the like product originating in or destined for the territories of all other contracting parties.

2. The provisions of paragraph 1 of this Article shall not require the elimination of any preferences in respect of import duties or charges which do not exceed the levels provided for in paragraph 4 of this Article and which fall within the following descriptions:

(a) Preferences in force exclusively between two or more of the territories listed in Annex A, subject to the conditions set forth therein;

(b) Preferences in force exclusively between two or more territories which on July 1, 1939, were connected by common sovereignty or relations of protection or suzerainty and which are listed in Annexes B, C and D, subject to the conditions set forth therein;

(c) Preferences in force exclusively between the United States of America and the Republic of Cuba;

(d) Preferences in force exclusively between neighbouring countries listed in Annexes E and F.

3. The provisions of paragraph 1 shall not apply to preferences between the countries formerly a part of the Ottoman Empire and detached from it on July 24, 1923, provided such preferences are approved under paragraph 5 of Article XXV, which shall be applied in this respect in the light of paragraph 1 of Article XXIX.

4. The margin of preference* on any product in respect of which a preference is permitted under paragraph 2 of this Article but is not specifically set forth as a maximum margin of preference in the appropriate Schedule annexed to this Agreement shall not exceed:

(a) in respect of duties or charges on any product described in such Schedule, the difference between the most-favoured-nation and preferential rates provided for therein; if no preferential rate is provided for, the preferential rate shall for the purposes of this paragraph be taken to be that in force on April 10, 1947, and, if no most-favoured-nation rate is provided for, the margin shall not exceed the difference between the most-favoured-nation and preferential rates existing on April 10, 1947;

(b) in respect of duties or charges on any product not described in the appropriate Schedule, the difference between the most-favoured-nation and preferential rates existing on April 10, 1947.

In the case of the contracting parties named in Annex G, the date of April 10, 1947, referred to in sub-paragraph (a) and (b) of this paragraph shall be replaced by the respective dates set forth in that Annex.

Article II Schedules of Concessions

1. (a) Each contracting party shall accord to the commerce of the other contracting parties treatment no less favourable than that provided for in the appropriate Part of the appropriate Schedule annexed to this Agreement.

(b) The products described in Part I of the Schedule relating to any contracting party, which are the products of territories of other contracting parties, shall, on their importation into the territory to which the Schedule relates, and subject to the terms, conditions or qualifications set forth in that Schedule, be exempt from ordinary customs duties in excess of those set forth and provided therein. Such products shall also be exempt from all other duties or charges of any kind imposed on or in connection with the importation in excess of those imposed on the date of this Agreement or those directly and mandatorily required to be imposed thereafter by legislation in force in the importing territory on that date.

(c) The products described in Part II of the Schedule relating to any contracting party which are the products of territories entitled under Article I to receive preferential treatment upon importation into the territory to which the Schedule relates shall, on their importation into such territory, and subject to the terms, conditions or qualifications set forth in that Schedule, be exempt from ordinary customs duties in excess of those set forth and provided for in Part II of that Schedule. Such products shall also be exempt from all other duties or charges of any kind imposed on or in connection with importation in excess of those imposed on the date of this Agreement or those directly or mandatorily required to be imposed thereafter by legislation in force in the importing territory on that date. Nothing in this Article shall prevent any contracting party from maintaining its requirements existing on the date of this Agreement as to the eligibility of goods for entry at preferential rates of duty.

2. Nothing in this Article shall prevent any contracting party from imposing at any time on the importation of any product:

(a) a charge equivalent to an internal tax imposed consistently with the provisions of paragraph 2 of Article III* in respect of the like domestic product or in respect of an article from which the imported product has been manufactured or produced in whole or in part;

(b) any anti-dumping or countervailing duty applied consistently with the provisions of Article VI;*

(c) fees or other charges commensurate with the cost of services rendered.

3. No contracting party shall alter its method of determining dutiable value or of converting currencies so as to impair the value of any of the concessions provided for in the appropriate Schedule annexed to this Agreement.

4. If any contracting party establishes, maintains or authorizes, formally or in effect, a monopoly of the importation of any product described in the appropriate Schedule annexed to this Agreement, such monopoly shall not, except as provided for in that Schedule or as otherwise agreed between the parties which initially negotiated the concession, operate so as to afford protection on the average in excess of the amount of protection provided for in that Schedule. The provisions of this paragraph shall not limit the use by contracting parties of any form of assistance to domestic producers permitted by other provisions of this Agreement.*

5. If any contracting party considers that a product is not receiving from another contracting party the treatment which the first contracting party believes to have been contemplated by a concession provided for in the appropriate Schedule annexed to this Agreement, it shall bring the matter directly

to the attention of the other contracting party. If the latter agrees that the treatment contemplated was that claimed by the first contracting party, but declares that such treatment cannot be accorded because a court or other proper authority has ruled to the effect that the product involved cannot be classified under the tariff laws of such contracting party so as to permit the treatment contemplated in this Agreement, the two contracting parties, together with any other contracting parties substantially interested, shall enter promptly into further negotiations with a view to a compensatory adjustment of the matter.

6. (a) The specific duties and charges included in the Schedules relating to contracting parties members of the International Monetary Fund, and margins of preference in specific duties and charges maintained by such contracting parties, are expressed in the appropriate currency at the par value accepted or provisionally recognized by the Fund at the date of this Agreement. Accordingly, in case this par value is reduced consistently with the Articles of Agreement of the International Monetary Fund by more than twenty per centum, such specific duties and charges and margins of preference may be adjusted to take account of such reduction; provided that the CONTRACTING PARTIES (i.e., the contracting parties acting jointly as provided for in Article XXV) concur that such adjustments will not impair the value of the concessions provided for in the appropriate Schedule or elsewhere in this Agreement, due account being taken of all factors which may influence the need for, or urgency of, such adjustments.
   (b) Similar provisions shall apply to any contracting party not a member of the Fund, as from the date on which such contracting party becomes a member of the Fund or enters into a special exchange agreement in pursuance of Article XV.
7. The Schedules annexed to this Agreement are hereby made an integral part of Part I of this Agreement.

PART II

Article III* National Treatment on Internal Taxation and Regulation

1. The contracting parties recognize that internal taxes and other internal charges, and laws, regulations and requirements affecting the internal sale, offering for sale, purchase, transportation, distribution or use of products, and internal quantitative regulations requiring the mixture, processing or use of products in specified amounts or proportions, should not be applied to imported or domestic products so as to afford protection to domestic production.*

2. The products of the territory of any contracting party imported into the territory of any other contracting party shall not be subject, directly or indirectly, to internal taxes or other internal charges of any kind in excess of those applied, directly or indirectly, to like domestic products. Moreover, no contracting party shall otherwise apply internal taxes or other internal charges to imported or domestic products in a manner contrary to the principles set forth in paragraph 1.*

3. With respect to any existing internal tax which is inconsistent with the provisions of paragraph 2, but which is specifically authorized under a trade agreement, in force on April 10, 1947, in which the import duty on the taxed product is bound against increase, the contracting party imposing the tax shall be free to postpone the application of the provisions of paragraph 2 to such tax until such time as it can obtain release from the obligations of such trade agreement in order to permit the increase of such duty to the extent necessary to compensate for the elimination of the protective element of the tax.

4. The products of the territory of any contracting party imported into the territory of any other contracting party shall be accorded treatment no less favourable than that accorded to like products of national origin in respect of all laws, regulations and requirements affecting their internal sale, offering for sale, purchase, transportation, distribution or use. The provisions of this paragraph shall not prevent the application of differential internal transportation charges which are based exclusively on the economic operation of the means of transport and not on the nationality of the product.

5. No contracting party shall establish or maintain any internal quantitative regulation relating to the mixture, processing or use of products in specified amounts or proportions which requires, directly or indirectly, that any specified amount or proportion of any product which is the subject of the regulation must be supplied from domestic sources. Moreover, no contracting party shall otherwise apply internal quantitative regulations in a manner contrary to the principles set forth in paragraph 1.*
6. The provisions of paragraph 5 shall not apply to any internal quantitative regulation in force in the territory of any contracting party on July 1, 1939, April 10, 1947, or March 24, 1948, at the option of that contracting party; Provided that any such regulation which is contrary to the provisions of paragraph 5 shall not be modified to the detriment of imports and shall be treated as a customs duty for the purpose of negotiation.
7. No internal quantitative regulation relating to the mixture, processing or use of products in specified amounts or proportions shall be applied in such a manner as to allocate any such amount or proportion among external sources of supply.
8. (a) The provisions of this Article shall not apply to laws, regulations or requirements governing the procurement by governmental agencies of products purchased for governmental purposes and not with a view to commercial resale or with a view to use in the production of goods for commercial sale.
   (b) The provisions of this Article shall not prevent the payment of subsidies exclusively to domestic producers, including payments to domestic producers derived from the proceeds of internal taxes or charges applied consistently with the provisions of this Article and subsidies effected through governmental purchases of domestic products.
9. The contracting parties recognize that internal maximum price control measures, even though conforming to the other provisions of this Article, can have effects prejudicial to the interests of contracting parties supplying imported products. Accordingly, contracting parties applying such measures shall take account of the interests of exporting contracting parties with a view to avoiding to the fullest practicable extent such prejudicial effects.
10. The provisions of this Article shall not prevent any contracting party from establishing or maintaining internal quantitative regulations relating to exposed cinematograph films and meeting the requirements of Article IV.

Article IV Special Provisions relating to Cinematograph Films

If any contracting party establishes or maintains internal quantitative regulations relating to exposed cinematograph films, such regulations shall take the form of screen quotas which shall conform to the following requirements:

(a) Screen quotas may require the exhibition of cinematograph films of national origin during a specified minimum proportion of the total screen time actually utilized, over a specified period of not less than one year, in the commercial exhibition of all films of whatever origin, and shall be computed on the basis of screen time per theatre per year or the equivalent thereof;
(b) With the exception of screen time reserved for films of national origin under a screen quota, screen time including that released by administrative action from screen time reserved for films of national origin, shall not be allocated formally or in effect among sources of supply;
(c) Notwithstanding the provisions of sub-paragraph (b) of this Article, any contracting party may maintain screen quotas conforming to the requirements of sub-paragraph (a) of this Article which reserve a minimum proportion of screen time for films of a specified origin other than that of the contracting party imposing such screen quotas; Provided that no such minimum proportion of screen time shall be increased above the level in effect on April 10, 1947;
(d) Screen quotas shall be subject to negotiation for their limitation, liberalization or elimination.

Article V Freedom of Transit

1. Goods (including baggage), and also vessels and other means of transport, shall be deemed to be in transit across the territory of a contracting party when the passage across such territory, with or without trans-shipment, warehousing, breaking bulk, or change in the mode of transport, is only a portion of a complete journey beginning and terminating beyond the frontier of the contracting party across whose territory the traffic passes. Traffic of this nature is termed in this article "traffic in transit".
2. There shall be freedom of transit through the territory of each contracting party, via the routes most convenient for international transit, for traffic in transit to or from the territory of other contracting parties. No distinction shall be made which is based on the flag of vessels, the place of origin, departure, entry, exit or destination, or on any circumstances relating to the ownership of goods, of vessels or of other means of transport.
3. Any contracting party may require that traffic in transit through its territory be entered at the proper custom house, but, except in cases of failure to comply with applicable customs laws and regulations, such traffic coming from or going to the territory of other contracting parties shall not be subject to any unnecessary delays or restrictions and shall be exempt from customs duties and from all transit duties or other charges imposed in respect of transit, except charges for transportation or those commensurate with administrative expenses entailed by transit or with the cost of services rendered.
4. All charges and regulations imposed by contracting parties on traffic in transit to or from the territories of other contracting parties shall be reasonable, having regard to the conditions of the traffic.
5. With respect to all charges, regulations and formalities in connection with transit, each contracting party shall accord to traffic in transit to or from the territory of any other contracting party treatment no less favourable than the treatment accorded to traffic in transit to or from any third country.*
6. Each contracting party shall accord to products which have been in transit through the territory of any other contracting party treatment no less favourable than that which would have been accorded to such products had they been transported from their place of origin to their destination without going through the territory of such other contracting party. Any contracting party shall, however, be free to maintain its requirements of direct consignment existing on the date of this Agreement, in respect of any goods in regard to which such direct consignment is a requisite condition of eligibility for entry of the goods at preferential rates of duty or has relation to the contracting party's prescribed method of valuation for duty purposes.
7. The provisions of this Article shall not apply to the operation of aircraft in transit, but shall apply to air transit of goods (including baggage).

Article VI Anti-dumping and Countervailing Duties

1. The contracting parties recognize that dumping, by which products of one country are introduced into the commerce of another country at less than the normal value of the products, is to be condemned if it causes or threatens material injury to an established industry in the territory of a contracting party or materially retards the establishment of a domestic industry. For the purposes of this Article, a product is to be considered as being introduced into the commerce of an importing country at less than its normal value, if the price of the product exported from one country to another

   (a) is less than the comparable price, in the ordinary course of trade, for the like product when destined for consumption in the exporting country, or,

   (b) in the absence of such domestic price, is less than either

      (i) the highest comparable price for the like product for export to any third country in the ordinary course of trade, or

      (ii) the cost of production of the product in the country of origin plus a reasonable addition for selling cost and profit.

Due allowance shall be made in each case for differences in conditions and terms of sale, for differences in taxation, and for other differences affecting price comparability.*

2. In order to offset or prevent dumping, a contracting party may levy on any dumped product an anti-dumping duty not greater in amount than the margin of dumping in respect of such product. For the purposes of this Article, the margin of dumping is the price difference determined in accordance with the provisions of paragraph 1.*

3. No countervailing duty shall be levied on any product of the territory of any contracting party imported into the territory of another contracting party in excess of an amount equal to the estimated bounty or subsidy determined to have been granted, directly or indirectly, on the manufacture, production or export of such product in the country of origin or exportation, including any special subsidy to the transportation of a particular product. The term "countervailing duty" shall be understood to mean a special duty levied for the purpose of offsetting any bounty or subsidy bestowed, directly, or indirectly, upon the manufacture, production or export of any merchandise.*

4. No product of the territory of any contracting party imported into the territory of any other contracting party shall be subject to anti-dumping or countervailing duty by reason of the exemption of such product from duties or taxes borne by the like product when destined for consumption in the country of origin or exportation, or by reason of the refund of such duties or taxes.

5. No product of the territory of any contracting party imported into the territory of any other contracting party shall be subject to both anti-dumping and countervailing duties to compensate for the same situation of dumping or export subsidization.

6. (a) No contracting party shall levy any anti-dumping or countervailing duty on the importation of any product of the territory of another contracting party unless it determines that the effect of the dumping or subsidization, as the case may be, is such as to cause or threaten material injury to an established domestic industry, or is such as to retard materially the establishment of a domestic industry.

(b) The CONTRACTING PARTIES may waive the requirement of sub-paragraph (a) of this paragraph so as to permit a contracting party to levy an anti-dumping or countervailing duty on the importation of any product for the purpose of offsetting dumping or subsidization which causes or threatens material injury to an industry in the territory of another contracting party exporting the product concerned to the territory of the importing contracting party. The CONTRACTING PARTIES shall waive the requirements of sub-paragraph (a) of this paragraph, so as to permit the levying of a countervailing duty, in cases in which they find that a subsidy is causing or threatening material injury to an industry in the territory of another contracting party exporting the product concerned to the territory of the importing contracting party.*

(c) In exceptional circumstances, however, where delay might cause damage which would be difficult to repair, a contracting party may levy a countervailing duty for the purpose referred to in sub-paragraph (b) of this paragraph without the prior approval of the CONTRACTING PARTIES; Provided that such action shall be reported immediately to the CONTRACTING PARTIES and that the countervailing duty shall be withdrawn promptly if the CONTRACTING PARTIES disapprove.

7. A system for the stabilization of the domestic price or of the return to domestic producers of a primary commodity, independently of the movements of export prices, which results at times in the sale of the commodity for export at a price lower than the comparable price charged for the like commodity to buyers in the domestic market, shall be presumed not to result in material injury within the meaning of paragraph 6 if it is determined by consultation among the contracting parties substantially interested in the commodity concerned that:

(a) the system has also resulted in the sale of the commodity for export at a price higher than the comparable price charged for the like commodity to buyers in the domestic market, and

(b) the system is so operated, either because of the effective regulation of production, or otherwise, as not to stimulate exports unduly or otherwise seriously prejudice the interests of other contracting parties.

Article VII Valuation for Customs Purposes

1. The contracting parties recognize the validity of the general principles of valuation set forth in the following paragraphs of this Article, and they undertake to give effect to such principles, in respect of all products subject to duties or other charges* or restrictions on importation and exportation based upon or regulated in any manner by value. Moreover, they shall, upon a request by another contracting party review the operation of any of their laws or regulations relating to value for customs purposes in the light of these principles. The CONTRACTING PARTIES may request from contracting parties reports on steps taken by them in pursuance of the provisions of this Article.

2. (a) The value for customs purposes of imported merchandise should be based on the actual value of the imported merchandise on which duty is assessed, or of like merchandise, and should not be based on the value of merchandise of national origin or on arbitrary or fictitious values.*

(b) "Actual value" should be the price at which, at a time and place determined by the legislation of the country of importation, such or like merchandise is sold or offered for sale in the ordinary course of trade under fully competitive conditions. To the extent to which the price of such or like merchandise is governed by the quantity in a particular transaction, the price to be considered should uniformly be related to either (i) comparable quantities, or (ii) quantities not less favourable to importers than those in which the greater volume of the merchandise is sold in the trade between the countries of exportation and importation.*

(c) When the actual value is not ascertainable in accordance with sub-paragraph (b) of this paragraph, the value for customs purposes should be based on the nearest ascertainable equivalent of such value.*

3. The value for customs purposes of any imported product should not include the amount of any internal tax, applicable within the country of origin or export, from which the imported product has been exempted or has been or will be relieved by means of refund.

4. (a) Except as otherwise provided for in this paragraph, where it is necessary for the purposes of paragraph 2 of this Article for a contracting party to convert into its own currency a price expressed in the currency of another country, the conversion rate of exchange to be used shall be based, for each currency involved, on the par value as established pursuant to the Articles of Agreement of the International Monetary Fund or on the rate of exchange recognized by the Fund, or on the par value established in accordance with a special exchange agreement entered into pursuant to Article XV of this Agreement.

(b) Where no such established par value and no such recognized rate of exchange exist, the conversion rate shall reflect effectively the current value of such currency in commercial transactions.

(c) The CONTRACTING PARTIES, in agreement with the International Monetary Fund, shall formulate rules governing the conversion by contracting parties of any foreign currency in respect of which multiple rates of exchange are maintained consistently with the Articles of Agreement of the International Monetary Fund. Any contracting party may apply such rules in respect of such foreign currencies for the purposes of paragraph 2 of this Article as an alternative to the use of par values. Until such rules are adopted by the CONTRACTING PARTIES, any contracting party may employ, in respect of any such foreign currency, rules of conversion for the purposes of paragraph 2 of this Article which are designed to reflect effectively the value of such foreign currency in commercial transactions.

(d) Nothing in this paragraph shall be construed to require any contracting party to alter the method of converting currencies for customs purposes which is applicable in its territory on the date of this Agreement, if such alteration would have the effect of increasing generally the amounts of duty payable.

5. The bases and methods for determining the value of products subject to duties or other charges or restrictions based upon or regulated in any manner by value should be stable and should be given

sufficient publicity to enable traders to estimate, with a reasonable degree of certainty, the value for customs purposes.

Article VIII Fees and Formalities connected with Importation and Exportation*

1. (a) All fees and charges of whatever character (other than import and export duties and other than taxes within the purview of Article III) imposed by contracting parties on or in connection with importation or exportation shall be limited in amount to the approximate cost of services rendered and shall not represent an indirect protection to domestic products or a taxation of imports or exports for fiscal purposes.
   (b) The contracting parties recognize the need for reducing the number and diversity of fees and charges referred to in sub-paragraph (a).
   (c) The contracting parties also recognize the need for minimizing the incidence and complexity of import and export formalities and for decreasing and simplifying import and export documentation requirements.*
2. A contracting party shall, upon request by another contracting party or by the CONTRACTING PARTIES, review the operation of its laws and regulations in the light of the provisions of this Article.
3. No contracting party shall impose substantial penalties for minor breaches of customs regulations or procedural requirements. In particular, no penalty in respect of any omission or mistake in customs documentation which is easily rectifiable and obviously made without fraudulent intent or gross negligence shall be greater than necessary to serve merely as a warning.
4. The provisions of this Article shall extend to fees, charges, formalities and requirements imposed by governmental authorities in connection with importation and exportation, including those relating to:
   (a) consular transactions, such as consular invoices and certificates;
   (b) quantitative restrictions;
   (c) licensing;
   (d) exchange control;
   (e) statistical services;
   (f) documents, documentation and certification;
   (g) analysis and inspection; and
   (h) quarantine, sanitation and fumigation.

Article IX Marks of Origin

1. Each contracting party shall accord to the products of the territories of other contracting parties treatment with regard to marking requirements no less favourable than the treatment accorded to like products of any third country.
2. The contracting parties recognize that, in adopting and enforcing laws and regulations relating to marks of origin, the difficulties and inconveniences which such measures may cause to the commerce and industry of exporting countries should be reduced to a minimum, due regard being had to the necessity of protecting consumers against fraudulent or misleading indications.
3. Whenever it is administratively practicable to do so, contracting parties should permit required marks of origin to be affixed at the time of importation.
4. The laws and regulations of contracting parties relating to the marking of imported products shall be such as to permit compliance without seriously damaging the products, or materially reducing their value, or unreasonably increasing their cost.
5. As a general rule, no special duty or penalty should be imposed by any contracting party for failure to comply with marking requirements prior to importation unless corrective marking is unreasonably delayed or deceptive marks have been affixed or the required marking has been intentionally omitted.
6. The contracting parties shall co-operate with each other with a view to preventing the use of trade names in such manner as to misrepresent the true origin of a product, to the detriment of such

distinctive regional or geographical names of products of the territory of a contracting party as are protected by its legislation. Each contracting party shall accord full and sympathetic consideration to such requests or representations as may be made by any other contracting party regarding the application of the undertaking set forth in the preceding sentence to names of products which have been communicated to it by the other contracting party.

Article X Publication and Administration of Trade Regulations

1. Laws, regulations, judicial decisions and administrative rulings of general application, made effective by any contracting party, pertaining to the classification or the valuation of products for customs purposes, or to rates of duty, taxes or other charges, or to requirements, restrictions or prohibitions on imports or exports or on the transfer of payments therefor, or affecting their sale, distribution, transportation, insurance, warehousing inspection, exhibition, processing, mixing or other use, shall be published promptly in such a manner as to enable governments and traders to become acquainted with them. Agreements affecting international trade policy which are in force between the government or a governmental agency of any contracting party and the government or governmental agency of any other contracting party shall also be published. The provisions of this paragraph shall not require any contracting party to disclose confidential information which would impede law enforcement or otherwise be contrary to the public interest or would prejudice the legitimate commercial interests of particular enterprises, public or private.

2. No measure of general application taken by any contracting party effecting an advance in a rate of duty or other charge on imports under an established and uniform practice, or imposing a new or more burdensome requirement, restriction or prohibition on imports, or on the transfer of payments therefor, shall be enforced before such measure has been officially published.

3. (a) Each contracting party shall administer in a uniform, impartial and reasonable manner all its laws, regulations, decisions and rulings of the kind described in paragraph 1 of this Article.

(b) Each contracting party shall maintain, or institute as soon as practicable, judicial, arbitral or administrative tribunals or procedures for the purpose, inter alia, of the prompt review and correction of administrative action relating to customs matters. Such tribunals or procedures shall be independent of the agencies entrusted with administrative enforcement and their decisions shall be implemented by, and shall govern the practice of, such agencies unless an appeal is lodged with a court or tribunal of superior jurisdiction within the time prescribed for appeals to be lodged by importers; Provided that the central administration of such agency may take steps to obtain a review of the matter in another proceeding if there is good cause to believe that the decision is inconsistent with established principles of law or the actual facts.

(c) The provisions of sub-paragraph (b) of this paragraph shall not require the elimination or substitution of procedures in force in the territory of a contracting party on the date of this Agreement which in fact provide for an objective and impartial review of administrative action even though such procedures are not fully or formally independent of the agencies entrusted with administrative enforcement. Any contracting party employing such procedures shall, upon request, furnish the CONTRACTING PARTIES with full information thereon in order that they may determine whether such procedures conform to the requirements of this sub-paragraph.

Article XI* General Elimination of Quantitative Restrictions

1. No prohibitions or restrictions other than duties, taxes or other charges, whether made effective through quotas, import or export licences or other measures, shall be instituted or maintained by any contracting party on the importation of any product of the territory of any other contracting party or on the exportation or sale for export of any product destined for the territory of any other contracting party.

2. The provisions of paragraph 1 of this Article shall not extend to the following:

(a) Export prohibitions or restrictions temporarily applied to prevent or relieve critical shortages of foodstuffs or other products essential to the exporting contracting party;
(b) Import and export prohibitions or restrictions necessary to the application of standards or regulations for the classification, grading or marketing of commodities in international trade;
(c) Import restrictions on any agricultural or fisheries product, imported in any form,* necessary to the enforcement of governmental measures which operate:
  (i) to restrict the quantities of the like domestic product permitted to be marketed or produced, or, if there is no substantial domestic production of the like product, of a domestic product for which the imported product can be directly substituted; or
  (ii) to remove a temporary surplus of the like domestic product, or, if there is no substantial domestic production of the like product, of a domestic product for which the imported product can be directly substituted, by making the surplus available to certain groups of domestic consumers free of charge or at prices below the current market level; or
  (iii) to restrict the quantities permitted to be produced of any animal product the production of which is directly dependent, wholly or mainly, on the imported commodity, if the domestic production of that commodity is relatively negligible.

Any contracting party applying restrictions on the importation of any product pursuant to sub-paragraph (c) of this paragraph shall give public notice of the total quantity or value of the product permitted to be imported during a specified future period and of any change in such quantity or value. Moreover, any restrictions applied under (i) above shall not be such as will reduce the total of imports relative to the total of domestic production, as compared with the proportion which might reasonably be expected to rule between the two in the absence of restrictions. In determining this proportion, the contracting party shall pay due regard to the proportion prevailing during a previous representative period and to any special factors* which may have affected or may be affecting the trade in the product concerned.

Article XII* Restrictions to Safeguard the Balance of Payments

1. Notwithstanding the provisions of paragraph 1 of Article XI, any contracting party, in order to safeguard its external financial position and its balance of payments, may restrict the quantity or value of merchandise permitted to be imported, subject to the provisions of the following paragraphs of this Article.

2. (a) Import restrictions instituted, maintained or intensified by a contracting party under this Article shall not exceed those necessary:
  (i) to forestall the imminent threat of, or to stop, a serious decline in its monetary reserves, or
  (ii) in the case of a contracting party with very low monetary reserves, to achieve a reasonable rate of increase in its reserves.

Due regard shall be paid in either case to any special factors which may be affecting the reserves of such contracting party or its need for reserves, including, where special external credits or other resources are available to it, the need to provide for the appropriate use of such credits or resources.

(b) Contracting parties applying restrictions under sub-paragraph (a) of this paragraph shall progressively relax them as such conditions improve, maintaining them only to the extent that the conditions specified in that sub-paragraph still justify their application. They shall eliminate the restrictions when conditions would no longer justify their institution or maintenance under that sub-paragraph.

3. (a) Contracting parties undertake, in carrying out their domestic policies, to pay due regard to the need for maintaining or restoring equilibrium in their balance of payments on a sound and lasting basis and to the desirability of avoiding an uneconomic employment of productive resources. They recognize that, in order to achieve these ends, it is desirable so far as possible to adopt measures which expand rather than contract international trade.

(b) Contracting parties applying restrictions under this Article may determine the incidence of the restrictions on imports of different products or classes of products in such a way as to give priority to the importation of those products which are more essential.

(c) Contracting parties applying restrictions under this Article undertake:

(i) to avoid unnecessary damage to the commercial or economic interests of any other contracting party;*

(ii) not to apply restrictions so as to prevent unreasonably the importation of any description of goods in minimum commercial quantities the exclusion of which would impair regular channels of trade; and

(iii) not to apply restrictions which would prevent the importations of commercial samples or prevent compliance with patent, trade mark, copyright, or similar procedures.

(d) The contracting parties recognize that, as a result of domestic policies directed towards the achievement and maintenance of full and productive employment or towards the development of economic resources, a contracting party may experience a high level of demand for imports involving a threat to its monetary reserves of the sort referred to in paragraph 2 (a) of this Article. Accordingly, a contracting party otherwise complying with the provisions of this Article shall not be required to withdraw or modify restrictions on the ground that a change in those policies would render unnecessary restrictions which it is applying under this Article.

4. (a) Any contracting party applying new restrictions or raising the general level of its existing restrictions by a substantial intensification of the measures applied under this Article shall immediately after instituting or intensifying such restrictions (or, in circumstances in which prior consultation is practicable, before doing so) consult with the CONTRACTING PARTIES as to the nature of its balance of payments difficulties, alternative corrective measures which may be available, and the possible effect of the restrictions on the economies of other contracting parties.

(b) On a date to be determined by them,* the CONTRACTING PARTIES shall review all restrictions still applied under this Article on that date. Beginning one year after that date, contracting parties applying import restrictions under this Article shall enter into consultations of the type provided for in sub-paragraph (a) of this paragraph with the CONTRACTING PARTIES annually.

(c) (i) If, in the course of consultations with a contracting party under sub-paragraph (a) or (b) above, the CONTRACTING PARTIES find that the restrictions are not consistent with provisions of this Article or with those of Article XIII (subject to the provisions of Article XIV), they shall indicate the nature of the inconsistency and may advise that the restrictions be suitably modified.

(ii) If, however, as a result of the consultations, the CONTRACTING PARTIES determine that the restrictions are being applied in a manner involving an inconsistency of a serious nature with the provisions of this Article or with those of Article XIII (subject to the provisions of Article XIV) and that damage to the trade of any contracting party is caused or threatened thereby, they shall so inform the contracting party applying the restrictions and shall make appropriate recommendations for securing conformity with such provisions within the specified period of time. If such contracting party does not comply with these recommendations within the specified period, the CONTRACTING PARTIES may release any contracting party the trade of which is adversely affected by the restrictions from such obligations under this Agreement towards the contracting party applying the restrictions as they determine to be appropriate in the circumstances.

(d) The CONTRACTING PARTIES shall invite any contracting party which is applying restrictions under this Article to enter into consultations with them at the request of any contracting party which can establish a prima facie case that the restrictions are inconsistent with the provisions of this Article or with those of Article XIII (subject to the provisions of Article XIV) and that its trade is adversely affected thereby. However, no such invitation shall be issued unless the CONTRACTING PARTIES have ascertained that direct discussions between the contracting parties concerned have not been successful. If, as a result of the consultations with the CONTRACTING PARTIES, no agreement is reached and they determine that the restrictions are being applied inconsistently with such provisions, and that damage to the trade of the contracting party initiating the procedure is caused or threatened thereby, they shall recommend the withdrawal or modification of the restrictions. If the restrictions are not withdrawn or modified within such time as the CONTRACTING PARTIES may prescribe, they may release the contracting party initiating the procedure from such obligations under this Agreement towards the contracting party applying the restrictions as they determine to be appropriate in the circumstances.

(e) In proceeding under this paragraph, the CONTRACTING PARTIES shall have due regard to any special external factors adversely affecting the export trade of the contracting party applying the restrictions.*

(f) Determinations under this paragraph shall be rendered expeditiously and, if possible, within sixty days of the initiation of the consultations.

5. If there is a persistent and widespread application of import restrictions under this Article, indicating the existence of a general disequilibrium which is restricting international trade, the CONTRACTING PARTIES shall initiate discussions to consider whether other measures might be taken, either by those contracting parties the balance of payments of which are under pressure or by those the balance of payments of which are tending to be exceptionally favourable, or by any appropriate intergovernmental organization, to remove the underlying causes of the disequilibrium. On the invitation of the CONTRACTING PARTIES, contracting parties shall participate in such discussions.

Article XIII* Non-discriminatory Administration of Quantitative Restrictions

1. No prohibition or restriction shall be applied by any contracting party on the importation of any product of the territory of any other contracting party or on the exportation of any product destined for the territory of any other contracting party, unless the importation of the like product of all third countries or the exportation of the like product to all third countries is similarly prohibited or restricted.

2. In applying import restrictions to any product, contracting parties shall aim at a distribution of trade in such product approaching as closely as possible the shares which the various contracting parties might be expected to obtain in the absence of such restrictions and to this end shall observe the following provisions:

(a) Wherever practicable, quotas representing the total amount of permitted imports (whether allocated among supplying countries or not) shall be fixed, and notice given of their amount in accordance with paragraph 3 (b) of this Article;

(b) In cases in which quotas are not practicable, the restrictions may be applied by means of import licences or permits without a quota;

(c) Contracting parties shall not, except for purposes of operating quotas allocated in accordance with sub-paragraph (d) of this paragraph, require that import licences or permits be utilized for the importation of the product concerned from a particular country or source;

(d) In cases in which a quota is allocated among supplying countries the contracting party applying the restrictions may seek agreement with respect to the allocation of shares in the quota with all other contracting parties having a substantial interest in supplying the product concerned. In cases in which this method is not reasonably practicable, the contracting party concerned shall allot to contracting parties having a substantial interest in supplying the product shares based upon the proportions, supplied by such contracting parties during a previous representative period, of the total quantity or value of imports of the product, due account being taken of any special factors which may have affected or may be affecting the trade in the product. No conditions or formalities shall be imposed which would prevent any contracting party from utilizing fully the share of any such total quantity or value which has been allotted to it, subject to importation being made within any prescribed period to which the quota may relate.*

3. (a) In cases in which import licences are issued in connection with import restrictions, the contracting party applying the restrictions shall provide, upon the request of any contracting party having an interest in the trade in the product concerned, all relevant information concerning the administration of the restrictions, the import licences granted over a recent period and the distribution of such licences among supplying countries; Provided that there shall be no obligation to supply information as to the names of importing or supplying enterprises.

(b) In the case of import restrictions involving the fixing of quotas, the contracting party applying the restrictions shall give public notice of the total quantity or value of the product or products which will be permitted to be imported during a specified future period and of any change in such quantity or value. Any supplies of the product in question which were en route at the time at which public notice was given shall not be excluded from entry; Provided that they may be counted so far as practicable, against the quantity permitted to be imported in the period in question, and also, where necessary, against the quantities permitted to be imported in the next following period or periods; and Provided further that if any contracting party customarily exempts from such restrictions products entered for consumption or withdrawn from warehouse for consumption during a period of thirty days after the day of such public notice, such practice shall be considered full compliance with this sub-paragraph.

(c) In the case of quotas allocated among supplying countries, the contracting party applying the restrictions shall promptly inform all other contracting parties having an interest in supplying the product concerned of the shares in the quota currently allocated, by quantity or value, to the various supplying countries and shall give public notice thereof.

4. With regard to restrictions applied in accordance with paragraph 2 (d) of this Article or under paragraph 2 (c) of Article XI, the selection of a representative period for any product and the appraisal of any special factors* affecting the trade in the product shall be made initially by the contracting party applying the restriction; Provided that such contracting party shall, upon the request of any other contracting party having a substantial interest in supplying that product or upon the request of the CONTRACTING PARTIES, consult promptly with the other contracting party or the CONTRACTING PARTIES regarding the need for an adjustment of the proportion determined or of the base period selected, or for the reappraisal of the special factors involved, or for the elimination of conditions, formalities or any other provisions established unilaterally relating to the allocation of an adequate quota or its unrestricted utilization.

5. The provisions of this Article shall apply to any tariff quota instituted or maintained by any contracting party, and, in so far as applicable, the principles of this Article shall also extend to export restrictions.

Article XIV* Exceptions to the Rule of Non-discrimination

1. A contracting party which applies restrictions under Article XII or under Section B of Article XVIII may, in the application of such restrictions, deviate from the provisions of Article XIII in a manner having equivalent effect to restrictions on payments and transfers for current international transactions which that contracting party may at that time apply under Article VIII or XIV of the Articles of Agreement of the International Monetary Fund, or under analogous provisions of a special exchange agreement entered into pursuant to paragraph 6 of Article XV.*

2. A contracting party which is applying import restrictions under Article XII or under Section B of Article XVIII may, with the consent of the CONTRACTING PARTIES, temporarily deviate from

the provisions of Article XIII in respect of a small part of its external trade where the benefits to the contracting party or contracting parties concerned substantially outweigh any injury which may result to the trade of other contracting parties.*

3. The provisions of Article XIII shall not preclude a group of territories having a common quota in the International Monetary Fund from applying against imports from other countries, but not among themselves, restrictions in accordance with the provisions of Article XII or of Section B of Article XVIII on condition that such restrictions are in all other respects consistent with the provisions of Article XIII.

4. A contracting party applying import restrictions under Article XII or under Section B of Article XVIII shall not be precluded by Articles XI to XV or Section B of Article XVIII of this Agreement from applying measures to direct its exports in such a manner as to increase its earnings of currencies which it can use without deviation from the provisions of Article XIII.

5. A contracting party shall not be precluded by Articles XI to XV, inclusive, or by Section B of Article XVIII, of this Agreement from applying quantitative restrictions:

(a) having equivalent effect to exchange restrictions authorized under Section 3 (b) of Article VII of the Articles of Agreement of the International Monetary Fund, or

(b) under the preferential arrangements provided for in Annex A of this Agreement, pending the outcome of the negotiations referred to therein.

Article XV Exchange Arrangements

1. The CONTRACTING PARTIES shall seek co-operation with the International Monetary Fund to the end that the CONTRACTING PARTIES and the Fund may pursue a co-ordinated policy with regard to exchange questions within the jurisdiction of the Fund and questions of quantitative restrictions and other trade measures within the jurisdiction of the CONTRACTING PARTIES.

2. In all cases in which the CONTRACTING PARTIES are called upon to consider or deal with problems concerning monetary reserves, balances of payments or foreign exchange arrangements, they shall consult fully with the International Monetary Fund. In such consultations, the CONTRACTING PARTIES shall accept all findings of statistical and other facts presented by the Fund relating to foreign exchange, monetary reserves and balances of payments, and shall accept the determination of the Fund as to whether action by a contracting party in exchange matters is in accordance with the Articles of Agreement of the International Monetary Fund, or with the terms of a special exchange agreement between that contracting party and the CONTRACTING PARTIES. The CONTRACTING PARTIES in reaching their final decision in cases involving the criteria set forth in paragraph 2 (a) of Article XII or in paragraph 9 of Article XVIII, shall accept the determination of the Fund as to what constitutes a serious decline in the contracting party's monetary reserves, a very low level of its monetary reserves or a reasonable rate of increase in its monetary reserves, and as to the financial aspects of other matters covered in consultation in such cases.

3. The CONTRACTING PARTIES shall seek agreement with the Fund regarding procedures for consultation under paragraph 2 of this Article.

4. Contracting parties shall not, by exchange action, frustrate* the intent of the provisions of this Agreement, nor, by trade action, the intent of the provisions of the Articles of Agreement of the International Monetary Fund.

5. If the CONTRACTING PARTIES consider, at any time, that exchange restrictions on payments and transfers in connection with imports are being applied by a contracting party in a manner inconsistent with the exceptions provided for in this Agreement for quantitative restrictions, they shall report thereon to the Fund.

6. Any contracting party which is not a member of the Fund shall, within a time to be determined by the CONTRACTING PARTIES after consultation with the Fund, become a member of the Fund, or, failing that, enter into a special exchange agreement with the CONTRACTING PARTIES.

A contracting party which ceases to be a member of the Fund shall forthwith enter into a special exchange agreement with the CONTRACTING PARTIES. Any special exchange agreement entered into by a contracting party under this paragraph shall thereupon become part of its obligations under this Agreement.

7. (a) A special exchange agreement between a contracting party and the CONTRACTING PARTIES under paragraph 6 of this Article shall provide to the satisfaction of the CONTRACTING PARTIES that the objectives of this Agreement will not be frustrated as a result of action in exchange matters by the contracting party in question.
   (b) The terms of any such agreement shall not impose obligations on the contracting party in exchange matters generally more restrictive than those imposed by the Articles of Agreement of the International Monetary Fund on members of the Fund.

8. A contracting party which is not a member of the Fund shall furnish such information within the general scope of section 5 of Article VIII of the Articles of Agreement of the International Monetary Fund as the CONTRACTING PARTIES may require in order to carry out their functions under this Agreement.

9. Nothing in this Agreement shall preclude:
   (a) the use by a contracting party of exchange controls or exchange restrictions in accordance with the Articles of Agreement of the International Monetary Fund or with that contracting party's special exchange agreement with the CONTRACTING PARTIES, or
   (b) the use by a contracting party of restrictions or controls in imports or exports, the sole effect of which, additional to the effects permitted under Articles XI, XII, XIII and XIV, is to make effective such exchange controls or exchange restrictions.

Article XVI* Subsidies

Section A _ Subsidies in General

1. If any contracting party grants or maintains any subsidy, including any form of income or price support, which operates directly or indirectly to increase exports of any product from, or to reduce imports of any product into, its territory, it shall notify the CONTRACTING PARTIES in writing of the extent and nature of the subsidization, of the estimated effect of the subsidization on the quantity of the affected product or products imported into or exported from its territory and of the circumstances making the subsidization necessary. In any case in which it is determined that serious prejudice to the interests of any other contracting party is caused or threatened by any such subsidization, the contracting party granting the subsidy shall, upon request, discuss with the other contracting party or parties concerned, or with the CONTRACTING PARTIES, the possibility oflimiting the subsidization.

Section B _ Additional Provisions on Export Subsidies*

2. The contracting parties recognize that the granting by a contracting party of a subsidy on the export of any product may have harmful effects for other contracting parties, both importing and exporting, may cause undue disturbance to their normal commercial interests, and may hinder the achievement of the objectives of this Agreement.

3. Accordingly, contracting parties should seek to avoid the use of subsidies on the export of primary products. If, however, a contracting party grants directly or indirectly any form of subsidy which operates to increase the export of any primary product from its territory, such subsidy shall not be applied in a manner which results in that contracting party having more than an equitable share of world export trade in that product, account being taken of the shares of the contracting parties in such

trade in the product during a previous representative period, and any special factors which may have affected or may be affecting such trade in the product.*

4. Further, as from 1 January 1958 or the earliest practicable date thereafter, contracting parties shall cease to grant either directly or indirectly any form of subsidy on the export of any product other than a primary product which subsidy results in the sale of such product for export at a price lower than the comparable price charged for the like product to buyers in the domestic market. Until 31 December 1957 no contracting party shall extend the scope of any such subsidization beyond that existing on 1 January 1955 by the introduction of new, or the extension of existing, subsidies.*

5. The CONTRACTING PARTIES shall review the operation of the provisions of this Article from time to time with a view to examining its effectiveness, in the light of actual experience, in promoting the objectives of this Agreement and avoiding subsidization seriously prejudicial to the trade or interests of contracting parties.

Article XVII State Trading Enterprises

1.* (a) Each contracting party undertakes that if it establishes or maintains a State enterprise, wherever located, or grants to any enterprise, formally or in effect, exclusive or special privileges,* such enterprise shall, in its purchases or sales involving either imports or exports, act in a manner consistent with the general principles of non-discriminatory treatment prescribed in this Agreement for governmental measures affecting imports or exports by private traders.

(b) The provisions of sub-paragraph (a) of this paragraph shall be understood to require that such enterprises shall, having due regard to the other provisions of this Agreement, make any such purchases or sales solely in accordance with commercial considerations,* including price, quality, availability, marketability, transportation and other conditions of purchase or sale, and shall afford the enterprises of the other contracting parties adequate opportunity, in accordance with customary business practice, to compete for participation in such purchases or sales.

(c) No contracting party shall prevent any enterprise (whether or not an enterprise described in sub-paragraph (a) of this paragraph) under its jurisdiction from acting in accordance with the principles of sub-paragraphs (a) and (b) of this paragraph.

2. The provisions of paragraph 1 of this Article shall not apply to imports of products for immediate or ultimate consumption in governmental use and not otherwise for resale or use in the production of goods* for sale. With respect to such imports, each contracting party shall accord to the trade of the other contracting parties fair and equitable treatment.

3. The contracting parties recognize that enterprises of the kind described in paragraph 1 (a) of this Article might be operated so as to create serious obstacles to trade; thus negotiations on a reciprocal and mutually advantageous basis designed to limit or reduce such obstacles are of importance to the expansion of international trade.*

4. (a) Contracting parties shall notify the CONTRACTING PARTIES of the products which are imported into or exported from their territories by enterprises of the kind described in paragraph 1 (a) of this Article.

(b) A contracting party establishing, maintaining or authorizing an import monopoly of a product, which is not the subject of a concession under Article II, shall, on the request of another contracting party having a substantial trade in the product concerned, inform the CONTRACTING PARTIES of the import mark-up* on the product during a recent representative period, or, when it is not possible to do so, of the price charged on the resale of the product.

(c) The CONTRACTING PARTIES may, at the request of a contracting party which has reason to believe that its interest under this Agreement are being adversely affected by the operations of an enterprise of the kind described in paragraph 1 (a), request the contracting party establishing, maintaining or authorizing such enterprise to supply information about its operations related to the carrying out of the provisions of this Agreement.

(d) The provisions of this paragraph shall not require any contracting party to disclose confidential information which would impede law enforcement or otherwise be contrary to the public interest or would prejudice the legitimate commercial interests of particular enterprises.

Article XVIII* Governmental Assistance to Economic Development

1. The contracting parties recognize that the attainment of the objectives of this Agreement will be facilitated by the progressive development of their economies, particularly of those contracting parties the economies of which can only support low standards of living* and are in the early stages of development.*

2. The contracting parties recognize further that it may be necessary for those contracting parties, in order to implement programmes and policies of economic development designed to raise the general standard of living of their people, to take protective or other measures affecting imports, and that such measures are justified in so far as they facilitate the attainment of the objectives of this Agreement. They agree, therefore, that those contracting parties should enjoy additional facilities to enable them

(a) to maintain sufficient flexibility in their tariff structure to be able to grant the tariff protection required for the establishment of a particular industry* and (b) to apply quantitative restrictions for balance of payments purposes in a manner which takes full account of the continued high level of demand for imports likely to be generated by their programmes of economic development.

3. The contracting parties recognize finally that, with those additional facilities which are provided for in Sections A and B of this Article, the provisions of this Agreement would normally be sufficient to enable contracting parties to meet the requirements of their economic development. They agree, however, that there may be circumstances where no measure consistent with those provisions is practicable to permit a contracting party in the process of economic development to grant the governmental assistance required to promote the establishment of particular industries* with a view to raising the general standard of living of its people. Special procedures are laid down in Sections C and D of this Article to deal with those cases.

4. (a) Consequently, a contracting party, the economy of which can only support low standards of living* and is in the early stages of development,* shall be free to deviate temporarily from the provisions of the other Articles of this Agreement, as provided in Sections A, B and C of this Article.

(b) A contracting party, the economy of which is in the process of development, but which does not come within the scope of sub-paragraph (a) above, may submit applications to the CONTRACTING PARTIES under Section D of this Article.

5. The contracting parties recognize that the export earnings of contracting parties, the economies of which are of the type described in paragraph 4 (a) and (b) above and which depend on exports of a small number of primary commodities, may be seriously reduced by a decline in the sale of such commodities. Accordingly, when the exports of primary commodities by such a contracting party are seriously affected by measures taken by another contracting party, it may have resort to the consultation provisions of Article XXII of this Agreement.

6. The CONTRACTING PARTIES shall review annually all measures applied pursuant to the provisions of Sections C and D of this Article.

Section A

7. (a) If a contracting party coming within the scope of paragraph 4 (a) of this Article considers it desirable, in order to promote the establishment of a particular industry* with a view to raising the general standard of living of its people, to modify or withdraw a concession included in the appropriate Schedule annexed to this Agreement, it shall notify the CONTRACTING PARTIES to this effect and enter into negotiations with any contracting party with which such

concession was initially negotiated, and with any other contracting party determined by the CONTRACTING PARTIES to have a substantial interest therein. If agreement is reached between such contracting parties concerned, they shall be free to modify or withdraw concessions under the appropriate Schedules to this Agreement in order to give effect to such agreement, including any compensatory adjustments involved.

(b) If agreement is not reached within sixty days after the notification provided for in sub-paragraph (a) above, the contracting party which proposes to modify or withdraw the concession may refer the matter to the CONTRACTING PARTIES which shall promptly examine it. If they find that the contracting party which proposes to modify or withdraw the concession has made every effort to reach an agreement and that the compensatory adjustment offered by it is adequate, that contracting party shall be free to modify or withdraw the concession if, at the same time, it gives effect to the compensatory adjustment. If the CONTRACTING PARTIES do not find that the compensation offered by a contracting party proposing to modify or withdraw the concession is adequate, but find that it has made every reasonable effort to offer adequate compensation, that contracting party shall be free to proceed with such modification or withdrawal. If such action is taken, any other contracting party referred to in sub-paragraph (a) above shall be free to modify or withdraw substantially equivalent concessions initially negotiated with the contracting party which has taken the action.*

Section B

8. The contracting parties recognize that contracting parties coming within the scope of paragraph 4 (a) of this Article tend, when they are in rapid process of development, to experience balance of payments difficulties arising mainly from efforts to expand their internal markets as well as from the instability in their terms of trade.

9. In order to safeguard its external financial position and to ensure a level of reserves adequate for the implementation of its programme of economic development, a contracting party coming within the scope of paragraph 4 (a) of this Article may, subject to the provisions of paragraphs 10 to 12, control the general level of its imports by restricting the quantity or value of merchandise permitted to be imported; Provided that the import restrictions instituted, maintained or intensified shall not exceed those necessary:

(a) to forestall the threat of, or to stop, a serious decline in its monetary reserves, or

(b) in the case of a contracting party with inadequate monetary reserves, to achieve a reasonable rate of increase in its reserves.

Due regard shall be paid in either case to any special factors which may be affecting the reserves of the contracting party or its need for reserves, including, where special external credits or other resources are available to it, the need to provide for the appropriate use of such credits or resources.

10. In applying these restrictions, the contracting party may determine their incidence on imports of different products or classes of products in such a way as to give priority to the importation of those products which are more essential in the light of its policy of economic development; Provided that the restrictions are so applied as to avoid unnecessary damage to the commercial or economic interests of any other contracting party and not to prevent unreasonably the importation of any description of goods in minimum commercial quantities the exclusion of which would impair regular channels of trade; and Provided further that the restrictions are not so applied as to prevent the importation of commercial samples or to prevent compliance with patent, trade mark, copyright or similar procedures.

11. In carrying out its domestic policies, the contracting party concerned shall pay due regard to the need for restoring equilibrium in its balance of payments on a sound and lasting basis and to the desirability of assuring an economic employment of productive resources. It shall progressively relax any restrictions applied under this Section as conditions improve, maintaining them only to the extent

necessary under the terms of paragraph 9 of this Article and shall eliminate them when conditions no longer justify such maintenance; Provided that no contracting party shall be required to withdraw or modify restrictions on the ground that a change in its development policy would render unnecessary the restrictions which it is applying under this Section.*

12.(a) Any contracting party applying new restrictions or raising the general level of its existing restrictions by a substantial intensification of the measures applied under this Section, shall immediately after instituting or intensifying such restrictions (or, in circumstances in which prior consultation is practicable, before doing so) consult with the CONTRACTING PARTIES as to the nature of its balance of payments difficulties, alternative corrective measures which may be available, and the possible effect of the restrictions on the economies of other contracting parties.

(b) On a date to be determined by them* the CONTRACTING PARTIES shall review all restrictions still applied under this Section on that date. Beginning two years after that date, contracting parties applying restrictions under this Section shall enter into consultations of the type provided for in sub-paragraph (a) above with the CONTRACTING PARTIES at intervals of approximately, but not less than, two years according to a programme to be drawn up each year by the CONTRACTING PARTIES; Provided that no consultation under this sub-paragraph shall take place within two years after the conclusion of a consultation of a general nature under any other provision of this paragraph.

(c) (i) If, in the course of consultations with a contracting party under sub-paragraph (a) or (b) of this paragraph, the CONTRACTING PARTIES find that the restrictions are not consistent with the provisions of this Section or with those of Article XIII (subject to the provisions of Article XIV), they shall indicate the nature of the inconsistency and may advise that the restrictions be suitably modified.

(ii) If, however, as a result of the consultations, the CONTRACTING PARTIES determine that the restrictions are being applied in a manner involving an inconsistency of a serious nature with the provisions of this Section or with those of Article XIII (subject to the provisions of Article XIV) and that damage to the trade of any contracting party is caused or threatened thereby, they shall so inform the contracting party applying the restrictions and shall make appropriate recommendations for securing conformity with such provisions within a specified period. If such contracting party does not comply with these recommendations within the specified period, the CONTRACTING PARTIES may release any contracting party the trade of which is adversely affected by the restrictions from such obligations under this Agreement towards the contracting party applying the restrictions as they determine to be appropriate in the circumstances.

(d) The CONTRACTING PARTIES shall invite any contracting party which is applying restrictions under this Section to enter into consultations with them at the request of any contracting party which can establish a prima facie case that the restrictions are inconsistent with the provisions of this Section or with those of Article XIII (subject to the provisions of Article XIV) and that its trade is adversely affected thereby. However, no such invitation shall be issued unless the CONTRACTING PARTIES have ascertained that direct discussions between the contracting parties concerned have not been successful. If, as a result of the consultations with the CONTRACTING PARTIES no agreement is reached and they determine that the restrictions are being applied inconsistently with such provisions, and that damage to the trade of the contracting party initiating the procedure is caused or threatened thereby, they shall recommend the withdrawal or modification of the restrictions. If the restrictions are not withdrawn or modified within such time as the CONTRACTING PARTIES may prescribe, they may release the contracting party initiating the procedure from such obligations under this Agreement towards the contracting party applying the restrictions as they determine to be appropriate in the circumstances.

(e) If a contracting party against which action has been taken in accordance with the last sentence of sub-paragraph (c) (ii) or (d) of this paragraph, finds that the release of obligations authorized by the CONTRACTING PARTIES adversely affects the operation of its programme and policy of economic development, it shall be free, not later than sixty days after such action is taken, to give written notice to the Executive Secretary to the CONTRACTING PARTIES of its intention to withdraw from this Agreement and such withdrawal shall take effect on the sixtieth day following the day on which the notice is received by him.

(f) In proceeding under this paragraph, the CONTRACTING PARTIES shall have due regard to the factors referred to in paragraph 2 of this Article. Determinations under this paragraph shall be rendered expeditiously and, if possible, within sixty days of the initiation of the consultations.

Section C

13. If a contracting party coming within the scope of paragraph 4 (a) of this Article finds that governmental assistance is required to promote the establishment of a particular industry* with a view to raising the general standard of living of its people, but that no measure consistent with the other provisions of this Agreement is practicable to achieve that objective, it may have recourse to the provisions and procedures set out in this Section.*

14. The contracting party concerned shall notify the CONTRACTING PARTIES of the special difficulties which it meets in the achievement of the objective outlined in paragraph 13 of this Article and shall indicate the specific measure affecting imports which it proposes to introduce in order to remedy these difficulties. It shall not introduce that measure before the expiration of the time-limit laid down in paragraph 15 or 17, as the case may be, or if the measure affects imports of a product which is the subject of a concession included in the appropriate Schedule annexed to this Agreement, unless it has secured the concurrence of the CONTRACTING PARTIES in accordance with provisions of paragraph 18; Provided that, if the industry receiving assistance has already started production, the contracting party may, after informing the CONTRACTING PARTIES, take such measures as may be necessary to prevent, during that period, imports of the product or products concerned from increasing substantially above a normal level.*

15. If, within thirty days of the notification of the measure, the CONTRACTING PARTIES do not request the contracting party concerned to consult with them,* that contracting party shall be free to deviate from the relevant provisions of the other Articles of this Agreement to the extent necessary to apply the proposed measure.

16. If it is requested by the CONTRACTING PARTIES to do so,* the contracting party concerned shall consult with them as to the purpose of the proposed measure, as to alternative measures which may be available under this Agreement, and as to the possible effect of the measure proposed on the commercial and economic interests of other contracting parties. If, as a result of such consultation, the CONTRACTING PARTIES agree that there is no measure consistent with the other provisions of this Agreement which is practicable in order to achieve the objective outlined in paragraph 13 of this Article, and concur* in the proposed measure, the contracting party concerned shall be released from its obligations under the relevant provisions of the other Articles of this Agreement to the extent necessary to apply that measure.

17. If, within ninety days after the date of the notification of the proposed measure under paragraph 14 of this Article, the CONTRACTING PARTIES have not concurred in such measure, the contracting party concerned may introduce the measure proposed after informing the CONTRACTING PARTIES.

18. If the proposed measure affects a product which is the subject of a concession included in the appropriate Schedule annexed to this Agreement, the contracting party concerned shall enter into

consultations with any other contracting party with which the concession was initially negotiated, and with any other contracting party determined by the CONTRACTING PARTIES to have a substantial interest therein. The CONTRACTING PARTIES shall concur* in the measure if they agree that there is no measure consistent with the other provisions of this Agreement which is practicable in order to achieve the objective set forth in paragraph 13 of this Article, and if they are satisfied:

(a) that agreement has been reached with such other contracting parties as a result of the consultations referred to above, or

(b) if no such agreement has been reached within sixty days after the notification provided for in paragraph 14 has been received by the CONTRACTING PARTIES, that the contracting party having recourse to this Section has made all reasonable efforts to reach an agreement and that the interests of other contracting parties are adequately safeguarded.*

The contracting party having recourse to this Section shall thereupon be released from its obligations under the relevant provisions of the other Articles of this Agreement to the extent necessary to permit it to apply the measure.

19. If a proposed measure of the type described in paragraph 13 of this Article concerns an industry the establishment of which has in the initial period been facilitated by incidental protection afforded by restrictions imposed by the contracting party concerned for balance of payments purposes under the relevant provisions of this Agreement, that contracting party may resort to the provisions and procedures of this Section; Provided that it shall not apply the proposed measure without the concurrence* of the CONTRACTING PARTIES.*

20. Nothing in the preceding paragraphs of this Section shall authorize any deviation from the provisions of Articles I, II and XIII of this Agreement. The provisos to paragraph 10 of this Article shall also be applicable to any restriction under this Section.

21. At any time while a measure is being applied under paragraph 17 of this Article any contracting party substantially affected by it may suspend the application to the trade of the contracting party having recourse to this Section of such substantially equivalent concessions or other obligations under this Agreement the suspension of which the CONTRACTING PARTIES do not disapprove;* Provided that sixty days' notice of such suspension is given to the CONTRACTING PARTIES not later than six months after the measure has been introduced or changed substantially to the detriment of the contracting party affected. Any such contracting party shall afford adequate opportunity for consultation in accordance with the provisions of Article XXII of this Agreement.

Section D

22. A contracting party coming within the scope of sub-paragraph 4 (b) of this Article desiring, in the interest of the development of its economy, to introduce a measure of the type described in paragraph 13 of this Article in respect of the establishment of a particular industry* may apply to the CONTRACTING PARTIES for approval of such measure. The CONTRACTING PARTIES shall promptly consult with such contracting party and shall, in making their decision, be guided by the considerations set out in paragraph 16. If the CONTRACTING PARTIES concur* in the proposed measure the contracting party concerned shall be released from its obligations under the relevant provisions of the other Articles of this Agreement to the extent necessary to permit it to apply the measure. If the proposed measure affects a product which is the subject of a concession included in the appropriate Schedule annexed to this Agreement, the provisions of paragraph 18 shall apply.*

23. Any measure applied under this Section shall comply with the provisions of paragraph 20 of this Article.

Article XIX Emergency Action on Imports of Particular Products

1. (a) If, as a result of unforeseen developments and of the effect of the obligations incurred by a contracting party under this Agreement, including tariff concessions, any product is being imported into the territory of that contracting party in such increased quantities and under such conditions as to cause or threaten serious injury to domestic producers in that territory of like or directly competitive products, the contracting party shall be free, in respect of such product, and to the extent and for such time as may be necessary to prevent or remedy such injury, to suspend the obligation in whole or in part or to withdraw or modify the concession.

(b) If any product, which is the subject of a concession with respect to a preference, is being imported into the territory of a contracting party in the circumstances set forth in sub-paragraph (a) of this paragraph, so as to cause or threaten serious injury to domestic producers of like or directly competitive products in the territory of a contracting party which receives or received such preference, the importing contracting party shall be free, if that other contracting party so requests, to suspend the relevant obligation in whole or in part or to withdraw or modify the concession in respect of the product, to the extent and for such time as may be necessary to prevent or remedy such injury.

2. Before any contracting party shall take action pursuant to the provisions of paragraph 1 of this Article, it shall give notice in writing to the CONTRACTING PARTIES as far in advance as may be practicable and shall afford the CONTRACTING PARTIES and those contracting parties having a substantial interest as exporters of the product concerned an opportunity to consult with it in respect of the proposed action. When such notice is given in relation to a concession with respect to a preference, the notice shall name the contracting party which has requested the action. In critical circumstances, where delay would cause damage which it would be difficult to repair, action under paragraph 1 of this Article may be taken provisionally without prior consultation, on the condition that consultation shall be effected immediately after taking such action.

3. (a) If agreement among the interested contracting parties with respect to the action is not reached, the contracting party which proposes to take or continue the action shall, nevertheless, be free to do so, and if such action is taken or continued, the affected contracting parties shall then be free, not later than ninety days after such action is taken, to suspend, upon the expiration of thirty days from the day on which written notice of such suspension is received by the CONTRACTING PARTIES, the application to the trade of the contracting party taking such action, or, in the case envisaged in paragraph 1 (b) of this Article, to the trade of the contracting party requesting such action, of such substantially equivalent concessions or other obligations under this Agreement the suspension of which the CONTRACTING PARTIES do not disapprove.

(b) Notwithstanding the provisions of sub-paragraph (a) of this paragraph, where action is taken under paragraph 2 of this Article without prior consultation and causes or threatens serious injury in the territory of a contracting party to the domestic producers of products affected by the action, that contracting party shall, where delay would cause damage difficult to repair, be free to suspend, upon the taking of the action and throughout the period of consultation, such concessions or other obligations as may be necessary to prevent or remedy the injury.

Article XX General Exceptions

Subject to the requirement that such measures are not applied in a manner which would constitute a means of arbitrary or unjustifiable discrimination between countries where the same conditions prevail, or a disguised restriction on international trade, nothing in this Agreement shall be construed to prevent the adoption or enforcement by any contracting party of measures:

(a) necessary to protect public morals;

(b) necessary to protect human, animal or plant life or health;

(c) relating to the importations or exportations of gold or silver;

(d) necessary to secure compliance with laws or regulations which are not inconsistent with the provisions of this Agreement, including those relating to customs enforcement, the enforcement of monopolies operated under paragraph 4 of Article II and Article XVII, the protection of patents, trade marks and copyrights, and the prevention of deceptive practices;
(e) relating to the products of prison labour;
(f) imposed for the protection of national treasures of artistic, historic or archaeological value;
(g) relating to the conservation of exhaustible natural resources if such measures are made effective in conjunction with restrictions on domestic production or consumption;
(h) undertaken in pursuance of obligations under any intergovernmental commodity agreement which conforms to criteria submitted to the CONTRACTING PARTIES and not disapproved by them or which is itself so submitted and not so disapproved;*
(i) involving restrictions on exports of domestic materials necessary to ensure essential quantities of such materials to a domestic processing industry during periods when the domestic price of such materials is held below the world price as part of a governmental stabilization plan; Provided that such restrictions shall not operate to increase the exports of or the protection afforded to such domestic industry, and shall not depart from the provisions of this Agreement relating to non-discrimination;
(j) essential to the acquisition or distribution of products in general or local short supply; Provided that any such measures shall be consistent with the principle that all contracting parties are entitled to an equitable share of the international supply of such products, and that any such measures, which are inconsistent with the other provisions of the Agreement shall be discontinued as soon as the conditions giving rise to them have ceased to exist. The CONTRACTING PARTIES shall review the need for this sub-paragraph not later than 30 June 1960.

Article XXI Security Exceptions
Nothing in this Agreement shall be construed
(a) to require any contracting party to furnish any information the disclosure of which it considers contrary to its essential security interests; or
(b) to prevent any contracting party from taking any action which it considers necessary for the protection of its essential security interests
  (i) relating to fissionable materials or the materials from which they are derived;
  (ii) relating to the traffic in arms, ammunition and implements of war and to such traffic in other goods and materials as is carried on directly or indirectly for the purpose of supplying a military establishment;
  (iii) taken in time of war or other emergency in international relations; or
(c) to prevent any contracting party from taking any action in pursuance of its obligations under the United Nations Charter for the maintenance of international peace and security.

Article XXII Consultation
1. Each contracting party shall accord sympathetic consideration to, and shall afford adequate opportunity for consultation regarding, such representations as may be made by another contracting party with respect to any matter affecting the operation of this Agreement.
2. The CONTRACTING PARTIES may, at the request of a contracting party, consult with any contracting party or parties in respect of any matter for which it has not been possible to find a satisfactory solution through consultation under paragraph 1.

Article XXIII Nullification or Impairment

1. If any contracting party should consider that any benefit accruing to it directly or indirectly under this Agreement is being nullified or impaired or that the attainment of any objective of the Agreement is being impeded as the result of

   (a) the failure of another contracting party to carry out its obligations under this Agreement, or

   (b) the application by another contracting party of any measure, whether or not it conflicts with the provisions of this Agreement, or

   (c) the existence of any other situation, the contracting party may, with a view to the satisfactory adjustment of the matter, make written representations or proposals to the other contracting party or parties which it considers to be concerned. Any contracting party thus approached shall give sympathetic consideration to the representations or proposals made to it.

2. If no satisfactory adjustment is effected between the contracting parties concerned within a reasonable time, or if the difficulty is of the type described in paragraph 1 (c) of this Article, the matter may be referred to the CONTRACTING PARTIES. The CONTRACTING PARTIES shall promptly investigate any matter so referred to them and shall make appropriate recommendations to the contracting parties which they consider to be concerned, or give a ruling on the matter, as appropriate. The CONTRACTING PARTIES may consult with contracting parties, with the Economic and Social Council of the United Nations and with any appropriate inter-governmental organization in cases where they consider such consultation necessary. If the CONTRACTING PARTIES consider that the circumstances are serious enough to justify such action, they may authorize a contracting party or parties to suspend the application to any other contracting party or parties of such concessions or other obligations under this Agreement as they determine to be appropriate in the circumstances. If the application to any contracting party of any concession or other obligation is in fact suspended, that contracting party shall then be free, not later than sixty days after such action is taken, to give written notice to the Executive Secretary to the CONTRACTING PARTIES of its intention to withdraw from this Agreement and such withdrawal shall take effect upon the sixtieth day following the day on which such notice is received by him.

PART III

Article XXIV Territorial Application – Frontier Traffic – Customs Unions and Free-trade Areas

1. The provisions of this Agreement shall apply to the metropolitan customs territories of the contracting parties and to any other customs territories in respect of which this Agreement has been accepted under Article XXVI or is being applied under Article XXXIII or pursuant to the Protocol of Provisional Application. Each such customs territory shall, exclusively for the purposes of the territorial application of this Agreement, be treated as though it were a contracting party; Provided that the provisions of this paragraph shall not be construed to create any rights or obligations as between two or more customs territories in respect of which this Agreement has been accepted under Article XXVI or is being applied under Article XXXIII or pursuant to the Protocol of Provisional Application by a single contracting party.

2. For the purposes of this Agreement a customs territory shall be understood to mean any territory with respect to which separate tariffs or other regulations of commerce are maintained for a substantial part of the trade of such territory with other territories.

3. The provisions of this Agreement shall not be construed to prevent:

   (a) Advantages accorded by any contracting party to adjacent countries in order to facilitate frontier traffic;

   (b) Advantages accorded to the trade with the Free Territory of Trieste by countries contiguous to that territory, provided that such advantages are not in conflict with the Treaties of Peace arising out of the Second World War.

4. The contracting parties recognize the desirability of increasing freedom of trade by the development, through voluntary agreements, of closer integration between the economies of the countries parties to such agreements. They also recognize that the purpose of a customs union or of a free-trade area should be to facilitate trade between the constituent territories and not to raise barriers to the trade of other contracting parties with such territories.

5. Accordingly, the provisions of this Agreement shall not prevent, as between the territories of contracting parties, the formation of a customs union or of a free-trade area or the adoption of an interim agreement necessary for the formation of a customs union or of a free-trade area; Provided that:

(a) with respect to a customs union, or an interim agreement leading to a formation of a customs union, the duties and other regulations of commerce imposed at the institution of any such union or interim agreement in respect of trade with contracting parties not parties to such union or agreement shall not on the whole be higher or more restrictive than the general incidence of the duties and regulations of commerce applicable in the constituent territories prior to the formation of such union or the adoption of such interim agreement, as the case may be;

(b) with respect to a free-trade area, or an interim agreement leading to the formation of a free-trade area, the duties and other regulations of commerce maintained in each if the constituent territories and applicable at the formation of such free-trade area or the adoption of such interim agreement to the trade of contracting parties not included in such area or not parties to such agreement shall not be higher or more restrictive than the corresponding duties and other regulations of commerce existing in the same constituent territories prior to the formation of the free-trade area, or interim agreement as the case may be; and

(c) any interim agreement referred to in sub-paragraphs (a) and (b) shall include a plan and schedule for the formation of such a customs union or of such a free-trade area within a reasonable length of time.

6. If, in fulfilling the requirements of sub-paragraph 5 (a), a contracting party proposes to increase any rate of duty inconsistently with the provisions of Article II, the procedure set forth in Article XXVIII shall apply. In providing for compensatory adjustment, due account shall be taken of the compensation already afforded by the reduction brought about in the corresponding duty of the other constituents of the union.

7. (a) Any contracting party deciding to enter into a customs union or free-trade area, or an interim agreement leading to the formation of such a union or area, shall promptly notify the CONTRACTING PARTIES and shall make available to them such information regarding the proposed union or area as will enable them to make such reports and recommendations to contracting parties as they may deem appropriate.

(b) If, after having studied the plan and schedule included in an interim agreement referred to in paragraph 5 in consultation with the parties to that agreement and taking due account of the information made available in accordance with the provisions of sub-paragraph (a), the CONTRACTING PARTIES find that such agreement is not likely to result in the formation of a customs union or of a free-trade area within the period contemplated by the parties to the agreement or that such period is not a reasonable one, the CONTRACTING PARTIES shall make recommendations to the parties to the agreement. The parties shall not maintain or put into force, as the case may be, such agreement if they are not prepared to modify it in accordance with these recommendations.

(c) Any substantial change in the plan or schedule referred to in paragraph 5 (c) shall be communicated to the CONTRACTING PARTIES, which may request the contracting parties concerned to consult with them if the change seems likely to jeopardize or delay unduly the formation of the customs union or of the free-trade area.

8. For the purposes of this Agreement:
   (a) A customs union shall be understood to mean the substitution of a single customs territory for two or more customs territories, so that
      (i) duties and other restrictive regulations of commerce (except, where necessary, those permitted under Articles XI, XII, XIII, XIV, XV and XX) are eliminated with respect to substantially all the trade between the constituent territories of the union or at least with respect to substantially all the trade in products originating in such territories, and,
      (ii) subject to the provisions of paragraph 9, substantially the same duties and other regulations of commerce are applied by each of the members of the union to the trade of territories not included in the union;
   (b) A free-trade area shall be understood to mean a group of two or more customs territories in which the duties and other restrictive regulations of commerce (except, where necessary, those permitted under Articles XI, XII, XIII, XIV, XV and XX) are eliminated on substantially all the trade between the constituent territories in products originating in such territories.

9. The preferences referred to in paragraph 2 of Article I shall not be affected by the formation of a customs union or of a free-trade area but may be eliminated or adjusted by means of negotiations with contracting parties affected.* This procedure of negotiations with affected contracting parties shall, in particular, apply to the elimination of preferences required to conform with the provisions of paragraph 8 (a)(i) and paragraph 8 (b).

10. The CONTRACTING PARTIES may by a two-thirds majority approve proposals which do not fully comply with the requirements of paragraphs 5 to 9 inclusive, provided that such proposals lead to the formation of a customs union or a free-trade area in the sense of this Article.

11. Taking into account the exceptional circumstances arising out of the establishment of India and Pakistan as independent States and recognizing the fact that they have long constituted an economic unit, the contracting parties agree that the provisions of this Agreement shall not prevent the two countries from entering into special arrangements with respect to the trade between them, pending the establishment of their mutual trade relations on a definitive basis.*

12. Each contracting party shall take such reasonable measures as may be available to it to ensure observance of the provisions of this Agreement by the regional and local governments and authorities within its territories.

Article XXV Joint Action by the Contracting Parties

1. Representatives of the contracting parties shall meet from time to time for the purpose of giving effect to those provisions of this Agreement which involve joint action and, generally, with a view to facilitating the operation and furthering the objectives of this Agreement. Wherever reference is made in this Agreement to the contracting parties acting jointly they are designated as the CONTRACTING PARTIES.

2. The Secretary-General of the United Nations is requested to convene the first meeting of the CONTRACTING PARTIES, which shall take place not later than March 1, 1948.

3. Each contracting party shall be entitled to have one vote at all meetings of the CONTRACTING PARTIES.

4. Except as otherwise provided for in this Agreement, decisions of the CONTRACTING PARTIES shall be taken by a majority of the votes cast.

5. In exceptional circumstances not elsewhere provided for in this Agreement, the CONTRACTING PARTIES may waive an obligation imposed upon a contracting party by this Agreement; Provided that any such decision shall be approved by a two-thirds majority of the votes cast and that such majority shall comprise more than half of the contracting parties. The CONTRACTING PARTIES may also by such a vote

(i) define certain categories of exceptional circumstances to which other voting requirements shall apply for the waiver of obligations, and
(ii) prescribe such criteria as may be necessary for the application of this paragraph.

Article XXVI Acceptance, Entry into Force and Registration
1. The date of this Agreement shall be 30 October 1947.
2. This Agreement shall be open for acceptance by any contracting party
which, on 1 March 1955, was a contracting party or was negotiating with a view to accession to this Agreement.
3. This Agreement, done in a single English original and a single French original, both texts authentic, shall be deposited with the Secretary-General of the United Nations, who shall furnish certified copies thereof to all interested governments.
4. Each government accepting this Agreement shall deposit an instrument of acceptance with the Executive Secretary to the CONTRACTING PARTIES, who will inform all interested governments of the date of deposit of each instrument of acceptance and of the day on which this Agreement enters into force under paragraph 6 of this Article.
5. (a) Each government accepting this Agreement does so in respect of its metropolitan territory and of the other territories for which it has international responsibility, except such separate customs territories as it shall notify to the Executive Secretary to the CONTRACTING PARTIES at the time of its own acceptance.
(b) Any government, which has so notified the Executive Secretary under the exceptions in sub-paragraph (a) of this paragraph, may at any time give notice to the Executive Secretary[1] that its acceptance shall be effective in respect of any separate customs territory or territories so excepted and such notice shall take effect on the thirtieth day following the day on which it is received by the Executive Secretary.
(c) If any of the customs territories, in respect of which a contracting party has accepted this Agreement, possesses or acquires full autonomy in the conduct of its external commercial relations and of the other matters provided for in this Agreement, such territory shall, upon sponsorship through a declaration by the responsible contracting party establishing the above-mentioned fact, be deemed to be a contracting party.
6. This Agreement shall enter into force, as among the governments which have accepted it, on the thirtieth day following the day on which instruments of acceptance have been deposited with Executive Secretary to the CONTRACTING PARTIES on behalf of governments named in Annex H, the territories of which account for 85 per centum of the total external trade of the territories of such governments, computed in accordance with the applicable column of percentages set forth therein, The instrument of acceptance of each other government shall take effect on the thirtieth day following the day on which such instrument has been deposited.
7. The United Nations is authorized to effect registration of this Agreement as soon as it enters into force.

Article XXVII Withholding or Withdrawal of Concessions
Any contracting party shall at any time be free to withhold or to withdraw in whole or in part any concession, provided for in the appropriate Schedule annexed to this Agreement, in respect of which such contracting party determines that it was initially negotiated with a government which has not become, or has ceased to be, a contracting party. A contracting party taking such action shall notify the CONTRACTING PARTIES and, upon request, consult with contracting parties which have a substantial interest in the product concerned.

Article XXVIII* Modification of Schedules

1. On the first day of each three-year period, the first period beginning on 1 January 1958 (or on the first day of any other period* that may be specified by the CONTRACTING PARTIES by two-thirds of the votes cast) a contracting party (hereafter in this Article referred to as the "applicant contracting party") may, by negotiation and agreement with any contracting party with which such concession was initially negotiated and with any other contracting party determined by the CONTRACTING PARTIES to have a principal supplying interest* (which two preceding categories of contracting parties, together with the applicant contracting party, are in this Article hereinafter referred to as the "contracting parties primarily concerned"), and subject to consultation with any other contracting party determined by the CONTRACTING PARTIES to have a substantial interest* in such concession, modify or withdraw a concession* included in the appropriate schedule annexed to this Agreement.

2. In such negotiations and agreement, which may include provision for compensatory adjustment with respect to other products, the contracting parties concerned shall endeavour to maintain a general level of reciprocal and mutually advantageous concessions not less favourable to trade than that provided for in this Agreement prior to such negotiations.

3. (a) If agreement between the contracting parties primarily concerned cannot be reached before 1 January 1958 or before the expiration of a period envisaged in paragraph 1 of this Article, the contracting party which proposes to modify or withdraw the concession shall, nevertheless, be free to do so and if such action is taken any contracting party with which such concession was initially negotiated, any contracting party determined under paragraph 1 to have a principal supplying interest and any contracting party determined under paragraph 1 to have a substantial interest shall then be free not later than six months after such action is taken, to withdraw, upon the expiration of thirty days from the day on which written notice of such withdrawal is received by the CONTRACTING PARTIES, substantially equivalent concessions initially negotiated with the applicant contracting party.

(b) If agreement between the contracting parties primarily concerned is reached but any other contracting party determined under paragraph 1 of this Article to have a substantial interest is not satisfied, such other contracting party shall be free, not later than six months after action under such agreement is taken, to withdraw, upon the expiration of thirty days from the day on which written notice of such withdrawal is received by the CONTRACTING PARTIES, substantially equivalent concessions initially negotiated with the applicant contracting party.

4. The CONTRACTING PARTIES may, at any time, in special circumstances, authorize* a contracting party to enter into negotiations for modification or withdrawal of a concession included in the appropriate Schedule annexed to this Agreement subject to the following procedures and conditions:

(a) Such negotiations* and any related consultations shall be conducted in accordance with the provisions of paragraph 1 and 2 of this Article.

(b) If agreement between the contracting parties primarily concerned is reached in the negotiations, the provisions of paragraph 3 (b) of this Article shall apply.

(c) If agreement between the contracting parties primarily concerned is not reached within a period of sixty days* after negotiations have been authorized, or within such longer period as the CONTRACTING PARTIES may have prescribed, the applicant contracting party may refer the matter to the CONTRACTING PARTIES.

(d) Upon such reference, the CONTRACTING PARTIES shall promptly examine the matter and submit their views to the contracting parties primarily concerned with the aim of achieving a settlement. If a settlement is reached, the provisions of paragraph 3 (b) shall apply as if agreement between the contracting parties primarily concerned had been reached. If no settlement is reached between the contracting parties primarily concerned, the applicant contracting party shall be free to modify or withdraw the concession, unless the CONTRACTING PARTIES determine that the applicant contracting party has unreasonably failed to offer adequate compensation.* If such action is taken, any contracting party with which the concession was initially negotiated, any contracting party determined under paragraph 4 (a) to have a principal supplying interest and any contracting party determined under paragraph 4 (a) to have a substantial interest, shall be free, not later than six months after such action is taken, to modify or withdraw, upon the expiration of thirty days from the day on which written notice of such withdrawal is received by the CONTRACTING PARTIES, substantially equivalent concessions initially negotiated with applicant contracting party.

5. Before 1 January 1958 and before the end of any period envisaged in paragraph 1 a contracting party may elect by notifying the CONTRACTING PARTIES to reserve the right, for the duration of the next period, to modify the appropriate Schedule in accordance with the procedures of paragraph 1 to 3. If a contracting party so elects, other contracting parties shall have the right, during the same period, to modify or withdraw, in accordance with the same procedures, concessions initially negotiated with that contracting party.

Article XXVIII bis Tariff Negotiations

1. The contracting parties recognize that customs duties often constitute serious obstacles to trade; thus negotiations on a reciprocal and mutually advantageous basis, directed to the substantial reduction of the general level of tariffs and other charges on imports and exports and in particular to the reduction of such high tariffs as discourage the importation even of minimum quantities, and conducted with due regard to the objectives of this Agreement and the varying needs of individual contracting parties, are of great importance to the expansion of international trade. The CONTRACTING PARTIES may therefore sponsor such negotiations from time to time.

2. (a) Negotiations under this Article may be carried out on a selective product-by-product basis or by the application of such multilateral procedures as may be accepted by the contracting parties concerned. Such negotiations may be directed towards the reduction of duties, the binding of duties at then existing levels or undertakings that individual duties or the average duties on specified categories of products shall not exceed specified levels. The binding against increase of low duties or of duty-free treatment shall, in principle, be recognized as a concession equivalent in value to the reduction of high duties.

(b) The contracting parties recognize that in general the success of multilateral negotiations would depend on the participation of all contracting parties which conduct a substantial proportion of their external trade with one another.

3. Negotiations shall be conducted on a basis which affords adequate opportunity to take into account:

(a) the needs of individual contracting parties and individual industries;

(b) the needs of less-developed countries for a more flexible use of tariff protection to assist their economic development and the special needs of these countries to maintain tariffs for revenue purposes; and

(c) all other relevant circumstances, including the fiscal,* developmental, strategic and other needs of the contracting parties concerned.

Article XXIX The Relation of this Agreement to the Havana Charter

1. The contracting parties undertake to observe to the fullest extent of their executive authority the general principles of Chapters I to VI inclusive and of Chapter IX of the Havana Charter pending their acceptance of it in accordance with their constitutional procedures.*

2. Part II of this Agreement shall be suspended on the day on which the Havana Charter enters into force.

3. If by September 30, 1949, the Havana Charter has not entered into force, the contracting parties shall meet before December 31, 1949, to agree whether this Agreement shall be amended, supplemented or maintained.

4. If at any time the Havana Charter should cease to be in force, the CONTRACTING PARTIES shall meet as soon as practicable thereafter to agree whether this Agreement shall be supplemented, amended or maintained. Pending such agreement, Part II of this Agreement shall again enter into force; Provided that the provisions of Part II other than Article XXIII shall be replaced, mutatis mutandis, in the form in which they then appeared in the Havana Charter; and Provided further that no contracting party shall be bound by any provisions which did not bind it at the time when the Havana Charter ceased to be in force.
5. If any contracting party has not accepted the Havana Charter by the date upon which it enters into force, the CONTRACTING PARTIES shall confer to agree whether, and if so in what way, this Agreement in so far as it affects relations between such contracting party and other contracting parties, shall be supplemented or amended. Pending such agreement the provisions of Part II of this Agreement shall, notwithstanding the provisions of paragraph 2 of this Article, continue to apply as between such contracting party and other contracting parties.
6. Contracting parties which are Members of the International Trade Organization shall not invoke the provisions of this Agreement so as to prevent the operation of any provision of the Havana Charter. The application of the principle underlying this paragraph to any contracting party which is not a Member of the International Trade Organization shall be the subject of an agreement pursuant to paragraph 5 of this Article.

Article XXX Amendments
1. Except where provision for modification is made elsewhere in this Agreement, amendments to the provisions of Part I of this Agreement or the provisions of Article XXIX or of this Article shall become effective upon acceptance by all the contracting parties, and other amendments to this Agreement shall become effective, in respect of those contracting parties which accept them, upon acceptance by two-thirds of the contracting parties and thereafter for each other contracting party upon acceptance by it.
2. Any contracting party accepting an amendment to this Agreement shall deposit an instrument of acceptance with the Secretary-General of the United Nations within such period as the CONTRACTING PARTIES may specify. The CONTRACTING PARTIES may decide that any amendment made effective under this Article is of such a nature that any contracting party which has not accepted it within a period specified by the CONTRACTING PARTIES shall be free to withdraw from this Agreement, or to remain a contracting party with the consent of the CONTRACTING PARTIES.

Article XXXI Withdrawal
Without prejudice to the provisions of paragraph 12 of Article XVIII, of Article XXIII or of paragraph 2 of Article XXX, any contracting party may withdraw from this Agreement, or may separately withdraw on behalf of any of the separate customs territories for which it has international responsibility and which at the time possesses full autonomy in the conduct of its external commercial relations and of the other matters provided for in this Agreement. The withdrawal shall take effect upon the expiration of six months from the day on which written notice of withdrawal is received by the Secretary-General of the United Nations.

Article XXXII Contracting Parties
1. The contracting parties to this Agreement shall be understood to mean those governments which are applying the provisions of this Agreement under Articles XXVI or XXXIII or pursuant to the Protocol of Provisional Application.
2. At any time after the entry into force of this Agreement pursuant to paragraph 6 of Article XXVI, those contracting parties which have accepted this Agreement pursuant to paragraph 4 of Article XXVI may decide that any contracting party which has not so accepted it shall cease to be a contracting party.

Article XXXIII Accession
A government not party to this Agreement, or a government acting on behalf of a separate customs territory possessing full autonomy in the conduct of its external commercial relations and of the other matters provided for in this Agreement, may accede to this Agreement, on its own behalf or on behalf of that territory, on terms to be agreed between such government and the CONTRACTING PARTIES. Decisions of the CONTRACTING PARTIES under this paragraph shall be taken by a two-thirds majority.

Article XXXIV Annexes
The annexes to this Agreement are hereby made an integral part of this Agreement.

Article XXXV Non-application of the Agreement between Particular Contracting Parties
1. This Agreement, or alternatively Article II of this Agreement, shall not apply as between any contracting party and any other contracting party if:
(a) the two contracting parties have not entered into tariff negotiations with each other, and
(b) either of the contracting parties, at the time either becomes a contracting party, does not consent to such application.
2. The CONTRACTING PARTIES may review the operation of this Article in particular cases at the request of any contracting party and make appropriate recommendations.

PART IV* TRADE AND DEVELOPMENT

Article XXXVI Principles and Objectives
1. * The contracting parties,
(a) recalling that the basic objectives of this Agreement include the raising of standards of living and the progressive development of the economies of all contracting parties, and considering that the attainment of these objectives is particularly urgent for less-developed contracting parties;
(b) considering that export earnings of the less-developed contracting parties can play a vital part in their economic development and that the extent of this contribution depends on the prices paid by the less-developed contracting parties for essential imports, the volume of their exports, and the prices received for these exports;
(c) noting, that there is a wide gap between standards of living in less-developed countries and in other countries;
(d) recognizing that individual and joint action is essential to further the development of the economies of less-developed contracting parties and to bring about a rapid advance in the standards of living in these countries;
(e) recognizing that international trade as a means of achieving economic and social advancement should be governed by such rules and procedures _ and measures in conformity with such rules and procedures _ as are consistent with the objectives set forth in this Article;
(f) noting that the CONTRACTING PARTIES may enable less-developed contracting parties to use special measures to promote their trade and development;
agree as follows.
2. There is need for a rapid and sustained expansion of the export earnings of the less-developed contracting parties.
3. There is need for positive efforts designed to ensure that less-developed contracting parties secure a share in the growth in international trade commensurate with the needs of their economic development.

4. Given the continued dependence of many less-developed contracting parties on the exportation of a limited range of primary products,* there is need to provide in the largest possible measure more favourable and acceptable conditions of access to world markets for these products, and wherever appropriate to devise measures designed to stabilize and improve conditions of world markets in these products, including in particular measures designed to attain stable, equitable and remunerative prices, thus permitting an expansion of world trade and demand and a dynamic and steady growth of the real export earnings of these countries so as to provide them with expanding resources for their economic development.
5. The rapid expansion of the economies of the less-developed contracting parties will be facilitated by a diversification* of the structure of their economies and the avoidance of an excessive dependence on the export of primary products. There is, therefore, need for increased access in the largest possible measure to markets under favourable conditions for processed and manufactured products currently or potentially of particular export interest to less-developed contracting parties.
6. Because of the chronic deficiency in the export proceeds and other foreign exchange earnings of less-developed contracting parties, there are important inter-relationships between trade and financial assistance to development. There is, therefore, need for close and continuing collaboration between the CONTRACTING PARTIES and the international lending agencies so that they can contribute most effectively to alleviating the burdens these less-developed contracting parties assume in the interest of their economic development.
7. There is need for appropriate collaboration between the CONTRACTING PARTIES, other intergovernmental bodies and the organs and agencies of the United Nations system, whose activities relate to the trade and economic development of less-developed countries.
8. The developed contracting parties do not expect reciprocity for commitments made by them in trade negotiations to reduce or remove tariffs and other barriers to the trade of less-developed contracting parties.*
9. The adoption of measures to give effect to these principles and objectives shall be a matter of conscious and purposeful effort on the part of the contracting parties both individually and jointly.

Article XXXVII Commitments
1. The developed contracting parties shall to the fullest extent possible – that is, except when compelling reasons, which may include legal reasons, make it impossible – give effect to the following provisions:
- (a) accord high priority to the reduction and elimination of barriers to products currently or potentially of particular export interest to less-developed contracting parties, including customs duties and other restrictions which differentiate unreasonably between such products in their primary and in their processed forms;*
- (b) refrain from introducing, or increasing the incidence of, customs duties or non-tariff import barriers on products currently or potentially of particular export interest to less-developed contracting parties; and
- (c) (i) refrain from imposing new fiscal measures, and
  - (ii) in any adjustments of fiscal policy accord high priority to the reduction and elimination of fiscal measures,

which would hamper, or which hamper, significantly the growth of consumption of primary products, in raw or processed form, wholly or mainly produced in the territories of less-developed contracting parties, and which are applied specifically to those products.
2. (a) Whenever it is considered that effect is not being given to any of the provisions of sub-paragraph (a), (b) or (c) of paragraph 1, the matter shall be reported to the CONTRACTING PARTIES either by the contracting party not so giving effect to the relevant provisions or by any other interested contracting party.

(b) (i) The CONTRACTING PARTIES shall, if requested so to do by any interested contracting party, and without prejudice to any bilateral consultations that may be undertaken, consult with the contracting party concerned and all interested contracting parties with respect to the matter with a view to reaching solutions satisfactory to all contracting parties concerned in order to further the objectives set forth in Article XXXVI. In the course of these consultations, the reasons given in cases where effect was not being given to the provisions of sub-paragraph (a), (b) or (c) of paragraph 1 shall be examined.

(ii) As the implementation of the provisions of sub-paragraph (a), (b) or (c) of paragraph 1 by individual contracting parties may in some cases be more readily achieved where action is taken jointly with other developed contracting parties, such consultation might, where appropriate, be directed towards this end.

(iii) The consultations by the CONTRACTING PARTIES might also, in appropriate cases, be directed towards agreement on joint action designed to further the objectives of this Agreement as envisaged in paragraph 1 of Article XXV.

3. The developed contracting parties shall:

(a) make every effort, in cases where a government directly or indirectly determines the resale price of products wholly or mainly produced in the territories of less-developed contracting parties, to maintain trade margins at equitable levels;

(b) give active consideration to the adoption of other measures* designed to provide greater scope for the development of imports from less-developed contracting parties and collaborate in appropriate international action to this end;

(c) have special regard to the trade interests of less-developed contracting parties when considering the application of other measures permitted under this Agreement to meet particular problems and explore all possibilities of constructive remedies before applying such measures where they would affect essential interests of those contracting parties.

4. Less-developed contracting parties agree to take appropriate action in implementation of the provisions of Part IV for the benefit of the trade of other less-developed contracting parties, in so far as such action is consistent with their individual present and future development, financial and trade needs taking into account past trade developments as well as the trade interests of less-developed contracting parties as a whole.

5. In the implementation of the commitments set forth in paragraph 1 to 4 each contracting party shall afford to any other interested contracting party or contracting parties full and prompt opportunity for consultations under the normal procedures of this Agreement with respect to any matter or difficulty which may arise.

Article XXXVIII Joint Action

1. The contracting parties shall collaborate jointly, with the framework of this Agreement and elsewhere, as appropriate, to further the objectives set forth in Article XXXVI.

2. In particular, the CONTRACTING PARTIES shall:

(a) where appropriate, take action, including action through international arrangements, to provide improved and acceptable conditions of access to world markets for primary products of particular interest to less-developed contracting parties and to devise measures designed to stabilize and improve conditions of world markets in these products including measures designed to attain stable, equitable and remunerative prices for exports of such products;

(b) seek appropriate collaboration in matters of trade and development policy with the United Nations and its organs and agencies, including any institutions that may be created on the basis of recommendations by the United Nations Conference on Trade and Development;

(c) collaborate in analysing the development plans and policies of individual less-developed contracting parties and in examining trade and aid relationships with a view to devising concrete measures to promote the development of export potential and to facilitate access to export markets for the products of the industries thus developed and, in this connection, seek appropriate collaboration with governments and international organizations, and in particular with organizations having competence in relation to financial assistance for economic development, in systematic studies of trade and aid relationships in individual less-developed contracting parties aimed at obtaining a clear analysis of export potential, market prospects and any further action that may be required;

(d) keep under continuous review the development of world trade with special reference to the rate of growth of the trade of less-developed contracting parties and make such recommendations to contracting parties as may, in the circumstances, be deemed appropriate;

(e) collaborate in seeking feasible methods to expand trade for the purpose of economic development, through international harmonization and adjustment of national policies and regulations, through technical and commercial standards affecting production, transportation and marketing, and through export promotion by the establishment of facilities for the increased flow of trade information and the development of market research; and

(f) establish such institutional arrangements as may be necessary to further the objectives set forth in Article XXXVI and to give effect to the provision of this Part.

ANNEX A LIST OF TERRITORIES REFERRED TO IN PARAGRAPH 2 (A) OF ARTICLE I

United Kingdom of Great Britain and Northern Ireland
Dependent territories of the United Kingdom of Great Britain and Northern Ireland
Canada
Commonwealth of Australia
Dependent territories of the Commonwealth of Australia New Zealand
Dependent territories of New Zealand
Union of South Africa including South West Africa Ireland
India (as on April 10, 1947) Newfoundland
Southern Rhodesia Burma
Ceylon

Certain of the territories listed above have two or more preferential rates in force for certain products. Any such territory may, by agreement with the other contracting parties which are principal suppliers of such products at the most-favoured-nation rate, substitute for such preferential rates a single preferential rate which shall not on the whole be less favourable to suppliers at the most-favoured-nation rate than the preferences in force prior to such substitution.

The imposition of an equivalent margin of tariff preference to replace a margin of preference in an internal tax existing on April 10, 1947 exclusively between two or more of the territories listed in this Annex or to replace the preferential quantitative arrangements described in the following paragraph, shall not be deemed to constitute an increase in a margin of tariff preference.

The preferential arrangements referred to in paragraph 5 (b) of Article XIV are those existing in the United Kingdom on 10 April 1947, under contractual agreements with the Governments of Canada, Australia and New Zealand, in respect of chilled and frozen beef and veal, frozen mutton and lamb, chilled and frozen pork and bacon. It is the intention, without prejudice to any action taken under sub-paragraph (h) of Article XX, that these arrangements shall be eliminated or replaced by tariff preferences, and that negotiations to this end shall take place as soon as practicable among the countries substantially concerned or involved.

The film hire tax in force in New Zealand on 10 April 1947, shall, for the purposes of this Agreement, be treated as a customs duty under Article I. The renters' film quota in force in New Zealand on April 10, 1947, shall, for the purposes of this Agreement, be treated as a screen quota under Article IV.

The Dominions of India and Pakistan have not been mentioned separately in the above list since they had not come into existence as such on the base date of April 10, 1947.

ANNEX B LIST OF TERRITORIES OF THE FRENCH UNION REFERRED TO IN PARAGRAPH 2 (B) OF ARTICLE I

France
French Equatorial Africa (Treaty Basin of the Congo and other territories)
French West Africa
Cameroons under French Trusteeship
French Somali Coast and Dependencies
French Establishments in Oceania
French Establishments in the Condominium of the New Hebrides
Indo-China
Madagascar and Dependencies
Morocco (French zone)
New Caledonia and Dependencies
Saint-Pierre and Miquelon
Togo under French Trusteeship
Tunisia

ANNEX C LIST OF TERRITORIES REFERRED TO IN PARAGRAPH 2 (B) OF ARTICLE I AS RESPECTS THE CUSTOMS UNION OF BELGIUM, LUXEMBURG AND THE NETHERLANDS

The Economic Union of Belgium and Luxemburg
Belgian Congo
Ruanda Urundi
Netherlands
New Guinea
Surinam
Netherlands Antilles
Republic of Indonesia

For imports into the territories constituting the Customs Union only.

ANNEX D LIST OF TERRITORIES REFERRED TO IN PARAGRAPH 2 (B) OF ARTICLE I AS RESPECTS THE UNITED STATES OF AMERICA

United States of America (customs territory)
Dependent territories of the United States of America
Republic of the Philippines

The imposition of an equivalent margin of tariff preference to replace a margin of preference in an internal tax existing on 10 April, 1947, exclusively between two or more of the territories listed in this Annex shall not be deemed to constitute an increase in a margin of tariff preference.

ANNEX E LIST OF TERRITORIES COVERED BY PREFERENTIAL ARRANGEMENTS BETWEEN CHILE AND NEIGHBOURING COUNTRIES REFERRED TO IN PARAGRAPH 2 (D) OF ARTICLE I

Preferences in force exclusively between Chile on the one hand, and
1. Argentina
2. Bolivia
3. Peru on the other hand.

ANNEX F LIST OF TERRITORIES COVERED BY PREFERENTIAL ARRANGEMENTS BETWEEN LEBANON AND SYRIA AND NEIGHBOURING COUNTRIES REFERRED TO IN PARAGRAPH 2 (D) OF ARTICLE I

Preferences in force exclusively between the Lebano-Syrian Customs Union, on the one hand, and
1. Palestine
2. Transjordan on the other hand.

ANNEX G DATES ESTABLISHING MAXIMUM MARGINS OF PREFERENCE REFERRED TO IN PARAGRAPH 4 OF ARTICLE I

Australia	October 15, 1946
Canada	July 1, 1939
France	January 1, 1939
Lebano-Syrian Customs Union	November 30, 1938
Union of South Africa	July 1, 1938
Southern Rhodesia	May 1, 1941

ANNEX H PERCENTAGE SHARES OF TOTAL EXTERNAL TRADE TO BE USED FOR THE PURPOSE OF MAKING THE DETERMINATION REFERRED TO IN ARTICLE XXVI

(based on the average of 1949-1953)

If, prior to the accession of the Government of Japan to the General Agreement, the present Agreement has been accepted by contracting parties the external trade of which under Column I accounts for the percentage of such trade specified in paragraph 6 of Article XXVI, column I shall be applicable for the purposes of that paragraph. If the present Agreement has not been so accepted prior to the accession of the Government of Japan, column II shall be applicable for the purposes of that paragraph.

	Column I (Contracting parties on 1 March 1955)	**Column II (Contracting parties on 1 March 1955 and Japan)**
Australia	3.1	3.0
Austria	0.9	0.8
Belgium-Luxemburg	4.3	4.2
Brazil	2.5	2.4
Burma	0.3	0.3
Canada	6.7	6.5
Ceylon	0.5	0.5
Chile	0.6	0.6
Cuba	1.1	1.1
Czechoslovakia	1.4	1.4
Denmark	1.4	1.4
Dominican Republic	0.1	0.1
Finland	1.0	1.0
France	8.7	8.5
Germany, Federal Republic of	5.3	5.2
Greece	0.4	0.4
Haiti	0.1	0.1
India	2.4	2.4
Indonesia	1.3	1.3
Italy	2.9	2.8
Netherlands, Kingdom of the	4.7	4.6
New Zealand	1.0	1.0
Nicaragua	0.1	0.1
Norway	1.1	1.1
Pakistan	0.9	0.8
Peru	0.4	0.4
Rhodesia and Nyasaland	0.6	0.6
Sweden	2.5	2.4
Turkey	0.6	0.6
Union of South Africa	1.8	1.8
United Kingdom	20.3	19.8
United States of America	20.6	20.1
Uruguay	0.4	0.4
Japan	-	2.3
	100.0	100.0

Note: These percentages have been computed taking into account the trade of all territories in respect of which the General Agreement on Tariffs and Trade is applied.

ANNEX I NOTES AND SUPPLEMENTARY PROVISIONS

Ad Article I

Paragraph 1

The obligations incorporated in paragraph 1 of Article I by reference to paragraphs 2 and 4 of Article III and those incorporated in paragraph 2 (b) of Article II by reference to Article VI shall be considered as falling within Part II for the purposes of the Protocol of Provisional Application.

The cross-references, in the paragraph immediately above and in paragraph 1 of Article I, to paragraphs 2 and 4 of Article III shall only apply after Article III has been modified by the entry into force of the amendment provided for in the Protocol Modifying Part II and Article XXVI of the General Agreement on Tariffs and Trade, dated September 14, 1948.

Paragraph 4

The term "margin of preference" means the absolute difference between the most-favoured-nation rate of duty and the preferential rate of duty for the like product, and not the proportionate relation between those rates. As examples:
(1) If the most-favoured-nation rate were 36 per cent *ad valorem* and the preferential rate were 24 per cent *ad valorem*, the margin of preference would be 12 per cent *ad valorem*, and not one-third of the most-favoured-nation rate;
(2) If the most-favoured-nation rate were 36 per cent *ad valorem* and the preferential rate were expressed as two-thirds of the most-favoured-nation rate, the margin of preference would be 12 per cent *ad valorem*;
(3) If the most-favoured-nation rate were 2 francs per kilogramme and the preferential rate were 1.50 francs per kilogramme, the margin of preference would be 0.50 franc per kilogramme.

The following kinds of customs action, taken in accordance with established uniform procedures, would not be contrary to a general binding of margins of preference:

(i) The re-application to an imported product of a tariff classification or rate of duty, properly applicable to such product, in cases in which the application of such classification or rate to such product was temporarily suspended or inoperative on April 10, 1947; and

(ii) The classification of a particular product under a tariff item other than that under which importations of that product were classified on April 10, 1947, in cases in which the tariff law clearly contemplates that such product may be classified under more than one tariff item.

Ad Article II

Paragraph 2 (a)

The cross-reference, in paragraph 2 (a) of Article II, to paragraph 2 of Article III shall only apply after Article III has been modified by the entry into force of the amendment provided for in the Protocol Modifying Part II and Article XXVI of the General Agreement on Tariffs and Trade, dated September 14, 1948.

Paragraph 2 (b)

See the note relating to paragraph 1 of Article I.

Paragraph 4
Except where otherwise specifically agreed between the contracting parties which initially negotiated the concession, the provisions of this paragraph will be applied in the light of the provisions of Article 31 of the Havana Charter.

Ad Article III

Any internal tax or other internal charge, or any law, regulation or requirement of the kind referred to in paragraph 1 which applies to an imported product and to the like domestic product and is collected or enforced in the case of the imported product at the time or point of importation, is nevertheless to be regarded as an internal tax or other internal charge, or a law, regulation or requirement of the kind referred to in paragraph 1, and is accordingly subject to the provisions of Article III.

Paragraph 1
The application of paragraph 1 to internal taxes imposed by local governments and authorities with the territory of a contracting party is subject to the provisions of the final paragraph of Article XXIV. The term "reasonable measures" in the last-mentioned paragraph would not require, for example, the repeal of existing national legislation authorizing local governments to impose internal taxes which, although technically inconsistent with the letter of Article III, are not in fact inconsistent with its spirit, if such repeal would result in a serious financial hardship for the local governments or authorities concerned. With regard to taxation by local governments or authorities which is inconsistent with both the letter and spirit of Article III, the term "reasonable measures" would permit a contracting party to eliminate the inconsistent taxation gradually over a transition period, if abrupt action would create serious administrative and financial difficulties.

Paragraph 2
A tax conforming to the requirements of the first sentence of paragraph 2 would be considered to be inconsistent with the provisions of the second sentence only in cases where competition was involved between, on the one hand, the taxed product and, on the other hand, a directly competitive or substitutable product which was not similarly taxed.

Paragraph 5
Regulations consistent with the provisions of the first sentence of paragraph 5 shall not be considered to be contrary to the provisions of the second sentence in any case in which all of the products subject to the regulations are produced domestically in substantial quantities. A regulation cannot be justified as being consistent with the provisions of the second sentence on the ground that the proportion or amount allocated to each of the products which are the subject of the regulation constitutes an equitable relationship between imported and domestic products.

Ad Article V

Paragraph 5
With regard to transportation charges, the principle laid down in paragraph 5 refers to like products being transported on the same route under like conditions.

Ad Article VI

Paragraph 1

1. Hidden dumping by associated houses (that is, the sale by an importer at a price below that corresponding to the price invoiced by an exporter with whom the importer is associated, and also below the price in the exporting country) constitutes a form of price dumping with respect to which the margin of dumping may be calculated on the basis of the price at which the goods are resold by the importer.
2. It is recognized that, in the case of imports from a country which has a complete or substantially complete monopoly of its trade and where all domestic prices are fixed by the State, special difficulties may exist in determining price comparability for the purposes of paragraph 1, and in such cases importing contracting parties may find it necessary to take into account the possibility that a strict comparison with domestic prices in such a country may not always be appropriate.

Paragraphs 2 and 3

1. As in many other cases in customs administration, a contracting party may require reasonable security (bond or cash deposit) for the payment of anti-dumping or countervailing duty pending final determination of the facts in any case of suspected dumping or subsidization.
2. Multiple currency practices can in certain circumstances constitute a subsidy to exports which may be met by countervailing duties under paragraph 3 or can constitute a form of dumping by means of a partial depreciation of a country's currency which may be met by action under paragraph 2. By "multiple currency practices" is meant practices by governments or sanctioned by governments.

Paragraph 6 (b)

Waivers under the provisions of this sub-paragraph shall be granted only on application by the contracting party proposing to levy an anti-dumping or countervailing duty, as the case may be.

Ad Article VII

Paragraph 1

The expression "or other charges" is not to be regarded as including internal taxes or equivalent charges imposed on or in connection with imported products.

Paragraph 2

1. It would be in conformity with Article VII to presume that "actual value" may be represented by the invoice price, plus any non-included charges for legitimate costs which are proper elements of "actual value" and plus any abnormal discount or other reduction from the ordinary competitive price.
2. It would be in conformity with Article VII, paragraph 2 (b), for a contracting party to construe the phrase "in the ordinary course of trade ... under fully competitive conditions", as excluding any transaction wherein the buyer and seller are not independent of each other and price is not the sole consideration.
3. The standard of "fully competitive conditions" permits a contracting party to exclude from consideration prices involving special discounts limited to exclusive agents.
4. The wording of sub-paragraphs (a) and (b) permits a contracting party to determine the value for customs purposes uniformly either (1) on the basis of a particular exporter's prices of the imported merchandise, or (2) on the basis of the general price level of like merchandise.

Ad Article VIII

1. While Article VIII does not cover the use of multiple rates of exchange as such, paragraphs 1 and 4 condemn the use of exchange taxes or fees as a device for implementing multiple currency practices; if, however, a contracting party is using multiple currency exchange fees for balance of payments reasons with the approval of the International Monetary Fund, the provisions of paragraph 9 (a) of Article XV fully safeguard its position.
2. It would be consistent with paragraph 1 if, on the importation of products from the territory of a contracting party into the territory of another contracting party, the production of certificates of origin should only be required to the extent that is strictly indispensable.

Ad Articles XI, XII, XIII, XIV and XVIII

Throughout Articles XI, XII, XIII, XIV and XVIII, the terms "import restrictions" or "export restrictions" include restrictions made effective through state-trading operations.

Ad Article XI

Paragraph 2 (c)
The term "in any form" in this paragraph covers the same products when in an early stage of processing and still perishable, which compete directly with the fresh product and if freely imported would tend to make the restriction on the fresh product ineffective.

Paragraph 2, last sub-paragraph
The term "special factors" includes changes in relative productive efficiency as between domestic and foreign producers, or as between different foreign producers, but not changes artificially brought about by means not permitted under the Agreement.

Ad Article XII
The CONTRACTING PARTIES shall make provision for the utmost secrecy in the conduct of any consultation under the provisions of this Article.

Paragraph 3 (c)(i)
Contracting parties applying restrictions shall endeavour to avoid causing serious prejudice to exports of a commodity on which the economy of a contracting party is largely dependent.

Paragraph 4 (b)
It is agreed that the date shall be within ninety days after the entry into force of the amendments of this Article effected by the Protocol Amending the Preamble and Parts II and III of this Agreement. However, should the CONTRACTING PARTIES find that conditions were not suitable for the application of the provisions of this sub-paragraph at the time envisaged, they may determine a later date; Provided that such date is not more than thirty days after such time as the obligations of Article VIII, Sections 2, 3 and 4, of the Articles of Agreement of the International Monetary Fund become applicable to contracting parties, members of the Fund, the combined foreign trade of which constitutes at least fifty per centum of the aggregate foreign trade of all contracting parties.

Paragraph 4 (e)
It is agreed that paragraph 4 (e) does not add any new criteria for the imposition or maintenance of quantitative restrictions for balance of payments reasons. It is solely intended to ensure that all

external factors such as changes in the terms of trade, quantitative restrictions, excessive tariffs and subsidies, which may be contributing to the balance of payments difficulties of the contracting party applying restrictions, will be fully taken into account.

Ad Article XIII

Paragraph 2 (d)

No mention was made of "commercial considerations" as a rule for the allocation of quotas because it was considered that its application by governmental authorities might not always be practicable. Moreover, in cases where it is practicable, a contracting party could apply these considerations in the process of seeking agreement, consistently with the general rule laid down in the opening sentence of paragraph 2.

Paragraph 4

See note relating to "special factors" in connection with the last sub-paragraph of paragraph 2 of Article XI.

Ad Article XIV

Paragraph 1

The provisions of this paragraph shall not be so construed as to preclude full consideration by the CONTRACTING PARTIES, in the consultations provided for in paragraph 4 of Article XII and in paragraph 12 of Article XVIII, of the nature, effects and reasons for discrimination in the field of import restrictions.

Paragraph 2

One of the situations contemplated in paragraph 2 is that of a contracting party holding balances acquired as a result of current transactions which it finds itself unable to use without a measure of discrimination.

Ad Article XV

Paragraph 4

The word "frustrate" is intended to indicate, for example, that infringements of the letter of any Article of this Agreement by exchange action shall not be regarded as a violation of that Article if, in practice, there is no appreciable departure from the intent of the Article. Thus, a contracting party which, as part of its exchange control operated in accordance with the Articles of Agreement of the International Monetary Fund, requires payment to be received for its exports in its own currency or in the currency of one or more members of the International Monetary Fund will not thereby be deemed to contravene Article XI or Article XIII. Another example would be that of a contracting party which specifies on an import licence the country from which the goods may be imported, for the purpose not of introducing any additional element of discrimination in its import licensing system but of enforcing permissible exchange controls.

Ad Article XVI

The exemption of an exported product from duties or taxes borne by the like product when destined for domestic consumption, or the remission of such duties or taxes in amounts not in excess of those which have accrued, shall not be deemed to be a subsidy.

Section B

1. Nothing in Section B shall preclude the use by a contracting party of multiple rates of exchange in accordance with the Articles of Agreement of the International Monetary Fund.
2. For the purposes of Section B, a "primary product" is understood to be any product of farm, forest or fishery, or any mineral, in its natural form or which has undergone such processing as is customarily required to prepare it for marketing in substantial volume in international trade.

Paragraph 3
1. The fact that a contracting party has not exported the product in question during the previous representative period would not in itself preclude that contracting party from establishing its right to obtain a share of the trade in the product concerned.
2. A system for the stabilization of the domestic price or of the return to domestic producers of a primary product independently of the movements of export prices, which results at times in the sale of the product for export at a price lower than the comparable price charged for the like product to buyers in the domestic market, shall be considered not to involve a subsidy on exports within the meaning of paragraph 3 if the CONTRACTING PARTIES determine that:
   (a) the system has also resulted, or is so designed as to result, in the sale of the product for export at a price higher than the comparable price charged for the like product to buyers in the domestic market; and
   (b) the system is so operated, or is designed so to operate, either because of the effective regulation of production or otherwise, as not to stimulate exports unduly or otherwise seriously to prejudice the interests of other contracting parties.

Notwithstanding such determination by the CONTRACTING PARTIES, operations under such a system shall be subject to the provisions of paragraph 3 where they are wholly or partly financed out of government funds in addition to the funds collected from producers in respect of the product concerned.

Paragraph 4
The intention of paragraph 4 is that the contracting parties should seek before the end of 1957 to reach agreement to abolish all remaining subsidies as from 1 January 1958; or, failing this, to reach agreement to extend the application of the standstill until the earliest date thereafter by which they can expect to reach such agreement.

Ad Article XVII

Paragraph 1
The operations of Marketing Boards, which are established by contracting parties and are engaged in purchasing or selling, are subject to the provisions of sub-paragraphs (a) and (b).

The activities of Marketing Boards which are established by contracting parties and which do not purchase or sell but lay down regulations covering private trade are governed by the relevant Articles of this Agreement.

The charging by a state enterprise of different prices for its sales of a product in different markets is not precluded by the provisions of this Article, provided that such different prices are charged for commercial reasons, to meet conditions of supply and demand in export markets.

Paragraph 1 (a)
Governmental measures imposed to insure standards of quality and efficiency in the operation of external trade, or privileges granted for the exploitation of national natural resources but which do not

empower the government to exercise control over the trading activities of the enterprise in question, do not constitute "exclusive or special privileges".

Paragraph 1 (b)
A country receiving a "tied loan" is free to take this loan into account as a "commercial consideration" when purchasing requirements abroad.

Paragraph 2
The term "goods" is limited to products as understood in commercial practice, and is not intended to include the purchase or sale of services.

Paragraph 3
Negotiations which contracting parties agree to conduct under this paragraph may be directed towards the reduction of duties and other charges on imports and exports or towards the conclusion of any other mutually satisfactory arrangement consistent with the provisions of this Agreement. (See paragraph 4 of Article II and the note to that paragraph.)

Paragraph 4 (b)
The term "import mark-up" in this paragraph shall represent the margin by which the price charged by the import monopoly for the imported product (exclusive of internal taxes within the purview of Article III, transportation, distribution, and other expenses incident to the purchase, sale or further processing, and a reasonable margin of profit) exceeds the landed cost.

Ad Article XVIII

The CONTRACTING PARTIES and the contracting parties concerned shall preserve the utmost secrecy in respect of matters arising under this Article.

Paragraphs 1 and 4
1. When they consider whether the economy of a contracting party "can only support low standards of living", the CONTRACTING PARTIES shall take into consideration the normal position of that economy and shall not base their determination on exceptional circumstances such as those which may result from the temporary existence of exceptionally favourable conditions for the staple export product or products of such contracting party.
2. The phrase "in the early stages of development" is not meant to apply only to contracting parties which have just started their economic development, but also to contracting parties the economies of which are undergoing a process of industrialization to correct an excessive dependence on primary production.

Paragraphs 2, 3, 7, 13 and 22
The reference to the establishment of particular industries shall apply not only to the establishment of a new industry, but also to the establishment of a new branch of production in an existing industry and to the substantial transformation of an existing industry, and to the substantial expansion of an existing industry supplying a relatively small proportion of the domestic demand. It shall also cover the reconstruction of an industry destroyed or substantially damaged as a result of hostilities or natural disasters.

Paragraph 7 (b)
A modification or withdrawal, pursuant to paragraph 7 (b), by a contracting party, other than the applicant contracting party, referred to in paragraph 7 (a), shall be made within six months of the day on which the action is taken by the applicant contracting party, and shall become effective on the thirtieth day following the day on which such modification or withdrawal has been notified to the CONTRACTING PARTIES.

Paragraph 11
The second sentence in paragraph 11 shall not be interpreted to mean that a contracting party is required to relax or remove restrictions if such relaxation or removal would thereupon produce conditions justifying the intensification or institution, respectively, of restrictions under paragraph 9 of Article XVIII.

Paragraph 12 (b)
The date referred to in paragraph 12 (b) shall be the date determined by the CONTRACTING PARTIES in accordance with the provisions of paragraph 4 (b) of Article XII of this Agreement.

Paragraphs 13 and 14
It is recognized that, before deciding on the introduction of a measure and notifying the CONTRACTING PARTIES in accordance with paragraph 14, a contracting party may need a reasonable period of time to assess the competitive position of the industry concerned.

Paragraphs 15 and 16
It is understood that the CONTRACTING PARTIES shall invite a contracting party proposing to apply a measure under Section C to consult with them pursuant to paragraph 16 if they are requested to do so by a contracting party the trade of which would be appreciably affected by the measure in question.

Paragraphs 16, 18, 19 and 22
1. It is understood that the CONTRACTING PARTIES may concur in a proposed measure subject to specific conditions or limitations. If the measure as applied does not conform to the terms of the concurrence it will to that extent be deemed a measure in which the CONTRACTING PARTIES have not concurred. In cases in which the CONTRACTING PARTIES have concurred in a measure for a specified period, the contracting party concerned, if it finds that the maintenance of the measure for a further period of time is required to achieve the objective for which the measure was originally taken, may apply to the CONTRACTING PARTIES for an extension of that period in accordance with the provisions and procedures of Section C or D, as the case may be.
2. It is expected that the CONTRACTING PARTIES will, as a rule, refrain from concurring in a measure which is likely to cause serious prejudice to exports of a commodity on which the economy of a contracting party is largely dependent.

Paragraph 18 and 22
The phrase "that the interests of other contracting parties are adequately safeguarded" is meant to provide latitude sufficient to permit consideration in each case of the most appropriate method of safeguarding those interests. The appropriate method may, for instance, take the form of an additional concession to be applied by the contracting party having recourse to Section C or D during such time as the deviation from the other Articles of the Agreement would remain in force or of the temporary suspension by any other contracting party referred to in paragraph 18 of a concession substantially equivalent to the impairment due to the introduction of the measure in question. Such contracting

party would have the right to safeguard its interests through such a temporary suspension of a concession; Provided that this right will not be exercised when, in the case of a measure imposed by a contracting party coming within the scope of paragraph 4 (a), the CONTRACTING PARTIES have determined that the extent of the compensatory concession proposed was adequate.

Paragraph 19
The provisions of paragraph 19 are intended to cover the cases where an industry has been in existence beyond the "reasonable period of time" referred to in the note to paragraphs 13 and 14, and should not be so construed as to deprive a contracting party coming within the scope of paragraph 4 (a) of Article XVIII, of its right to resort to the other provisions of Section C, including paragraph 17, with regard to a newly established industry even though it has benefited from incidental protection afforded by balance of payments import restrictions.

Paragraph 21
Any measure taken pursuant to the provisions of paragraph 21 shall be withdrawn forthwith if the action taken in accordance with paragraph 17 is withdrawn or if the CONTRACTING PARTIES concur in the measure proposed after the expiration of the ninety-day time limit specified in paragraph 17.

Ad Article XX

Sub-paragraph (h)
The exception provided for in this sub-paragraph extends to any commodity agreement which conforms to the principles approved by the Economic and Social Council in its resolution 30 (IV) of 28 March 1947.

Ad Article XXIV

Paragraph 9
It is understood that the provisions of Article I would require that, when a product which has been imported into the territory of a member of a customs union or free-trade area at a preferential rate of duty is re-exported to the territory of another member of such union or area, the latter member should collect a duty equal to the difference between the duty already paid and any higher duty that would be payable if the product were being imported directly into its territory.

Paragraph 11
Measures adopted by India and Pakistan in order to carry out definitive trade arrangements between them, once they have been agreed upon, might depart from particular provisions of this Agreement, but these measures would in general be consistent with the objectives of the Agreement.

Ad Article XXVIII

The CONTRACTING PARTIES and each contracting party concerned should arrange to conduct the negotiations and consultations with the greatest possible secrecy in order to avoid premature disclosure of details of prospective tariff changes. The CONTRACTING PARTIES shall be informed immediately of all changes in national tariffs resulting from recourse to this Article.

Paragraph 1
1. If the CONTRACTING PARTIES specify a period other than a three-year period, a contracting party may act pursuant to paragraph 1 or paragraph 3 of Article XXVIII on the first day following

the expiration of such other period and, unless the CONTRACTING PARTIES have again specified another period, subsequent periods will be three-year periods following the expiration of such specified period.
2. The provision that on 1 January 1958, and on other days determined pursuant to paragraph 1, a contracting party "may modify or withdraw a concession" means that on

such day, and on the first day after the end of each period, the legal obligation of such contracting party under Article II is altered; it does not mean that the changes in its customs tariff should necessarily be made effective on that day. If a tariff change resulting from negotiations undertaken pursuant to this Article is delayed, the entry into force of any compensatory concessions may be similarly delayed.
3. Not earlier than six months, nor later than three months, prior to 1 January 1958, or to the termination date of any subsequent period, a contracting party wishing to modify or withdraw any concession embodied in the appropriate Schedule, should notify the CONTRACTING PARTIES to this effect. The CONTRACTING PARTIES shall then determine the contracting party or contracting parties with which the negotiations or consultations referred to in paragraph 1 shall take place. Any contracting party so determined shall participate in such negotiations or consultations with the applicant contracting party with the aim of reaching agreement before the end of the period. Any extension of the assured life of the Schedules shall relate to the Schedules as modified after such negotiations, in accordance with paragraphs 1, 2, and 3 of Article XXVIII. If the CONTRACTING PARTIES are arranging for multilateral tariff negotiations to take place within the period of six months before 1 January 1958, or before any other day determined pursuant to paragraph 1, they shall include in the arrangements for such negotiations suitable procedures for carrying out the negotiations referred to in this paragraph.
4. The object of providing for the participation in the negotiation of any contracting party with a principle supplying interest, in addition to any contracting party with which the concession was originally negotiated, is to ensure that a contracting party with a larger share in the trade affected by the concession than a contracting party with which the concession was originally negotiated shall have an effective opportunity to protect the contractual right which it enjoys under this Agreement.

On the other hand, it is not intended that the scope of the negotiations should be such as to make negotiations and agreement under Article XXVIII unduly difficult nor to create complications in the application of this Article in the future to concessions which result from negotiations thereunder. Accordingly, the CONTRACTING PARTIES should only determine that a contracting party has a principal supplying interest if that contracting party has had, over a reasonable period of time prior to the negotiations, a larger share in the market of the applicant contracting party than a contracting party with which the concession was initially negotiated or would, in the judgement of the CONTRACTING PARTIES, have had such a share in the absence of discriminatory quantitative restrictions maintained by the applicant contracting party. It would therefore not be appropriate for the CONTRACTING PARTIES to determine that more than one contracting party, or in those exceptional cases where there is near equality more than two contracting parties, had a principal supplying interest.
5. Notwithstanding the definition of a principal supplying interest in note 4 to paragraph 1, the CONTRACTING PARTIES may exceptionally determine that a contracting party has a principal supplying interest if the concession in question affects trade which constitutes a major part of the total exports of such contracting party.
6. It is not intended that provision for participation in the negotiations of any contracting party with a principal supplying interest, and for consultation with any contracting party having a substantial interest in the concession which the applicant contracting party is seeking to modify or withdraw, should have the effect that it should have to pay compensation or suffer retaliation greater than the withdrawal or modification sought, judged in the light of the conditions of trade at the time of the proposed withdrawal or modification, making allowance for any discriminatory quantitative restrictions maintained by the applicant contracting party.

7. The expression "substantial interest" is not capable of a precise definition and accordingly may present difficulties for the CONTRACTING PARTIES. It is, however, intended to be construed to cover only those contracting parties which have, or in the absence of discriminatory quantitative restrictions affecting their exports could reasonably be expected to have, a significant share in the market of the contracting party seeking to modify or withdraw the concession.

Paragraph 4

1. Any request for authorization to enter into negotiations shall be accompanied by all relevant statistical and other data. A decision on such request shall be made within thirty days of its submission.
2. It is recognized that to permit certain contracting parties, depending in large measure on a relatively small number of primary commodities and relying on the tariff as an important aid for furthering diversification of their economies or as an important source of revenue, normally to negotiate for the modification or withdrawal of concessions only under paragraph 1 of Article XXVIII, might cause them at such time to make modifications or withdrawals which in the long run would prove unnecessary. To avoid such a situation the CONTRACTING PARTIES shall authorize any such contracting party, under paragraph 4, to enter into negotiations unless they consider this would result in, or contribute substantially towards, such an increase in tariff levels as to threaten the stability of the Schedules to this Agreement or lead to undue disturbance of international trade.
3. It is expected that negotiations authorized under paragraph 4 for modification or withdrawal of a single item, or a very small group of items, could normally be brought to a conclusion in sixty days. It is recognized, however, that such a period will be inadequate for cases involving negotiations for the modification or withdrawal of a larger number of items and in such cases, therefore, it would be appropriate for the CONTRACTING PARTIES to prescribe a longer period.
4. The determination referred to in paragraph 4 (d) shall be made by the CONTRACTING PARTIES within thirty days of the submission of the matter to them unless the applicant contracting party agrees to a longer period.
5. In determining under paragraph 4 (d) whether an applicant contracting party has unreasonably failed to offer adequate compensation, it is understood that the CONTRACTING PARTIES will take due account of the special position of a contracting party which has bound a high proportion of its tariffs at very low rates of duty and to this extent has less scope than other contracting parties to make compensatory adjustment.

Ad Article XXVIII bis

Paragraph 3

It is understood that the reference to fiscal needs would include the revenues aspect of duties and particularly duties imposed primarily for revenue purpose, or duties imposed on products which can be substituted for products subject to revenue duties to prevent the avoidance of such duties.

Ad Article XXIX

Paragraph 1

Chapters VII and VIII of the Havana Charter have been excluded from paragraph 1 because they generally deal with the organization, functions and procedures of the International Trade Organization.

Ad Part IV

The words "developed contracting parties" and the words "less-developed contracting parties" as used in Part IV are to be understood to refer to developed and less-developed countries which are parties to the General Agreement on Tariffs and Trade.

Ad Article XXXVI

Paragraph 1
This Article is based upon the objectives set forth in Article I as it will be amended by Section A of paragraph 1 of the Protocol Amending Part I and Articles XXIX and XXX when that Protocol enters into force.[1]

Paragraph 4
The term "primary products" includes agricultural products, vide paragraph 2 of the note ad Article XVI, Section B.

Paragraph 5
A diversification programme would generally include the intensification of activities for the processing of primary products and the development of manufacturing industries, taking into account the situation of the particular contracting party and the world outlook for production and consumption of different commodities.

Paragraph 8
It is understood that the phrase "do not expect reciprocity" means, in accordance with the objectives set forth in this Article, that the less-developed contracting parties should not be expected, in the course of trade negotiations, to make contributions which are inconsistent with their individual development, financial and trade needs, taking into consideration past trade developments.

This paragraph would apply in the event of action under Section A of Article XVIII, Article XXVIII, Article XXVIII bis (Article XXIX after the amendment set forth in Section A of paragraph 1 of the Protocol Amending Part I and Articles XXIX and XXX shall have become effective), Article XXXIII, or any other procedure under this Agreement.

Ad Article XXXVII

Paragraph 1 (a)
This paragraph would apply in the event of negotiations for reduction or elimination of tariffs or other restrictive regulations of commerce under Articles XXVIII, XXVIII bis (XXIX after the amendment set forth in Section A of paragraph 1 of the Protocol Amending Part I and Articles XXIX and XXX shall have become effective[1]), and Article XXXIII, as well as in connection with other action to effect such reduction or elimination which contracting parties may be able to undertake.

Paragraph 3 (b)
The other measures referred to in this paragraph might include steps to promote domestic structural changes, to encourage the consumption of particular products, or to introduce measures of trade promotion.

PROTOCOL OF PROVISIONAL APPLICATION OF THE GENERAL AGREEMENT ON TARIFFS AND TRADE

1. The Governments of the COMMONWEALTH OF AUSTRALIA, the KINGDOM OF BELGIUM (in respect of its metropolitan territory), CANADA, the FRENCH REPUBLIC (in respect of its metropolitan territory), the GRAND-DUCHY OF LUXEMBURG, the KINGDOM OF THE NETHERLANDS (in respect of its metropolitan territory), the UNITED KINGDOM OF GREAT BRITAIN AND NORTHERN IRELAND (in respect of its metropolitan territory), and the UNITED STATES OF AMERICA undertake, provided that this Protocol shall have been signed on behalf of all the foregoing Governments not later than 15 November 1947, to apply provisionally on and after 1 January 1948:

(a) Parts I and III of the General Agreement on Tariffs and Trade, and

(b) Part II of that Agreement to the fullest extent not inconsistent with existing legislation.

2. The foregoing Governments shall make effective such provisional application of the General Agreement, in respect of any of their territories other than their metropolitan territories, on or after 1 January 1948, upon the expiration of thirty days from the day on which notice of such application is received by the Secretary-General of the United Nations.

3. Any other government signatory to this Protocol shall make effective such provisional application of the General Agreement, on or after 1 January 1948, upon the expiration of thirty days from the day of signature of this Protocol on behalf of such Government.

4. This Protocol shall remain open for signature at the Headquarters of the United Nations (a) until 15 November 1947, on behalf of any government named in paragraph 1 of this Protocol which has not signed it on this day, and (b) until 30 June 1948, on behalf of any other Government signatory to the Final Act adopted at the conclusion of the Second Session of the Preparatory Committee of the United Nations Conference on Trade and Employment which has not signed it on this day.

5. Any government applying this Protocol shall be free to withdraw such application, and such withdrawal shall take effect upon the expiration of sixty days from the day on which written notice of such withdrawal is received by the Secretary-General of the United Nations.

6. The original of this Protocol shall be deposited with the Secretary-General of the United Nations, who will furnish certified copies thereof to all interested Governments.

In WITNESS WHEREOF the respective Representatives, after having communicated their full powers, found to be in good and due form, have signed the Protocol.

DONE at Geneva, in a single copy, in the English and the French languages, both texts authentic, this thirtieth day of October one thousand nine hundred and forty-seven.

10.1.8 General Agreement On Trade In Services ('GATS') (1994)

Signed 15 April 1994 entered into force 1 January 1995.

Members,

Recognizing the growing importance of trade in services for the growth and development of the world economy;

Wishing to establish a multilateral framework of principles and rules for trade in services with a view to the expansion of such trade under conditions of transparency and progressive liberalization and as a means of promoting the economic growth of all trading partners and the development of developing countries;

Desiring the early achievement of progressively higher levels of liberalization of trade in services through successive rounds of multilateral negotiations aimed at promoting the interests of all participants on a mutually advantageous basis and at securing an overall balance of rights and obligations, while giving due respect to national policy objectives;

Recognizing the right of Members to regulate, and to introduce new regulations, on the supply of services within their territories in order to meet national policy objectives and, given asymmetries existing with respect to the degree of development of services regulations in different countries, the particular need of developing countries to exercise this right;

Desiring to facilitate the increasing participation of developing countries in trade in services and the expansion of their service exports including, inter alia, through the strengthening of their domestic services capacity and its efficiency and competitiveness;

Taking particular account of the serious difficulty of the least-developed countries in view of their special economic situation and their development, trade and financial needs;

Hereby *agree* as follows:

PART I SCOPE AND DEFINITION

Article I Scope and Definition

1. This Agreement applies to measures by Members affecting trade in services.
2. For the purposes of this Agreement, trade in services is defined as the supply of a service:
   (a) from the territory of one Member into the territory of any other Member;
   (b) in the territory of one Member to the service consumer of any other Member;
   (c) by a service supplier of one Member, through commercial presence in the territory of any other Member;
   (d) by a service supplier of one Member, through presence of natural persons of a Member in the territory of any other Member.
3. For the purposes of this Agreement:
   (a) "measures by Members" means measures taken by:
   (i) central, regional or local governments and authorities; and
   (ii) non-governmental bodies in the exercise of powers delegated by central, regional or local governments or authorities;

In fulfilling its obligations and commitments under the Agreement, each Member shall take such reasonable measures as may be available to it to ensure their observance by regional and local governments and authorities and non-governmental bodies within its territory;

(b) "services" includes any service in any sector except services supplied in the exercise of governmental authority;

(c) "a service supplied in the exercise of governmental authority" means any service which is supplied neither on a commercial basis, nor in competition with one or more service suppliers.

PART II GENERAL OBLIGATIONS AND DISCIPLINES

Article II Most-Favoured-Nation Treatment

1. With respect to any measure covered by this Agreement, each Member shall accord immediately and unconditionally to services and service suppliers of any other Member treatment no less favourable than that it accords to like services and service suppliers of any other country.
2. A Member may maintain a measure inconsistent with paragraph 1 provided that such a measure is listed in, and meets the conditions of, the Annex on Article II Exemptions.
3. The provisions of this Agreement shall not be so construed as to prevent any Member from conferring or according advantages to adjacent countries in order to facilitate exchanges limited to contiguous frontier zones of services that are both locally produced and consumed.

Article III Transparency

1. Each Member shall publish promptly and, except in emergency situations, at the latest by the time of their entry into force, all relevant measures of general application which pertain to or affect the operation of this Agreement. International agreements pertaining to or affecting trade in services to which a Member is a signatory shall also be published.
2. Where publication as referred to in paragraph 1 is not practicable, such information shall be made otherwise publicly available.
3. Each Member shall promptly and at least annually inform the Council for Trade in Services of the introduction of any new, or any changes to existing, laws, regulations or administrative guidelines which significantly affect trade in services covered by its specific commitments under this Agreement.
4. Each Member shall respond promptly to all requests by any other Member for specific information on any of its measures of general application or international agreements within the meaning of paragraph 1. Each Member shall also establish one or more enquiry points to provide specific information to other Members, upon request, on all such matters as well as those subject to the notification requirement in paragraph 3. Such enquiry points shall be established within two years from the date of entry into force of the Agreement Establishing the WTO (referred to in this Agreement as the "WTO Agreement"). Appropriate flexibility with respect to the time-limit within which such enquiry points are to be established may be agreed upon for individual developing country Members. Enquiry points need not be depositories of laws and regulations.
5. Any Member may notify to the Council for Trade in Services any measure, taken by any other Member, which it considers affects the operation of this Agreement.

Article III bis Disclosure of Confidential Information

Nothing in this Agreement shall require any Member to provide confidential information, the disclosure of which would impede law enforcement, or otherwise be contrary to the public interest, or which would prejudice legitimate commercial interests of particular enterprises, public or private.

Article IV Increasing Participation of Developing Countries

1. The increasing participation of developing country Members in world trade shall be facilitated through negotiated specific commitments, by different Members pursuant to Parts III and IV of this Agreement, relating to:

(a) the strengthening of their domestic services capacity and its efficiency and competitiveness, inter alia through access to technology on a commercial basis;

(b) the improvement of their access to distribution channels and information networks; and

(c) the liberalization of market access in sectors and modes of supply of export interest to them.

2. Developed country Members, and to the extent possible other Members, shall establish contact points within two years from the date of entry into force of the WTO Agreement to facilitate the access of developing country Members' service suppliers to information, related to their respective markets, concerning:

(a) commercial and technical aspects of the supply of services;

(b) registration, recognition and obtaining of professional qualifications; and

(c) the availability of services technology.

3. Special priority shall be given to the least-developed country Members in the implementation of paragraphs 1 and 2. Particular account shall be taken of the serious difficulty of the least-developed countries in accepting negotiated specific commitments in view of their special economic situation and their development, trade and financial needs.

Article V Economic Integration

1. This Agreement shall not prevent any of its Members from being a party to or entering into an agreement liberalizing trade in services between or among the parties to such an agreement, provided that such an agreement:

(a) has substantial sectoral coverage, and

(b) provides for the absence or elimination of substantially all discrimination, in the sense of Article XVII, between or among the parties, in the sectors covered under subparagraph (a), through:

(i) elimination of existing discriminatory measures, and/or

(ii) prohibition of new or more discriminatory measures,

either at the entry into force of that agreement or on the basis of a reasonable time-frame, except for measures permitted under Articles XI, XII, XIV and XIV bis.

2. In evaluating whether the conditions under paragraph 1(b) are met, consideration may be given to the relationship of the agreement to a wider process of economic integration or trade liberalization among the countries concerned.

3. (a) Where developing countries are parties to an agreement of the type referred to in paragraph 1, flexibility shall be provided for regarding the conditions set out in paragraph 1, particularly with reference to subparagraph (b) thereof, in accordance with the level of development of the countries concerned, both overall and in individual sectors and subsectors.

(b) Notwithstanding paragraph 6, in the case of an agreement of the type referred to in paragraph 1 involving only developing countries, more favourable treatment may be granted to juridical persons owned or controlled by natural persons of the parties to such an agreement.

4. Any agreement referred to in paragraph 1 shall be designed to facilitate trade between the parties to the agreement and shall not in respect of any Member outside the agreement raise the overall level of barriers to trade in services within the respective sectors or subsectors compared to the level applicable prior to such an agreement.

5. If, in the conclusion, enlargement or any significant modification of any agreement under paragraph 1, a Member intends to withdraw or modify a specific commitment inconsistently with the terms and conditions set out in its Schedule, it shall provide at least 90 days advance notice of such

modification or withdrawal and the procedure set forth in paragraphs 2, 3 and 4 of Article XXI shall apply.

6. A service supplier of any other Member that is a juridical person constituted under the laws of a party to an agreement referred to in paragraph 1 shall be entitled to treatment granted under such agreement, provided that it engages in substantive business operations in the territory of the parties to such agreement.

7. (a) Members which are parties to any agreement referred to in paragraph 1 shall promptly notify any such agreement and any enlargement or any significant modification of that agreement to the Council for Trade in Services. They shall also make available to the Council such relevant information as may be requested by it. The Council may establish a working party to examine such an agreement or enlargement or modification of that agreement and to report to the Council on its consistency with this Article.
   (b) Members which are parties to any agreement referred to in paragraph 1 which is implemented on the basis of a time-frame shall report periodically to the Council for Trade in Services on its implementation. The Council may establish a working party to examine such reports if it deems such a working party necessary.
   (c) Based on the reports of the working parties referred to in subparagraphs (a) and (b), the Council may make recommendations to the parties as it deems appropriate.

8. A Member which is a party to any agreement referred to in paragraph 1 may not seek compensation for trade benefits that may accrue to any other Member from such agreement.

Article V bis Labour Markets Integration Agreements

This Agreement shall not prevent any of its Members from being a party to an agreement establishing full integration of the labour markets between or among the parties to such an agreement, provided that such an agreement:

(a) exempts citizens of parties to the agreement from requirements concerning residency and work permits;

(b) is notified to the Council for Trade in Services.

Article VI Domestic Regulation

1. In sectors where specific commitments are undertaken, each Member shall ensure that all measures of general application affecting trade in services are administered in a reasonable, objective and impartial manner.

2. (a) Each Member shall maintain or institute as soon as practicable judicial, arbitral or administrative tribunals or procedures which provide, at the request of an affected service supplier, for the prompt review of, and where justified, appropriate remedies for, administrative decisions affecting trade in services. Where such procedures are not independent of the agency entrusted with the administrative decision concerned, the Member shall ensure that the procedures in fact provide for an objective and impartial review.
   (b) The provisions of subparagraph (a) shall not be construed to require a Member to institute such tribunals or procedures where this would be inconsistent with its constitutional structure or the nature of its legal system.

3. Where authorization is required for the supply of a service on which a specific commitment has been made, the competent authorities of a Member shall, within a reasonable period of time after the submission of an application considered complete under domestic laws and regulations, inform the applicant of the decision concerning the application. At the request of the applicant, the competent authorities of the Member shall provide, without undue delay, information concerning the status of the application.

4. With a view to ensuring that measures relating to qualification requirements and procedures, technical standards and licensing requirements do not constitute unnecessary barriers to trade in services, the Council for Trade in Services shall, through appropriate bodies it may establish, develop any necessary disciplines. Such disciplines shall aim to ensure that such requirements are, *inter alia*:
   (a) based on objective and transparent criteria, such as competence and the ability to supply the service;
   (b) not more burdensome than necessary to ensure the quality of the service;
   (c) in the case of licensing procedures, not in themselves a restriction on the supply of the service.
5. (a) In sectors in which a Member has undertaken specific commitments, pending the entry into force of disciplines developed in these sectors pursuant to paragraph 4, the Member shall not apply licensing and qualification requirements and technical standards that nullify or impair such specific commitments in a manner which:
      (i) does not comply with the criteria outlined in subparagraphs 4(a), (b) or (c); and
      (ii) could not reasonably have been expected of that Member at the time the specific commitments in those sectors were made.
   (b) In determining whether a Member is in conformity with the obligation under paragraph 5(a), account shall be taken of international standards of relevant international organizations applied by that Member.
6. In sectors where specific commitments regarding professional services are undertaken, each Member shall provide for adequate procedures to verify the competence of professionals of any other Member.

Article V II Recognition

1. For the purposes of the fulfilment, in whole or in part, of its standards or criteria for the authorization, licensing or certification of services suppliers, and subject to the requirements of paragraph 3, a Member may recognize the education or experience obtained, requirements met, or licenses or certifications granted in a particular country. Such recognition, which may be achieved through harmonization or otherwise, may be based upon an agreement or arrangement with the country concerned or may be accorded autonomously.
2. A Member that is a party to an agreement or arrangement of the type referred to in paragraph 1, whether existing or future, shall afford adequate opportunity for other interested Members to negotiate their accession to such an agreement or arrangement or to negotiate comparable ones with it. Where a Member accords recognition autonomously, it shall afford adequate opportunity for any other Member to demonstrate that education, experience, licenses, or certifications obtained or requirements met in that other Member's territory should be recognized.
3. A Member shall not accord recognition in a manner which would constitute a means of discrimination between countries in the application of its standards or criteria for the authorization, licensing or certification of services suppliers, or a disguised restriction on trade in services.
4. Each Member shall:
   (a) within 12 months from the date on which the WTO Agreement takes effect for it, inform the Council for Trade in Services of its existing recognition measures and state whether such measures are based on agreements or arrangements of the type referred to in paragraph 1;
   (b) promptly inform the Council for Trade in Services as far in advance as possible of the opening of negotiations on an agreement or arrangement of the type referred to in paragraph 1 in order to provide adequate opportunity to any other Member to indicate their interest in participating in the negotiations before they enter a substantive phase;
   (c) promptly inform the Council for Trade in Services when it adopts new recognition measures or significantly modifies existing ones and state whether the measures are based on an agreement or arrangement of the type referred to in paragraph 1.

5. Wherever appropriate, recognition should be based on multilaterally agreed criteria. In appropriate cases, Members shall work in cooperation with relevant intergovernmental and non-governmental organizations towards the establishment and adoption of common international standards and criteria for recognition and common international standards for the practice of relevant services trades and professions.

Article VIII Monopolies and Exclusive Service Suppliers

1. Each Member shall ensure that any monopoly supplier of a service in its territory does not, in the supply of the monopoly service in the relevant market, act in a manner inconsistent with that Member's obligations under Article II and specific commitments.
2. Where a Member's monopoly supplier competes, either directly or through an affiliated company, in the supply of a service outside the scope of its monopoly rights and which is subject to that Member's specific commitments, the Member shall ensure that such a supplier does not abuse its monopoly position to act in its territory in a manner inconsistent with such commitments.
3. The Council for Trade in Services may, at the request of a Member which has a reason to believe that a monopoly supplier of a service of any other Member is acting in a manner inconsistent with paragraph 1 or 2, request the Member establishing, maintaining or authorizing such supplier to provide specific information concerning the relevant operations.
4. If, after the date of entry into force of the WTO Agreement, a Member grants monopoly rights regarding the supply of a service covered by its specific commitments, that Member shall notify the Council for Trade in Services no later than three months before the intended implementation of the grant of monopoly rights and the provisions of paragraphs 2, 3 and 4 of Article XXI shall apply.
5. The provisions of this Article shall also apply to cases of exclusive service suppliers, where a Member, formally or in effect, (a) authorizes or establishes a small number of service suppliers and (b) substantially prevents competition among those suppliers in its territory.

Article IX Business Practices

1. Members recognize that certain business practices of service suppliers, other than those falling under Article VIII, may restrain competition and thereby restrict trade in services.
2. Each Member shall, at the request of any other Member, enter into consultations with a view to eliminating practices referred to in paragraph 1. The Member addressed shall accord full and sympathetic consideration to such a request and shall cooperate through the supply of publicly available non-confidential information of relevance to the matter in question. The Member addressed shall also provide other information available to the requesting Member, subject to its domestic law and to the conclusion of satisfactory agreement concerning the safeguarding of its confidentiality by the requesting Member.

Article X Emergency Safeguard Measures

1. There shall be multilateral negotiations on the question of emergency safeguard measures based on the principle of non-discrimination. The results of such negotiations shall enter into effect on a date not later than three years from the date of entry into force of the WTO Agreement.
2. In the period before the entry into effect of the results of the negotiations referred to in paragraph 1, any Member may, notwithstanding the provisions of paragraph 1 of Article XXI, notify the Council on Trade in Services of its intention to modify or withdraw a specific commitment after a period of one year from the date on which the commitment enters into force; provided that the Member shows cause to the Council that the modification or withdrawal cannot await the lapse of the three-year period provided for in paragraph 1 of Article XXI.
3. The provisions of paragraph 2 shall cease to apply three years after the date of entry into force of the WTO Agreement.

Article XI Payments and Transfers

1. Except under the circumstances envisaged in Article XII, a Member shall not apply restrictions on international transfers and payments for current transactions relating to its specific commitments.

2. Nothing in this Agreement shall affect the rights and obligations of the members of the International Monetary Fund under the Articles of Agreement of the Fund, including the use of exchange actions which are in conformity with the Articles of Agreement, provided that a Member shall not impose restrictions on any capital transactions inconsistently with its specific commitments regarding such transactions, except under Article XII or at the request of the Fund.

Article XII Restrictions to Safeguard the Balance of Payments

1. In the event of serious balance-of-payments and external financial difficulties or threat thereof, a Member may adopt or maintain restrictions on trade in services on which it has undertaken specific commitments, including on payments or transfers for transactions related to such commitments. It is recognized that particular pressures on the balance of payments of a Member in the process of economic development or economic transition may necessitate the use of restrictions to ensure, inter alia, the maintenance of a level of financial reserves adequate for the implementation of its programme of economic development or economic transition.

2. The restrictions referred to in paragraph 1:
   (a) shall not discriminate among Members;
   (b) shall be consistent with the Articles of Agreement of the International Monetary Fund;
   (c) shall avoid unnecessary damage to the commercial, economic and financial interests of any other Member;
   (d) shall not exceed those necessary to deal with the circumstances described in paragraph 1;
   (e) shall be temporary and be phased out progressively as the situation specified in paragraph 1 improves.

3. In determining the incidence of such restrictions, Members may give priority to the supply of services which are more essential to their economic or development programmes. However, such restrictions shall not be adopted or maintained for the purpose of protecting a particular service sector.

4. Any restrictions adopted or maintained under paragraph 1, or any changes therein, shall be promptly notified to the General Council.

5. (a) Members applying the provisions of this Article shall consult promptly with the Committee on Balance-of-Payments Restrictions on restrictions adopted under this Article.
   (b) The Ministerial Conference shall establish procedures for periodic consultations with the objective of enabling such recommendations to be made to the Member concerned as it may deem appropriate.
   (c) Such consultations shall assess the balance-of-payment situation of the Member concerned and the restrictions adopted or maintained under this Article, taking into account, inter alia, such factors as:
      (i) the nature and extent of the balance-of-payments and the external financial difficulties;
      (ii) the external economic and trading environment of the consulting Member;
      (iii) alternative corrective measures which may be available.
   (d) The consultations shall address the compliance of any restrictions with paragraph 2, in particular the progressive phaseout of restrictions in accordance with paragraph 2(e).
   (e) In such consultations, all findings of statistical and other facts presented by the International Monetary Fund relating to foreign exchange, monetary reserves and balance of payments, shall be accepted and conclusions shall be based on the assessment by the Fund of the balance-of-payments and the external financial situation of the consulting Member.

6. If a Member which is not a member of the International Monetary Fund wishes to apply the provisions of this Article, the Ministerial Conference shall establish a review procedure and any other procedures necessary.

Article XIII Government Procurement

1. Articles II, XVI and XVII shall not apply to laws, regulations or requirements governing the procurement by governmental agencies of services purchased for governmental purposes and not with a view to commercial resale or with a view to use in the supply of services for commercial sale.
2. There shall be multilateral negotiations on government procurement in services under this Agreement within two years from the date of entry into force of the WTO Agreement.

Article XIV General Exceptions

Subject to the requirement that such measures are not applied in a manner which would constitute a means of arbitrary or unjustifiable discrimination between countries where like conditions prevail, or a disguised restriction on trade in services, nothing in this Agreement shall be construed to prevent the adoption or enforcement by any Member of measures:

(a) necessary to protect public morals or to maintain public order;
(b) necessary to protect human, animal or plant life or health;
(c) necessary to secure compliance with laws or regulations which are not inconsistent with the provisions of this Agreement including those relating to:
 (i) the prevention of deceptive and fraudulent practices or to deal with the effects of a default on services contracts;
 (ii) the protection of the privacy of individuals in relation to the processing and dissemination of personal data and the protection of confidentiality of individual records and accounts;
 (iii) safety;
(d) inconsistent with Article XVII, provided that the difference in treatment is aimed at ensuring the equitable or effective imposition or collection of direct taxes in respect of services or service suppliers of other Members;
(e) inconsistent with Article II, provided that the difference in treatment is the result of an agreement on the avoidance of double taxation or provisions on the avoidance of double taxation in any other international agreement or arrangement by which the Member is bound.

Article XIV bis Security Exceptions

1. Nothing in this Agreement shall be construed:
 (a) to require any Member to furnish any information, the disclosure of which it considers contrary to its essential security interests; or
  (i) apply to non-resident service suppliers in recognition of the fact that the tax obligation of non-residents is determined with respect to taxable items sourced or located in the Member's territory; or
  (ii) apply to non-residents in order to ensure the imposition or collection of taxes in the Member's territory; or
  (iii) apply to non-residents or residents in order to prevent the avoidance or evasion of taxes, including compliance measures; or
  (iv) apply to consumers of services supplied in or from the territory of another Member in order to ensure the imposition or collection of taxes on such consumers derived from sources in the Member's territory; or
  (v) distinguish service suppliers subject to tax on worldwide taxable items from other service suppliers, in recognition of the difference in the nature of the tax base between them; or

(vi) determine, allocate or apportion income, profit, gain, loss, deduction or credit of resident persons or branches, or between related persons or branches of the same person, in order to safeguard the Member's tax base.

Tax terms or concepts in paragraph (d) of Article XIV and in this footnote are determined according to tax definitions and concepts, or equivalent or similar definitions and concepts, under the domestic law of the Member taking the measure.

(b) to prevent any Member from taking any action which it considers necessary for the protection of its essential security interests:

(i) relating to the supply of services as carried out directly or indirectly for the purpose of provisioning a military establishment;

(ii) relating to fissionable and fusionable materials or the materials from which they are derived;

(iii) taken in time of war or other emergency in international relations; or

(c) to prevent any Member from taking any action in pursuance of its obligations under the United Nations Charter for the maintenance of international peace and security.

2. The Council for Trade in Services shall be informed to the fullest extent possible of measures taken under paragraphs 1(b) and (c) and of their termination.

Article XV Subsidies

1. Members recognize that, in certain circumstances, subsidies may have distortive effects on trade in services. Members shall enter into negotiations with a view to developing the necessary multilateral disciplines to avoid such trade-distortive effects. The negotiations shall also address the appropriateness of countervailing procedures. Such negotiations shall recognize the role of subsidies in relation to the development programmes of developing countries and take into account the needs of Members, particularly developing country Members, for flexibility in this area. For the purpose of such negotiations, Members shall exchange information concerning all subsidies related to trade in services that they provide to their domestic service suppliers.

2. Any Member which considers that it is adversely affected by a subsidy of another Member may request consultations with that Member on such matters. Such requests shall be accorded sympathetic consideration.

PART III SPECIFIC COMMITMENTS

Article XVI Market Access

1. With respect to market access through the modes of supply identified in Article I, each Member shall accord services and service suppliers of any other Member treatment no less favourable than that provided for under the terms, limitations and conditions agreed and specified in its Schedule.

2. In sectors where market-access commitments are undertaken, the measures which a Member shall not maintain or adopt either on the basis of a regional subdivision or on the basis of its entire territory, unless otherwise specified in its Schedule, are defined as:

(a) limitations on the number of service suppliers whether in the form of numerical quotas, monopolies, exclusive service suppliers or the requirements of an economic needs test;

(b) limitations on the total value of service transactions or assets in the form of numerical quotas or the requirement of an economic needs test;

(c) limitations on the total number of service operations or on the total quantity of service output expressed in terms of designated numerical units in the form of quotas or the requirement of an economic needs test;

(d) limitations on the total number of natural persons that may be employed in a particular service sector or that a service supplier may employ and who are necessary for, and directly related to, the supply of a specific service in the form of numerical quotas or the requirement of an economic needs test;

(e) measures which restrict or require specific types of legal entity or joint venture through which a service supplier may supply a service; and

(f) limitations on the participation of foreign capital in terms of maximum percentage limit on foreign shareholding or the total value of individual or aggregate foreign investment.

Article XVII National Treatment

1. In the sectors inscribed in its Schedule, and subject to any conditions and qualifications set out therein, each Member shall accord to services and service suppliers of any other Member, in respect of all measures affecting the supply of services, treatment no less favourable than that it accords to its own like services and service suppliers.

2. A Member may meet the requirement of paragraph 1 by according to services and service suppliers of any other Member, either formally identical treatment or formally different treatment to that it accords to its own like services and service suppliers.

3. Formally identical or formally different treatment shall be considered to be less favourable if it modifies the conditions of competition in favour of services or service suppliers of the Member compared to like services or service suppliers of any other Member.

Article XVIII Additional Commitments

Members may negotiate commitments with respect to measures affecting trade in services not subject to scheduling under Articles XVI or XVII, including those regarding qualifications, standards or licensing matters. Such commitments shall be inscribed in a Member's Schedule.

PART IV PROGRESSIVE LIBERALIZATION

Article XIX Negotiation of Specific Commitments

1. In pursuance of the objectives of this Agreement, Members shall enter into successive rounds of negotiations, beginning not later than five years from the date of entry into force of the WTO Agreement and periodically thereafter, with a view to achieving a progressively higher level of liberalization. Such negotiations shall be directed to the reduction or elimination of the adverse effects on trade in services of measures as a means of providing effective market access. This process shall take place with a view to promoting the interests of all participants on a mutually advantageous basis and to securing an overall balance of rights and obligations.

2. The process of liberalization shall take place with due respect for national policy objectives and the level of development of individual Members, both overall and in individual sectors. There shall be appropriate flexibility for individual developing country Members for opening fewer sectors, liberalizing fewer types of transactions, progressively extending market access in line with their development situation and, when making access to their markets available to foreign service suppliers, attaching to such access conditions aimed at achieving the objectives referred to in Article IV.

3. For each round, negotiating guidelines and procedures shall be established. For the purposes of establishing such guidelines, the Council for Trade in Services shall carry out an assessment of trade in services in overall terms and on a sectoral basis with reference to the objectives of this Agreement, including those set out in paragraph 1 of Article IV. Negotiating guidelines shall establish modalities for the treatment of liberalization undertaken autonomously by Members since previous negotiations, as well as for the special treatment for least-developed country Members under the provisions of paragraph 3 of Article IV.

4. The process of progressive liberalization shall be advanced in each such round through bilateral, plurilateral or multilateral negotiations directed towards increasing the general level of specific commitments undertaken by Members under this Agreement.

Article XX Schedules of Specific Commitments

1. Each Member shall set out in a schedule the specific commitments it undertakes under Part III of this Agreement. With respect to sectors where such commitments are undertaken, each Schedule shall specify:

(a) terms, limitations and conditions on market access;
(b) conditions and qualifications on national treatment;
(c) undertakings relating to additional commitments;
(d) where appropriate the time-frame for implementation of such commitments; and
(e) the date of entry into force of such commitments.

2. Measures inconsistent with both Articles XVI and XVII shall be inscribed in the column relating to Article XVI. In this case the inscription will be considered to provide a condition or qualification to Article XVII as well.

3. Schedules of specific commitments shall be annexed to this Agreement and shall form an integral part thereof.

Article XXI Modification of Schedules

1. (a) A Member (referred to in this Article as the "modifying Member") may modify or withdraw any commitment in its Schedule, at any time after three years have elapsed from the date on which that commitment entered into force, in accordance with the provisions of this Article.
(b) A modifying Member shall notify its intent to modify or withdraw a commitment pursuant to this Article to the Council for Trade in Services no later than three months before the intended date of implementation of the modification or withdrawal.

2. (a) At the request of any Member the benefits of which under this Agreement may be affected (referred to in this Article as an "affected Member") by a proposed modification or withdrawal notified under subparagraph 1(b), the modifying Member shall enter into negotiations with a view to reaching agreement on any necessary compensatory adjustment. In such negotiations and agreement, the Members concerned shall endeavour to maintain a general level of mutually advantageous commitments not less favourable to trade than that provided for in Schedules of specific commitments prior to such negotiations.
(b) Compensatory adjustments shall be made on a most-favoured-nation basis.

3. (a) If agreement is not reached between the modifying Member and any affected Member before the end of the period provided for negotiations, such affected Member may refer the matter to arbitration. Any affected Member that wishes to enforce a right that it may have to compensation must participate in the arbitration.
(b) If no affected Member has requested arbitration, the modifying Member shall be free to implement the proposed modification or withdrawal.

4. (a) The modifying Member may not modify or withdraw its commitment until it has made compensatory adjustments in conformity with the findings of the arbitration.
(b) If the modifying Member implements its proposed modification or withdrawal and does not comply with the findings of the arbitration, any affected Member that participated in the arbitration may modify or withdraw substantially equivalent benefits in conformity with those findings. Notwithstanding Article II, such a modification or withdrawal may be implemented solely with respect to the modifying Member.

5. The Council for Trade in Services shall establish procedures for rectification or modification of Schedules. Any Member which has modified or withdrawn scheduled commitments under this Article shall modify its Schedule according to such procedures.

PART V INSTITUTIONAL PROVISIONS

Article XXII Consultation

1. Each Member shall accord sympathetic consideration to, and shall afford adequate opportunity for, consultation regarding such representations as may be made by any other Member with respect to any matter affecting the operation of this Agreement. The Dispute Settlement Understanding (DSU) shall apply to such consultations.
2. The Council for Trade in Services or the Dispute Settlement Body (DSB) may, at the request of a Member, consult with any Member or Members in respect of any matter for which it has not been possible to find a satisfactory solution through consultation under paragraph 1.
3. A Member may not invoke Article XVII, either under this Article or Article XXIII, with respect to a measure of another Member that falls within the scope of an international agreement between them relating to the avoidance of double taxation. In case of disagreement between Members as to whether a measure falls within the scope of such an agreement between them, it shall be open to either Member to bring this matter before the Council for Trade in Services. The Council shall refer the matter to arbitration. The decision of the arbitrator shall be final and binding on the Members.

Article XXIII Dispute Settlement and Enforcement

1. If any Member should consider that any other Member fails to carry out its obligations or specific commitments under this Agreement, it may with a view to reaching a mutually satisfactory resolution of the matter have recourse to the DSU.
2. If the DSB considers that the circumstances are serious enough to justify such action, it may authorize a Member or Members to suspend the application to any other Member or Members of obligations and specific commitments in accordance with Article 22 of the DSU.
3. If any Member considers that any benefit it could reasonably have expected to accrue to it under a specific commitment of another Member under Part III of this Agreement is being nullified or impaired as a result of the application of any measure which does not conflict with the provisions of this Agreement, it may have recourse to the DSU. If the measure is determined by the DSB to have nullified or impaired such a benefit, the Member affected shall be entitled to a mutually satisfactory adjustment on the basis of paragraph 2 of Article XXI, which may include the modification or withdrawal of the measure. In the event an agreement cannot be reached between the Members concerned, Article 22 of the DSU shall apply.

Article XXIV Council for Trade in Services

1. The Council for Trade in Services shall carry out such functions as may be assigned to it to facilitate the operation of this Agreement and further its objectives. The Council may establish such subsidiary bodies as it considers appropriate for the effective discharge of its functions.
2. The Council and, unless the Council decides otherwise, its subsidiary bodies shall be open to participation by representatives of all Members.
3. The Chairman of the Council shall be elected by the Members.

Article XXV Technical Cooperation

1. Service suppliers of Members which are in need of such assistance shall have access to the services of contact points referred to in paragraph 2 of Article IV.

2. Technical assistance to developing countries shall be provided at the multilateral level by the Secretariat and shall be decided upon by the Council for Trade in Services.

Article XXVI Relationship with Other International Organizations

The General Council shall make appropriate arrangements for consultation and cooperation with the United Nations and its specialized agencies as well as with other intergovernmental organizations concerned with services.

PART VI FINAL PROVISIONS

Article XXVII Denial of Benefits

A Member may deny the benefits of this Agreement:

(a) to the supply of a service, if it establishes that the service is supplied from or in the territory of a non-Member or of a Member to which the denying Member does not apply the WTO Agreement;

(b) in the case of the supply of a maritime transport service, if it establishes that the service is supplied:

  (i) by a vessel registered under the laws of a non-Member or of a Member to which the denying Member does not apply the WTO Agreement, and

  (ii) by a person which operates and/or uses the vessel in whole or in part but which is of a non-Member or of a Member to which the denying Member does not apply the WTO Agreement;

(c) to a service supplier that is a juridical person, if it establishes that it is not a service supplier of another Member, or that it is a service supplier of a Member to which the denying Member does not apply the WTO Agreement.

Article XXVIII Definitions

For the purpose of this Agreement:

(a) "measure" means any measure by a Member, whether in the form of a law, regulation, rule, procedure, decision, administrative action, or any other form;

(b) "supply of a service" includes the production, distribution, marketing, sale and delivery of a service;

(c) "measures by Members affecting trade in services" include measures in respect of

  (i) the purchase, payment or use of a service;

  (ii) the access to and use of, in connection with the supply of a service, services which are required by those Members to be offered to the public generally;

  (iii) the presence, including commercial presence, of persons of a Member for the supply of a service in the territory of another Member;

(d) "commercial presence" means any type of business or professional establishment, including through

  (i) the constitution, acquisition or maintenance of a juridical person, or

  (ii) the creation or maintenance of a branch or a representative office, within the territory of a Member for the purpose of supplying a service;

(e) "sector" of a service means,

  (i) with reference to a specific commitment, one or more, or all, subsectors of that service, as specified in a Member's Schedule,

  (ii) otherwise, the whole of that service sector, including all of its subsectors;

(f) "service of another Member" means a service which is supplied,

  (i) from or in the territory of that other Member, or in the case of maritime transport, by a vessel registered under the laws of that other Member, or by a person of that other Member which supplies the service through the operation of a vessel and/or its use in whole or in part; or

(ii) in the case of the supply of a service through commercial presence or through the presence of natural persons, by a service supplier of that other Member;

(g) "service supplier" means any person that supplies a service;

(h) "monopoly supplier of a service" means any person, public or private, which in the relevant market of the territory of a Member is authorized or established formally or in effect by that Member as the sole supplier of that service;

(i) "service consumer" means any person that receives or uses a service;

(j) "person" means either a natural person or a juridical person;

(k) "natural person of another Member" means a natural person who resides in the territory of that other Member or any other Member, and who under the law of that other Member:

(i) is a national of that other Member; or

(ii) has the right of permanent residence in that other Member, in the case of a Member which:

1. does not have nationals; or
2. accords substantially the same treatment to its permanent residents as it does to its nationals in respect of measures affecting trade in services, as notified in its acceptance of or accession to the WTO Agreement, provided that no Member is obligated to accord to such permanent residents treatment more favourable than would be accorded by that other Member to such permanent residents. Such notification shall include the assurance to assume, with respect to those permanent residents, in accordance with its laws and regulations, the same responsibilities that other Member bears with respect to its nationals;

(l) "juridical person" means any legal entity duly constituted or otherwise organized under applicable law, whether for profit or otherwise, and whether privately-owned or governmentally-owned, including any corporation, trust, partnership, joint venture, sole proprietorship or association;

(m) "juridical person of another Member" means a juridical person which is either:

(i) constituted or otherwise organized under the law of that other Member, and is engaged in substantive business operations in the territory of that Member or any other Member; or

(ii) in the case of the supply of a service through commercial presence, owned or controlled by:

1. natural persons of that Member; or
2. juridical persons of that other Member identified under subparagraph (i);

(n) a juridical person is:

(i) "owned" by persons of a Member if more than 50 per cent of the equity interest in it is beneficially owned by persons of that Member;

(ii) "controlled" by persons of a Member if such persons have the power to name a majority of its directors or otherwise to legally direct its actions;

(iii) "affiliated" with another person when it controls, or is controlled by, that other person; or when it and the other person are both controlled by the same person;

(o) "direct taxes" comprise all taxes on total income, on total capital or on elements of income or of capital, including taxes on gains from the alienation of property, taxes on estates, inheritances and gifts, and taxes on the total amounts of wages or salaries paid by enterprises, as well as taxes on capital appreciation.

Article XXIX Annexes

The Annexes to this Agreement are an integral part of this Agreement.

ANNEX ON ARTICLE II EXEMPTIONS

Scope

1. This Annex specifies the conditions under which a Member, at the entry into force of this Agreement, is exempted from its obligations under paragraph 1 of Article II.
2. Any new exemptions applied for after the date of entry into force of the WTO Agreement shall be dealt with under paragraph 3 of Article IX of that Agreement.

Review

3. The Council for Trade in Services shall review all exemptions granted for a period of more than 5 years. The first such review shall take place no more than 5 years after the entry into force of the WTO Agreement.
4. The Council for Trade in Services in a review shall:
   (a) examine whether the conditions which created the need for the exemption still prevail; and
   (b) determine the date of any further review.

Termination

5. The exemption of a Member from its obligations under paragraph 1 of Article II of the Agreement with respect to a particular measure terminates on the date provided for in the exemption.
6. In principle, such exemptions should not exceed a period of 10 years. In any event, they shall be subject to negotiation in subsequent trade liberalizing rounds.
7. A Member shall notify the Council for Trade in Services at the termination of the exemption period that the inconsistent measure has been brought into conformity with paragraph 1 of Article II of the Agreement.

Lists of Article II Exemptions

[The agreed lists of exemptions under paragraph 2 of Article II will be annexed here in the treaty copy of the WTO Agreement.]

ANNEX ON MOVEMENT OF NATURAL PERSONS SUPPLYING SERVICES UNDER THE AGREEMENT

1. This Annex applies to measures affecting natural persons who are service suppliers of a Member, and natural persons of a Member who are employed by a service supplier of a Member, in respect of the supply of a service.
2. The Agreement shall not apply to measures affecting natural persons seeking access to the employment market of a Member, nor shall it apply to measures regarding citizenship, residence or employment on a permanent basis.
3. In accordance with Parts III and IV of the Agreement, Members may negotiate specific commitments applying to the movement of all categories of natural persons supplying services under the Agreement. Natural persons covered by a specific commitment shall be allowed to supply the service in accordance with the terms of that commitment.
4. The Agreement shall not prevent a Member from applying measures to regulate the entry of natural persons into, or their temporary stay in, its territory, including those measures necessary to protect the integrity of, and to ensure the orderly movement of natural persons across, its borders, provided that such measures are not applied in such a manner as to nullify or impair the benefits accruing to any Member under the terms of a specific commitment.

ANNEX ON AIR TRANSPORT SERVICES

1. This Annex applies to measures affecting trade in air transport services, whether scheduled or non-scheduled, and ancillary services. It is confirmed that any specific commitment or obligation assumed under this Agreement shall not reduce or affect a Member's obligations under bilateral or multilateral agreements that are in effect on the date of entry into force of the WTO Agreement.
2. The Agreement, including its dispute settlement procedures, shall not apply to measures affecting:
   (a) traffic rights, however granted; or
   (b) services directly related to the exercise of traffic rights, except as provided in paragraph 3 of this Annex.
3. The Agreement shall apply to measures affecting:
   (a) aircraft repair and maintenance services;
   (b) the selling and marketing of air transport services;
   (c) computer reservation system (CRS) services.
4. The dispute settlement procedures of the Agreement may be invoked only where obligations or specific commitments have been assumed by the concerned Members and where dispute settlement procedures in bilateral and other multilateral agreements or arrangements have been exhausted.
5. The Council for Trade in Services shall review periodically, and at least every five years, developments in the air transport sector and the operation of this Annex with a view to considering the possible further application of the Agreement in this sector.
6. Definitions:
   (a) "Aircraft repair and maintenance services" mean such activities when undertaken on an aircraft or a part thereof while it is withdrawn from service and do not include so-called line maintenance.
   (b) "Selling and marketing of air transport services" mean opportunities for the air carrier concerned to sell and market freely its air transport services including all aspects of marketing such as market research, advertising and distribution. These activities do not include the pricing of air transport services nor the applicable conditions.
   (c) "Computer reservation system (CRS) services" mean services provided by computerised systems that contain information about air carriers' schedules, availability, fares and fare rules, through which reservations can be made or tickets may be issued.
   (d) "Traffic rights" mean the right for scheduled and non-scheduled services to operate and/or to carry passengers, cargo and mail for remuneration or hire from, to, within, or over the territory of a Member, including points to be served, routes to be operated, types of traffic to be carried, capacity to be provided, tariffs to be charged and their conditions, and criteria for designation of airlines, including such criteria as number, ownership, and control.

ANNEX ON FINANCIAL SERVICES

1. Scope and Definition
   (a) This Annex applies to measures affecting the supply of financial services. Reference to the supply of a financial service in this Annex shall mean the supply of a service as defined in paragraph 2 of Article I of the Agreement.
   (b) For the purposes of subparagraph 3(b) of Article I of the Agreement, "services supplied in the exercise of governmental authority" means the following:
      (i) activities conducted by a central bank or monetary authority or by any other public entity in pursuit of monetary or exchange rate policies;
      (ii) activities forming part of a statutory system of social security or public retirement plans; and

(iii) other activities conducted by a public entity for the account or with the guarantee or using the financial resources of the Government.

(c) For the purposes of subparagraph 3(b) of Article I of the Agreement, if a Member allows any of the activities referred to in subparagraphs (b)(ii) or (b)(iii) of this paragraph to be conducted by its financial service suppliers in competition with a public entity or a financial service supplier, "services" shall include such activities.

(d) Subparagraph 3(c) of Article I of the Agreement shall not apply to services covered by this Annex.

2. Domestic Regulation

(a) Notwithstanding any other provisions of the Agreement, a Member shall not be prevented from taking measures for prudential reasons, including for the protection of investors, depositors, policy holders or persons to whom a fiduciary duty is owed by a financial service supplier, or to ensure the integrity and stability of the financial system. Where such measures do not conform with the provisions of the Agreement, they shall not be used as a means of avoiding the Member's commitments or obligations under the Agreement.

(b) Nothing in the Agreement shall be construed to require a Member to disclose information relating to the affairs and accounts of individual customers or any confidential or proprietary information in the possession of public entities.

3. Recognition

(a) A Member may recognize prudential measures of any other country in determining how the Member's measures relating to financial services shall be applied. Such recognition, which may be achieved through harmonization or otherwise, may be based upon an agreement or arrangement with the country concerned or may be accorded autonomously.

(b) A Member that is a party to such an agreement or arrangement referred to in subparagraph (a), whether future or existing, shall afford adequate opportunity for other interested Members to negotiate their accession to such agreements or arrangements, or to negotiate comparable ones with it, under circumstances in which there would be equivalent regulation, oversight, implementation of such regulation, and, if appropriate, procedures concerning the sharing of information between the parties to the agreement or arrangement. Where a Member accords recognition autonomously, it shall afford adequate opportunity for any other Member to demonstrate that such circumstances exist.

(c) Where a Member is contemplating according recognition to prudential measures of any other country, paragraph 4(b) of Article VII shall not apply.

4. Dispute Settlement

Panels for disputes on prudential issues and other financial matters shall have the necessary expertise relevant to the specific financial service under dispute.

5. Definitions

For the purposes of this Annex:

(a) A financial service is any service of a financial nature offered by a financial service supplier of a Member. Financial services include all insurance and insurance-related services, and all banking and other financial services (excluding insurance). Financial services include the following activities:

Insurance and insurance-related services

(i) Direct insurance (including co-insurance):
  (A) life
  (B) non-life

(ii) Reinsurance and retrocession;

(iii) Insurance intermediation, such as brokerage and agency;

(iv) Services auxiliary to insurance, such as consultancy, actuarial, risk assessment and claim settlement services.

Banking and other financial services (excluding insurance)

(v) Acceptance of deposits and other repayable funds from the public;
(vi) Lending of all types, including consumer credit, mortgage credit, factoring and financing of commercial transaction;
(vii) Financial leasing;
(viii) All payment and money transmission services, including credit, charge and debit cards, travellers cheques and bankers drafts;
(ix) Guarantees and commitments;
(x) Trading for own account or for account of customers, whether on an exchange, in an over-the-counter market or otherwise, the following:
  (A) money market instruments (including cheques, bills, certificates of deposits);
  (B) foreign exchange;
  (C) derivative products including, but not limited to, futures and options;
  (D) exchange rate and interest rate instruments, including products such as swaps, forward rate agreements;
  (E) transferable securities;
  (F) other negotiable instruments and financial assets, including bullion.
(xi) Participation in issues of all kinds of securities, including underwriting and placement as agent (whether publicly or privately) and provision of services related to such issues;
(xii) Money broking;
(xiii) Asset management, such as cash or portfolio management, all forms of collective investment management, pension fund management, custodial, depository and trust services;
(xiv) Settlement and clearing services for financial assets, including securities, derivative products, and other negotiable instruments;
(xv) Provision and transfer of financial information, and financial data processing and related software by suppliers of other financial services;
(xvi) Advisory, intermediation and other auxiliary financial services on all the activities listed in subparagraphs (v) through (xv), including credit reference and analysis, investment and portfolio research and advice, advice on acquisitions and on corporate restructuring and strategy.

(b) A financial service supplier means any natural or juridical person of a Member wishing to supply or supplying financial services but the term "financial service supplier" does not include a public entity.

(c) "Public entity" means:
  (i) a government, a central bank or a monetary authority, of a Member, or an entity owned or controlled by a Member, that is principally engaged in carrying out governmental functions or activities for governmental purposes, not including an entity principally engaged in supplying financial services on commercial terms; or
  (ii) a private entity, performing functions normally performed by a central bank or monetary authority, when exercising those functions.

SECOND ANNEX ON FINANCIAL SERVICES

1. Notwithstanding Article II of the Agreement and paragraphs 1 and 2 of the Annex on Article II Exemptions, a Member may, during a period of 60 days beginning four months after the date of entry into force of the WTO Agreement, list in that Annex measures relating to financial services which are inconsistent with paragraph 1 of Article II of the Agreement.

2. Notwithstanding Article XXI of the Agreement, a Member may, during a period of 60 days beginning four months after the date of entry into force of the WTO Agreement, improve, modify or withdraw all or part of the specific commitments on financial services inscribed in its Schedule.
3. The Council for Trade in Services shall establish any procedures necessary for the application of paragraphs 1 and 2.

ANNEX ON NEGOTIATIONS ON MARITIME TRANSPORT SERVICES

1. Article II and the Annex on Article II Exemptions, including the requirement to list in the Annex any measure inconsistent with most-favoured-nation treatment that a Member will maintain, shall enter into force for international shipping, auxiliary services and access to and use of port facilities only on:
  (a) the implementation date to be determined under paragraph 4 of the Ministerial Decision on Negotiations on Maritime Transport Services; or,
  (b) should the negotiations not succeed, the date of the final report of the Negotiating Group on Maritime Transport Services provided for in that Decision.
2. Paragraph 1 shall not apply to any specific commitment on maritime transport services which is inscribed in a Member's Schedule.
3. From the conclusion of the negotiations referred to in paragraph 1, and before the implementation date, a Member may improve, modify or withdraw all or part of its specific commitments in this sector without offering compensation, notwithstanding the provisions of Article XXI.

ANNEX ON TELECOMMUNICATIONS

1. Objectives

Recognizing the specificities of the telecommunications services sector and, in particular, its dual role as a distinct sector of economic activity and as the underlying transport means for other economic activities, the Members have agreed to the following Annex with the objective of elaborating upon the provisions of the Agreement with respect to measures affecting access to and use of public telecommunications transport networks and services. Accordingly, this Annex provides notes and supplementary provisions to the Agreement.

2. Scope
  (a) This Annex shall apply to all measures of a Member that affect access to and use of public telecommunications transport networks and services.
  (b) This Annex shall not apply to measures affecting the cable or broadcast distribution of radio or television programming.
  (c) Nothing in this Annex shall be construed:
  (i) to require a Member to authorize a service supplier of any other Member to establish, construct, acquire, lease, operate, or supply telecommunications transport networks or services, other than as provided for in its Schedule; or
  (ii) to require a Member (or to require a Member to oblige service suppliers under its jurisdiction) to establish, construct, acquire, lease, operate or supply telecommunications transport networks or services not offered to the public generally.

3. Definitions

For the purposes of this Annex:
  (a) "Telecommunications" means the transmission and reception of signals by any electromagnetic means.
  (b) "Public telecommunications transport service" means any telecommunications transport service required, explicitly or in effect, by a Member to be offered to the public generally. Such

services may include, inter alia, telegraph, telephone, telex, and data transmission typically involving the real-time transmission of customer-supplied information between two or more points without any end-to-end change in the form or content of the customer's information.

(c) "Public telecommunications transport network" means the public telecommunications infrastructure which permits telecommunications between and among defined network termination points.

(d) "Intra-corporate communications" means telecommunications through which a company communicates within the company or with or among its subsidiaries, branches and, subject to a Member's domestic laws and regulations, affiliates. For these purposes, "subsidiaries", "branches" and, where applicable, "affiliates" shall be as defined by each Member. "Intra-corporate communications" in this Annex excludes commercial or non-commercial services that are supplied to companies that are not related subsidiaries, branches or affiliates, or that are offered to customers or potential customers.

(e) Any reference to a paragraph or subparagraph of this Annex includes all subdivisions thereof.

4. Transparency

In the application of Article III of the Agreement, each Member shall ensure that relevant information on conditions affecting access to and use of public telecommunications transport networks and services is publicly available, including: tariffs and other terms and conditions of service; specifications of technical interfaces with such networks and services; information on bodies responsible for the preparation and adoption of standards affecting such access and use; conditions applying to attachment of terminal or other equipment; and notifications, registration or licensing requirements, if any.

5. Access to and use of Public Telecommunications Transport Networks and Services

(a) Each Member shall ensure that any service supplier of any other Member is accorded access to and use of public telecommunications transport networks and services on reasonable and non-discriminatory terms and conditions, for the supply of a service included in its Schedule. This obligation shall be applied, inter alia, through paragraphs (b) through (f).

(b) Each Member shall ensure that service suppliers of any other Member have access to and use of any public telecommunications transport network or service offered within or across the border of that Member, including private leased circuits, and to this end shall ensure, subject to paragraphs (e) and (f), that such suppliers are permitted:

(i) to purchase or lease and attach terminal or other equipment which interfaces with the network and which is necessary to supply a supplier's services;

(ii) to interconnect private leased or owned circuits with public telecommunications transport networks and services or with circuits leased or owned by another service supplier; and

(iii) to use operating protocols of the service supplier's choice in the supply of any service, other than as necessary to ensure the availability of telecommunications transport networks and services to the public generally.

(c) Each Member shall ensure that service suppliers of any other Member may use public telecommunications transport networks and services for the movement of information within and across borders, including for intra-corporate communications of such service suppliers, and for access to information contained in data bases or otherwise stored in machine-readable form in the territory of any Member. Any new or amended measures of a Member significantly affecting such use shall be notified and shall be subject to consultation, in accordance with relevant provisions of the Agreement.

(d) Notwithstanding the preceding paragraph, a Member may take such measures as are necessary to ensure the security and confidentiality of messages, subject to the requirement that such measures are not applied in a manner which would constitute a means of arbitrary or unjustifiable discrimination or a disguised restriction on trade in services.

(e) Each Member shall ensure that no condition is imposed on access to and use of public telecommunications transport networks and services other than as necessary:

(i) to safeguard the public service responsibilities of suppliers of public telecommunications transport networks and services, in particular their ability to make their networks or services available to the public generally;

(ii) to protect the technical integrity of public telecommunications transport networks or services; or

(iii) to ensure that service suppliers of any other Member do not supply services unless permitted pursuant to commitments in the Member's Schedule.

(f) Provided that they satisfy the criteria set out in paragraph (e), conditions for access to and use of public telecommunications transport networks and services may include:

(i) restrictions on resale or shared use of such services;

(ii) a requirement to use specified technical interfaces, including interface protocols, for inter-connection with such networks and services;

(iii) requirements, where necessary, for the inter-operability of such services and to encourage the achievement of the goals set out in paragraph 7(a);

(iv) type approval of terminal or other equipment which interfaces with the network and technical requirements relating to the attachment of such equipment to such networks;

(v) restrictions on inter-connection of private leased or owned circuits with such networks or services or with circuits leased or owned by another service supplier; or

(vi) notification, registration and licensing.

(g) Notwithstanding the preceding paragraphs of this section, a developing country Member may, consistent with its level of development, place reasonable conditions on access to and use of public telecommunications transport networks and services necessary to strengthen its domestic telecommunications infrastructure and service capacity and to increase its participation in international trade in telecommunications services. Such conditions shall be specified in the Member's Schedule.

6. Technical Cooperation

(a) Members recognize that an efficient, advanced telecommunications infrastructure in countries, particularly developing countries, is essential to the expansion of their trade in services. To this end, Members endorse and encourage the participation, to the fullest extent practicable, of developed and developing countries and their suppliers of public telecommunications transport networks and services and other entities in the development programmes of international and regional organizations, including the International Telecommunication Union, the United Nations Development Programme, and the International Bank for Reconstruction and Development.

(b) Members shall encourage and support telecommunications cooperation among developing countries at the international, regional and sub-regional levels.

(c) In cooperation with relevant international organizations, Members shall make available, where practicable, to developing countries information with respect to telecommunications services and developments in telecommunications and information technology to assist in strengthening their domestic telecommunications services sector.

(d) Members shall give special consideration to opportunities for the least-developed countries to encourage foreign suppliers of telecommunications services to assist in the transfer of technology, training and other activities that support the development of their telecommunications infrastructure and expansion of their telecommunications services trade.

7. Relation to International Organizations and Agreements

(a) Members recognize the importance of international standards for global compatibility and inter-operability of telecommunication networks and services and undertake to promote such standards through the work of relevant international bodies, including the International Telecommunication Union and the International Organization for Standardization.

(b) Members recognize the role played by intergovernmental and non-governmental organizations and agreements in ensuring the efficient operation of domestic and global telecommunications services, in particular the International Telecommunication Union. Members shall make appropriate arrangements, where relevant, for consultation with such organizations on matters arising from the implementation of this Annex.

ANNEX ON NEGOTIATIONS ON BASIC TELECOMMUNICATIONS

1. Article II and the Annex on Article II Exemptions, including the requirement to list in the Annex any measure inconsistent with most-favoured-nation treatment that a Member will maintain, shall enter into force for basic telecommunications only on:

(a) the implementation date to be determined under paragraph 5 of the Ministerial Decision on Negotiations on Basic Telecommunications; or,

(b) should the negotiations not succeed, the date of the final report of the Negotiating Group on Basic Telecommunications provided for in that Decision.

2. Paragraph 1 shall not apply to any specific commitment on basic telecommunications which is inscribed in a Member's Schedule.

10.1.9 The Agreement on Subsidies and Countervailing Measures ('SCM Agreement') (1994)

Signed 15 April 1994 entered into force 1 January 1995.

Members hereby agree as follows:

PART I: GENERAL PROVISIONS

Article 1 Definition of a Subsidy

1.1 For the purpose of this Agreement, a subsidy shall be deemed to exist if:

(a) (1) there is a financial contribution by a government or any public body within the territory of a Member (referred to in this Agreement as "government"), i.e. where:

(i) a government practice involves a direct transfer of funds (e.g. grants, loans, and equity infusion), potential direct transfers of funds or liabilities (e.g. loan guarantees);

(ii) government revenue that is otherwise due is foregone or not collected (e.g. fiscal incentives such as tax credits);

(iii) a government provides goods or services other than general infrastructure, or purchases goods;

(iv) a government makes payments to a funding mechanism, or entrusts or directs a private body to carry out one or more of the type of functions illustrated in (i) to (iii) above which would normally be vested in the government and the practice, in no real sense, differs from practices normally followed by governments;

or

(a) (2) there is any form of income or price support in the sense of Article XVI of GATT 1994;

and

(b) a benefit is thereby conferred.

1.2 A subsidy as defined in paragraph 1 shall be subject to the provisions of Part II or shall be subject to the provisions of Part III or V only if such a subsidy is specific in accordance with the provisions of Article 2.

Article 2 Specificity

2.1 In order to determine whether a subsidy, as defined in paragraph 1 of Article 1, is specific to an enterprise or industry or group of enterprises or industries (referred to in this Agreement as "certain enterprises") within the jurisdiction of the granting authority, the following principles shall apply:

(a) Where the granting authority, or the legislation pursuant to which the granting authority operates, explicitly limits access to a subsidy to certain enterprises, such subsidy shall be specific.

(b) Where the granting authority, or the legislation pursuant to which the granting authority operates, establishes objective criteria or conditions governing the eligibility for, and the amount of, a subsidy, specificity shall not exist, provided that the eligibility is automatic and that such criteria and conditions are strictly adhered to. The criteria or conditions must be clearly spelled out in law, regulation, or other official document, so as to be capable of verification.

(c) If, notwithstanding any appearance of non-specificity resulting from the application of the principles laid down in subparagraphs (a) and (b), there are reasons to believe that the subsidy may in fact be specific, other factors may be considered. Such factors are: use of a subsidy programme by a limited number of certain enterprises, predominant use by certain enterprises, the granting of disproportionately large amounts of subsidy to certain enterprises, and the manner in which discretion has been exercised by the granting authority in the decision to grant a subsidy. In applying this subparagraph, account shall be taken of the extent of diversification of economic activities within the jurisdiction of the granting authority, as well as of the length of time during which the subsidy programme has been in operation.

2.2 A subsidy which is limited to certain enterprises located within a designated geographical region within the jurisdiction of the granting authority shall be specific. It is understood that the setting or change of generally applicable tax rates by all levels of government entitled to do so shall not be deemed to be a specific subsidy for the purposes of this Agreement.

2.3 Any subsidy falling under the provisions of Article 3 shall be deemed to be specific.

2.4 Any determination of specificity under the provisions of this Article shall be clearly substantiated on the basis of positive evidence.

PART II: PROHIBITED SUBSIDIES

Article 3 Prohibition

3.1 Except as provided in the Agreement on Agriculture, the following subsidies, within the meaning of Article 1, shall be prohibited:

(a) subsidies contingent, in law or in fact, whether solely or as one of several other conditions, upon export performance, including those illustrated in Annex I;

(b) subsidies contingent, whether solely or as one of several other conditions, upon the use of domestic over imported goods.

3.2 A Member shall neither grant nor maintain subsidies referred to in paragraph 1.

Article 4 Remedies

4.1 Whenever a Member has reason to believe that a prohibited subsidy is being granted or maintained by another Member, such Member may request consultations with such other Member.

4.2 A request for consultations under paragraph 1 shall include a statement of available evidence with regard to the existence and nature of the subsidy in question.

4.3 Upon request for consultations under paragraph 1, the Member believed to be granting or maintaining the subsidy in question shall enter into such consultations as quickly as possible. The purpose of the consultations shall be to clarify the facts of the situation and to arrive at a mutually agreed solution.

4.4 If no mutually agreed solution has been reached within 30 days of the request for consultations, any Member party to such consultations may refer the matter to the Dispute Settlement Body ("DSB") for the immediate establishment of a panel, unless the DSB decides by consensus not to establish a panel.

4.5 Upon its establishment, the panel may request the assistance of the Permanent Group of Experts (referred to in this Agreement as the "PGE") with regard to whether the measure in question is a prohibited subsidy. If so requested, the PGE shall immediately review the evidence with regard to the existence and nature of the measure in question and shall provide an opportunity for the Member applying or maintaining the measure to demonstrate that the measure in question is not a prohibited subsidy. The PGE shall report its conclusions to the panel within a time-limit determined by the panel. The PGE's conclusions on the issue of whether or not the measure in question is a prohibited subsidy shall be accepted by the panel without modification.

4.6 The panel shall submit its final report to the parties to the dispute. The report shall be circulated to all Members within 90 days of the date of the composition and the establishment of the panel's terms of reference.

4.7 If the measure in question is found to be a prohibited subsidy, the panel shall recommend that the subsidizing Member withdraw the subsidy without delay. In this regard, the panel shall specify in its recommendation the time-period within which the measure must be withdrawn.

4.8 Within 30 days of the issuance of the panel's report to all Members, the report shall be adopted by the DSB unless one of the parties to the dispute formally notifies the DSB of its decision to appeal or the DSB decides by consensus not to adopt the report.

4.9 Where a panel report is appealed, the Appellate Body shall issue its decision within 30 days from the date when the party to the dispute formally notifies its intention to appeal. When the Appellate Body considers that it cannot provide its report within 30 days, it shall inform the DSB in writing of the reasons for the delay together with an estimate of the period within which it will submit its report. In no case shall the proceedings exceed 60 days. The appellate report shall be adopted by the DSB and unconditionally accepted by the parties to the dispute unless the DSB decides by consensus not to adopt the appellate report within 20 days following its issuance to the Members.

4.10 In the event the recommendation of the DSB is not followed within the time-period specified by the panel, which shall commence from the date of adoption of the panel's report or the Appellate Body's report, the DSB shall grant authorization to the complaining Member to take appropriate countermeasures, unless the DSB decides by consensus to reject the request.

4.11 In the event a party to the dispute requests arbitration under paragraph 6 of Article 22 of the Dispute Settlement Understanding ("DSU"), the arbitrator shall determine whether the countermeasures are appropriate.

4.12 For purposes of disputes conducted pursuant to this Article, except for time-periods specifically prescribed in this Article, time-periods applicable under the DSU for the conduct of such disputes shall be half the time prescribed therein.

PART III: ACTIONABLE SUBSIDIES

Article 5 Adverse Effects

No Member should cause, through the use of any subsidy referred to in paragraphs 1 and 2 of Article 1, adverse effects to the interests of other Members, i.e.:

(a) injury to the domestic industry of another Member;

(b) nullification or impairment of benefits accruing directly or indirectly to other Members under GATT 1994 in particular the benefits of concessions bound under Article II of GATT 1994;

(c) serious prejudice to the interests of another Member.

This Article does not apply to subsidies maintained on agricultural products as provided in Article 13 of the Agreement on Agriculture.

Article 6 Serious Prejudice

6.1 Serious prejudice in the sense of paragraph (c) of Article 5 shall be deemed to exist in the case of:

(a) the total ad valorem subsidization of a product exceeding 5 per cent;

(b) subsidies to cover operating losses sustained by an industry;

(c) subsidies to cover operating losses sustained by an enterprise, other than one-time measures which are non-recurrent and cannot be repeated for that enterprise and which are given merely to provide time for the development of long-term solutions and to avoid acute social problems;

(d) direct forgiveness of debt, i.e. forgiveness of government-held debt, and grants to cover debt repayment.

6.2 Notwithstanding the provisions of paragraph 1, serious prejudice shall not be found if the subsidizing Member demonstrates that the subsidy in question has not resulted in any of the effects enumerated in paragraph 3.

6.3 Serious prejudice in the sense of paragraph (c) of Article 5 may arise in any case where one or several of the following apply:

(a) the effect of the subsidy is to displace or impede the imports of a like product of another Member into the market of the subsidizing Member;

(b) the effect of the subsidy is to displace or impede the exports of a like product of another Member from a third country market;

(c) the effect of the subsidy is a significant price undercutting by the subsidized product as compared with the price of a like product of another Member in the same market or significant price suppression, price depression or lost sales in the same market;

(d) the effect of the subsidy is an increase in the world market share of the subsidizing Member in a particular subsidized primary product or commodity as compared to the average share it had during the previous period of three years and this increase follows a consistent trend over a period when subsidies have been granted.

6.4 For the purpose of paragraph 3(b), the displacement or impeding of exports shall include any case in which, subject to the provisions of paragraph 7, it has been demonstrated that there has been a change in relative shares of the market to the disadvantage of the non-subsidized like product (over an appropriately representative period sufficient to demonstrate clear trends in the development of the market for the product concerned, which, in normal circumstances, shall be at least one year). "Change in relative shares of the market" shall include any of the following situations: (a) there is an increase in the market share of the subsidized product; (b) the market share of the subsidized product remains constant in circumstances in which, in the absence of the subsidy, it would have declined; (c) the market share of the subsidized product declines, but at a slower rate than would have been the case in the absence of the subsidy.

6.5 For the purpose of paragraph 3(c), price undercutting shall include any case in which such price undercutting has been demonstrated through a comparison of prices of the subsidized product with prices of a non-subsidized like product supplied to the same market. The comparison shall be made at the same level of trade and at comparable times, due account being taken of any other factor affecting price comparability. However, if such a direct comparison is not possible, the existence of price undercutting may be demonstrated on the basis of export unit values.

6.6 Each Member in the market of which serious prejudice is alleged to have arisen shall, subject to the provisions of paragraph 3 of Annex V, make available to the parties to a dispute arising under Article 7, and to the panel established pursuant to paragraph 4 of Article 7, all relevant information that can be obtained as to the changes in market shares of the parties to the dispute as well as concerning prices of the products involved.

6.7 Displacement or impediment resulting in serious prejudice shall not arise under paragraph 3 where any of the following circumstances exist during the relevant period:

(a) prohibition or restriction on exports of the like product from the complaining Member or on imports from the complaining Member into the third country market concerned;

(b) decision by an importing government operating a monopoly of trade or state trading in the product concerned to shift, for non-commercial reasons, imports from the complaining Member to another country or countries;

(c) natural disasters, strikes, transport disruptions or other force majeure substantially affecting production, qualities, quantities or prices of the product available for export from the complaining Member;

(d) existence of arrangements limiting exports from the complaining Member;

(e) voluntary decrease in the availability for export of the product concerned from the complaining Member (including, inter alia, a situation where firms in the complaining Member have been autonomously reallocating exports of this product to new markets);

(f) failure to conform to standards and other regulatory requirements in the importing country.

6.8 In the absence of circumstances referred to in paragraph 7, the existence of serious prejudice should be determined on the basis of the information submitted to or obtained by the panel, including information submitted in accordance with the provisions of Annex V.

6.9 This Article does not apply to subsidies maintained on agricultural products as provided in Article 13 of the Agreement on Agriculture.

Article 7 Remedies

7.1 Except as provided in Article 13 of the Agreement on Agriculture, whenever a Member has reason to believe that any subsidy referred to in Article 1, granted or maintained by another Member, results in injury to its domestic industry, nullification or impairment or serious prejudice, such Member may request consultations with such other Member.

7.2 A request for consultations under paragraph 1 shall include a statement of available evidence with regard to (a) the existence and nature of the subsidy in question, and (b) the injury caused to the domestic industry, or the nullification or impairment, or serious prejudice caused to the interests of the Member requesting consultations.

7.3 Upon request for consultations under paragraph 1, the Member believed to be granting or maintaining the subsidy practice in question shall enter into such consultations as quickly as possible. The purpose of the consultations shall be to clarify the facts of the situation and to arrive at a mutually agreed solution.

7.4 If consultations do not result in a mutually agreed solution within 60 days, any Member party to such consultations may refer the matter to the DSB for the establishment of a panel, unless the DSB decides by consensus not to establish a panel. The composition of the panel and its terms of reference shall be established within 15 days from the date when it is established.

7.5 The panel shall review the matter and shall submit its final report to the parties to the dispute. The report shall be circulated to all Members within 120 days of the date of the composition and establishment of the panel's terms of reference.

7.6 Within 30 days of the issuance of the panel's report to all Members, the report shall be adopted by the DSB unless one of the parties to the dispute formally notifies the DSB of its decision to appeal or the DSB decides by consensus not to adopt the report.

7.7 Where a panel report is appealed, the Appellate Body shall issue its decision within 60 days from the date when the party to the dispute formally notifies its intention to appeal. When the Appellate Body considers that it cannot provide its report within 60 days, it shall inform the DSB in writing of the reasons for the delay together with an estimate of the period within which it will submit its report. In no case shall the proceedings exceed 90 days. The appellate report shall be adopted by the DSB and unconditionally accepted by the parties to the dispute unless the DSB decides by consensus not to adopt the appellate report within 20 days following its issuance to the Members.

7.8 Where a panel report or an Appellate Body report is adopted in which it is determined that any subsidy has resulted in adverse effects to the interests of another Member within the meaning of Article 5, the Member granting or maintaining such subsidy shall take appropriate steps to remove the adverse effects or shall withdraw the subsidy.

7.9 In the event the Member has not taken appropriate steps to remove the adverse effects of the subsidy or withdraw the subsidy within six months from the date when the DSB adopts the panel report or the Appellate Body report, and in the absence of agreement on compensation, the DSB shall grant authorization to the complaining Member to take countermeasures, commensurate with the degree and nature of the adverse effects determined to exist, unless the DSB decides by consensus to reject the request.

7.10 In the event that a party to the dispute requests arbitration under paragraph 6 of Article 22 of the DSU, the arbitrator shall determine whether the countermeasures are commensurate with the degree and nature of the adverse effects determined to exist.

PART IV: NON-ACTIONABLE SUBSIDIES

Article 8 Identification of Non-Actionable Subsidies

8.1 The following subsidies shall be considered as non-actionable:

(a) subsidies which are not specific within the meaning of Article 2;

(b) subsidies which are specific within the meaning of Article 2 but which meet all of the conditions provided for in paragraphs 2(a), 2(b) or 2(c) below.

8.2 Notwithstanding the provisions of Parts III and V, the following subsidies shall be non-actionable:

(a) assistance for research activities conducted by firms or by higher education or research establishments on a contract basis with firms if:

the assistance covers not more than 75 per cent of the costs of industrial research or 50 per cent of the costs of pre-competitive development activity;

and provided that such assistance is limited exclusively to:

(i) costs of personnel (researchers, technicians and other supporting staff employed exclusively in the research activity);

(ii) costs of instruments, equipment, land and buildings used exclusively and permanently (except when disposed of on a commercial basis) for the research activity;

(iii) costs of consultancy and equivalent services used exclusively for the research activity, including bought-in research, technical knowledge, patents, etc.;

(iv) additional overhead costs incurred directly as a result of the research activity;

(v) other running costs (such as those of materials, supplies and the like), incurred directly as a result of the research activity.

(b) assistance to disadvantaged regions within the territory of a Member given pursuant to a general framework of regional development and non-specific (within the meaning of Article 2) within eligible regions provided that:

(i) each disadvantaged region must be a clearly designated contiguous geographical area with a definable economic and administrative identity;

(ii) the region is considered as disadvantaged on the basis of neutral and objective criteria, indicating that the region's difficulties arise out of more than temporary circumstances; such criteria must be clearly spelled out in law, regulation, or other official document, so as to be capable of verification;

(iii) the criteria shall include a measurement of economic development which shall be based on at least one of the following factors:

- one of either income per capita or household income per capita, or GDP per capita, which must not be above 85 per cent of the average for the territory concerned;
- unemployment rate, which must be at least 110 per cent of the average for the territory concerned;

as measured over a three-year period; such measurement, however, may be a composite one and may include other factors.

(c) assistance to promote adaptation of existing facilities to new environmental requirements imposed by law and/or regulations which result in greater constraints and financial burden on firms, provided that the assistance:

(i) is a one-time non-recurring measure; and

(ii) is limited to 20 per cent of the cost of adaptation; and

(iii) does not cover the cost of replacing and operating the assisted investment, which must be fully borne by firms; and

(iv) is directly linked to and proportionate to a firm's planned reduction of nuisances and pollution, and does not cover any manufacturing cost savings which may be achieved; and

(v) is available to all firms which can adopt the new equipment and/or production processes.

8.3 A subsidy programme for which the provisions of paragraph 2 are invoked shall be notified in advance of its implementation to the Committee in accordance with the provisions of Part VII. Any such notification shall be sufficiently precise to enable other Members to evaluate the consistency of the programme with the conditions and criteria provided for in the relevant provisions of paragraph 2. Members shall also provide the Committee with yearly updates of such notifications, in particular by supplying information on global expenditure for each programme, and on any modification of the programme. Other Members shall have the right to request information about individual cases of subsidization under a notified programme.

8.4 Upon request of a Member, the Secretariat shall review a notification made pursuant to paragraph 3 and, where necessary, may require additional information from the subsidizing Member concerning the notified programme under review. The Secretariat shall report its findings to the Committee. The Committee shall, upon request, promptly review the findings of the Secretariat (or, if a review by the Secretariat has not been requested, the notification itself), with a view to determining whether the conditions and criteria laid down in paragraph 2 have not been met. The procedure provided for in this paragraph shall be completed at the latest at the first regular meeting of the Committee following the notification of a subsidy programme, provided that at least two months have elapsed between such notification and the regular meeting of the Committee. The review procedure described in this paragraph shall also apply, upon request, to substantial modifications of a programme notified in the yearly updates referred to in paragraph 3.

8.5 Upon the request of a Member, the determination by the Committee referred to in paragraph 4, or a failure by the Committee to make such a determination, as well as the violation, in individual cases, of the conditions set out in a notified programme, shall be submitted to binding arbitration. The arbitration body shall present its conclusions to the Members within 120 days from the date when the matter was referred to the arbitration body. Except as otherwise provided in this paragraph, the DSU shall apply to arbitrations conducted under this paragraph.

Article 9 Consultations and Authorized Remedies

9.1 If, in the course of implementation of a programme referred to in paragraph 2 of Article 8, notwithstanding the fact that the programme is consistent with the criteria laid down in that paragraph, a Member has reasons to believe that this programme has resulted in serious adverse effects to the domestic industry of that Member, such as to cause damage which would be difficult to repair, such Member may request consultations with the Member granting or maintaining the subsidy.

9.2 Upon request for consultations under paragraph 1, the Member granting or maintaining the subsidy programme in question shall enter into such consultations as quickly as possible. The purpose of the consultations shall be to clarify the facts of the situation and to arrive at a mutually acceptable solution.

9.3 If no mutually acceptable solution has been reached in consultations under paragraph 2 within 60 days of the request for such consultations, the requesting Member may refer the matter to the Committee.

9.4 Where a matter is referred to the Committee, the Committee shall immediately review the facts involved and the evidence of the effects referred to in paragraph 1. If the Committee determines that such effects exist, it may recommend to the subsidizing Member to modify this programme in such a way as to remove these effects. The Committee shall present its conclusions within 120 days from the date when the matter is referred to it under paragraph 3. In the event the recommendation is not followed within six months, the Committee shall authorize the requesting Member to take appropriate countermeasures commensurate with the nature and degree of the effects determined to exist.

PART V: COUNTERVAILING MEASURES

Article 10 Application of Article VI of GATT 1994

Members shall take all necessary steps to ensure that the imposition of a countervailing duty on any product of the territory of any Member imported into the territory of another Member is in accordance with the provisions of Article VI of GATT 1994 and the terms of this Agreement. Countervailing duties may only be imposed pursuant to investigations initiated and conducted in accordance with the provisions of this Agreement and the Agreement on Agriculture.

Article 11 Initiation and Subsequent Investigation

11.1 Except as provided in paragraph 6, an investigation to determine the existence, degree and effect of any alleged subsidy shall be initiated upon a written application by or on behalf of the domestic industry.

11.2 An application under paragraph 1 shall include sufficient evidence of the existence of (a) a subsidy and, if possible, its amount, (b) injury within the meaning of Article VI of GATT 1994 as interpreted by this Agreement, and (c) a causal link between the subsidized imports and the alleged injury. Simple assertion, unsubstantiated by relevant evidence, cannot be considered sufficient to meet the requirements of this paragraph. The application shall contain such information as is reasonably available to the applicant on the following:

(i) the identity of the applicant and a description of the volume and value of the domestic production of the like product by the applicant. Where a written application is made on behalf of the domestic industry, the application shall identify the industry on behalf of which the application is made by a list of all known domestic producers of the like product (or associations of domestic producers of the like product) and, to the extent possible, a description of the volume and value of domestic production of the like product accounted for by such producers;

(ii) a complete description of the allegedly subsidized product, the names of the country or countries of origin or export in question, the identity of each known exporter or foreign producer and a list of known persons importing the product in question;

(iii) evidence with regard to the existence, amount and nature of the subsidy in question;

(iv) evidence that alleged injury to a domestic industry is caused by subsidized imports through the effects of the subsidies; this evidence includes information on the evolution of the volume of the allegedly subsidized imports, the effect of these imports on prices of the like product in the domestic market and the consequent impact of the imports on the domestic industry, as demonstrated by relevant factors and indices having a bearing on the state of the domestic industry, such as those listed in paragraphs 2 and 4 of Article 15.

11.3 The authorities shall review the accuracy and adequacy of the evidence provided in the application to determine whether the evidence is sufficient to justify the initiation of an investigation.

11.4 An investigation shall not be initiated pursuant to paragraph 1 unless the authorities have determined, on the basis of an examination of the degree of support for, or opposition to, the application expressed by domestic producers of the like product, that the application has been made by or on behalf of the domestic industry. The application shall be considered to have been made "by or on behalf of the domestic industry" if it is supported by those domestic producers whose collective output constitutes more than 50 per cent of the total production of the like product produced by that portion of the domestic industry expressing either support for or opposition to the application. However, no investigation shall be initiated when domestic producers expressly supporting the application account for less than 25 per cent of total production of the like product produced by the domestic industry.

11.5 The authorities shall avoid, unless a decision has been made to initiate an investigation, any publicizing of the application for the initiation of an investigation.

11.6 If, in special circumstances, the authorities concerned decide to initiate an investigation without having received a written application by or on behalf of a domestic industry for the initiation of such investigation, they shall proceed only if they have sufficient evidence of the existence of a subsidy, injury and causal link, as described in paragraph 2, to justify the initiation of an investigation.

11.7 The evidence of both subsidy and injury shall be considered simultaneously (a) in the decision whether or not to initiate an investigation and (b) thereafter, during the course of the investigation, starting on a date not later than the earliest date on which in accordance with the provisions of this Agreement provisional measures may be applied.

11.8 In cases where products are not imported directly from the country of origin but are exported to the importing Member from an intermediate country, the provisions of this Agreement shall be fully applicable and the transaction or transactions shall, for the purposes of this Agreement, be regarded as having taken place between the country of origin and the importing Member.

11.9 An application under paragraph 1 shall be rejected and an investigation shall be terminated promptly as soon as the authorities concerned are satisfied that there is not sufficient evidence of either subsidization or of injury to justify proceeding with the case. There shall be immediate termination in cases where the amount of a subsidy is *de minimis*, or where the volume of subsidized imports, actual or potential, or the injury, is negligible. For the purpose of this paragraph, the amount of the subsidy shall be considered to be *de minimis* if the subsidy is less than 1 per cent ad valorem.

11.10 An investigation shall not hinder the procedures of customs clearance.

11.11 Investigations shall, except in special circumstances, be concluded within one year, and in no case more than 18 months, after their initiation.

Article 12 Evidence

12.1 Interested Members and all interested parties in a countervailing duty investigation shall be given notice of the information which the authorities require and ample opportunity to present in writing all evidence which they consider relevant in respect of the investigation in question.

12.1.1 Exporters, foreign producers or interested Members receiving questionnaires used in a countervailing duty investigation shall be given at least 30 days for reply. Due consideration should be given to any request for an extension of the 30-day period and, upon cause shown, such an extension should be granted whenever practicable.

12.1.2 Subject to the requirement to protect confidential information, evidence presented in writing by one interested Member or interested party shall be made available promptly to other interested Members or interested parties participating in the investigation.

12.1.3 As soon as an investigation has been initiated, the authorities shall provide the full text of the written application received under paragraph 1 of Article 11 to the known exporters and to the authorities of the exporting Member and shall make it available, upon request, to other interested parties involved. Due regard shall be paid to the protection of confidential information, as provided for in paragraph 4.

12.2. Interested Members and interested parties also shall have the right, upon justification, to present information orally. Where such information is provided orally, the interested Members and interested parties subsequently shall be required to reduce such submissions to writing. Any decision of the investigating authorities can only be based on such information and arguments as were on the written record of this authority and which were available to interested Members and interested parties participating in the investigation, due account having been given to the need to protect confidential information.

12.3 The authorities shall whenever practicable provide timely opportunities for all interested Members and interested parties to see all information that is relevant to the presentation of their cases, that is not confidential as defined in paragraph 4, and that is used by the authorities in a countervailing duty investigation, and to prepare presentations on the basis of this information.

12.4 Any information which is by nature confidential (for example, because its disclosure would be of significant competitive advantage to a competitor or because its disclosure would have a significantly adverse effect upon a person supplying the information or upon a person from whom the supplier acquired the information), or which is provided on a confidential basis by parties to an investigation shall, upon good cause shown, be treated as such by the authorities. Such information shall not be disclosed without specific permission of the party submitting it.

12.4.1 The authorities shall require interested Members or interested parties providing confidential information to furnish non-confidential summaries thereof. These summaries shall be in sufficient detail to permit a reasonable understanding of the substance of the information submitted in confidence. In exceptional circumstances, such Members or parties may indicate that such information is not susceptible of summary. In such exceptional circumstances, a statement of the reasons why summarization is not possible must be provided.

12.4.2 If the authorities find that a request for confidentiality is not warranted and if the supplier of the information is either unwilling to make the information public or to authorize its disclosure in generalized or summary form, the authorities may disregard such information unless it can be demonstrated to their satisfaction from appropriate sources that the information is correct.

12.5 Except in circumstances provided for in paragraph 7, the authorities shall during the course of an investigation satisfy themselves as to the accuracy of the information supplied by interested Members or interested parties upon which their findings are based.

12.6 The investigating authorities may carry out investigations in the territory of other Members as required, provided that they have notified in good time the Member in question and unless that Member objects to the investigation. Further, the investigating authorities may carry out investigations on the premises of a firm and may examine the records of a firm if (a) the firm so agrees and (b) the Member in question is notified and does not object. The procedures set forth in Annex VI shall apply to investigations on the premises of a firm. Subject to the requirement to protect confidential information, the authorities shall make the results of any such investigations available, or shall provide disclosure thereof pursuant to paragraph 8, to the firms to which they pertain and may make such results available to the applicants.

12.7 In cases in which any interested Member or interested party refuses access to, or otherwise does not provide, necessary information within a reasonable period or significantly impedes the investigation, preliminary and final determinations, affirmative or negative, may be made on the basis of the facts available.

12.8 The authorities shall, before a final determination is made, inform all interested Members and interested parties of the essential facts under consideration which form the basis for the decision whether to apply definitive measures. Such disclosure should take place in sufficient time for the parties to defend their interests.

12.9 For the purposes of this Agreement, "interested parties" shall include:

(i) an exporter or foreign producer or the importer of a product subject to investigation, or a trade or business association a majority of the members of which are producers, exporters or importers of such product; and

(ii) a producer of the like product in the importing Member or a trade and business association a majority of the members of which produce the like product in the territory of the importing Member.

This list shall not preclude Members from allowing domestic or foreign parties other than those mentioned above to be included as interested parties.

12.10 The authorities shall provide opportunities for industrial users of the product under investigation, and for representative consumer organizations in cases where the product is commonly sold at the retail level, to provide information which is relevant to the investigation regarding subsidization, injury and causality.

12.11 The authorities shall take due account of any difficulties experienced by interested parties, in particular small companies, in supplying information requested, and shall provide any assistance practicable.

12.12 The procedures set out above are not intended to prevent the authorities of a Member from proceeding expeditiously with regard to initiating an investigation, reaching preliminary or final determinations, whether affirmative or negative, or from applying provisional or final measures, in accordance with relevant provisions of this Agreement.

Article 13 Consultations

13.1 As soon as possible after an application under Article 11 is accepted, and in any event before the initiation of any investigation, Members the products of which may be subject to such investigation shall be invited for consultations with the aim of clarifying the situation as to the matters referred to in paragraph 2 of Article 11 and arriving at a mutually agreed solution.

13.2 Furthermore, throughout the period of investigation, Members the products of which are the subject of the investigation shall be afforded a reasonable opportunity to continue consultations, with a view to clarifying the factual situation and to arriving at a mutually agreed solution.

13.3 Without prejudice to the obligation to afford reasonable opportunity for consultation, these provisions regarding consultations are not intended to prevent the authorities of a Member from proceeding expeditiously with regard to initiating the investigation, reaching preliminary or final determinations, whether affirmative or negative, or from applying provisional or final measures, in accordance with the provisions of this Agreement.

13.4 The Member which intends to initiate any investigation or is conducting such an investigation shall permit, upon request, the Member or Members the products of which are subject to such investigation access to non-confidential evidence, including the non-confidential summary of confidential data being used for initiating or conducting the investigation.

Article 14 Calculation of the Amount of a Subsidy in Terms of the Benefit to the Recipient

For the purpose of Part V, any method used by the investigating authority to calculate the benefit to the recipient conferred pursuant to paragraph 1 of Article 1 shall be provided for in the national legislation or implementing regulations of the Member concerned and its application to each particular case shall be transparent and adequately explained. Furthermore, any such method shall be consistent with the following guidelines:

(a) government provision of equity capital shall not be considered as conferring a benefit, unless the investment decision can be regarded as inconsistent with the usual investment practice (including for the provision of risk capital) of private investors in the territory of that Member;

(b) a loan by a government shall not be considered as conferring a benefit, unless there is a difference between the amount that the firm receiving the loan pays on the government loan and the amount the firm would pay on a comparable commercial loan which the firm could actually obtain on the market. In this case the benefit shall be the difference between these two amounts;

(c) a loan guarantee by a government shall not be considered as conferring a benefit, unless there is a difference between the amount that the firm receiving the guarantee pays on a loan guaranteed by the government and the amount that the firm would pay on a comparable commercial loan absent the government guarantee. In this case the benefit shall be the difference between these two amounts adjusted for any differences in fees;

(d) the provision of goods or services or purchase of goods by a government shall not be considered as conferring a benefit unless the provision is made for less than adequate remuneration, or the purchase is made for more than adequate remuneration. The adequacy of remuneration shall be determined in relation to prevailing market conditions for the good or service in question in the country of provision or purchase (including price, quality, availability, marketability, transportation and other conditions of purchase or sale).

Article 15 Determination of Injury

15.1 A determination of injury for purposes of Article VI of GATT 1994 shall be based on positive evidence and involve an objective examination of both (a) the volume of the subsidized imports and the effect of the subsidized imports on prices in the domestic market for like products and (b) the consequent impact of these imports on the domestic producers of such products.

15.2 With regard to the volume of the subsidized imports, the investigating authorities shall consider whether there has been a significant increase in subsidized imports, either in absolute terms or relative to production or consumption in the importing Member. With regard to the effect of the subsidized imports on prices, the investigating authorities shall consider whether there has been a significant price undercutting by the subsidized imports as compared with the price of a like product of the importing Member, or whether the effect of such imports is otherwise to depress prices to a significant degree or to prevent price increases, which otherwise would have occurred, to a significant degree. No one or several of these factors can necessarily give decisive guidance.

15.3 Where imports of a product from more than one country are simultaneously subject to countervailing duty investigations, the investigating authorities may cumulatively assess the effects of such imports only if they determine that (a) the amount of subsidization established in relation to the imports from each country is more than de minimis as defined in paragraph 9 of Article 11 and the volume of imports from each country is not negligible and (b) a cumulative assessment of the effects of the imports is appropriate in light of the conditions of competition between the imported products and the conditions of competition between the imported products and the like domestic product.

15.4 The examination of the impact of the subsidized imports on the domestic industry shall include an evaluation of all relevant economic factors and indices having a bearing on the state of the industry, including actual and potential decline in output, sales, market share, profits, productivity, return on investments, or utilization of capacity; factors affecting domestic prices; actual and potential negative effects on cash flow, inventories, employment, wages, growth, ability to raise capital or investments and, in the case of agriculture, whether there has been an increased burden on government support programmes. This list is not exhaustive, nor can one or several of these factors necessarily give decisive guidance.

15.5 It must be demonstrated that the subsidized imports are, through the effects of subsidies, causing injury within the meaning of this Agreement. The demonstration of a causal relationship between the subsidized imports and the injury to the domestic industry shall be based on an examination of all relevant evidence before the authorities. The authorities shall also examine any known factors other than the subsidized imports which at the same time are injuring the domestic industry, and the injuries caused by these other factors must not be attributed to the subsidized imports. Factors which may be relevant in this respect include, inter alia, the volumes and prices of non-subsidized imports of the product in question, contraction in demand or changes in the patterns of consumption, trade restrictive practices of and competition between the foreign and domestic producers, developments in technology and the export performance and productivity of the domestic industry.

15.6 The effect of the subsidized imports shall be assessed in relation to the domestic production of the like product when available data permit the separate identification of that production on the basis of such criteria as the production process, producers' sales and profits. If such separate identification of that production is not possible, the effects of the subsidized imports shall be assessed by the examination of the production of the narrowest group or range of products, which includes the like product, for which the necessary information can be provided.

15.7 A determination of a threat of material injury shall be based on facts and not merely on allegation, conjecture or remote possibility. The change in circumstances which would create a situation in which the subsidy would cause injury must be clearly foreseen and imminent. In making a determination regarding the existence of a threat of material injury, the investigating authorities should consider, inter alia, such factors as:

(i) nature of the subsidy or subsidies in question and the trade effects likely to arise therefrom;
(ii) a significant rate of increase of subsidized imports into the domestic market indicating the likelihood of substantially increased importation;
(iii) sufficient freely disposable, or an imminent, substantial increase in, capacity of the exporter indicating the likelihood of substantially increased subsidized exports to the importing Member's market, taking into account the availability of other export markets to absorb any additional exports;
(iv) whether imports are entering at prices that will have a significant depressing or suppressing effect on domestic prices, and would likely increase demand for further imports; and
(v) inventories of the product being investigated.

No one of these factors by itself can necessarily give decisive guidance but the totality of the factors considered must lead to the conclusion that further subsidized exports are imminent and that, unless protective action is taken, material injury would occur.

15.8 With respect to cases where injury is threatened by subsidized imports, the application of countervailing measures shall be considered and decided with special care.

Article 16 Definition of Domestic Industry

16.1 For the purposes of this Agreement, the term "domestic industry" shall, except as provided in paragraph 2, be interpreted as referring to the domestic producers as a whole of the like products or to those of them whose collective output of the products constitutes a major proportion of the total domestic production of those products, except that when producers are related to the exporters or importers or are themselves importers of the allegedly subsidized product or a like product from other countries, the term "domestic industry" may be interpreted as referring to the rest of the producers.

16.2. In exceptional circumstances, the territory of a Member may, for the production in question, be divided into two or more competitive markets and the producers within each market may be regarded as a separate industry if (a) the producers within such market sell all or almost all of their production of the product in question in that market, and (b) the demand in that market is not to any substantial degree supplied by producers of the product in question located elsewhere in the territory. In such circumstances, injury may be found to exist even where a major portion of the total domestic industry is not injured, provided there is a concentration of subsidized imports into such an isolated market and provided further that the subsidized imports are causing injury to the producers of all or almost all of the production within such market.

16.3 When the domestic industry has been interpreted as referring to the producers in a certain area, i.e. a market as defined in paragraph 2, countervailing duties shall be levied only on the products in question consigned for final consumption to that area. When the constitutional law of the importing Member does not permit the levying of countervailing duties on such a basis, the importing Member may levy the countervailing duties without limitation only if (a) the exporters shall have been given an opportunity to cease exporting at subsidized prices to the area concerned or otherwise give assurances pursuant to Article 18, and adequate assurances in this regard have not been promptly given, and (b) such duties cannot be levied only on products of specific producers which supply the area in question.

16.4 Where two or more countries have reached under the provisions of paragraph 8(a) of Article XXIV of GATT 1994 such a level of integration that they have the characteristics of a single, unified market, the industry in the entire area of integration shall be taken to be the domestic industry referred to in paragraphs 1 and 2.

16.5 The provisions of paragraph 6 of Article 15 shall be applicable to this Article.

Article 17 Provisional Measures

17.1 Provisional measures may be applied only if:

(a) an investigation has been initiated in accordance with the provisions of Article 11, a public notice has been given to that effect and interested Members and interested parties have been given adequate opportunities to submit information and make comments;

(b) a preliminary affirmative determination has been made that a subsidy exists and that there is injury to a domestic industry caused by subsidized imports; and

(c) the authorities concerned judge such measures necessary to prevent injury being caused during the investigation.

17.2 Provisional measures may take the form of provisional countervailing duties guaranteed by cash deposits or bonds equal to the amount of the provisionally calculated amount of subsidization.

17.3 Provisional measures shall not be applied sooner than 60 days from the date of initiation of the investigation.

17.4 The application of provisional measures shall be limited to as short a period as possible, not exceeding four months.

17.5 The relevant provisions of Article 19 shall be followed in the application of provisional measures.

Article 18 Undertakings

18.1 Proceedings may be suspended or terminated without the imposition of provisional measures or countervailing duties upon receipt of satisfactory voluntary undertakings under which:

(a) the government of the exporting Member agrees to eliminate or limit the subsidy or take other measures concerning its effects; or

(b) the exporter agrees to revise its prices so that the investigating authorities are satisfied that the injurious effect of the subsidy is eliminated. Price increases under such undertakings shall not be higher than necessary to eliminate the amount of the subsidy. It is desirable that the price increases be less than the amount of the subsidy if such increases would be adequate to remove the injury to the domestic industry.

18.2 Undertakings shall not be sought or accepted unless the authorities of the importing Member have made a preliminary affirmative determination of subsidization and injury caused by such subsidization and, in case of undertakings from exporters, have obtained the consent of the exporting Member.

18.3 Undertakings offered need not be accepted if the authorities of the importing Member consider their acceptance impractical, for example if the number of actual or potential exporters is too great, or for other reasons, including reasons of general policy. Should the case arise and where practicable, the authorities shall provide to the exporter the reasons which have led them to consider acceptance of an undertaking as inappropriate, and shall, to the extent possible, give the exporter an opportunity to make comments thereon.

18.4 If an undertaking is accepted, the investigation of subsidization and injury shall nevertheless be completed if the exporting Member so desires or the importing Member so decides. In such a case, if a negative determination of subsidization or injury is made, the undertaking shall automatically lapse, except in cases where such a determination is due in large part to the existence of an undertaking. In such cases, the authorities concerned may require that an undertaking be maintained for a reasonable period consistent with the provisions of this Agreement. In the event that an affirmative determination of subsidization and injury is made, the undertaking shall continue consistent with its terms and the provisions of this Agreement.

18.5 Price undertakings may be suggested by the authorities of the importing Member, but no exporter shall be forced to enter into such undertakings. The fact that governments or exporters do not offer such undertakings, or do not accept an invitation to do so, shall in no way prejudice the consideration of the case. However, the authorities are free to determine that a threat of injury is more likely to be realized if the subsidized imports continue.

18.6 Authorities of an importing Member may require any government or exporter from whom an undertaking has been accepted to provide periodically information relevant to the fulfilment of such an undertaking, and to permit verification of pertinent data. In case of violation of an undertaking, the authorities of the importing Member may take, under this Agreement in conformity with its provisions, expeditious actions which may constitute immediate application of provisional measures using the best information available. In such cases, definitive duties may be levied in accordance with this Agreement on products entered for consumption not more than 90 days before the application of such provisional measures, except that any such retroactive assessment shall not apply to imports entered before the violation of the undertaking.

Article 19 Imposition and Collection of Countervailing Duties

19.1 If, after reasonable efforts have been made to complete consultations, a Member makes a final determination of the existence and amount of the subsidy and that, through the effects of the subsidy, the subsidized imports are causing injury, it may impose a countervailing duty in accordance with the provisions of this Article unless the subsidy or subsidies are withdrawn.

19.2 The decision whether or not to impose a countervailing duty in cases where all requirements for the imposition have been fulfilled, and the decision whether the amount of the countervailing duty to be imposed shall be the full amount of the subsidy or less, are decisions to be made by the authorities of the importing Member. It is desirable that the imposition should be permissive in the territory of all Members, that the duty should be less than the total amount of the subsidy if such lesser duty would be adequate to remove the injury to the domestic industry, and that procedures should be established which would allow the authorities concerned to take due account of representations made by domestic interested parties whose interests might be adversely affected by the imposition of a countervailing duty.

19.3 When a countervailing duty is imposed in respect of any product, such countervailing duty shall be levied, in the appropriate amounts in each case, on a non-discriminatory basis on imports of such product from all sources found to be subsidized and causing injury, except as to imports from those sources which have renounced any subsidies in question or from which undertakings under the terms of this Agreement have been accepted. Any exporter whose exports are subject to a definitive countervailing duty but who was not actually investigated for reasons other than a refusal to cooperate, shall be entitled to an expedited review in order that the investigating authorities promptly establish an individual countervailing duty rate for that exporter.

19.4 No countervailing duty shall be levied on any imported product in excess of the amount of the subsidy found to exist, calculated in terms of subsidization per unit of the subsidized and exported product.

Article 20 Retroactivity

20.1 Provisional measures and countervailing duties shall only be applied to products which enter for consumption after the time when the decision under paragraph 1 of Article 17 and paragraph 1 of Article 19, respectively, enters into force, subject to the exceptions set out in this Article.

20.2 Where a final determination of injury (but not of a threat thereof or of a material retardation of the establishment of an industry) is made or, in the case of a final determination of a threat of injury, where the effect of the subsidized imports would, in the absence of the provisional measures, have led to a determination of injury, countervailing duties may be levied retroactively for the period for which provisional measures, if any, have been applied.

20.3 If the definitive countervailing duty is higher than the amount guaranteed by the cash deposit or bond, the difference shall not be collected. If the definitive duty is less than the amount guaranteed by the cash deposit or bond, the excess amount shall be reimbursed or the bond released in an expeditious manner.

20.4 Except as provided in paragraph 2, where a determination of threat of injury or material retardation is made (but no injury has yet occurred) a definitive countervailing duty may be imposed only from the date of the determination of threat of injury or material retardation, and any cash deposit made during the period of the application of provisional measures shall be refunded and any bonds released in an expeditious manner.

20.5 Where a final determination is negative, any cash deposit made during the period of the application of provisional measures shall be refunded and any bonds released in an expeditious manner.

20.6 In critical circumstances where for the subsidized product in question the authorities find that injury which is difficult to repair is caused by massive imports in a relatively short period of a product benefiting from subsidies paid or bestowed inconsistently with the provisions of GATT 1994 and of this Agreement and where it is deemed necessary, in order to preclude the recurrence of such injury, to assess countervailing duties retroactively on those imports, the definitive countervailing duties may be assessed on imports which were entered for consumption not more than 90 days prior to the date of application of provisional measures.

Article 21 Duration and Review of Countervailing Duties and Undertakings

21.1 A countervailing duty shall remain in force only as long as and to the extent necessary to counteract subsidization which is causing injury.

21.2 The authorities shall review the need for the continued imposition of the duty, where warranted, on their own initiative or, provided that a reasonable period of time has elapsed since the imposition of the definitive countervailing duty, upon request by any interested party which submits positive information substantiating the need for a review. Interested parties shall have the right to request the authorities to examine whether the continued imposition of the duty is necessary to offset subsidization, whether the injury would be likely to continue or recur if the duty were removed or varied, or both. If, as a result of the review under this paragraph, the authorities determine that the countervailing duty is no longer warranted, it shall be terminated immediately.

21.3 Notwithstanding the provisions of paragraphs 1 and 2, any definitive countervailing duty shall be terminated on a date not later than five years from its imposition (or from the date of the most recent review under paragraph 2 if that review has covered both subsidization and injury, or under this paragraph), unless the authorities determine, in a review initiated before that date on their own initiative or upon a duly substantiated request made by or on behalf of the domestic industry within a reasonable period of time prior to that date, that the expiry of the duty would be likely to lead to continuation or recurrence of subsidization and injury. The duty may remain in force pending the outcome of such a review.

21.4 The provisions of Article 12 regarding evidence and procedure shall apply to any review carried out under this Article. Any such review shall be carried out expeditiously and shall normally be concluded within 12 months of the date of initiation of the review.

21.5 The provisions of this Article shall apply mutatis mutandis to undertakings accepted under Article 18.

Article 22 Public Notice and Explanation of Determinations

22.1 When the authorities are satisfied that there is sufficient evidence to justify the initiation of an investigation pursuant to Article 11, the Member or Members the products of which are subject to such investigation and other interested parties known to the investigating authorities to have an interest therein shall be notified and a public notice shall be given.

22.2 A public notice of the initiation of an investigation shall contain, or otherwise make available through a separate report, adequate information on the following:

(i) the name of the exporting country or countries and the product involved;
(ii) the date of initiation of the investigation;
(iii) a description of the subsidy practice or practices to be investigated;
(iv) a summary of the factors on which the allegation of injury is based;
(v) the address to which representations by interested Members and interested parties should be directed; and
(vi) the time-limits allowed to interested Members and interested parties for making their views known.

22.3 Public notice shall be given of any preliminary or final determination, whether affirmative or negative, of any decision to accept an undertaking pursuant to Article 18, of the termination of such an undertaking, and of the termination of a definitive countervailing duty. Each such notice shall set forth, or otherwise make available through a separate report, in sufficient detail the findings and conclusions reached on all issues of fact and law considered material by the investigating authorities. All such notices and reports shall be forwarded to the Member or Members the products of which are subject to such determination or undertaking and to other interested parties known to have an interest therein.

22.4 A public notice of the imposition of provisional measures shall set forth, or otherwise make available through a separate report, sufficiently detailed explanations for the preliminary determinations on the existence of a subsidy and injury and shall refer to the matters of fact and law which have led to arguments being accepted or rejected. Such a notice or report shall, due regard being paid to the requirement for the protection of confidential information, contain in particular:

(i) the names of the suppliers or, when this is impracticable, the supplying countries involved;
(ii) a description of the product which is sufficient for customs purposes;
(iii) the amount of subsidy established and the basis on which the existence of a subsidy has been determined;
(iv) considerations relevant to the injury determination as set out in Article 15;
(v) the main reasons leading to the determination.

22.5 A public notice of conclusion or suspension of an investigation in the case of an affirmative determination providing for the imposition of a definitive duty or the acceptance of an undertaking shall contain, or otherwise make available through a separate report, all relevant information on the matters of fact and law and reasons which have led to the imposition of final measures or the acceptance of an undertaking, due regard being paid to the requirement for the protection of confidential information. In particular, the notice or report shall contain the information described in paragraph 4, as well as the reasons for the acceptance or rejection of relevant arguments or claims made by interested Members and by the exporters and importers.

22.6 A public notice of the termination or suspension of an investigation following the acceptance of an undertaking pursuant to Article 18 shall include, or otherwise make available through a separate report, the non-confidential part of this undertaking.

22.7 The provisions of this Article shall apply mutatis mutandis to the initiation and completion of reviews pursuant to Article 21 and to decisions under Article 20 to apply duties retroactively.

Article 23 Judicial Review

Each Member whose national legislation contains provisions on countervailing duty measures shall maintain judicial, arbitral or administrative tribunals or procedures for the purpose, inter alia, of the prompt review of administrative actions relating to final determinations and reviews of determinations within the meaning of Article 21. Such tribunals or procedures shall be independent of the authorities responsible for the determination or review in question, and shall provide all interested parties who participated in the administrative proceeding and are directly and individually affected by the administrative actions with access to review.

PART VI: INSTITUTIONS

Article 24 Committee on Subsidies and Countervailing Measures and Subsidiary Bodies

24.1 There is hereby established a Committee on Subsidies and Countervailing Measures composed of representatives from each of the Members. The Committee shall elect its own Chairman and shall meet not less than twice a year and otherwise as envisaged by relevant provisions of this Agreement at the request of any Member. The Committee shall carry out responsibilities as assigned to it under this Agreement or by the Members and it shall afford Members the opportunity of consulting on any matter relating to the operation of the Agreement or the furtherance of its objectives. The WTO Secretariat shall act as the secretariat to the Committee.

24.2 The Committee may set up subsidiary bodies as appropriate.

24.3 The Committee shall establish a Permanent Group of Experts composed of five independent persons, highly qualified in the fields of subsidies and trade relations. The experts will be elected by the Committee and one of them will be replaced every year. The PGE may be requested to assist a panel, as provided for in paragraph 5 of Article 4. The Committee may also seek an advisory opinion on the existence and nature of any subsidy.

24.4 The PGE may be consulted by any Member and may give advisory opinions on the nature of any subsidy proposed to be introduced or currently maintained by that Member. Such advisory opinions will be confidential and may not be invoked in proceedings under Article 7.

24.5 In carrying out their functions, the Committee and any subsidiary bodies may consult with and seek information from any source they deem appropriate. However, before the Committee or a subsidiary body seeks such information from a source within the jurisdiction of a Member, it shall inform the Member involved.

PART VII: NOTIFICATION AND SURVEILLANCE

Article 25 Notifications

25.1 Members agree that, without prejudice to the provisions of paragraph 1 of Article XVI of GATT 1994, their notifications of subsidies shall be submitted not later than 30 June of each year and shall conform to the provisions of paragraphs 2 through 6.

25.2 Members shall notify any subsidy as defined in paragraph 1 of Article 1, which is specific within the meaning of Article 2, granted or maintained within their territories.

25.3 The content of notifications should be sufficiently specific to enable other Members to evaluate the trade effects and to understand the operation of notified subsidy programmes. In this connection, and without prejudice to the contents and form of the questionnaire on subsidies, Members shall ensure that their notifications contain the following information:

(i) form of a subsidy (i.e. grant, loan, tax concession, etc.);
(ii) subsidy per unit or, in cases where this is not possible, the total amount or the annual amount budgeted for that subsidy (indicating, if possible, the average subsidy per unit in the previous year);
(iii) policy objective and/or purpose of a subsidy;
(iv) duration of a subsidy and/or any other time-limits attached to it;
(v) statistical data permitting an assessment of the trade effects of a subsidy.

25.4 Where specific points in paragraph 3 have not been addressed in a notification, an explanation shall be provided in the notification itself.

25.5 If subsidies are granted to specific products or sectors, the notifications should be organized by product or sector.

25.6 Members which consider that there are no measures in their territories requiring notification under paragraph 1 of Article XVI of GATT 1994 and this Agreement shall so inform the Secretariat in writing.

25.7 Members recognize that notification of a measure does not prejudge either its legal status under GATT 1994 and this Agreement, the effects under this Agreement, or the nature of the measure itself.

25.8 Any Member may, at any time, make a written request for information on the nature and extent of any subsidy granted or maintained by another Member (including any subsidy referred to in Part IV), or for an explanation of the reasons for which a specific measure has been considered as not subject to the requirement of notification.

25.9 Members so requested shall provide such information as quickly as possible and in a comprehensive manner, and shall be ready, upon request, to provide additional information to the requesting Member. In particular, they shall provide sufficient details to enable the other Member to assess their compliance with the terms of this Agreement. Any Member which considers that such information has not been provided may bring the matter to the attention of the Committee.

25.10 Any Member which considers that any measure of another Member having the effects of a subsidy has not been notified in accordance with the provisions of paragraph 1 of Article XVI of GATT 1994 and this Article may bring the matter to the attention of such other Member. If the alleged subsidy is not thereafter notified promptly, such Member may itself bring the alleged subsidy in question to the notice of the Committee.

25.11 Members shall report without delay to the Committee all preliminary or final actions taken with respect to countervailing duties. Such reports shall be available in the Secretariat for inspection by other Members. Members shall also submit, on a semi-annual basis, reports on any countervailing duty actions taken within the preceding six months. The semi-annual reports shall be submitted on an agreed standard form.

25.12 Each Member shall notify the Committee (a) which of its authorities are competent to initiate and conduct investigations referred to in Article 11 and (b) its domestic procedures governing the initiation and conduct of such investigations.

Article 26 Surveillance

26.1 The Committee shall examine new and full notifications submitted under paragraph 1 of Article XVI of GATT 1994 and paragraph 1 of Article 25 of this Agreement at special sessions held every third year. Notifications submitted in the intervening years (updating notifications) shall be examined at each regular meeting of the Committee.

26.2 The Committee shall examine reports submitted under paragraph 11 of Article 25 at each regular meeting of the Committee.

PART VIII: DEVELOPING COUNTRY MEMBERS

Article 27 Special and Differential Treatment of Developing Country Members

27.1 Members recognize that subsidies may play an important role in economic development programmes of developing country Members.

27.2 The prohibition of paragraph 1(a) of Article 3 shall not apply to:

(a) developing country Members referred to in Annex VII.

(b) other developing country Members for a period of eight years from the date of entry into force of the WTO Agreement, subject to compliance with the provisions in paragraph 4.

27.3 The prohibition of paragraph 1(b) of Article 3 shall not apply to developing country Members for a period of five years, and shall not apply to least developed country Members for a period of eight years, from the date of entry into force of the WTO Agreement.

27.4 Any developing country Member referred to in paragraph 2(b) shall phase out its export subsidies within the eight-year period, preferably in a progressive manner. However, a developing country Member shall not increase the level of its export subsidies, and shall eliminate them within a period shorter than that provided for in this paragraph when the use of such export subsidies is inconsistent with its development needs. If a developing country Member deems it necessary to apply such subsidies beyond the 8-year period, it shall not later than one year before the expiry of this period enter into consultation with the Committee, which will determine whether an extension of this period is justified, after examining all the relevant economic, financial and development needs of the developing country Member in question. If the Committee determines that the extension is justified, the developing country Member concerned shall hold annual consultations with the Committee to determine the necessity of maintaining the subsidies. If no such determination is made by the Committee, the developing country Member shall phase out the remaining export subsidies within two years from the end of the last authorized period.

27.5 A developing country Member which has reached export competitiveness in any given product shall phase out its export subsidies for such product(s) over a period of two years. However, for a developing country Member which is referred to in Annex VII and which has reached export competitiveness in one or more products, export subsidies on such products shall be gradually phased out over a period of eight years.

27.6 Export competitiveness in a product exists if a developing country Member's exports of that product have reached a share of at least 3.25 per cent in world trade of that product for two consecutive calendar years. Export competitiveness shall exist either (a) on the basis of notification by the developing country Member having reached export competitiveness, or (b) on the basis of a computation undertaken by the Secretariat at the request of any Member. For the purpose of this paragraph, a product is defined as a section heading of the Harmonized System Nomenclature. The Committee shall review the operation of this provision five years from the date of the entry into force of the WTO Agreement.

27.7 The provisions of Article 4 shall not apply to a developing country Member in the case of export subsidies which are in conformity with the provisions of paragraphs 2 through 5. The relevant provisions in such a case shall be those of Article 7.

27.8 There shall be no presumption in terms of paragraph 1 of Article 6 that a subsidy granted by a developing country Member results in serious prejudice, as defined in this Agreement. Such serious prejudice, where applicable under the terms of paragraph 9, shall be demonstrated by positive evidence, in accordance with the provisions of paragraphs 3 through 8 of Article 6.

27.9 Regarding actionable subsidies granted or maintained by a developing country Member other than those referred to in paragraph 1 of Article 6, action may not be authorized or taken under Article 7 unless nullification or impairment of tariff concessions or other obligations under GATT 1994 is found to exist as a result of such a subsidy, in such a way as to displace or impede imports of a like product of another Member into the market of the subsidizing developing country Member or unless injury to a domestic industry in the market of an importing Member occurs.

27.10 Any countervailing duty investigation of a product originating in a developing country Member shall be terminated as soon as the authorities concerned determine that:

(a) the overall level of subsidies granted upon the product in question does not exceed 2 per cent of its value calculated on a per unit basis; or

(b) the volume of the subsidized imports represents less than 4 per cent of the total imports of the like product in the importing Member, unless imports from developing country Members whose individual shares of total imports represent less than 4 per cent collectively account for more than 9 per cent of the total imports of the like product in the importing Member.

27.11 For those developing country Members within the scope of paragraph 2(b) which have eliminated export subsidies prior to the expiry of the period of eight years from the date of entry into force of the WTO Agreement, and for those developing country Members referred to in Annex VII, the number in paragraph 10(a) shall be 3 per cent rather than 2 per cent. This provision shall apply from the date that the elimination of export subsidies is notified to the Committee, and for so long as export subsidies are not granted by the notifying developing country Member. This provision shall expire eight years from the date of entry into force of the WTO Agreement.

27.12 The provisions of paragraphs 10 and 11 shall govern any determination of de minimis under paragraph 3 of Article 15.

27.13 The provisions of Part III shall not apply to direct forgiveness of debts, subsidies to cover social costs, in whatever form, including relinquishment of government revenue and other transfer of liabilities when such subsidies are granted within and directly linked to a privatization programme of a developing country Member, provided that both such programme and the subsidies involved are granted for a limited period and notified to the Committee and that the programme results in eventual privatization of the enterprise concerned.

27.14 The Committee shall, upon request by an interested Member, undertake a review of a specific export subsidy practice of a developing country Member to examine whether the practice is in conformity with its development needs.

27.15 The Committee shall, upon request by an interested developing country Member, undertake a review of a specific countervailing measure to examine whether it is consistent with the provisions of paragraphs 10 and 11 as applicable to the developing country Member in question.

PART IX: TRANSITIONAL ARRANGEMENTS

Article 28 Existing Programmes

28.1 Subsidy programmes which have been established within the territory of any Member before the date on which such a Member signed the WTO Agreement and which are inconsistent with the provisions of this Agreement shall be:

(a) notified to the Committee not later than 90 days after the date of entry into force of the WTO Agreement for such Member; and

(b) brought into conformity with the provisions of this Agreement within three years of the date of entry into force of the WTO Agreement for such Member and until then shall not be subject to Part II.

28.2 No Member shall extend the scope of any such programme, nor shall such a programme be renewed upon its expiry.

Article 29 Transformation into a Market Economy

29.1 Members in the process of transformation from a centrally-planned into a market, free-enterprise economy may apply programmes and measures necessary for such a transformation.

29.2 For such Members, subsidy programmes falling within the scope of Article 3, and notified according to paragraph 3, shall be phased out or brought into conformity with Article 3 within a period of seven years from the date of entry into force of the WTO Agreement. In such a case, Article 4 shall not apply. In addition during the same period:

(a) Subsidy programmes falling within the scope of paragraph 1(d) of Article 6 shall not be actionable under Article 7;

(b) With respect to other actionable subsidies, the provisions of paragraph 9 of Article 27 shall apply.

29.3 Subsidy programmes falling within the scope of Article 3 shall be notified to the Committee by the earliest practicable date after the date of entry into force of the WTO Agreement. Further notifications of such subsidies may be made up to two years after the date of entry into force of the WTO Agreement.

29.4 In exceptional circumstances Members referred to in paragraph 1 may be given departures from their notified programmes and measures and their time-frame by the Committee if such departures are deemed necessary for the process of transformation.

PART X: DISPUTE SETTLEMENT

Article 30

The provisions of Articles XXII and XXIII of GATT 1994 as elaborated and applied by the Dispute Settlement Understanding shall apply to consultations and the settlement of disputes under this Agreement, except as otherwise specifically provided herein.

PART XI: FINAL PROVISIONS

Article 31 Provisional Application

The provisions of paragraph 1 of Article 6 and the provisions of Article 8 and Article 9 shall apply for a period of five years, beginning with the date of entry into force of the WTO Agreement. Not later than 180 days before the end of this period, the Committee shall review the operation of those provisions, with a view to determining whether to extend their application, either as presently drafted or in a modified form, for a further period.

Article 32 Other Final Provisions

32.1 No specific action against a subsidy of another Member can be taken except in accordance with the provisions of GATT 1994, as interpreted by this Agreement.

32.2 Reservations may not be entered in respect of any of the provisions of this Agreement without the consent of the other Members.

32.3 Subject to paragraph 4, the provisions of this Agreement shall apply to investigations, and reviews of existing measures, initiated pursuant to applications which have been made on or after the date of entry into force for a Member of the WTO Agreement.

32.4 For the purposes of paragraph 3 of Article 21, existing countervailing measures shall be deemed to be imposed on a date not later than the date of entry into force for a Member of the WTO Agreement, except in cases in which the domestic legislation of a Member in force at that date already included a clause of the type provided for in that paragraph.

32.5 Each Member shall take all necessary steps, of a general or particular character, to ensure, not later than the date of entry into force of the WTO Agreement for it, the conformity of its laws, regulations and administrative procedures with the provisions of this Agreement as they may apply to the Member in question.

32.6 Each Member shall inform the Committee of any changes in its laws and regulations relevant to this Agreement and in the administration of such laws and regulations.

32.7 The Committee shall review annually the implementation and operation of this Agreement, taking into account the objectives thereof. The Committee shall inform annually the Council for Trade in Goods of developments during the period covered by such reviews.

32.8 The Annexes to this Agreement constitute an integral part thereof.

ANNEX I ILLUSTRATIVE LIST OF EXPORT SUBSIDIES

(a) The provision by governments of direct subsidies to a firm or an industry contingent upon export performance.
(b) Currency retention schemes or any similar practices which involve a bonus on exports.
(c) Internal transport and freight charges on export shipments, provided or mandated by governments, on terms more favourable than for domestic shipments.
(d) The provision by governments or their agencies either directly or indirectly through government-mandated schemes, of imported or domestic products or services for use in the production of exported goods, on terms or conditions more favourable than for provision of like or directly competitive products or services for use in the production of goods for domestic consumption, if (in the case of products) such terms or conditions are more favourable than those commercially available on world markets to their exporters.
(e) The full or partial exemption remission, or deferral specifically related to exports, of direct taxes or social welfare charges paid or payable by industrial or commercial enterprises.
(f) The allowance of special deductions directly related to exports or export performance, over and above those granted in respect to production for domestic consumption, in the calculation of the base on which direct taxes are charged.
(g) The exemption or remission, in respect of the production and distribution of exported products, of indirect taxes58 in excess of those levied in respect of the production and distribution of like products when sold for domestic consumption.
(h) The exemption, remission or deferral of prior-stage cumulative indirect taxes58 on goods or services used in the production of exported products in excess of the exemption, remission or deferral of like prior-stage cumulative indirect taxes on goods or services used in the production of like products when sold for domestic consumption; provided, however, that prior-stage cumulative indirect taxes may be exempted, remitted or deferred on exported products even when not exempted, remitted or deferred on like products when sold for domestic consumption, if the prior-stage cumulative indirect taxes are levied on inputs that are consumed in the production of the exported product (making normal allowance for waste). This item shall be interpreted in accordance with the guidelines on consumption of inputs in the production process contained in Annex II.
(i) The remission or drawback of import charges in excess of those levied on imported inputs that are consumed in the production of the exported product (making normal allowance for waste); provided, however, that in particular cases a firm may use a quantity of home market inputs equal to, and having the same quality and characteristics as, the imported inputs as a substitute for them in order to benefit from this provision if the import and the corresponding export operations both occur within a reasonable time period, not to exceed two years. This item shall be interpreted in accordance with the guidelines on consumption of inputs in the production process contained in Annex II and the guidelines in the determination of substitution drawback systems as export subsidies contained in Annex III.
(j) The provision by governments (or special institutions controlled by governments) of export credit guarantee or insurance programmes, of insurance or guarantee programmes against increases in the cost of exported products or of exchange risk programmes, at premium rates which are inadequate to cover the long-term operating costs and losses of the programmes.
(k) The grant by governments (or special institutions controlled by and/or acting under the authority of governments) of export credits at rates below those which they actually have to pay for the funds so employed (or would have to pay if they borrowed on international capital markets in order to obtain funds of the same maturity and other credit terms and denominated in the same currency as the export credit), or the payment by them of all or part of the costs incurred by exporters or financial

institutions in obtaining credits, in so far as they are used to secure a material advantage in the field of export credit terms.

Provided, however, that if a Member is a party to an international undertaking on official export credits to which at least twelve original Members to this Agreement are parties as of 1 January 1979 (or a successor undertaking which has been adopted by those original Members), or if in practice a Member applies the interest rates provisions of the relevant undertaking, an export credit practice which is in conformity with those provisions shall not be considered an export subsidy prohibited by this Agreement.

(l) Any other charge on the public account constituting an export subsidy in the sense of Article XVI of GATT 1994.

ANNEX II GUIDELINES ON CONSUMPTION OF INPUTS IN THE PRODUCTION PROCESS

I

1. Indirect tax rebate schemes can allow for exemption, remission or deferral of prior-stage cumulative indirect taxes levied on inputs that are consumed in the production of the exported product (making normal allowance for waste). Similarly, drawback schemes can allow for the remission or drawback of import charges levied on inputs that are consumed in the production of the exported product (making normal allowance for waste).

2. The Illustrative List of Export Subsidies in Annex I of this Agreement makes reference to the term "inputs that are consumed in the production of the exported product" in paragraphs (h) and (i). Pursuant to paragraph (h), indirect tax rebate schemes can constitute an export subsidy to the extent that they result in exemption, remission or deferral of prior-stage cumulative indirect taxes in excess of the amount of such taxes actually levied on inputs that are consumed in the production of the exported product. Pursuant to paragraph (i), drawback schemes can constitute an export subsidy to the extent that they result in a remission or drawback of import charges in excess of those actually levied on inputs that are consumed in the production of the exported product. Both paragraphs stipulate that normal allowance for waste must be made in findings regarding consumption of inputs in the production of the exported product. Paragraph (i) also provides for substitution, where appropriate.

II

In examining whether inputs are consumed in the production of the exported product, as part of a countervailing duty investigation pursuant to this Agreement, investigating authorities should proceed on the following basis:

1. Where it is alleged that an indirect tax rebate scheme, or a drawback scheme, conveys a subsidy by reason of over-rebate or excess drawback of indirect taxes or import charges on inputs consumed in the production of the exported product, the investigating authorities should first determine whether the government of the exporting Member has in place and applies a system or procedure to confirm which inputs are consumed in the production of the exported product and in what amounts. Where such a system or procedure is determined to be applied, the investigating authorities should then examine the system or procedure to see whether it is reasonable, effective for the purpose intended, and based on generally accepted commercial practices in the country of export. The investigating authorities may deem it necessary to carry out, in accordance with paragraph 6 of Article 12, certain practical tests in order to verify information or to satisfy themselves that the system or procedure is being effectively applied.

2. Where there is no such system or procedure, where it is not reasonable, or where it is instituted and considered reasonable but is found not to be applied or not to be applied effectively, a further examination by the exporting Member based on the actual inputs involved would need to be carried out in the context of determining whether an excess payment occurred. If the investigating authorities deemed it necessary, a further examination would be carried out in accordance with paragraph 1.
3. Investigating authorities should treat inputs as physically incorporated if such inputs are used in the production process and are physically present in the product exported. The Members note that an input need not be present in the final product in the same form in which it entered the production process.
4. In determining the amount of a particular input that is consumed in the production of the exported product, a "normal allowance for waste" should be taken into account, and such waste should be treated as consumed in the production of the exported product. The term "waste" refers to that portion of a given input which does not serve an independent function in the production process, is not consumed in the production of the exported product (for reasons such as inefficiencies) and is not recovered, used or sold by the same manufacturer.
5. The investigating authority's determination of whether the claimed allowance for waste is "normal" should take into account the production process, the average experience of the industry in the country of export, and other technical factors, as appropriate. The investigating authority should bear in mind that an important question is whether the authorities in the exporting Member have reasonably calculated the amount of waste, when such an amount is intended to be included in the tax or duty rebate or remission.

ANNEX III GUIDELINES IN THE DETERMINATION OF SUBSTITUTION DRAWBACK SYSTEMS AS EXPORT SUBSIDIES

I

Drawback systems can allow for the refund or drawback of import charges on inputs which are consumed in the production process of another product and where the export of this latter product contains domestic inputs having the same quality and characteristics as those substituted for the imported inputs. Pursuant to paragraph (i) of the Illustrative List of Export Subsidies in Annex I, substitution drawback systems can constitute an export subsidy to the extent that they result in an excess drawback of the import charges levied initially on the imported inputs for which drawback is being claimed.

II

In examining any substitution drawback system as part of a countervailing duty investigation pursuant to this Agreement, investigating authorities should proceed on the following basis:
1. Paragraph (i) of the Illustrative List stipulates that home market inputs may be substituted for imported inputs in the production of a product for export provided such inputs are equal in quantity to, and have the same quality and characteristics as, the imported inputs being substituted. The existence of a verification system or procedure is important because it enables the government of the exporting Member to ensure and demonstrate that the quantity of inputs for which drawback is claimed does not exceed the quantity of similar products exported, in whatever form, and that there is not drawback of import charges in excess of those originally levied on the imported inputs in question.
2. Where it is alleged that a substitution drawback system conveys a subsidy, the investigating authorities should first proceed to determine whether the government of the exporting Member has in place and applies a verification system or procedure. Where such a system or procedure is determined to be

applied, the investigating authorities should then examine the verification procedures to see whether they are reasonable, effective for the purpose intended, and based on generally accepted commercial practices in the country of export. To the extent that the procedures are determined to meet this test and are effectively applied, no subsidy should be presumed to exist. It may be deemed necessary by the investigating authorities to carry out, in accordance with paragraph 6 of Article 12, certain practical tests in order to verify information or to satisfy themselves that the verification procedures are being effectively applied.
3. Where there are no verification procedures, where they are not reasonable, or where such procedures are instituted and considered reasonable but are found not to be actually applied or not applied effectively, there may be a subsidy. In such cases a further examination by the exporting Member based on the actual transactions involved would need to be carried out to determine whether an excess payment occurred. If the investigating authorities deemed it necessary, a further examination would be carried out in accordance with paragraph 2.
4. The existence of a substitution drawback provision under which exporters are allowed to select particular import shipments on which drawback is claimed should not of itself be considered to convey a subsidy.
5. An excess drawback of import charges in the sense of paragraph (i) would be deemed to exist where governments paid interest on any monies refunded under their drawback schemes, to the extent of the interest actually paid or payable.

ANNEX IV CALCULATION OF THE TOTAL AD VALOREM SUBSIDIZATION (PARAGRAPH 1(A) OF ARTICLE 6)

1. Any calculation of the amount of a subsidy for the purpose of paragraph 1(a) of Article 6 shall be done in terms of the cost to the granting government.
2. Except as provided in paragraphs 3 through 5, in determining whether the overall rate of subsidization exceeds 5 per cent of the value of the product, the value of the product shall be calculated as the total value of the recipient firm's sales in the most recent 12-month period, for which sales data is available, preceding the period in which the subsidy is granted.
3. Where the subsidy is tied to the production or sale of a given product, the value of the product shall be calculated as the total value of the recipient firm's sales of that product in the most recent 12- month period, for which sales data is available, preceding the period in which the subsidy is granted.
4. Where the recipient firm is in a start-up situation, serious prejudice shall be deemed to exist if the overall rate of subsidization exceeds 15 per cent of the total funds invested. For purposes of this paragraph, a start-up period will not extend beyond the first year of production.
5. Where the recipient firm is located in an inflationary economy country, the value of the product shall be calculated as the recipient firm's total sales (or sales of the relevant product, if the subsidy is tied) in the preceding calendar year indexed by the rate of inflation experienced in the 12 months preceding the month in which the subsidy is to be given.
6. In determining the overall rate of subsidization in a given year, subsidies given under different programmes and by different authorities in the territory of a Member shall be aggregated.
7. Subsidies granted prior to the date of entry into force of the WTO Agreement, the benefits of which are allocated to future production, shall be included in the overall rate of subsidization.
8. Subsidies which are non-actionable under relevant provisions of this Agreement shall not be included in the calculation of the amount of a subsidy for the purpose of paragraph 1(a) of Article 6.

ANNEX V PROCEDURES FOR DEVELOPING INFORMATION CONCERNING SERIOUS PREJUDICE

1. Every Member shall cooperate in the development of evidence to be examined by a panel in procedures under paragraphs 4 through 6 of Article 7. The parties to the dispute and any third-country Member concerned shall notify to the DSB, as soon as the provisions of paragraph 4 of Article 7 have been invoked, the organization responsible for administration of this provision within its territory and the procedures to be used to comply with requests for information.

2. In cases where matters are referred to the DSB under paragraph 4 of Article 7, the DSB shall, upon request, initiate the procedure to obtain such information from the government of the subsidizing Member as necessary to establish the existence and amount of subsidization, the value of total sales of the subsidized firms, as well as information necessary to analyze the adverse effects caused by the subsidized product. This process may include, where appropriate, presentation of questions to the government of the subsidizing Member and of the complaining Member to collect information, as well as to clarify and obtain elaboration of information available to the parties to a dispute through the notification procedures set forth in Part VII.

3. In the case of effects in third-country markets, a party to a dispute may collect information, including through the use of questions to the government of the third-country Member, necessary to analyse adverse effects, which is not otherwise reasonably available from the complaining Member or the subsidizing Member. This requirement should be administered in such a way as not to impose an unreasonable burden on the third-country Member. In particular, such a Member is not expected to make a market or price analysis specially for that purpose. The information to be supplied is that which is already available or can be readily obtained by this Member (e.g. most recent statistics which have already been gathered by relevant statistical services but which have not yet been published, customs data concerning imports and declared values of the products concerned, etc.). However, if a party to a dispute undertakes a detailed market analysis at its own expense, the task of the person or firm conducting such an analysis shall be facilitated by the authorities of the third-country Member and such a person or firm shall be given access to all information which is not normally maintained confidential by the government.

4. The DSB shall designate a representative to serve the function of facilitating the information-gathering process. The sole purpose of the representative shall be to ensure the timely development of the information necessary to facilitate expeditious subsequent multilateral review of the dispute. In particular, the representative may suggest ways to most efficiently solicit necessary information as well as encourage the cooperation of the parties.

5. The information-gathering process outlined in paragraphs 2 through 4 shall be completed within 60 days of the date on which the matter has been referred to the DSB under paragraph 4 of Article 7. The information obtained during this process shall be submitted to the panel established by the DSB in accordance with the provisions of Part X. This information should include, inter alia, data concerning the amount of the subsidy in question (and, where appropriate, the value of total sales of the subsidized firms), prices of the subsidized product, prices of the non-subsidized product, prices of other suppliers to the market, changes in the supply of the subsidized product to the market in question and changes in market shares. It should also include rebuttal evidence, as well as such supplemental information as the panel deems relevant in the course of reaching its conclusions.

6. If the subsidizing and/or third-country Member fail to cooperate in the information-gathering process, the complaining Member will present its case of serious prejudice, based on evidence available to it, together with facts and circumstances of the non-cooperation of the subsidizing and/or third-country Member. Where information is unavailable due to non-cooperation by the subsidizing and/or third-country Member, the panel may complete the record as necessary relying on best information otherwise available.

7. In making its determination, the panel should draw adverse inferences from instances of non-cooperation by any party involved in the information-gathering process.
8. In making a determination to use either best information available or adverse inferences, the panel shall consider the advice of the DSB representative nominated under paragraph 4 as to the reasonableness of any requests for information and the efforts made by parties to comply with these requests in a cooperative and timely manner.
9. Nothing in the information-gathering process shall limit the ability of the panel to seek such additional information it deems essential to a proper resolution to the dispute, and which was not adequately sought or developed during that process. However, ordinarily the panel should not request additional information to complete the record where the information would support a particular party's position and the absence of that information in the record is the result of unreasonable non-cooperation by that party in the information-gathering process.

ANNEX VI PROCEDURES FOR ON-THE-SPOT INVESTIGATIONS PURSUANT TO PARAGRAPH 6 OF ARTICLE 12

1. Upon initiation of an investigation, the authorities of the exporting Member and the firms known to be concerned should be informed of the intention to carry out on-the-spot investigations.
2. If in exceptional circumstances it is intended to include non-governmental experts in the investigating team, the firms and the authorities of the exporting Member should be so informed. Such non-governmental experts should be subject to effective sanctions for breach of confidentiality requirements.
3. It should be standard practice to obtain explicit agreement of the firms concerned in the exporting Member before the visit is finally scheduled.
4. As soon as the agreement of the firms concerned has been obtained, the investigating authorities should notify the authorities of the exporting Member of the names and addresses of the firms to be visited and the dates agreed.
5. Sufficient advance notice should be given to the firms in question before the visit is made.
6. Visits to explain the questionnaire should only be made at the request of an exporting firm. In case of such a request the investigating authorities may place themselves at the disposal of the firm; such a visit may only be made if (a) the authorities of the importing Member notify the representatives of the government of the Member in question and (b) the latter do not object to the visit.
7. As the main purpose of the on-the-spot investigation is to verify information provided or to obtain further details, it should be carried out after the response to the questionnaire has been received unless the firm agrees to the contrary and the government of the exporting Member is informed by the investigating authorities of the anticipated visit and does not object to it; further, it should be standard practice prior to the visit to advise the firms concerned of the general nature of the information to be verified and of any further information which needs to be provided, though this should not preclude requests to be made on the spot for further details to be provided in the light of information obtained.
8. Enquiries or questions put by the authorities or firms of the exporting Members and essential to a successful on-the-spot investigation should, whenever possible, be answered before the visit is made.

ANNEX VII DEVELOPING COUNTRY MEMBERS REFERRED TO IN PARAGRAPH 2(A) OF ARTICLE 27

The developing country Members not subject to the provisions of paragraph 1(a) of Article 3 under the terms of paragraph 2(a) of Article 27 are:

(a) Least-developed countries designated as such by the United Nations which are Members of the WTO.

(b) Each of the following developing countries which are Members of the WTO shall be subject to the provisions which are applicable to other developing country Members according to paragraph 2(b) of Article 27 when GNP per capita has reached $1,000 per annum: Bolivia, Cameroon, Congo, Côte d'Ivoire, Dominican Republic, Egypt, Ghana, Guatemala, Guyana, India, Indonesia, Kenya, Morocco, Nicaragua, Nigeria, Pakistan, Philippines, Senegal, Sri Lanka and Zimbabwe.

10.2 Model Legislation

10.2.1 Dutch Model Bilateral Investment Agreement ('Dutch Model BIT 2019')

Agreement on reciprocal promotion and protection of investments between
______
and
the Kingdom of the Netherlands.

The______ and the Kingdom of the Netherlands,

hereinafter referred to as the Contracting Parties,

Desiring to strengthen their traditional ties of friendship and to extend and intensify economic relations between them by creating conditions with a view to attract and promote responsible foreign investment of the Contracting Parties in their respective territories that contribute to sustainable economic development;

Recognizing that fostering an open and transparent policy environment and protecting investments of investors of one Contracting Party in the territory of the other Contracting Party are conducive to the stimulation of mutually beneficial economic activity and intensification of economic cooperation;

Reaffirming their commitment to sustainable development and to enhancing the contribution of international trade and investment to sustainable development;

Recognizing the importance of equality between men and women when formulating, implementing and reviewing measures within the field of international trade and investment;

Considering that these objectives can be achieved without compromising the right of the Contracting Parties to regulate within their territories through measures necessary to achieve legitimate policy objectives, such as the protection of public health, safety, environment, public morals, labor rights, animal welfare, social or consumer protection or for prudential financial reasons;

Have agreed as follows:

SECTION 1: DEFINITIONS AND SCOPE

Article 1 Definitions
For the purposes of this Agreement:
(a) "investment" means every kind of asset that has the characteristics of an investment, which includes a certain duration, the commitment of capital or other resources, the expectation of gain or profit, and the assumption of risk. Forms that an investment may take include:

(i) movable and immovable property as well as any other property rights in rem in respect of every kind of asset, such as mortgages, liens and pledges;
(ii) rights derived from shares, bonds and other kinds of interests in companies and joint ventures;
(iii) claims to money, to other assets or to any contractual performance having an economic value;
(iv) rights in the field of intellectual property, technical processes, goodwill and know-how;
(v) rights granted under public law or under contract, including rights to prospect, explore, extract and exploit natural resources.

'Claims to money' within the meaning of sub (iii) does not include claims to money that arise solely from commercial contracts for the sale of goods or services by a natural or legal in the territory of a Contracting Party to a natural or legal person in the territory of the other Contracting Party, the domestic financing of such contracts, or any related order, judgment, or arbitral award.

Returns that are invested shall be treated as investments and any alteration of the form in which assets are invested or reinvested shall not affect their qualification as investments.

(b) "investor" means with regard to either Contracting Party:
(i) any natural person having the nationality of that Contracting Party under its applicable law;
(ii) any legal person constituted under the law of that Contracting Party and having substantial business activities in the territory of that Contracting Party; or
(iii) any legal person that is constituted under the law of that Contracting Party and is directly or indirectly owned or controlled by a natural person as defined in (i) or by a legal person as defined in (ii).

A natural person who has the nationality of the Kingdom of the Netherlands and the other Contracting Party is deemed to be exclusively a natural person of the Contracting Party of his or her dominant and effective nationality.

(c) Indications of having 'substantive business activities' in a Contracting Party may include:
(i) the undertaking's registered office and/or administration is established in that Contracting Party;
(ii) the undertaking's headquarters and/or management is established in that Contracting Party;
(iii) the number of employees and their qualifications based in that Contracting Party;
(iv) the turnover generated in that Contracting Party; and
(v) an office, production facility and/or research laboratory is established in that Contracting Party;

These indications should be assessed in each specific case, taking into account the total number of employees and turnover of the undertaking concerned, and take account of the nature and maturity of the activities carried out by the undertaking in the Contracting Party in which it is established.

(d) "freely convertible currency" means a currency which is widely traded in international foreign exchange markets and widely used in international transactions.

(e) "territory" means the territory of the Contracting Party concerned, including [if applicable] its territorial sea and any area beyond and adjacent to its territorial sea within which it exercises jurisdiction or sovereign rights in accordance with international law.

Article 2 Scope and application

1. This Agreement shall apply to an investment, made in accordance with the applicable law of the host Contracting Party at the time the investment is made, that is directly or indirectly owned or controlled by an investor of the other Contracting Party and existing on the date of entry into force of this Agreement or made thereafter.

2. The provisions of this Agreement shall not affect the right of the Contracting Parties to regulate within their territories necessary to achieve legitimate policy objectives such as the protection of public health, safety, environment, public morals, labor rights, animal welfare, social or consumer protection or for prudential financial reasons. The mere fact that a Contracting Party regulates,

including through a modification to its laws, in a manner which negatively affects an investment or interferes with an investor's expectations, including its expectation of profits, is not a breach of an obligation under this Agreement.
3. The Contracting Parties reserve the right to introduce or maintain nondiscriminatory, appropriate and necessary measures for the purpose of preventing investors who, alone or together, have the ability to affect materially the terms of participation in the relevant market as a result of their position in the market, from engaging in or continuing anti-competitive practices.
4. Nothing in this Agreement shall be construed as preventing a Contracting Party from discontinuing the granting of a subsidy and/or requesting its reimbursement, where such measure is necessary in order to comply with international obligations between the Contracting Parties or where it has been ordered by a competent court, administrative tribunal or other competent authority, or requiring that Contracting Party to compensate the investor therefor.
5. No provision of this Agreement shall be construed as to prevent a Contracting Party from fulfilling its obligations as a member of an economic integration agreement such as a free trade area, customs union, common market, economic community, monetary union, e.g. the European Union, or as to oblige a Contracting Party to extend to the investors of the other Contracting Party and to their investments or returns the present or future benefit of any treatment, preference of privilege by virtue of its membership in such an agreement.

SECTION 2: INVESTMENT PROMOTION AND FACILITATION

Article 3 Favorable conditions for investment
1. Each Contracting Party shall, within the framework of its laws and regulations and in accordance with its international obligations, promote economic cooperation and encourage the creation of favorable conditions for responsible investment in its territory that contribute to sustainable economic development.
2. Subject to its right to exercise powers conferred by its laws and regulations, each Contracting Party shall admit foreign investments.
3. The Contracting Parties affirm the G20 Guiding Principles for Global Investment Policymaking.
4. The Contracting Parties strive to strengthen the promotion and facilitation of investments that contribute to sustainable development, including but not limited through regular consultations between investment promotion and facilitation agencies and the exchange of information regarding investment opportunities.

Article 4 Transparency
Each Contracting Party shall ensure that its laws, regulations, judicial decisions, procedures and administrative rulings of general application with respect to any matter covered by this Agreement are promptly published or made available in such a manner as to enable interested persons and the other Contracting Party to become acquainted with them. Whenever possible, such instruments will be made available through the internet in English.

Article 5 Rule of law
1. The Contracting Parties shall guarantee the principles of good administrative behavior, such as consistency, impartiality, independence, openness and transparency, in all issues that relate to the scope and aim of this Agreement.
2. Each Contracting Party shall ensure that investors have access to effective mechanisms of dispute resolution and enforcement, such as judicial, quasi-judicial or administrative tribunals or procedures for the purpose of prompt review, which mechanisms should be fair, impartial, independent, transparent and based on the rule of law.

3. As part of their duty to protect against business-related human rights abuse, the Contracting Parties must take appropriate steps to ensure, through judicial, administrative, legislative or other appropriate means, that when such abuses occur within their territory and/or jurisdiction those affected have access to effective remedy. These mechanisms should be fair, impartial, independent, transparent and based on the rule of law.

SECTION 3: SUSTAINABLE DEVELOPMENT

Article 6 Sustainable development

1. The Contracting Parties are committed to promote the development of international investment in such a way as to contribute to the objective of sustainable development.
2. Each Contracting Party shall ensure that its investment laws and policies provide for and encourage high levels of environmental and labor protection and shall strive to continue to improve those laws and policies and their underlying levels of protection.
3. The Contracting Parties emphasize the important contribution by women to economic growth through their participation in economic activity, including in international investment. They acknowledge the importance of incorporating a gender perspective into the promotion of inclusive economic growth. This includes removing barriers to women's participation in the economy and the key role that gender-responsive policies play in achieving sustainable development. The Contracting Parties commit to promote equal opportunities and participation for women and men in the economy. Where beneficial, the Contracting Parties shall carry out cooperation activities to improve the participation of women in the economy, including in international investment.
4. The Contracting Parties recognize that it is inappropriate to lower the levels of protection afforded by domestic environmental or labor laws in order to encourage investment.
5. A Contracting Party shall not adopt and apply domestic laws contributing to the objective of sustainable development in a manner that would constitute unjustifiable discrimination or a disguised restriction on trade and investment.
6. Within the scope and application of this Agreement, the Contracting Parties reaffirm their obligations under the multilateral agreements in the field of environmental protection, labor standards and the protection of human rights to which they are party, such as the Paris Agreement, the fundamental ILO Conventions and the Universal Declaration of Human Rights. Furthermore, each Contracting Party shall continue to make sustained efforts towards ratifying the fundamental ILO Conventions that it has not yet ratified.
7. The Contracting Parties are committed to cooperate as appropriate on investment- related sustainable development matters of mutual interest in multilateral fora.

Article 7 Corporate Social Responsibility

1. Investors and their investments shall comply with domestic laws and regulations of the host state, including laws and regulations on human rights, environmental protection and labor laws.
2. The Contracting Parties reaffirm the importance of each Contracting Party to encourage investors operating within its territory or subject to its jurisdiction to voluntarily incorporate into their internal policies those internationally recognized standards, guidelines and principles of corporate social responsibility that have been endorsed or are supported by that Party, such as the OECD Guidelines for Multinational Enterprises, the United Nations Guiding Principles on Business and Human Rights, and the Recommendation CM/REC(2016) of the Committee of Ministers to Member States on human rights and business.
3. The Contracting Parties reaffirm the importance of investors conducting a due diligence process to identify, prevent, mitigate and account for the environmental and social risks and impacts of its investment.

4. Investors shall be liable in accordance with the rules concerning jurisdiction of their home state for the acts or decisions made in relation to the investment where such acts or decisions lead to significant damage, personal injuries or loss of life in the host state.
5. The Contracting Parties express their commitment to the international framework on Business and Human Rights, such as the United Nations Guiding Principles on Business and Human Rights and the OECD Guidelines for Multinational Enterprises, and commit to strengthen this framework.

SECTION 4: INVESTMENT PROTECTION

Article 8 Non-discriminatory treatment

1. Each Contracting Party shall accord to an investor of the other Contracting Party and to an investment of an investor of the other Contracting Party, treatment no less favorable than the treatment it accords, in like situations, to its own investors and to their investments with respect to conduct, operation, management, maintenance, use, enjoyment and sale or disposal of their investments in its territory.
2. Each Contracting Party shall accord to an investor of the other Contracting Party and/or to an investment of an investor of the other Contracting Party, treatment no less favorable than the treatment it accords in like situations, to investors of a third country and to their investments with respect to the conduct, operation, management, maintenance, use, enjoyment and sale or disposal of their investments in its territory.
3. Substantive obligations in other international investment and trade agreements do not in themselves constitute "treatment", and thus cannot give rise to a breach of paragraph 2 of this Article, absent measures adopted or maintained by a Contracting Party pursuant to those obligations. Furthermore, the "treatment" referred to in paragraph 2 of this Article does not include procedures for the resolution of investment disputes between investors and States provided for in other international investment and trade agreements.

Article 9 Treatment of investors and of covered investments

1. Each Contracting Party shall ensure fair and equitable treatment of the investments of investors of the other Contracting Party. In addition, each Contracting Party shall accord to such investments full physical security and protection.
2. A Contracting Party breaches the aforementioned obligation of fair and equitable treatment where a measure or series of measures constitutes:
   (a) Denial of justice in criminal, civil or administrative proceedings;
   (b) Fundamental breach of due process, including a fundamental breach of transparency, in judicial and administrative proceedings;
   (c) Manifest arbitrariness;
   (d) Direct or targeted indirect discrimination on wrongful grounds, such as gender, race, nationality, sexual orientation or religious belief;
   (e) Abusive treatment of investors such as harassment, coercion, abuse of power, corrupt practices or similar bad faith conduct; or
   (f) A breach of any further elements of the fair and equitable treatment obligation adopted by the Contracting Parties in accordance with paragraph 3 of this Article.
3. The Contracting Parties shall, upon request of a Contracting Party, review the content of the obligation to provide fair and equitable treatment and may complement this list through a joint interpretative declaration within the meaning of Article 31, paragraph 3, sub a, of the Vienna Convention on the Law of Treaties.
4. When applying paragraph 2 of this Article, a Tribunal may take into account whether a Contracting Party made a specific representation to an investor to induce an investment that created a legitimate

expectation, and upon which the investor relied in deciding to make or maintain that investment, but that the Contracting Party subsequently frustrated.
5. When a Contracting Party has entered into a written commitment with investors of the other Contracting Party regarding a specific investment, that Contracting Party shall not, either itself or through an entity exercising governmental authority, breach the said commitment through the exercise of governmental authority in a way that causes loss or damage to the investor or its investment.
6. For greater certainty, a breach of another provision of this Agreement or of any other international agreement does not constitute a breach of this Article. In addition, the fact that a measure breaches domestic law does not, in and of itself, establish a breach of this Article.

Article 10 Fiscal Treatment
1. With respect to taxes, fees, charges and to fiscal deductions and exemptions, each Contracting Party shall, regarding the operation, management, maintenance, use, enjoyment and disposal of the investment, accord to investors of the other Contracting Party who are engaged in any economic activity in its territory, treatment not less favorable than that accorded to its own investors or to those of any third State who are in like situations, whichever is more favorable to the investors concerned.

For this purpose, however, any tax benefits granted by that Contracting Party pursuant to the following obligations shall not be taken into account:

(a) under an agreement for the avoidance of double taxation; or
(b) by virtue of its participation in a customs union, economic union, monetary union or similar institution, such as the European Union, or on the basis of interim agreements leading to such unions or institutions; or
(c) on the basis of reciprocity with a third State.

2. Nothing in this Agreement shall be construed to prevent a Party from adopting or maintaining any taxation measure aimed at preventing the avoidance or evasion of taxes pursuant to its tax laws or its agreements for the avoidance of double taxation.
3. This Agreement does not affect the rights and obligations of a Party under an agreement for the avoidance of double taxation. In the event of inconsistency between such agreement and this Agreement, the agreement for the avoidance of double taxation prevails to the extent of the inconsistency.

Article 11 Treatment related to free transfer
1. The Contracting Parties shall guarantee that payments relating to an investment may be transferred. The transfers shall be made in a freely convertible currency, without restriction or delay, and at the market rate of exchange applicable on the date of transfer. Such transfers include in particular though not exclusively:

(a) profits, interests, dividends and other current income;
(b) funds necessary;
  (i) for the acquisition of raw or auxiliary materials, semi-fabricated or finished products, or
  (ii) to replace capital assets in order to safeguard the continuity of an investment;
(c) additional funds necessary for the development of an investment;
(d) funds in repayment of loans;
(e) royalties or fees;
(f) earnings of natural persons;
(g) the proceeds of sale or liquidation of the investment;
(h) payments arising under Articles 12 and 13 of this Agreement.

2. This Agreement shall not be construed so as to prevent the Contracting Parties from fulfilling, in good faith, its international obligations for the purpose of maintaining international peace and security.

3. Notwithstanding paragraph 1, nothing in this Article shall be construed to prevent a Contracting Party from applying in an equitable and non-discriminatory manner and not in a way that would constitute a disguised restriction on transfers, its laws relating to:

(a) bankruptcy, insolvency, bank recovery and resolution, or the protection of the rights of creditors, and the prudential supervision of financial institutions;
(b) issuing, trading, or dealing in financial instruments;
(c) financial reporting or record keeping of transfers where necessary to assist law enforcement or financial regulatory authorities;
(d) criminal or penal offenses, deceptive or fraudulent practices;
(e) the satisfaction of judgments in adjudicatory proceedings.
(f) social security, public retirement or compulsory savings schemes.

Article 12 Expropriation

1. Neither Contracting Party shall nationalize or take any other measures depriving, directly or indirectly, the investors of the other Contracting Party of their investments, unless the following conditions are complied with:

(a) the measure is taken in the public interest;
(b) the measure is taken under due process of law;
(c) the measure is taken in a non-discriminatory manner; and
(d) the measure is taken against prompt, adequate and effective compensation.

2. Direct expropriation occurs when an investment is nationalised or otherwise directly taken through formal transfer of title or outright seizure.

3. Indirect expropriation occurs if a measure or a series of measures of a Contracting Party has an effect equivalent to direct expropriation, in that it substantially deprives the investor of the fundamental attributes of property in its investment, including the right to use, enjoy and dispose of its investment, without formal transfer of title or outright seizure.

4. The determination of whether a measure or a series of measures by a Contracting Party, in a specific factual situation, constitutes an indirect expropriation requires a case-by-case, fact-based inquiry that considers, amongst other factors:

(a) the economic impact of the measure or series of measures, although the sole fact that a measure or a series of measures of a Contracting Party has an adverse effect on the economic value of an investment does not establish that an indirect expropriation has occurred;
(b) the duration of the measure or series of measures by a Contracting Party; and
(c) the character of the measure or series of measures, notably their object and context.

5. The compensation referred to in paragraph 1 of this Article shall amount to the fair market value of the investment at the time immediately before the expropriation or the impending expropriation became known, whichever is earlier. For greater certainty, this method to evaluate the compensation also applies in case of unlawful expropriation. Valuation criteria shall include going concern value, asset value including the declared tax value of tangible property, and other criteria, as appropriate, to determine fair market value.

6. In addition to paragraph 5 of this Article, the compensation shall include interest at a normal commercial rate from the date of expropriation until the date of payment and shall, in order to be effective for the investor, be paid and made transferable, without delay, to the State designated by the investor and in the currency of the State of which the investor is a national or in any freely convertible currency accepted by the investor.

7. The affected investor shall have the right, under the law of the expropriating Contracting Party, to a prompt review of its claim and of the valuation of its investment, by a judicial or other independent authority of that Contracting Party, in accordance with the principles set out in this Article.

8. Except in the rare circumstance when the impact of a measure or series of measures is so severe in light of its purpose that it appears manifestly excessive, nondiscriminatory measures of a Contracting Party that are designed and applied in good faith to protect legitimate public interests, such as the protection of public health, safety, environment or public morals, social or consumer protection or promotion and protection of cultural diversity, do not constitute indirect expropriations.
9. This Article does not apply to the issuance of compulsory licences granted in relation to intellectual property rights, to the extent that such issuance is consistent with the Agreement on Trade-Related Aspects of Intellectual Property Rights in Annex 1C to the WTO Agreements.

Article 13 Compensation for losses
1. Investors of a Contracting Party who suffer losses in respect of their investments owing to war or other armed conflict, revolution, a state of national emergency, revolt, insurrection or riot in the territory of the other Contracting Party shall be accorded by the latter Contracting Party treatment, as regards restitution, indemnification, compensation or other settlement, no less favorable than that accorded by that Contracting Party to its own investors or to investors of any third State, whichever is more favorable to the investor concerned.
2. Without prejudice to paragraph 1 of this Article, investors of a Contracting Party who, in any of the situations referred to in that paragraph, suffer losses in the territory of the other Contracting Party resulting from:
(a) requisitioning of their investment or a part thereof by the latter's armed forces or authorities; or
(b) destruction of their investment or a part thereof by the latter's armed forces or authorities, which was not required by the necessity of the situation;

shall be accorded prompt, adequate and effective restitution or compensation by the other Party. The amount of such compensation shall be determined in accordance with the provisions of Article 12.

Article 14 Subrogation
If the investment of an investor of a Contracting Party is insured against noncommercial risks or otherwise give rise to payment of indemnification in respect of such investment under a system established by law, regulation or government contract, any subrogation of the insurer or re-insurer or agency designated by that Contracting Party to the rights of the said investor pursuant to the terms of such insurance or under any other indemnity given shall be recognized by the other Contracting Party.

SECTION 5: SETTLEMENT OF DISPUTES BETWEEN AN INVESTOR OF A CONTRACTING PARTY AND THE OTHER CONTRACTING PARTY

Article 15 Multilateral investment court
1. The Parties shall pursue with each other and other interested partners the multilateral reform of ISDS. Upon the entry into force between the Contracting Parties of an international agreement providing for a multilateral investment court applicable to disputes under this Agreement, the relevant provisions set out in this Section shall cease to apply.
2. The Contracting Parties shall, if necessary, adopt transitional arrangements taking into account the legitimate expectations of investors in ongoing disputes under the procedures set out under this Section.

Article 16 Scope of application
1. This Section shall apply to a dispute between, on the one hand, an investor of one Contracting Party and, on the other hand, the other Contracting Party concerning treatment alleged to be a breach of a

provision in Section 4 of this Agreement, which breach allegedly causes loss or damage to the investor or its investment(s).
2. The Tribunal shall decline jurisdiction if the investment has been made through fraudulent misrepresentation, concealment, corruption, or similar bad faith conduct amounting to an abuse of process.
3. The Tribunal shall decline jurisdiction if an investor within the meaning of Article 1(b) of this Agreement, which has changed its corporate structure with a main purpose to gain the protection of this Agreement at a point in time where a dispute had arisen or was foreseeable. This particularly includes situations where an investor has changed its corporate structure with a main purpose to submit a claim to its original home state.

Article 17 Alternative dispute resolution
1. Any dispute should, as far as possible, be settled amicably through negotiations, conciliation or mediation. Such settlement may be agreed at any time, including after proceedings under this Section have been commenced. A disputing party shall give favorable consideration to a request for negotiations, conciliation or mediation by the other disputing party.
2. Mutually agreed solutions shall be made publicly available. However, the version disclosed to the public may not contain any information that a disputing party has designated as confidential.

Article 18 Consultations
1. Where a dispute has not been resolved in a manner as provided for under Article 17, an investor of a Contracting Party alleging a breach of a provision in Section 4 of this Agreement, may submit a written request for consultations to the other Contracting Party. During these consultations, the disputing parties may use non-binding third party procedures, such as good offices, conciliation or mediation.
2. A request for consultations within the meaning of this Article shall contain the following information:
 (a) the name and address of the investor and, where such request is submitted on behalf of a locally established company, the name, address and place of incorporation of the locally established company;
 (b) the provision(s) in Section 4 of this Agreement, alleged to have been breached;
 (c) the legal and factual basis for the claim, including the treatment alleged to be inconsistent with the provision(s) in Section 4 of this Agreement;
 (d) the relief sought and the estimated amount of damages claimed; and
 (e) evidence establishing that the claimant is an investor of the other Party and that it owns or controls the investment and, where it acts on behalf of a locally established company, that it owns or controls the locally established company.

Where a request for consultations is submitted by more than one investor or on behalf of more than one locally established company, the information in (a) and (e) shall be submitted for each investor or each locally established company, as the case may be.
3. Unless the disputing parties agree to a longer period, consultations shall be held within 60 days of the submission of the request for consultations under paragraph 2.
4. The request for consultations must be submitted within:
 (a) five years of the date on which the investor first acquired, or should have first acquired, knowledge of the treatment alleged to be inconsistent with a provision in Section 4 of this Agreement, and of the loss or damage alleged to have been incurred thereby; or
 (b) two years of the date on which the investor or, as applicable, the locally established company, exhausts or ceases to pursue claims or proceedings before a tribunal or court under the domestic law of a Contracting Party; and, in any event, no later than ten years after the date on which the investor first acquired, or should have first acquired knowledge, of the treatment alleged to be

inconsistent with a provision in Section 4 of this Agreement, and of the loss or damage alleged to have been incurred thereby.

5. In the event that the claimant has not submitted a claim pursuant to Article 19 of this Agreement within eighteen months of submitting the request for consultations, the investor shall be deemed to have withdrawn its request for consultations. This period may be extended by agreement between the parties involved in the consultations.

6. The time periods in paragraphs 4 and 5 shall not render a claim inadmissible where the investor can demonstrate that the failure to request consultations or submit a claim is due to the investor's inability to act as a result of actions taken by the other disputing party, provided that the investor acts as soon as reasonably possible after it is able to act.

Article 19 Submission of a claim

1. If a request for consultations has been submitted according to the procedures laid down in Article 18 and where such consultations do not result in a resolution of the claim within six months from the date of the written request for consultations, the investor may submit a claim under one of the following sets of rules on dispute settlement:

(a) the Convention on the Settlement of Investment Disputes between States and Nationals of Other States of 18 March 1965 (ICSID Convention) or in accordance with the Rules on the Additional Facility for the Administration of Proceedings by the Secretariat of the Centre (ICSID Additional Facility), where the conditions for proceedings pursuant to the ICSID Convention do not apply;

(b) the arbitration rules of the United Nations Commission on International Trade Law (UNCITRAL Arbitration Rules), with the understanding that the Permanent Court of Arbitration (PCA) shall administer the proceedings;

The rules on dispute settlement according to which a claim has been submitted, shall apply subject to the rules in this Section and the other relevant procedures laid down in this Agreement.

2. All the claims identified by the investor in the submission of its claim pursuant to this Article must be related to treatment identified in its request for consultations pursuant to Article 18, paragraph 2 of this Agreement, or to treatment that occurred after the request for consultations was submitted.

3. The responding Contracting Party hereby unconditionally consents to the submission of a claim as provided under this Section.

4. The consent under paragraph 3 of this Article and the submission of a claim under paragraph 1 of this Article shall be deemed to satisfy the requirements of:

(a) Article 25 of the ICSID Convention or the ICSID Additional Facility Rules for written consent of the parties to the dispute; and

(b) Article I of the New York Convention for "arising out of a commercial relationship".

(c) Article II of the New York Convention for an "agreement in writing".

5. A claim may only be referred to a Tribunal pursuant to paragraph 1 of this Article if the investor withdraws or discontinues any existing proceeding before a tribunal or court under domestic or international law with respect to a measure alleged to constitute a breach referred to in its claim and waives its right to initiate any claim or proceeding before a tribunal or court under domestic or international law with respect to a measure alleged to constitute a breach referred to in its claim.

6. A claim with respect to restructuring of debt issued by a Contracting Party may only be submitted under this Section in accordance with the Protocol on public debt.

7. If two or more claims have been submitted separately to arbitration under this Article and the claims have a question of law or fact in common and arise out of the same events or circumstances, either party to the dispute may seek a consolidation order at either Tribunal. After giving all disputing parties the opportunity to be heard, the Tribunal shall in principle accept such request for consolidation, especially where the claimants are small and medium sized enterprises.

8. The claimant shall disclose to the other disputing party and to the Tribunal the name and address of a third party funder. The disclosure shall be made at the time of the submission of a claim, or as soon as possible if the funding has been granted after the submission of a claim.

Article 20 Constitution and functioning of the Tribunal

1. All Members of the Tribunal under this Agreement shall be appointed by an appointing authority. In the event that the claimant chooses arbitration pursuant to the ICSID Convention or the Additional Facility in accordance with Article 19, paragraph 1, subparagraph a, the Secretary-General of ICSID shall serve as appointing authority for arbitration under this Agreement. In the event that the claimant chooses arbitration pursuant to the UNCITRAL Arbitration Rules in accordance with Article 19, paragraph 1, subparagraph b, the Secretary-General of the Permanent Court of Arbitration shall serve as appointing authority for arbitration under this Agreement.
2. The appointing authority shall appoint Members of the Tribunal that fulfill the conditions set out in paragraphs 5 and 6 of this Article, after thoroughly consulting the disputing parties. In appointing the Members of the Tribunal, the appointing authority shall strive for gender and geographic diversity. For greater certainty, in making appointments the Secretary General of ICSID is not limited to the Panel of Arbitrators.
3. The Tribunal shall be composed of three Members. After consulting the disputing parties, the appointing authority may decide that the Tribunal consists of one Member taking into account the complexity of the case, the amount of damages claimed and the desirability of keeping the costs of the procedure as low as possible, especially for small and medium sized enterprises.
4. The appointing institution shall publish the composition of each Tribunal on its website together with the date of the constitution of the Tribunal, the name of the disputing parties, the legal basis for the claim, and the relief sought.
5. The Members of the Tribunal shall possess the qualifications required in their respective countries for appointment to judicial office, or be jurists of recognized competence. The appointing authority shall make every effort to ensure that the members of the Tribunal, either individually or together, possess the necessary expertise in public international law, which includes environmental and human rights law, international investment law as well as in the resolution of disputes arising under international agreements. In addition, Members of the Tribunal shall not act as legal counsel or shall not have acted as legal counsel for the last five years in investment disputes under this or any other international agreement.
6. Members of the Tribunal and their staff shall be independent of, and not be affiliated with or take instructions from, either disputing party or Contracting Party with regard to matters related to the dispute. They shall not participate in the consideration of any dispute that would create a direct or indirect conflict of interest, including as a party-appointed expert or witness. Arbitrators shall comply with the International Bar Association Guidelines on Conflicts of Interest in International Arbitration and any supplemental rules agreed upon by the Contracting Parties. The Contracting Parties will negotiate a Code of Conduct with the aim to include in this Agreement additional requirements on ethics for the Members of the Tribunal.
7. If a disputing party considers that a Member of the Tribunal has a conflict of interest, it shall send to the President of the International Court of Justice a notice of challenge to the appointment. The notice of challenge shall be sent within 15 days of the date on which the composition of the division of the Tribunal has been communicated to the disputing party, or within 15 days of the date on which the relevant facts came to its knowledge, if they could not have reasonably been known at the time of composition of the division. The notice of challenge shall state the grounds for the challenge.
8. If, within 15 days from the date of the notice of challenge, the challenged Member of the Tribunal has elected not to resign from the division, the President of the International Court of Justice shall, after hearing the disputing parties and after providing the Member of the Tribunal an opportunity

to submit any observations, issue a decision within 45 days of receipt of the notice of challenge and notify the disputing parties and the other Members of the division. A vacancy resulting from the disqualification or resignation of a Member of the Tribunal shall be filled promptly.
9. The fees and expenses of Members of the Tribunal as well as of witnesses and experts involved in the procedure shall be governed by ICSID Administrative and Financial Regulation 14.
10. The Tribunal shall determine whether the treatment subject to the claim is inconsistent with the provisions in Section 4 of this Agreement. In making its determination, the Tribunal shall apply the provisions of this Agreement and other rules of international law applicable between the Contracting Parties. It shall interpret this Agreement in accordance with customary rules of interpretation of public international law, as codified in the Vienna Convention on the Law of Treaties.
11. Without prejudice to preliminary objections raised in accordance with Article 21 of this Agreement and absent a different agreement between the disputing parties, the arbitral proceedings shall, in the interest of an expeditious resolution of the dispute and in order to prevent unnecessary bifurcation of the proceedings, in general consider issues of jurisdiction and merits together.
12. The Tribunal shall not have jurisdiction to determine the legality of a measure, alleged to constitute a breach of this Agreement, under the domestic law of the disputing Contracting Party. In determining the consistency of a measure with this Agreement, the Tribunal may consider, as appropriate, the domestic law of the disputing Party as a matter of fact. In doing so, the Tribunal shall follow the prevailing interpretation given to the domestic law by the court or authorities of that Contracting Party and any meaning given to domestic law by the Tribunal shall not be binding upon the courts or the authorities of that Contracting Party.
13. The "UNCITRAL Transparency Rules" shall apply to disputes under this Section. The Tribunal and the disputing parties shall give positive consideration to a request from a third party to submit as an amicus curiae oral or written submissions in accordance with Article 4 of these Rules. The Tribunal shall give the reasons for a decision to deny such request.

Article 21 Preliminary objections

1. Any objection that the dispute or any ancillary claim is not within the jurisdiction of the Tribunal shall be made as early as possible. The respondent shall file the objection no later than the expiration of the time limit fixed for the filing of the counter-memorial, or, if the objection relates to an ancillary claim, for the filing of the rejoinder - unless the facts on which the objection is based are unknown to the respondent at that time.
2. The respondent may, no later than 30 days after the constitution of the division of the Tribunal, and in any event before its first session, file an objection that a claim is manifestly without legal merit. The respondent shall specify as precisely as possible the basis for the objection. On receipt of such an objection the Tribunal shall suspend the proceedings on the merits and establish a schedule for considering such an objection consistent with its schedule for considering any other preliminary question. The Tribunal, after giving the disputing parties an opportunity to present their observations, shall at its first session of promptly thereafter, issue a decision or award stating the grounds therefor. In doing so, the Tribunal shall assume the alleged facts to be true. This paragraph is without prejudice to the Tribunal's authority to address other objections as a preliminary question or to the right of the respondent to object, in the course of the proceeding, that a claim lacks legal merit.

Article 22 Final award

1. The Tribunal and the disputing parties shall make every effort to ensure that the dispute settlement process is carried out in a timely manner. The Tribunal shall endeavor to issue its final award within 24 months of the date the claim is submitted pursuant to Article 19 of this Agreement. If the Tribunal requires additional time to issue its final award, it shall provide the disputing parties the reasons for the delay.

2. An award issued by a Tribunal pursuant to this Agreement shall be final and binding between the disputing parties and in respect of that particular case. The respondent shall comply with the award with undue delay.
3. An award can only result in compensation for damages, unless the disputing parties agree on restitution. Monetary compensation shall include the applicable interest at a normal commercial rate from the date of expropriation until the date of payment.
4. The Tribunal shall not award punitive damages. Monetary damages shall not be greater than the loss suffered by the investor, reduced by any prior damages or compensation already provided in relation to the same factual dispute. For the calculation of monetary damages, the Tribunal shall also reduce the damages to take into account any restitution of property or repeal or modification of the measure.
5. The Tribunal shall order that reasonable costs incurred by the successful disputing party shall be borne by the unsuccessful disputing party, unless the Tribunal determines that such allocation is unreasonable in the circumstances of the case. Such a determination may take into account whether the successful disputing party has acted improperly, for example by raising manifestly frivolous objections or improperly invoking preliminary objections, and whether the unsuccessful disputing party is a small or medium sized enterprise. If only some parts of the claims have been successful the costs shall be adjusted, proportionately, to the number or extent of the successful parts of the claims.

Article 23 Behavior of the investor
Without prejudice to national administrative or criminal law procedures, a Tribunal, in deciding on the amount of compensation, is expected to take into account noncompliance by the investor with its commitments under the UN Guiding Principles on Business and Human Rights, and the OECD Guidelines for Multinational Enterprises.

SECTION 6: CONSULTATIONS AND DISPUTE SETTLEMENT BETWEEN THE CONTRACTING PARTIES

Article 24 Consultations of Contracting Parties
1. Either Contracting Party may propose to the other Contracting Party that consultations be held on any matter concerning the interpretation or application of this Agreement. The other Contracting Party shall accord sympathetic consideration to the proposal and shall afford adequate opportunity for such consultations. Such consultations shall be held at a place and at a time agreed upon through diplomatic channels by the Contracting Parties.
2. A joint interpretative declaration adopted as result of consultations by the Contracting Parties shall be binding on a Tribunal established under Section 5 of this Agreement. Such joint interpretative declaration is not applicable in cases where a claim has been submitted by an investor under Section 5 of this Agreement.

Article 25 Settlement of Disputes between the Contracting Parties
1. Any dispute between the Contracting Parties concerning the interpretation or application of this Agreement, which cannot be settled within a reasonable amount of time by means of diplomatic negotiations, shall, unless the Contracting Parties have otherwise agreed, be submitted, at the request of either Contracting Party, to an arbitral tribunal, composed of three members. Each Contracting Party shall appoint one arbitrator and the two arbitrators thus appointed shall together appoint a third arbitrator as their chairman who is not a national of either Contracting Party and who is a national of a third State that has diplomatic relations with both Contracting Parties.
2. If one of the Contracting Parties fails to appoint an arbitrator and has not proceeded to do so within two months after an invitation from the other Contracting Party to make such appointment, the latter Contracting Party may invite the President of the International Court of Justice to make the necessary

appointment. The President shall consult both Parties which consultations shall not take no longer than one month.
3. If the two core arbitrators are unable to agree on the chair person in the two months following their appointment, either Contracting Party may invite the President of the International Court of Justice to make the necessary appointment.
4. If, in the cases provided for in the paragraphs 2 and 3 of this Article, the President of the International Court of Justice is prevented from discharging the said function or is a national of either Contracting Party, the Vice-President shall be invited to make the necessary appointments. If the Vice-President is prevented from discharging the said function or is a national of either Contracting Party, the most senior member of the Court available who is not a national of either Contracting Party shall be invited to make the necessary appointments.
5. In making its determination the Tribunal shall decide the dispute in accordance with customary rules of interpretation of public international law, as codified in the Vienna Convention on the Law of Treaties. Before the Tribunal decides, it may at any stage of the proceedings propose to the Contracting Parties to settle the dispute amicably. The foregoing provisions shall not prejudice settlement of the dispute *ex aequo et bono* if the Contracting Parties so agree.
6. Unless the Contracting Parties decide otherwise, the Tribunal shall determine its own procedure.
7. The Tribunal shall reach its decision by a majority of votes. Such decision shall be final and binding on the Contracting Parties.
8. Each Contracting Party shall bear the costs of its appointed member of the Tribunal and of its representation in the arbitration proceedings and half of the costs of the chairman and the remaining costs. The Tribunal may, however, in its decision direct that a higher proportion of the costs shall be borne by one of the two Contracting Parties. Such decision shall be binding on both Contracting Parties.

SECTION 7: FINAL PROVISIONS

Article 26 Entry into Force, Duration and Termination

1. The present Agreement shall enter into force on the first day of the second month following the date on which the Contracting Parties have notified each other in writing that their constitutionally required procedures have been complied with, and shall remain in force for a period of fifteen years.
2. Unless notice of termination has been given by either Contracting Party at least six months before the date of its expiry, the present Agreement shall be extended tacitly for periods of five years, whereby each Contracting Party reserves the right to terminate the Agreement upon notice of at least six months before the date of expiry of the current period of validity.
3. In respect of investments made before the date of the termination of the present Agreement, this Agreement shall continue to be in effect for a further period of fifteen years from that date.
4. Subject to the period mentioned in paragraph 2 of this Article, the Kingdom of the Netherlands shall be entitled to terminate the application of the present Agreement separately in respect of any of the parts of the Kingdom of the Netherlands.

Article 27 Territorial Application

As regards the Kingdom of the Netherlands, the present Agreement shall apply to the European part of the Netherlands, to Aruba, Curaçao, Sint Maarten and the Caribbean part of the Netherlands (the islands of Bonaire, Sint Eustatius and Saba), unless the notification provided for in Article 26, paragraph 1 provides otherwise.

IN WITNESS WHEREOF, the undersigned representatives, duly authorized thereto, have signed the present Agreement.

DONE in two originals at , on , in the ..., Netherlands and English languages, the [...] texts being authentic.

In case of difference of interpretation, the English text shall prevail.

For ....

For the Kingdom of the Netherlands:

PROTOCOL ON PUBLIC DEBT

On the signing of the Agreement on reciprocal encouragement and protection of investments between [...] and the Kingdom of the Netherlands, the undersigned representatives have agreed on the following provisions, which constitute an integral part of the Agreement:
1. No claim that a restructuring of public debt of a Contracting Party breaches an obligation of this Agreement may be submitted to, or if already submitted, be pursued under Article 19 of this Agreement if the restructuring is a negotiated restructuring at the time of submission, or becomes a negotiated restructuring after such submission.
2. Subject to paragraph 1 of this Protocol, an investor may not submit a claim under Article 19 of this Agreement that a restructuring of debt of a Contracting Party breaches the provisions of this Agreement, unless 270 days have elapsed from the date of submission by the claimant of the written request for consultations pursuant to Article 18 of this Agreement.
3. A breach of Article 8, paragraph 1, does not occur merely by virtue of a different treatment provided by a Contracting Party to certain categories of investors or investments on grounds of a different macroeconomic impact, for instance to avoid systemic risks or spillover effects, or on grounds of eligibility for debt restructuring.

For the purposes of this Protocol:
(a) 'negotiated restructuring' means the restructuring or rescheduling of debt of a Contracting Party that has been effected through:
  (i) a modification or amendment of debt instruments, as provided for under their terms, including their governing law, or
  (ii) a debt exchange or other similar process in which the holders of no less than 66% of the aggregate principal amount of the outstanding debt subject to restructuring, excluding debt held by that Contracting Party or by entities owned or controlled by it, have consented to such debt exchange or other process.

(b) "governing law" of a debt instrument means a Contracting Party's legal and regulatory framework applicable to that debt instrument.

www.ingramcontent.com/pod-product-compliance
Lightning Source LLC
Chambersburg PA
CBHW061352240926
51846CB00007B/1377
* 9 7 8 9 0 4 7 3 0 1 6 4 6 *